The
John Ireland
Companion

John Ireland, November 1917. Pencil drawing by Jane Emmet de Glehn (1873–1961).

The
John Ireland
Companion

Edited by
Lewis Foreman

With a Foreword by Julian Lloyd Webber

THE BOYDELL PRESS

First published 2011
The Boydell Press, Woodbridge

ISBN 978 1 84383 686 5

The Boydell Press is an imprint of Boydell & Brewer Ltd
PO Box 9, Woodbridge, Suffolk IP12 3DF, UK
and of Boydell & Brewer Inc.
668 Mount Hope Ave, Rochester, NY 14620, USA
website: www.boydellandbrewer.com

A catalogue record for this book is available
from the British Library

The publisher has no responsibility for the continued existence or
accuracy of URLs for external or third-party internet websites referred
to in this book, and does not guarantee that any content on such
websites is, or will remain, accurate or appropriate.

Papers used by Boydell & Brewer Ltd are natural, recyclable
products made from wood grown in sustainable forests

Designed and typeset in Adobe Warnock Pro by
David Roberts, Pershore, Worcestershire

Printed in Great Britain by
CPI Antony Rowe, Chippenham and Eastbourne

Contents

Illustrations

(All from the Archive of the John Ireland Trust unless otherwise acknowledged)

Frontispiece: John Ireland, November 1917.
Pencil drawing by Jane Emmet de Glehn (1873–1961).

Illustrations in the text

Plates

The plates appear between pp. 254 and 255.

Musical Examples

Contributors & Authors of Reprinted Articles

Felix Aprahamian (1914–2005) was a celebrated music critic, for nearly forty years on the *Sunday Times*. A notable champion of French music, and organiser of the French concerts in London during the war and a champion of Delius, whom he met in 1933, becoming President of the Delius Society.

Richard Arnell (1917–2009) was a British composer whose career was established in the USA during the Second World War, afterwards enjoying a relatively short-lived career as a leading composer in London. His music was revived by the Dutton Epoch record company during the last few years of his life.

Jocelyn Brooke (1908–66), educated at Bedales and Oxford, wrote literary criticism for leading journals. His four novels and a study of British wild orchids were crowned by four autobiographical books which combine fiction and memoirs in a unique way, culminating in *The Dog at Clambercrown* (1955).

Alan Bush (1900–95), composer and pianist, was also celebrated for his communist views. He taught composition at the Royal Academy of Music for fifty years. His music includes operas, symphonies and orchestral music, chamber music, choral and piano music.

Geoffrey Bush (1920–98) was a composer and teacher with a specialist interest in extra-mural education. As a pianist and editor of the music of Stanford he championed the Stanford generation of British composers and orchestrated Stanford's Third Piano Concerto for the Lyrita recording.

George Dannatt (1915–2009) was an artist and a chartered surveyor. He had also published as a music critic on the *News Chronicle*. A friend of Sir Arthur Bliss, his Tantris series of paintings inspired Bliss's *Metamorphic Variations*, which was dedicated to Dannatt and his wife.

Julie Deller, a niece of the late Alfred Deller, remembers John Ireland coming in to the Deal music shop of Goulden & Wind where she worked for the manager in her school holidays. She wrote her article on 'Ireland in Deal' in 1997 and still lives in the town.

Jeremy Dibble is Professor of Music at the University of Durham. His specialist interests in the Victorian, Edwardian and Georgian eras are reflected in his major studies of *C. Hubert H. Parry: His Life and Music* (1992; rev. 1998), *Charles Villiers Stanford: Man and Musician* (2002) and *John Stainer: A Life in Music*.

Edwin Evans (1874–1945), a celebrated music critic, was the son of a music critic of the same name. He was a champion of the new music between the wars and adviser to Diaghilev. His library is the foundation collection of Central Music Library at Westminster Public Library.

Lewis Foreman, librarian and author of many books on music including *Bax: A Composer and his Times*. A Trustee of various composer trusts and repertoire adviser to record companies.

Susan Foreman, educated at Bedales and St Anne's College Oxford, librarian, editor and indexer. Author of books on the history of Whitehall, consumerism and, with her husband, Lewis Foreman, *London – A Musical Gazetteer* (2005).

Norah Kathleen Kirby (1895–1982), née de Peyer, was the daughter of Emile Victor de Peyer, a London spice broker born in 1858. She became Ireland's housekeeper at 14 Gunter Grove. In 1953 she moved with him to Rock Mill, Washington, Sussex, and took over all his correspondence and affairs. Later she founded the John Ireland Trust and commissioned the first full-length biography of the composer.

Frederic Lamond (1868–1948) was a legendary Scottish pianist and composer who studied with von Bülow and Liszt. Celebrated for his performances of Beethoven, he enjoyed a widespread European career, living in Germany for much of his life, though forced to leave by the two World Wars.

Philip Lancaster is a singer, researcher and writer specialising in the study of British music and poetry of the early twentieth century. One of the main focuses of this is the work of Ivor Gurney, whose music he has edited for performance, recording and publication, and whose complete poems he is co-editing, with Tim Kendall, for Oxford University Press.

Stephen Le Prevost is Organist and Director of Music at the Town Church, St Peter Port, Guernsey. He previously held appointments at Ely Cathedral and Westminster Abbey.

Stephen Lloyd has recently completed (2011) an extensive study of Constant Lambert for the Boydell Press. His previous books include volumes on Balfour Gardiner, Dan Godfrey, William Walton and a collection of Eric Fenby's writings on Delius.

Charles Markes (1900–86) was one of Ireland's choristers at St Luke's from 1908 and later his deputy as organist. His musical career was largely on the variety stage in England and abroad. After a gap of several decades he became close to Ireland again during the composer's later years.

Robert Matthew-Walker was a private composition pupil of Darius Milhaud (Paris, 1962–3); author of 22 books; editor *Music & Musicians*, 1984–8; editor and publisher *Musical Opinion*, 2009–; editor and publisher *The Organ*, 2009–; editorial consultant *International Record Review*; producer of over 150 records; awarded Grand Prix du Disque 1978 (Brian Ferneyhough Sonatas for String Quartet).

E. J. Moeran (1894–1950), pupil of Stanford and John Ireland, was a composer and folksong collector. His music includes three orchestral rhapsodies, violin and cello concertos, a Symphony in G minor, a Sinfonietta and other orchestral music, chamber music and many songs and folksong settings.

Angus Morrison (1902–76) was a concert pianist, teacher and Professor of Piano at the Royal College of Music for over fifty years (1926–76).

Eric Parkin studied and taught at Trinity College of Music, London, and is known as a specialist in the music of John Ireland, whose piano works he studied with the composer and recorded over a period of over fifty years. His repertoire of recordings includes piano music as varied as Bridge, Bax, Hurlstone, Baines, Moeran, Peter Dickinson, Billy Mayerl, Gershwin, Chaminade, Copland, Rosza, Jerome Kern, George Shearing and Robert Farnon.

Bruce Phillips read Modern Languages at Oxford and worked at Oxford University Press for thirty years. He has been a Trustee of the John Ireland Charitable Trust for over thirty years and is now its director.

Fiona Richards is Senior Lecturer in Music at the Open University. She has previously published *The Music of John Ireland* (2000) and also works on Australian music, as seen in her edited volume *The Soundscapes of Australia: Music, Place, and Spirituality*.

Alan Rowlands started professional life as a scientist but became a student at the Royal College of Music at the age of twenty-six, meeting John Ireland during this time. He subsequently taught at the College for thirty-five years and was the first person to participate in the recording of Ireland's complete solo piano music and songs.

Murray Schafer is a distinguished Canadian composer and an innovative writer on music. His interviews with sixteen British composers were conducted during 1961 for the Canadian Broadcasting Corporation and were first printed in 1963.

Marion Scott (1877–1953) was a violinist and writer who championed the cause of composer Ivor Gurney. She studied the violin at the RCM with Arbos and composition with Stanford. Later she edited the *RCM Magazine*. Ill health interrupted her playing career, and she achieved success as a writer and critic, becoming an international authority on Haydn.

Colin Scott-Sutherland wrote the first book-length study of Arnold Bax (1973), and made a collected edition of Bax's poems (*Ideala*). Later volumes include studies of Edward Thomas and John Ireland, the songs of Frances George Scott, Ronald Stevenson and the Scottish painter and craftswoman Elizabeth Mary Watt. His study of composer Cedric Thorpe Davie is forthcoming.

Humphrey Searle (1915–82) was the first British composer successfully to adopt serial technique in widely accepted concert works. A pupil of Webern as well as John Ireland, his output include three operas including a setting of *Hamlet*, ballets and orchestral music, much chamber music and vocal settings. In his earlier career he was a BBC music producer.

Freda Swain (1902–85) was a composer, teacher and pianist. She studied the piano with Matthay, and was Stanford's last female pupil. (She remembered that he always referred to her as 'm'bhoy'!) With her husband, the pianist Arthur Alexander, she was long associated with the musical circles round Bax and Ireland between the wars.

Kenneth Thompson (1904–1991) was a Church of England vicar who met Ireland in the early 1930s and was his confidant for half his life. He served successively at St Cuthbert's, Kensington, as Assistant Chaplain at Lancing College, and later at St Philip's, Philbeach Gardens, Kensington. He buried both Ireland and Norah Kirby at Shipley Church.

Roderick Williams is a well-known baritone, internationally active in the opera house and on the concert platform. His wide repertoire of operatic roles includes many new operas and the role of Pilgrim in Vaughan Williams' *The Pilgrim's Progress*. He is well known for his championship of English songs, including those of John Ireland. He orchestrated Ireland's recitation *Annabel Lee* for his Dutton recording.

Kenneth A. Wright (1899–1975) was a very long-standing member of the music staff at the BBC, including periods as Assistant Director of Music, Overseas Director of Music and acting Director of Music. He is the dedicatee of Ireland's *A Downland Suite*.

For Richard Itter
whose pioneering Lyrita Recorded Edition
succeeded in completely relaunching
John Ireland's music

Foreword

Julian Lloyd Webber

JOHN Ireland – what does that name mean to music-lovers fifty years after his death? Sadly not as much as it should, for he is a wonderful composer whose music really does – for once – merit that oft-abused phrase 'unjustly neglected'.

I have a special liking for the extraordinary group of composers that emerged from the 'land without music' (as the Germans had so smugly dubbed England) in the years after Elgar laid down his self-taught gauntlet.

Yet 'group' can hardly be the right word to describe a collection of individuals who resolutely pursued their own distinctive paths. Unlike the French 'Les Six' (who more-or-less declared a similar direction of purpose), Frank Bridge, Gustav Holst, Frederick Delius, Ralph Vaughan Williams and John Ireland – not to mention more peripheral figures such as John Foulds and Cyril Scott – followed singular musical visions.

One of my most memorable musical experiences is of playing – fresh out of college – Ireland's wonderful Cello Sonata in a converted railway shed in Curitiba, Brazil! A thunderstorm struck in the middle of the performance and the music felt visceral, alive. That is the spirit of John Ireland. Forget 'English pastoral' – although there is nothing wrong with that – but *Ireland's* passion is to be found elsewhere. So I would like to direct your attention, in this impressively comprehensive collection of 'All Things Ireland', to Colin Scott-Sutherland's essay 'Ireland and Machen'. For Ireland was hugely affected by the work of the Welsh supernatural writer Arthur Machen, to the extent of asking 'How can people understand my music if they've never read Machen?' It is a key question because, as Vincent Starrett remarks in his monograph *Arthur Machen – A novelist of Ecstasy and Sin*: 'Machen is a novelist of the soul. He writes of a strange borderland, lying somewhere between Dreams and Death'. And there, I would suggest, is where the essence of John Ireland's music lies.

Editor's Introduction

APART from Stewart Craggs's invaluable *Catalogue*[1] published in its second edition in 2007, there have only been three book-length accounts of John Ireland's life and music.[2] They have all faced the same problem: the absence of documentation of Ireland's early and middle years, and the strong suspicion that the companion of his later years, Norah Kirby, who was the sole beneficiary of his estate, had sanitised the archive, suppressing letters and documents of which she did not approve. The circumstances of Mrs Kirby's death in 1982 further interrupted any possibility of research into Ireland's life, when the owners of her care home were prosecuted after her death and the resolution of the probate on her estate was completed only with difficulty by the John Ireland Trust buying out a disputed last will. This is formally documented by Bruce Phillips in his chapter on the John Ireland Charitable Trust (hereafter referred to as John Ireland Trust) in Chapter 13. During this time much of the John Ireland paper archive was inaccessible. At the time I was told it was being stored in black plastic bin bags at a police station.

I was first commissioned by the John Ireland Trust to write a full biography of Ireland when this material was returned to the John Ireland Trust and again became available for research, and Peter Taylor (1913–2003), his wife Margaret (1920–2004) and especially their very efficient daughter-in-law Jane, were wonderfully helpful in assembling documents and an extensive archive of photocopies. However, it rapidly became obvious to me that owing to the gaps in the documentary record it would not be possible to write a conventional full musical life-and-works study on the lines of my own *Bax: A Composer and his Times*. I therefore opted to start with a volume of selected letters, since long delayed, which I hope, after some twenty years, will finally be completed after this *Companion* has appeared.

Following the success of *The Percy Grainger Companion*[3] and Penelope Thwaites' recent *The New Percy Grainger Companion*,[4] and similar volumes about other composers, this seemed an excellent format in which to present a variety of accounts of Ireland and his music, shining a succession of searchlights onto the often hazy Ireland scene, and presenting the fruits of the latest research in the light of performances and recordings of almost all the music. This process encompasses newly written chapters by various writers of today, together with reprints of

---

[1] *John Ireland: A Catalogue, Discography and Bibliography*, 2nd revised and enlarged edition compiled by Stewart R. Craggs (Aldershot: Ashgate, 2007).

[2] A short commissioned volume by Peter Crossley-Holland, a composition pupil of John Ireland, was written in the 1940s for publication by Éditions de L'Oiseau-Lyre but was never issued. Edited by the present author, the surviving manuscript was finally published in the journal *Manchester Sounds*, vol. 7 (2007–8), pp. 5–73. There is also *The Correspondence of Alan Bush and John Ireland, 1927–1961*, compiled by Rachel O'Higgins (Aldershot: Ashgate, 2006).

[3] *The Percy Grainger Companion*, ed. Lewis Foreman (London: Thames Publishing, 1981).

[4] *The New Percy Grainger Companion*, ed. Penelope Thwaites (Woodbridge: Boydell Press, 2010).

material variously published but generally inaccessible, and all of Ireland's writings on music, much of it previously unpublished. In trying to make this volume helpful to newcomers to Ireland as well as a source book for those familiar with the music I have also included chapters which are basically intended as straightforward introductions to the music for the music lover, including my own account of the orchestral music, essentially a collection of programme notes.

In assembling such a volume the editor is confronted by a problem more acute than it would have been in the case of many other composers: that of the repetition of a limited number of stories and anecdotes. In a volume not intended to be read from cover to cover at one go, but to provide informative accounts of different aspects of his life and music, and including all Ireland's own rather small number of essays on music, it has been felt that a controlled measure of repetition is preferable to compromising the integrity of any specific chapter. Furthermore, the chapters vary very considerably in length, and alongside a number of substantial essays I have included a variety of much shorter contributions which will place on record accounts of those who knew Ireland at first hand.

This volume is being produced to mark the fiftieth anniversary of John Ireland's death in 1962 and will, I hope, be of most value to those wanting to play and enjoy the music, as well as those wishing to research the life and art of a remarkably idiosyncratic character, and the vibrant musical period in which he flourished.

The moving spirit behind the gestation and promotion of this *Companion* has been Bruce Phillips of the John Ireland Trust, and I have to thank him and the Trust most sincerely for their unstinting assistance and patience over more than a quarter of a century, as my various strands of Ireland research have evolved. I have to thank Bruce and the Trust for sponsoring the present volume and for supplying much of the archive material, including photographs, that appears in it, and various friends and helpers, notably Alan Rowlands and Stephen Lloyd, for taking a close interest in the project and for their expert and helpful criticism and commentary. Thanks, too, to Alan, Stephen and Graham Parlett for their detailed reading of the proofs.

My very first interview (with the critic Felix Aprahamian) concerning John Ireland dates back to 1969, and over the intervening years alongside my research for a variety of other books I have been fortunate enough to interview many of those who had been personally involved with the composer, but who have now passed on. My first awareness of the personalities concerned came when the composer was still alive and he appeared at the Arts Council Drawing Room, then in St James's Square, for the first modern performance of his glorious Sextet. Later, after Ireland had died, again at that elegant St James's Square location, I attended a memorial concert under the auspices of the short-lived John Ireland Society and found myself sitting next to Anna Instone of the BBC. There was a minor flurry at the door when a rather rustically dressed elderly lady appeared, and I was all agog when Anna Instone's husband, the broadcaster Julian Herbage, returned to his seat almost laughing out loud, and I could not avoid hearing him gasp out to his wife: 'It's Norah – she's wearing John's gum boots and trousers!' They both laughed knowingly.[5] Thus Norah Kirby entered my consciousness. Later, Lawrence

---

[5] See p. 39 for Alan Rowland's recollection of this episode.

Norcross,[6] the instigator of the short-lived John Ireland Society, consulted me about issuing a Society recording of one of the early Ireland string quartets, only to be foiled at the last hurdle when Mrs Kirby insisted on retaining the tape and not allowing its issue. He was furious. It seemed to me at that point, as someone then very much on the fringe of Ireland matters, that Mrs Kirby was probably someone to be avoided, and I never interviewed her. Nevertheless, I should perhaps emphasise that Mrs Kirby, despite her indiosyncrasies, was the key factor in the safe transmission of the bulk of Ireland's papers and manuscripts after his death and, through the foundation of the John Ireland Trust, the later promotion and dissemination of the music

Later, as well as Felix Aprahamian, I interviewed (on tape) Geoffrey Bush, Charles Markes, Angus Morrison and Freda Swain, all of whom were fluent and bright in their recall. There was also Father Kenneth Thompson and the composer Alan Bush, both of whom by the time I visited them were losing their memories and were beginning to be extremely hazy in their reminiscences. My wife and I visited John Longmire and his wife at their home on Guernsey on 25–6 June 1985, but it was soon after John's devastating stroke and he was unable to contribute anything useful, though I am very grateful to Viviane Longmire for guiding us round places of Ireland interest on the island. Not least of my memories of that visit was the bust of John Ireland by sculptor Nigel Konstam, illustrated in Plate 49, which the Longmires had placed so that the composer appeared to be looking through their sitting room window and out to sea, above his favourite Le Catioroc, a place he evoked so successfully in his piano suite *Sarnia*. Baritone Roderick Williams' chapter originates from an extended and wide-ranging discussion I had with him about Ireland's songs in the summer of 2010, which was recorded and later transcribed. I am delighted to include it here for its many insights, vivid conversational feel and exuberant evocative hyperbole. Transcripts of extracts from interviews with the composer's contemporaries appear at the appropriate places in the *Companion*.

Finally, my interest in John Ireland has been primarily driven by performances and recordings of the music, and I have tried to make this *Companion* as helpful as possible both to music-lovers and to intending performers. Thus I have included surveys of the orchestral music and songs that are more programme notes than academic analysis, with the objective of attracting both listeners and performers. The pre-eminent historical catalogue of Ireland's music is that by Stewart Craggs, already cited, but the catalogue that appears in the *Companion* is aimed at the performer and is alphabetically arranged. I hope it will be found to be comprehensive and it indicates what forces are required and from where the music can be obtained. Similarly, I am grateful to Stephen Lloyd for all matters discographical, for his encyclopaedic knowledge acquired over the many years I have known him, and for compiling what is the most comprehensive discography of Ireland's music ever assembled. This includes details of those very early recordings, both acoustic and electric, that have eluded other discographies,

---

[6] For Lawrence Norcross (1927–2010), a leading educationalist of his time, see his obituary in the *Times Educational Supplement*, 26 February 2010.

together with the multiplicity of recordings of hymn tunes and church works that sometimes escape conventional current trade discographies.

To music lovers in the UK, John Ireland was a familiar composer in his lifetime. Yet that was for the relatively small proportion of his output which was frequently played on the radio and at orchestral concerts, and in songs or piano recitals. A few of his easier piano pieces regularly appeared in graded piano examinations. Yet the majority of his music was rarely heard and until it was recorded few could have made an authoritative overview of his music and his achievement as a composer. It seems strange now to realise that when Richard Itter started his Lyrita Recorded Edition in 1959 and opted to record a complete cycle of John Ireland's piano music with Alan Rowlands[7] as the pianist, he was making an unknown repertoire available to the wider musical public. Later, as an early project for the John Ireland Trust, he moved on to the orchestral music with Sir Adrian Boult conducting, to the chamber music and still later to the complete songs. It is only now when these have all been reissued, the piano music and songs in boxed sets, that one can appreciate the breadth of his achievement, in recognition of which I have dedicated the *Companion* to him.

In viewing Ireland's music in the context of twentieth-century music there was once a temptation to consider it as old-fashioned, doubtless how it was seen by the new musical management at the BBC in the early 1960s. A limited repertoire of orchestral works, including the Piano Concerto, had been regularly heard every summer at the Proms, and the music had what appears to have been an enthusiastic following by a wide audience. Then suddenly Ireland's orchestral music disappeared from the Proms and almost as quickly vanished from the regular concert repertoire both in London and the provinces. It would only be on records – initially LPs, later CDs – that the music would be re-evaluated by a new and younger audience, and, in the case of the piano music and the songs, by a new generation of talented performers.

So here, in what I hope is one convenient volume, I offer a range of newly written chapters, the fruits of varied and wide-spanning research. I have also been fortunate in gathering a number of previously unpublished texts often by those who knew him, now printed for the first time. In support of these accounts of the music and the times in which Ireland lived, I have included reprints of valuable articles which have perhaps not been as easily and conveniently available as they should have been.

Acknowledgements

This book is the culmination of research which has gradually accumulated over many years, running alongside my interest in Arnold Bax. Many have contributed during this time and I have to record my deep-felt thanks to those many helpers whose knowledge and insights informed both interests, not forgetting those who

---

[7] Alan Rowlands' first recording sessions with Lyrita took place on 12 and 14 January 1959. Subsequently he was the pianist for the Lyrita collected *John Ireland Songs*, recorded at St Johns Smith Square on 8–10 August 1972 and in July and November 1973.

assisted in the earlier stages. All authors and editors of a book such as this have a debt owing to previous performers, researchers and journalist running back decades. My personal debt in exploring the music of John Ireland started with those who had known him in his prime, and I am particularly grateful to Felix Aprahamian, Alan Bush, Geoffrey Bush, David Dunhill, Charlie Markes, Angus Morrison, Freda Swain, Father Kenneth Thompson and Patrick Piggott, all of whom have now passed on, for their time, memories and hospitality. Visiting them all was to catch the last fading vision of a world now lost.

In addition to the John Ireland Trust and my own ever-expanding collection, the majority of research for this book was carried in the British Library, the Central Music Library collection (at Westminster Music Library), the Royal College of Music (with thanks to Peter Horton and Mariarosaria Canzonieri) and the BBC Written Archives at Caversham. Most of the literary sources were found in the ever-reliable London Library, what would we do without it! I am grateful to Nicholas Bell at the British Library for many kindnesses and for explaining that letters here footnoted as being in the British Library collection, though without additional manuscript numbers, are from 'Music Deposit 2005/31', eight boxes of correspondence, press cuttings, concert programmes and other papers of and relating to the composer and pianist John Ireland. They are expected to be catalogued formally in due course.

I have to thank many copyright owners for permission to reproduce material quoted here. The largest single collection of such items is that owned by the John Ireland estate, and I thank Bruce Phillips representing the John Ireland Trust who commissioned the book for providing many of these and giving permission for their reproduction. I have to thank authors and publishers for articles previously published elsewhere, and these include Colin Scott-Sutherland for his two articles revised by him for their appearance here (with thanks to Triad Press for Chapter 1, which first appeared as a pamphlet, and the Friends of Arthur Machen for Chapter 10, which first appeared in their journal *Faunus*). Murray Schafer's interview with John Ireland first appeared in his book *British Composers in Interview* and is reproduced by permission of Faber & Faber and the John Ireland Trust, who now own the original recorded interview on which it is based. Julie Deller's article, Chapter 8, originally appeared in the journal *Bygone Kent* and is reproduced with due acknowledgement to author and publisher. The late George Dannatt had planned to write his own biography of Ireland, unhappily never completed; his article on Charles Markes, first published in the British Music Society's journal *British Music*, is reproduced with grateful thanks to the Society, the editor Jonathan Woolf and the estate of George Dannatt. The article by Eric Parkin first appeared in the now no-longer published journal *Music and Musicians* and is reproduced with acknowledgement to its publisher and author.

For the various reminiscences of Ireland I am grateful to Jennifer Johnson (for permission to use her father Richard Arnell's account of Ireland), Oscar Rook representing the Trustees of the Arabesque Trust (for my interview with Felix Aprahamian), Julie Bush (for her late husband, Geoffrey Bush's account of Ireland first published by the late John Bishop of Thames Publishing), Fiona Searle (for permission to use an extract from her late husband's autobiography *Quadrille With a Raven*, the full text of which is also available via the Internet), Rachel O'Higgins (for permission to reproduce my interview with her father Alan Bush and for his account of Ireland), Chris Grogan representing the Britten–Pears Foundation (for all material by Benjamin Britten, specifically extracts from Britten's diaries formerly published in *Journeying Boy: The Diaries of the Young Benjamin Britten, 1928–1938* selected and edited by John Evans, Faber & Faber, 2009, and letters from the Britten–Pears Library), Philip Roberts for material relating to the Chelsea Arts Club, Eric Wickham-Ruffle, Executor of the Estate of Freda Swain (for letters by Freda Swain, and for allowing me to photograph and reproduce the painting of Freda Swain which now hangs in his house at Wendover), and the residual estates of Charles Markes and Kenneth Thompson for their accounts of Ireland.

Dr Fiona Richards joins me in recording her thanks to Kenneth Adie for permission to use all material relating to Helen Perkin. The composer E. J. Moeran's accounts of Ireland were made available by the inheritor of the Moeran Estate, the late Walter Knott. Liz Cowlin gave the BBC Worldwide's permission to reproduce C. B. Rees article 'Ireland the Man' from *Radio Times*, and Antony Bye for articles from past issues of the *Musical Times*. An article from *The Times* newspaper appears with acknowledgement to Times Newspapers, and last, and most importantly, Trish Hayes at Caversham, whose assistance with my research in the BBC Archives cannot be overestimated, gave permission on behalf of the BBC Written Archives Centre for all material from BBC Archives. I would also like to record my thanks to Stephen Laing, Curator of the Heritage Motor Centre at Gaydon, for advice on Talbot cars in the 1920s. Thanks also to Michael Bryant who advised on all matters to do with clarinets, to Malcolm Walker for the dating of 78 rpm recordings, and Pamela Blevins who supplied the review by Marion Scott.

The majority of the poems quoted are by authors now out of copyright, but for Aldous Huxley's poem 'The Trellis' we wish to thank the Estate of Huxley, and the Estate of John Masefield for an extract from his poem 'Sea Fever'. Quotations from the novels of Arthur Machen are reprinted with acknowledgement to the Machen Estate. The three quotations from the works of Jocelyn Brooke (*The Dog at Clambercrown* © Jocelyn Brooke 1955; an article from *The London Magazine* © Jocelyn Brooke 1965; *The Birth of a Legend* © Jocelyn Brooke 1964) are reprinted by permission of A. M. Heath & Co. Ltd.

I am grateful to my publisher the Boydell Press for agreeing to several of my authors using a large number of musical examples, and for permissions for them to quote short extracts from the music I have to record our thanks. I am grateful to Andy Chan and James Egglestone at Boosey & Hawkes for their assistance and sympathetic consideration of Boosey & Hawkes copyrights, mainly but not exclusively of music by Ireland, as follows (*The Cost* © Copyright 1917 by Winthrop Rogers Ltd. Reproduced by permission of Boosey & Hawkes Music Publishers Ltd.; *Ex Ore Innocentium* © Copyright 1944 by Boosey & Co. Ltd. Reproduced by permission of Boosey & Hawkes Music Publishers Ltd.; *Fantasy Sonata in E Flat* © Copyright 1945 by Hawkes & Son (London) Ltd. Reproduced by permission of Boosey & Hawkes Music Publishers Ltd.; *Fire of Spring* © Copyright 1918 by Winthrop Rogers Ltd. Reproduced by permission of Boosey & Hawkes Music Publishers Ltd.; *The Holy Boy* © Copyright 1918 by Winthrop Rogers Ltd.

Reproduced by permission of Boosey & Hawkes Music Publishers Ltd.; *A London Overture* © Copyright 1937 by Hawkes & Son (London) Ltd.; Reproduced by permission of Boosey & Hawkes Music Publishers Ltd.; *Rhapsody* © Copyright 1917 by Winthrop Rogers Ltd. Reproduced by permission of Boosey & Hawkes Music Publishers Ltd.; *Sarnia* © Copyright 1941 by Hawkes & Son (London) Ltd. Reproduced by permission of Boosey & Hawkes Music Publishers Ltd.; *These Things Shall Be* © Copyright 1937 by Hawkes & Son (London) Ltd. Reproduced by permission of Boosey & Hawkes Music Publishers Ltd.; *The Undertone* © Copyright 1918 by Winthrop Rogers Ltd. Reproduced by permission of Boosey & Hawkes Music Publishers Ltd.; *Violin Sonata No. 2* © Copyright 1917 by Winthrop Rogers Ltd. Reproduced by permission of Boosey & Hawkes Music Publishers Ltd. And the following non-Ireland extracts: *Peter Grimes* (Britten) © Copyright 1944 by Boosey & Hawkes Music Publishers Ltd. Reproduced by permission of Boosey & Hawkes Music Publishers Ltd.; *Elektra* (Richard Strauss) © Copyright 1908, 1909 by Adolph Furstner. U. S. copyright renewed. Copyright assigned 1943 to Hawkes & Son (London) Ltd., a Boosey & Hawkes company, for the world excluding Germany, Italy, Portugal and the former territories of the USSR (excluding Estonia, Latvia and Lithuania) Reproduced by permission of Boosey & Hawkes Music Publishers Ltd.; *Salome* (Strauss) © Copyright 1905 by Adolph Furstner. U. S. copyright renewed. Copyright assigned 1943 to Hawkes & Son (London) Ltd., a Boosey & Hawkes company, for the world excluding Germany, Italy, Portugal and the former territories of the USSR (excluding Estonia, Latvia and Lithuania) Reproduced by permission of Boosey & Hawkes Music Publishers Ltd.; *Petrouchka* (Stravinsky) © Copyright 1912 by Hawkes & Son (London) Ltd. Revised version: © Copyright 1948 by Hawkes & Son (London) Ltd. U. S. copyright renewed. Reproduced by permission of Boosey & Hawkes Music Publishers Ltd.; *The Rite of Spring* (Stravinsky) © Copyright 1912, 1921 by Hawkes & Son (London) Ltd. Reproduced by permission of Boosey & Hawkes Music Publishers Ltd.

For quotations from the published copyright music of John Ireland from other music publishers we have to thank: Stainer & Bell (incorporating the former catalogues of Augener, Goodwin & Tabb, Joseph Williams and Galliard), J. & W. Chester, Novello, Oxford University Press, Schott and Feldman (now EMI Music Publishing) and Schirmer. To Stainer & Bell for extracts from Ireland's Piano Sonata, *Sea Fever*, *Month's Mind*, *London Pieces*, *The Land of Lost Content*, *The Forgotten Rite*, *Satyricon*, *Bergomask*, *Decorations*, *The Trellis*, *My True Love Hath My Heart*, *The Darkened Valley*, *Equinox*, Cello Sonata, *Vexilla Regis*, *Fraternity*, *Capriccio*, and Piano Trio No. 2. To J. & W. Chester for Ireland's Piano Concerto and *The Adoration*; to Novello for 'Response' and 'Sanctus', *Vesper Hymn* and the *Elegiac Romance* and *Sursum Corda* for organ; to Schott for the *Legend* and *February's Child*; to Schirmer for 'Youth's Spring-Tribute' and 'Spleen' from *Marigold*; to Warner Chappell for *Merry Andrew* originally published by Ascherberg, Hopwood & Crew, EMI Music for the *Meditation on John Keble's Rogationtide Hymn* originally published by Feldman and here quoted from Robert Gower's Album published by Stainer & Bell; and finally Oxford University Press for *We'll to the Woods No More*, *In My Sage Moments*, the Sonatina for piano and *We'll to the Woods No More*, and also to Oxford University Press for brief incipits from Vaughan Williams's *Flos Campi* and Walton's *Portsmouth Point* and *Belshazzar's*

Feast. Ireland's setting of Psalm 42 is copyright the John Ireland Estate, a page of which is reproduced by permission of the John Ireland Trust. It was wonderful to attend the Dutton Epoch recording of Martin Yates' orchestration of *Sarnia* with the Royal Scottish National Orchestra, and I thank Martin, the John Ireland Trust and Boosey & Hawkes for the page from the full score of 'Le Catioroc'.

A feature of this book is the illustrations, and I have to thanks Bruce Phillips and the John Ireland Trust for making available a rich selection relating to Ireland. I have supplemented these with a variety of my own photographs of places and documents. Other permissions not already mentioned are due to: Julie Deller and Pat Moody in respect of illustrations from Deal, the estate of Juliet Pannett for three drawings, Fiona Richards for the studio photo of Helen Perkin, the BBC for two photographs and handbills from Written Archive Centre files, Ron Bleach of the Bantock Society for a group photograph from 1942, Tully Potter for illustrations relating to Antoni Sala and Albert Sammons, Alan Rowlands and Colin Scott-Sutherland for one photograph each and Central Music Library Ltd and Westminster Public Libraries for allowing me to photograph the painting of Edwin Evans by Mary Eristoff which hangs on the stairs to the library. Nigel Konstam's bust of John Ireland was photographed by me through the good offices of Bruce Phillips, the photograph reproduced with the sculptor's enthusiastic permission. Thanks to Bruce Phillips and Valerie Langfield for assistance in the identification of the artist of the frontispiece as being Jane Emmet de Glehn (1873–1961), and I have to thank Valerie, Carol Tee and David Messum for facilitating copyright permission by David Messum, London W1, to use it here.

Finally, I am particularly grateful to David Roberts who has given such elegant effect to my concept by designing and setting this book, as he did my earlier book on Bax; and to Jenny Roberts who prepared and formatted the musical examples, and to all my contributors for their enthusiasm, expertise and patience. I must also thank all at Boydell & Brewer for their helpful and welcoming treatment of my proposal. Finally, my thanks and love to my daughter Tamsin for much scanning and typing of documents, and to my wife, Susan, for her patience, forensic proof reading and long hours spent compiling the index using the Macrex programme.

LEWIS FOREMAN
Rickmansworth
September 2011

Chronology

1879 (13 August) John Nicholson Ireland born at 'Inglewood', Bowdon (described on the birth certificate as Dunham Massey)

1893 (January) Enrols at Leeds Grammar School

1893 (28 September) Enrols at Royal College of Music as a student

1893 (4 October) Death of mother, Ann Elizabeth Ireland, at 31 Mauldeth Road, Fallowfield, Withington

1894 (7 December) Death of father, Alexander Ireland, at 31 Mauldeth Road, Fallowfield, Withington

1895 (2 February) Attends Saturday Popular Concert at St James's Hall and hears Mühlfeld play the new Brahms Clarinet Quintet

1896 (Easter) Awarded ARCM

1897 (3 May) Becomes a scholar and composition pupil of Stanford at the Royal College of Music

1898 (January) Successful at Royal College of Organists Fellowship examination (FRCO)

1899 *Vexilla Regis* performed at Holy Trinity, Sloane Street

1900 (8 March) Performs his *Sea Idyll* at a RCM concert at Alexandra House

1901 (21 March) College Concert at Alexandra House opens with *Symphonic Prelude* (later known as *Tritons*)

1901 (30 March) Leaves the Royal College of Music

1902 Communion Service in A♭ major published by Houghton & Co.

1904 (July) Appointed organist and choirmaster at St Luke's Church, Chelsea

1904 Schott publish Ireland's viola and piano reduction of Cecil Forsyth's Viola Concerto

1904 Moves to 54 Elm Park Mansions, Park Walk and remains until 1915

1906 Purchases *The House of Souls* by Arthur Machen from station bookstall

1908 (28 February) Completes setting of Psalm 42 for his Durham Mus.Bac., and submits it with a declaration dated 21 March 1908

1909 (26 January) Phantasie Trio [no. 1] first performed by the London Trio at Steinway Hall

1911 Publishes ballads 'Billie Bowline'; 'Love's Window' and 'Hillo, My Bonny' over the pseudonym Turlay Royce. ['Porto Rico' followed in 1913.]

1912 (6 January) Ballads *Hope the Hornblower* and *Here's to the Ships* sung at Royal Albert Hall by Ivan Foster and Harry Dearth (baritones)

1914 (9 June) Plays the piano in first performance of his Clarinet Trio in D at Steinway Hall

1914 (4 August) War declared

1915 Purchases 'The Studio' at 14A Gunter Grove, Chelsea

1915 (July) First account of John Ireland as a composer published in *Monthly Musical Record*

1916 (January) Introduction of conscription (Ireland rejected)

1916 Purchases a Morgan three-wheeler car

1917 (6 March) Violin Sonata no. 2 played by Albert Sammons and William Murdoch at the Aeolian Hall, Bond Street; Ireland 'woke up famous'

1917 (12 June 1917) First performance of Piano Trio no. 2 at Wigmore Hall (Albert Sammons (violin), Felix Salmond (cello) and John Ireland) and *The Heart's Desire* (Housman), *The Cost* (Cooper) and *The Soldier* (Brooke) sung by Muriel Foster with John Ireland (piano)

1918 (7 June) Gives first performance of *Four Preludes*, 'Chelsea Reach' and 'Ragamuffin' at Aeolian Hall

1918 (11 November) Armistice announced – end of the First World War

1922 Appointed as temporary professor at the RCM

1922 (summer) Visits Norfolk with Arthur Miller and E. J. Moeran

1923 Appointed Professor of Composition at the RCM

1923 Acquires a Talbot 8/18 car, holidays in Dorset in it with Arthur Miller

1924 (4 April) First performance of Cello Sonata (Beatrice Harrison (cello) and Evlyn Howard-Jones (piano) at Aeolian Hall

1926 Writes *Five Poems by Thomas Hardy*

1926 (1 May) General Strike starts

1926 (29 October) Resigns from St Luke's Church as organist and choirmaster

1926 (17 December) Marries Dorothy Phillips at Chelsea Register Office

1927 (February) Writes *We'll to the Woods No More* dedicated 'To Arthur: in memory of the darkest days'

1927 (December) Ireland's first report on Helen Perkin as his composition pupil

1928 (19 April) Broadcasts his new Sonatina

1928 (19 September) Dissolution of his marriage to Dorothy Phillips is made absolute on grounds of non-consummation

1928 (25 October) Records his Cello Sonata with Antoni Sala for Columbia

1929 (7 April) Plays his Sonatina at the 7th ISCM Festival in Geneva

1930 (4 April) Helen Perkin is soloist in Prokofiev's Third Piano Concerto at the RCM, Malcolm Sargent conducting

1930 (September) Benjamin Britten becomes Ireland's composition pupil

1930 (2 October) First performance of Piano Concerto at Queen's Hall Promenade Concert with Helen Perkin as soloist

1930 (7 October) Records Violin Sonata no. 2 with Albert Sammons for Columbia but recording remains unissued until 1999

1932 (July) Hon D.Mus. from University of Durham

1933 (4 January) Crisis in relationship with pupil Benjamin Britten; writes apologetic letter to Britten's father

1934 (12 January) Helen Perkin soloist in first performance of the *Legend* for piano and orchestra at Queen's Hall

1935 (21 August) First meets Elizabeth Needham (1899–1979) who, until Mrs Kirby came on the scene, became a self-appointed general factotum in looking after his affairs

1936 (June) Sudden and unexpected death of Ireland's friend Percy Bentham (obituary in *The Times*, 19 June 1936, p. 11)

1936 (1 September) Rubinstein plays the Ireland Piano Concerto at the Proms at Queen's Hall

1936 (23 September) *A London Overture* first performed at Queen's Hall Promenade Concert

1937 (12 May) Coronation of King George VI and Queen Elizabeth

1937 (13 May) First (broadcast) performance of *These Things Shall Be* commissioned to celebrate the Coronation

1937 (27 August) Conducts *The Forgotten Rite* and *Mai-Dun* in the same concert at the Proms

1937 (1 December) First concert performance of *These Things Shall Be* at Queen's Hall

1939 (5 April) The third concert of the Festival of Music for the People at Queen's Hall conducted by Constant Lambert; Ireland's *These Things Shall Be* sung alongside the first performance of Britten's *A Ballad of Heroes*

1939 (3 July) With John Longmire moves to Guernsey

1939 (3 September) Outbreak of Second World War

1940 (22 June) Evacuated from Guernsey on SS *Antwerp*, the last boat to leave

1940 (23 June) Lands at Weymouth

1940 (30 June) Germany invades Guernsey

1940 (July) Moves to the house of Mrs Alice Bush, Alan Bush's mother, 'Clifton', Loom Lane, Radlett, Herts

1940 (August) Moves to Alan Bush's house, 25 Christchurch Crescent, Radlett, Herts

1940 (Autumn) Moves to 15 Calthorpe Road, Banbury, Oxon

1941 (night of 10 May) Destruction of Queen's Hall by enemy bombing

1942 (14 January) Houldsworth Hall, Manchester: Eileen Joyce/ Hallé Orchestra/ Leslie Heward record Piano Concerto

1942 (27 June) Ireland's *Epic March* opens the Proms at the Royal Albert Hall

1942 (July) Moves to Little Sampford Rectory, Saffron Walden, Essex

1942 (26 August) As part of wartime cultural diplomacy, Ireland, Bantock, Bax and Britten deliver a letter to the wife of the Soviet Ambassador sending greetings from British composers to their Soviet counterparts (See plate 50.)

1942 (Autumn) Joins BBC Reading panel and remains on it until the autumn of 1944

1943 (31 July) First Prom performance of *These Things Shall Be* at the Royal Albert Hall

1944 (29 January) First performance of Fantasy Sonata at Wigmore Hall by Frederick Thurston and Kendall Taylor (Ireland was the accompanist for Thurston's subsequent broadcast on 6 February)

1944 (11 April) Philharmonic Hall, Liverpool: Liverpool Philharmonic Orchestra/ Sargent record *A London Overture*

1945 (February) Boosey & Hawkes end their publishing contract with Ireland on the grounds he cannot produce enough new works to justify a retainer

1945 (8 May) VE Day

1945 Moves to the White House, Great Sampford, Saffron Walden, Essex

1945 (22 & 23 November) Records First Violin Sonata at Hampstead for Decca with Frederick Grinke (violin)

1946 (March–April) Writes music for the film *The Overlanders* (opens London October)

1947 Norah Kirby becomes Ireland's personal assistant and companion

1948 (1 May) Abbey Road, Studio 1: Hallé Orch/ Barbirolli record *These Things Shall Be*

1949 (31 May) Abbey Road, Studio 1: Hallé Orch/ Barbirolli record *The Forgotten Rite* and *Mai-Dun*

1949 (10 September) BBC promotes a '70th birthday Prom' [issued on CD on LPO 0041]

1951 (4 May) Wigmore Hall Ireland concert, Ireland accompanying Peter Pears, broadcast by the BBC

1953 (2 June) Coronation of Queen Elizabeth II; issue of recording of *A Garland for the Queen* by CUMS/Boris Ord

1953 (October) Moves into Rock Mill, Washington, W. Sussex

1954 (13 August) 75th birthday concert at Royal Albert Hall

1959 (12 & 14 January) Alan Rowlands records Ireland piano music for Lyrita

1959 (14 August) 80th birthday concert at Royal Albert Hall

1960 (25 March) Modern revival of the Sextet at the Arts Council Drawing Room, Ireland [and the Editor] present

1961 (7 October) 82nd birthday concert at Arts Council Drawing Room

1962 (12 June) Dies at Rock Mill

1962 (16 June) Funeral and burial at the Church of St Mary the Virgin, Shipley, West Sussex celebrated by the Rev. Kenneth Thompson

PART I

The Man, his Circle and his Times

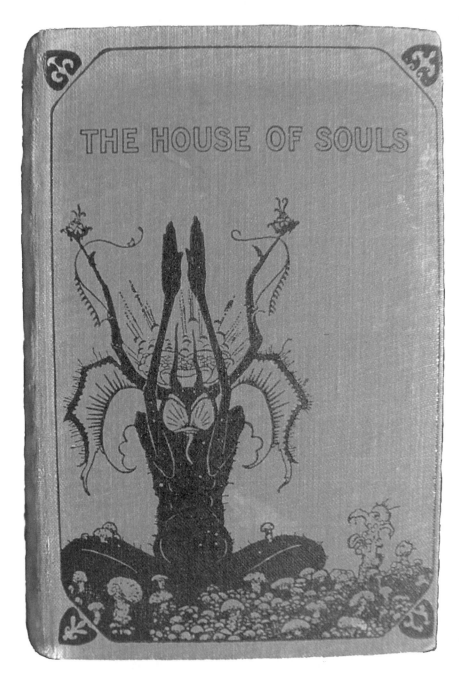

Fig. 1 The cover design blocked on the front board of the first edition
of Arthur Machen's *The House of Souls*, 1906

CHAPTER 1

John Ireland: A Life in Music

Colin Scott-Sutherland

The one adventure of the holidays was the visit to the Roman fort, to that
fantastic hill about whose steep bastions and haggard oaks he had seen the
flames of sunset writhing nearly three years before. Ever since that Saturday
evening in January the lonely valley had been a desirable place to him; he
had watched the green battlements in summer and winter weather, had
seen the heaped mounds rising dimly amidst the drifting rain, had marked
the violent height swim up from the ice-white mists of summer evenings:
had watched the fairy bulwarks glimmer and vanish in hovering April
twilight.

Arthur Machen, The Hill of Dreams

JOHN Nicholson Ireland was born at Bowdon, Cheshire, on 13 August 1879. His
father, Alexander Ireland from Fife, was seventy years old when John was born
and his second wife, Anne Elizabeth Nicholson from Cumberland, some thirty
years younger and of delicate health. John was the youngest by seven years of a
family of five children and, being of a sensitive disposition, suffered considerably.
(Ireland was reticent about his life and especially about his childhood. Nevertheless, enough can be gauged of the effect that these early years may have had upon
his life from those recollections he confided to his friends Mrs Norah Kirby and
John Longmire.)

In spite of the difficulties of his early childhood the young Ireland, encouraged
by his mother, began to show a love of poetry and a musical talent. And perhaps
because of these difficulties he developed, at first inwardly, a sensitive taste in literature and a highly aware fastidious critical judgment that were to mark the first
important years of his development as a composer. By birth he had inherited a
shyness and reserve that betokened his northerly descent, traits that were sharpened by the unhappier experiences in childhood. Perhaps also because of this he
must often have sought his own company and the kind of solace that can only be
found in nature.

After preliminary education at a dame school, and at Leeds Grammar School,
Ireland came to London to begin organ study with Sir Walter Parratt, and piano
with Frederic Cliffe in September 1893. The break with his home life in Bowdon
was to be a permanent one, for within a year both Alexander Ireland and his wife
died. The young boy was left in the care of a succession of landladies who ministered, albeit kindly, to his comforts. On his parents' death Ireland was left comfortably off, but since the control of his financial affairs was placed in the hands of

conservatively minded guardians[1] he was obliged, for the small extravagances of student life, to take jobs such as accompanying at smoking concerts and in restaurants.

His studies therefore proved a discipline in which he was not untutored. After the first performance of an early string quartet he was allowed to begin composition lessons with Stanford, and took a small flat nearer the centre of London.

In 1896 he was appointed assistant to Sir W. G. Alcock at the organ of Holy Trinity, Sloane Street, and later became organist of St Jude's, and of St Luke's, the parish church of Chelsea, where he remained from 1904 until 1926. Chelsea was a richly formative influence with something of the artistic atmosphere of Paris – its embankment, its parks, taverns and accessible company amongst fellow artists and students – the Chelsea of Whistler, one of the nerve centres of London's cultural life, the home of the visual arts and a district which presented many colourful and aesthetic experiences to the observant eye.

The habit of fastidiousness dictated his first compositional efforts and, severely self-critical, he sought simplicity and sincerity in equal measure. The Phantasie Trio (1906) was published in 1908 and was the first representative work exposed to the public. The first Violin Sonata successfully carried off the coveted Cobbett prize (amongst 134 entries) in 1909. In those early chamber works Ireland's growing individuality gradually asserted itself against the strong influence of Brahms, and between these works, and the *Rhapsody* for piano (1915), two events had occurred that were to have far-reaching consequences for his development. The first, and perhaps most important, was in 1906, when Ireland chanced, on a station bookstall, on the writings of Arthur Machen. In *The Hill of Dreams* and *The Great God Pan* Ireland immersed himself deeply, finding himself drawn to this writer who seemed conscious of, even in contact with, something supernatural. The remote peace of the countryside that had for so long attracted him took on now a mysterious and sinister significance. Machen's writing awakened some long-dormant race memory within Ireland that drove him again and again, restlessly, from the city to those districts where this feeling was strongest – to the Sussex Downs, Stonehenge, Maiden Castle and to the Channel Isles. So captivated was Ireland with the Channel Isles that he later accepted the post of organist at the church of St Stephen's, making the islands his home for periods of time and estab-lishing particularly a deep affinity with a rather forbidding part of the Guernsey coast at Rocquaine. Into the music that was taking shape in his mind, Ireland

---

[1] EDITOR'S NOTE: Alexander Ireland appointed as executors and trustees his brother Edmund Kell Blyth, solicitor; Henry Dunckley of Manchester; and his nephew Charles Frederick Tolmé Blyth writing 'I desire that the gift in favour of each of my sons Walter Alleyne and John Nicholson ... shall be subject to the following provision namely that if at any time when the division of my estate comes into operation my trustees should be of opinion that it is undesirable that such son should have sole control of his share then I direct my trustees to hold the share of such son Upon trust for him for life or until he shall do or suffer some act whereby the same would but for this condition be received by some other person ... subject to such conditions and restrictions as my trustees shall determine ...' His inheritance was thus controlled by third parties for years.

infused this new and powerful feeling. By November 1913 he had completed *The Forgotten Rite* for orchestra and the set of piano pieces *Decorations*. The tragic days of 1914 and their aftermath left no less an impression on the composer, and an indelible mark on the music, most apparent in the Second Trio, and in the Second Violin Sonata. At the latter's first performance (by Albert Sammons and William Murdoch) Ireland was widely acclaimed – no chance success, for at a performance of this same work at Kilkenny so enthusiastic was its reception the performance had to be repeated. Ireland had overnight become one of the foremost composers of the day. And with the success of the Sonata – enshrining a feeling both patriotic and serene, characterised by that fervour associated with the Georgian poets – Ireland's career was assured.

In 1923 he was established on the staff of his old College, numbering amongst his pupils in his teaching career Britten, Alan Bush, E. J. Moeran and Richard Arnell. Though he retained his house at 14 Gunter Grove, Chelsea, until 1953, he also lived in various parts of the South of England – at Deal, Radlett, Banbury and the Sampfords – with continual yearning for the Channel Islands, where he made his home for short periods, finally disturbed by the war in 1940. Although he returned in 1947, domestic reasons and worsening health prevented his settling there, and in 1953 he gave up the Chelsea house and moved to Sussex, where, he bought Rock Mill, a converted windmill on the Downs, where he lived until his death in 1962.

His life outwardly at least was uneventful, with much of his time spent in composition and teaching. A disastrous marriage and an unsatisfactory relationship with a young pupil[2] marred the withdrawn tenor of his domestic life. John Longmire's monograph[3] reveals a strange, complex, sensitive and sometimes unapproachable character – distrustful of human relationships, apprehensive of pain and rebuff – yet loved by those who were permitted to know his shy personality. Few honours earned him headlines – and only in his music can we discern the inmost thoughts, the deepest experiences that brought him both joy and sorrow.

John Ireland's formative years belong to the close of a century – and to the close of an era. The roots of his creative impulses run deep, through the cultural top-soil of the present day, through the disturbed strata of world wars, into that ground that nourished the seeds of the renaissance of an expressly English nationalist spirit in music. Of this renaissance John Ireland's work is an essential part, having something of its prophetic and of its retrospective character and probing as deeply to the fount of that nationalism as the music of any other British composer.

Renaissance is an apt context. For no other music expresses in quite such a striking way the idea of dormant yet vibrant life that, as in its natural counterpart of the recurring seasons, has strength, freshness, and harmony of colour in its reburgeoning and flowering. In 1913 Ireland set, in *Youth's Spring-Tribute*, these words of D. G. Rossetti:

[2] See pp. 46–7.

[3] John Longmire, *Portrait of a Friend* (London: John Baker, 1969).

On these debatable borders of the year
  Spring's foot half falters: scarce she yet may know
  The leafless blackthorn-blossom from the snow:
And through her bowers the wind's way still is clear.[4]

And in 1915 he expressed this urge in *Fire of Spring*, a piece whose exuberance speaks of the natural energy released by the earth in response to the call of the sun and the awakening year:

Ex. 1 Ireland, *Fire of Spring*

Ireland's music belongs almost exclusiveoly in spirit to those years immediately preceding the war of 1914–18. And to this period also (in spite of his self-confessed interest in the sounds of such music as Webern – and his enthusiasm for the motor car, which he first owned in 1916) belongs the figure of the composer himself. In the converted mill on the chalk downs of Sussex where he made his last home, the walls were hung with delicate Chelsea scenes and Japanese prints – and his bookshelves with Machen, Hardy, Housman and *The Yellow Book*. Of this period and atmosphere his music is a part.[5] The acclaim accorded him in later years, which he appeared alternately to court and distrust, is due less perhaps to his musical stature in this latter half of a fast-moving century than to the great personal esteem, even affection, in which his music has always been held by those who know it well.

Ireland's popularity is paradoxical. If the music publisher were to do for music what the verse anthologist has done for the poetry reader, Ireland's name above all

---

[4] 'Youth's Spring-Tribute' (*The House of Life* – Sonnet XIV).

[5] Ireland in fact is almost completely 'Georgian' – and the rather nebulous literary movement for which Edward Marsh coined the title displays far more important and strong characteristics than are derived from the merely historical. It was a brief movement, intensely nationalist, wholly democratic in mood, yet at the same time possessed of a sensitivity that marked a high achievement in our artistic expression.

others should be conspicuous. For just as such lines as 'Everyone suddenly burst out singing', 'I have come to the borders of sleep' and 'I must go down to the seas again' ring with a magic in no way dimmed by familiarity, so do the most characteristic bars of Ireland's music evoke the recognition that accompanies every significant and valued artistic experience. The paradox is to some extent explained by the fact that much of Ireland's public are perhaps amateur musicians not in a position to make their allegiance widely known except by the continuous traffic in the sales ledgers of his publishers.

Ireland's songs reinforce the poetic analogy. His selectivity in choice of texts might itself constitute the basis of an anthology of some of the finest, though not always the best known, English poetry. His reaction to poets such as Masefield or Rossetti was immediate and spontaneous. There are deeper parallels – with Hardy (whose understanding of the harsh and beautiful reality of life aroused sympathetic echoes in Ireland) – and with Housman (whose poetry fuelled much of the English revival in music). If we may trace the inner melancholy of Ireland's music through these poets we are closer to Ireland the nature mystic in the verse of Edward Thomas (though Ireland set none of his lines). Edward Thomas's 'delicate yet vigorous intuition', of which Walter de la Mare speaks,[6] closely parallels that of Ireland. So also does Thomas's fastidious use of language, accenting by reticent understatement what was most potent in the mood encountered in his 'daily, almost common experience'.[7] Both were supremely aware of the moods of nature. Both were able to express in down-to-earth language the characteristics of these moods and their own reaction to them. Both were aware of the promise of renewing Spring, the green pulse held in Winter's thrall. And both were conscious of the melancholy tints which the retrospective memory infused into that promise.

The two most vital characteristics of John Ireland's music are the essential humanity of its appeal, and a less common nature mysticism whose fires were fed by the early discovery of the writings of Arthur Machen and the composer's sojournings in the Channel Isles and on lonely heights peopled by the wind-scourged phantoms of our earliest pre-history. In the long light of early Spring, fleeting wraiths of some distant past are awakened which find expression in the orchestral works *The Forgotten Rite* and *Mai-Dun*. This 'druidical' element is Ireland's most recognisable characteristic. Listen to those awe-filled chords in the D minor Violin Sonata, with their Dorian colour (Ex. 2). And to the portentous clamour of the Piano Sonata, the last movement of which is haunted by the woodland shadows of Chanctonbury whose green crown raises itself beyond the windows of Rock Mill, an eternal reminder of those depths in Ireland's work (Ex. 3).

At the other end of the scale, Ireland's down-to-earth vein of musical imagery revels in the robust and unaffected joyousness of *On a Birthday Morning*, *Ragamuffin* and *Merry Andrew* – a rumbustious catalogue of truly vulgar[8] merriment that is the nearest thing to unrestrained emotion in his work. And, like many

---

[6] Introduction to *Collected Poems* (London: Faber & Faber, 1949).

[7] Ibid.

[8] 'Vulgar' is used strictly in the literal and derivative sense as of the common people and of humanity.

Ex. 2 Ireland, Violin Sonata in D minor

composers of his generation, Ireland had a vein of what comes dangerously near to sentimentality, closely akin to that of the drawing-room ballad – that directness of emotional appeal that marks much of MacDowell and other contemporary popular composers. This ballad influence of the popular song is near the surface in much of Ireland's music (Ex. 4).

His music is at the same time often uncompromising, with a forthrightness that, in such pieces as the *Rhapsody* and *Ballade*, approaches downright harshness, especially in moments of climactic stress. Nor is the resolution of that stress an easily found release. Unlike those of Bax, Ireland's emotional climaxes never lose control or become over-passionate. While Bax's disintegrate in chromatic star bursts, Ireland's descents from this peak are always strictly controlled. His harmonic luxuriance has none of the cloying qualities of late romanticism. It is masculine and vigorous and leads to passages of almost gratuitous harshness that often just escape ugliness. This is the very antithesis of sentiment, chromatic

Ex. 3 Ireland, Piano Sonata

Ex. 4 Ireland, Violin Sonata no. 2

ruggedness impelling the ear to seek ultimate resolution. This harshness, however, does not always lead to obvious resolution but frequently poses new problems of its own. In the centre section of *Aubade* – and elsewhere – it is sometimes made to sound an aggressive triumph.

His impulses are lyrical – yet it is a lyricism influenced by penetrating sadness, underlined by the sharp tang of modal dissonance (not only in obvious places such as *The Holy Boy* and 'The Boy Bishop' but in the major/minor clashes of *Spring will not Wait* and elsewhere). The A♯ (Lydian fourth in the key of E) which decorates the final bars of the Piano Sonata, added, according to the composer, to make it sound more festive, seems only to reinforce the rising minor third and add that tinge of melancholy that is so characteristic. In *Fire of Spring* after intense chromaticism we come suddenly across a common-chord resolution (bars 10–12) whose translucency, much decorated with sparkles of light, suggests the kind of impressionism that derives from Grieg. And the whole-tone scale that imparts an aerial wildness to *Amberley Wild Brooks* also imparts the dark melancholy to *Spring will not Wait*. The cast of his melodic and harmonic language is basically diatonic and takes its colouring, often rough with the mannered speech of dialect, from those added notes and inflexions, used in much the same way as that of the English water colourists, who used tints to enrich emotively their fundamentally classical draughtsmanship. From these inflexions many recognisable passages derive.

Much of the apparent chromaticism is decorative, colouring rather than obscuring the pull of the underlying tonality, and despite the colour there remains a feeling of an austere purpose. There is nothing indulgent about the *Rhapsody* or the *Ballade*. And in many of the shorter pieces, despite a superficial impressionism, the imagery belongs to a bare and windswept musical heath-land rather than to some lush surroundings. Even those pieces in sharp keys are tinged with an indefinable melancholy.

Each bar of Ireland's music carries his imprint. The descending–ascending third which opens *The Forgotten Rite* is also found in the opening bars of *Chelsea Reach*, the final movement of the Sonata, in *On a Birthday Morning*, *Aubade*, *Blow out, you Bugles* and is the principal assertion of *These Things Shall Be*. There are many such recurrent figures. One of those, the drop of a fifth at the end of a phrase or line, is not exclusively a melodic figure, as the succession of chords built upon the dominant pedal-point resolve by this movement to the tonic below. (The harmonic basis of the dominant, however, by its nature, implies ambivalence as if the visual source of his inspiration were, in nature, hinged upon this great natural axis to reveal either the light or the dark aspects at will.)

In all his work there is restless urgency of movement, both rhythmic and harmonic, contrasting with its deep inner serenity. The two are allied, as for instance in *Ragamuffin* (p. 3) and the Piano Sonata (p. 28) where there are passages of a sequential nature, marked with incomplete resolution of the seventh, repeating and rising by the interval of a third, ending on the home tonic, impelled towards this point of rest. His music has also a strong sense of organic unity. (He could easily have written a symphony – he did not, and we must accept his reasons – yet his ideas have organic life, dramatic content, and are eminently suitable for development. But his was a gruff, terse speech, and he felt the need for terseness and compression rather than expansion.) The tautness of structure has also an almost classical sense of proportion. The architecture is instinctive and nowhere does the form dictate the musical content or rob it of its spontaneity. Yet so direct is his approach, so pared to essentials, that the listener is sometimes left behind by the swift and sure exposition of the material (as in both the Piano and the Cello Sonatas). In *The Forgotten Rite* formal unity A–B–A (an arch-like mound or tumulus in music) is delineated by the central theme, is echoed in the insistence of the flute motif (rising from mediant to upper tonic and falling back to dominant) and is worked in every bar, with even the seemingly decorative and atmospheric harp glissandi conforming to the pattern. There are also instances where he makes use of a strict pattern of notes (*Moon-glade* is one, *Cypress* another).

There is unity of expression too in the whole corpus of his work. There is a sense of stylistic development, but periods are hard to establish. Several works would appear to indicate turning points – the *Rhapsody*, the Second Trio, the Sonatina – but these seem to have less to do with internal formal principles of evolution than with some strong emotional experience. And after the Piano Concerto, *Legend* and *February's Child*, the *Concertino Pastorale* defies classification by appearing in 1939.

Ireland seems rightly to belong to the Romantic/Impressionist category in the renaissance of English music after 1900. There are certainly romantic and impressionistic elements in his work. Yet his romanticism is thin-blooded, his impressionism too deeply conscious of the depths of his visual inspiration. As a composer for the piano – for which instrument most of his music was written – he indulged neither in impassioned bravura, nor in the incandescent skein of sound for its own sake. The music, despite superficial similarities, echoes neither Liszt nor Debussy, but rather demonstrates its allegiance through Brahms to Beethoven.

Ireland is predominantly a lyrical composer. The implications of lyrical need not necessarily lead to song-like melodic lines. Yet melody, even with the asperities of *Mai-Dun* and the Piano Concerto, is the principal element in his music. Despite its characteristic harmonic dress it is the melodic inflexion which identifies his voice. Few composers have a more readily recognisable speech. Palgrave, in his preface to the *Golden Treasury*, defines the lyrical as 'implying that each poem shall turn upon a single thought, feeling or situation'. The definition applies equally well to the short piano compositions of Ireland, whose predominantly ternary form involves melodic identity and unity of impression as well as of poetic impulse. One must not be too conscious of the titles added, like those of Schumann, to enable the listener to come near to the intended mood. Yet whatever the musical validity of such a process, such titles as *February's Child* (and one might add *The Blossoming Idyll*, *Red Autumn* and *Through the Eaves* in other composers of the period) have more evocative power than *The Merry Peasant* and must add something to the musical experience. Two pieces, 'Cypress' and 'The Cherry Tree' (from *Green Ways*), were originally entitled 'The Intruder' and 'Indian Summer', the knowledge of which must add another dimension to the music. And if the Sonata needs no embellishment it must nonetheless colour the musical experience to learn that the final movement was conceived after a visit to Chanctonbury. The poetic impulse, however, remains within the music itself, and is transmuted by a method more subtle than mere impressionism. The evocation of such scarcely defined imagery goes deeper than the mere addition of a title, often enigmatic

Fig. 2 Chanctonbury Ring (1920s photograph)

enough to do no more than hint at the kind of impressionism found in Debussy, but with a more parochial, more earthy application. The inspiration of much of his music, if the titles may be taken as some indication of the composer's predilections, is twofold: firstly the world of Nature (*April, Moonglade, Equinox*) and secondly, and perhaps more significantly, of place ('Amberley Wild Brooks', 'Le Catioroc', *The Towing Path*).

The expression of this identity through the medium of the pianoforte has given Ireland's music a very characteristic sound that also owes a great deal to the peculiarities of the instrument itself. Although the purely personal elements in his language are readily recognisable as the musical equivalent of certain subjective reactions he has experienced to the source of his inspiration, many of those elements are specifically related to the keyboard, as if certain idiosyncrasies of the instrument such as are derived from its sonorities, the placing of chords and even simply the manipulative problems of fingers were directly related to the musical idea. Ireland was himself a considerable pianist (with an equally distinctive style in performance, an almost clumsy quality that is as much his own as the melodic line)[9] and could perhaps have allowed matters of technical expertise to dictate the shape of the piano writing. His creative technique is more subtly poetic. The presentation of virtuosity, often a facile habit in a composer who is also a gifted pianist, was not a part of Ireland's technique. This is nowhere more clearly recognised than in the Piano Sonata, whose difficulties lie more in the assimilation and realisation

[9] To make a first-hand assessment of Ireland's pianism see the CDs of historical recordings issued by Dutton on CDBP 9799 (piano music, songs, Cello Sonata and Fantasy Sonata) and CDLX 7103 (both violin sonatas).

of the musical idea than in the execution of the more demanding passages. Even in the Concerto, virtuosity is made to serve an artistic purpose. This is unquestionably piano music, by a pianist, for a pianist – it lies under the hand, exploiting to the full the sonorities of the keyboard, decorated with passagework that depends for its effect upon the piano's percussive nature. The texture seemingly crowded with clustered harmonies is full of a paradoxical clarity, illuminated rather than clouded by chromatic additions. This very clarity of expression is that of the lyric poet for whom economy in carefully chosen words must spark the train of associative thought yet leave the main impulse clear. The hollow doubling (in, for instance, *Ballade*), the sharp sonorities of second and diminished octave, the 'tangy' runs of the Concerto and the Sonata, the harmonic delicacy of the upper parts in *Ballade of London Nights* sparkling like the lights of a Whistler Nocturne in the waters by the Embankment, the sparing pedal indications – all are elements of Ireland's technique and of his inspiration.

The Darkened Valley, prefaced by a line from Blake, is typical of Ireland's many short lyrical piano compositions. The opening phrase is delicate and simple, leading into a reflective middle section which in turn resolves into a varied form of the opening material. This kind of ternary form, with the opening material subtly varied in mood on its return, is characteristic of many of his short pieces such as *The Towing Path*. Its fragrance, far from cloying, has an atmosphere of infinite sweetness, tinged with a trace of melancholy. The limpid reflection of the opening is disturbed in the middle section, as if the waters had been ruffled by the passing of barge and draught horse, and in the resumption of the opening material the mood is somehow subtly changed. Few composers can create such an atmosphere with such simplicity of material.

In spite of the common humanity of *On a Birthday Morning* and the *London Pieces*, which abound in an extrovert cheerfulness, most of Ireland's short works evoke a feeling of lonely contemplation. 'Amberley Wild Brooks' (that green alluvial plain north of Amberley in Sussex where the River Arun spreads its valley into a wild-flower-haunted marsh – wild refers to weald) is full of this atmosphere, the peace of solitariness. And the mood of contemplation is often shot through with impassioned anguish, the agony of transient beauty. Despite the moments of passion there is nothing in Ireland reminiscent of the surges of Strauss's *Don Juan* – nothing ecstatic. For all Ireland's impassioned moments have their origins in disillusionment, the expression of which is forced from him in an anguish from which tears, though unshed, are not far. Even the climax of the last movement of the Piano Sonata bears with it, in its drooping phrases, the seeds of its own destruction. The modal inflexions which impart the minor colour are symptomatic of a deeper unease. Yet it is not altogether a human sadness, for in such moments Ireland comes nearest to the source of his inspiration in nature. The communing of 'Amberley Wild Brooks' is with a spirit that, unseen, is free as air, and as devoid of sexuality. This same spirit's darker and more demonic counterpart appears in *The Scarlet Ceremonies*, where nature is haunted by something from a human past that suggests pantheistic origins. The warmth of *The Towing Path* and *Chelsea Reach* is engendered by sun on water – the aerial loveliness of the Wild Brooks and the landscapes of *February's Child* (whose ambivalent gender suggests some elfin creature) and *On a Birthday Morning* by the interchanging elements of a vernal landscape, begetting the intuitive yearning of the young pre-adolescent, his sexual passions unawakened, who strays by the river bank to trace the yet unknowable in the reflections and sounds of Nature.

This lonely contemplation is also of self reflected in nature – a narcissism that is echoed in 'A Grecian Lad' (which was originally entitled 'Hyacinthus') and in the central piece of *Sarnia*, 'In a May Morning' (again originally entitled 'Boyslove', the name of the plant Southernwood – though Ireland subsequently changed the title to *In a Maytime Garden*). *Equinox* sweeps its gusty course *poco agitato* in irregular groups of semiquavers, a virtuosic study – yet here also are hints of a darker vision. *April's* springlike clarity casts its colder reflection into the companion piece *Bergomask* (two pieces which according to the composer should be played together). The four Preludes (*Fire of Spring, Undertone, Obsession*, and *The Holy Boy*) are full of this pantheistic element, despite the cloistered simplicity of *The Holy Boy*.

Ireland wrote another Prelude – in E♭, and given no other title. The term 'Prelude' has little relation to Chopin or Scriabin, but is used by Ireland as if it were a programmatic title, implying the opening of some sombre ritual with its dark incantations. *Month's Mind*, too, is prefaced by a quotation from Brand's *Observations on Popular Antiquities*[10] running thus: 'days which our ancestors called their month's mind as being the days whereon their souls (after death) were had in special remembrance – hence the expression having a month's mind to imply a longing desire.'

This longing desire is amply evident in the music. 'The Boy Bishop' evokes a seemingly innocent yet mysterious ceremony, the solemn processional theme in the central section delineated in the inner parts. Despite the quasi-modal melodic element which gives the impression of a Christian observance, the origins of the ritual seem lost in an antiquity that is pagan and the vision has a hint of none-too-Anglican, almost bizarre, sensuality. (Similar pagan origins are hinted at in the writings of Jocelyn Brooke, appearing simply as old customs and practices with no more than a symbolic meaning whose origins are forgotten – yet which in practice suddenly seem menacing and dangerous.) Ireland was a devout, if doubting, Anglo-Catholic. He confessed himself a pagan – but the origins of this paganism in nature were inmixed with a kind of reverence for the outward and visible signs of ecclesiastical practice. He found, in the Mass, and in the physical ritual of its performance, the significance that assured him of its functional efficacy. This is in no way to be thought of as superstitious observance – for the spiritual benefits he derived therefrom in later life were not always the certain ease of mind that the superstitious derive from the practice of their observances. He returns to his doubtings.

Ireland wrote no really extended orchestral work apart from the Piano Concerto. Yet his expression is by no means a slight talent for the colourful miniature. In miniature he distils his colour and expression to a tense concentrate – yet nowhere are the large spaces (for they are there, even if they take but a few bars in the telling) filled with a mere wash of colour. The highly personal elements that are reticently exposed in the short lyrical works are shown in the larger-scale compositions to

[10] London: Chatto & Windus, 1913.

be matters of considerable moment. Even in the longer piano works, the *Rhapsody*, *Ballade*, *Sarnia* and the Sonata, expansiveness is not a matter of time-scale but of intensity.

Like Brahms, Ireland was concerned with content and not with superficial effect. The opening of the *Rhapsody* with its strangely heavy-footed rhythms, its hollow dual chords, is set in a characteristic rhythmic pattern. It has its dark and light sides – the first and second subjects in embryonic form (droop A–G–F contrasting with the rise G–E♭–F, as if the first rose from the darkness to the light of the second, yet with its implied harmonies unresolved). A darker treatment (in broken semiquaver chords) gives vigorous melodic purpose to the idea, its essence distilled in a *dolce* passage. The skeletal variant of this theme which emerges suggests, with its deep penetrating pulse, some ancient incantation as of Druids unveiled in the midst of ritual and ancient evils.

The *Ballade*, a dark evocation connected with those quiet downlands amidst whose sunny undulations Ireland experienced the mysterious events that inspired the *Legend* for piano and orchestra,[11] never becomes wholly lyrical. Its opening motif is transformed by some mighty and awful experience and achieves a kind of nobility. Yet this has age-old sorrow, made serene by the passage of time. Its dark-ness is broken by flashes of coruscating brilliance but the landscape thus illumined is a daunting one. It is the outcome of some deeply felt spiritual encounter.

The heavy silences and hidden terrors of 'Le Catioroc' (from *Sarnia*) reflect his awareness of the remoter parts of Guernsey, where he had been physically conscious of that dark, impenetrable, yet tangible, reality beyond. This piece, the first of the set, was originally entitled 'Aegipans Headland' and the music broods, heavy with the threat of unknown fears. These are banished in the sultry warmth of the second piece yet its mood is more late summery than the May of the title. Only in the final 'Song of the Springtides' does the composer's gaze rise to the limitless horizon (echoing the fresh colour, exposed melody notes, downward sweeping left-hand passages and elaborate arabesque of *The Palm and May*), an image which recurs in the Piano Concerto. Ireland's biggest work for the piano is the Sonata in E minor (October 1915–January 1920.) Here are all the facets of his art – the lyrical, the dramatic, the extrovert and the melancholy – the intense self-questioning and the open, almost naive, avowals. It is an enormous fresco, a landscape shrill with birdsong, shrouded in summer's haze, yet dark with the leafy umbrage of groves where secrets are hid. From its thickets, through the light of high summer, floods a dark foreboding:

> The dominant image evoked (by Ireland's music) is of a wooded and remote countryside, silent and frost-bound in the early twilight of a winter's evening. It is the dead season, yet there is a subtle, half-realised feeling of Spring in the air: a stirring of bird-life in the woods, the catkins lengthening upon the hazels, the first celandine, perhaps, gleaming precociously in the shel-tered hedgerow. After a day of rain and unbroken cloud, the western sky is suddenly clear, a broad rift of brightness palely green over the humped outline of the woods: the days are 'drawing out', and the land itself seems to extend with the lengthening days, one is suddenly aware of far, illimitable

---

[11] See Jocelyn Brooke's account in Chapter 26.

distances. The dimension of Time, also, is extended in this country of the mind; Uricon or Camelot lie beyond those farther woods: and on the beech-crowned hill, where the cromlech rises stark against the rainy sunset, the ancient and bloody rites are celebrated anew, and the beacon fires lit for Beltane or Samhain.[12]

At its heart is the *non troppo lento* slow movement. Its seven-bar theme moves like a stately soliloquy, punctuated by chords. Its repeated plea culminates in a powerful chordal passage in E♭ major, the central focal point of the Sonata, in which is revealed something dimly recognised, from the past experience of man. The climax dies to a deep hush. The experience has seared the soul and a new but related theme in 3/4 arises in the inner parts like some new awareness in the consciousness. This is the fullest expression of Ireland's music and the movement ends in an atmosphere of utter serenity, a coda of exquisite beauty like some colossal sunset over Stonehenge. It is the serenity of time itself – and surely one of the finest and most eloquent pages ever written for the piano.

However conservative, Ireland was not unaware of the impulses that were directing the course of events both here and abroad. He studied closely both Ravel and Stravinsky, to both of whom he owed much. There are traces of French influence, not only in the piano writing but in the overtones of *The Forgotten Rite*, a kind of English *L'Après-midi* – and in the similarities between the Trio and *Introduction and Allegro* of Ravel, and the Second Trio and the Sonatina of Ireland. The technique, if not always the matter, of the impressionists Ireland found significant, showing itself as early as the piano pieces entitled *Decorations*. Ireland's impressionism is more earthy, as a comparison between the opening bars of the Piano Concerto and 'La Cathédrale engloutie' or 'Canope' will show.

The lurid, even bizarre, colours that develop from this become darker and more menacing as Ireland came under the influence of early Stravinsky. Writing of *Le Sacre du printemps*, Ireland said, 'I always feel that the musical sounds Stravinsky makes in this work – the musical ideas themselves – seem to have the power of calling up something from the subconscious mind: some racial memory perhaps of things long hidden and belonging to a remote and forgotten past.'[13]

Though the fruits of the study of Stravinsky are apparent in the Piano Concerto, the influence is a very much deeper one – and despite those sounds, it is from this date (1930) that Ireland, from being a modern composer, seems somehow to join the ranks of those to whom we are all too impetuously liable to refer in the past tense. Events, as it happened, moved all too swiftly. Ireland was essentially of his generation – and in spite of a further twelve years or more of composition he could not be emotionally in key with the developments of contemporary art. The choral work *These Things Shall Be* suggests an unfulfilled social optimism that in 1939 was to be cruelly swept aside. To turn as he did then to the realms of the *Concertino Pastorale* was to avert his face from the contemporary scene.

John Ireland died in June 1962, at a season of the year to which his music had always driven for fulfilment – Spring turning gradually into full Summer.

[12] Jocelyn Brooke, *The Dog at Clambercrown* (New York: Vanguard Press, 1955), pp. 100–1. This quotation is from a section in Brooke's book entitled 'Month's Mind'.

[13] BBC broadcast, see pp. 411–12.

CHAPTER 2

John Ireland: A Personal Discovery

Bruce Phillips

I FIRST became aware of John Ireland's music in 1961, when I was sixteen. My piano teacher at school, John Alston, placed in front of me a piano piece called *Month's Mind* and said that if I learned to play the piece properly he would take me to meet the composer, then living not far from the school in a converted windmill just outside the village of Washington, between Steyning and Storrington in West Sussex. I struggled with the piece but became completely captivated by its atmosphere of nostalgic yearning conveyed through harmonies that reminded me of Ravel's *Sonatine*, a piece I had attempted to add to my rather restricted repertoire. Here, though, was music that seemed as quintessentially English as Ravel's was French, and moreover evoking a rather different Englishness from that of my then musical god, Ralph Vaughan Williams.

In June 1962 I read the obituaries of John Ireland, who had died at the age of eighty-two. Much mention was made of the Sussex windmill in which he had passed the last nine years of his life. My relief at not being compelled to visit him and perform his piece to him in person – he would by that time have been unable to see me – was mixed with intense sadness at the news of his death and curiosity to know more about him than was revealed in Percy Scholes's *Oxford Companion to Music*, in which was printed at thumbnail size that well-known photograph of the composer gazing downwards to his right and looking for all the world like a bank manager or headmaster. Acting on impulse a few days later I went to the one phone booth in the school and looked him up in the local directory. There he was: Ireland, Dr John, Rock Mill, Washington, with an Ashington number. I rang the number without of course knowing whether anyone would answer or what I would say if anyone did. I heard a woman's voice at the other end, pressed Button A, and found myself speaking to a lady who introduced herself as Mrs Norah Kirby. I introduced myself as a schoolboy speaking from nearby Lancing College and said that I had been greatly moved and saddened by the news of John Ireland's passing and that I had come to love his piece *Month's Mind* above all other music that I knew.

I discovered in the course of our conversation that Norah Kirby had been John Ireland's (or as she always referred to him, Dr. Ireland's) companion, secretary and housekeeper for more or less twenty years. I learned later that she divided the world into those who loved his music and those who did not. By revealing that I had fallen completely in love with *Month's Mind* I had fortunately placed myself in the former category. On hearing that I had not heard anything else he had written and that I knew no more about him than had been included in Scholes or the main obituaries, she invited me to lunch, promising to meet me in Steyning and drive me westwards past the foot of Chanctonbury Ring to the beautiful converted windmill named Rock Mill in which he had spent nearly the last decade of his life.

I obtained leave from my housemaster and met Norah in Steyning High Street. She was driving Ireland's last car, a green Ford Popular which she later told me he had bought in the 1950s through contacts in Guernsey, which was then an export market for cars. We drove past Chanctonbury and turned right along a small slip road that led to a drive flanked by pine trees. There at the end of the drive was the windmill, minus its sails but with an adjoining two-storey building erected when it had been converted from a working mill into a residential house. Norah told me that Ireland had been aware of it for a number of years. When it came on the market in 1953 he had asked her whether she would move from London, where she had been running his household at 14 Gunter Grove for several years, and perform the same function at Rock Mill. He had made it clear that had she not accepted, he would have been unable to contemplate purchasing it and living there. Fortunately she had agreed. At that first meeting Norah was in good health. She told me about Ireland's funeral that had taken place at Shipley, a village between Washington and Horsham. She showed me round the main part of the Mill, especially the octagonal room at the base of the tower, and we walked out of one of the doors through the sun lounge into a beautiful garden from which one could see straight up towards Chanctonbury Ring, a large circle of beech trees cresting a promontory jutting out from the line of the South Downs. I was shown Ireland's study and bedroom and then taken up to the very top of the Mill, from which one could see all around below the results of the extensive sand and gravel extraction that had caused Ireland and Norah so much annoyance almost from the moment they had moved in. I also made the acquaintance of Smoky and Laddin, two Siamese cats that had played an important part in Ireland's last years and remained for Norah a living link with him.

Over lunch she asked me what pieces of Ireland's music I knew (at that time only *Month's Mind* and 'Ragamuffin', the music of which I had found I had at home). She played me the 10-inch LP of Boyd Neel's recording of the Minuet from *A Downland Suite*, and presented me with a copy. She showed me the leather-bound autograph book presented to Ireland on his seventy-fifth birthday in which a wide range of musicians and other friends and admirers had written messages of congratulations and memories. Prominent among these was one from Ralph Vaughan Williams. This book is now in the British Library along with the majority of Ireland's autograph manuscripts and correspondence.

Later that summer Norah suffered a series of strokes, doubtless brought on by the stress of Ireland's death. She made a pretty good recovery except for her left arm, which was paralysed in such a way that it was very difficult for her to use her left hand despite constant physiotherapy. I for my part had left school at the end of December, leaving myself about ten months' 'gap year' (as it was not then called) until I went up to Christ Church, Oxford. I had no plans for how to spend this time until I received, via the good offices of Rev. Kenneth Thompson, then Rector of Great Haseley in Oxfordshire, an invitation from Norah to go and stay at the Mill and assist her in matters such as cooking, cleaning and general domestic duties, as well as to provide a sympathetic companion and fellow listener to the many private recordings which had been made of performances and broadcasts of Ireland's music. I would also be able to meet many of the musicians and friends who regularly visited the Mill. I accepted without hesitation, and was driven down to Sussex by Kenneth through the snow and ice of that legendary winter of 1962–3.

For the next three months, under Norah's supervision, I acquired rudimentary skills in cooking and cleaning, and learned to drive well enough to accompany Norah to the places she associated with Ireland: Shipley churchyard, Storrington (where Ireland had been wont in earlier times to meet Arnold Bax in the bar of the White Horse), Steyning and Pulborough (where lived Mary and Percy Turnbull, the third composer besides Ireland and John Longmire to be on board the SS *Antwerp* when it left Guernsey for Weymouth a few days before Germany invaded in 1940). I also met the pianists Eric Parkin and Alan Rowlands, the critic Scott Goddard, the broadcaster Alec Robertson, the writer Jocelyn Brooke, the artist Juliet Pannett, and Charlie Markes, whose friendship with Ireland had begun when Markes was a choirboy at St Luke's before the First World War and had survived a long interruption based on a misunderstanding between them (see pp. 72 and 155–6). Another frequent visitor was Lawrence Norcross, who in 1959 with John Steel had formed the John Ireland Society that had done so much to rescue Ireland's music from a period of neglect in the 1950s. Other visitors included Peter and Margaret Taylor, friends of Norah's from the days even before she had met Ireland and later the principal members of the Trust which she set up in the 1970s.

From this period dates my admiration for John Ireland the composer and interest in John Ireland the man. The picture I gained of him at that time was inevitably influenced by Norah Kirby, whose regard for him bordered on idolatry. There were times when, even then, I realised that he could not have been quite the perfect human being portrayed by Norah. A forceful and articulate person herself, she brooked not a single word of criticism or questioning of any aspect of his life or music, and viewed any failure to further his cause as evidence of malicious conspiracy, as for example his exclusion from the Proms after the BBC music department was taken over by William Glock and Hans Keller (though she much appreciated the hoax perpetrated by Keller and Susan Bradshaw when they recorded and broadcast on the BBC Third Programme music alleged to have been by the Polish composer Piotr Zak). She could take against perfectly good performances or recordings if she thought Ireland would not have approved of them, as for example the singer John Shirley-Quirk, whose Saga LP of songs elicited her constant disparagement. Yet it was Norah who from the mid-1940s, when Ireland had returned to London after the war, had brought order and comfort into the last two decades of his life.

In the month after I left the Mill I was a Hesse student at the 1963 Aldeburgh Festival, one of a group of young people who helped with things like ferrying musicians to rehearsals and concerts, setting out chairs, and the like. A high point while I was there was a party for all the Hesse students given by Imogen Holst at her house. Britten and Pears both came. Bursting with adolescent pride and curiosity I told Britten what I had been doing at Rock Mill, then knowing only that he had studied composition with Ireland and not knowing of the difficult relationship that seems to have existed between them. I asked Britten for his opinion on Ireland's music. I ought to have written down what he said immediately after the party, but did not. All I can remember of what he said was, first that Ireland's piano music was difficult to play because it had fistfuls of notes (he made much the same comment to Alan Rowlands), and that in his answer to my question as to what Ireland was like to meet, Britten replied that he had a strong personality but a weak character.

Ireland was once asked, so the story goes, whether he thought he was a great composer (what a question!). He is said to have replied after some thought: 'No, but I think I'm a significant one.' This perhaps tells us something about Ireland's character. Born the fifth and by some years the last child of Victorian parents – his father was seventy when he was born – his childhood seems not to have been happy (some evidence of being teased by his siblings, remote father but loving and supportive mother). Details of his early schooling are sparse, but what is clear is that somehow at the age of thirteen Ireland was sufficiently certain of his interest and ability in music to take himself unaided to the Royal College of Music, sit whatever entrance examination or audition was required, and return to Manchester to tell his mother what he had done.

His original intention was to become a professional pianist, but the two string quartets that he wrote well before he began full-time composition lessons with Stanford bear witness to a precocious gift for composition. This is confirmed by the Sextet for clarinet, horn and string quartet that he wrote shortly after starting composition lessons. Saturated as all these works are in Brahms – an influence which Stanford sought to overcome, sometimes it seems rather cruelly – they bear witness to Ireland's serious intentions as a composer. The fact that he withdrew them and several other studentship works until towards the end of his life when he was persuaded to relent suggests a high degree of self-criticism.

Ireland was never exactly a prolific composer. He once described himself as 'England's most laborious composer'. His peak years were between 1910 and 1930, with the apex coming in 1913–23, the years in which *The Forgotten Rite*, the second piano trio and second violin sonata, the piano sonata, the cello sonata, the Housman cycle *The Land of Lost Content* and *Mai-Dun* were written. The 1930s saw the production of Ireland's two great works for piano and orchestra, the Piano Concerto and *Legend*, plus *A Downland Suite*, *A London Overture*, the *Concertino Pastorale* for strings, and his one extended work for chorus and orchestra, his setting of John Addington Symonds poem 'A Vista' entitled *These Things Shall Be*, in which Ireland, with more than a little help from his friend and pupil Alan Bush, expressed an optimistic hope for an Utopian future seemingly at odds with his innately pessimistic outlook. During the Second World War came two masterpieces, *Sarnia*, begun in his beloved Guernsey, and the Fantasy Sonata for clarinet and piano. His *Epic March* was written in response to a BBC commission for a patriotic march. After the war came the overture *Satyricon*, a piece that deserves to be played more often if for nothing else than for its glorious clarinet tune in the middle section. The immediate postwar period also brought Ireland's only film score, *The Overlanders*.

In England we tend not to celebrate our native composers enough unless they have produced a string of symphonies, concertos, large scale choral works and operas – and perhaps not even then. Ireland's music is never going to achieve the same degree of popularity, admiration and wide exposure as, say, Elgar, Vaughan Williams, Britten, or Walton. He is often described as a miniaturist, sometimes in rather patronising terms. We can regret that he did not write more orchestral music given his mastery of orchestral colouring. His legacy is that of an intensely self-critical perfectionist who has given us some exquisite pieces for piano, many beautiful and deeply moving songs, some splendid sonatas and piano trios, and a handful of arguably great pieces for orchestra. It is to be hoped that this book will contribute towards explaining some of the background to the life and music of this very significant composer.

A T a very late stage in the preparation of this book we received via the good offices of Nicolas Bell, in the Music Division of the British Library, copies of a series of letters from Ireland to the composer Martin Shaw. This extract from a letter dated 2 April 1916 (one of Ireland's very few surviving letters written during the First World War) demonstrates that Ireland's misgivings about the state of music and the musical profession – a recurring theme of his later years – were already present in the early stages of his life as a composer.

But the real question is Art, which we have so placidly accepted from our youth upwards & your "Joys of War" or my "Sea Fever" are just as definitely Art as the works of Schoenberg – only they are one kind of art – the kind we like. The more I think of it, the more I think the bottom drops out of the whole thing the moment one ceases to think of it from the point of view of a professional musician – a specialist in purveying or dealing with the commodity of civilization which we call music. Really Martin, I see no end to all this, if one begins to think clearly and analytically and on broad lines.

I feel the more at sea since talking to Frank Bridge – he thinks, and I suppose 99 per cent of composers would think, that a man who cannot show a good modern symphonic poem or chamber work is "amateurish" – & therefore, one concludes that composing music is a profession, like surgery. I think it follows that the best composer, like the best surgeon, is the one who can do the most elaborate and complex work successfully.

Well Martin, I have said enough to suggest to you that this subject is a much longer one than any of the "Restorationists" think, & as I can see no solution at present, I think I shall have to sit on the fence and watch the combat.

It is to me a very ominous sign in myself that I find listening to music more and more irksome & intolerable – unless it is music which expresses what I feel to be true, and that is very, very little. To hear Brahms' C minor Trio for instance does not merely bore me – it makes me furious at the time & makes me hate music for days afterwards – yet it is a very good work, according to the canons of the art, & one which stirs most musicians very deeply. Even the Ravel Trio, which I really enjoyed learning & playing, gives me no pleasure to listen to. Quite the contrary.

CHAPTER 3

Meeting John Ireland:
An Interview with Alan Rowlands

This interview took place in Summer 2010.

INTERVIEWER You must be one of the few people still alive who knew John Ireland quite well.

ALAN ROWLANDS Yes, I think so. In fact the only other person I can think of is the pianist Eric Parkin, and he is even further into his eighties than I am and seems to have retired from the scene.

INTERVIEWER When did you first meet Ireland?

ALAN ROWLANDS It was in 1957 when he was seventy-eight and I was twenty-eight. I found it rather a nerve-wracking experience as I had never met anyone so distinguished before and I felt quite apprehensive at the thought of playing him some of his own music.

INTERVIEWER I'd like to hear more about that. But how had you become drawn to Ireland's music in the first place?

ALAN ROWLANDS Through my upbringing in Swansea. My father was the conductor of the local choral society and had broadcast some of Ireland's part-songs, such as *Twilight Night*. He was an enthusiast for English music and had amassed quite a good library and I soon discovered songs like *Sea Fever* and *The Bells of San Marie* and loved them. I suppose the first piano piece I played was *The Holy Boy*. Another factor was our friendship with the composer Percy Turn-bull who was living in Swansea at the time and visited our house regularly. He had actually known Ireland and could imitate his very characteristic voice – that rather querulous monotone in which he would make self-deprecating remarks about himself or his music in the hope that you would, as Percy put it, 'pump him up again'. He regaled us with many stories, including the one about how he, John Longmire and Ireland had escaped from the Channel Islands just before the German invasion in 1940. They had got on one of the last boats from Guernsey and endured a hazardous and overcrowded crossing to Weymouth, where Ireland arrived in a highly nervous state, the unfinished manuscript of *Sarnia* among his few possessions. Percy told us that Longmire had gone to the Captain and said of Ireland, 'He's mad, you know', thereby enabling Ireland to leave the boat ahead of the normal disembarkation procedures.

INTERVIEWER Did he play Ireland's music to you?

ALAN ROWLANDS Yes, and he used to bring other pieces for me to look at, such as the Sonata and *Sarnia*. I was quite swept away by *Song of the Springtides*.

INTERVIEWER Was it at Rock Mill that you met Ireland?

ALAN ROWLANDS Yes, but that was not the first time I had seen the Mill. I'd like to tell you about that, because the experience mirrors one which Ireland later told me he had expressed musically near the end of his piano piece *Rhapsody*. In the summer of 1954 I was staying with a friend near Brighton and we went for an extended ramble in the Sussex Downs. We started from the coast and went north over Cissbury Ring and towards Chanctonbury Ring. On both these summits you can see the earth ramparts where prehistoric peoples had built their hill-top forts – places haunted by that kind of ancient and pagan atmosphere which, I later learned, had always stirred Ireland deeply. We toiled up towards Chanctonbury and at the summit the ground fell away and within a few steps we could see a vast expanse of the Sussex weald spread out in the sunshine like a map. My companion pointed downwards and said, 'Do you see that windmill?' I could just see about a mile and a half away the dark shape of a windmill. He said, 'That's where the composer John Ireland lives.' I was fascinated by this – I had already read of how the composer had found a windmill home, but having escaped the traffic noise of a busy street in London now found him disturbed by the nearby noise of sand-mining machinery. I could have had no idea that within three years I would be sitting in that windmill, talking to John Ireland and looking back up at Chanctonbury Ring – to say nothing of the fact that he would later recommend me to be the first person to record his complete works for solo piano. Still, these unlikely events did happen.

By the way, this is the passage from *Rhapsody* which Ireland later told me was like coming to the top of a hill and then seeing the view opening out on the other side – I can remember the way he held up his hands horizontally and wiggled his fingers as he described this:

Ex. 1 Ireland, *Rhapsody*

INTERVIEWER So how did you come to visit the Mill?

ALAN ROWLANDS Well, I had developed my playing of Ireland at Oxford, where I took a degree in chemistry and then did four year's research in peptide synthesis. I practised in Taphouse's music studios, which then cost 1s 6d an hour – about

8p. I played the Sonata and *Sarnia* in the Holywell Music Room, and took part in a great deal of other musical activities as well, my interest in science meanwhile steadily declining. When Dr Thomas Armstrong finally persuaded my father that I could make a go of it in music, I went to the Royal College of Music at the age of twenty-six and studied piano with Angus Morrison. He was another person who had known Ireland, and had played his Piano Concerto several times, including at the Proms. He had a few more Ireland stories, one relating to how he had questioned the composer as to why he had introduced an A♯ into this passage near the end of the Piano Sonata – it is after all foreign to the key, E major. Ireland had said, in his gloomiest voice, 'I think it sounds more *festive*':

Ex. 2 Ireland, Piano Sonata

Perhaps Benjamin Britten, Ireland's pupil at the RCM, had also noticed the festive effect of a sharpened fourth at the opening of this Sea Interlude from *Peter Grimes*:

Ex. 3 Benjamin Britten 'Sunday Morning' – interlude from *Peter Grimes*

INTERVIEWER So did Angus Morrison introduce you to Ireland?

ALAN ROWLANDS Yes, eventually. I worked hard again on *Sarnia* and the Sonata – these were my first piano lessons since the age of sixteen – and Angus wondered whether Ireland would like to hear me play them. He wrote to the composer at Rock Mill and received an encouraging reply, saying that Ireland would write to me about a visit. And then nothing happened for several months and I began to think nothing would. But suddenly a letter arrived saying, 'Take the Worthing coach from Victoria Coach Station and get off at the village of Washington; Mrs Kirby will meet you.' So I worked hard again and the great day arrived.

INTERVIEWER What was your first impression?

ALAN ROWLANDS Oddly enough, his dewlap – it shook slightly as he spoke. Earlier photographs show him as quite full in the region of the double chin, but by the time I knew him he had shrunk a little.

INTERVIEWER But his manner?

ALAN ROWLANDS He was the soul of old-world courtesy in receiving me. I was in some awe of him, though. I had heard stories about the pungency of his views and the dryness of his wit – that much-imitated voice could take on a rasping edge when he wanted to mock something or make one of his characteristically morose observations. I remember my surprise that he would not sit down, but came and stood by my chair – Mrs Kirby had given me a seat in the sun-lounge facing Chanctonbury Ring. Perhaps it was because of his slight hardness of hearing. He smoked a small cigar and talked for about two hours, standing all the while and quizzing me at length about my musical tastes and preferences. At one point I expressed my great enthusiasm for Vaughan Williams's Sixth Symphony. He cut me short with three words: 'I detest that.' I was totally taken aback and felt I must have chosen the wrong symphony – VW's Sixth is after all a very warlike and violent work. So I began to enthuse about the merits of the Fifth – that epitome of peace and reflective meditation. This elicited the same response: 'I detest that.' Was there a touch of mischief in his voice? Was he trying to provoke me? At any rate I didn't have the nerve to question his views and knew nothing at the time of his somewhat ambivalent attitude to Vaughan Williams. He then went on to tell me that he thought VW's finest work was *Flos Campi*, though he thought it odd that the passage relating to 'the beloved's bed' should be in dry consecutive fourths and an angular rhythm. I looked up this score recently and though there is a reference to Solomon's bed, it also mentions that it is surrounded by threescore valiant men with swords, so I think VW was thinking of the militaristic rather than the amorous potentialities of the scene:

Ex. 4 Ralph Vaughan Williams, *Flos Campi*

It was a slight relief to me that Mrs Kirby then called us through for lunch, which meant going through the main music-room on the ground floor of the Mill to the dining-room in the adjacent buildings. Lunch was pleasant, even convivial, but slow and protracted, and merged imperceptibly into a similarly protracted tea, for which we had to go back into the music-room. Mrs Kirby gave a certain sense of formality to these proceedings and I began to sense that these meal rituals were an important part of life at the Mill. I wondered when I was going to be asked to play, if at all. But finally Ireland pottered over to the piano, lifted the keyboard lid of the Bechstein grand and said, 'Perhaps you'd like to play something.' Though I was by this time getting rather tired, I had a go at *Song of the Springtides* and I remember that I had the bright idea of handing Dr Ireland a pencil and suggesting he might like to write his comments in the score. (I had by this time picked up from Mrs Kirby that he liked to be addressed as 'Dr'.) This was a step I soon regretted, for the pencil was a rather noisy one and it was not long before I was aware of vigorous scratchings coming from the depths of Dr Ireland's armchair. My mind went instantly to the first act of *Die Meistersinger* where Walther is singing his

Trial Song and having his faults noisily chalked up on the slate by the invisible Beckmesser.

INTERVIEWER That must have been rather off-putting.

ALAN ROWLANDS It was, because I kept thinking, 'I wonder what I've done wrong.' But it turned out his comments were by no means devastating – things like 'no dim yet', or 'fuller tone' – this last applying to the central section in E♭, which he wanted to be 'like the ocean swell'. That theme at the bottom of the first page, a kind of second subject, he wanted to be played in a robust manner, and not to sound dainty nor effeminate. By the way, I noticed recently that it bears a strong family resemblance to the second subject in the Piano Concerto:

Ex. 5 Ireland, 'Song of the Springtides' (*Sarnia*)

Ex. 6 Ireland, Piano Concerto

I think on the whole he did like my playing and said I must come again, which I did, and soon my visits became regular. Before long we had been through the whole of the Sonata and *Sarnia* in some detail, and other pieces as well.

INTERVIEWER Did he play to you?

ALAN ROWLANDS Hardly ever, but he did illustrate the rugged style he wanted at the opening of the Piano Sonata – he played it with strongly marked accents and emphatic rhythms. There was one piece he played all the way through – *Month's Mind*. He had practised it in order to play it to the writer Jocelyn Brooke, who was fascinated by it and had written about it in one of his books. He also wrote a poem with the same title. So Ireland played it to me too, using the music and wearing the green celluloid eye-shade he often used to relieve the strain on his eyes. Another thing he played was that passage of strange chords from *The Rite of Spring*, of which he had heard the first London performance in 1913 [Ex. 7]. He never forgot that first performance and described the breathless silence before it began and the eerie sound that emerged. He told me that they could hardly make out what that instrument was – nobody had heard the bassoon like that before. He also showed me an exercise he used to do to improve his stretch – holding down

Ex. 7 Igor Stravinsky, *Rite of Spring*

the notes of the dominant ninth, G–B–D–F–A, and exercising each finger in turn. As Benjamin Britten once told me, you need 'a good fist' to play Ireland.

INTERVIEWER What was the Mill like to live in?

ALAN ROWLANDS Quite wonderful, I should think. To begin with it was in a spectacular situation, on an eminence some 400 feet above sea-level, with a lovely view of the Downs and directly opposite Chanctonbury Ring. There was quite a large garden, lovingly tended by Mrs Kirby – with the help of a gardener whom Ireland liked to call Harry Harry Harry. When I asked her about this she said the man's name actually was Harry Harry but Ireland liked to add one more Harry for luck. The Mill had been marvellously converted into a residence, almost luxuriously – a fact which struck me forcibly again on a recent visit to the very similar smock mill at Shipley which is still in its original working condition. It was masonry up to the first floor, with walls three feet thick and octagonal in shape – Mrs Kirby would sometimes say, when she wanted to impart something confidential, '*within these eight walls* ...' This became the main music-room and above it was her room which had its own bathroom. Above this was a room used for listening to gramophone records, then a spare room with a wonderful view, then an attic. Ireland's quarters were adjacent to the main part of the Mill, above the dining-room and kitchen. He had a study, containing a smaller Broadwood grand, then a bedroom and bathroom. I only saw this part of the premises after Ireland had died, when I would sometimes go and stay with Norah Kirby.

The Mill had an intensely personal atmosphere, which one felt immediately on entering. Beside the doorbell was a small brass plate with the single word in Latin, AEQUANIMITAS – and perhaps the composer had indeed now entered a safe harbour after a life not without its share of inner torment. He was in a part of the country that had meant so much to him, devotedly looked after by Mrs Kirby and surrounded by the objects he loved. I remember the antique furniture and china, much of it collected in Sussex, the haunting pictures of old Chelsea, the Japanese prints, the grandfather clock that chimed most melodiously on every quarter, the cherubic sculpted boy's head on the piano and the much loved books of poetry and writings of Arthur Machen. Particularly vivid in my mind are a pair of bronze figures, faun-like or Dionysian, with drinking-horns, and a picture of strange children in medieval garb, one of whom seemed to be appearing or disappearing in a shower of rose-petals. (I later found that this was an illustration taken from a book of Ireland's called *The Romaunt of the Rose*.) These objects conveyed an atmosphere of something pagan and magical – feelings often to be found in his music.

We once captured the atmosphere of the Mill very effectively on tape. I had a friend called John Chaffer whom I had met at Oxford through a mutual passion for the music of Delius. He revelled in added note harmonies and the higher dominant discords which he found in abundance in Ireland's music also. He begged me to take him to visit the composer. I was a little reluctant at first as I felt John's puppyish and over-exuberant manner might seem out of place. But the two got on very well and the older John almost basked in the younger John's adulation. One day he brought a tape-recorder, which Ireland noticed. Mrs Kirby had told us that she didn't think Dr Ireland would agree to be recorded, so with her active connivance we quietly placed the tape-recorder behind the composer's armchair at tea-time and turned it on. Pleasant conversation ensued, but owing to Chaffer's over-obvious feeding Ireland with leading questions, he twigged the situation and barked, 'Is that thing on?' 'Well, yes sir, I am afraid it is', said Chaffer. 'Well will you please turn it off *at once!*' So that was that. The next day John received a letter from Ireland asking him to destroy the tape, which he did, but not before we had listened to it. It was quite magical, with all our voices sounding clear and the delicate chink of china tea-cups and the ticking and chiming of the grandfather clock in the background.

INTERVIEWER So there's no copy?

ALAN ROWLANDS No. I think Ireland was highly sensitive to the possibility of this being listened to by other people, not knowing what he had said, and of course we shouldn't have practised that deception. A happier occasion was when John Chaffer and I played the composer his own four-hand arrangement of *Mai-Dun* – we had worked very hard on that. Incidentally, my performance of this piece with Adrian Sims has just come out on an Albion Records CD – which also includes Ireland's similar arrangement of *The Forgotten Rite*. (I felt, in rehearsing these, that I was able to considerably enhance Ireland's versions by restoring various runs, twiddles or glissandi that the composer had thought it more prudent to leave out!)

My friend was quite taken by what he called Ireland's 'Edwardian' pronunciation, for instance in the word 'permission' – he put an unusual emphasis on the first syllable. Dr Ireland had told us that when he was a student at the RCM, men and women had to go in by separate entrances and you couldn't be in a practice room with a member of the opposite sex without permission. There was a Lady Superintendent called Mrs Binden who would snoop around the practice rooms and if she found mixed-sex occupants would say, 'Have you had *per*-mission to be in this room?'

There were other young people who were enthusiastic about Ireland's music at that time, including the tenor John Steel and Lawrence Norcross, who formed the John Ireland Society. I think that must have pleased him. Quite a number of concerts were given in and around London from 1960–67, including two in the Wigmore Hall and several in the Great Drawing Room of 4 St James's Square when the Arts Council was there. Harold Rutland was the President. Eric Parkin and I played in most of them, in various capacities. Ireland came to several of the earlier ones, driven up from the Mill by Norah Kirby. I remember one when his early Sextet was done and he shouted out 'Steady!' in the last movement. In another one he came to I played the Sonatina and had the worst memory lapse of my entire life. The second subject comes quite early in the first movement and when I got to it I realised that I was playing it in the key of the recapitulation rather than the exposition. If I had gone on I would have come to the end having omitted the major part of the movement. So there was nothing to do but stop and say, 'I'm so sorry, I've taken a wrong turning, I'll start again.' The awful thing was that when I got to the same place I found I was again playing in the wrong key – and I knew I couldn't possibly stop a second time! So I sent up a fervent prayer to heaven and somehow managed to wrench the music back on to its right tracks. People said at the end how well I had handled the emergency, but they didn't know I had been through just about the worst agony I've ever known on the concert platform.

INTERVIEWER Did Ireland comment?

ALAN ROWLANDS No, not at all. It was the same at the Mill – he never paid any attention to my slips or wrong notes. But if I had made a misreading he dropped on it at once – he always knew the difference. Another thing I remember is that if I had been in any doubt as to the interpretation of a passage, and had thought I would ask him about it, it often seemed to be settled by his mere presence in the room: when I came to that place it would simply go the right way.

One of the most memorable concerts at St James's Square was in honour of Ireland's eighty-second birthday in 1961. I think that must have been the last time he came to London and he was quite frail then. Sir Arthur Bliss spoke, referring to Ireland as 'our finest writer for piano', and congratulatory telegrams were read out. After Ireland died the following year another concert was given there in his memory and Sir Adrian Boult spoke. The last concert of the John Ireland Society was in 1967, but after that Norcross and Mrs Kirby found that they couldn't get on so it petered out and then she formed the John Ireland Trust in 1968.

INTERVIEWER When did you begin to record Ireland's music?

ALAN ROWLANDS That would have been in 1959. It was one of the greatest surprises of my life when Richard Itter of Lyrita Recorded Edition contacted me with the idea of my recording Ireland's piano output on the composer's recommendation. After all, I was completely unknown at the time, still a student at the RCM, and there were other people who could have done it. I believe Itter had first considered Iris Loveridge, who had already recorded Bax for him. But Ireland was not very keen on women playing his music, in spite of his earlier relationship with Helen Perkin. Regarding this particular form of musical misogyny, I recall Ruth Dyson at the RCM telling me that when she and two women string players had gone to play Ireland one of his trios he had said afterwards, 'I'm afraid you ladies are insufficiently acquainted with the devil to play my music.' And when she had offered him a pair of tickets for the concert 'for you and your wife' he said, 'Wife? – I don't have *wives!*' – this in spite of the fact that in 1926 he had married the seventeen-year-old Dorothy Phillips, though I suppose that was not a marriage in the fullest sense of the term.

INTERVIEWER So they didn't use Iris Loveridge. But what about Eric Parkin?

ALAN ROWLANDS Yes, indeed. Eric had got to know Ireland several years before I did and played his music extremely well, including a performance of the Concerto at the Proms in 1953. I believe Ireland had worked extensively with him and he had recorded the Sonata and *Sarnia* for Argo with the composer present in the studio. Eric told me that the recording sessions were so intense that at the end his fingers were bleeding. Why Ireland didn't choose Eric for Lyrita, I don't know. He had a more fluent and reliable technique than mine – I always found technical matters difficult, perhaps because of that late start. I think it may have been something to do with my musicianship. Ireland never praised me to my face, but said some extremely complimentary things about me in letters to other people, like Angus Morrison, often mentioning my 'musical brain'. I only saw these letters recently, when Angus's daughter passed them on to me, when I realised that Ireland was quite right in predicting that I might not have the right temperament for the life of a concert pianist.

But perhaps I could relate a telling incident at the Royal Albert Hall. Ireland had come up for the rehearsal of one of his works and during an intermission groups of us were standing in one of those curving corridors, Ireland with Julian Herbage, Anna Instone and others. They were praising Eric's playing of his music and Ireland agreed. But then he turned and pointed his stick at me, standing a few feet away, and said, 'But this is the finer musician.' He then went on to tell them how I had played large sections of orchestral works on the piano, including chunks of Wagner and Delius. It is true that I was a good score-reader and enjoyed making piano transcriptions of works I loved – I had arranged Ravel's *La Valse* for solo piano before I realised that the composer had done this himself!

I remember one occasion at the Mill when I was playing *Brigg Fair* while waiting for Ireland to come down from his study – which often took quite a time. When I had finished I realised he had been standing in the doorway all the time, just listening. He said, with great reverence in his voice, 'I could never have written anything like that.' Of course, Eric did go on to make fine recordings of Ireland's works in stereo (mine were in mono) for both Lyrita and Chandos subsequently, including the Piano Concerto. I went on to record all the songs with several different singers.

INTERVIEWER I notice all your recordings have come out recently on CD. How do you feel about them now?

ALAN ROWLANDS I think they sound remarkably well, considering their age. Perhaps the digital remastering has something to do with it. Listening to them now after so many years, I feel they give a good account of how Ireland wanted his music done, though one or two details worry me. He was always insistent that his music should not be played too fast – the finale of the Sonatina being a frequent casualty in this respect – but I do now feel that the tempo I adopted for the opening of the last movement of the Sonata is too slow, even though it is marked 'with breadth'. And then *Sea Fever*! Ireland had told me that he did not like it sung in a rumbustious, get-up-and-go kind of manner, but when I passed this on to Benjamin Luxon he emphasised the reflective element so much that we ended up at an extreme of meditative nostalgia. I was severely taken to task for this by Charles Markes, who had known Ireland at the time he wrote *Sea Fever* and well knew the composer's intentions. He was one of Ireland's favourite choirboys during his time at St Luke's, Chelsea, and I think it was he who chose the present modal ending of *Spring Sorrow* out of the three that the composer had devised. He was also Ireland's companion when, coming back over Battersea Bridge in his Morgan motor one evening in 1917, they were suddenly struck by the extraordinary beauty of the scene, with the flickering gas-lamps reflected in the dark waters of the Thames. This was the origin of the piano piece *Chelsea Reach*.

Concerning *Sea Fever*, Ireland told me that the singer Betty Chester, who had done so much to popularise the song in its early days, could never get the ending of each verse right. She would ignore the tie and come down a beat early to the final E♭:

Ex. 8 Ireland, *Sea Fever* (deliberately misquoted)

I expect you know that this song was voted the most popular in a BBC poll in the 1920s.

INTERVIEWER Did you enjoy making the recordings?

ALAN ROWLANDS Well, yes and no. It was a wonderful project to be working on, but a tough one – I have a letter from Ireland in which he refers to 'this particular form of hard labour'. The first of the five solo LPs had to be done without editing facilities, so we had to get complete performances. I won't easily forget the sinking feeling of going back into Richard Itter's studio at Burnham Beeches to attempt yet another take of *Equinox*, but we did finally get a good version of this concert-study-like piece. I'm glad Ireland lived long enough to hear the first of those LPs.

INTERVIEWER Did he help you in the preparation?

ALAN ROWLANDS Well, whenever possible I would play through to him what I was going to record and he usually had a few hints. Of course he died before the series was complete.

INTERVIEWER Do you remember any?

ALAN ROWLANDS His most common adjuration was 'Don't hurry', which I remember in both the following instances, where I must have been guilty of imparting too much forward movement [Exx. 9 and 10]:

Ex. 9 Ireland, 'Song of the Springtides' (*Sarnia*)

Ex. 10 Ireland, *Month's Mind*

I was also sometimes guilty of the cardinal sin of cutting rests – something for which I must have admonished many of my own pupils – for instance, in *The Holy Boy*, where Ireland would count the rests out loud with punctilious regularity:

Ex. 11 Ireland, *The Holy Boy*

He felt the opening triplet in *April* should not be quite regular – the first note needed a slight expressive lengthening. In *The Undertone* he wanted an intensely smooth and quiet *legato* and came and put his hands over mine to ensure the least possible movement. That unexpected bass B♭ on the last page of *The Towing-Path* he wanted brought out strongly. He told me he had taken out the added sixth, C♯, in the last chord of the first movement of the Sonata in a new edition: it was 'stronger' that way. He was very keen that I should play his *Rhapsody* – I didn't know it when I first met him but he said, 'Oh, you must play my *Rhapsody*', so I did learn it and then he described that opening-out-of-a-view effect near the end. He said that this passage from *Soho Forenoons* should suggest 'an alcoholically unsteady gait' – a gait with which I later learnt he himself had not been unacquainted. (I believe he had once apologised for bumping into a lamp-post with the words, 'I really shouldn't be like this after only ten Johnnie Walkers.')

Ex. 12 Ireland, *Soho Forenoons*

I'm not sure I ever got the right kind of lurching *rubato* for this. I once tried out a *rubato* that I had heard on one of Ireland's own recordings of *Ragamuffin,* but he didn't like it.

When I was studying *Soliloquy*, I felt a strong resemblance of the opening phrase to something else – was it Vaughan Williams? I asked Dr Ireland. He wrote to me later, saying 'The phrase you refer to was cribbed by me not from VW but from Butterworth's setting of Housman's *Is my team ploughing?*', whose opening phrase it indeed greatly resembles. He had also used the same five-note figure in *The Lent Lily*:

Ex. 13 Ireland, *Soliloquy*

Ex. 14 George Butterworth, 'Is My Team Ploughing?'

Ex. 15 Ireland, 'The Lent Lily' (*The Land of Lost Content*)

He commented in this letter on the fact that VW had 'committed the crime' of leaving out one stanza in his setting of *Is my team ploughing?*, though he owned up to having done the same thing himself in *The Heart's Desire*. There is another slight dig at VW in this letter where he says that the 'august editor' of *The English Hymnal* had 'elected' to put his hymn-tune *Eastergate* to words other than those for which it had been written.

He told me that one of the things that linked the movements of *Sarnia* was the following chord progression, which occurs in all three:

Ex. 16 Ireland, 'Le Catioroc' (*Sarnia*)

Ex. 17 Ireland, 'In a May Morning' (*Sarnia*)

Ex. 18 Ireland, 'Song of the Springtides' (*Sarnia*)

When it came to *In a May Morning* he said, 'Play it as if you were looking at something so beautiful you could hardly bear it.' I did my best to conjure up a picture of the loveliness of Nature in May, not realising at that stage that one of the objects of beauty which had so inspired him was the young boy Michael Rayson, to whom it is dedicated. Michael was the son of the proprietors of the Birnam Court Hotel in Guernsey where Ireland was staying at the time, and was described by him, in a letter to Kenneth Thompson, as being 'beautiful … with long curling eyelashes'. I now feel, following Fiona Richards, that this piece is almost a love-song, and don't think it is any coincidence that the opening so closely resembles *Drink to me only with thine eyes* and that the middle section has something in common with the music of the dancing children in *Legend*:

Ex. 19 Ireland, 'In a May Morning'

Ex. 20 Ireland, *Legend*

It also contains a chordal progression very similar to one in *Spring will not wait* which seems to express an unassuagable longing:

Ex. 21 Ireland, 'In a May Morning'

Ex. 22 Ireland, 'Spring will not Wait'

INTERVIEWER Do you think of some of Ireland's music as paederastic?

ALAN ROWLANDS Well, it is not the word I would have chosen. But it is obvious that his attraction towards boys played an enormous part in his inspiration, possibly even more than in the case of Britten. He originally wanted to call the middle movement of *Sarnia* 'Boyslove' and the Fantasy Sonata for clarinet and piano *Ode to Giton* (the boy in the *Satyricon*). He was deeply moved by Thomas Mann's *Death in Venice*, which he read in the 1930s. As Kenneth Thompson, his closest friend and confidante in these matters, wrote to Colin Scott-Sutherland, 'John was a romantic Invert ... and an innocent lover of boys (again I emphasise innocent).' I think that's all that need be said. Perhaps it's worth mentioning that his friendship with the choirboy Arthur Miller continued into the boy's adult years and became perhaps the most inspirational relationship in the composer's life.

INTERVIEWER Do you remember any more of Ireland's conversation?

ALAN ROWLANDS I wish I had kept a diary of those years! One or two things come back to me. During the time I knew him his sight was gradually deteriorating – once he was trying to read with something that looked like a pair of binoculars.

He spoke of an arterial degeneration that affected his sight, hearing and mobility. I once asked him hopefully whether his sight varied a little from day to day. He thought for a moment and then said, 'Yes. I usually think it gets *worse*.'

I remember his fascination with the strange discord that haunts the pages of Strauss's *Elektra*. He played it at the piano and said he couldn't make up his mind whether to think of it as added-note harmony – E♭ major with an added major sixth and minor ninth, or as an example of bitonality – E♭ major plus C major. On my next visit I was able to show him that I had discovered the identical chord (a semitone higher) in Schubert – it comes in the piano duet *Lebensstürme*, D947, where it has an entirely different meaning and a remarkably simple resolution:

Ex. 23 Richard Strauss, *Elektra*

Ex. 24 Franz Schubert, Sonata Movement in A minor, *Lebensstürme*, D947

He does use this chord several times in his music, for example in the piano piece *Obsession*:

Ex. 25 Ireland, *Obsession*

Elektra chord

He had met Elgar more than once, though I don't think he got to know him well. He told me that on one occasion Elgar looked over one of his scores and said, 'You needn't hold that bassoon note as long as that – you can end it earlier and it will still remain in the mind.'

Once at lunch we were discussing the speed of light and I described one of the ways it was first measured. With my scientific background I thought I gave a good account of how, if you project a narrow beam of light through one of the gaps in a cogged wheel towards a mirror some distance away, the returning beam will, if the wheel is rotating fast enough, hit one of the cogs instead of coming back through the gap. This gives one enough data, if you know the distance of the mirror and the speed of the wheel, to calculate the speed of the light-beam. Ireland considered this for a while, and then said, in his usual gloomy voice, 'I don't understand it.'

Often, towards the end of my day's visits to Rock Mill, Ireland would potter over to a chest of drawers and get out some of his unpublished compositions. I remember the two songs *What art thou thinking of?* and *If we must part* – both in his mature style. I thought them beautiful and asked why he had not published them. He replied that there had been no market for such things, but perhaps there were other reasons – the second bears the words 'for 25 July 1929' and the music is redolent of some personal anguish. Both were included in the Lyrita recording of Ireland's songs.

There were also a number of works from Ireland's student days, for which he obviously still held considerable affection – early tone-poems, two string quartets and a sextet for horn, clarinet and strings. It was of this last work that Stanford had said, 'The last movement's not organic, me bhoy.' But it is remarkably well composed and mellifluous in sound and, with a string quartet, was given a hearing at one of the early concerts of the John Ireland Society.

As time went on Ireland's mental powers did decline and he spoke less and less. Towards the end his conversation was often limited to three words: 'What?', 'Oh', and 'Well'. He had a very characteristic way of saying 'Oh' which retained some trace of the North (his Manchester roots) and with a slight downward inflection seemed to imply that he was not much impressed by what he had just heard. The sequence would go something like this: you would make some comment and Ireland would say, 'What?' (with a rising inflection). You would then repeat your comment a bit louder and after a pause he would say, 'Oh' (with that downward inflection). Then there would then be another pause, after which Ireland would say, '*Well ...*' (in a tone of dismissive exasperation).

Mrs Kirby would not allow that Ireland's mind had lost anything of its power. I once arrived shortly after the visit of a doctor and found her quite furious at something he had said. She said she had told him, 'Never use that word in this house again! Dr Ireland has more brains in his little finger than you have in the whole of your body!' One can only imagine what the word might have been – perhaps it began with an s.

INTERVIEWER Do you think he really disliked the music of Vaughan Williams?

ALAN ROWLANDS Not altogether, though he did have this way of making provocative remarks. He once told me that whenever he passed the house in Cheyne Walk where VW used to live he felt he ought to raise his hat. He wrote in a letter to Alan Bush that he had been 'bored up to top D' by *The Lark Ascending*, but in another letter to Kenneth Thompson he said that 'Vaughan Williams at his best knocks Bax into a cocked hat.' So what can one say?

He and VW had been great friends when they were students together under Stanford. There was a tea-shop in Kensington High Street called Wilkins where they and other students including Dunhill, Howard-Jones and Holst used to meet and discuss everything under the sun, from music to philosophy. After they had finished their day's work at the RCM, they would sing to the tune of the scherzo of Brahms's Fourth Symphony, 'Shall we go to Wilkins? Shall we go to Wilkins? – YES!!':

Ex. 26 Johannes Brahms, Symphony no. 4 – *Scherzo*

Of the two, VW and Ireland, my impression is that it was Ireland who was the more compositionally gifted in those early days – think of those early chamber works, so fluent and expertly written. But as time went on he was overtaken by the older man and Stanford rubbed his nose in the fact by saying, after a VW item at an RCM concert in which works by both men had been played, 'That's better than anything you could write, me bhoy.' Ireland quotes this remark in a letter to VW for his eightieth birthday, adding that 'Its truth is borne in upon me whenever I hear your works.' The rest of the letter is extremely generous in tone and is quoted by Ursula in her biography of VW. I have no doubt that Ireland inwardly recognised VW's greatness, yet there was something, perhaps his own inner insecurity, that led him to take this rather mischievous stance of wanting to deflate the older man.

Of course, Norah Kirby considered Ireland's stature in every way comparable to VW's, and felt that he should have received the OM, as VW had done. She put in some spadework to this end, getting people like Bax to write supportive letters, but I think this was unrealistic. On the other hand, Ireland considered the CBE beneath him and turned it down some time in the 1950s.

INTERVIEWER What was Norah Kirby like?

ALAN ROWLANDS She was rather mannish to look at – short hair and tweedy clothes – and her heavily rimmed spectacles gave her face a somewhat owlish appearance. I could never quite fathom how musical she was, but she was knowledgeable and extremely well read. She was particularly interested in the literature of the 1890s – *The Yellow Book*, Beardsley and so on. She had encountered Ireland's music for the first time during the Second World War when the *Phantasie Trio* had been broadcast, and thought it the most beautiful music she had ever heard. I would say she was intelligent, except that she had a one-track mind – that track being devoted solely to the well-being and spotless reputation of John Ireland. She had her own view of the happenings in Ireland's life, and often would not countenance other people's versions. For instance, John Longmire says in his book that Ireland referred to Helen Perkin as his 'Madonna', but Norah denied any such possibility, saying 'He would *never* have said such a thing.' But how could she know? She certainly did not know something that Longmire once told me – that in their early days Ireland would refer to her as 'the horse'. She was certainly a devoted helper and had come to his rescue when he was ill and uncared for during the last period at Gunter Grove and told me how he had asked her, if he took over the Mill, whether she would come and 'look after things', at the same time making it clear there could be no question of marriage.

She did look after him wonderfully, became his agent and promoted his interests unflaggingly, but with such single-minded intensity that in the process she became almost unbalanced. She could take violent antipathies to some people, especially singers, and would scrawl vehement derogatory comments in heavy handwriting all over the covers of their LPs. I remember that John Shirley-Quirk, who had made quite a decent recording of Ireland's songs with Eric Parkin, came in for this treatment. Another hearty dislike was Roy Henderson – I'm not sure why.

She had a slow and persuasive way of talking which seemed to draw one into her mental orbit, as though one shared a common understanding which was never quite openly stated. There was a drawing in the Mill of what Norah called 'the Amberley boy' – he had a round face and a somewhat wistful expression. I don't know what Norah thought privately about Ireland's interest in boys, but she spoke of his relationship with 'the Amberley boy' almost in a tone of reverence. She certainly would not have attributed Ireland's involvement to anything but a paternal interest or a spirit of generosity, yet who was it who blacked out several of the dedicatory words in Ireland's manuscripts, particularly those associated with Arthur Miller? – it was she who presented the manuscripts to the British Museum (as it then was).

After Ireland's death she became even more identified with him. She would take on his views and even his way of talking. After she had had her stroke her face began to sag in a way that made her almost look like him – it was quite weird. She wrote me letters in which she referred to Him or His works with the capital H. At one of the London concerts she came to, Lawrence Norcross whispered to me, 'Isn't she wearing Ireland's corduroy trousers?'[1] I was once practising some Bax on the upstairs piano at the Mill – and here I should say that one of Ireland's favourite words in describing Bax's music was 'diffuse' – and she looked in and said, 'That sounds rather nice, what is it?' When I said it was Bax, she said 'Oh' (with that downward inflection) – and then, as she went out, 'I thought it sounded rather *diffuse.*'

Another thing I remember her telling me about this time is that in the Green Room after the first performance of *Satyricon*, Walton had 'looked daggers' at Ireland. She spoke as if this had been a matter of personal malevolence, but I think there is a more likely explanation. There is an undoubted air of Waltonesque busyness about the brisker parts of *Satyricon*, but in addition there are two musical figures which bear an uncomfortable resemblance to figures from *Portsmouth Point* and *Belshazzar's Feast* [Exx. 27 and 28].

I don't think Walton would have appreciated being imitated or quoted – though I feel sure this must have been unconscious on Ireland's part. But Waltonesque or not, *Satyricon* is a highly successful piece and the middle section is, as Barbirolli once said to me, 'ravishing, absolutely ravishing!'

[1] See p. xxiii for the editor's experience of this episode.

Ex. 27 (a) Ireland, *Satyricon*; (b) Walton, *Portsmouth Point*

Ex. 28 (a) Ireland, *Satyricon*; (b) Walton, *Belshazzar's Feast*

INTERVIEWER What happened to the Mill after Ireland's death?

ALAN ROWLANDS Norah stayed on for some time. Ireland had realised his debt to her and left her almost his entire estate (it would otherwise have gone to Arthur Miller, though he had already benefited on many occasions from Ireland's financial generosity). It was during this time that Norah invited a party of schoolboys from nearby Lancing College to come over to the Mill and hear me give a talk about Ireland and play some of his music. That was how I first met Bruce Phillips, now the director of the John Ireland Trust. Norah had had a stroke, as I've said, and it was Bruce who helped her to keep things going for a few months at the Mill, this being during what would now be called his gap year.

INTERVIEWER Did Norah recover from the stroke?

ALAN ROWLANDS She worked at it with great determination and recovered the use of her leg well enough to walk again, though not without effort. She never regained the use of one arm. She realised she would not be able to stay on at the Mill and bought a house in Steyning, no. 106, High Street, now a bookseller's (where they have had great difficulty in getting rid of the smell of cats). There was one large reception room which she set up as a John Ireland Memorial Room, with all his most treasured possessions arranged as nearly as possible to the way they were at the Mill. On almost every available horizontal surface she placed a framed photograph of Ireland – on one visit I think I counted twenty-three. In the early years at Steyning interested visitors would come to look at this room, though as time went on and Norah became less able it fell into some neglect. On a later visit I went in and found all twenty-three photographs literally linked by cobwebs, a dismaying and Havisham-like spectacle.

Nevertheless, during those years Norah continued to work assiduously in the interests of Ireland's music and reputation. She instigated the beautiful John Ireland Memorial Window, designed by Brian Thomas CBE, in the Musician's Chapel of St Sepulchre's, the musicians' church of London. She commissioned the first formal biography of Ireland from Muriel Searle, who did as well as could be expected, considering that behind almost every page one seems to hear the voice of Norah Kirby. She continued to attend the meetings of the John Ireland Trust, though I have been told that she could be almost impossible to work with, her irrational behaviour eventually causing two members to resign.[2] And of course she attended all the events of the John Ireland Centenary Festival in 1979, of which she had largely been the driving force – four concerts and a competition in the Wigmore Hall.

INTERVIEWER Who bought the Mill?

ALAN ROWLANDS After Norah Kirby decided in the mid-1960s that she could not continue to live there on her own, a potential buyer was the well-known artist Juliet Pannett, who had visited the Mill towards the end of Ireland's life in order to make drawings of him. At that time Norah had planned to move to St Mawes in Cornwall where she had spent holidays. However, Mrs Pannett was advised by a chartered surveyor that the Mill was a fire risk and furthermore that the extensive quarrying at Rock Common virtually surrounding the Mill was likely to be a source of permanent environmental pollution and disruption. Mrs Pannett decided against the purchase and instead moved to Angmering, West Sussex, where she died in 2005.

The Mill passed through a number of private owners including a property developer, a pilot[3] working for British Caledonian, and a chartered accountant. The external fabric of the Mill, a Grade 2 listed building, was maintained and various modifications made to the Mill itself, the adjoining house and the garden. At one time the owners of the land on which the Mill stood and of the surrounding quarry, the Wiston Estate, working in conjunction with the firm of Veolia Environmental Services, obtained permission from West Sussex County Council to use one part of the site for landfill. Rock Mill was sold to Veolia who have used it for offices.

In 2006 an application was made by Veolia, backed by the Wiston Estate, for a major expansion of landfill use. This was vigorously opposed by Washington Parish Council and by other bodies including the Environment Agency, and was finally rejected by West Sussex County Council in 2009. The area is now part of the newly created South Downs National Park. The future of Rock Mill itself is uncertain. The view of Chanctonbury Ring, so loved by Ireland, is now completely obscured by tall trees, the garden so carefully nurtured by Norah a wilderness, and the public is barred from admission. The stone plaque outside the front door commemorates Ireland's last ten happy years there, and I wish someone would come and rescue it from further decline and decay.

---

[2] One was Father Kenneth Thompson; see his account on p. 78.

[3] In the summer of 1967 I accompanied an American friend, Richard Brodhead, on a visit to West Sussex. Richard wanted to photograph Rock Mill, and when we arrived we found the path from the gate obscured by a density of overgrown bushes and trees. As we went up the path a teenage boy appeared and asked what we wanted. As we explained we could see a family group sitting on the extensive lawn. A man called out in notably well-modulated tones: 'Can you handle it?' The boy assured his father (presumably the airline pilot) that he could and we took our photographs and left. So in 1967 it appears to have been a family home. – EDITOR.

CHAPTER 4

John Ireland's Personal World

Fiona Richards

M ORE than many other composers, John Ireland's personal world is played out in his music, with a complex system of musical symbols, images and ideas woven into almost everything he wrote. There is a rich tapestry of extra-musical layers of meanings, with pieces closely linked to dates, places, people and literature. While he spent most of his life living either alone or only with a dedicated housekeeper, nonetheless his private loves and friendships were many and varied. His family and friends played a huge role, and there are many surviving letters and dedications in his compositions which allow the investigator to create a map of the family members, composers, performers, officials and ordinary people who circle, detour and cross the linear narrative of Ireland's life.

People come and go and have different roles in this narrative. For example, Ireland's long associations with Geoffrey Shaw (1879–1943) are the catalyst for his hymn tunes. There are performers whose associations with the composer are significant, among them violinist Albert Sammons (1886–1957) and cellist Carl Fuchs (1865–1951). Edwin Evans (1871–1945) was a critic and close friend of the composer, and letters to him span a long period. Harold Rutland (1900–77) was a musician and writer who knew Ireland from the 1920s until his death, and became the president of the John Ireland Society. In his later life the composer became friendly with composer Geoffrey Bush (1920–98) and pianists Alan Rowlands and Eric Parkin and developed a friendship with the writer Jocelyn Brooke (1908–66). There are thumbnail roles (Guernsey flautist Albert Sebire), people who are important at particular moments (Sylvia Townsend Warner [1893–1978] and Peter Warlock [1894–1930])[1] and those who stay with him for many years (Alan Bush [1900–95]).

Close friends, such as John Longmire (1902–86), E. J. Moeran (1894–1950) and Thomas Dunhill (1877–1946), for whom Ireland had stood as best man, were loyal and supportive, and have left memories of his kindness and integrity. But Ireland also suffered from difficult personal relationships, and there are other recollections of a grumpy, antisocial man prone to alcoholism. The composer wrote of himself and his family that 'we are liable every few years to some kind of "crisis", when everything in life seems impossible and unbearable, and one feels unable to face up to anything. I have had it several times ...'[2]

Even with no supporting biographical evidence, the programmatic and literary nature of Ireland's output suggests an innate homosexuality, though there is no evidence of his having had a sexual relationship with another man. This would in any case have been prohibited in his day; such secrets were closely guarded, and confessions were never committed to paper. Just as Housman's poetry has often

---

[1] Ireland was involved in the inquest into Warlock' death.

[2] Ireland to Silvio Ireland, 30 June 1948: John Ireland Trust.

been treated as a cryptic diary, so Ireland's music is inherently autobiographical. Even before one looks at the notes of the music, there are many clues to his sexuality, including the composer's interest in symbols such as Pan the goat-god and in the poetry of Housman and Rupert Brooke. Then there are more suggestive indications in the musical expression of homoerotic passions aroused by the First World War and the Anglican Church. There are hints and ambiguities in his choice of words by homosexual icon, John Addington Symonds. There are song settings of the highly charged, secretive love poetry of Sidney and Huxley. And there are also enigmatic dedications and carefully chosen literary epigraphs attached to many of his works.

The dedications on his manuscripts reveal much about the people who passed through his life. On the one hand each of the three lyric pieces for solo piano, *Green Ways* (1937) is dedicated to a different person: 'The Cherry Tree' to Ireland's legal advisor Herbert Brown, 'Cypress' to his accountant Alfred Chenhalls and 'The Palm and May' to pianist Harriet Cohen. At a different level, there are a number of works with much more personal dedications and heavily deleted annotations on the scores. For example, the six songs composed between 1929 and 1931 that were published as *Songs Sacred and Profane*, were described by the composer as 'a very personal document.'[3] The second song, 'Hymn for a Child', was dedicated to the brilliant young pianist Helen Perkin. The third, 'My Fair', carries no dedication. It was composed in July 1929, a time of great personal crisis for the composer. The manuscript has an inscription that has been heavily deleted. Within Ireland's manuscripts, it is only the pieces intended for a young man, Arthur Miller, that carry these frenzied obliterations. The song itself is a fervent declaration of love.

Ireland was a prolific letter-writer, and there is much surviving correspondence, though unfortunately very little from the 1920s, the decade in which he was producing his most intense, intimate music. Of the large number of letters from the 1940s that have survived, some are to close friends, others to musicians. They are one of the main ways in which it is possible to build a picture of Ireland's personality, as they contain information on his composing methods, remarks on the political situation, descriptions of places and little throwaway lines that often give much away. Letters to singer George Parker, for example, span a long period starting from 1913, and contain comments on the composer's music and personal situation – such as a comment that his private affairs are involving him in 'endless worry.'[4]

J OHN Nicholson Ireland was born on 13 August 1879 in Bowdon, a prosperous suburb of south Manchester. His father, Alexander Ireland (1809–94), was born in Edinburgh, his family having moved from Orkney some generations earlier. He moved to Manchester in *c.* 1846 to become manager and publisher of the recently established *Manchester Examiner*, and in 1865 married his second wife, Anne (Annie) Elizabeth Nicholson (1839–93), already having a son (Alexander) by a first wife. Annie was born in Penrith, and was herself an author and critic. Her father,

---

[3] Ireland to George Parker, 24 October 1934: John Ireland Trust.
[4] Ireland to George Parker, 17 October 1928: John Ireland Trust.

Dr John Nicholson, was a scholar of oriental languages at Queen's College, Oxford; her brother Alleyne Nicholson a Professor in Aberdeen.

In 1866 Alexander and Annie were living in 'Alder Bank', Ashley Road, Altrincham. Their first child, Lucy, was born in October that year, followed by another girl, Alice, in February 1868. The family then moved to Bowdon. Walter Alleyne (known always as Alleyne) was born in January 1871, and a third girl, Edith (Ethel), in January 1873. By 1871 the family were in the large house 'Inglewood', in Bowdon, with a household of five servants. There was a gap of a few years before the birth of John in 1879, when his father was seventy and his mother forty years old. Ireland's mother Annie was the most influential figure in the early part of his life. Although in poor health, she lectured and published on literature.

Of the three sisters, Ireland never mentioned either Lucy or Alice in any correspondence with anyone: it is almost as though they never existed. The youngest, Ethel, was the only one to maintain contact with John. She studied at the Royal Academy of Music, had some musical and literary works published, and moved to Switzerland after her marriage. She was divorced during the First World War, and John was in touch with her at least until the Second World War, when she was living first in Venice, in 1939, and then in France, in Menton and Juan-les-Pins in 1940. She had two sons, the eldest of whom, Silvio (*b.* 1904), after an education at the King's College Choir School, Cambridge, and at King William's School in the Isle of Man, did remain in contact with his uncle, visiting him in Chelsea in the 1920s. Silvio moved to San Francisco, where he took a new name, Henri Lenoir, and settled first as the owner of a café and eventually as a collector and dealer in fine art. Throughout Ireland's life there is affectionate and often lengthy correspondence between them. Silvio sent what were evidently very generous food parcels on a regular basis during and after the Second World War. Ethel's other son, Anthony (1906–89), worked for some time as a language teacher. He married and had three children, Nicholas (*b.* 1939), Caroline (*b.* 1941) and Adrian (*b.* 1945).

On 28 September 1893, at the age of just fourteen, Ireland enrolled at the Royal College of Music. His sister Ethel was already at the RAM and he moved in with her for a short time. Less than a week after he had started at the RCM their mother died, followed a year later by their father. Ireland and his sister were left in the charge of a guardian, and the next few years saw them moving frequently around different lodgings. Ireland lived in London for most of his life, from 1893 until 1953, though within this period he did spend spells away from the city, some of them quite lengthy. The first home in which he lived for any length of time, from *c.* 1904 until 1915, was 54 Elm Park Mansions, Park Walk. In 1915 he bought a studio, 14A Gunter Grove, Chelsea, and in 1923 purchased the whole house. For sixty years Ireland lived in a road leading off the Kings Road, the main artery that connected his homes and other significant places such as St Luke's, Holy Trinity, and Chelsea Arts Club, of which he was an honorary member for many years, from 1925 to at least 1941.

In July 1904 Ireland took up an appointment as organist and choirmaster at St Luke's Church. Clearly he viewed this as a very significant part of his life as in the 1911 census entry he signs himself 'John Ireland, organist', and he left the post only in 1926. St Luke's introduced him to figures who were to play important roles in his career outside the Church. These included the curate Paul Walde, who became a lifelong friend, and also the cleric A. R. Lee Gardner, who was a friend from *c.* 1908 to at least 1954; Gardner later gave up Holy Orders to become a crime writer. A number of the choirboys also played significant roles in Ireland's life and music, three in particular. These were Charles Markes (1900–85), Bobby Glassby (*c.* 1900–34) and Arthur George Miller (1905–86).

Markes was the son of an alcoholic, living in very poor circumstances, who joined St Luke's as a chorister in 1908, exchanging singing for duties as Ireland's deputy at the organ when his voice broke in 1915. Markes, whose uncle was a chorister at Southwark Cathedral and at St Anne's, Soho, was a natural musician, and was taken on as a piano pupil by Ireland *c.* 1911. Ireland, with assistance from St Luke's, also contributed to Markes's school fees. The two gradually developed a close friendship, and the boy spent much time in his teacher's company. Markes was called up in 1918. On his return to London in 1919 he found employment as a music hall artist. In 1920 a misunderstanding (a moment of misinterpretation as Ireland appeared to cut Markes in the street) led to the end of his friendship with the composer, and this was not renewed until 1948. The rediscovered intimacy saw Markes once again working closely with Ireland, correcting the proofs of the score of *Satyricon* and preparing the editions of the early string quartets.

Bobby Glassby (Robert McLean Glassby) joined St Luke's choir in about 1911 at the instigation of Markes. In 1913 Ireland wrote what has become one of his most frequently performed pieces, 'The Holy Boy'. At first glance the piece is about Christmas and the birth of Christ, the 'holy boy', but a real 'holy boy' may also have lain behind the work, this being the young Bobby Glassby, a sculpted head of whom was a treasured possession of the composer. Glassby was still in contact with Ireland in 1920, as a signed photograph testifies (see Plate 31). He died in tragic circumstances, his body recovered from the River Ouse, near York, in 1934.

In the first two months of 1920 Ireland wrote two songs, 'The Trellis' and 'My True Love Hath my Heart', which embody his positive musical declarations of love during the first part of this decade. The first of these songs, 'The Trellis', is one of the most idyllic and rapturous of all Ireland's works. For the second song, the dreamy euphoria of 'The Trellis' gives way to an absolute affirmation of love. Horace Randerson (1892–1992), a pupil of Ireland at this time, wrote in his diary: 'Stayed with Ireland till 11.45 pm.! – discussed education, the Church, marriage, friendship & life in general. He played over his new song "My true love hath my heart" before publishing – he was hesitating about it as to whether it would be understood. Walt Whitman – he advised me to read "Leaves of Grass".'[5] The implication is that 1920 was a year of personal rapture, though whether this was in hope or in reality remains a mystery. Soon after this date Ireland must have begun to experience a different type of love, one that was to cause him anguish, and which was not to be fulfilled, as he never again wrote a song in such affirmative and passionate vein.

The year 1920 was the start of a period of creative intensity, and a time when Ireland's personal passions were most obviously played out in his music. In 1922 he wrote the piano solo *On a Birthday Morning*. This bore the dedication 'Pro amicitia' ('for friendship'), and was dated 22 February 1922. It was a present for

---

[5] Horace Randerson, notes from diary, February 1920: John Ireland Trust.

Arthur George Miller, who was seventeen on that day. Between 1922 and 1929 Ireland dedicated a series of works to Miller, most of which were intended as birthday gifts, and thus dated 22 February. This young man was a central figure in Ireland's life, the person behind the composer's most intense music. Born in 1905, Miller was the eldest son of Arthur Miller and Maud Major. There were three younger siblings: Ruby, Charles and Rene. According to Markes, Miller 'became a choirboy at St Luke's towards the end of my years there. He was the son of an antique dealer who had a small "antique" shop a few doors from where the Chelsea Palace used to be.'[6] Miller probably joined the choir in about 1915.

The initial St Luke's connection swiftly flowered into a much closer companionship, with Miller spending much time with the composer. In 1922, the year of the first dedication, for example, they holidayed together in Norfolk, a habit that was continued over the next few years. There are no known extant letters from Ireland to Miller, only one from Miller to Ireland, and very few surviving details of this friendship. It is not clear whether Miller was aware what Ireland felt for him, and there is no evidence that their relationship was a sexual one. But it is clear from the recurrence of the dedications to Miller and the intense nature of the works that, for Ireland at least, this relationship was of the utmost significance.

On a Birthday Morning is the first of four piano works dedicated to Miller. There was no work specifically dedicated to him in 1923, and Ireland spent much of this year working on his large-scale Cello Sonata. There are, however, musical links between this sonata and the pieces written for Miller. In this year the two men travelled together to Dorset, Somerset and Wiltshire, visiting the type of historic sites that interested Ireland. In 1924 Ireland dedicated another piano piece, the Prelude in E♭, to Miller, and the year after that, 'Bergomask'. 'Bergomask' was not the only piece dedicated to Miller in 1925. In 1924 Ireland had turned to Christina Rossetti's verse to set the frequently-used poem, 'When I am dead, my dearest', a passage from 'Song' in *Goblin Market and other poems*. The following year he inscribed the song 'To A.G.M.: Cerne Abbas, June, 1925'. Presumably a trip to the pagan site at Cerne Abbas had been a memorable one, and the wistful nostalgia of Rossetti's words must have been in some way connected to the feelings kindled at this time. This was the first song that Ireland dedicated to Miller. In the following year, 1926, Ireland produced a cycle of *Three Songs*. Completed in July, the work was then retrospectively headed 'for February 22, 1926'.

1926 was a momentous year for Ireland, and the start of a period of bleak despair, reflected in his music. In October he left St Luke's. On 17 December he married a seventeen-year-old pianist and student at the Royal Academy of Music, Dorothy Phillips (*b.* 1909)[7], Arthur Miller acting as his witness. This turned out

---

[6] Charles Markes to George Dannatt, 2 November 1974.

[7] EDITOR'S NOTE: Among the Longmire papers at the John Ireland trust we find the following account of Dorothy Phillips which was not included in Longmire's published book on John Ireland. Despite its novelletish tone Longmire paints a vivid portrait: Ireland's friend, the amusingly cynical Christopher à Beckett Williams took John Ireland to a party. 'The party was held in the studio of a professor, eminent in his day, and included a bevy of his young lady students. ... It was in this smoke-laden, irresponsible atmosphere that John met his first heart throb. She was dark and slim – he had always admired the boyish figure. Full of fun, tomboy like,

to be a disastrous move, and Ireland developed an extreme antipathy for the girl. Why Ireland ever chose to marry Phillips remains a mystery. Perhaps he was going through some sort of mid-life crisis, and saw marriage as a conventional and proper thing to do, a way of presenting himself to the public as a respectable married man.

The Miller work of two months later, February 1927, was the song-cycle *We'll to the Woods No More*. The dedication in the printed music merely says 'To Arthur', with the additional inscription 'for February 22 1927' at the end of the work. The manuscript version offers a fuller dedication, reading 'To Arthur: in memory of the darkest days', with some further words heavily scratched out. The cycle is axiomatic of the problems surrounding Ireland's sexuality: there are many ambiguities and subtle connections at play here.

The composer's disastrous marriage in 1926 was shortly followed by Miller's own marriage to a twenty-one-year-old Chelsea girl, Emmeline Orriss, which took place in St Luke's Church on 26 June 1927, this time with Ireland acting as witness. No compositions were dedicated to Miller in 1928, and in March of that year Ireland's marriage ended. There is virtually nothing known of his relationship with Phillips in the intervening months. It may have been unconsummated, but in fact there was a divorce, which was made absolute on 19 September 1928.

In 1929 Ireland wrote *Two Pieces* for piano: 'February's child' and 'Aubade'. To the first of these were appended the words 'To AGM for 22 February, 1929', but as with *We'll to the Woods No More*, the manuscript carries a fuller dedication, deleted by another hand. However, it is possible to read through the obliteration to find these words, those marked in square brackets showing alternatives at the points where the words are difficult to discern:

> ... whatsoever things are grave [gone] ...
> whatsoever things are lovely ...
> So [I'll] think on these things.

These words are a personal eulogy to Miller, but are also a transformation of a biblical text from the Letter of Paul to the Philippians 4:8. There are other pieces that seem to belong to this sequence of Miller works, and which are expressions of Ireland's state of mind at this time. The song, 'If We Must Part', bears no dedication, but just the words 'for 25 July 1929'. July 1929 was also the date of the song 'My Fair', which, though not dedicated to Arthur, like many of the known Miller pieces, bears a heavily deleted inscription. In August Ireland wrote to Randerson from his Sussex retreat of 'the worst worries which have confronted me (an aftermath of previous disturbances)'.[8]

Despite his issues with Arthur Miller, Ireland had acquired another beautiful

she fascinated him. Her sparkling eyes always seemed to be smiling invitingly at him whenever he dared steel a glance in her direction. Her dancing was more vital, her laughter more gay, her legs more slim than any of the other guests. John was at this time in his middle forties, often lonely, and for all his misogynistic outbursts he envied his more sociable colleagues with their wives and families. He found himself obsessed by his memory of this young girl, and invited himself to the next party ...'

[8] Ireland to H. O. Randerson, 29 August 1929: John Ireland Trust

young protégée, this time a woman, with whom he enjoyed a happier and much more productive relationship than he had with his wife, albeit temporarily. This was the pianist, Helen Perkin (1909–96). As with Miller, it is difficult to ascertain the nature of Ireland's relationship with Perkin. Longmire saw it as 'devoted and disinterested love.'[9] Thompson repudiated Longmire's account, on the grounds that he believed Ireland could not possibly have had an intense personal relationship with a woman, and that his interests in her were purely musical.[10] Perkin herself said that they were inseparable between 1928 and 1930, and that their relationship was 'one of the highest forms of love that I have ever known.'[11] The most significant product of this relationship was the Piano Concerto, one of Ireland's most uplifting and beautiful works.

Ireland's association with Helen Perkin appears to have been his last important relationship with a woman until his latter years in the company of Norah Kirby. Although he thought so highly of Perkin's playing, Ireland was often critical of performances of his music undertaken by women, and after the demise of his friendship with Perkin he increasingly expressed a dislike for women performers. After this friendship ended, Ireland was not closely involved with any single individual, male or female, for some time, with the exception of Father Kenneth Thompson (1904–91).

By about 1932 Ireland had become a regular worshipper at St Cuthbert's, Kensington, along with another friend Percy Bentham (1883–1936).[12] Bentham was one of many professional sculptors working in Chelsea. In 1926 he moved into The Studio, 8 Gunter Grove, a few doors away from Ireland, and knew the composer from this time. During this period, according to Ireland, they 'met almost daily.'[13] The Priest-in-Charge at this church was Kenneth Thompson, who swiftly became a close friend of the composer. His position as a cleric and his obvious empathy with Ireland's music and sexuality were powerful attractions, and from 1936 to 1962 the two met regularly and corresponded frequently. Fourteen years after Ireland's death, Thompson wrote to Scott-Sutherland that the composer 'regarded me as his Chaplain, so to speak – and one to whom he could talk intimately about his personal affairs.'[14]

In 1936 Thompson left St Cuthbert's and moved to Sussex to be assistant chaplain at Lancing College, and the following year added to this post that of lecturer and librarian at Chichester Theological College. From this date up to 1961 the two

---

[9] John Longmire, *John Ireland – Portrait of a Friend* (London: John Baker, 1969), p. 29.

[10] Kenneth Thompson to Colin Scott-Sutherland, 20 September 1976: John Ireland Trust.

[11] Helen Perkin, notes to Colin Scott-Sutherland: John Ireland Trust.

[12] Bentham died in tragic circumstances and the composer's *London Overture* is dedicated to him, carrying within it a quote from Schumann's 'Widmung', which song opens with the words 'Du meine Seele, du mein Herz' ('You my soul, you my heart'). See also p. 207 and Plate 39

[13] Ireland to Ethel Ireland, 17 June 1936: John Ireland Trust.

[14] Kenneth Thompson to Colin Scott-Sutherland, 20 September 1976: John Ireland Trust.

men corresponded frequently. The correspondence was painstakingly conserved by Thompson, who gave the material to the British Library in 1979, where it is now preserved as two large volumes of letters (Additional MSS 60535 and 60536), presented chronologically. Into this correspondence Thompson has periodically inserted explanatory notes or diary entries of his own on brown paper, some written retrospectively, some concurrent with the letters they accompany. The correspondence, which began on 18 May 1936, was extensive, comprising 143 letters and cards, often long and detailed. On average Ireland wrote once a month, though there were also periods, the 1950s in particular, when he corresponded much more frequently. And there were times when there would be a gap of a few months, for example in 1942, when there were only two letters, and in 1948 and 1949. From August 1960, when his eyesight was deteriorating, he was forced to use a typewriter, and from 1961 Norah Kirby had to write on his behalf. Sadly the archived Ireland–Thompson correspondence is almost entirely one-sided: few letters from Thompson to Ireland survive, with just five held by the John Ireland Trust. In addition to the discussion of religious and literary issues, the tone and content of Ireland's letters to him revealed aspects of his most private side. Thompson's own sympathies with Ireland's sexuality and his position as a cleric seemed to enable Ireland to offload some of his desires and fantasies. There is an informality and an honesty about these letters that is rarely seen elsewhere. Below is a good example of the style and content of these letters:

> … my music does not appeal to <u>women</u>: who form the majority of listeners. They know instinctively that it is not inspired by their charms – and for the same reason, I do not think what I write is acceptable to the majority of men.
>
> Well, when you return from your present trip, or, at any rate, when the war is over, you must take a country living…in a small town, where we can work up a large choir & I will be your organist & choirmaster. I really mean this. I will live with you in the Rectory or Vicarage. You will not be such a fool as to marry the good lady who is thirsty for your blood. Marriage is not for Uranians. It only creates the most ghastly strife and horrible unhappiness for <u>both</u> parties, believe me.
>
> … Although living here is by no means ideal, it might be much worse. I shall have to try to put up with it till hostilities cease. You must not think I am being quite idle. I have nearly completed a Fantasy-Sonata for Clarinet and Piano – it is in one movement, & will last 14 or 15 minutes. I have been at it for quite 6 months! The clarinet is a remarkable instrument, & I have been most impressed by the playing of Thurston – hence the choice of this combination … I'm afraid it will have very few performances – works for wind instruments are seldom heard. I will have to concoct some 'bread-&-butter' (ie uninspired) works. Life without romance is really dull – one lives only on memories, and even these are marred by the fact that one did not make the most of one's opportunities. 'Gather ye rosebuds while ye may' is a maxim to be instilled into the young – though I know this to be contrary to ecclesiastical principles![15]

---

[15] Ireland to Kenneth Thompson, 25 November 1943: *GB-Lbl*, Add. MSS 60535–6.

For a short period, in 1936, Ireland rented a room in a house in Middle Street, Deal. At this time his friend and solicitor, Herbert Brown, was living in Shepherds-well near Dover, and introduced Ireland to the Hulke family, the owners of a large Georgian house, Comarques, in the High Street, Deal. Ireland rented part of the top floor of this house between 1936 and 1939. From 1937 he stayed in this flat on an increasingly regular basis, and did much of his writing here, producing his *Concertino Pastorale* for the Boyd Neel String Orchestra, for a performance in the 1939 Canterbury Festival. Ireland wrote to Neel several times after this performance expressing his feelings about the piece and the current political situation.

In June 1939 Ireland decided to shut Gunter Grove, vacate the Deal rooms and leave England for Guernsey. On 3 July, along with John Longmire, he travelled from Southampton to St Peter Port. According to Longmire[16] this was a project which had been discussed for some time. From October 1939 they lived in a marvellous, spacious house, Fort Saumarez. The brief time in Guernsey introduced new friends into Ireland's life. He became the organist at St Stephen's church, and the song 'Boys' Names' is dedicated to a Guernsey boy, Peter Lihou, who had been in the St Stephen's choir for only a short time.

In April 1940 Ireland moved from the west coast of the island to the Birnam Court Hotel in St Peter Port, owned by an ex-naval man, George Davy Rayson, and his wife, Margaret. They had a nine-year-old son, Michael (1930–2011), described by Ireland as 'beautiful, clever & alert, with perfect manners – & being well educated at one of the best schools here. Not, alas, musical. But lovely, long, curling eyelashes. Here comes out the stifled paternal instinct.'[17] In a slightly later letter Ireland enclosed a photograph of the boy, saying that he was 'attractive, but not at all affectionate, wh: is perhaps as well!'[18]

The central movement of Ireland's subsequent three-movement piano work, *Sarnia*, is about this young boy Michael Rayson.[19] This is made clear by the dedication, references in letters, and the Victor Hugo poem attached to the movement. Ireland originally contemplated calling this piece 'Boyslove' (a word much used by the Uranian poets, a group of male poets who produced romantic works concerned with the beauty and attraction of young boys and Greek homoerotic themes), but eventually settled on 'In a May Morning' as being less overt and more holistically appropriate to the piece.

Just over a month later Ireland was forced to leave Guernsey. On 19 June the Channel Islands were demilitarized, and evacuation was soon under way. Ireland was still there on the morning of 22 June, waiting for transport off the island. Boult and the BBC had become involved in urging the War Office[20] to secure a passage for him, and he was on one of the last boats to leave Guernsey, the SS *Antwerp*, along with Longmire and Percy Turnbull (1902–76), the latter a composer friend who had been visiting. On his arrival in Weymouth later that day, Ireland wrote to Thompson, describing his ordeal. Guernsey was bombed by the Luftwaffe on

---

[16] Longmire, *John Ireland*, p. 40.

[17] Ireland to Kenneth Thompson, 29 April 1940: *GB-Lbl*, Add. MSS 60535–6.

[18] Ireland to Kenneth Thompson, 18 May 1940: *GB-Lbl*, Add. MSS 60535–6.

[19] Later Air Commodore Michael Rayson LVO (Retd) died Surrey, 12 August 2011.

[20] See p. 93.

28 June, and invaded on 30 June. Jersey surrendered the next day, followed by Alderney on 2 July and Sark on 3 July. Many hotels were commandeered, as was Fort Saumarez.

Ireland's circumstances on his return to England were in great contrast to his situation on Guernsey. He could not return to Gunter Grove, and his Deal flat was in a hazardous spot on the exposed and vulnerable south coast of England. Thenceforth he spent the war years relying on the hospitality of friends. He went first to Alan Bush's home in Radlett, a town which was itself heavily bombed, and from there to Banbury, where he completed *Sarnia*. In July 1942 Ireland moved to Little Sampford Rectory, in a village near Saffron Walden, Essex, to stay with his old friend Paul Walde. Later this year Ireland moved to The White House, Great Sampford, to stay with the Hutcheson family, friends from some years earlier. Gunter Grove was then repaired following bomb damage, and in 1945 he was moving between London and the Sampford addresses.

During the years 1940–45 Ireland was surprisingly productive. His pieces for piano, *Three Pastels*, all bear titles suggesting a mythical or historical youth. His return to Greek subject matter in this set of pieces demonstrated a continued interest in a subject that had always lurked behind his music, a subject there for its homoerotic, more specifically paederastic connotations. 'Greek love' became progressively more present in his thoughts, as expressed in the later letters to and from Thompson. In 1943 he wrote his Fantasy Sonata for Clarinet and Piano, the sole work of this year. The Fantasy Sonata was written for the renowned clarinettist Frederick Thurston (1901–53), a figure who had a significant impact on the work of a number of British composers, inspiring many works for the clarinet. Thurston was principal clarinet with the BBC Symphony Orchestra from 1930 until 1946. As far as Ireland was concerned, this was a very fruitful partnership, and the prominence of the clarinet part in both *Satyricon* and *The Overlanders* was a direct result of his work with Thurston on the Fantasy Sonata. Ireland worked closely with him on the composition of the piece. As well as extant letters to Thurston, which discuss technical issues, there are also some clues to hidden meanings. Another friend of the 1940s was former cleric A. R. Lee Gardner. A handful of letters to him from Ireland survive. Though neither so wide-ranging nor so personal, these letters have similarities with those to Thompson, in that Ireland makes reference to Greek influences and to his attraction to boys, and talks of the two of them (that is, Gardner and Ireland) as being of the same persuasion. In a letter to Gardner of August 1943, Ireland writes of the Fantasy-Sonata as: 'really about some aspects of <u>Gito</u> – the boy in the "Satyricon" – I should like to call it "The Song of Gito" – but, of course, <u>I dare not!</u>'[21]

Throughout this time, and despite the anguish expressed in *We'll to the Woods No More*, Ireland had maintained his relationship with Arthur Miller. There is a letter from Ireland to Alan Bush in which he asks Bush to find employment for Arthur: 'I trust there is still some hope, as he is in rather a bad way at present, and suffering more & more from his enforced idleness.'[22] In 1940 Miller married for

---

[21] Ireland to Lee Gardner, 5 August 1943: John Ireland Trust.

[22] Ireland to Alan Bush, 31 March 1933, in *The Correspondence of Alan Bush and John Ireland, 1927–1961*, ed. Rachel O'Higgins (Aldershot: Ashgate, 2006), p. 43.

a second time, to Rita. He already had one child from his first marriage, and the second produced two sons and two daughters. Miller and Ireland continued to stay in touch, and during the 1940s and 1950s Ireland lent him sums of money on several occasions, purchased businesses for him (a practice that had begun some years earlier) and acted as mortgage guarantor for a family home in 1948. Ireland's solicitor friend, Herbert Brown, was closely involved with the financial dealings between Miller and Ireland. There no longer appeared to be any trauma in the relationship between the two men, as the only extant letter from Miller to Ireland[23] seems to testify. In this Miller thanks him for money and tells him that he is about to sail either to Australia or to Singapore, Hong Kong and Japan in his new P. & O. job. Miller then goes on to describe his financial problems and to ask for more money. In 1952 Ireland was again bailing out Miller, clearing his debts. Astonishingly, Ireland's letters to Thompson never mention Miller, perhaps because the reality of the relationship was too far removed from the fantasies that Ireland preferred to impart to his friend, though at one point Thompson had been involved in the drafting of Ireland's will.

Here there are many uncertainties and ambiguities. In the John Ireland Trust there is a surviving document in the hand of Ireland's solicitor, Herbert Brown, dating from *c.* 1940–42. This is a piece of paper listing the proposed recipients of Ireland's estate. In it £1,500 is left to his sister Ethel, small sums to several other people and the residue to Arthur G. Miller. At about this time Brown referred to Miller as being Ireland's legatee.[24] In 1952, largely on account of Ethel's death in 1948, Ireland wrote to Thompson that he was thinking of making a new will, and asked him to help deal with things, as he would 'hate the idea of all my papers, letters, etc. passing through the hands of a normal (heterosexual) person'.[25] In 1953 Ireland was clearly thinking about his family and his will, as he wrote to a number of distant relatives asking them for biographical information. On 17 July 1953 Ireland drew up his new will, leaving everything bar a small sum of money to Norah Kirby, his housekeeper, whom he had known for only six years. Perhaps this was a curious decision, given that he had two living nephews with whom he stayed in touch, and that there were also Arthur Miller (though he had received substantial sums of money over the previous years, and especially in 1952) and Kenneth Thompson.

After producing the film score for *The Overlanders* in 1946, Ireland composed very little music, and what he did write is insubstantial, and was produced to commission only. In his latter years he suffered increasingly from health problems, including arteriosclerosis and worsening hearing and eyesight. Nevertheless, during this period Ireland continued to read extensively, and to write regularly to friends and colleagues. Much of his time in 1947 was taken up with the appointment of Norah Kirby to be his housekeeper, but there were also two short pieces in this year. 1949 was the year of Ireland's seventieth birthday. This was marked with an impressive autograph book presented to the composer, which had been signed with greetings from many important figures, among them Ralph Vaughan

---

[23] Arthur Miller to John Ireland, 29 December 1949: John Ireland Trust.

[24] Herbert Brown to John Ireland, 8 December 1940: John Ireland Trust.

[25] Ireland to Kenneth Thompson, 30 December 1952: *GB-Lbl*, Add. MSS 60535–6.

Williams (1872–1958), Alan Rawsthorne (1905–71) and Malcolm Sargent (1895–1967). In June of the following year, though still primarily based in London, he took a flat at The Old Rectory, Ashington.

In the autumn of 1953 he purchased Rock Mill in Sussex. The early months at the mill seemed to bring a tranquillity of spirit to the composer, and although he found the winter of 1954 extremely cold, the tone of his letters of these first few months is quite mellow. However, by April 1954 Ireland was suffering 'a period of <u>hideous</u> depression'[26] brought about by the fact that Rock Mill was bounded by invasive and noisy sand quarrying activities. During the late 1950s Ireland wrote nothing, though continued to attend concerts which included his music. August 1959 saw him celebrate his eightieth birthday, with performances at the Proms of the Piano Concerto, *The Forgotten Rite* and *Satyricon*.[27] In 1960 the John Ireland Society was formed, though it was comparatively short-lived. Its chairman was long-time friend Harold Rutland, and Lawrence Norcross (1927–2010), a teacher[28] and former sailor, was secretary to the society.

Ireland died on 12 June 1962 at the age of 82. He was buried in the Church of St Mary the Virgin, Shipley, West Sussex. The choice of burial place was symbolic and appropriate. It is a small church in an idyllic setting, tucked away in the Sussex countryside. Ireland lies buried outside, his grave marked by pagan Sarsen stones brought from Dorset to West Sussex. Those present at the funeral perhaps provide a closing snapshot of his personal world. Kenneth Thompson officiated at the service, and Ireland's nephew Anthony was an attending family member. Former choirboys Charlie Markes and Arthur Miller were both there, as were long-standing musician friends, including Alan Bush, Ernest Chapman, Peter Crossley-Holland, Scott Goddard, John Longmire, Horace Randerson and Percy Turnbull, and performers of his music Eric Parkin and Alan Rowlands. Finally, his devoted housekeeper Norah Kirby had helped to make the arrangements for the event, and some years later was buried beside him.

---

[26] Ireland to Kenneth Thompson, 27 April 1954: *GB-Lbl*, Add. MSS 60535–6.

[27] That year *A London Overture* was also given during the Proms, on 25 July.

[28] Norcross was a major contributor to papers produced by the Centre for Policy Studies and to Kenneth Baker's national curriculum in the 1970s and 80s.

CHAPTER 5

Interview with John Ireland

Murray Schafer

This interview was first published in British Composers in Interview *(London: Faber & Faber, 1963). The interview on which it is based is now in the possession of the John Ireland Trust, representing the John Ireland Estate. A correlation between the tape and the printed interview reveals no revision is required for its reappearance here.*

BORN 1879, studied composition with Stanford. When Dr. Ireland says 'You must remember that when I was young Brahms was the greatest living composer', he lets us in on a musical period now legendary for most. True, Dr. Ireland's reflections deal mostly with musical life in England before and after the turn of the century, but was this not a time when this country was firmly under the Teutonic spell? Her liberation, the encouragement of a less sophisticated and more individual music took the combined efforts of many composers, Dr. Ireland not the least of them. He died in June 1962. During the last years of his life, retired, the composer lived in a converted windmill on the Sussex Downs.

In the spacious interior of the windmill, three large armchairs were drawn up round the fire. Dr. Ireland relaxed in the largest and smoked a cigar. He spoke slowly but appeared eager, and in replying to questions employed a wide range of dynamics; these varied in proportion to the interest the questions aroused in him. His boldest remarks were accompanied by sideward glances to register the impression they were producing. Kind to his critics, he was modest about his own work, but he was intensely curious about the new music of others, towards which he was remarkably tolerant.

SCHAFER When you were born in 1879, Brahms had just finished his second symphony, Tchaikovsky his opera *Eugene Onegin* and César Franck his F minor piano quintet. Your early childhood must seem remote even to you now, but I would like to begin by asking you what you recall of your first experiences with music.

IRELAND Oh, I was always interested in music from early childhood. My sisters used to play the piano – Chopin and various things like that. And my mother, although she was not a professional musician, took a deep interest in music. I started playing the piano when I was seven or eight, but it wasn't until I came to London in 1893 that I began my serious studies. I can't remember precisely when I began composing, probably at an early age in my head, though I didn't put any of it down on paper until much later. I began writing music before I had any lessons in composition or any of the fundamentals. That would have been before my fifteenth year when I came to the Royal College of Music.

SCHAFER   Your piano lessons took first place in the early stages, did they?

IRELAND   Yes. I have the most unpleasant memories attached to my first piano teachers. They used to use a round, black and quite hefty ruler which would descend on my fingers the moment they got into trouble. But the difficulties didn't disappear as a result of the ruler treatment; they only became worse, and I became more and more terrified. At the age of ten I associated Beethoven with suffering and punishment. The crowning catastrophe occurred after I had come to London to study. I was studying the piano then with Frederic Cliffe[1] in a group lesson where each student would play the piano for twenty minutes and spend the remainder of the time listening, it was hoped, with profit. On one occasion I arrived for my lesson badly prepared and broke down completely. 'Where do you live?' thundered Mr. Cliffe. 'West Hampstead, sir', I replied. 'Go home at once, practise that passage three hours and come straight back here to me!' And such was the discipline in those days that I didn't dream of disobeying him.[2]

SCHAFER   Were all your earlier experiences such frightening ones?

IRELAND   Oh no. Later they became more pleasant. I recall the first time I heard Beethoven's Eighth Symphony played by the College orchestra. It made a fantastic impression. It was quite unlike the Beethoven I had known. It was wild, exciting, full of a divine sort of mirth – almost wicked.

SCHAFER   Both your parents were literary people. They must have stimulated an early interest in good literature.

IRELAND   Both my parents wrote books – not novels, books of criticism. My father was the editor of an important Manchester newspaper. My mother published a book on Jane Welsh Carlyle upon whom she was an authority.

SCHAFER   In fact, many celebrated literary people of the day were friends of your parents, Carlyle and Emerson among them.

IRELAND   Oh yes, especially the younger men who came to see my father because he was in a position to help them. I remember Richard le Gallienne coming, and Sir William Watson, before he was Sir William. There is a story told that Emerson came to visit us when I was very young and left his top hat in the hall. I took it and filled it with daisies for him. I have vague impressions of all these people, but too vague to put into words.

SCHAFER   This early association with literature must have been invaluable for you when you later came to choose texts for your many songs.

IRELAND   Oh undoubtedly. I've always been interested in literature as a consequence of my home life, particularly poetry. I have the greatest admiration for A. E. Housman because he managed to say so much in such a condensed way. I mean, when you think of Wordsworth or Tennyson, they turned out such a tremendous lot of stuff, some good, some not so good; but Housman has such a small output

[1] Frederic Cliffe (1857–1931). Ireland was probably never aware of Cliffe's brief fame between 1889 and 1906 as a composer; to Ireland he was his piano professor at the RCM. – EDITOR

[2] Ireland's radio talk on this subject must have still been fresh in his mind, for it is almost word-for-word the same; see pp. 398 and the historical CD, track 2. – EDITOR

and yet he has said everything. Swinburne was a great master of words and I used to admire him too.

SCHAFER Have you any outstanding memories of your student days at the Royal College of Music?

IRELAND Do you mean musical memories? The most vivid recollection I have is that there used to be two entrances to the College, one for male students and one for female. One day, when I was about seventeen, I was caught practising with a student of the opposite sex without permission. I was reported to the principal by a lady superintendent who used to peer in rooms through the glass-panelled doors. It was regarded as a very serious offence and I was nearly sent down.

SCHAFER You studied composition with Stanford.

IRELAND Yes, but not until I had already been at the College about four years. I began studying with a very clever man of the old school – the thorough school – by the name of James Higgs, who wrote a book on fugue that is still in use today. After I had had a solid grounding in the rudiments, I went to Stanford. Stanford, of course, was very much influenced by Brahms and Brahms formed the basis of his teaching method. I had studied a great deal of Brahms before I went to him and this may have displeased him a little. He said to me, 'Your music is all Brahms and water, me boy. I shall have to do something with you which I have never done with anybody else.' He put me to work on sixteenth-century style and methods and I wrote music in the style of Palestrina for a year. After that he made me study Dvořák.

I think the best quality Stanford possessed as a teacher was that he made you feel nothing but the best would do. He wouldn't let you write in pencil. He held that you would have more respect for what you did if you wrote in ink. He could be severely critical, almost cruel at times. I recall once writing something for orchestra for him. He looked at it and must have known at once that there were all kinds of errors in it, but he told me to go home and copy the parts. When I brought them back he tried it over with the College orchestra and made me stand on the rostrum beside him. The orchestra made the most appalling sounds. Everything went wrong and I was utterly humiliated. But Stanford played it through in its entirety. Then he turned to me and, handing me the score, said, 'Well you see, my boy, it won't do will it? You'll have to find some other way.' And one did, you know.

SCHAFER One of the curious things about 'good taste' in art is the way in which art is constantly being revalued according to the spirit of the time. The number of supporters for an artist is never the same through two successive generations. During your long career you must have had a good chance to observe this. Who were considered to be the composers with the brightest prospects for the future during your days as a student?

IRELAND When I first went to Stanford his most admired pupils were William Hurlstone and Coleridge-Taylor, both of whom unhappily died young. My fellow students were Holst, Vaughan Williams and, at a slightly later period, though it overlapped, Frank Bridge. I couldn't say which of these Stanford considered the most talented. They all had something individual to say, and with the later years

Vaughan Williams grew to be the most powerful personality. Then Cyril Scott was a composer many thought exciting. You see, he was the first to break away from the academic school. Scott, of course, got his advanced training in Germany, not here. In his later years Stanford thought all his students had gone mad.

SCHAFER If you had a chance to rescue a composer who has fallen into what you feel to be unjust neglect, who would this be?

IRELAND Well, I think Holbrooke's neglect is unfortunate because he was a very clever composer, but was apt to write for very large combinations of instruments and wanted things in an orchestra that weren't usually there, concertinas and saxophones and things like that.

SCHAFER It is strange that you should defend Holbrooke. His ideas on the forces necessary to make a musical effect appear alien to your own.

IRELAND Well, my idea is that you ought to try and get the utmost out of the least and that the means you use ought never to be used just to fill up. If you use triple woodwind I think you ought to be able to do with double woodwind. Do you see what I mean? I remember the first time I heard Sibelius's first or second symphony – I can't remember which – I was so impressed with it that I went round to Sir Henry Wood and spoke to him. 'Well there certainly must have been triple woodwind in that.' 'Oh no', he replied, 'only double woodwind.' You see, Sibelius had made do with the smallest means. He knew precisely what every instrument was like in every part of its compass. There is a lesson in that.

SCHAFER I think most younger composers today have already learned that lesson.

IRELAND I don't know very much about the young generation of composers, especially those under thirty or thirty-five. I very seldom go up to London these days and I hear music mostly on the wireless. But I like trying to follow everything that is being done and always make a point of listening to the latest things.

SCHAFER I would be interested in hearing your impressions of Boulez's *Improvisation sur Mallarmé II* which I believe you listened to in a broadcast recently.

IRELAND Oh, interesting. He makes rather odd sounds. I liked the little clusters of sounds he obtained from the piano, celesta and the other instruments he used. It was very difficult to make anything of it. I don't know anything about the twelve-note system you know. It seems to me it destroys the composer's freedom of choice over his material, but I wouldn't like to criticize it without understanding it. Everybody seems to be turning that way today, even Stravinsky. I'd like to know something about it as a matter of interest because I'm always interested in new trends in music. But I think it may only be a phase. Of course it's not possible to shock the ears any more these days. Boulez's sounds didn't shock me, but I found them interesting.

SCHAFER Is this all you ask of music, that it be interesting?

IRELAND I think music ought to express some kind of emotion. Bach had tremendous skill and he was able to express the greatest emotions in the strictest forms. I think the older composers had more to say, but I don't like to criticize things I don't understand. I would have made an eminently bad music critic you know. I think composers are still serious and do their best. You must remember that when

I was young Brahms was the greatest living composer, and in questions of this kind I am always inclined to measure things up against Brahms. Today Stravinsky is a composer of great talent, and I suppose genius in a way, but I don't think he has as much to say as Brahms had.

SCHAFER   The training composers receive today is different. This may partly account for them wishing to say different things.

IRELAND   Well, students aren't trained as well these days. They don't receive anything like the thorough training in the fundamentals that we had. Today you start composing in the free forms and write what you like. In my day if you were given ten counterpoint exercises a week, well, you had to do them. There were no excuses. If you didn't do them you got into trouble. Today the teaching of strict counterpoint has been abolished. I think this is a great pity.

SCHAFER   Would you give some advice to young composers?

IRELAND   Advice? No. I don't believe in giving advice to anyone, especially young people. If you advise them it prompts them to go in the opposite direction.

SCHAFER   Was it that way in your case?

IRELAND   Oh no, not in my days. You had to do what you were told. You couldn't say, 'Oh well, it's too much trouble', or 'I've had a toothache this week and haven't had a chance to do my exercises'. It's no longer that way today. I know that for a fact. Students won't put up with hard work these days.

SCHAFER   But you must have advised people in the past. Many British composers have passed through your hands including: Alan Bush, Benjamin Britten, Humphrey Searle and E. J. Moeran.

IRELAND   During the period when I taught I never endeavoured to force my ideas on any of my students; I think it is a great mistake.

SCHAFER   Were there any of your students that gave you particular pleasure to work with?

IRELAND   I enjoyed working with them all. Benjamin Britten was very industrious. When he came to the Royal College of Music I knew that his was one of the finest musical brains the College had seen for many years. Frank Bridge, whose friend he was, wrote to me asking if I would accept him as a pupil. I attempted to secure a scholarship for him. The other two adjudicators were against it and one of them even went so far as to say, 'What is an English public school boy doing writing music of this kind?' But eventually I managed to convince them, and I don't think the academic world ever quite forgave me for it.

Humphrey Searle was also very clever and individual. He wasn't with me for very long though. He went and studied with Webern in Vienna and that influenced him a lot.

SCHAFER   Are you disappointed about that?

IRELAND   Certainly not. I like to see people develop in the way they feel they must.

SCHAFER   You told me once you didn't think Britain had produced a composer of the stature of Elgar since that time.

IRELAND Yes, I feel that way. Elgar was a serious, first-class composer.

SCHAFER Is music less interesting today then?

IRELAND That's difficult to say. You see, when I first encountered new music in those days I was young and impressionable – probably less prejudiced, though I have always tried to remain as unprejudiced as possible. My most pleasant memories of musical events are naturally connected with my younger days. I heard the first performance in this country of Brahms's Clarinet Quintet with the original clarinettist Brahms wrote it for. I also heard the first performance in this country of Tchaikovsky's Sixth Symphony. We all, students and teachers alike, went mad about it. It was quite different from anything we had heard before. Of course it has now become a sort of hobby-horse for conductors and you seldom hear a good performance of it. Another work which made a tremendous impression was Stravinsky's *Le Sacre du printemps*. Sometimes a new work today makes an overwhelming impression on me, comparable with those. Shostakovich's Eleventh Symphony, for example, struck me as a work that came from the heart, a work that had to be written.

Sometimes I get bored with the classics. You hear them too often. Harmonically they are limited and you know what is coming next. I can still enjoy them if they are well played, but generally they are not well played these days. There is a tendency to play everything too fast. I've heard quite famous conductors take Beethoven much faster than he ought to be taken.

SCHAFER Is British music becoming less British today?

IRELAND That's a difficult question to answer isn't it? I mean, what *is* British music? Vaughan Williams has made his music English by using a great deal of folk song or at least he has imitated folk songs. That's a thing I've never gone in for at all. I've never been conscious of my music being excessively English. It is true, my past is in this country and the traditions I was brought up on were English, but all that only affects you unconsciously. The rediscovery of Tudor church music about the turn of the century has had as great an influence on my music as anything. This is true of all the composers of my generation.

SCHAFER Did folk music never interest you?

IRELAND It was a question perhaps of opportunity. My teachers never discussed it at all.

SCHAFER You have lived an outwardly uneventful life, quietly consolidating your reputation as a composer without doing much about publicizing yourself.

IRELAND Yes, that's quite true. I've travelled very little and there haven't been many spectacular events.

SCHAFER But have there been any?

IRELAND I went to Geneva in 1929 to play my Sonatina for Piano at an I.S.C.M. festival. I don't think it got very good notices though, and when I returned I found a threatening note in my letter box telling me to stop writing such music or the author would shoot me!

SCHAFER Rachmaninov wasn't very flattering either when he heard some of your music.

IRELAND Oh I didn't blame him. It was quite amusing. There used to be a Society for English Music, and at one of their concerts there were to be some works by Vaughan Williams and myself. Someone had persuaded Rachmaninov to come. It turned out that a certain song of Vaughan Williams's was to be performed which he himself considered to be one of his worst. As soon as it was announced Vaughan Williams jumped up, cursed loudly and walked out. Next followed my piano piece *Chelsea Reach*, but the pianist played it as though it were a dirge. You couldn't imagine how slowly and rigidly he took it. My song *Sea Fever* followed. When it was over Rachmaninov turned to me and said, 'Yes, zat *Zea Fever* is good, but really, Mr. Ireland, you don't zink much of zat *Chelsea Reach* do you?'[3]

SCHAFER Although you have written important orchestral, chamber, choral and church music, as well as some forty-six works for piano and about ninety songs (including song cycles) you have never written a symphony. Is there any accountable reason for this?

IRELAND Oh, I don't think so. You see, I've only composed when I have had the urge to do so, and have never tried to convince myself I ought to write something unless I had something to say. Money didn't enter into it, and I never made a steady habit of composing to a daily schedule. Also we didn't have commissions for large orchestral works and operas in my day. All those things may have had something to do with it. I never had any prejudice against writing a symphony.

SCHAFER It has been said that Stravinsky has influenced your work but I find this difficult to believe.

IRELAND I hardly think so. Any composer must be influenced to some extent by the people of his time. It is the early Stravinsky that I like. Most of what he has done since *Le Sacre* seems to me dry, cerebral perhaps. I was probably more influenced by Ravel.

SCHAFER You met Ravel, didn't you?

IRELAND I was once at a party with Ravel. I don't remember what we ate but I do recall having eaten exceptionally well. Afterwards Ravel went to the piano and played his *Sonatine*. I don't think I ever heard it played worse than on that occasion. There is something to be learned from that. Food, alcohol and music don't mix.

SCHAFER There is also an amusing story told about an encounter you had with George Gershwin.

IRELAND I met Gershwin many years ago on one of his visits to this country. Almost as soon as we met he said, 'I hear you've written a *rrr*hapsody. How many performances does it get a year?' 'Two or three', I replied. 'I wrote a *rrr*hapsody that gets about ten performances a day!'[4]

SCHAFER Many of your compositions bear descriptive titles. Names like: *Moon-glade, Island Spell, Darkened Valley*. You must not be averse to programme music.

IRELAND At the time many of my works were published, publishers liked titles.

---

[3] The Music Club, 17 May 1922. The pianist was Evlyn Howard-Jones. See *Musical Times*, June 1922.

[4] *Rhapsody in Blue* – see p. 367.

I don't mean to imply they invented them, but they liked to have them. Brahms could write six intermezzi and get away with it. Well, in England at that time they liked to do things differently. The titles don't imply a programme, they just give some idea of the emotions involved.

SCHAFER But do you object to your music being listened to programmatically?

IRELAND Object? Of course not. A composer never objects to his music being listened to. I think myself that music ought to be complete on its own without a programme. What is programme music after all? There are so many ways of appreciating music. For instance, take that piece of Boulez's that I was listening to recently. I didn't have the slightest idea what he had in mind when he wrote it, but I was interested in the sounds he made. It didn't convey anything to me pictorially or even emotionally, it wasn't sad or merry, but it did hold my attention. That is the important thing, that music should hold our attention.

SCHAFER Nature has always been very important in your life. Until recently you used to take long walks over the Downs. Could you attempt to explain to what extent it has influenced your music?

IRELAND No, I don't think I could, except to say that there are a good many traces of the ancient on the Sussex Downs, the burial mounds and so forth, and I've always felt moved by that sort of thing. My *Legend for Piano and Orchestra* was inspired by an experience of that kind. I was intrigued by an old track leading to the ruins of an ancient church. During the Middle Ages the track was used by lepers. Although they were not allowed to mix with ordinary people they could not be denied the right to worship God, and so they were allowed to enter the church by another entrance and to peer through an opening in the wall called 'The Lepers' Squint'. Things like that would often start up certain thoughts and images, and these would be reflected in my music.

SCHAFER You are no longer writing music today?

IRELAND No. My eyesight makes it very difficult to put music down on paper properly. Besides, I think that, although there have been exceptional cases like Verdi, who wrote his best music towards the end of his life, most of us reach the highest peak much earlier. The last piece I wrote was a work for organ about three years ago.

SCHAFER Does this bother you?

IRELAND Not really. Fashions have changed so much lately that I don't think I could write in any of the present styles with anything approaching sincerity.

SCHAFER Are you satisfied with what you have accomplished?

IRELAND Oh, well, yes, I suppose so. It's very difficult to say exactly. I've not written a great many large-scale works but I have always written what I wanted to write when I had something to say, and have always tried to express myself sincerely.

SCHAFER Have you any complaints?

IRELAND Complaints? Oh no. I listen to everything that is new and find a good deal of it interesting. Whether I could say I really like it or not is another matter. At least I'm still keenly interested in musical trends.

CHAPTER 6

Interviews with Friends and Contemporaries of John Ireland

Felix Aprahamian, Alan Bush, Charles Markes, Angus Morrison and Rev. Kenneth Thompson

Lewis Foreman

This chapter consists of extracts from recorded interviews with five of those who met Ireland and knew him well. As will be seen three had good recall of the composer, but when the interviews were conducted with Alan Bush and Rev. Kenneth Thompson they had began to be somewhat hazy in their memory. The extracts from the latter reproduced here have been included because of the importance of each in the life of John Ireland.

1 *Felix Aprahamian* (11 September 1985)

FA I suppose the earliest possible date of my acquaintance with Ireland's music – because it all began there – was as an organ composer. There were two pieces published by Novello:[1] *Alla Marcia* and *Sursum Corda* – which are, in fact, organ pieces I learnt with my teacher. Long before I became aware of Ireland as a composer generally – as a composer of songs or chamber music – I knew him as an organ composer. Then early in the '30s or the late '20s I came to know John Stuart Archer – then organist of the Third Church of Christ Scientist, Curzon Street, Mayfair – who knew Ireland from the old days, because he had been his assistant organist in Chelsea. So there was another connection. I'd actually met the man who was his assistant organist. Archer, by the way, was older than Ireland, he was very tall, distinguished, a handsome man who had been a civil engineer till he was thirty-three and then went over to music. And, I suppose, [he] took on this assistant organist's job and then progressed through various churches until he finished up in Curzon Street. I don't think he'd kept in touch with Ireland. Stuart Archer was very much in the organ world – buddy of Henry Willis the organ builder – while Ireland, of course, was better known to a wider public for his more general music.

Another early work I became aware of was when people who swooned over choirboys singing in cathedrals and such places, used to rave about *Many Waters Cannot Quench Love* – an anthem of Ireland's which I don't know whether I would recognise today, but this was one of the anthems which were widely sung. There was also Ireland in F. So I suppose I became aware of Ireland the composer at about the same time as I perhaps first became aware of *Sea Fever*. And then of course, by 1931 when I attended the contemporary

[1] *Alla Marcia* and *Sursum Corda* were composed in 1911 and were published by Novello the same year.

music festival which was that year held in London and Oxford – I went to the London concerts[2] – he was already a well-known London musician. I can't say that I recognised him *then*, but in 1938 he was a very prominent figure at that Festival – for reasons that I will tell you.

I became aware of his chamber music – and another item which brought Ireland's name at that time to wide attention, [came when] he was asked to do one of the competition test pieces for the *Daily Express* Piano Competition. It was actually won by Cyril Smith. He won a piano. And the Ireland test piece was the Rondo from his Piano Sonatina. And I got this. I was fascinated. I thought, 'This is quite modern in its tonal, in its percussive way, Bartók-like.' I was aware that Ireland even then recognised the piano not only for its romantic and singing qualities, but also – almost Bartók-like – as a percussion instrument. I was fascinated by this Rondo. There was an early Columbia recording by William Murdoch[3] as a guide to competitors. This was long before I became aware that this was, in fact, part of a tripartite Sonatina published as such by the Oxford University Press and dedicated to Edward Clark – who was a great buddy of Ireland in the '30s and very much in the contemporary music field. And arguably the Piano Sonatina showed the most contemporary music side of Ireland.[4] It was published separately with a sort of pink and white cover saying 'Daily Express Piano Competition.'

During the '30s I got to know him because the London Contemporary Music Centre used to hold study circles. They were looked after by Frank Merrick and these study circles took place on the 17th of every month – irrespective of the day of the week on which it fell. Once, I remember, it happened to be on a Bank Holiday. At one of these, John Ireland came with his manuscript of *Songs Sacred and Profane*.[5] Even then, it wasn't one single manuscript. It

---

[2] The 1931 ISCM festival was held during July.

[3] Columbia 4944.

[4] In Felix Aprahamian's Diary for 26 January 1934 he describes seeing Ireland at a concert of modern orchestral music including the suite from Shostakovitch's *The Nose*. He writes: 'It was a really fascinating noise. Ireland was as happy as a sandboy and clapped his hands like a two year old at the end. He is a dear chap – never afraid to learn anything new! He takes a keen interest in contemporary music yet the <u>musical</u> content of his own works is not tainted in any way by these outside influences.'

[5] Felix Aprahamian's Diary for 17 February 1933: 'I … chose [the] Study Circle where Ireland was to bring along his six new songs & John Armstrong was to sing them. I arrived with Ernest [Chapman] and together with Ireland waited on the landing while Mr Merrick finished playing Prokofiev V. There were not many people present. … After laboriously cleaning his specs Ireland prepared to accompany his songs. He is certainly a very sensitive player & is undoubtedly a good pianist. He does however emit great heavings and whistlings through his nose while playing – one has to get used to it. … Now a little mystery – just before leaving Ireland went up to the studio to collect his MSS and I followed. I asked him where his songs were to be published – he said he had not thought of publication. I then mentioned Boosey & Hawkes & said that I felt sure Mr Ralph Hawkes would jump at them. Ireland said times were bad & that no one wanted to buy a song. [18.2.33]: …

was obviously a portfolio of Psalms, with the manuscript showing that they had been written at different times. And he came along with John Armstrong – one of those typically English high baritones, not the Voice Beautiful, but one of extraordinary intelligence and expressive power. And Ireland rejoiced in accompanying him. I suppose it was a 'run through' of *Songs Sacred and Profane* with John Armstrong – who disappeared after the war. He did a recording of *The Curlew* by Warlock. He was a singer of English Song, in the days when the English art song was, I would say, flourishing. I think I even turned over for Ireland then. I always chatted up any composer I came into contact with.

And then of course, I used to have regular news of Ireland through my friend Ernest Chapman,[6] who worked at Boosey & Hawkes. He was Ralph Hawkes's assistant. I would hear whether Ireland had been in the shop. He was published all over the place, but the Winthrop Rogers pieces were published by Boosey & Hawkes. Then, one unforgettable incident was at one of the Boosey & Hawkes concerts, where the Trio – not the Phantasy Trio but the one published by Booseys – was performed, I think by Florence Hooton, Dorothy Manley and David Martin.[7] These concerts took place in the room at the back of Boosey & Hawkes – the Studio. I think they sell electronic organs there now.[8]

I got invited because I was a close buddy of Ernest Chapman, and I was then on the reading committee of the London Contemporary Music Centre and took part in every one of those '17th of the month' study circles. They were always held at the Robert Mayer Studio. The Mayers would be away and they would make available their studio at wherever it might be – St James's Square, Holland Park, or, latterly, in Greville Place off Loudoun Road. These were sort of socials. There would be lemonade or coffee or something, but the main thing was meeting composers who happened to be there or people who turned up with manuscripts and played them through. And if there was nothing like that – if Ireland wasn't there to play through his latest song cycle – Arthur Alexander or Frank Merrick would sight-read any music that was brought along. They were prodigious sight-readers.

Ernest told me that he had mentioned the Ireland songs to Ralph Hawkes who said Ireland had shown him the songs some years back when he had offered to accept them on the spot – the songs are apparently six years old. Ireland had hummed and hahed and havered so nothing was done. – Hawkes told Ernest that of all their composers Ireland was the most difficult to deal with – 'he never gives a direct answer and leads publishers up the garden path.'

[6] Ernest Chapman lived just a few doors down Gunter Grove, Chelsea from Ireland who lived at no. 14.

[7] This must have been the performance at the 1938 ISCM Festival, on 20 June 1938. After over forty years Felix misremembers the names of the performers, who were Frederick Grinke (violin), Florence Hooton (cello) and John Ireland himself at the piano.

[8] This would have been at 295 Upper Regent Street. Since then Boosey & Hawkes have moved from these long-established premises.

Ireland was at this concert in Boosey & Hawkes's Studio where his Trio was given for the first time, and it was quite obvious to everybody that it was an earlier Ireland piece which he'd refurbished. Frank Bridge was there at the time and I remember Frank Bridge saying – certainly within my earshot and the earshot of a few others – 'Hello John: What's this? Some old piece you've taken out of the bottom drawer and tarted up?' Which was absolutely true and good natured. It didn't make the music any less good. But Ireland was absolutely hurt to the quick, he was mortified. I don't believe that he spoke to Frank Bridge after that. And it went around for days, I know that because this Boosey & Hawkes concert coincided with the ISCM Festival, which that year was in London.

LF   That would have been in 1938, would it?

FA   1938. So it was just about the same time – within days of this – after the final Queen's Hall concert. We always used to repair to Pagani's[9] on the ground floor – [it was] an L-shaped room – we used to go round the corner. They were all separate tables. The hierarchy of the ISCM was there. Ernest and I – you know – below the salt with the lesser mortals nearer the door. We'd just got there. And there was Messiaen and Roberto Gerhard – young then.

The concert was over and there was drinking, snacks. It must have been well after 11 o'clock. And suddenly Ireland appears at the door, absolutely pissed, wearing his boater – his straw hat – and whites, his ducks as it were, like something out of a musical comedy. He was swaying from side to side and had obviously been drinking heavily. Still what was riling him was Frank Bridge's remark. Ernest, who represented his publisher, didn't want Ireland to make an exhibition of himself among all the Europeans. It was a storm in a teacup as far as they were concerned. They were not aware of it. They hadn't all been at the Boosey & Hawkes concert, which was much more of an English affair – although I believe some Bartók and some Lopatnikov had been given at the same time. Ernest beckoned him and we got him to sit at our table. He said, 'Did you hear what that *rotter* Bridge said to me the other day? In front of our publisher? He heard it. Did you hear what he said?' Well, of course, we consoled him as best we could. It was true, and that hurt Ireland all the more.

Our main concern was to save Ireland from making an absolute ass of himself higher up in the room. So we sobered him up. I think we got him black coffee and that sort of thing. And finally we decided, as people were moving, the best thing would be to get him home – he lived in Gunter Grove. So I went out and hailed a taxi. It was open at the back – this I remember distinctly. It must have been a carriage of some kind. It must have been cab with the hood down, because it wasn't a private car – there were no mini cabs in those days. I have a distinct recollection of Ireland being conveyed down Great Portland Street standing in the back of this vehicle, waving his straw hat at us and trying

---

[9] Pagani's restaurant in Great Portland Street, was a short step from Queen's Hall and the BBC and had been the meeting place for artists and musicians for over half a century. It was severely damaged in the Second World War and never re-established itself after the war.

to keep himself from collapsing, and being taken home. We gave the address and he got home to Gunter Grove. He was a very human being.

LF Do you remember when Mrs Kirby first came on the scene?

FA Yes, she took over from a friend of mine, a strange lady called Elizabeth Needham who looked after Ireland, and was absolutely crazy about him. She was interested in early music and practised the harpsichord. She was a red-faced, short-sighted woman, full of British music, English music and worked – I mean *slaved* – for the cause of British music – certainly earlier than Francis Chagrin founded the Committee for the Promotion of New Music. The music that she was devoted to was Ireland particularly. Somehow or other – of course she lived round the corner in Gunter Grove – she got Ireland under her influence and looked after him.

LF His housekeeper, in other words.

FA Yes. And I think she was replaced by Mrs Kirby because Elizabeth was an indomitable, inexorable woman; she wouldn't take no for an answer. We put her in charge at the LPO of writing the letters to all those who sent instruments when all the orchestra's instruments were blown up in the Queen's Hall. And she had a job in the office, for a mere pittance I'm sure – and she was put in charge of organising the instruments and acknowledging them. I think it was a shambles. She didn't have the remotest idea, because that was not her interest. Her interest was English music and Ireland in particular. And I do remember – it must have been one of the reasons that she was dismissed or there was a sudden rupture – that Ernest and I discovered in Foyles [Bookshop] some music by Sorabji with inscriptions to John Ireland. I forget whether Ernest bought them or reported the matter to Ireland. Of course Ireland hadn't sent them, but Elizabeth Needham was so jealous of any British composer, [and] probably thought that here was John Ireland housing this impossible music by a wog who was able to have it published at his own expense and beautifully engraved. She was so possessive that she turned it all out and got it sold to Foyles. You know – clearing out on behalf of Ireland. God knows what she may have cleared out. But obviously she was a kind of chauvinist who probably thought that a man with a name like Sorabji had absolutely no right to give inscribed copies of his music to Ireland. It was no use anyway, and quite unplayable, and so out it goes. Now you see, this must have put Ireland in an awkward spot, because if this reached Sorabji's ear, he would – quite rightly – have been hurt and might well have taken Ireland to task for it. Well, this is not the way one behaves. And that other side of Ireland which was very prim and proper about not doing anything untoward might have realised that he'd been put into an awkward spot through the overzealous Elizabeth Needham. So Miss Needham was out and the next thing we were aware of was a Mrs Norah Kirby had come swanning to the rescue.

This is after the war. I didn't know Elizabeth Needham until the war. She was the sister-in-law of one of the horn players, one of our extra horns. I came across him and one of his extra horn colleagues the other day. And this horn player's wife was the sister – a much more sane and balanced music-lover than her sister – of Elizabeth Needham. Through that connection – through the orchestral players – she was working in this capacity, cataloguing all the instruments that had been sent to the London Philharmonic Orchestra and sending out letters of thanks. That was her way into the LPO. I think the Needham influence went on possibly until the end of the war, and that's when I became aware of Mrs Kirby.

I remember that Mrs Kirby was with Ireland at a concert of something of his that we went to hear – it might have been *Songs Sacred and Profane* sung by somebody or another – George Parker, perhaps. It was at the Suffolk Street Galleries of the Society of British water colourists. Anyway, a concert was given there. I remember that then, already, Mrs Kirby was in attendance on 'Doctor Ireland'. That was when he was all over me and Mrs Kirby – 'Mr Aprahamian'. It may well have been when I had just begun to write for the papers. Strange, you know, it embarrassed me because I may have been black-bearded and mono-cled then – a sort of utility Edward Clark or Nubar Gulbenkian – but not at all myself so terribly respectful and admiring of John Ireland, whose *music* I loved so much. But Ernest was closer to him. Ernest knew the Needham and he knew Norah Kirby. One of the reasons why Ernest left Boosey & Hawkes was that *his* loyalty to composers like John Ireland and Arthur Benjamin made his position there untenable. He saw the whole firm was being given over to Britten. It was right – I mean Britten's music was making money – that was at the top of the queue always and always had priority. And the influence of [Erwin] Stein was such that no other composer got a look-in, or was even considered. This may have been commercially expedient, but I think that Ernest probably thought that a firm as big and as affluent as that should have a more paternalistic atti-tude towards its less favoured composers. After all, they'd done very well out of Ireland and they'd done very well out of Arthur Benjamin's *Jamaican Rumba* etc. And this is why, of course, that Britten had it in for Ernest.

2 *Alan Bush* (6 September 1986)

AB In 1918 I was seventeen years old. (I go with the years, but right at the very end of them!) So I finished school in the summer term of 1918, when I was seventeen years old, and went to the Royal Academy of Music and started in that academic year; that is, I started in September of 1918. I had lessons in composition and I had an extra in piano, I had two first subjects – composition and piano. I studied composition with a man called Frederick Corder – I don't know whether you ever heard of him?

LF Bax's teacher.

AB That's quite right. Well I was his pupil for composition. At that time, English piano teaching was dominated by a Mr Tobias Matthay of unspeakable memory, who ruined English piano playing for forty years. He had only two pupils who ever got anywhere, and they were Myra Hess and Harriet Cohen, you could say.

LF And Scharrer.

AB I'd forgotten Irene Scharrer. But those were the only people that he produced. He didn't produce a male concert pianist of the slightest distinction at all – not anywhere. He really didn't.

LF What about people like York Bowen and Benjamin Dale?

AB York Bowen was a very talented musician altogether and was quite a good composer, but wasn't a concert pianist of rank. Frank Bridge was a viola player of course, a very fine one, but he didn't profess to be a pianist. No, that is very unfortunately a fact about the piano playing of my youth you see. Then I got to know – quite by chance – another young composer, whose name was Bush spelt with a 'c' – you will never have heard of him.

LF William Busch.

AB Ah yes. Well I got to know him. We became very friendly and he said 'You should learn the piano with a good teacher.' And of course the 'good teacher' was Benno Moiseiwitsch, who was a Leschetizky pupil. Anyway, I went to him and he said he would teach me. Of course I would have to go to his assistant who was also a pupil of Leschetizky, a Miss Mabel Lander, who was an absolutely systematic and devastating teacher of the piano and she taught me the Leschetizky method systematically. That enabled me to begin to play the piano quite decently. I haven't been a concert pianist – I have played concertos by people other than myself many years ago, but I never made a career as a concert pianist. I used to appear in my own works and in modern music and that kind of thing.

Then the teacher that I went to was a woman called Miss Lily West. She was a middle-aged lady, a very good teacher, although she had been a pupil with Matthay but had disregarded his music altogether. And she came to the Academy to take the place of a piano teacher whose name was Percy Waller – who you will never have heard of – who was my teacher and so she took his pupils, you see. I went to her and she began to teach me systematically and I realised, this is it! This is the beginning of something! She introduced me to John Ireland because she had played his compositions in public, and I knew some of them and I knew him as he was becoming a famous composer – and also as a very systematic teacher of composition, you see. So as soon as I left the Academy, which was in 1922, I went to him and had lessons with him more or less regularly for five years from 1922–7. The first thing he did was – he said, 'You must learn something about the history of music. You will study the works of Palestrina.' And I had to write music in the style of Palestrina. I wasn't expected to write in the style of Johann Sebastian Bach. Not at all! Palestrina was the beginning of West European music in a way. It developed – the style of Palestrina and one or two other composers like William Byrd and that kind of thing – from then on. Then, of course, we were dominated entirely by German music for 200 years and we composers – English composers – composed in the major and minor scales exclusively. And at the end of the nineteenth century a group of composers who were not at the Academy – but they were at the College – said, 'This is no good at all, we mustn't be dominated by Central Europe, we must develop our own style.' And Vaughan Williams and Holst formed a sort of group of students. I was never a pupil of Vaughan Williams, but I realised that that was absolutely right.

LF Do you feel that your music is self-evidently British?

AB I don't know. My early music was not. It was West European. It had no English character.

LF But your later stuff?

AB I think so, yes. Well I tried very hard to study the English folk songs: the kind of intervals. I, of course, wrote vocal music in which the vocal intervals were very carefully developed. John Ireland was a very good teacher, there's no doubt about that at all.

LF So, would you say that John Ireland was a self-evidently British composer?

AB Yes he was. But for different reasons. He also started as a West European composer and developed out of that into a national composer of English style in principle and practice too.

LF But without folk songs.

AB Well he knew a little bit about it, yes. He doesn't use folk song, he doesn't use the actual tunes, no. But he uses a great deal of the idiom of folk song. Some of it is very chromatic. I studied with him for five years. Before 1930 – well that was the time when I studied with him, of course. I studied with him from 1922–7. I accompanied him on various occasions. He went to Geneva and appeared in an ISCM festival. He played his Sonatina. It was in the year 1929. A devoted young woman who was a pupil of his at the time called Patience Ross. She was the daughter of a very famous theatre man called Adrian Ross who was a leading theatre personality of England at that moment. He wasn't a writer; he was an organiser of theatre. She was a very intelligent girl and when I went to the ISCM festival in Geneva, I went with him and she came as well. We went as three people. [Before] then of course he married. Well, it was not consummated. I can't remember whether I ever met his wife; I think I must have met his wife. Well, they were not married at all in a sexual way, apart from on paper. Then she brought an action, not for restitution of conjugal rights – she'd never had them – but for the dissolution of the marriage. Which he perfectly agreed – he didn't oppose it. He met her because she was a student at the RCM, she was a student of his. Then he became very friendly with Patience Ross after that, and also with a lady called Mrs Norah Kirby. You know about her I suppose? Well I got to know both those quite well, especially Mrs Kirby. She was his dominating life-organiser for quite a number of years. John Ireland actually stayed – when the war came – he was very nervous of air raids – he actually came to stay in my house [in Radlett, Herts] and in my mother's house in the next road for about two or three months. [After the war] he went to Rock Mill, near Washington in Sussex and lived there for the rest of his life really. Mrs Kirby lived there; they lived in the same house. He left Gunter Grove finally in 1953. When I was with him, I had my lessons at Gunter Grove.

LF Can you describe how John Ireland looked?

AB He was very well educated – I mean that in all seriousness. He went to an excellent school and he knew languages; he knew French and Latin quite well and had read a great deal on all sorts of subjects, you know. He was I should say, intellectually quite irreligious. He didn't believe in orthodox Christianity.

LF But he was a choir master for forty years!

AB Well, he didn't believe in it. No, it was an economic question. He had to earn money and he very sensibly realised that he wasn't going to earn money as a composer as a young man – it would take a long time to earn enough to live on anyway. And so he became a church organist in Chelsea, in a big church where the standard of music was already rather high before he went to it.

He was very diligent and he was serious in the sense that he attended regularly. He didn't let them down. He appeared when he had to appear at choir practices and played at services. He had an assistant organist, whose name I've forgotten[10] – a young man who was his pupil actually, he taught him the organ and then he became his assistant. So he didn't have to play at every service, but I should think out of fifty-two Sundays in the year he probably played for forty-eight. He didn't go away for long holidays or anything like that away from the church. He would go away for short times and he was very fond of the Channel Islands.

LF As far as politics was concerned, his sympathies seem to be vaguely somewhere to the left of centre, but in fact his actual inclinations seem more concerned with respectability than principle.

AB Yes, you're quite right. He was on the whole progressive in politics rather than reactionary. He wasn't active in elections; he didn't take part in general elections so far as I know or even in local elections in Chelsea. His interests there were [at] the Chelsea Arts Club, he went there regularly, at least once a week for some meal or other, more or less as a normal thing. He had some friends who were among the painters, yes he did.

LF How did you actually get sent to him in the first place?

AB I was a pupil of this Leschetizky teacher, Miss Lily West, who'd been a Matthay pupil. She knew John Ireland. She'd played some of his compositions at recitals and that kind of thing. It was when I began to compose. After about two or three years at the RAM as a composer, I began to have compositions performed, you see. One afternoon she said, 'I would like you to meet John Ireland. You've played his works. Perhaps he might be interested to hear some of your songs. You could play them to him.' So we had a little evening at her studio. I went along and played one or two of my compositions and that was how I got to know him. I found out that he was a serious teacher of composition, you see. So after I'd finished at the Academy I went to see him and said, 'I should like to become your pupil if you would be so kind.' And he agreed. I knew that I wanted to go to a composer for lessons. The only composer that I knew slightly personally was Arnold Bax, in fact.

3 *Charles Markes* (16 January 1985)

I visited Charles Markes at his home the year before he died, and we started by discussing how Ireland used to improvise during services at St Luke's, Chelsea, and how Ireland discovered him as a child pianist.

CM [Ireland] was prepared to play some Bach or something like that and I said, 'Don't play that, play some real music.' He said 'You'll get me the ruddy sack!' and he used to extemporise, you see.

LF On the organ.

CM It was my job [playing for choir practices] in the First World War – I don't remember a time when I didn't play the piano. And he discovered this when I was about eleven, because there was a full choir practice and he was late

---

[10] Bush is presumably referring to Charlie Markes.

and I gathered the choir around the piano and was more or less conducting a rehearsal, do you see. In the middle of this he came in but didn't say anything. After it was over he said, 'Charlie I want you.' So he took me back home. We lived in Chelsea in those days. And he got my mother out of bed, because my mother had to go out to work, and he said, 'What are you going to do about this boy?' Mother had to explain that she had two sons, and to have music lessons for me was quite out of the question. Then John Ireland said, 'I'll have to teach him myself.' And that's how it all started. During the First World War – you see I was with him constantly from the age of eight until I went into the Army in 1918.

LF   When were you actually born?

CM   I was born in 1900, the last year of Queen Victoria's reign.

LF   Can you remember how Ireland seemed, how he looked to you when you first saw him?

CM   He was always a bit of a hypochondriac. He used to say 'Charlie, I'll be dead before I'm forty with kidney disease. Rub my back will you?' And while he played I used to rub his back – pain in his back and so on. Of course, he eventually died of cancer.

My job in the First World War, when I had become sufficiently proficient on the organ, was to go to church when the maroon sounded. There weren't sirens in those days; they were called maroons and made a loud bang. I'd go into the church and play the organ to the people sheltering in the crypt while the Zeppelins droned overhead. A rather alarming experience for a sixteen-year-old boy, but it was very, very interesting.

LF   What did Ireland do in the First World War?

CM   He was composing.

LF   Did he have a post then?

CM   He was Organist and Choir Master at St Luke's in Chelsea.

LF   All through the war?

CM   Yes. He was there until 1926. He had a very decrepit organ, but he used to extemporise wonderfully with a running comment all the time. 'Don't use the Cornopean on the swell – it sounds like frying a plate of sausages.' Or 'Don't use a Vox Humana with a Tremulant – it sounds like a bleating goat.' There was a running commentary all the time.

In 1940 my wife and I were having lunch here when we heard the bomb come down which destroyed Chelsea Old Church. It's been restored very carefully, but in those days I lived at Chelsea, about five minutes walk from the church.

LF   Where did John Ireland live at this time, when he was Organist?

CM   Elm Park Road in Chelsea. When I first met him, I went to tea with him when I was ten. He lived in Elm Park Mansions. Then he moved to the Studio where most of his best music was written, in Gunter Grove. When I was called up in 1918 he was writing the Piano Sonata.

LF   Did he tell you about the music he was working on at any particular time?

CM   Well I knew because I was with him every day. I have lots of letters from him, most of them his personal notes like 'Can you take the 6 o'clock for me as I don't leave the Royal College until 6.' 'I went to church last night but no parson turned up.' And I've lots of old programmes and things going back to the old London Trio. I was official accompanist to the London Trio, consisting of Louis Pax, Giammina Goodwin and Charles Woodhouse, a cellist. But all that is very remote, long long ago now.

L F I was rather hoping you could fill me in on some of the background.

C M Well one of his earliest works is *Bed in Summer*, a little song that we used to sing at St Luke's in 1908.[11] I was with him every day up until I was eighteen and went into the army. He carried on there until 1926, but we had an estrangement which lasted for thirty years. I lived in Australia and New Zealand most of that time. When I was demobilised from the First World War I had to get a job pretty damned quick and I went on the music halls playing the piano. He was disgusted with this. I was crossing the road in Argyll Street, going to the London Palladium one day, and he cut me dead. And when I re-met him some thirty years later we met through a local butcher who remarked that a well-known Chelsea resident had come back to live in Gunter Grove. I said, 'Oh yes, who's that?' 'John Ireland.' So I said, 'Well, if his secretary, Norah Kirby, comes in, tell her that Charlie Markes sends his regards.' I hadn't been in five minutes before the phone went. So I went straight round to Gunter Grove and Norah Kirby let me in. She wondered who the hell I was, of course, because she'd never seen or heard of me before. I went upstairs to the Music Room, and he said, 'Where have you been the last thirty years? I was going to advertise in *The Times* for you!' And I said, 'Well, it was your fault. You cut me dead in Great Marlborough Street.' We quickly sorted that out and resumed our old friendship, which persisted until the day he died.

L F During the First World War he had a number of performances which were celebrated – like the Second Violin Sonata.

C M I was with him when they were being composed.

L F I wondered what sort of reception they got?

C M Well I went to the second performance of the Second Violin Sonata performed by Albert Sammons and William Murdoch, and sitting in front of us was Frank Bridge, who looked like a prosperous family butcher.

In later years – after the age of seventy he considered that voluntary euthanasia should be available to all. He considered it no fun when your faculties decline, as they inevitably do. I went down to the Mill just before he died and he said, 'Charlie, my bottom is so sore.' On his bedside table I noticed a tube of ointment – Capsicum, which is hot as hell. I said, 'Has Norah been giving you this? Don't use any more. I'm going to wash your bottom and get rid of it. In the meantime I've got some soothing ointment called Nupacainer which contains a local anaesthetic which will soothe you.' So I carefully washed his private parts and got rid of this Capsicum ointment. 'Oh,' he said, 'that's better.'

L F How did he first encounter Norah Kirby?

C M Norah Kirby was the most unfeminine woman. She was secretary to a man called Ralph Hill, who was Musical Editor of the *Radio Times*, and she brought some music from Ralph Hill to John Ireland at Gunter Grove and found John

---

[11] Craggs ascribes the date 1912 to this unison song, which was not published until 1915.

Ireland ill in bed. Ireland was as ill as he could be with influenza, and he let Norah Kirby in and she ministered to him. Eventually they got to the question of her taking up residence in Gunter Grove, which she did after a trial period. They hit it off all right, so she took up residence and was there until the day he died. When he died, he left his estate to Norah Kirby. He had £11,000 in cash and estimated royalties over the next twenty years which were terrible. Then of course, poor Norah had a stroke. Now in that picture,[12] Norah Kirby and John Ireland are together and sitting next to them is Father Kenneth Thompson, who buried both of them in Shipley. Father Thompson used to be Vicar of a local church here, just up the road – St Philip's in Philbeach Gardens.

John Ireland sometimes found it difficult to make up his mind regarding a certain passage and he'd be umming and ahhing. Of course he wrote music with his heart's blood. He found composition very difficult. When I'd played a service, I'd dash back from St Luke's and knock on the door of the Studio in Gunter Grove. He'd say, 'Come up Charlie, the door is open.' He'd be sitting at a high desk writing, and he'd say, 'I think I'd better give up writing, it's such hard work!' At that time he was writing *Mai-Dun*. John Ireland leads you up the garden musically. He writes a most enticing slow movement and then suddenly forgets it and goes to something else.

He used to love my piano. Of course music is finished as far as I am concerned, because I cannot hear. I can't hear whether the piano is in tune or out of tune, let alone play. But the piano is still there and I've got all this music. Very, very sad.

LF Tell me about his writing for orchestra.

CM He wrote *A London Overture*, which is supposed to be about London after dark and a policeman exploring the byways with a lantern. That beginning – everybody knows that tune. It became known as the 'Piccadilly Incident'! You see, musical taste changes so much. John Ireland is now almost a forgotten composer. I see him sometimes in the *Evening News* and wish I could hear it. There's been music for clarinet and piano at the Barbican but it's no good my going because I can't hear it. He had certain dislikes. He didn't like the chord of the dominant ninth or the diminished seventh very much. He always used to do something about the dominant ninth; he'd disguise it in some way and turn it into something else.

LF He was very keen on the Impressionists, wasn't he? Ravel was one of his enthusiasms.

CM Oh yes. I was talking to him one day round at Gunter Grove, and I said, 'I love the Ravel Trio.' 'Oh,' he said, 'that's the work I hold up to my students as a model of what a Trio should be.'[13]

LF Tell me about his students. Were you around when Benjamin Britten was his student?

CM He's the one who he fought for his admission to the Royal College. He said 'This boy's got more talent in his little finger than the other students have in the

---

[12] See Plate 5.

[13] Ireland played the piano in one of the first British performances of the Ravel Trio. The John Ireland Trust own the copy used in this performance, but see p. 21.

whole of their bodies and unless you admit him I will resign!' I think he would have resigned too. But you see Britten hasn't paid him the necessary due. He always referred to Frank Bridge, not to John Ireland. It was John Ireland who fought for his admission into the Royal College.

LF How did he think Britten developed afterwards?

CM He wrote to me in one of his letters: 'I don't like the music, but what Britten does with thirteen instruments [in *The Turn of the Screw*] is simply magical.' Britten had what John Ireland hadn't got – that facility.

Father Thompson lived up the road from here and when John Ireland was plagued by indecision, he'd ring him up and he would cycle down to Gunter Grove and John Ireland would unburden himself to him and say, 'Now, what do you like about this, that and the other?' And Father Thompson would make up his mind for him. For instance, John Ireland had a song called *Spring Sorrow* which has a three-bar ending and it had three versions. He said, 'Which do you like?' I said, 'That one'. 'Why?' 'Because of that flat.' There were many ways it could have ended, but that was the ending he gave it.

LF There's almost a touch of the Blues in it, isn't there?

CM He thought Gershwin was a genius. They met once and Gershwin said to him 'How often is your Concerto performed?' John Ireland said: 'Maybe once or twice a year'. Gershwin said 'Good Lord! Mine's performed three or four times every week', referring to the *Rhapsody in Blue*.

There's a tune Gershwin wrote called *The Man I Love* that Ireland thought was quite genius.[14] There's a super melody and lots down in the left hand. Ireland said 'You're making that up!' I said: 'It's not a question of making it up, it's how that sort of music is played. It's not as per copy, it's left in the hands of the performers. Those are just the bare bones.'

LF Did he approve of the style?

CM No, I don't think he did altogether. He set about playing it the way he thought Gershwin would play it. But Gershwin would have played it with all sorts of things going on in the left hand. John Ireland was a very good performer, especially of his own music. He gave things on the BBC, but not recitals as such. Eventually he decided he hadn't got what it takes to become a recital pianist, and so, I imagine, switched to composition. After all, if you're going to be a solo performer in the highest echelon it's hard work – practice, practice, practice – and that just wasn't John Ireland's cup of tea. He hated piano practice!

LF Tell me about the organ at St Luke's.

CM He left some notes in 1926: 'I did away with the old organ and installed a new one.' When we met again in 1945 he said to me: 'Have you tried that wonderful machine we've got at St. Luke's these days? It's built by John Compton and a very fine instrument. But it is not authentic; to me it sounds muddy. It borrows: the 8-foot diapason would be the top octave of the 16-foot diapason or something like that. It's all borrowed.'

LF The previous organ was a much smaller organ?[15]

---

[14] See also p. 367.

[15] The organ was rebuilt in 1932 by John Compton incorporating the original casework and some of the pipes that John Ireland would have known. For the organ today see Plate 10.

CM Oh yes. It was very old-fashioned. Here's a photograph of the choir at St. Luke's as it was when I was eleven years old.[16] John Ireland gave me this picture. There's Ireland, that's me, that's my boy friend Bobby Glassby who became the model for 'The Holy Boy'. That man would only blow the organ – it was a hand-blown organ – when he was wearing his Crimea Medal.

LF The man on the right. And who's next to him?

CM One of the sidesmen.

LF Who was the Vicar then?

CM A man called Bevan, H. E. J. Bevan. This man was a solicitor who used to live down the bottom of the road here. He's been dead many years now. Huw Bevan became a bishop. He became a bishop in Jerusalem. Gardner[17] lost his faith and died of alcoholic poisoning.

The last piece of music he ever wrote to me was this *Meditation*. He wrote to me, 'I've been commissioned to write a piece for organ by an American company but I desperately need two copies. Will you make them for me?' So I made the two copies for him.

[Before that] he wrote two pieces together – writing at the same time [as *The Overlanders* film music] the *Satyricon Overture*. He said he kept himself going on Benzedrine and brandy. I was round at Gunter Grove one day and he said to me, 'The proofs for *Satyricon* have come back. They're on the piano.' So I took a quick look and said, 'There's a mistake.' 'What?' 'There's a mistake.' He said, 'Alec Rowley's just corrected these and he's found 500 mistakes.' I said, 'Well, there's another one.' I looked further down the page and found another. He jumped at it and tore my hands off the paper and shouted, 'Don't look any more, I can't bear it!' 'But they can't go back to Joseph Williams like this,' I said. He was going back to Guernsey just after the war, and he said, 'I'll leave them with you. Will you look at them and I'll have a good look at them when I come back?' So I had a look through the proofs and I found 113 more mistakes including one or two composer's errors which are, of course, very difficult to spot. In the second trombone part there was a gigantic hiccup. When he came back I had them all over here and said to him: 'That's going to sound like hell.' He said 'Good Heavens! I've left the clef out!' Because, of course, the trombone vacillates between the bass clef and the tenor clef. He left the clef out and made a ghastly hiccup.

LF Why was it such a labour?

CM Because he was writing *Overlanders* at the same time.

LF When you first encountered him he wasn't very well known. But later he became very well known. How did this affect him?

CM What made him was the Second Violin Sonata. He wrote the First Violin Sonata, but the Second hit the nail on the head. It was played by two men in Service uniform – Sammons and Murdoch – and the mood of the composition – well the first edition was sold out next morning. It made him.

LF What was the impulse behind writing the Sonata, do you know?

CM Because he deplored the wastage of youthful life during the First World War.

---

[16] See Plate 9.

[17] Arthur R. Lee Gardner.

He felt the loss of youth terribly and the slaughter of trench warfare in the First World War. Do you know the two songs called *Blind* and *The Cost*? They're beautiful songs.

> I felt him catch his breath;
> Oh God if only this could be,
> Let this be given back to me!

A man's best friend stood beside him in the trench warfare, do you see.

LF Did Ireland lose any friends in the War? Presumably he must have done.

CM Rupert Brooke – yes. He was not a close friend. I met him once at the Studio in Gunter Grove. He died in 1915.

4 *Angus Morrison* (18 February 1987)

In talking to Angus Morrison I did not have to ask many questions. Once he was launched on his reminiscences it was almost a monologue.

LF Tell me about Ireland's Piano Concerto.

AM It was written for Helen Perkin, and the next year [actually 1933] I played it at the Proms. It was also broadcast in the 30s from the studio, and then I played it again after the War in Manchester with the BBC.

LF When did you meet Ireland?

AM I met John Ireland when I was fifteen, in 1917. It is a long story. Does the name Betty Chester mean anything to you? There was a show in the '20s called The Co-Optimists. It wasn't a review; it was a thing that stemmed from the old Follies, which was pre-First World War. A troupe who did songs, who did sketches – it wasn't a review because they were all in the same costumes, like pierrots. Betty was one of them and she, in the middle of this rather light thing, used to sing *Sea Fever*. Betty's name really was Betty Grundwig. Her mother was my godmother. She lived in Chester Square. She was in those days well-to-do; nowadays she wouldn't be rich. They lived very comfortably, but she was not in high grades of finance, so to speak. Betty was her only daughter. During the First War she had a very lovely, completely untrained, but absolutely natural *very lovely* voice. She used to sing to soldiers and charities which did so much during the First World War. Well, with a German-sounding name – though it was actually Danish – she called herself 'Betty Chester' because she lived in Chester Square. Quite simple! (Laughs.)

LF Oh, I see!

AM My godmother was a great musical amateur. A really knowledgeable person and knew lots of musicians, and played quite well herself. She was a great friend of John's long before he was famous. How she got to know him – that I don't know, but he became famous almost overnight with his Second Violin Sonata. It took everybody tremendously. Then all his early works started being played, and his songs. Betty Chester popularised *Sea Fever*. It went to an audience which would never have heard of John Ireland. I think it did have a good sale. When I was fifteen my godmother asked me to dinner to meet him; the idea [was] that he might teach me composition. Then when he heard I was studying with Harold Samuel and doing a certain amount of harmony and counterpoint, he said, 'You are in wonderful hands I won't step in.'

Over the years I did not know him at all well, but rather at the end, after the Second World War, I seemed to get in touch with him again and saw a lot of him in those last few years. I introduced Alan Rowlands, who was my pupil. I only really could say I knew him well in those last years, but my knowledge of him goes back through my life.

He was very poor. People's life was not so spectacular in those days. They didn't get performing rights; they didn't make a lot of money. The days when Britten and all these people set up Trusts because so much comes in the way of royalties was non-existent. He had to have this job at St Luke's Chelsea to help with the bread and butter.

He lived very simply in Gunter Grove. The World's End was the slums of the slums. Anything beyond World's End was pretty seedy, run down. He had that half a house with a studio in the garden. He lived on a shoestring.[18] You must remember that life was very cheap then. He didn't make money. He was very lucky if he just managed to get by.

When I played his concerto I went through it with him and saw him, and he was always terribly warm with me, because of that link with Mary Grundwig whom he was awfully fond of. There are certain things that put you in relation with somebody very quickly. But it was only after the war when he was down at the Mill, I went down a few times and saw him.

5 *The Rev Kenneth Thompson* (1986)

When I interviewed Father Thompson at the end of 1986 his memory for names was beginning to go. The prime source for Father Thompson's relationship with Ireland is to be found in Ireland's letters 1936–62, now in the British Library, Add. Mss. 60535/6. This is only a brief extract from our conversation.

LF John Ireland knew Philip Heseltine – Peter Warlock – in Chelsea?

KT Philip Heseltine, or Peter Warlock as he called himself – they were interested in Black Magic. At that time in Chelsea you had to watch when you gave communion to people. Make quite sure they received the Sacrament, if possible into their mouth like Roman Catholics, for fear they might steal the Sacrament away, d'you see, because part of the Black Mass is to have the Sacrament desecrated, as something that will please the Devil. Though of course, you are just playing about with the externals aren't you? Warlock, you know, is represented by Aldous Huxley in *Antic Hay*. John knew him very well and, I think, liked him. But he didn't think much of his music. He thought his music was somewhat amateurish.

Well, Warlock and a painter friend of some merit (and I think it was John

[18] While there is certainly more than an element of truth in Angus Morrison's assessment of Ireland's income and the cost of living in the first two or three decades of the twentieth century, Ireland, who could afford to run a car in the early 1920s, before the days of performing rights, was certainly never on the breadline.

Goss) were out in the country, John told me, and they were in a village and came to a beautiful church. They went into the church, it was very beautiful. It was very quiet and someone said: 'Let's say a Black Mass.' So they went up to the altar and turned the cross upside down and got a prayer book, placed it on the altar and started saying the Lord's Prayer backwards. And as they began, out of a clear sky there was a vast crack of thunder and the tower of the church was struck. They were absolutely petrified. They rushed out of the church. What did Heseltine do? He rushed to a telephone to get the story in the papers. That's all the effect it had on him. As Our Lord said: if they rose from the dead they will not be converted. Of no importance, but an interesting story from John. These rivalries between composers are very odd aren't they? He didn't think much of Walton, who was greatly supported by the Sitwells.

LF When he came back from Guernsey when the Germans arrived he had trouble finding somewhere to live?

KT Well, he had his house at Gunter Grove, of course. He went to live at Ashington. There is a rectory there and he stayed there quite frequently. He could come up to London when he wished. He was a member of the Savage Club. I did visit him there once; he had a room there. He had a house in the village in earlier times when he was a much younger man.

Norah [Kirby] was a widow. She lived by running a private taxi service. He engaged her. She used to drive for him. She never lived at Ashington with him, but when he moved, and they found Rock Mill and he bought it she went as his housekeeper there. She became completely devoted to him and looked after him at Rock Mill. I used to visit him there. One of the things that disturbed John very much at Rock Mill was the development of this tremendous excavation all round. He tried to get it stopped – the noise of the excavation was a background of unhappiness.

I gave up the John Ireland Trust because travelling to London became rather burdensome, though they paid all your expenses. Really it was difficult. Norah was very devoted and always attended the meetings, but really she wanted to decide everything herself. If you have a committee and you have formed a trust they are really in command. None of them wanted to offend Norah at all. They wanted to make a recording of his Violin Sonata and in one of my parishes I had a very distinguished violinist, Manoug Parikian. I said I would ask if he would play it for the recording. He agreed but he said, 'I would have to have my own pianist.' Norah wouldn't have this. Norah really became so strong. She didn't want him at all, so it fell through. So it created rather a difficult situation for me.

CHAPTER 7

John Ireland and the BBC

Lewis Foreman

F ROM the outset in 1922, the British Broadcasting Company gave music a significant role and the founding music director, L. Stanton Jefferies, was quickly succeeded by Percy Pitt, then known as an opera conductor and as a composer. He joined the BBC from the British National Opera Company in 1923 and remained until 1929 when he was succeeded by Adrian Boult. Music was well established by the time of the formation of the British Broadcasting Corporation in 1927, although unfortunately few of the Company's papers survive from before the time the Corporation came into being. Afterwards a records filing system based on Civil Service practice was quickly implemented, which filed almost all correspondence and internal papers and preserved them. This remains a particularly rich source for the researcher until late in the twentieth century.[1] The John Ireland files are particularly useful, including many Ireland letters to the BBC, and carbon copies of theirs to him, as well as file copies of his contracts, press cuttings and his longhand assessments of new music by others submitted to the BBC seeking broadcast. The latter, while confidential in their day and for long afterwards, are now available for research. These assessments of submitted scores are particularly illuminating in establishing what the assessors really thought about the music before them, and also occasionally they give us an insight into their own personal foibles and blind-spots.

The John Ireland files comprise a wide range of government-style manila file covers, the contents all secured by Treasury tags.[2] Helen Perkin is the subject of

---

[1] For the BBC Written Archives see Jacqueline Kavanagh's article 'The BBC's written archives', in *Information Sources in Music*, ed. Lewis Foreman (Munich: K. G. Saur, 2003), pp 325–37. Jacqueline Kavanagh is the long-standing Head of the BBC Written Archives Centre. The BBC WAC may be found at Peppard Road, Caversham Park, Reading RE4 8TZ.

[2] RCONT1 COMPOSER IRELAND, JOHN 1930–1938 File 1A
RCONT1 COMPOSER IRELAND, JOHN 1939–1941 File 2A
RCONT1 COMPOSER IRELAND, JOHN 1942–1943 File 2B
RCONT1 COMPOSER IRELAND, JOHN 1944–1947 File 2C
RCONT1 COMPOSER IRELAND, JOHN 1948–1962 File 3

RCONT1 COMPOSER IRELAND, JOHN 1932–1935 File 1A
RCONT1 COMPOSER IRELAND, JOHN 1936–1939 File 1B
RCONT1 COMPOSER IRELAND, JOHN 1940–1941 File 2A
RCONT1 COMPOSER IRELAND, JOHN 1942–1943 File 2B
RCONT1 COMPOSER IRELAND, JOHN 1944–1956 File 3
RCONT1 COMPOSER IRELAND, JOHN 1957–1962 File 4

RCONT9 GRAMOPHONE RECITALS (MISC) 1922–1962 JOHN IRELAND
[Excerpt for 1942–1949] *(continues overleaf)*

separate files in her own right, and it is worth noting that when Helen Perkin's orchestral work *Pageant* was submitted to the Reading Panel (then consisting of Benjamin Dale, S. P. Waddington and Edmund Rubbra) it was rejected. However, the conductor Clarence Raybould wrote[3] that he liked it 'sufficiently to be willing to do it'. Helen Perkin must have contacted John Ireland as she later resubmitted it with his support (22 February 1943), but it was again rejected. On the Perkin file we find a handbill for her 1949 Wigmore Hall concert at which three of her own works were on the programme. (See Fig. 3.)

The following chapter quotes selectively from the documents preserved in these BBC files. These documents can always be supplemented by reference to the very substantial surviving Ireland correspondence in the British Library or that retained (as photocopies) by the John Ireland Trust. Although John Ireland could be vitriolic about what he perceived as his neglect by the BBC, keenly feeling every apparent slight, and constantly challenging what he thought to be inadequate payment or incompetent administration, viewed historically his links with the BBC were longstanding and were actually remarkably cordial, with a golden period in the mid-1930s and during the Second World War. He was dealing with some of the leading names of the BBC Music Department, several of whom were personal friends. In fact John Ireland's relationship with the BBC, which ran from the mid-1920s almost until his death in 1962, was a major focus of his professional life from the late 1920s onwards. It was the BBC that established and maintained his standing as a significant British composer of orchestral music, despite his small catalogue of orchestral works. Indeed, they commissioned several of his most popular works, music which it is unlikely he would have written if he had not had the incentive of a BBC deadline and fee.

This relationship with the BBC falls into three clear areas: (1) as a composer: including BBC commissions and the performance of his music at the Proms; (2) as a performer: pianist, speaker and occasional conductor of his own music; and (3) participation in the BBC's Music Advisory Panel as a panel reader of submitted scores.

R27/55/1 MUSIC – GENERAL/ COMMISSIONED WORKS
R27/58 MUSIC – GENERAL. COMMISSIONED WORKS. PATRIOTIC SONGS
     1940–1944. [Main featured composers are Vaughan Williams, Dyson, Ireland]
R27/249/3 MUSIC GEN MUSIC PROGRAMME. ADVISORY PANEL FILE 3 1941–1945
R27/546–553 MUSIC – GENERAL. MUSIC REPORTS A–BON
R27/554–560 MUSIC – GENERAL. MUSIC REPORTS BOW–COK etc. for the rest of the
     alphabet
RCONT1 ARTIST PERKIN, HELEN FILE 1 1937–54 [There is no earlier file]
ARTIST PERKIN, HELEN File 2 1955–1962
COMPOSER PERKIN, HELEN 1941–1962

[3] 18 April 1941.

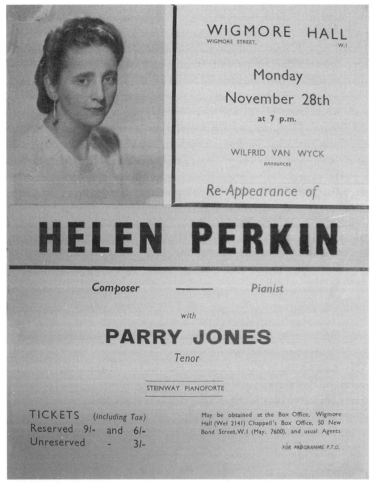

Fig. 3 Handbill for Helen Perkin's Wigmore Hall recital, 28 November, 1949

THE earliest John Ireland letter surviving at the BBC Written Archives Centre dates from 1926 but was clearly part of an established correspondence and relationship. The WAC holds John Ireland contracts onward from 1932. These are listed at the end of this article in Table 3.[4] A count of these shows a fairly steady spread of dates, in most years up to the late 1940s Ireland having several engagements. These were largely for him to appear as a pianist, almost always playing his own music.

The earliest surviving letter to the BBC[5] is addressed to Kenneth A. Wright, and untypically is typed, a sure sign Ireland was intending it to be formal.

---

[4] I am most grateful to my wife, Susan Foreman, for transcribing these from the Contract files at Caversham.

[5] BBC WAC file RCONT1 COMPOSER IRELAND, JOHN 1930–38 file 1

Sept 3, 1926

My dear Wright,

I have recently been paid approximately £6 by the P.R.S. for the broadcast of my works for the last six months of 1927. This is only, roughly speaking, about one-sixth of the amount paid to me for the preceding six months. This in itself seems odd. What makes me definitely mistrustful of these figures is that I know for a fact that there have been two performances of my first Violin Sonata at London and another Station during that period, neither of which occur on the list. Further, I have seen "Island Spell" in the programmes several times, and "Sea Fever" has of my own knowledge been broadcast frequently, as in previous periods. Neither of these items appear on the list. Similarly, it seems strange to me that such popular items as "Ragamuffin", "Chelsea Reach", and my Trios, which are frequently played in the ordinary way, do not occur on the list.

My first thought was to write to the P.R.S. at once, but knowing you personally, I though I would lay the matter before you, and ask you to take it up in the quarter concerned, with the B.B.C. I do not wish to do anything which will prejudice the interests of myself as a composer, or as a member of the P.R.S. Board, but I strongly feel there must be something very wrong with this return, which I herewith enclose.

I should be glad if, as a first step, the B.B.C. could confirm that it is reasonably accurate, or otherwise.

The fact that no stations or dates are quoted on the return makes the position still more unsatisfactory.

May I therefore hope to hear from you as soon as convenient, meanwhile leaving the matter in your good hand?"

Yours sincerely

John Ireland

We can only sample Ireland's extensive correspondence with the BBC here. A number of themes are recurrent, largely to do with the practical organisation of appearing as a performer or speaker, especially in wartime, with Ireland's perennial arguments over money, and also with the commissioning of new works. Later they document his assessments of manuscripts seeking performance submitted to the BBC. Alongside this we find a file of the BBC's contracts with Ireland, mainly relating to his appearances as pianist, or later, as speaker on the radio.

TABLE 1 Surviving contracts between the BBC and John Ireland, 1932–51

1932	4	1937	5	1942	6	1947	5
1933	3	1938	2	1943	4	1948	4
1934	4	1939	1	1944	6	1949	2
1935	3	1940	2	1945	3	1950	–
1936	3	1941	6	1946	4	1951	1

Fig. 4 Sir Henry Wood   Fig. 5 Sir Adrian Boult

T HE first substantial new work produced by the BBC was the Piano Concerto in
E♭. It had its world première performance at a Promenade Concert conducted,
as were all Ireland's early Prom performances, by Sir Henry Wood. This was at
Queen's Hall on 2 October 1930, when the soloist at Ireland's recommendation was
Helen Perkin.[6] While it was not formally commissioned by the BBC it was very
much written for the BBC and the Proms. Julian Herbage, his friend and producer
at the BBC over many years, remembered:[7]

> I first met John in the spring of 1930, in connection with his Piano Concerto,
> which was to get its first performance at the Proms that year. I was invited
> down one evening to his Chelsea studio, and when I arrived the sun was
> slanting into the room onto the hair of Helen Perkin, who was sitting at the
> piano playing John's "April". It all seemed too good to be true. Anyway John
> soon came on the scene, Helen played through as much of the Concerto
> as had been written, and we later adjourned to the nearby pub where he
> often used to eat. A few months later I got an urgent letter from John saying
> the Concerto couldn't be finished in time for the Proms … I replied firmly
> "No concerto by Ireland, no concerto for Helen". The concerto was, of course,
> duly completed.

It was a considerable success and is a remarkable example of the BBC cham-
pioning a specific work when new; it would be heard twenty-two times at the

[6] For Helen Perkin see Chapter 11.

[7] Julian Herbage to John Longmire, 19 March 1963.

TABLE 2 Piano Concerto in E♭ at the Proms

1930	Helen Perkin	1948	Eileen Joyce
1931	Helen Perkin	1949	Eileen Joyce
1933	Angus Morrison	1950	[Winter] Kendall Taylor
1934	Helen Perkin	1950	Colin Horsley
1936	Artur Rubinstein	1951	Kendall Taylor
1938	Clifford Curzon	1952	Colin Horsley
[1939]	Clifford Curzon*	1953	Eric Parkin
1941	*Destruction of Queen's Hall*	1954	Eric Parkin
1942	Clifford Curzon	1955	Gina Bachauer
1943	Clifford Curzon	1958	Colin Horsley
1944	Moura Lympani	1959	Eric Parkin
1945	Clifford Curzon	1979	Philip Fowke
1946	Kendall Taylor	1982	Kathryn Stott
1947	Kendall Taylor	1993	Kathryn Stott

*The aborted 1939 performance was announced for 16 September but the Proms were abandoned on 1 September owing to the outbreak of war.

Proms over the thirty years 1930–59. It was only heard a further three times at the Proms during the succeeding half century, and was clearly a victim of a conscious change of artistic policy in the 1960s, despite being a work which appeared to have a substantial and active public following.

When it was new the Piano Concerto was frequently played, Ireland noting in a letter to Kenneth Wright dated 20 March 1932 that it 'is down for performance at Belfast in May, this will make its 9th (& probably <u>last</u>!) performance, in 18 months'.[8]

The programmes for all BBC public concerts, including the Proms, are filed at Caversham together with press cuttings for each concert. The programme note by 'D.M.C.'[9] for the third Prom performance of the Concerto at Queen's Hall on 5 September 1933, when the soloist was Angus Morrison, clearly stated Ireland's position[10] at that date as far as the orchestral repertoire was concerned:

> John Ireland's name does not appear very often in orchestral programmes. While others court the glamour and publicity of orchestral performance, he prefers to work in the more secluded world of chamber music, where he has won the highest honours; the only orchestral works he has brought before the public are "The Forgotten Rite" and the Rhapsody, "Mai-Dun", both of which have already won assured places of their own among contemporary orchestral music of that poetic and pictorial order on which Ireland is not modern enough in his sympathies to turn a disdainful back.

This concerto, which made its first appearance in the Promenade

[8] Ireland from Chelsea Arts Club 20 March 1932; BBC WAC RCONT 1.

[9] David Millar Craig (1878–1965).

[10] Promenade Concerts, Queen's Hall, Tuesday 5 September 1933, pp. 9–10.

Concerts in 1930, is his first work of the kind: it brings into the concerto form a style of pianoforte writing highly personal to the composer, one in which the showy devices of most concertos have no place; and it displays a charm and amenability that have not always been noticeable in Ireland's music. Since its introduction by Miss Helen Perkin, the work has earned for itself a renown as nearly popular as any music of such an order may hope to win. It adheres neither to the classical sonata form nor to the cyclic form beloved of Liszt, though elements of both have gone into its design. There are three movements; of which the first stands alone, the third following on the second without a break.

Performances of the Piano Concerto continued throughout the 1930s, largely but not entirely promoted by the BBC. Even after the outbreak of war, when the promised 1939 Proms performance had been abandoned when the series ended prematurely, it was broadcast in October 1939 by Clifford Curzon conducted by Clarence Raybould. Ireland wrote from Guernsey: 'It is always a great pleasure to hear performances conducted by you, & the performance of my Piano Concerto the other night with yourself & Curzon was no exception. ... The slow movement was particularly beautifully played, & the difficult transition & opening of the Finale (which are sometimes rather rushed) very successful.'[11]

In the early 1930s Ireland still had few orchestral works to his name, so when he was actually engaged on a new one he tended to announce he was working on it, ostensibly to ensure that a performance was assured when he had finished it.

March 30 1932

My dear Boult

I am writing to let you know that I am at work on a second piano concerto, which will be ready for performance next season.

The experience I have had with my first concerto, thanks to the B.B.C., has made me anxious to write another work for the same combination in a totally different mood, tho' I hope, as direct in manner. I feel it is a form in which there is still a great deal to be said.

I am writing again for a Beethoven orchestra with the solo instrument definitely to the fore – I mean, the work will not be a Symphonie Concertante.

I expect this work to be rather more concise & economical, & so last about 20 minutes, certainly well under 25 minutes and altho' there will be a sense of 3 movements, it will probably be continuous, & with one break at the most. At any rate, I think it will be a work of significance and serious intention! I should certainly wish that its first performance is in the hands of the B.B.C.

Kindest regards from

Yrs vy sincerely

John Ireland

---

[11] Ireland, Fort Saumarez, L'Érée, Guernsey, C.I. to Clarence Raybould, 28 October 1939.

Wednesday, 1 October

BRAHMS CONCERT

Two Minuets from Serenade in D	*Brahms*
Concerto in A minor, for Violin, Violoncello and Orchestra	*Brahms*
Songs (*a*) "Ständchen" (Op. 106, No. 1)	
(*b*) "Die Schnur" (Op. 57)	*Brahms*
(*c*) "Wehe, so willst du mich" (Op. 32)	
Symphony No. 1, in C minor	*Brahms*
Suite "El Amor Brujo"	*de Falla*
Overture di Ballo	*Sullivan*

OLGA HALEY

Solo Violin   -   ARTHUR CATTERALL

Solo Violoncello   -   -   LAURI KENNEDY

Thursday, 2 October

BRITISH COMPOSERS CONCERT

Trumpet Voluntary	*Purcell*
Oboe Concerto	*Eugene Goossens*
Songs with Orchestra	
(*a*) "The Vagabond"	
(*b*) "The Road-side Fire" (Songs of Travel)	*Vaughan Williams*
Pianoforte Concerto	*John Ireland*
Symphony No. 2, in E flat	*Elgar*
Concerto Grosso No. 12, in B minor	*Handel*
Overture "Ruy Blas"	*Mendelssohn*

GEORGE PARKER

Solo Oboe   -   LEON GOOSSENS

Solo Pianoforte   -   HELEN PERKIN

Friday, 3 October

BEETHOVEN CONCERT

Overture "Namensfeier" ("Name Day")	*Beethoven*
Two Romances for Violin and Orchestra, No. 1, in G	
No. 2, in F	*Beethoven*
Symphony No. 9, in D minor ("The Choral")	*Beethoven*
Roumanian Rhapsody No. 1, in A	*Enesco*
Motet "Be not afraid"	*Bach*
Cossack Dance (Mazeppa)	*Tchaikovsky*

ELSIE SUDDABY

MARGARET BALFOUR

FRANCIS RUSSELL

HORACE STEVENS

Solo Violin   -   ORREA PERNEL

THE NATIONAL CHORUS

Fig. 6 The BBC prospectus for the 1930 season of Promenade Concerts at Queen's Hall, showing the programme in which John Ireland's Piano Concerto would first be performed. The Oboe Concerto by Eugene Goossens which preceded it was also a first performance.

The second piano concerto in fact became the one-movement *Legend* for piano and orchestra, running around a quarter of an hour and first performed by Helen Perkin during the BBC's British Music Festival on 12 January 1934. It was announced for a Promenade Concert at Queen's Hall in August 1934, but Perkin declined the date and less than two months before the performance the BBC sent a wire to Ireland, then at the Adelphi Hotel, Liverpool, asking him to recommend a soloist. He replied:

June 26 1934 8 p.m.
Dear Mr Wynn
I only got your wire on arrival here this evening. I have suggested Harriet Cohen & Harold Samuel for performances by them could be good for the work. I also suggested Kathleen Long because she very much wants to do it, & I dare say she w^ld do it well. I suppose it w^ld be impossible to get Myra Hess to do it, tho' Clark[12] suggested that last year.

If the worst comes to the worst, Angus Morrison could do it again, but his performance is not a striking one, sound enough as it is.

I certainly do not wish it done by Cyril Smith, Clifford Curzon or Laffitte or Howard-Jones, or Clark's German-American friend whose name I forget. It is somewhat unfortunate that Perkin cannot change the date, but maybe she thinks she has made enough London appearances with that work, or she may have arranged her holidays for September.

It is a pity I am not in town to see you about it, but that cannot be helped. Samuel has seen the work, & thought of playing it in America, tho' whether it would really suit him, I don't know.

Sorry to be so verbose:
Yrs. Sincerely
John Ireland

Thus we find Ireland having very definite views on the pianists of his day. Later he performed the work himself on at least two occasions, but for the Prom he conducted and Harriet Cohen appeared in the solo part.

Similarly a few weeks later on 7 July, 1934, he writes, at remarkably short notice, to discuss the choice of the singer for a broadcast of his songs from the BBC's Northern Station:

Dear Mr Wynn
In regard to my Manchester date on Aug: 7, I have suggest[ed] to the regional Director there the following singers:
John Armstrong
or (2) Alfred Reed
& as an alternative (3) George Parker
I consider Reed is <u>good</u>, a real <u>lieder</u> singer with a very nice voice, & that he sh^ld be encouraged, & if that could be arranged, he w^ld in many ways be the best for this purpose. So could you go for that? I do not know if (1) or (2) have Northern connections, but could not that be waived??
Parker is experienced & <u>has</u> Northern connections, but, <u>entre nous</u>,

---

[12] Edward Clark.

I do not like either his voice or his style, & his personality on wireless is uncouth. ...

While Ireland was someone quick to ingratiate himself with authority when he thought it would be beneficial, his attitude towards Adrian Boult could be ambivalent. Yet he had much to thank Boult for, and when he writes to congratulate him after hearing a performance by the then still new BBC Symphony Orchestra he is clearly responding honestly to the notable achievement of the new orchestra:

> May 7th 1931
> My dear Boult
> I listened-in last night (in the country) to the B.B.C. Symphony concert. The pitch to which you have worked up the B.B.C. orchestra is simply amazing, and, well as I know the Elgar variations, this performance even through a loud speaker was by far the finest & most thrilling I have ever heard. It was simply epoch-making, both as a piece of orchestral playing & as an exposition of the composer's thought.
> I felt I must write to thank you for this experience:
> Yrs very sincerely
> John Ireland

Also notable from the BBC files is his response to any affront. Ireland was quick to notice any slight, whether real or imaginery. For example on 30 May 1937 he writes to Julian Herbage from Deal:

> My dear Julian
> I see by "Radio Times" that a feature called "English Song Writers" is being carried out, in this case June 2, (Vaughan Williams).
> Now, I have heard nothing about this, & I ought to have been involved, as I consider I am by a long way the most important "English Song Writer". If I do not get a display in this series it is a public scandal. Will you see what you & Kenneth can do about it? I shall be away & unavailable from July 3 to July 10:
> Excuse haste:
> Yrs. Always
> John Ireland

> PS. My last group of songs "Songs Sacred & Profane" has not been given for ages – & there are 72 others.

Not only could he be impatient if he thought he was being ignored, he was constantly developing new contacts if he thought he had found someone who would promote his music.

In his later years Ireland broadcast as speaker, usually in reminiscent mood, and his surviving radio talks about Stanford and his youthful encounters with Beethoven at the keyboard appear later in these pages.

There is no doubt that Ireland found orchestral composition a heavy labour. In this respect three works from the period 1936–42, *A London Overture, These Things Shall Be* for baritone, chorus and orchestra and the wartime *Epic March* followed a similar pattern. Their production was documented by Ireland's letters.

In view of their subsequent success, all three promoted by the BBC, it is illuminating briefly to consider them here. First came *A London Overture*. This originated from a proposal in May 1936 to orchestrate, for that year's Proms at Queen's Hall, Ireland's *Comedy Overture* for brass band, which had been first performed at Crystal Palace on 29 September 1934. In the event Ireland completely recomposed it and had to ask that the first performance be put back to 23 September in order for him to deliver. He wrote to Adrian Boult on 6 September:

My dear Boult

Promenade Concerts, 1936

In regard to your suggestion of May 16th that an orchestral version of my Overture for Brass band should be included in this season's Promenade Concerts, I am writing to tell you that it is only a day or two since I have been able to complete the Score, which has cost me upwards of 300 hours' labour. After serious reflection, and a survey of the work as it now stands, I find it necessary to put the following facts before you.

The Overture in its present form is no mere transcription, which could have been made by some clever arranger, say, Gordon Jacob, but an entirely fresh creation, called forth by the orchestral medium, for which the Brass Band material provides only the basis. As you can readily believe, the piece is now of far greater artistic significance, more complex in detail, technically difficult and subtle in style, than in its original form.

Taking all this into account, and the fact that the conductor and the orchestra will have M.S. material to contend with, it is important for me to know definitely what amount of rehearsal time has been allotted to the preparation of this work, and I shall be grateful if you will kindly let me know this.

Yours sincerely
John Ireland

Such was the success of the new work, almost immediately he was sounded out to consider writing a choral work for a Coronation concert. The Coronation was announced for 12 May 1937. John Ireland was immediately concerned about the financial arrangements, the issues best seen in a letter to Kenneth A. Wright written on 22 February 1937 from Deal:

Dear Kenneth

I have had a letter from M. T. Candler in regard to what we discussed about a choral piece.

I saw Herbage soon after your last letter reached me, & he appeared to be handling the matter in your absence, but I am writing to you now, as the matter cannot be settled without further discussion.

There is very little time left, & if this work is to be written & got ready (vocal score printed, etc) I sh^{ld} have to start on it at once, & give up all my ordinary work for 5 or 6 weeks. In these circumstances, the actual financial loss thereby w^{ld} by no means be made up to me by the fee offered (50 guineas). If the B.B.C. really wish for this work from me, I think the fee sh^{ld} be 100 guineas, in which case I shall not make a direct profit, but shld be compensated for work cancelled.

As most composers here are men of means & leisure,[13] no doubt they think £50 handsome as a reward, but I really cannot afford to be a loser in this way – & I do not think the Copyright Department understand the labour involved in a work of this sort. It is not like a <u>pièce d'occasion</u>, such as a Coronation March, which could be dished up in a few days (& no doubt <u>will</u> be.)[14]

At any rate, after everything is decided, perhaps you will be able to see me, & in any case, it cannot be settled without discussion. The piece w^{ld} have to be done in time to get vocal score into print, parts copied, etc. – & in any case, Mr: Candler [in fact, *Miss* Candler] does not make it clear that the B.B.C. w^{ld} pay for copies or hire of material. However, the matter is important, and if it is to materialise, I shall have to start on it at once, by March 1 at the very latest.

I am very sorry to hear you had such a bad time with lumbago, & hope you are now recovered. I shall come up to town tomorrow or Wednesday, & perhaps you will write meanwhile (to Gunter Grove)

Yrs always

J. Ireland

Ireland started sketching the music but at that stage they had not agreed terms. We find John Ireland writing to Julian Herbage on 14 March 1937

My dear Julian

I have spent practically all my time, in a very concentrated way, since I saw you, in getting the choral work sketched – it was no use saying anything as to whether it could be done, or not, in the time, until I could see my way clearly through to the end – which now I do, & can estimate the work involved.

I have written to Miss Candler about the business side of it, & no doubt you will see the letter. I am just off to Edinburgh for 10 days of examining, etc: I simply could not get out of. After that, if the matter goes through with the B.B.C. I shall devote my whole time to the work – & I think you will not be very disappointed. By the way, the work will be nearer 15 minutes rather than 12[15] at the pace I think of it.

Excuse haste – Yrs. Always

John Ireland

Bearing in mind how near the proposed performance was, Ireland ran it very close. Comparison with Elgar's late delivery of major choral works to Edwardian choral festivals is immediately apposite. Probably both needed the pressure of the impending high profile performance to get the writing actually done, and both relied on a supporting body of music copying and engraving professionals to get

---

[13] He is referring to his friends Vaughan Williams and Arnold Bax.

[14] He is taking a swipe at Walton's commission for *Crown Imperial*.

[15] In practice the finished work can vary enormously in duration. Richard Hickox's Chandos recording runs a little over 22 minutes, but the first commercial recording conducted by Barbirolli was made to fit on four 78 rpm sides, and times at only 16′05″.

them through. This is vividly seen in Ireland's letter to Julian Herbage dated 11 April 1937.

My dear Julian

Thanks for yr. letter. I will forward you a copy of my version of the poem of "These things shall be". In course of the work I have decided to add yet one more verse!

I have tried to 'phone you today without success. The position now is this. The work divides itself into 2 parts. I will let you have a copy of the <u>chorus</u> part of the 1st section to-morrow – this covers 8 minutes & is about ½ the work, so they (copyists) can get going at once. The corresponding section of the full score sh^{ld} be in your hands by next Monday, April 19th, & the remainder by Monday April 26 – <u>at latest</u>. This ought to give plenty of time for copying – the other half of the <u>chorus</u> part will be ready by April 17, I expect, perhaps sooner.

I am relying on you to get everything in train, & meanwhile I am working hell for leather.

I think the B.B.C. ought to undertake, <u>as a part of the contract</u>, to give a public performance with the complete choir in the Autumn, tho' I cannot insist on this, of course, It is laid out for large chorus, & one verse is for a baritone solo – not bass, as it goes up to G.

I shall be extremely surprised if the work is not a popular success, as it is very striking & effective.

I enclose particulars of the orchestration.

I have seen Willie's march, wh: seems good – he has gone off to Italy.

I w^{ld} call & see you, but you can understand every hour matters now to me.

About "A London Overture", I hope Hawkes has handed over the printed score & ms: material. As this is the <u>first</u> <u>broadcast</u> performance, I sh^{ld} have thought the Radio Times w^{ld} have asked me for some particulars – but, dear me, not a word.! The loss of publicity over that work is lamentable, & I hope "These things" will not be treated with the same contempt & indifference.

By the way, I must attend one rehearsal of the Overture – as I do not want a repetition of the "Prom" fiasco – & I trust Sir A.B. will be interested enough to rehearse the work properly – it is well worth it – I have made a lot of improvements since you heard it.

Yrs ever

John:

Three weeks later it was completed, though we do not have firsthand accounts to illustrate the pressure on the copyists and engravers required to complete the music for performance on 13 May. Ireland wrote to Owen Mase on 6 May 1937:

Dear Mr: Mase

I am sorry for delay in replying to yours of Ap. 22, but I [am] only just recovering from the terrific strain of completing my new choral work in the short time allotted.

I do not mind being photographed on Sunday, providing

(1) that is it <u>not</u> with Miss Reiss[16] in the picture

(2) that you will not use the photograph unless I am satisfied with it.

Now there is something much more urgent for which I must ask your attention. The B.B.C. <u>commissioned</u> me to write this choral work, for a highly important occasion – presumably the B.B.C. w[ld] have wished to make some publicity about this in the press generally, but there has been absolutely none – in fact, I have only seen the title of the work mentioned in an official list supplied by the B.B.C. There has been some publicity for Walton's March, but no doubt he & his publishers saw to that.

This new work of mine is of first importance – not merely as coming from my pen but in the sentiments it expresses, which carry out exactly the ideals of the B.B.C. motto, "Nation shall speak unto nation"[17] etc: – & what all sane people are feeling at the present moment.

It ought to be the business of somebody, in a case like this, to get into contact with the newspapers ...

Its first performance came in a broadcast the day after the Coronation, on 13 May, but the first concert performance, at Queen's Hall, did not follow until 1 December. It was scheduled to have its first Proms performance on 19 September 1939, but this did not take place owing to the outbreak of the war. It tended to feature in anti-war or pacifist programmes and was featured in the first of many Anglo-Soviet programmes after Hitler declared war on Russia. This was at Westminster Central Hall on 11 October 1941. (See illustration, p. 208.) However, once it had been heard at the Proms – in July 1943, it became a popular favourite there and reappeared each season until 1949 and again in 1951 and 1952, 1954, 1955 and 1957, but has not been heard again since.

As can be seen from the table of contracts John Ireland's regular, if not frequent, invitations to perform his own music continued. We might, perhaps note two typical exchanges from 1937 and 1938:

Nov 14th 1937

Dear Mr Philips

I rather hoped for an acknowledgement of my last letter to you. It was to let you know that I have 3 new piano pieces [i.e. *Greenways*] that are to be published, & that I wish to give the first broadcast performance myself. I have no doubt that other performers may wish to broadcast these for the first time, hence my letter. So will you kindly bear this in mind. I w[d] suggest that the 3 new pieces, wh: take about 8 minutes, sh[d] form part of a short recital, at which I could play also the <u>Sonatina</u> & say, 2 other single pieces, if desired. I shall be in town on Thursday and will ring you up:

Yrs. Sincerely

John Ireland

---

[16] Thelma Reiss, cellist, who had recently broadcast Ireland's Cello Sonata with him at the piano. He did not warm to her or her playing.

[17] The BBC motto is actually 'National shall speak peace unto nation'.

May 15 1938

Dear Mrs Waterman

I have been laid up, & you sh^ld have had the new "Neptune"[18] score earlier. Mr: Colin Deane of the Year Book Press told me to send the score to the B.B.C., & that you are arranging to have the parts copied. There must be no delay about this, but as the composition is short (58 bars), it ought to be quite easy to get the job completed in a day or two. At any rate, will you get into touch with Mr: Deane immediately on receipt of this, so that the copying can be commenced <u>at</u> <u>once</u> – as Sir W. Davies[19] is very anxious about it.

Yours sincerely

John Ireland

I thought everyone at the B.B.C. knew that I am only in London on Thursdays and Fridays?

At the beginning of the Second World War Ireland went to live in Guernsey – presumably thinking he was well away from the war and clearly not anticipating the German invasion. He does not appear to have realised the way the BBC had attempted to ensure he was on the list of notable residents to be repatriated to England before the Germans arrived. On 24 June the Director General of the BBC had written to Major-General Beith at the War Office.[20]

> May I venture to trouble you on a point that may seem rather trivial in the present circumstances? We would very much like to secure your help in the evacuation of John Ireland from Courthouse Place, Guernsey, where apparently he is experiencing difficulty in securing permission to leave.
>
> John Ireland is, as you know, one of our foremost living composers, a person much loved and respected in the music profession, and there have been many expressions of anxiety about him. It is possible that his difficulties may be due to a prophet not being honoured in his own place of residence, and I wondered whether anything could be done to press the local authorities to give him the necessary permit for evacuation. ...

In fact Ireland had left Guernsey on 22 June and had arrived safely in England.

Ireland in his most sarcastic and acerbic vein may be amusing to us today but in one or two instances he seriously upset his BBC correspondents and had to repair fences with alacrity. One example will suffice:

---

[18] Ireland had orchestrated an SATB version of his 1911 patriotic unison song *In Praise of Neptune*, words by Thomas Campion.

[19] Sir Henry Walford Davies.

[20] B. E. Nicolls to Major-General J. H. Beith, 24 June. 'Private and confidential. *Sent by hand*.'

January 5th, 1942

Dear Dr. Thatcher,

Thank you for your note, with enclosure, dated the 18th of December. I have delayed replying until I could find out what I had said in an unofficial letter to Mr. Murrill which caused the resentment of which you spoke.

I have now written to him making clear, I hope, that the part of my letter to which exception was taken was not intended by me at all in the sense of a complaint, and deploring that it was so worded as to be susceptible of being interpreted as such.

No doubt Mr. Murrill will show you my letter, but meanwhile I cannot but express sincere regret that I should have unintentionally conveyed an impression which is quite contrary to the feelings I have always entertained for the B.B.C. and such members of its personnel as I have been privileged to meet and to number as friends.

Yours sincerely,

John Ireland

January 5th, 1942

Dear Mr Murrill

In reply to yours dated January 1st, may I say that my previous letter to you was, apart from my enquiry about the timing of "Sarnia", of a purely personal and unofficial nature, and I can only deplore that what was intended by me as merely a light (if, as now appears, misplaced) comment on passing musical events should have been taken at all seriously, or construed as expressing dissatisfaction with the presentation of my own works in the B.B.C. programmes. But in re-reading this thoughtless remark I can see that in cold typescript it may have tended to convey something which was quite absent from my mind.

In any case, I deeply regret having written anything which could be open to the interpretation placed on it, particularly as I am the last person to suggest, even remotely, that the B.B.C. fails to do justice to my music, when the contrary is so obviously the case.

Perhaps you will be kind enough to ensure that any such erroneous impression created by my remark may be dispelled.

With kind regards,

Yours sincerely,

John Ireland

John Ireland's *Epic March* was first performed at the Proms on 27 June 1942, and as the John Ireland Composer file for 1939–41 makes clear it had been first mooted by the Ministry of Information. A typed file note gives an administrative view of the commission after Ireland tried to raise the fee.

PATRIOTIC MARCH

Mr. Pick then of the Ministry of Information, suggested that the B.B.C. should arrange for a Patriotic March to be written. I have not yet discovered to whom this suggestion came in the B.B.C. but on 28th November, 1940, D.M. wrote to John Ireland making the suggestion and mentioning that it came from the Ministry of Information. Ireland expressed himself as willing to do it and said that the idea appealed strongly to him. It was agreed that D.M. should tell Ireland that the business side would be handled by Administration Division, and he did so on 9th December.

Programme Copyright wrote to John Ireland on 20th December offering 40 guineas which is the normal payment in such cases. The arrangement is that the Corporation obtains no rights other than first performance and permission to reproduce parts of the score in its journals for publicity purposes. (We could not obtain any other rights from a member of the P.R.S. if we wanted to.) The composer obtains his fees from the P.R.S. as he does for all his compositions and can publish the score.

Ireland put the matter into the hands of his agent and publisher, Ralph Hawkes, who on the telephone told Miss Candler that Ireland was making a long story about the Income Tax he had to pay and wanted 80 guineas. A few days later (31st December) Hawkes wrote a letter asking £100. This is the fee previously paid him for a much larger work which we asked him to do in a hurry laying aside all his other work.

D.D.M. and D.M. felt that we ought to go to 80 guineas, but both agreed that £100 was too much. It seems to the Administration that 50 guineas is ample as an addition to normal income from such compositions, especially in view of the fact that we give the composer the idea and will publicise the work and play it a number of times (thus increasing his P.R.S. fees). Any increase will operate for any other schemes of this kind, of which there may be several and fees are likely to go up all round.

Hawkes understands our view and simply says that Ireland just wants to stand out for as much as he can get. Incidentally Hawkes appeared surprised at our idea of asking Ireland to do this particular work. He, as the man's publisher, would obviously not have proposed such work to his client.

We suggest that a more suitable way of making the gesture of initiating the production of a patriotic march for full orchestra would be to offer a prize for the best march sent in. This will produce all the desired goodwill – much more than giving only one composer a chance – and will ensure that the material is accepted on its merits. Under the original scheme if Ireland does not produce what we want, which is quite possible, we shall have to play it and pretend it is excellent. This will not be good for our reputation in the musical world.

The commissioning of the march from Ireland did not proceed with any speed, probably largely to do with the non-agreement on terms. The following summer Ireland wrote to Sir Adrian Boult (3 June 1941):

… Now I have not forgotten your letter of last November in reference to the MARCH you suggested. I have thought the matter over carefully, and it is certain that I cannot do anything on the lines of "Pomp and Circumstance" No 1. It is not what I feel appropriate at the present time. That is to say, I personally cannot feel that kind of music as my own reaction to the position. I have evolved some ideas, but before working them out I think it would be best if I submit to you the opening fanfare and the first theme, in short score,

Fig. 7 The short score sketch of Epic March that Ireland sent to Sir Adrian Boult at the BBC

and then you can tell me candidly if you think it is the sort of thing which will be suitable. If you do, then I will carry on, but if not (and I must ask you to be perfectly frank) I will abandon the idea. What I have in mind is stern and purposeful rather than jolly or complacent – however, you will see at once the sort of thing it will be, when fully carried out, as soon as you have looked at my sketch of the opening section.

As to the business side, I left this in the hands of Ralph Hawkes, and he rather suddenly left for U.S.A., leaving this matter in the air, and up to the present I cannot obtain any reply from the Executive Department, and do not know what the position is. Maybe some other composer has been approached, in which case I think they might let me know, otherwise I can neither go forward nor withdraw.

The practical difficulties of broadcasting, often only in short-running programmes, were exacerbated by their always being live. Only later in the war did recording become a possibility, so if Ireland was broadcasting to a distant time-zone, in South America or the Pacific, he had to be in the studio during the night. Whether living at Bedford or Saffron Walden, and without a car, this meant much use of hotels, or if with the BBC at Bedford of BBC hostel accommodation. Ireland was constantly writing to make the necessary arrangements, typical examples of which are:

Feb 1st 1945 [misdated by Ireland, probably 1942]
Dear Mr: Wynn,

In regard to the engagement suggested for March 8th, 7–7.15 is not enough time for the programme suggested & I have written to Mr: Phillips about it. The actual time required is 18m 55sec: but I have explained this & asked him to wire me, wh: I will communicate with you at once –

Yrs. Sincerely
John Ireland

February 1st 1942
Dear Mr. St. George Phillips,

I have received a letter from Mr. Wynn offering me a broadcast on March 8, 7 – 7.15 p.m., in wh. he says you wish me to play my Sonatina and the 3 Pastels. I think I sent you the timings of these pieces, & you will see that 15 minutes is too little time.

The actual playing time of the 3 Pastels is 8m. 25s. & the "captions" will take quite 1m. to read. The Sonatina is 9m. 30s. – this makes 18m. 55s: so this programme wld. be a tight fit even in 20 minutes – it leaves only 1m. 5s. over for announcing, etc:

Has Mr. Wynn made a mistake, or did you wish the programme changed? Please send me a wire about this, as if I do this broadcast I shall have to get out of another engagement – though I am prepared to do so, as the B.B.C. is more important, only I must let the other people know at once.

In regard to Mr. Pauer's performance of my 'cello sonata, I really must ask you not to convey my private criticism to him, especially as I see the slow movement is marked metronomically too fast. I could let him know this myself, if you like.

Please excuse a somewhat hasty letter: The order of the programme wld. be:

```
        ms     Three Pastels:
        2.45       A Grecian Lad ⎫
3.55               The Boy Bishop ⎬ first performance
        1.45       Puck's Birthday ⎭
        1.0    Captions
        9.25 (sic)

        9.30   Sonatina
                   Moderato
                   Quasi lento leading to
                   Rondo
        18.55
        m.s.
```

Yours sincerely,
John Ireland

February 3rd 1942
Dear St. George Phillips,

You will have received my wire, I also telegraphed my acceptance of March 8 to Mr. Wynn.

If it meets your views, I would propose to play the 3 Pastels first, & then "The Island Spell" – I often receive requests to broadcast this piece, & it is a contrast to the others – so please let me know if this will be all right.

This makes the actual performing time 11m. 30s which will allow time for the "captions" to be ready by the Announcer, & any necessary introductory remarks. I enclose the exact particulars. I am sorry we have to omit the "Sonatina", but perhaps some occasion may arise later on for that.

Yours sincerely
John Ireland

February 15th 1942
Dear Miss Ware,

In reference to the recital I am giving next Friday/Saturday, Feb 20/21, I note I am to catch the 12.50 bus, & shld. be glad if I can be able to use the piano before the time stated (1.30 a.m.) – I suppose an earlier bus is not available?

I note you have booked a room for me at the Northwick Arms, though I greatly prefer the "Crown", which is far more comfortable.

Can you let me have the telephone number of your department, as I shall arrive by lunch time & may be glad to come up in the afternoon to get some practice, if possible.

Yours sincerely,
John Ireland

February 17th 1942

Dear Miss Duncan,

I am broadcasting from Bedford on Sunday March 8th at 7 p.m. There does not appear to be a satisfactory train connection on a Sunday from here to Bedford – so perhaps it will be best if you can arrange for me to spend Saturday night (March 7) as well as Sunday night (March 8) at Bedford. I suppose you will book me at the "Swan" – On hearing from you I will let you know the time of my train's arrival.

Yours very truly,   John Ireland

March 1st 1942

Dear St. George Phillips,

Forgive my delay in sending you the enclosed material about "Three Pastels".

I believe there <u>is</u> a monument of a "Boy Bishop" in Salisbury Cathedral.

I broadcast those pieces in the Latin-American transmission on Feb: 21, so it will be almost the only example of a British work being heard for the <u>first</u> time in S. America.

I shall look forward to meeting you at Bedford, where I shall arrive on the Saturday afternoon – perhaps you wld. dine with me, if free, on the Saturday – or lunch on the Sunday – I shld. like to meet Mr. Val Drewry, too – perhaps he could join us? or meet afterwards?

I have shown these pieces to Ralph Hill, & he may have a few words about them in Radio Times.

With kind regards,

Yrs. sincerely,
John Ireland

P.S. I shall be glad if I can get an hour or two of piano practice (preferably on the piano I am to use) on Sunday.

Even in the 1950s we find Ireland in his BBC relations still engaged in his customary challenging of fees offered and arrangements made:

May 25, 1952

Dear Mr Tillett

In regard to the engagement suggested for June 20th, I must say I do not consider a fee of £10.10. adequate.

I receive very few engagements from the B.B.C. and for me to play in my own works is a special feature for the public, which ought to be paid for at a higher rate. I know something of the fees paid to some British & foreign artists, which I do

Analysis of the frequency with which John Ireland's music appeared at the Henry Wood Promenade Concerts has been made easier by the BBC Proms' Archive online.[21] Thus we can quickly establish that there were 137 performances

---

[21] www.bbc.co.uk/proms/archive. This invaluable database needs to be used with caution. For example on 10 January 1935 *The Forgotten Rite* at the Winter Prom is billed as being conducted by Sir Henry Wood, but as a review in *The Times* and a

documented, and ignoring the three that in reality never took place, 134 comprising 11 songs, 1 part-song, 1 solo piano piece and 10 orchestral works[22] between 1912 and 2007. Ireland was first represented at the Proms, at Queen's Hall, by single songs with piano accompaniment. Even when Ireland had orchestrated the song, the piano version was given at the Proms. Continuing the ballad concert tradition, the songs chosen were always sung by a man and except on one occasion by a baritone. In 1912 and 1913 the preferred song was *Hope the Hornblower*. In 1919 it was *Sea Fever*, and the same year *When Lights Go Rolling Round the Sky*, the latter repeated in 1921, 1923, 1925 and 1926. In 1925 it was so popular that it appeared on two separate programmes six weeks apart. All told, it enjoyed eight Prom performances.

Ireland had been first represented at the Proms by an orchestral work – in 1917 – when *The Forgotten Rite* had its world premiere. His music featured every year until 1962 except for 1941, when the BBC was not running the concerts, and in 1961, when he was still alive but new management at the BBC Music Department were not sympathetic. Subsequently he was not heard again at the Proms for thirteen years, and only then with a brass band performance of *A Downland Suite*. In 1979 his Piano Concerto returned after an absence of twenty years, played by the pianist Philip Fowke. The sudden dropping of popular composers like Ireland and Delius reflected new policies initiated by (Sir) William Glock.

As Ireland's orchestral music was completed it was almost immediately given at the Proms. The next after *The Forgotten Rite* was *Mai-Dun* in 1922, this eventually being heard a total of ten times up to 1956 but then remaining unplayed for over fifty years. Ireland's songs were sung almost every year in the 1920s, doubtless because of the then small size of Ireland's orchestral catalogue.

During a brief period in the mid-1930s, John Ireland appeared four times as a performer at the Proms, on three occasions as conductor, once as a pianist. He conducted the tone poem *Mai-Dun* in 1934, which was repeated by him the following year, and later the same year he was the pianist in the second Prom appearance of the *Legend* for piano and orchestra. In 1935 he conducted the Winter Prom performance of *The Forgotten Rite*[23] and in 1937 he conducted *The Forgotten Rite* and *Mai-Dun* consecutively in the same programme, setting a precedent which only rarely have other conductors since emulated, despite the remarkable effectiveness of hearing them played thus.

---

surviving acetate recording make clear *The Forgotten Rite* was, in fact, conducted by Ireland himself, the only surviving recording of him conducting one of his orchestral works, and valuable as an artistic exemplar in view of his slow tempi. Later an announced performance of the Piano Concerto for the 1939 Prom Season is listed as having taken place when the series had been abandoned by the date concerned owing to the outbreak of the Second World War.

[22] Including one by brass band and a late (2007) performance of one movement from his film score for *The Overlanders*.

[23] See n. 21.

O N midsummer's day 1942 Ireland responded to a letter from (Sir) Arthur Bliss, newly appointed as Director of Music, inviting him to call:

Dear Arthur Bliss,

Many thanks for your note, which I received here this morning. I shall be delighted to come and have a talk with you. I am coming up to town tomorrow, and will ring up so that we can fix a time for meeting in the course of the next three or four days.

May I take this opportunity of saying how much I enjoyed and admired your new String Quartet which I heard broadcast recently? It was a real pleasure to hear from an English composer a work so direct, so optimistic and full of vitality, and, if I may venture to say so, in such a personal and characteristic idiom. It is to be hoped that the Music Department will give us the opportunity of hearing this work again soon, though their policy in recent years has been to give a new work a long rest, instead of following up the first performance with a second, to clinch the impression made. In these days of de-centralisation, ... when so many of us are living out of London, and therefore unable to hear concert performances, one is particularly dependent on the B.B.C. in getting to know new works, don't you agree?

I look forward to the pleasure of meeting you again.

Yours very sincerely,

John Ireland

Ireland was clearly pleased at what he took to be recognition from the BBC's new Director of Music, as we may see from a letter written to Lee Gardner dated 31 August.

I have been asked by the B.B.C. to undertake a rather responsible job – to sit on a Music Advisory panel, involving a good deal of work – but I am in a quandary because the remuneration offered is so ludicrously small that I calculate my <u>net</u> profit would be about £18 a year – if that. I shall have to see the Music Director, who suggested it, but he has nothing to do with the money side. I have also undertaken to play the piano part of my 2nd violin sonata[24] at a Boosey & Hawkes Concert on Sept 23. – wh. is rather rash, perhaps, as the strain might cause me to drop dead on the platform!

In characteristic fashion Ireland took up the issue of remuneration with Bliss, writing on 7 September. We do not need to follow the whole of the negotiation but it is useful to see Ireland's argument in putting his case. Unknown to him Bliss would, in fact, have been sympathetic to his position as he had undertaken a similar negotiation when he had been offered his BBC post.[25]

I felt honoured and delighted when, a few weeks ago, you asked me to act as Chairman of an Advisory Panel to examine modern scores and report on

---

[24] With the violinist Eda Kersey.

[25] For Bliss's relations with the BBC see my article 'In Search of a Progressive Music Policy: Arthur Bliss at the BBC', in *Arthur Bliss: Music and Literature*, ed. Stewart R. Craggs (Aldershot: Ashgate, 2002), pp. 227–65.

them to you. Naturally it was a pleasure to accept the work, if it meant this would be of some little help to you personally and of use to the Corporation.

Recently I have received a letter dealing with the business side (herewith enclosed) which I must ask you to read, and on which I venture to submit a few comments for your consideration.

Supposing there are twelve sessions of the Panel in the course of the year, the proposed remuneration would amount to about £87 in all. Calculated on the most modest scale, my actual expenses incurred in attending the meetings (travelling and subsistence) would amount to at least £25. Income-tax in round figures would account for another £44, making £69 to deduct from the gross amount, thus leaving me actually £18 in pocket for the work, which would involve:

(1) An unspecified amount of time spent in listening-in to programmes and writing reports on these.
(2) Advising the Corporation generally on musical matters.
(3) Attending the Panel sessions to read and report on MS scores.
(4) "casual" score reading not included in (3).

Taking all the above into consideration, I feel sure you will agree that Mr. Streeton's proposition is not an economic one, and that it shows little if any sense of values in relation to the responsible and highly specialised qualifications involved – <u>unless</u> the position is to be regarded as a purely honorary one, in which case that should have been made clear, and the financial consideration definitely scheduled as representing expenses only, which, as such would not be liable to taxation.

I have heard (though of course I may have been misinformed) that the members of the previous Advisory Panel, who I believe did not have to report on programmes broadcast, were paid at the rate of £250 per annum, which would seem a more reasonable valuation of the work; but in any case I cannot reply to Mr. Streeton until I have some ruling from yourself, when you have been able to look into the matter.

With best wishes, and hoping to see you again soon,

Yours always,
John Ireland

Fortunately Ireland was keen to dispel any misapprehensions about his role on the score reading panel, and writing[26] to Kilham Roberts of the Society of Authors, he left this useful first-hand account of how he viewed it:

This Panel meets about once a month, and our work is to look at and report upon MS scores sent in to the B.B.C. with a view to broadcasting.

99 per cent of these MS works are by quite unknown composers. Beyond sending in reports on these works, which are, in some cases, recommendations, we have nothing whatever to do with the building of the B.B.C. programmes. It does not follow that works recommended by us are included

---

[26] 8 November (1944?)

in the programmes, nor, conversely, does it follow that works we turn down are excluded.

I therefore resent the suggestion that the B.B.C. programme department is "guided in its choice" by the Music Advisory Panel. It certainly is not "guided". But, in any case, the Panel has nothing to say as regards the programme policy, nor is it ever consulted about programmes.

As panel chairman Ireland was constantly assessing music written by his musical contemporaries in London and the BBC. One score he saw twice was by Hubert Clifford, an Australian who was then the BBC's Empire Director of Music. Ireland clearly approved, a positive assessment not to be reinforced for the wider public until the score was recorded for Chandos[27] by the BBC Philharmonic conducted by Vernon Handley in 1999:

HUBERT CLIFFORD: Symphony
Well-written and effective – should be welcomed by listeners overseas and at home.
    J. Ireland 13/1/44

It is curious that at that date the BBC had already recorded two movements of the work for dissemination overseas as a BBC 'Special Music recording'. This was presumably because Clifford was Australian, but Ireland and his fellow panel members seem to have made no effort to have the discs played at their assessment sessions.

Without having heard the recording[28] of this work, it is easy to discover it is the most competent of its size & scope which has been before the panel. The vitality & interest are well sustained for the 40 minutes it occupies in performance. It is not the first British Symphony to show the influence of Sibelius, but it has a personality of its own, of a fine, open-air quality. I certainly recommend it for broadcasting – and public performance.
    J. Ireland 16/3/44

A colleague and fellow-countryman of Hubert Clifford was John Gough, also a BBC official during the war, in this case as Pacific Director of Music. (Both Gough and Clifford can be seen standing beside Sir Henry Wood in the ruins of Queen's Hall, in a famous photograph.)

JOHN GOUGH: Love Song for Strings in form of a Rondo
An unusual sort of work, formally. Quite effective & well-written for the medium.
    J. Ireland 14/10/43

An ongoing issue for panel members was the assessment of music by their colleagues on the panel and in the wider music profession. It is interesting to see

[27] Chandos CHAN 9757.

[28] The Symphony 1940 had been partially recorded by the BBC for overseas distribution as a 'Special Music recording' – the first movement by the BBC SO/ Clarence Raybould (16/1/43 AOBR 5362–3) and the fourth movement conducted by Boult (AOBR 4872–3 18/10/42).

how impartial Ireland was able to be when assessing music submitted by such friends and contemporaries, for example, in his treatment of scores by Alan Bush and William Busch.

ALAN BUSH: Violin Concerto
This work is highly competent, & has <u>style</u> & <u>personality</u>. I strongly recommend that it should be broadcast at an early date. It could not fail to make an impression. It is concise, emphatic & written with directness.
    John Ireland 14/10/43

ALAN BUSH: Freedom on the March for solo voice, chorus, piano and percussion[29]
I am afraid this is unsuitable for broadcasting – musically & politically – though undoubtedly sincere.
    John Ireland 14/10/43

WILLIAM BUSCH: Violoncello Concerto
The intentions of the composer are serious, but he has only succeeded in producing a dull work unrelieved by colour or any striking musical features. While competently written within its limitations, one can hardly feel there is enough invention or feeling there to justify taking up programme time with a work which though sincere, is lacking in distinction.
    John Ireland 18/3/43

The case of the concerto by William Busch, an Ireland student from the Royal College of Music, is a fascinating one, in that Ireland and his colleagues were reading manuscript scores. Quite why it was before the panel, when it had already been performed by Florence Hooton at a 1941 Prom, must have been because it had only been heard at one of the non-BBC Promenade Concert seasons.[30] Ireland was not impressed, but we are in the fortunate position of being able to second-guess his assessment from a commercial recording. In Busch's case this is the Lyrita recording played by Raphael Wallfisch and the RPO conducted by Vernon Handley.[31] The *Gramophone*'s reviewer, who declared he was new to William Busch, wrote of the reissue: 'The Cello Concerto ... proves a beautifully wrought, enviably terse yet warm-hearted score, its modal lyricism and appealingly ruminative manner strikingly prescient of Finzi's gorgeous Cello Concerto (lovers of the latter should most certainly lend an ear).'[32]

The problem of having to assess a piece by a colleague who was actually on the panel occasionally had to be addressed. Lennox Berkeley was a case in point when his Sonatina for Violin and Piano came before them:

I have nothing to add to the above assessments [Walton and Jacob had turned it down], and I agree that one is placed in rather an invidious

---

[29] The other members of the panel were Walton and Gordon Jacob. Walton wrote: 'Freedom, not to mention the workers, deserves something better than this.'
[30] The BBC did not run the Promenade Concerts in 1940 and 1941.
[31] Lyrita SRCD 320.
[32] *Gramophone*, February 2008, p. 61.

position if one has to assess works by members of BBC programme builders. <u>Without prejudice</u>.

John Ireland 30/9/43

Curiously in this case Berkeley's Sonatina became an accepted work and was later recorded for Decca by Grinke and the composer.

However, Ireland clearly took his task seriously and was not above changing his assessment if circumstances demanded it, as we can see from a letter dated 30 November 1942 written about a work submitted by a recent student at the Royal College of Music now in the army:

> In regard to MSS by NORMAN DEMUTH. If you still have any of these wh: have been before the Panel, I think we ought to reconsider them before they are returned to the composer, in view of the very successful performance of his "two War Poems" for pfte & orchestra last Sunday.[33]

When he came to the music of Eric Fogg, whom Ireland had known as a fellow Mancunian and the BBC's Empire Director of Music who earlier had commissioned him to broadcast to overseas listeners, he was dealing with a musician who had tragically died in 1939 when he fell under a tube train at Waterloo:

> ERIC FOGG: The Seasons for chorus and orchestra
> As this evidently had a good start (Leeds Festival, 1931) one wonders what has become of it since then, if it is so good as the previous reports indicate.[34]
>
> It is effective enough, though inadequate as a setting of Blake's early but remarkable poems. It might be performed as a gesture to the memory of Eric Fogg, if the B.B.C. wishes to make one.
>
> J.I. 29/4/44

At this date a continuous sprinkling of works of a previous generation, often works that had been performed in their day and were then well received, came before the panel and were often rejected, usually on the grounds of outmoded style, without recognition of their earlier history. Two of these that came to Ireland for adjudication were by Learmont Drysdale, who had died in 1909, and Samuel Alman, who was still alive at the date of the assessment but died in 1947 at the age

---

[33] In fact the Demuth file shows the BBC had already written on 29 November: 'whilst we are unable to include this work in a programme we should like to offer a place in a rehearsal for it'. The BBC then ran rehearsals to assess new works for possible broadcasting. The two movements by Demuth were: 'Lament for a Great City' and 'Mêlée Infernale'.

[34] *The Seasons* had the misfortune to be premiered in the same programme as the first performance of Walton's *Belshazzar's Feast*, and consequently was ignored. *The Seasons* was not performed after the panel's dismissal of the score and subsequently the orchestral full score was lost although the printed vocal score remained. It was not heard again until reorchestrated by the composer and later BBC producer David Ellis and sung, first with reduced orchestration by the Broadheath Singers and Windsor Sinfonia conducted by Garry Humphreys in a concert at Slough in September 2003 and subsequently revived by the BBC Philharmonic in a concert at Leeds Town Hall on 25 March 2006. It was revealed to be a delightful score, if, in the movement called 'Summer', a demanding sing.

of sixty-eight. Drysdale's overture *Herondean* dated from 1893, and for Ireland that was still too recent for him to be able to take an objective view:

LEARMONT DRYSDALE: Herondean – Concert overture for orchestra
Uninspired and dated. Little more than the musical platitudes current at the time it was written.
    John Ireland 20/5/43

Similarly in the case of an opera by the Jewish composer Samuel Alman that in its day had been widely sung:

SAMUEL ALMAN: [Opera] King Ahaz[35]
Far too rudimentary and immature for consideration, whatever claims the composer may make for its basis on Jewish material. One regrets having to dismiss in these terms a MS which represents so much labour on the composer's part.
    John Ireland 28/4/43

Ireland's assessments could be informed by his memory of names familiar to him from yesteryear, and he is notable for his sense of fairness in assessing works submitted by complete unknowns. Two examples will illustrate his approach. First, a setting for chorus and orchestra of A. E. Housman's poem 'Hell Gate' by P. M. Temple Bevan. His co-assessors had both found it 'amateurish and immature'. Ireland wrote:

Temple Bevan became a Captain during the last war and is now in the War Office. He is a son of the late Archdeacon of Middlesex. Though always fond of music and ambitious to compose, it is to be feared that he has attempted something quite beyond his capabilities – which in directions other than music, are by no means negligible. I would add that he has never studied with me or shown me any of his work.
    J. Ireland 16/3/44

Secondly, two short orchestral *Poems* by Allan Hawthorne Baker – 1. Aubade, 2. Nocturne. Ireland wrote:

---

[35] In their assessments none of the panel appear to have had any recognition of who the Russian-born Samuel Alman was – a pioneering British Jewish composer and conductor of synagogue music. It is difficult to believe that Ireland, in particular, had no memory of the favourable press coverage that *King Ahaz*, the first Yiddish grand opera, had received when it was premiered at the People's Palace in the Mile End Road in 1912, and subsequently performed at the 'Temple of the Arts' in the Commercial Road and on tour. In his assessment of the opera Gordon Jacob, probably too young to recall this history, wrote – 'This purports to be genuine Jewish music, and perhaps the melodic line may be so, (as regards its insistence on augmented 2nd etc.) but the harmonisation can only be described as puerile, destroying by its commonplace character any distinction there might have been in the melodies. It would be doing no service to the composer to broadcast such a manifestly immature work.' Extracts from the opera, with piano accompaniment, were once available on a pre-recorded cassette on Bnai Brith Records BB 001.

Some poetry and musical feeling – quite a sense of orchestral colour. Contemplative, and English in feeling. I think the two pieces should be considered either separately or together. There is still room for such music. There is a genuine impulse behind it, if not a very deep one. Properly placed, these could well be heard in Home Programmes.

John Ireland

2/9/43

Ireland was also not above a little musical politicking, especially when it concerned his pupil Benjamin Britten, whose brilliance he acknowledged but whose success in securing performances and adulation he clearly found irritating.[36] As an example we might note his minute to Arthur Bliss, then still Director of Music, dated 7 October 1943:

In my capacity as Chairman of the Music Advisory Panel I wish to protest against the re-broadcasting of Britten's string quartet at a date quite near its first broadcast, when a far finer and more important work, the Goossens Quartet, first broadcast last February, has not yet received its second performance.

It is eminently desirable that important new works by British composers should be broadcast a second (and even a <u>third</u>) time within a month or two of their first appearance so that listeners can get to know something about them before they are put on the shelf and forgotten, but this principle should be applied impartially, and not only in the case of one or two specially boosted composers, as is the case at present, especially in the section embracing chamber music, piano music and songs. I think you should look into this, if I may say so, as things of this sort do not pass unnoticed by listeners.

G RADUALLY Ireland appeared in public less frequently. In retrospect we might judge that this period of his life reached a climax when he accompanied Peter Pears in programmes of his songs. The first of these was a studio performance in 1947, the second in 1951 at the Wigmore Hall.[37] Fortunately these programmes were recorded, not only by the BBC, but also by a studio instructed by Ireland himself, and so we can still hear Ireland's playing as reissued on an historical CD from the Dutton label.[38]

Poignantly, the very last document on the John Ireland contract file for 1957–1962 is the bill for a wreath for the funeral of the 'late Dr John Ireland'.

[36] For Britten and Ireland see also pp. 337–43.

[37] *Ibid.*

[38] Dutton CDBP 9799. John Ireland (piano): *Amberley Wild Brooks*; *The Undertone*; *Ragamuffin*; *Soho Forenoons*; *Songs Sacred and Profane*: Peter Pears (tenor); Sonata in G minor for Cello & Piano: Antoni Sala (cello); *The Land of Lost Content*: Peter Pears (tenor); Fantasy Sonata for Clarinet & Piano Frederick Thurston (clarinet); *Hawthorn Time* ("'Tis time I think by Wenlock Town'); *I have Twelve Oxen*; *The Trellis*: Peter Pears (tenor).

This documented a BBC expenditure of £4/4/0 for the wreath and 4/– for its delivery to the funeral, which took place at 12:00 noon on Saturday 16 June 1962 at the Church of St Mary the Virgin at Shipley, Sussex.

TABLE 3 John Ireland: surviving BBC contracts

22/2/32	'Programme as arranged'
17/5/32	Concerto and short orchestral work [not 'Forgotten Rite'], of the 'Mai Dun' type, Ulster Hall, Belfast
20/6/32	Recital with May Harrison, including Sonata no. 1 in D minor for Violin & Pianoforte
12/12/32	Sonata recital with Douglas Cameron
30/3/33	To accompany Ireland songs: The Advent (Alice Meynell), Hymn for a Child (Sylvia Townsend Warner), My Fair (Meynell), The Salley Gardens (Yeats), The Soldier's Return (Townsend Warner), The Scapegoat (Townsend Warner) NB *This concert was cancelled as singer John Armstrong ill* [see 29/5/33]
29/5/33	Rearranged performance of Ireland songs (rearranged again 30/5/33)
12/8/34	Manchester. Programme of own works incl. a Trio, piano solos and songs
26/8/34	Chamber music: *April*, 'Ragamuffin', short songs – *Sea Fever, Bells of St Marie, Vagabond Love* [sic], *Trio No 2, Hawthorn Time, Land of Lost Content, Heart's Desire*
7/12/34	Cello Sonata
16/12/34	*Legend*
21/4/35	Special Chamber Music concert and to accompany Songs [NB Ireland ill and Alan Bush was asked to stand by in case he could not play – the outcome not noted]
19/8/35	*Mai-Dun* – [no actual contract on file, just memo 'Please … arrange']
28/9/35	*Legend* [no contract]
20/2/36	To accompany a 22 minute group of Ireland songs on an Empire broadcast to Shanghai and the Far East
2/4/36	Programme of own works with Parry Jones: *Hawthorn Time, Land of Lost Content, Amberley Wild Brooks, Month's Mind, Merry Andrew, If There Were Dreams to Sell, Weather, The Trellis, My True Love Hath My Heart, Santa Chiara, The Heart's Desire, Great Things*
11/9/36	Sonata recital with May Harrison to play own and Moeran [violin] sonatas, *April, The Holy Boy, Ragamuffin*
26/1/37	Violin and Piano Sonata and Trio, *Land of Lost Content*, Sonata no. 1 in D minor; Songs: *If There Were Dreams to Sell, Weather, The Trellis, Remember, Santa Chiara, The Heart's Desire*, Trio no. 2 in one movement
9/5/37	Sonata for Cello and Piano
27/8/37	*The Forgotten Rite* and *Mai-Dun*
22/10/37	Sonata for Cello and Piano
2/12/37	*Legend* for Piano and Orchestra

TABLE 3 *continued*

5/2/38	First performance of 3 new piano pieces: *The Cherry Tree, Cypress, The Palm and May*; Songs: 'Ladslove', 'Hawthorn Time', 'The Heart's Desire', *Remember, Weather, The Sacred Flame*. As programme is 2 or 3 minutes short, could add 'The Island Spell'.
4/4/38	Trio no. 3 in E
6/3/39	Recital: From 4 Preludes: 'The Undertone', 'Obsession', 'Fire of Spring', *Green Ways, Three Lyric Pieces*: 'The Cherry Tree', 'Cypress', 'Palm and May'
2 & 3/6/40 2/6	Sonata recital, Cello and Piano Sonata. [Ireland cancelled due to travel disruption but BBC found 2 other pianists – 3/6: 'The Cherry Tree', 'Palm and May', Sonatina for Piano, *Three London Pieces, Soliloquy, Equinox* (Howard-Jones)
3/11/40	Songs: *Hawthorn Time, Weather, Land of Lost Content, I Have Twelve Oxen*
5/1/41	Piano and Cello Sonata
11/5/41	Interview with Albert Sammons, partly on 2nd Violin Sonata
18/8/41	Accompanies Wm. Parsons and plays one group of solos. 5 songs: *April, Ragamuffin, Oh, Happy Land, Bells of San Marie, Great Things, I Have Twelve Oxen*
25/9/41	Songs: *Oh, Happy Land, Great Things, Sea Fever, When Lights Go Rolling Round the Sky, Ragamuffin,*
6 & 7/10/41	*Hope the Horn Blower, Oh, Happy Land, Great Things*
17 & 18/11/41	Cello Sonata
9/2/42	[Violin] Sonata no. 1 in D minor
20 & 21/2/42	*Boyhood Scene, Three Pastels*
8/3/42	*Three Pastels*
4 & 5/5/42	'Composer at the Piano' with Arthur Catterall. Sonata no. 1 for Piano and Violin
3 & 4/10/42	Sonatina for Piano
14/12/42	Cello sonata (extra, if required: 'The Holy Boy')
1/10/43	British Piano Music: Sonatina
18 & 19/4/43	Recital of Ireland works
13/9/43	Sonata recital with Lionel Tertis including Cello Sonata arranged for Viola [This may have been cancelled. There are three contract forms on file of which one says 'Cancelled']
20 & 21/10/43	Recital of own work
6/2/44	Phantasy sonata (*sic*)
28/4/44	Phantasy sonata (*sic*)
3 & 4/5/44	Recital
21/11/44	Sonata recital – Cello Sonata
2/12/44	*Legend*

TABLE 3 *continued*

11/12/44	Cello Sonata, 'The Holy Boy'
25/1/45	Recital. 'Island Spell', 'Chelsea Reach', 'Ragamuffin', *Equinox*
11/4/45	'British Composers of Our Time'
9/12/45	*Sarnia*
24/4/46	Sonata no. 1 in D minor, 'Island Spell'
17 & 18/6/46	Own music
2/10/46	Sonata recital – A minor Violin Sonata [i.e. no. 2]
7/11/46	Clarinet Sonata, 'The Undertone', *February's Child*, *Aubade*
9 & 10/2/47	Clarinet Sonata
28/3/47	Cello Sonata, 'Holy Boy'
12 & 15/5/47	Recording session with Pini
22/10/47	Cello Sonata with F. Hooton
8/12/47	Songs with Peter Pears: *Love and Friendship* (Emily Bronte), *Hawthorn Time* (Housman), *I Have Twelve Oxen* (anon), *The Trellis* (Huxley), *Down by the Salley Gardens* (Yeats), *My True Love Hath my Heart* (Sidney) *Land of Lost Content*
8/1/48	Clarinet Fantasy Sonata
4/2/48	Sonata in D minor for Violin and Piano [No. 1] with Grinke
6/2/48	As item above
6/3/48	As above, pre-recording for 24/3/48
27/3/49	Music Magazine
10/9/49	70th birthday Prom: *A London Overture*, Prelude: *The Forgotten Rite*, Pianoforte Concerto, *These Things Shall Be*
14/5/51	*Land of Lost Content* with Peter Pears. Songs with William Parsons: *Songs Sacred and Profane*
27/12/54	'Personal Call' interview with Stephen Black
24/1/56	Eric Parkin: Piano Sonata, *The Undertone*
10/1/56	Violin Sonata no. 2
20/11/56	Harry Isaacs Trio: Trio no. 3
3/2/56	Eleanor Warren and Paul Hamburger Cello Sonata
7/2/56	F. Merrick Piano Sonatina and William Parsons Songs
21/2/56	Clarinet Sonata, Songs
2/3/56	Harry Isaacs Trio: Trios nos. 1 and 2 and *Five Poems of Thomas Hardy*
11/3/56	*The Trellis, My True Love Hath my Heart, Land of Lost Content*
13/3/56	Eric Parkin: *Sarnia, April, Bergomask, Summer Schemes, Rest, Salley Gardens, Soldier's Return, Bells of St Marie, Great Things*
6/6/57	Recorded interview for 'The Composer Speaks' with Joseph Cooper
22/7/58	Interview with Jonah Barrington in 'Town & Country' magazine
1/10/59	Interview with David Lloyd Jones for 'Music Club'
6/10/61	Interview with Robert Cradock for the 'Today' programme

14/12/45	'Music Magazine' talk
24/4/46	Violin Sonata no. 1 in D minor, 'Island Spell'
7/11/46	Clarinet Fantasy Sonata, *February's Child*, *Aubade*

PERFORMANCES WITHOUT CONTRACT NOTE

7/5/32	Piano Concerto, *Mai-Dun*
12/1/33	*Legend* for Piano and Orchestra
10/1/35	Prelude: *The Forgotten Rite*
Sept 1936	Overture for Brass Band
5/6/38	Grinke Trio: Trio in E (no. 3)

TABLE 4 The Music of John Ireland at the Proms

20 Aug. 1912	*Hope the Hornblower* (with piano)	Proms premiere
21 Aug. 1913	*Hope the Hornblower* (with piano)	
13 Sept. 1917	*The Forgotten Rite*	World premiere
3 Sept. 1919	*Sea Fever* (with piano)	
10 Oct. 1919	*When Lights Go Rolling Round the Sky* (with piano)	
23 Sept. 1920	*The Forgotten Rite*	
17 Oct. 1921	*When Lights Go Rolling Round the Sky* (with piano)	
27 Sept. 1922	*Mai-Dun*	Proms premiere
20 Aug. 1923	*When Lights Go Rolling Round the Sky* (with piano)	
8 Oct. 1924	*The Forgotten Rite*	
21 Aug. 1925	*When Lights Go Rolling Round the Sky* (with piano)	
14 Oct. 1925	*When Lights Go Rolling Round the Sky* (with piano)	
26 Aug. 1926	*When Lights Go Rolling Round the Sky* (with piano)	
9 Sept. 1926	*Mai-Dun*	
26 Aug. 1927	*Sea Fever* (with piano)	
28 August 1928	*The Soldier* (with piano)	
31 Aug. 1928	*When I am Dead My Dearest* (with piano)	
7 Sept. 1928	*The Cost* (with piano)	
19 Sept. 1928	*Sea Fever* (with piano)	

TABLE 4 *continued*

17 Aug. 1929	*Sea Fever* (with piano)	
5 Sept. 1929	*Mai-Dun*	
20 Sept. 1929	*Songs to Poems by Thomas Hardy* (with piano)	
9 Aug. 1930	*Sea Fever* (with piano)	
15 Aug. 1930	*Spring Sorrow* (with piano)	
21 Aug. 1930	*Mai-Dun*	
26 Aug. 1930	*Twilight Night* (8 named singers without piano)	
2 Oct. 1930	Piano Concerto in E♭	soloist Helen Perkin; World premiere
2 Oct. 1930	*Santa Chiara* (with piano)	
24 Sept. 1931	Piano Concerto in E♭	soloist Helen Perkin
8 Sept. 1932	*Mai-Dun*	
5 Sept. 1933	Piano Concerto in E♭	soloist Angus Morrison
28 Aug. 1934	*Legend* for Piano and Orchestra	soloist Harriet Cohen
26 Sept. 1934	*Mai-Dun*	conducted by Ireland
29 Sept. 1934	Piano Concerto in E♭	soloist Helen Perkin
7 January 1935	*The Soldier* (with piano)	Winter Proms
10 January 1935	*The Forgotten Rite*	conducted by Ireland; Winter Proms
19 Aug. 1935	*Mai-Dun*	conducted by Ireland
28 Sept. 1935	*Legend* for piano and orchestra	soloist Ireland
29 Aug. 1936	*A London Overture*	Did not take place, postponed to 23 Sept.
1 Sept. 1936	Piano Concerto in E♭	soloist Rubinstein
23 Sept. 1936	*A London Overture*	World premiere
7 Aug. 1937	*A London Overture*	
27 Aug. 1937	*The Forgotten Rite*	conducted by Ireland
27 Aug. 1937	*Mai-Dun*	conducted by Ireland
14 Sept. 1937	*Twilight Night* (8 voices)	
12 Aug. 1938	*Rhapsody* (solo piano)	Proms premiere
30 Aug. 1938	*The Forgotten Rite*	
1 Oct. 1938	Piano Concerto in E♭	soloist Clifford Curzon
18 Aug. 1939	*Concertino Pastorale*	London premiere
22 Aug. 1939	*The Bells of San Marie* (with piano)	
22 Aug. 1939	*When Lights Go Rolling Round the Sky* (with piano)	

TABLE 4 *continued*

16 Sept. 1939	Piano Concerto in E♭	soloist Clifford Curzon. Did not take place.
19 Sept. 1939	*These Things Shall be*	Did not take place.
7 Oct. 1939	*A London Overture*	Did not take place.
21 Aug. 1940	*The Bells of San Marie* (with piano)	
21 Aug. 1940	*When Lights Go Rolling Round the Sky* (with piano)	
24 Aug. 1940	*Sea Fever* (with piano)	
12 Sept. 1940	*A London Overture*	
27 June 1942	*Epic March*	World premiere
30 July 1942	Piano Concerto in E♭	soloist Clifford Curzon; first time Boult conducts Ireland at Prom
19 Aug. 1942	*The Forgotten Rite*	
24 June 1943	*Epic March*	
10 July 1943	Piano Concerto in E♭	soloist Clifford Curzon
24 July 1943	*A London Overture*	
31 July 1943	*These Things Shall Be*	
22 July 1944	*These Things Shall Be*	
5 Aug. 1944	Piano Concerto in E♭	soloist Moura Lympany
7 Aug. 1944	*A London Overture*	
21 July 1945	*The Forgotten Rite*	
6 Aug. 1945	*A London Overture*	
16 Aug. 1945	Piano Concerto in E♭	soloist Clifford Curzon
25 Aug. 1945	*These Things Shall Be*	
8 Sept. 1945	*Epic March*	
15 Aug. 1946	*These Things Shall Be*	
17 Aug. 1946	*Epic March*	
29 Aug. 1946	*Mai-Dun*	conducted by Constant Lambert
7 Sept. 1946	Piano Concerto in E♭	soloist Kendall Taylor
11 Sept. 1946	Overture *Satyricon*	conducted by Constant Lambert; world premiere
6 January 1946	Overture *Satyricon*	Winter Proms
29 July 1947	Piano Concerto in E♭	soloist Kendall Taylor
11 Aug. 1947	Overture *Satyricon*	
12 Sept. 1947	*These Things Shall Be*	

TABLE 4 *continued*

16 January 1948	*The Forgotten Rite*	
11 Aug. 1948	*A London Overture*	
10 Sept. 1948	*Legend* for piano and orchestra	soloist Kyla Greenbaum
14 Sept. 1948	*These Things Shall Be*	
18 Sept. 1948	Piano Concerto in E♭	soloist Eileen Joyce
22 Jan. 1949	*A London Overture*	Winter Proms
2 Aug. 1949	Overture *Satyricon*	
10 Sept. 1949	*A London Overture*	
10 Sept. 1949	*These Things Shall Be*	
10 Sept. 1949	*The Forgotten Rite*	
10 Sept. 1949	Piano Concerto in E♭	soloist Eileen Joyce
11 Jan. 1950	Piano Concerto in E♭	soloist Kendall Taylor; Winter Proms
21 Jan. 1950	*A London Overture*	Winter Proms
22 Aug. 1950	Piano Concerto in E♭	soloist Colin Horsley
25 Aug. 1950	*Concertino Pastorale*	
26 Aug. 1950	*A London Overture*	
11 Sept. 1950	*The Forgotten Rite*	
17 Jan. 1951	Overture *Satyricon*	Winter Proms
31 July 1951	Piano Concerto in E♭	soloist Kendall Taylor
25 Aug. 1951	Overture *Satyricon*	
17 Sept. 1951	*The Forgotten Rite*	
20 Sept. 1951	*These Things Shall Be*	
22 Sept. 1951	*A London Overture*	
31 July 1952	*Concertino Pastorale*	
2 Aug. 1952	Piano Concerto in E♭	soloist Colin Horsley
28 Aug. 1952	Overture *Satyricon*	
30 Aug. 1952	*These Things Shall Be*	
5 Sept. 1953	Piano Concerto in E♭	soloist Eric Parkin
24 July 1954	*A London Overture*	
13 Aug. 1954	*These Things Shall Be*	
13 Aug. 1954	Piano Concerto in E♭	soloist Eric Parkin
16 Sept. 1955	*These Things Shall Be*	
17 Sept. 1955	Piano Concerto in E♭	soloist Gina Bachauer
10 Aug. 1956	*The Forgotten Rite*	
10 Aug. 1956	*Mai-Dun*	

TABLE 4 *continued*

7 Sept. 1956	Overture *Satyricon*	
19 Aug. 1957	*Legend* for piano and orchestra	soloist Eric Parkin
6 Sept. 1957	*These Things Shall Be*	
22 Aug. 1958	Overture *Satyricon*	
20 Sept. 1958	Piano Concerto in E♭	soloist Colin Horsley
25 July 1959	*A London Overture*	
14 Aug. 1959	Piano Concerto in E♭	soloist Eric Parkin
14 Aug. 1959	Overture *Satyricon*	
14 Aug. 1959	*The Forgotten Rite*	
25 July 1960	*A London Overture*	
14 Aug. 1962	*A London Overture*	
13 Sept. 1975	*A Downland Suite* for Brass Band	Black Dyke Band
13 Aug. 1979	Piano Concerto in E♭	soloist Philip Fowke
15 Sept. 1979	Overture *Satyricon*	
14 Aug. 1982	Piano Concerto in E♭	soloist Kathryn Stott
7 Aug. 1984	*A London Overture*	
22 Aug. 1993	Piano Concerto in E♭	soloist Kathryn Stott
10 Aug. 1994	*A London Overture*	conducted by Vernon Handley
18 July 2005	*Sea Fever* (with piano)	
14 July 2007	*The Overlanders* – 'Scorched Earth' [march] only	
	JOHN IRELAND AS PERFORMER AT THE PROMS	
26 Sept. 1934	*Mai-Dun*	conducted by Ireland
10 January 1935	*The Forgotten Rite*	conducted by Ireland*
18 Aug. 1935	*Mai-Dun*	conducted by Ireland
28 Sept. 1935	*Legend* for piano and orchestra	soloist Ireland
27 Aug. 1937	*The Forgotten Rite*	conducted by Ireland
27 Aug. 1937	*Mai-Dun*	conducted by Ireland

* The BBC's Proms database shows this Winter Prom billed as conducted by Sir Henry Wood, but, as a review in *The Times* and a surviving acetate recording make clear, *The Forgotten Rite* was, in fact, conducted by Ireland himself.

Fig. 8 'Comarques' at Deal. Ireland occupied the top flat during the 1930s.
Photograph by Sally Hulke.

CHAPTER 8

Sea Fever: John Ireland and Deal

Julie Deller

Originally published in Bygone Kent, *October 1991, pp. 617–24. Reproduced here with acknowledgement.*

'IT IS a strange experience to see Deal again – and the sea.' So wrote John Ireland, the composer of *Sea Fever,* when he returned to the town at the end of the Second World War. There were 'hedges' of barbed-wire along the promenade and iron sea defences protruded from the pebbled beach. Deal was his favourite Kent coastal resort and he noted the war damage. The flat he had occupied in the 1930s had been damaged by enemy action, as had the offices of his solicitor and friend, Herbert Sydney Brown, but he still had old friends to visit.

The King's Head on Beach Street was still attracting interesting customers who discussed literature and music with the licensee, Miss Norah Miles. A woman of great character and a fine musician, Miss Miles was popular with everyone and a very dear friend to a chosen few. Her baby grand piano had, somehow, been installed in the bar and, indeed, the place would not have seemed right without it! On the evenings when Miss Miles played, the low beamed ceilings, darkly coloured with the tobacco smoke of years, glowed from the log fires of winter

Fig. 9 The King's Head,
Beach Street, Deal, 1949.
Drawing by Pat Moody.

and that little bar became as a concert-room. In recent years this establishment has undergone modernisation. In the time of Norah Miles it was a cramped cosy place with a special kind of magic. John Ireland enjoyed the whole atmosphere and was a frequent caller, introducing the delights of Deal to 'Willie' Walton.

In nearby Middle Street John Ireland had good friends living in one of the fascinating small cottages. Here Mrs Phyllis Thompson always welcomed his visits – whatever his mood, for he could be changeable – and her daughter treasures the many letters he sent on his return to his work, as Professor at the Royal College of Music in London. 'I think of you often', he wrote in 1944, when he had heard that she had thought of moving and asked, 'perhaps I could have first refusal of your cottage?'

John Ireland first saw Deal in 1906 when, as a young organist to St Jude's Church in Chelsea, he and the Curate were placed in charge of the choir's annual holiday. Not for them the one-day trip to the seaside, but a two-week stay at a local school which rented dormitory accommodation when closed for the summer. The London boys ran with joy into the sea and through the countryside and they followed in the footsteps of countless pilgrims on a visit to Canterbury Cathedral. Thirty-three years later, as an important twentieth-century composer, Ireland would attend a broadcast of his own music from the cathedral. Fate had much in store for the young man, born in 1879 to literary parents. His father was editor of the *Manchester Examiner and Times* and his mother was a writer.

In 1932 the University of Durham conferred upon Ireland the degree of Doctor of Music *honoris causa*. He was already a Bachelor of Music of that university in his own right. His name appears in the Street Directory for Deal of 1938 as 'Dr. John Ireland'. This was what he was pleased to called his 'Out-of-Town Pied-à-terre'. He travelled to London each week to carry out his duties at the RCM, and toured for the Royal Schools of Music as an Examiner and at all times he was pleased to feel the freshness of sea air as the train left Ashford. Deal and his peaceful retreat were not far away!

Friends joked that John Ireland's topographical affections were akin to love affairs with places, but they were quick to acknowledge his gift of deep feeling which almost amounted to clairvoyance. On entering a house he would know at once if it was a happy place, or otherwise. His Deal home was very much in harmony with his feelings at a time when he needed to relax, meditate and write more music.

The fine Georgian house named 'Comarques' provided Ireland with a spacious top flat, originally the nursery. This property has been owned and occupied by the Hulke family for over two centuries. Local history records the name of Hulke as Mayors of Deal, bankers, land owners, physicians and surgeons since the reign of Queen Anne. Almost directly opposite stands another house, originally in the ownership of the Hulke family and a passageway, far below street level, once connected the two properties. (There is a bricked-up entrance in the cellars of both). Such a passageway could be used at night, to avoid the Press gangs which frequented Deal in the eighteenth century and the ladies would find it conveniently cleaner to their dainty footwear and long dresses, than walking across the muddy street above.

Number 127 – across the street – housed the offices of the well-known Deal solicitor, Herbert Sydney Brown. Known to his friends as HSB, he was a man of rare musical ability and artistic appreciation. (He it was who made the anonymous gift to the Deal Borough Council of a Turner watercolour, depicting the beach in a rough sea, luggers and hovellers.) HSB was Ireland's contemporary and had long admired the composer's work, discussing details of the music on equal terms. During the late 1930s Ireland's piano music formed an impressive body of work, together with almost a hundred songs. He was established as a leading English composer who combined advanced musical ideas whilst keeping faith with the traditional. Obviously Ireland was someone about whom music lovers wished to know more. His biography needed to be written and HSB was asked, by Ireland, to accept the task and a very difficult task it proved to be.

At this time Mr and Mrs Brown, with their young family, lived in Shepherd-swell, near Dover, where they entertained Ireland, talked of music and worked on an early (1913) piano Prelude which, with words by Brown, became a carol for the Nativity and entitled 'The Holy Boy'. This was dedicated to Trevor Harvey and the BBC Singers. Ireland had other compositions for which he needed titles and Brown, being attuned to his lyrical style, suggested words to suit both music and musician. In return Ireland dedicated the 'Cherry Tree', from his piano suite *Green Ways*, to H. S. Brown and in this period of happy collaboration work began on the biography.

Night after night Ireland talked. Although a shy man, in congenial company he would become especially alert and exhibited a wry sense of humour, but in attempting to recount his memoirs Brown found him unable to provide any substantial information. His early honours at the Royal College were only lightly touched upon, as were his successful pupils (Benjamin Britten was one) and his memory for dates tended to be most uncertain. Reluctant to speak of his early childhood, or his marriage, of which even close friends had been unaware (by this time it had been annulled) Ireland would suddenly change the subject. At best his story was disjointed and at worst he would entirely stray from the point. Brown was not a man to 'suffer' anyone this difficult 'gladly' and he agreed to abandon the project.[1] He had admired Ireland's music, but, sadly, the man was – to quote Mrs Brown – 'rather trying'. It was disappointing, but the Browns continued to extend hospitality to Ireland and Mrs Brown helped with curtains for the High Street flat. She said that his taste was impeccable. The flat was furnished with the greatest care, the centrepiece being the baby grand piano which had been presented to him by Chappell. It was rumoured that the understanding was that Ireland would promote sales for the firm; something that John Ireland was not at pains to do!

From the main body of the old house the wife of Dr Hulke would hear Ireland play the occasional chord and expressed surprise that he could sit in his study for hours and compose music with so little use of the piano.

[1] John Longmire is one contemporary of the composer whose memoir – *John Ireland: Portrait of a Friend* – was actually completed. Muriel Searle's biography *John Ireland – The Man and his Music*, was written with Mrs Kirby's assistance and published in her lifetime.

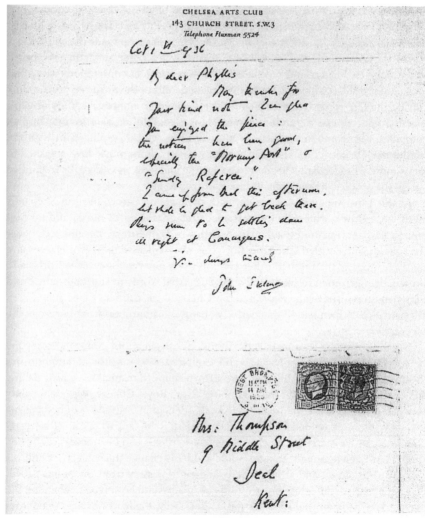

Fig. 10 Letter of 1 October 1936 to Mrs Phyllis Thompson of 9 Middle Street, Deal

CHELSEA ARTS CLUB
143 CHURCH STREET S.W.3
Telephone Flaxman 5524

Oct. 1ˢᵗ 1936

My dear Phyllis

Many thanks for your kind note. I am glad you enjoyed the piece. [He had obtained seats for her to hear his music played at a Promenade Concert.] The notices have been good, especially the "Morning Post" & "Sunday Referee."

I came up from Deal this afternoon, but shall be glad to get back there. Things seem to be settling down all right at Comarques.

Yrs always, sincerely,
John Ireland

Whilst he was at 'Comarques' John Ireland's Concerto for Pianoforte and Orchestra was again given at the Henry Wood Promenade Concerts in Queen's Hall. It had first been performed there in 1930. This concert, on 1st September 1936, was conducted by Sir Henry J. Wood, with Artur Rubinstein as the soloist. Mrs Gladys Hulke was, of course, a guest of honour and kept the programme as a memento. The programme notes mention Ireland's having 'won the highest honours' in the more secluded field of chamber music and continues, at some length, in describing the piano concerto themes as 'lyrical' and 'joyous', 'merry, mischievous' and the last movement 'brilliant'.

In May 1937 the BBC broadcast Ireland's Coronation work, a setting of the poem by J. A. Symonds, 'These Things Shall Be'. This work was requested late in 1936 and Ireland worked under pressure to complete this – a passionate expression of his own hopes and fears for mankind and for peace – to be included in the concert of celebration at the Coronation of King George VI. He wrote the work at 'Comarques' although he was still engaged in teaching in London. 'These Things Shall Be' never quite left his mind and he was with the composer Alan Bush (to whom he dedicated the work) awaiting the train to Deal, from Charing Cross, when a melody came to mind. Alan Bush wrote the notes on the back of an envelope as the two musicians sat in Charing Cross Buffet. This hurried scribble was, in fact, the first four bars of the *Internationale*, composed by a French musician *c.* 1895. It was later to become the National Anthem of the Soviet Union, as it was at the time of the Coronation in 1937.

Symonds' poem is perhaps even more moving now with the verse:

> These things shall be! A loftier race
> Than e'er the world hath known, shall rise.
> With flame of freedom in their souls
> And light of science in their eyes ...
> ... Nation with nation, land with land
> Unarmed[2] shall live as comrades free;
> In every brain and heart shall throb
> The pulse of one fraternity ...

Ireland's Deal flat was close to the Congregational church and the sounds of the organ would have pleased him. It was his first love and he had become an organist and FRCO at the early age of eighteen. Whenever he fell into a low humour he would become nostalgic about his time as an organist (twenty-two years at St Luke's, the Parish Church of Chelsea) saying that he regretted 'pretending to compose', even when, in 1925, *Sea Fever* had been voted by listeners to be the most popular song heard on the wireless (as we called the radio in those days).

In June 1939 Boyd Neel was to be at the Canterbury Festival for Choral and Orchestral Music and Ireland, a long-time admirer of Neel, promised him a new work. So it was that his last pre-war music was composed at Deal and dedicated to Boyd Neel. It was *Concertino Pastorale*, a work almost nineteenth century in style. The late Sir Adrian Boult was always deeply moved by the beauty of its slow movement and it has become one of Ireland's best-remembered compositions, although

---

[2] Actually *Inarmed*, meaning arm-in-arm.

the song *Sea Fever*, set to the poem by John Masefield, may be more familiar to the people of our island race.

The first performance of *Concertino Pastorale* was given and broadcast from the Cloisters of Canterbury Cathedral on 14 June 1939. John Ireland was present, but as the weather was less than kind he sat wrapped in a travelling rug, saying that people would hear the sheet music flapping in the wind. (They did!) In those anxious times the work aroused a great emotional response from all who heard it and after the premiere many letters were received expressing the gratitude felt for the priceless beauty of the music.

Although it has been said that Ireland wrote music for musicians, it also reached a wider audience with his film score for *The Overlanders*, which captured the atmosphere of Australia so successfully.

John Ireland is considered to be one of the six foremost British composers of the twentieth century. He died in 1962 having willed most of his estate to his house-keeper and secretary, Mrs Norah Kirby who, like Ireland, lived into her eighties. Both shared a liking for Kentish seaside resorts. Mrs Kirby died at Westgate in November 1982, in an old folks' home known as 'The Cabin'. She had devoted the latter years of her life to the charitable trust which preserved John Ireland's home at Steyning as a memorial to the composer. His was not the 'vagrant gypsy life' of which baritones sing in *Sea Fever*, but one in which he sought and finally found an ordered peace, due mainly to the protective care of Mrs Kirby. Who would doubt the truth of Masefield's poem with:

> And all I ask is a merry yarn from a laughing fellow rover,
> And quiet sleep and a sweet dream when the long trick's over.

CHAPTER 9

Remembering John Ireland and his World

Freda Swain

I QUITE expect that you will differ from various things I[1] have said. My only excuse is that I speak from the dual point of view of composer *and* pianist. I have performed many of the people (in all classes) both here and abroad and have always promoted the cause of British piano music, so perhaps you will bear with what I have said. If there was *some* way in which invidious classifications of 'greater' and 'lesser' composers could be avoided it might perhaps be good?

Not only did we[2] know John Ireland well but I have promoted, taught and performed his piano music for very many years and have a very great regard for the songs, many of the best of which are seldom heard. I played his Piano Concerto under his baton in Birmingham and also played the very taxing Piano Sonata at a Wigmore Hall recital – the *Rhapsody* also, a fine work. So I claim to have an all-round knowledge of the composer and his work. In fact I have promoted and performed British composers for more years than I care to remember, both here and abroad.[3]

When we went to see John Ireland at Rock Mill he was very guarded and although we were alone part of the time we noticed that when he began to enquire if we had news of Helen Perkin he dropped the subject at once when his house-keeper came in! A pity, as he never really recovered from losing her, in spite of having made in anger an irrevocable break.

Strangely enough, although the 'sense' of Sussex – the Downs and Chanctonbury Ring – was all around and familiar to me – the site of the new house, and the house itself, gave me nothing. No. 14 Gunter Grove, Chelsea, where he had a house and a big outside studio, was far more 'in' (no not in beer although that did play a large part in his life!), but in an atmosphere and influences of all kinds. Not *always* good, but always potent, a curious and complex person. I always felt a profound pity for him as an unhappy, discontented, ungrateful, capricious, both weak and aggressive, emotionally unstable being. Capable of true affection for a few, generosity and protectiveness and possessiveness would spill over them, but for the rest of mankind (and especially womankind) he had no time, as they say, other than as they could be useful to him. This sounds a terrible indictment, but

---

[1] Freda Swain (1902–85), composer and pianist, and one of the last surviving pupils of Sir Charles Villiers Stanford at the RCM. This text is extracted from letters written by Freda Swain to Colin Scott-Sutherland between April 1980 and October 1981, copies of the letters in the John Ireland Trust archive.

[2] When Freda Swain refers to 'we' she is including her husband the pianist and teacher Arthur Alexander.

[3] For many years Freda Swain ran the NEMO concerts. They promoted then modern British music in programmes which also included Swain's own music, the latter rarely being heard elsewhere.

one always has to remember that we all bring our particular stage of evolution with us – *including* gifts we have acquired with much labour and *specialisation* (to the detriment of other qualities).

However, in spite of the evidence – ([directed] towards us and to many people and colleagues) – of many of these negative destructive qualities I have mentioned, we managed to retain some friendly feeling towards him and helped to 'push the boat out' by playing, teaching and promoting his music whenever possible, over a very long period of years. This music was the best part of him: his love of Nature unquestionable – also his appreciation of poetry and literature. He was always courteous (except in drink) and had much charm – all of which hid what he was really feeling and thinking about those he had to deal with. I think he took 'hero-worship' for granted and had little understanding of the genuine feeling others had for his music. So often we have heard him say nice and appreciative things to people, and immediately they were out of hearing, snarl out the opposite! Truly a tormented soul, probably had some devil in him!

The only two books on John Ireland so far[4] are very inadequate, and so far as Norah Kirby's financial backing of the young journalist[5] who wrote the last of these carefully dictated by N.K. and with only biographical stuff and glossed-over personal details – I think it poor. I got a good laugh over some of it – all so 'prettied' up. But I am never in favour of publicly 'debunking' a person no longer in this world when so much of artistic merit has been contributed by that person. Therefore in John Ireland's case, perhaps it would be best to confine oneself to his music and what it means to one. After all, that is what matters and if one cannot honestly praise a person's character, it is best to say nothing!

Helen Perkin: that affair, if it can be called such, went very deep with J.I. and apart from possessiveness, brought out what of better nature he had. Hence, some music, notably the Concerto (not a lot else, I believe) was inspired by that period. But perhaps the tenderest and most loving inspiration was in the music he wrote *earlier* than the H.P. episode – and connected with quite another person.

But his music conveyed all the things I love, and most [particularly] nature and the countryside. My favourite piano works were *Amberley Wild Brooks*, the *Rhapsody* and the Sonata, to which I would add *April*, which touches me very nearly still. Of course, never having confined myself to the love and appreciation of piano music only, the songs particularly have meant a lot to me – chamber and orchestral works next.

J.I. was inspired mostly by Sussex and to some extent the Channel Islands. Sussex is not a soft gentle country, although it has its softer side. Some of it is extremely sturdy and steeped in early, occult and even bloody history. I agree that most of one's reactions must be largely subjective but the fact that others do not always hear or feel the things in music that you do must mostly depend on their varying stages of spiritual, musical and cultural evolution. Some may even hear or

---

[4] Freda Swain is writing in March 1981.

[5] Muriel Searle, *John Ireland – The Man and his Music* (Tunbridge Wells: Midas Books, 1979). Muriel Searle worked for HMSO at the time the editor was also there, but he did not know of Searle's interest in John Ireland until her book appeared.

feel things that are beyond us. This does not often occur because speaking rather egotistically, the qualities of imagination and perception are not often advanced enough in so many.

Fig. 11 Freda Swain in the 1930s. The signature on this painting is illegible, though we are told it was by a woman artist. This portrait used to hang over Freda Swain's piano in her music room.

CHAPTER 10

Arthur Machen and John Ireland

Colin Scott-Sutherland

JOHN Ireland's first encounter with the writings of Arthur Machen was his discovery, on a station bookstall, of *The House of Souls* – strangely reminiscent of Machen's own discovery of De Quincey:

> ... and another event of like importance was my seeing De Quincey's *Confessions of an English Opium Eater* at Pontypool Road Station. *This* also I instantly bought and as instantly loved and still love very heartily. He (the critic) is quite aware since he is, ex hypothesi, an able critic, that De Quincey deliberately used our tongue as if it had been a mighty organ in a mightier cathedral, so that the very stones of the far-lifted vault and the hollow spaces of the tower re-echo and reverberate and thrill with tremendous fugal harmonies.

It has been noted in numerous places that John Ireland's discovery of Machen occurred at Charing Cross station in London. But in a letter dated 28 September 1957 to Aidan Reynolds, he makes quite clear that it was at Penrith station:

> I first came across Machen's work some time in 1906 when I saw the first edition of *The House of Souls* as a Mackie's library 'remainder' on a bookstall at Penrith station in Cumberland. Some fate led me to pounce on it, and I have been a worshipper of Machen ever since. I did not meet him personally till 1933, when I was in my fifty-fourth year. I could say a good deal about his work, its influence on myself and my own work and something on the Master as I met him. I expect you possess the first edition of *The Hill of Dreams*. In it there is printed a remarkable criticism of *The House of Souls* by Sir (then Mr) John Masefield[1] who seems to have perceived the astounding qualities of *A Fragment of Life* and *The White People* at which I never cease to marvel. Machen told me something about *The White People* which I think, is not known to anyone except myself.

How tantalising that this last sentence was never revealed by the composer.

It is generally assumed that the first signs of the influence of Machen in the music of John Ireland appeared in 1912–13 with the three piano pieces entitled *Decorations*, and with the orchestral tone-poem *The Forgotten Rite*. Ireland had discovered Machen in 1906. On reflection I feel that Machen is not so much an influence as an impact – a catalyst that brought to the surface that spirit of place which Ireland, perhaps even unconsciously, had felt from quite an early date. He had encountered the Channel Islands in 1900 when he visited Jersey with choristers from the church at Holy Trinity, Sloane Street, where he was assistant organist.

Though it is apparent that during the years 1906 to 1912 he concentrated on

---

[1] Masefield was never knighted.

songs and part songs — and the lovely motet *Greater Love hath No Man* — as if storing up and assimilating the impact made upon him by Machen, and reading all of his work that he could lay his hands on, he wrote also the first of his two violin sonatas — which contains a druidical passage in the Dorian mode (see Ex. 2 of Chapter 1, p. 8). I am reminded of the description of Machen's tales by Anthony Lejeune: 'they hinted at dark things, at half-remembered rituals and evil powers which might still be lingering among the foxgloves and hawthorn around some mossy stone ...'

In 1913 came the three piano pieces entitled *Decorations*, and here there is no question about the influence of Machen. The third piece, 'The Scarlet Ceremonies', is prefaced by a quotation from *The White People*. The specifically musical influences in his work are recognisably derived from the French of Ravel and Debussy – although, apart from 'The Island Spell' (the first piece of *Decorations*), it is a mistake to pigeonhole his work as impressionistic – that would be a superficial judgment.

The principal characteristics of his music stem from, first, a very personal use of harmony and, second, the recurrence of several readily identifiable fingerprints. The first I can only describe in lay terms as basically diatonic – taking its colour from the added notes and modal inflexions that he uses as tints in something of the same way as the English watercolourists. The second characteristic, that of recognisable fingerprints, is easier to demonstrate — although a much more detailed examination of character and meaning of each phrase than is possible here would be needed to discern their import. Suffice it to say that they are like the inflexions of a well-kept voice. To the listener they will very quickly become recognisable — the drop of a fifth at the end of a phrase: a descending pattern of four notes, sometimes fast sometimes slow, the melodies sometimes in the inner parts, in a curious way related to the characteristics of the keyboard. One of the most prevalent fingerprints is also, strangely enough, one of the earliest and principal evocations of the spirit aroused by the writings of Machen. I can think of several passages in *The Hill of Dreams* that might evoke just this sort of imagery (Ex. 1).

The tone poem *The Forgotten Rite*, his first published orchestral work, was written in 1913 though not performed until 1917. From a melodic point of view the opening fragment shown in Ex. 1 recurs in many places – in the Piano Sonata's last movement (conceived after a visit to

Fig. 12 Arthur Machen
in silhouette

Ex. 1 Ireland, *The Forgotten Rite*, opening fragment

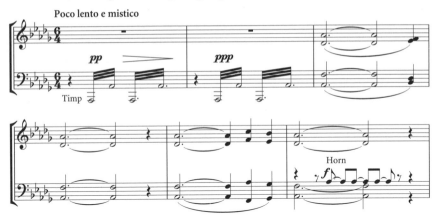

Chanctonbury Ring) – in *Month's Mind*, *Ragamuffin*, *Aubade*, and *Chelsea Reach*. It is also the principal motif in the choral work *These Things Shall Be*. But here, in *The Forgotten Rite*, it assumes a darker significance. It is poised above a dominant pedal, evocatively, even sinisterly echoed on the horn and becomes, in essence, a kind of tumulus in musical terms. The use of this dominant pedal, a 6-4 chord – a chord of the second inversion – also occurs in the Cello Sonata, the E♭ Prelude and in many other places. It evokes here a strange pagan symbolism. Its essence is sexual – certainly occult – recalling perhaps the chalk giant of Cerne Abbas, where St Augustine resorted to his own magic to counter the old powers. This kind of pantheistic element – related to the spirit of place – occurs again and again in the music of John Ireland.

Ireland kept the emotional side of his life private. It is, however, very evident from his letters (especially those to his close friend and confidant of the later years, the Rev. Kenneth Thompson), that despite the apparently boyish streak in his character, his was a very complex personality. 'As you know', he wrote, 'I am a rather bad sort of Anglo-Catholic. I am a Pagan.' (He uses the capital letter.) 'A Pagan I was born and a Pagan I shall remain – that is the foundation of religion.'

In religious matters he was very conscious of ritual. At his friend Percy Bentham's cremation he found the ceremony, or lack of it, horrible. 'There is absolutely no ritual', he complained. And in the dark years of 1940 he told of how he had been to confession, saying, 'It will not do to neglect one's religious duties in these days.' He always kept a book of Bible readings given him by his mother, with portions for each day, called 'Daily Light on the Daily Path'. Significantly the portion for 3 October is 'Many Waters cannot quench Love', the text of his motet *Greater Love Hath No Man*. However, the pagan in him was easily aroused by the atmosphere of these places – like Chanctonbury Ring and Maiden Castle – where he was conscious of early pagan rituals.

He was also conscious of strong, even demonic forces. He once purchased a ring with a curious priapic device from a Chelsea antique shop. He began to sense a malevolent influence from this ring, and eventually gave it to a friend. The friend, however, became convinced that this brought him bad luck, and returned the ring

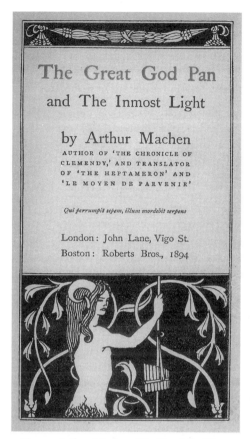

Fig. 13 Arthur Machen, *The Great God Pan*:
title page of the first edition

Fig. 14 Arthur Machen, *The House of Souls*:
frontispiece of the first edition

to Ireland. Knowing that you can only get rid of a spell-bound object to a willing recipient, or by casting it into running water, Ireland took the ring to Chelsea Bridge and threw it into the waters of the Thames. This pagan element in his nature was certainly aroused by Machen's writings. There is little doubt that the strongest impulses in his music stem from the experience of Nature, the wild bird-haunted marshes of Amberley, the placid waters beside the Towing path – and more particularly these places where there is a marked atmosphere of something strange, full of the dark associations of pre-history and foreboding. This is most aptly described by Jocelyn Brooke in his *The Dog at Clambercrown*:

> The dominant image evoked is of a wooded and remote countryside, silent and frostbound in the early twilight of a winter's evening. It is the dead season, yet there is a subtle half-realised feeling of Spring in the air: a stirring of bird life in the woods, the catkins lengthening upon the hazels, the first celandine perhaps gleaming precociously in the sheltered hedgerow. After a day of rain and unbroken cloud, the western sky is suddenly clear, a broad rift of brightness palely green over the humped outline of the woods: the days are drawing out and the land itself seems to extend with

the lengthening days, one is suddenly aware of far illimitable distances. The dimension of Time also is extended in this country of the mind: Uricon or Camelot lie beyond those further woods: and the beech-crowned hill, where the cromlech rises stark against the rainy sunset, the ancient and bloody rites are celebrated anew, and the beacon fires lit for Beltane or Samhain.

Something of the emotional turmoil that resulted from the unhappy excursion into matrimony in 1927 can be gauged from the rather bitter expressions of the Sonatina for piano – and from the Thomas Hardy settings of those years. His conception of beauty was of a kind of idealised youth expressed in many of his piano pieces – with an almost classical grace and elegance of phrase, more sensuous than sensual – *The Holy Boy, A Grecian Lad, The Boy Bishop, February's Child* and also in several places, as *On a Birthday Morning*, which refer mysteriously to a date – 22 February (which we now know to be the birthday of Arthur Miller). This is expressed, perhaps less explicitly, in the Suite *Sarnia* (the old name for Guernsey). The second movement, 'On a May Morning', he had wished to call 'Boyslove', which, of course, is the name of the plant Southernwood. 'Do you think this would cause comment?' he wrote. 'It is such a delightful word.' It is essential that this element in Ireland's makeup is properly understood and it is to be hoped that future biographers in this sensation-seeking age will deal with this aspect with the sensitivity it demands.

The pattern of his life did not take him to exotic places, content as he was to live in Southern England and the Channel Isles. I have stressed his feeling for the spirit of place – and gradually London with its increasing noise and traffic became untenable. His love for the Channel Isles would have led him to settle there but for the war of 1939–45. Moving more and more to the country of Sussex, he established a pied-à-terre there from 1940. He spent the latter years of his life in Sussex – finally moving in 1953 to the old converted mill which was his idyllic last home.

It was in Sussex that he had one of the most curious experiences connected with Arthur Machen. Whilst picnicking on the Sussex Downs Ireland was conscious of a number of children, dressed in white and, in complete silence, dancing and playing. He glanced away for a moment – and the children had vanished. He wrote to Machen about it – whose response was a laconic 'O, so you've seen them too.' This is described by Jocelyn Brooke in his 'The Birth of a Legend'[2] and resulted in Ireland's *Legend* for piano and orchestra. Ireland's encounter with Machen's writing, however, did not immediately ripen into a close friendship with the writer. It was in fact 1933, when *Legend* was performed, before Ireland's initial approach to Machen was returned with that enigmatic postcard. It seems as if Ireland, not really knowing the man, was somewhat put out by this apparently cool reception, for in a letter of September of that year Machen writes to Ireland: 'I have wondered now and again whether I should issue another summons: but concluded, to use your own phrase, that life was complex; that you had your reasons for silence.'

This letter is full of interest – first because he invited Ireland to Amersham when the fair, 'an ancient, noisy and gaudy business', was in full swing – little knowing that this accords well with that almost 'vulgar' (I use the word strictly in its real sense of 'of the people') streak that is heard often in Ireland's music – in

[2] See Chapter 26.

On a Birthday Morning, Merry Andrew, Soho Forenoons and elsewhere. Not for Ireland the somewhat 'twee' works of the folk-song revival. His sense of the rumbustious is more closely related to burlesque. Even more interesting is the following paragraph:

> It is indeed hard to deal with the mysteries. Hard, as you and I know to express them in art: hard even to speak of them. It was St Paul, I think, who heard things that it is not lawful to utter. And it is to be remembered that only a hairsbreadth divides the mysteries from the blasphemies.

For the ensuing years Ireland was to wrestle with all those driving forces in his music. Such pieces as the *Rhapsody*, the four Preludes, the Prelude in E♭, and the songs 'Earth's Call' and 'Marigold' – as well as the later Cello Sonata, develop these strange haunting elements.

Two compositions put Ireland, for a time, squarely on the musical map: the song *Sea Fever* (Masefield), probably one of the most popular English songs ever. The other was his second Violin Sonata which, coming at a time of intensely nationalist feeling, seemed to enshrine something of that fervent spirit, and it found immediate acceptance with a wide public. This same spirit I hear in the lovely second Trio – especially in the beautiful slow central section.

Over the years 1918–29 Ireland produced some of his finest, most mature works. The symphonic poem *Mai-Dun* is also redolent of that spirit of place with dark prehistoric associations, evoked in John Cowper Powys's *Maiden Castle*. This period included the fine Cello Sonata, the Piano Sonata and the dark-hued *Ballade*. The Piano Sonata surely expresses that 'ecstasy' of which Machen was in pursuit. In many quarters Ireland is considered a miniaturist: he wrote no symphony, and we must accept his reasons for this. But surely the intense concentration of idea in such works as the above Sonatas is evidence enough of the scope of his musical thought. No musical expression could be more concentrated, or more symphonic in nature than in the *Ballade* of 1929 – a dark tale indeed!

In the introduction to Machen's *The Shining Pyramid* Jorge Luis Borges considers Machen as 'a minor poet', explaining that he considers him a poet because his prose has the intensity and sense of isolation characteristic of poetry. He considers him minor because minor poetry is a particular genre, not an inferior one. It has a lesser range but a more intimate tone. How aptly these words apply to the music of John Ireland.

CHAPTER 11

Helen Perkin: Pianist, Composer and Muse of John Ireland

Fiona Richards[1]

A SHORT article on Helen Perkin (1909–96) is included in this book not only for her role as an important figure in the life and music of John Ireland, but also because she was a very significant performer in her own right throughout the 1930s, and to a lesser extent after the Second World War. As a pianist, Perkin worked in Britain, Europe and Australia. As a composer, she produced a range of works including songs, chamber music, orchestral and brass band pieces, ballet and film scores and a large repertory for solo piano.

The youngest of six children, Helen Craddock Perkin was born in Hackney on 25 February 1909. Her father, Joseph Craddock Perkin (*b.* 1862), worked as an architect and surveyor. Her mother, Gertrude Helen Garlick (*b.* 1866) studied as a pianist at the Royal College of Music (RCM) and her maternal grandfather, George Garlick (*b.* 1837), was a music hall entertainer and the owner of a music shop in Stratford-upon-Avon, registered as a teacher of music in the 1881 census. The family in which Helen Perkin grew up was a fairly affluent one, as census records list domestic servants living in the household. As can be deduced from the dates above, Perkin, like Ireland, was born to relatively elderly parents, her mother forty-three, her father forty-seven when she was born. Her first piano lessons came from her mother; from the age of eleven she also studied with Arthur Alexander, a noted teacher in London at that time, and a close associate of Ireland. She showed musical promise at an early age, winning Associated Board gold medals in 1923 and 1925.

In September 1925 her mother died, and at the age of 16 Perkin entered the RCM, becoming an exhibitioner in 1926 and a scholar in 1927. She continued to study with Alexander, and by 1928 was already regarded as a gifted student, performing the solo part in the Saint-Saëns Piano Concerto no. 2 in G minor, conducted by Boult. In 1927 she first took composition lessons with Ireland, whose March 1928 report of her early pieces read 'her work is fresh & interesting'. Her association with this composer was to provide a tremendous impetus for her professional career.

During the late 1920s Perkin was building up a portfolio of work in much the same manner as any young pianist today. Surviving programmes and other documents give some idea of her repertoire, of the types of works favoured and taught

---

[1] With the exception of the sources referenced as belonging to the John Ireland Trust, all of the documents used in this article exist in a private archive of Helen Perkin's musical manuscripts, programmes, contracts and other miscellaneous items now in Australia and belonging to her son Kenneth Adie (*b.* 1940). Some parts of this article were substantially rewritten from an earlier piece, 'Changing Identities: The Pianist and Composer Helen Perkin', *Australasian Music Research* 7 (2002), 15–30.

at the RCM at this time, and also of the other figures performing alongside Perkin. Her concert programmes included pieces by Chopin, Liszt and Ravel, but she was also performing lesser-known works by composers such as Szymanowski, her own pieces and many works by British composers, above all Ireland. Her intense relationship with the composer was one of companionship based around their shared musical interests, with him as the revered teacher, she the beautiful young muse.[2] Her close connection with him may also have been motivated by shared elements in their background circumstances, both losing their mother at a similarly young age just before entering the RCM. Perkin accompanied him to concerts and dinners and often acted as his page-turner, for example at a BBC 'John Ireland' evening on 19 April 1928, where writer Sylvia Townsend Warner described her as 'a very beautiful serious child'.[3]

In 1929 Ireland dedicated his song 'Hymn for a child' from *Songs Sacred and Profane* to Perkin. By now she was beginning to develop her work as a composer, and in July of this year wrote a Sonata for Piano in one movement. During 1929 she was also working on a one-movement Phantasy for string quartet, completed in December. This quartet went on to win the prestigious Cobbett Chamber Music Prize in 1930, previously won by Frank Bridge and by Ireland himself, and then, in 1932, by Britten. Perkin's quartet was broadcast by the eminent Spencer Dyke String Quartet. The dense, contrapuntal textures seen in the opening bars of this piece embody her personal compositional style (Ex. 1). In terms of the rhapsodic, evolving structures, soaring melodies and modal harmonies, Ireland's influence on Perkin's music is evident in this piece, and remained with her for the rest of her life.

Ireland's impact on Perkin's career as a performer was even more significant. On 4 April 1930 she was the soloist in Prokofiev's Third Piano Concerto at the RCM, when Malcolm Sargent was conductor. One cannot imagine that this was other than enormously influential on Ireland and the concerto he was then writing. He spent much of 1930 working on the new Piano Concerto, with Perkin in mind. This work is closely associated with her for a number of reasons, one of which is that the principal theme of its first movement is related musically to Perkin's Phantasy. Ireland's opening Eb–Bb–C, shares its shape and tonality with a motif in the viola line in Perkin's quartet, as shown in bars 56–7 and bar 59 of Ex. 2.[4]

In addition, the whole piece resonates with the brilliance and energy of her youthful manner, and was surely conceived with the best aspects of her playing in mind, especially her brilliant fingerwork, often commended in reviews. The premiere took place on 2 October, as part of the 'British Composers' Night' series

[2] Among the John Longmire papers gathered when he was writing his book *John Ireland: Portrait of a Friend* is the following description of Helen Perkin when Ireland met her, unsigned but probably written by Longmire himself: 'Helen was of medium height, fine boned, delicate, dark hair in a coil in the nape of a slender neck, and classical features. The Patrician type of beauty that would appeal to an artist.. I am sure she will forgive me if I say I was in love with her myself, as were most of my fellow-students! I always thought of her as a Madonna-type. Her manner was as fascinating as her appearance.' – EDITOR.

[3] Claire Harman, *The Diaries of Sylvia Townsend Warner* (London: Virago, 1994), p. 16.

[4] See Helen Perkin's analysis of this and the influence of the Prokofiev on p. 369.

Ex. 1 Helen Perkin, Phantasy for string quartet

at the Promenade Concerts, an event which served to fill the Queen's Hall 'to over-flowing'[5], probably because the second half of the concert featured Elgar's Second Symphony conducted by the composer.

The reviews of Perkin's playing at this first performance were glowing. The *Observer* described her as a soloist '… that many would have wished for a new work' as 'she evidently understood the work wholly, and was in great sympathy with it'.[6] The earlier review in the *Daily Telegraph* was equally vociferous in its praise:[7]

> Mr. Ireland's Concerto was a revelation. The revelation lies in the development of self-expression, of self-understanding, in a composer now past 50 years of age. Both technically and aesthetically this Concerto is a work of rare beauty. The solo part, played with surpassing skill and understanding by Helen Perkin, is pianistic to the highest degree; and I doubt if in the whole literature of this form of orchestral music there is a slow movement of more charm.

[5] *Daily Telegraph*, 3 October 1930.

[6] *Observer*, 5 October 1930.

[7] *Daily Telegraph*, 3 October 1930.

Ex. 2 Helen Perkin, Phantasy for string quartet

Fig. 15 Helen Perkin with John Ireland at the time of the Piano Concerto (from an unidentified press cutting)

Ireland himself wrote of her repeat performance of the work at the Proms in the following year, on 24 September 1931:

> Believe me or not, what carried the whole thing thro'… was the outstanding quality of Helen's playing. She held the audience in a way I have seldom known even with pianists of twice her age & fame… the slow movement was absolutely electrifying, Helen playing the long phrases in the most intimate way, long drawn out, & holding the audience by the short hairs, in a way I have heard many pianists fail over – & pianists with very big names, too. I have known her for nearly four years & any time she plays in public (the bigger the occasion the better) the more she surprises & astounds me.[8]

The Concerto seems to have been a turning point for Perkin, and further performances and broadcasts of the work were swiftly followed by BBC radio recitals of piano sonatas by Haydn and eighteenth-century French keyboard music. Throughout 1930 and 1931 she was also beginning to expand her portfolio of compositions, the spring and summer months of 1930 seeing a collection of lyrical settings for voice and piano of poems by Walter de la Mare and a Ballade for piano. Perkin's period of study at the RCM was extremely successful. She won many of the major awards and prizes, including the Signor Foli composition scholarship (1929) (previous recipients being Tippett, Elizabeth Maconchy and Grace Williams), the Arthur Sullivan Prize (1930), the Dannreuther Prize (1930) and a Blumenthal scholarship that lasted from 1930 until her departure from the college in June 1933. By this point Perkin was studying with Gordon Jacob in addition to her continuing lessons with Ireland.

In May 1933 Perkin spent some weeks studying and playing in Paris, working with violinist André Mangeot, whom she accompanied in Delius's Violin Sonata no. 3 in the presence of the composer. Her own 1931 Piano Trio was performed at the Société Nationale, reviewed by Rollo Myers: 'Not only is it an astonishingly mature piece of work for a young girl: judged by any standard it can hold its own. To call it brilliant would be misleading, for it reveals a genuine and imaginative musical temperament, as well as considerable technical facility and a sureness of touch that delights as much as it surprises.'[9]

In the late summer of 1933 Perkin won an Octavia travelling scholarship (as had Imogen Holst and Grace Williams three years earlier) and left London for Vienna. She used the endowment for a consultation with Berg, and then to study composition with Webern and piano with Eduard Steuermann. The study abroad helped her to develop a performing career in Europe, with concerts and broadcasts following in Vienna, Budapest, Frankfurt and Leipzig, and for the next few years she appeared as frequently in Germany and Austria as she did in Britain. However, in the compositions that followed there was no sign of the impact of the teaching of either Berg or Webern. In October 1933 she was back in London as soloist with the BBC Symphony Orchestra in that year's Promenade season, in Beethoven's Concerto no. 3. Her appearances as a soloist at the Proms spanned several years:

[8] Ireland to Edward Clark, 30 September 1931, *GB-Lbl*, Add. Ms. 52256.
[9] *Daily Telegraph*, 6 May 1933.

1930	Ireland	Concerto
1931	Ireland	Concerto
1932	Prokofiev	Concerto no. 3
1933	Beethoven	Concerto no. 3
1934	Ireland	Concerto
1935	Prokofiev	Concerto no. 3
1936	Haydn	Concerto in G (with cadenza by Perkin)
	Beethoven	Concerto no. 1
1937	Prokofiev	Concerto no. 3

Each time Perkin appeared at the Proms her appearances were reviewed very positively, for example in 1932: 'She gave an exceedingly fine performance, balanced, controlled, brilliant, and in every way, I should say, well-nigh perfect. This evening should have made this young player's reputation.'[10] The 1937 Prokofiev 'bubbled and spurted with irrepressible high spirits and fascinated the mind by its distinctive kind of pianism.'[11] In addition to the Proms appearances, Perkin performed concertos in many other venues, for example Beethoven's Concerto no. 3 in Bournemouth Pavilion under Sir Dan Godfrey (October 1933) and the same work in Eastbourne (November 1933).

Perkin's developing European reputation as a composer was beginning to have an impact on her success in Britain, with the publishing company Schott taking on her music, including a set of four Preludes for piano which were performed in November 1933 alongside works by her slightly older RCM colleagues, Elizabeth Maconchy and Grace Williams. This particular event formed part of the recently-established Macnaghten-Lemare concert series, founded by violinist Anne Macnaghten, along with Iris Lemare and Elisabeth Lutyens, to perform works by young or little-known British composers. In January 1934 Perkin played the solo part in the first performance of Ireland's *Legend* for piano and orchestra at a Queen's Hall concert. Her work in this year continued in a similar manner to the previous one, with some new publications (such as *Village Fair* for piano) and many performances.

In 1935 she married George Mountford Adie (1901–89), an affluent architect and partner in a major firm, Adie, Button & Partners, founded in 1933. The firm now forms part of the well-known company Waterhouse. Adie was renowned for his avant-garde designs. Three notable surviving buildings include a striking art deco apartment block in Princes Gate, South Kensington; a 1930s mansion, 'Charters', in Sunningdale, which was used as a country retreat by Edward, Duke of Windsor and Wallis Simpson; and, in the 1950s, Stockwell Garage, a large bus garage which is now a listed building.

After her marriage Perkin at first succeeded in maintaining a public profile as both pianist and composer. Her engagements in 1935 included many BBC radio broadcasts, and an appearance with the BBC Symphony Orchestra as Proms soloist in Prokofiev's Piano Concerto no. 3 in a Russian programme conducted

---

[10] *Music Lover*, 17 September 1932.

[11] *The Times*, 2 September 1937.

by Sir Henry Wood (19 September 1935). She was also continuing to develop her career as a composer. In 1936 she was living at 3 Camp View, a large house situated in the heart of Wimbledon Park, and wrote of her working methods:

> Actually, however, I only know that I am thinking or living in a musical form as opposed to a normal condition of thinking in words. When this occurs I compose, and find that I must compose. It is imperative and cannot be overlooked. I, therefore, say for myself that [for] this form of expression music is natural, inevitable and possibly inspirational. I cannot imagine inventing or forcing musical thought nor disobeying the urge to compose when the conditions arise. This does not mean that I do not make great effort and use great concentration in composing. I do make great effort but the effort is to deliberate and express what is there and not to find something to put there. My studio is a large and lofty room facing South and looking across Wimbledon Common to silver birches and woods in the background and in the distance the trees of Richmond Park. There are no visible houses and the view is uninterrupted. The wind howls round the large square bay-window and moans through the cracks in winter. The furniture and walls are all light in colour and simple in design. They were in fact designed by my husband. There are no pictures on the walls; the main interest is the view from the window and in winter the large open fire. Bright cushions of primary colours and flowers provide the necessary colour. The proportions of the room and furniture are conducive to thought and work and calm.[12]

It seems that Ireland was shocked by the Adie–Perkin marriage, as his friendship with Perkin had been a demanding and possessive one, and he perhaps thought that it might hamper the development of her promising career. In 1935 Ireland wrote to his sister of Perkin that 'she has detached herself from me entirely, & I do not blame her – circumstances probably dictated her actions, & she probably was not able to consider what effect on me her rather ruthless behaviour might have'.[13]

The two ceased to communicate, and when, in 1936, Perkin broadcast English music from Frankfurt, Leipzig and Hamburg, there was no Ireland in the programme, but rather works by Sterndale Bennett and E. J. Moeran, and her own *Episode*, a piece dedicated to her husband and indicative of the philosophical path she was to take, described by her as 'the moment which properly understood contains the entire truth for all time, as the understanding of the microcosm contains the truth of the Macrocosm' (Perkin's autobiographical notes, 1936). Grand words, but *Episode* is a tightly constructed piece, once again in the mould of Ireland with its evident subscription to the notion of contrasting musical topics within a single movement.

Perkin was again a soloist at the Proms in 1936, this time in Beethoven's Piano Concerto no. 3: 'Her performance had a captivating air of thoughtful care. But the care was devoted to the avoidance of anything like an emphatic statement. Nothing stood out unduly; every movement was dealt with conscientiously and

[12] Helen Perkin, typed notes, 1936.

[13] John Ireland to Ethel Ireland, 5 April 1935: John Ireland Trust.

with seeming ease'.[14] In this year she wrote a *Spring Rhapsody* for violin and piano, and also worked closely with other leading young British virtuosi such as clarinettist Frederick Thurston and horn-player Aubrey Brain. In November 1936 she booked the Aeolian Hall for an entire concert of her compositions, which included the Phantasy for string quartet, the new *Spring Rhapsody*, a piano trio and a number of other chamber works, including songs and piano solos, with a reviewer writing that 'Her piano writing is never without interest and, often, also terse and effective'.[15] This recital of her own works followed a concert the previous month in which she performed Ireland's Preludes and music by Chopin, Ravel and Ibert. Her strengths were identified as the French repertory and an 'exceptionally strong' left hand, her weakness Chopin miniatures in which 'the emotion seemed forced'.[16] (This reviewer liked her best in the more brilliant pianistic works, especially Ravel's *Jeux d'eau* and 'Ondine' from *Gaspard de la nuit*.)

In January 1937 Perkin was the subject of a British BBC television programme, part of a new series with the title 'Music-Makers'. At this time she was renowned in Britain and Europe both as a pianist and as a composer. Her Piano Sonata was premiered at Queen's Hall, London, in October, attracting the comment that 'there was ingenuity in the way the moods, sombre and frivolous, in the first movement were contrasted and then brought together. The slow movement and the cheerful finale included some attractive invention'.[17] The piece was equally well received in other reviews, for example: 'Clever technically, the sonata is melodious and ingeniously original'.[18] She also had a busy broadcasting schedule, with numerous engagements for BBC radio, embracing a large and diverse repertory of piano music. At the same time she was a wife and mother living in a large suburban house in Farnham Royal, near Maidenhead, having moved there from Wimbledon in that year.

Thus her career both in Britain and in Europe was flourishing, and she seemed set to develop a profile as a significant musician. However, at this point Perkin already had one son, George (*b.* 1936) and two further children, Timothy and Kenneth, were born before 1940. The combination of the outbreak of the Second World War and the birth of three children in the space of five years meant an inevitable break in her career. She was able to continue with commitments such as broadcasts in 1938 (with a continued focus on Ireland's piano music, for example with a BBC Empire broadcast for South Africa of a programme of Ireland's music on 19 January 1938), but 1939 was the last busy year for some time and featured only a few events such as performing Schumann in a six-part BBC radio programme on Robert and Clara Schumann's lives and work. She did attempt to resume her relationship with Ireland in this year, and indeed was engaged to perform the Concerto in Belfast in May 1939. However, what might have been a temporary quarrel with Ireland had become a major rift which only worsened over the next decade. Writing retrospectively in 1962, Perkin said that 'although every

---

[14] *Daily Telegraph*, 19 September 1936.

[15] *Daily Telegraph*, 13 November 1936.

[16] *The Times*, 24 October 1936.

[17] *The Times*, 11 October 1937.

[18] *The Star*, 11 October 1937.

effort was made on the part of all concerned to have a friendly relation, it was too difficult, and the situation became so impossible that a complete break had to be made'.[19]

Perkin spent the war years looking after her children, while her husband undertook unpaid work for the army, designing barracks for soldiers. When she attempted to renew her career as a professional musician after the war, she began with occasional concerts, and some new compositions of her own. In 1947, for example, she wrote two large-scale piano works, *Impressions* and a second Ballade. A Suite for string quartet followed in 1949.

It was initially through her associations with John Ireland that the rejuvenation of her performing career took place, and in 1951, the year of the Festival of Britain, she was invited by the BBC to give a recital of his piano music. For some reason, quite possibly the intervention of his protective housekeeper, Norah Kirby, Ireland's letters to her in the early 1950s became increasingly vitriolic, telling her that she was 'intensely ego-centric' and saying how totally she lacked 'self-criticism in [her] activities as a musician'.[20] It was also a great shock to Perkin to find that Ireland had removed the dedication to her from the score of the Concerto (undated notes by Perkin, John Ireland Trust).

For a variety of reasons Perkin's opportunities as a pianist were not what they had been in the 1930s. The break in her career, with a period of some ten years in which her name disappeared from public circulation, seriously affected her opportunities, given that she had not yet made the transition from brilliant rising star to mature soloist. Whereas Perkin's almost exact contemporary, Eileen Joyce, sustained a career in Britain throughout and beyond the Second World War (for example, Joyce recorded the Ireland Concerto in 1942), and Myra Hess's career was strengthened by her involvement with London's National Gallery concerts, Perkin instead devoted herself to her young sons during the war years.

Perkin left a number of recordings of her compositions and of her own performances, some commercial, some private. Among the private surviving recordings are her chamber ballet *King's Cross* and a version of her Cello Sonata in which Florence Hooton is accompanied by Perkin. There are nine recordings listed in the National Sound Archive catalogue, which feature the performance of Ireland's Sonatina included with this book, songs by Stanford with her at the piano and some of her works for brass band. Her 1935 accompaniment of Walter Widdop in Elgar's 'The Shepherd's Song' was issued in 2010 in the Elgar Society's 'Interpreters on Record' set, volume 5, EECD003005.

Across 1951 and 1952 Perkin continued to revitalize her solo career. A concert in the Reardon Smith Lecture Theatre, Cardiff,[21] included Ireland's *Ragamuffin*, *April* and *Equinox*. The early 1950s saw Perkin working as accompanist to two international cellists, Antoni Sala and André Navarra, the latter an acquaintance dating from a meeting in Paris in 1933. With Navarra she developed a wide knowledge of the repertory for cello and piano, and their recitals included works by Beethoven, Chopin, Debussy and Ireland's Sonata, as well as Perkin's own music for this duo

---

[19] Perkin to John Longmire, 26 January 1962: John Ireland Trust.

[20] Ireland to Perkin, 21 October 1954: John Ireland Trust.

[21] 25 March 1952.

Ex. 3 Helen Perkin, *Three Impressions* for cello and piano, second movement, 'Far niente',

combination, as seen in a Wigmore Hall programme of 24 September 1951. Perkin's involvement with Navarra led in 1953 to her *Siesta* and *Three Impressions* for cello and piano, both performed by him. The latter work is a series of French-influenced mood pieces, which reveal some of the same topics that appear in Ireland's music. For example, the second movement, 'Far niente', is a lilting pastoral miniature (Ex. 3).

Perkins's associations with cellists also extended to Helen Just, with whom she performed on a number of occasions in programmes featuring Perkin's Sonata and other sonatas by Kodály, Handel and Brahms. In 1956 she produced a large-scale Cello Sonata, one of her best and most substantial works, which she recorded with Florence Hooton, and which owes a debt to Ireland's 1923 Sonata for cello and piano and to a number of his other chamber works. The first movement, for example, opens with a rhapsodic and richly-scored Andante with soaring melodies strongly influenced by Ireland (Ex. 4).

The central movement of her work is a delicate French-influenced scherzo (Ex. 5) whose gradual changing time signatures can be traced back to Ireland's 1938 Piano Trio no. 3. The finale opens with a melodic statement over the same big, parallel chords that feature so often in Ireland's chamber music (Ex. 6) before swiftly moving into an Allegro con fuoco (Ex. 7), which has the greatest affinity

Ex. 4 Helen Perkin, Sonata for cello and piano, first movement

Ex. 5 Helen Perkin, Sonata for cello and piano, second movement

with the final section of Ireland's 1943 Fantasy-Sonata for clarinet and piano. There are many other traits learnt from her first composition teacher, in particular the way in which fragments from one movement infiltrate another and little references to musical topics appear and disappear. The shifting web of changing time and key signatures creates a fluid, narrative structure.

Perkin's composing career in the 1950s had become increasingly diverse, including two 1955 BBC commissions of ballets for children's television, *King's Cross* and *Calamity at Court*. These display deft handling of a small ensemble in a style which is very typical of 1950s' children's entertainment, and show her natural ability to write simple 'character' music to accompany a spoken script. In 1955 she also wrote the score for a short film for a live BBC recording in the London Playhouse, part of a series which ran weekly from 29 September 1955 to 16 February 1956. The Perkin episode, *The Inward Eye*, was a story of a girl suddenly afflicted by blindness, and was broadcast on 10 November 1955, produced by Peter Coates (1912–98) and with William Hartnell (1908–75) playing a lead role.

A number of brass band works followed this. Perkin's brass band music was and remains widely acclaimed, and chosen on a number of occasions as the test music for British national band competitions: *Carnival Suite*, in three movements, was the test piece at the 105th Annual British Open Championship Brass Band Contest held in the Kings Hall, Belle Vue, Manchester in September 1957. On this occasion sixteen bands competed for the title, with Black Dyke Mills taking first place. On 15 September 1962 her *Island Heritage* was the test piece for the 110th Championships at Belle Vue, in which Besses o' th' Barn won the top prize. These works are among her most accomplished in terms of their understanding of the instruments deployed, and were in part brought about because her son Timothy played the French horn as a pupil at Highgate School – the *Cordell Suite* was performed by the school in 1956 in an early version for horn and orchestra. Her chamber music of the late 1950s included a String Quartet in C minor (1958), a Suite for violin, cello, piano (1959) and a second Piano Sonata (1959).

The 1960s saw Perkin spending long periods travelling, living in Grenada and also visiting Venezuela and Peru as part of an increasing involvement with the Gurdjieff esoteric movement. One interesting source of information on these years is a series of letters written to the English composer John Longmire. In the early 1960s Longmire started work on a biography of Ireland. Wanting to include a section on the relationship between Perkin and Ireland he began to correspond with Perkin. Most of her letters to him date from 1963, and as well as showing her enthusiasm for reflections on the 1930s, reveal her lifestyle and feelings at this time.

In 1965 she and her husband emigrated to Sydney for a number of reasons, principal among them the poor pulmonary health of George Adie. The family swiftly settled into life in Grandview Drive, Newport Beach, where Perkin then lived from 31 March 1966 until her death in 1996. For a short time she resumed a career as a pianist broadcasting on the Australian Broadcasting Commission's second network, and as a soloist and accompanist, playing in such venues as Everett House, Wahroonga for the Wahroonga District Music Club (in March 1967). There are surviving records of a number of engagements in 1966 and 1967, though these decreased gradually as other interests took over. In 1968 her reassessment audition

Ex. 6 Helen Perkin, Sonata for cello and piano, third movement

Ex. 7 Helen Perkin, Sonata for cello and piano, third movement

to continue as a regular performer for the ABC saw her performing Ireland again, this time *The Towing Path*.

Perhaps the most striking aspect of Perkin's life in Australia was her commitment to the Gurdjieff movement. Interestingly, there was already some history of family interest in spiritual or religious groups: her father was a Wesleyan Methodist, and her older brother Noel (1893–1979) had earlier emigrated to the USA, becoming the director of world missions for the Pentecostal church, Assemblies of God. Perkin had been involved with Gurdjieff as early as the late 1930s, attending group meetings in London, the impetus for this again coming from her husband. In 1922 George Ivanovich Gurdjieff had established his Institute for the Harmonious Development of Man at the Château du Prieuré in Paris, the aim of this school being self-knowledge and the development of consciousness. Perkin and her husband met Gurdjieff in Paris in 1948, and after the latter's death, George Adie continued as one of the leaders of the Gurdjieff Work in England, which in 1950 included a woman called Jane Heap among its members. Heap became a lifelong student and teacher in the Gurdjieff Work, and also a friend of Perkin.

Music played an important role in the Institute's activities. Gurdjieff's close associate in Paris in the 1920s was the Russian composer Thomas de Hartmann, (1885–1956) and between them they composed music for the group. This included contemplative hymns, often drawing on the idiom of the Russian Orthodox liturgy, and dance movements, utilising the component features of Russian folk melodies. Perkin was introduced to de Hartmann by another Gurdjieff follower, Jeanne de Salzmann (herself an accomplished pianist), and after her move to Australia remained in regular contact with her. She had already performed music by de Hartmann in her 1950s revival, including his *Lumière noire*, op. 74, in a Wigmore Hall recital on 17 March 1951.

In the latter part of her life Perkin was closely involved with the Gurdjieff movement in Australia, with her husband running the Newport Beach group. Perkin's part in the group was essentially as the composer and performer of dance music, with a large volume of her own rhythmic 'movements' published posthumously. The characteristics of de Hartmann's Gurdjieff music were taken up by Perkin in her own musical compositions at a late point in her life. His stylistic features: simplicity of structure, undulating melodies and underpinning drones are echoed in her 'movement' music, which was aimed to 'bring intellect, feeling and body into a harmonious state.'[22]

Even in her 70s and early 80s Perkin was still performing in public and continuing to travel to Europe, though now only in association with Gurdjieff meetings. Although she developed some memory loss following invasive treatment for arteriosclerosis brought about by years of heavy smoking, she was recorded performing the music of Gurdjieff and de Hartmann in Paris in 1990. Perkin died in Sydney in 1996.

From the evidence of contemporary reviews, and more importantly of a good range of surviving historic recordings, Perkin was an extremely good pianist.

---

[22] J. George Adie Azize, *A Gurdjieff Pupil in Australia* (Cambridge: Lighthouse Editions., 2007), p. 25.

She was also a skilled composer, who could turn her hand to an array of musical mediums. Her musical eclecticism was perhaps born of personal circumstances, and she enjoyed a long and varied career for a married woman with three children living through the Second World War. While she is an example of someone whose changing life was heavily influenced by the spirit of the ages, people and places she crossed, she was without question a very interesting and talented woman, whose relationship with John Ireland's music lasted for a period of over thirty years.

CHAPTER 12

John Ireland and Charles Markes:
A Creative Relationship

George Dannatt

This article was first published in British Music, *the annual journal of the British Music Society, vol. 28 (2006). It is reproduced here by permission of the Estate of George Dannatt and the editor of* British Music.

T HROUGH my meetings with John Ireland, more particularly between 1940 and 1945 (and these were not just brief encounters), I got to know, and can still hear, the very personal timbre of that voice. His was an intonation especially noticeable when in ironic mood, or when exchanging some quip about fellow musicians; this he had the generosity to do without being malicious. His very personal voice was, I think, due in the main to the laconicism of his observations, frequently uttered through only part of his mouth, his lips pressed together to retain his pipe.

I have introduced this personal observation to these recollections of Charles Markes because when he and I were together, surrounded by a group of photographs, the floor and the piano littered with the music, it was our experience that we had, in fact, evoked something of the personality of the composer and the spirit of his music. As it happened, both Markes and I were good mimics, so that from time to time our reminiscences were interrupted by some quizzical observation such as Ireland himself might have made.[1]

From Markes I obtained a strong sense of the past, of his and Ireland's past, in particular of Chelsea at the turn of the century through to 1918, and of the Edwardian era. From these reminiscences, by playing from the music, seeing the photographs, we did seem to evoke the presence of the composer himself, indeed to such an extent that Charles Markes has fallen quiet, in that sort of stillness which can so mysteriously descend on a room in the very centre of London (it was at my then home in Belgravia) and has quietly said, 'How I wish he could walk into this room just now.' I remained silent and let the thought follow through.

My mention of the impact of photographs upon a mind striving truly to re-create a personality and a period may possibly strike the reader as unusual, even as sentimental. In a history of the Second World War there is a reference to the then General Montgomery having in his headquarters-caravan a photograph of Rommel with the aim of 'getting to know his man, of getting inside the mind and personality of his adversary'. For me, this is good psychology, and through the co-operation of Charles Markes and of Mrs Norah Kirby[2] I have been able, when

---

[1] Hear Ireland's voice on the accompanying compact disc, tracks 1 and 2.

[2] [George Dannatt's footnote] This enigmatic personality has to be linked with the name of Ralph Hill and to myself in regard to Norah's request that I should write a biography of John Ireland. Readers will know of Ralph's editing of the Penguin series

working on this book,[3] to place in my study many photographs of the composer from his earliest to his last years. One photograph in particular which stands out is that of the group showing the clergy and choir of St. Luke's, Chelsea, *circa*

– on *The Concerto*, on *The Symphony*, as editor of the *Penguin Music Magazine*. He was music critic of the *Daily Mail* as well as music editor of the *Radio Times*. I had written for him on the *Mail*, but more extensively on the 'Concerts in London' section of *Penguin Music Magazine*. Although I think I was originally introduced to Ireland by Scott Goddard (with whom I shared music criticism on the London liberal daily, the *News Chronicle*), continuation of the 'contacts' was more due to Ralph Hill, and I well remember all five of us (Hill, Ireland, Kirby, Goddard and myself) conferring together after an Albert Hall Promenade Concert at which a work of Ireland had been performed. This was the occasion on which I was introduced to Kirby.

My recollection is that, after Norah had been bombed out, she was housed at Ralph's house, and it was there that she first heard Ireland's music in any depth through Ralph's enthusiasm for the composer. It would be not too much to say that Norah came to idolize Ireland and his music almost frenetically. She became his 'housekeeper' at Rock Mill (Steyning) and virtually his right hand in all practical matters, established the Ireland Charitable Trust and was an immense force in getting his music performed and his status maintained. As one fellow critic said to me: 'Norah Kirby has done an immense amount of good in furthering Ireland's music, but also quite a degree of harm.' The public gets tired of relentless 'pushers' of an artist's work. To some extent Ireland himself regretted the constant helper and 'do-gooder', particularly in that several visitors to Rock Mill were, as was Ireland, homosexual. 'Is she anywhere about?' Ireland whispered to Scott Goddard on one of his fairly regular visits! It was an incredible fact that Norah would not, could not, admit Ireland's sexuality; this even to the extent that, when one very distinguished critic and broadcaster mentioned that fact to her, she refused ever to meet or speak with him again. Hers was an obstinate blindness that could hardly help the constant 'companionship' at Rock Mill.

[3] [George Dannatt's footnote] As mentioned above, Norah Kirby commissioned me to write a full biography of Ireland. To do this, during a period of making constant notes, I spent virtually a couple of years in obtaining copies of everything he had written – not an easy task where so many songs were concerned, many out of print or republished by different publishers. When I commenced to write, I found Norah regularly 'at my elbow' with the implied warning that a certain characteristic should not appear! Norah's 'interventions' took the form of a stream of letters, as well as telephone calls. The situation became impossible, my interest in the project diminished, so that eventually I did just write the article about the relationship between Ireland and Markes and shoved it aside with accumulated piano and orchestral scores, and notes and drafts which I had collected together. It was when handing over all the material to Bruce Phillips, who now curates many of Ireland's possessions and all the archival material within the Trust, that my article came to light. Bruce felt that it could prove of interest for publication, and I therefore 'updated' it in some respects into the form in which it is here presented. It might be mentioned that some of the material which I was able to forward to the care of Bruce Phillips is unique – for instance, Adrian Boult's notes upon Ireland's comments on the interpretation of the orchestral works (which Boult gladly gave me) and, secondly, copies of all the legal material regarding Ireland's mistaken marriage, its non-consummation, and its nullification.

1911–1912, in which John Ireland as Choirmaster and Charles Markes and Robert Glassby as choirboys, an inseparable trio for nearly a decade, are portrayed in close proximity to each other. Inevitably, this stimulating friendship was subject to the vicissitudes of love and hate and of joy and sorrow inherent in any close human relationship; though Charles Markes confessed his jealousy of the very good looking 'Bobby' Glassby – soon to become the inspiration for *The Holy Boy* – we can only surmise that the latter might, in his turn, have envied the highly superior musicianship of 'Charlie' Markes. It was as 'Bobby' and 'Charlie' that Ireland knew them.

Charles Stafford Markes, whose unusual second name is derived from that of his maternal uncle, Victor Stafford, who was to play an important part in the child's musical development, was born on 1 July 1900 in Pimlico, the year of the relief of Ladysmith, the production of *The Dream of Gerontius*, and the deaths of Ruskin and Nietzsche. One month later John Nicholson Ireland became twenty-one, took leave of his guardians and assumed control of his own finances, including the management of the comparatively small sum of money which his mother had settled on him before his fourteenth year when she realized that the whole impetus of his life was towards becoming a musician – a pianist and, perhaps, a composer.

By 1900 Ireland had written the two string quartets[4] and the Sextet for clarinet, horn and string quartet and, characteristically, had written and destroyed much else. Joseph Holbrooke, astonishingly uncritical of his own voluminous output, recorded in his crusading book *Contemporary British Composers* that Ireland

> is one of our strong men, and we have not got too many in music. His first essays in composing seem to have been of no great mark. He has agreed to this verdict by suppressing a lot of his early work. Very few have seen any of it ... he published no important work until he was aged twenty-nine, and he has destroyed quartets, sextets, sonatas, trios, etc.

Neither Charles, the new child, nor his parents, nor the young composer could have known that, within four years of that twenty-first birthday, he would become organist at St Luke's, and that, within another four years, when the child was in his ninth year, he would become a chorister at that church, and that from this slender beginning would develop an intimate friendship in which each became mentor to the other; nor could they have known that this close and constantly renewed friendship would last from 1908 to 1920, would come to grief through an unpremeditated incident one day in 1920, yet flourish again from 1948 until the composer's death in 1962.[5]

To Charles Lewis and Edith Constance Markes a second son was born some four years later and christened Lawrence. The Markes family was very poor and,

---

[4] Dannatt: 'It is highly unlikely that these two early student works (*circa* 1890), the D minor and the C minor Quartets, would ever have appeared if I had not urged and encouraged Markes to complete the missing parts, and for us jointly to go to Boosey & Hawkes and persuade them that the scores should be printed; thus it is rewarding that the beautifully produced scores recognize Markes's contribution in the publisher's note.'

[5] See also Charles Markes interview with Lewis Foreman, pp. 70–76

as happened so frequently in the late Victorian and the Edwardian eras, up to 1914, that age of extremes of poverty and wealth, illness and good health, inadequate and splendid housing conditions, the father became an alcoholic. And, as also happened so often under these circumstances, the desperate mother had an upright spinster sister, Jessie Rose Stafford; together they made a home for themselves and the two boys in a house in Chichester Street, Paddington (later named Sussex Street) on the condition – no doubt a condition of the sisterly partnership laid down by Aunt Jessie – that the mother would see no more of the erring drunkard; he was 'evicted' and might not return in any circumstances – thus the stage was set at that early date for the desire for a father figure, for masculine society, as some twelve to fifteen years earlier had been the case with John Ireland, whose mother had died in 1893 when he was just fourteen years old, and whose father was to die a year later, leaving the boy for a time in an almost exclusively feminine society of sisters, teachers and governesses.

An intense friendship was to develop between the composer and his pupil which, as the boy grew, led to endless talks upon a diversity of subjects, with music and poetry always in the foreground; constructive, creative talk such as is probably only fully experienced in the intimate friendship of two males. Such creative masculine friendships have existed since time immemorial and, as also occurs so frequently when they do develop, the mother of the younger man disliked the elder and was, no doubt, jealous of him and of his influence; yet this was understandable, for the pupil adored his master and was fascinated and captivated by his musical thinking and the highly personal music which he produced in his improvisations and in his compositions, and, clearly, he kept far too late hours for a boy of his sensitivity and musical precocity. No doubt, too, Uncle Victor Stafford had his say as to the relationship.

But Uncle Victor – an alto chorister at Southwark Cathedral and St. Anne's, Soho – was interested in his nephew's passionate enthusiasm for music, the boy having industriously set himself to work at the piano, virtually unaided, from the age of four, and took him, when he was some eight years old, for an audition to Sir Walter Alcock, then assistant organist at Westminster Abbey. He was not accepted by Alcock, being considered too young, with the result that the uncle then took him to see John Ireland, organist at St Luke's, with J. Stuart Archer as assistant organist. To Ireland he sang *Love Divine, All Loves Excelling*, and was accepted for the choir. Meanwhile, he continued with his self-imposed task of learning the piano, which he had commenced by experimenting first of all with the black notes only, then with the white notes, then with a combination of the two 'in order to get the sounds right'.

Charles Markes recalled that for the first year or two he was not particularly noticed by Ireland, the Choirmaster and Organist, for he was simply a new choir boy. But the boy noticed the master and was moved beyond words by this maker of magical sounds on the organ, especially during extemporizations, for Ireland 'chose stops with great care and was very aware of what went with what, in order to produce a careful selection of colour through which his unique harmony evolved'. What Charles Markes lacked in beauty of voice, he made up for as a sight reader of uncanny ability, as, indeed, he remained. Inevitably, Ireland became aware of the boy's talent and, thus, of his worth in leading the choir in unfamiliar music. After some two or three years he asked him if he knew of any other boys who might like to join the choir. 'Yes', said Charles Markes, 'my friend, Bobby Glassby.'

Bobby was brought along and accepted; though he was a rather poor musician, he was a very beautiful child. The Glassby family had a lasting influence upon the composer, for the father died suddenly, and his sculpture studio at the rear of 14 Gunter Grove became the composer's own studio from 1915 to 1938. A highly competent head-and-shoulders sculpture of the boy by his father was soon acquired by Ireland and stood near one of his pianos all his life; there, also, stood the small Greek male sculptures which Charles Markes remembered from the very earliest days and to which Ireland used to point from time to time in extolling the beauty of the male form. A little later, Ireland occupied the lower part of the Glassbys' house, whilst the widowed mother and her family lived in the upper part; from 1945 to 1953 he occupied the whole property.

At one Friday evening choir practice, in the continued absence of their choirmaster, Charles Markes gathered the choir round the piano, and a full choir practice developed, to be interrupted only by the dry voice and characteristic sniff and foot tapping of the choirmaster with: 'When you have quite finished, Charlie, perhaps you would allow me to take over.' Charles Markes tried to slip away at the end of the practice, but, no, 'I am going home with you my boy.' At home, contrary to the 'wigging' which the boy had expected, Mrs Markes was urged to allow him to have proper piano lessons, 'as he has real musical talent'. She demurred; she could not arrange this, for she had two boys to bring up and there was no spare money available.

The result was that Ireland took him as a pupil at Elm Park Gardens where, after tea served by one of Ireland's succession of dour housekeepers, he played a little piece called *Pamela*.[6] Ireland pointed out his mistakes, then placed another piece of music in front of him, and said, 'Play that.' The boy played it, but it sounded so dissonant that he commenced to 'correct' the harmonies, to Ireland's annoyance who snapped out, 'Play what you see written, not how you think it should sound.' It was probably, Charles Markes seemed to remember, a piece by Bax or Bridge who, to a boy of that age, employed exceptionally 'modern' harmonies.

The Markes family was then living in two rooms on the top floor of a house in Tadema Road, and Charles Markes recalled this as an horrific time illuminated only by his passion for music and for that of Ireland's in particular and, indeed, for his love for John Ireland himself, who had become a sort of second father to him; although Charles Markes did not know until many years later, Ireland had, with the assistance of the church, paid his school fees, and probably contributed to other expenses. In one of these rooms the aunt took some two years to die of cancer, existing, so it seemed, on the Fremlin's stout which the doctor prescribed and on *Hymns Ancient and Modern* which Charles Markes played to her from the adjoining room.

Charles Markes records how blunt and forthright Ireland would be with the choir, for he was entirely unable to equivocate. But after choir practice, or after a piano lesson, he became a different person; then they would go out for a meal

---

[6] Probably *Pamela: Petite Serenade pour piano* by Paul Graener (Schott, 1904). – EDITOR

together, or talk in the studio far into the night about the musical and other experiences which they had encountered since they last met. More often than not, the piano lessons developed into an exchange of ideas, in musical appreciation and appraisals. Ireland generally played something of what he had recently written; often he played Ravel and battled with his *Gaspard de la nuit*, which he was never able to play really well, and this led, to Charles Markes's amusement, to furious oaths supplanting the running commentary with which he larded almost any piece he was playing in the intimacy of his studio. At one time Charles Markes was given the 'Arietta' from Book I of the Grieg *Lyric Pieces* to learn; he was so intrigued with the music that he learned the lot and played them right through at his next lesson. 'You play Grieg very well', said Ireland through his half-closed lips. 'Give it to me', and then he inscribed the volume to Charles Markes. Later, he wanted to send him to Tobias Matthay for proper lessons, remarking: 'If you work hard for three or four years, you could be a very good pianist', but Charles Markes did not want to leave his true master and refused to go.

He worked his way through the choir until he became leader of the Cantoris side, probably about 1913, and he was, in fact, a member of the choir from 1908 to 1915, when his voice broke. On that occasion he was the soloist in Mendelssohn's *Hear my Prayer* and, when he reached for the top B in 'Oh! God, hear my Cry', nothing happened; no sound came. The organ loft curtains were torn apart, and an enquiring face looked down on him. In the vestry afterwards he was inconsolable; Ireland put his arms round him and said, 'Never mind my boy, come to Church just the same and I know what we must do, we must have you taught the organ and then you can relieve me sometimes.'

So he was coached a little by Ireland and took over for the Thursday evening services 'for about six old women in the congregation'; proving his ability, he was then sent to Stuart Archer for proper lessons at the Curzon Street Church of Christ Science where there was a splendid Norman and Beard organ. At this he worked diligently, and frequently practised throughout his lunch hour; after a year or so he was pronounced capable of becoming assistant at St Luke's, where he gradually assumed duties in helping out the busy composer from time to time; more and more frequently little notes popped through his letterbox, such as:

[June 2nd 1917]
Dear Charlie, I had to come here today (St. Luke's) as you did not reply to my letter. Please reply on this card <u>at once</u> to say if you can play the children's Service on Whit Sunday at 3.15, also if you can finish the 6.30 for me on Sunday evening – letting me go after the sermon?
    Yours ever JI.

'You can play an Amen this evening', he said on an earlier occasion and gave explicit instructions as to how the keys were to be released in order to get the right effect – taking off from left to right; at Evening Prayer there is in the general confession a nice trap for an eager organist, and Charles Markes fell into it, playing a beautiful 'Amen' at the end of the words 'Unto Mankind in Christ Jesus our Lord', instead of a few lines later after 'To the Glory of thy Holy Name'; a tremendous sigh from Ireland and a sibilant 'You'll get me the sack.'

On another occasion, there came a boy with curly hair clutching a note, 'This is

Master Woodgate', it said 'Will you please see if he can play', and Charles Markes's report was favourable; many years later there came this from the composer:

> [September 5th 1951]
> I have three Prom performances during the final week beginning Monday, the 17th instant. What *These Things* will sound like under the masterly direction of Master Woodgate, I dread to think.

In fact, it sounded very well, as I myself recall, Leslie Woodgate conducting with his customary verve and aplomb.

'Bobby', 'Charlie' and their master did not forget their little jokes together, and Charles Markes told of a nice one from during the First World War which Ireland remembered and joked about again after the Second World War, in 1948. The three friend were returning from a choir practice and a meal, their arms linked, as was customary ('Trioism' they called it) when they found themselves following a lamp-lighter with his pole; 'Do you know what that is?' said Ireland. 'That's an anti-aircraft zeppelin protector!' Charles Markes could give many examples of Ireland's discipline and wry humour during the St Luke's days. At the first rehearsals of his Service in C, for instance, when the choir found themselves quite unable to go straight into the Credo on the third beat after the organ's unison C, as usual on such occasions, an irate face looked down on the choir from the organ loft and a particularly dry voice said, 'Charlie, could you possibly take yourself to the piano and contrive to play the chord of C major', which the frightened but rather proud boy proceeded to do, but so quietly as to call forth even more scornful remarks from above.

I have mentioned the slender beginnings from which this intimate friendship arose, a friendship which was by no means restricted to the older man giving and the younger one taking; they were truly mentors to each other, and both were keenly aware of the agonies and satisfactions involved in the creation of music, indeed, in the creation of any work of art. During the day the boy would be thinking of what the composer might have written for him to hear that evening; during the evening the composer would, more often than not, play through the few bars which he had produced so laboriously and submit these to the boy for his comments. Charles Markes gives a vivid description of how the few bars were tested out on him:

> I would stand just behind the piano stool listening intently; frequently I was so moved that I could say nothing, but when something struck me as being out of place, I would raise one of my hands slightly in a gesture which seemed to be forced out of me; then Ireland would growl: 'Well, what is wrong with that?' I don't know how I answered, but it would be something such as 'What you just played, that last bar, that last chord in that last bar, doesn't seem quite right to me' – or words to that effect.

Sometimes the composer had four or five different versions of one or two bars and these would all be propped up on the music rack and tried out over and over again for the approval of Charles's eager and discerning ear; the decision for the G flat in the third bar before the end of the song *Spring Sorrow* is a case in point, as also the sequence of chords at the climax of the *Rhapsody* for piano of March

1915. On one occasion, rather later in their friendship, Ireland played to his critical friend a song (one of two songs which remain, for some inexplicable reason, still unpublished) which Charles Markes then went through at the piano and remarked, apropos a point which occurred to him where it seemed the composer had missed the opportunity of allowing one 'voice' to imitate another, 'Why don't you do this?'; Ireland pounced on it, 'What's that you did?' he said and proceeded to make the alteration in the manuscript. 'Don't alter it because I say so', Charles Markes protested; 'I am not altering it because of what you say, but because it is better' came back swiftly from the composer.

On another occasion, an earlier one this time, Charles Markes went round to Gunter Grove and found Ireland labouring over some orchestral scoring; he looked up, 'Oh! this is hard work', he said, to which Charles Markes replied, 'Yes, there are always half-a-dozen ways of scoring anything.' 'Twenty; you mean twenty', replied the composer with that particular intonation which embraced pleasure, dislike and irony at the same time – as 'twaentee' it might best be expressed phonetically. Ireland did not care for the total involvement of orchestration and made it abundantly clear to Charles Markes that he felt no great compulsion to write for the orchestra, or for large bodies of performers.

As a young man, soon after he had commenced to earn a small wage, Charles Markes purchased for his friend a Japanese print; mingled with his gratified thanks Ireland could not help saying, as, indeed, any older man in those circumstances would have reacted: 'You shouldn't buy this sort of thing for me; does your mother know?' Ireland's collection of Japanese prints stemmed from this incident.

Many years later, when they had been to see an open-air sculpture exhibition, which included works by Henry Moore and Rodin, on learning Charles Markes's reaction that there was nothing in it, Ireland replied so very much more constructively: 'All you can say is you don't understand it, not that there is nothing in it.' Like many dedicated creative thinkers, he was a perceptive critic, even though impatient of the general trend in the contemporary music scene – the contemporary scene of the post-World War I years, that is – and, inevitably, more so of the post-World War II years when combinations of notes which he would not have dared to use were accepted without comment, and the amplification of dissonance had become almost a virtue. But it is interesting to record, from a letter to Charles Markes of October 13th 1954, his considered views on Benjamin Britten's opera *The Turn of the Screw*:

> I am no judge of opera as such, but this contains the most remarkable and original music I have ever heard from the pen of a British composer and it is on a purely diatonic and tonal basis. Also, what he has accomplished in sound by the use of only thirteen instruments was, to me, inexplicable, almost miraculous. This is not to say I liked the music, but it is gripping, vital and often terrifying.

It is difficult to believe that the 'daring' harmonies which Ireland himself had used really did upset some people, particularly in relation to his work as an organist and church musician. Charles Markes would often ask him to extemporize on the organ, 'to play some *real* music' – by which he meant Ireland's own particular blend of bittersweet harmonies, and he would occasionally do so, muttering meanwhile, 'The Archdeacon won't like this.' As with the piano playing in the studio, Ireland provided his pupil and assistant in the organ loft with a running commentary, often humorous and generally useful, such as 'The full swell on this organ is rather like frying a pan of sausages', or, apropos the *vox humana* stop, 'Bah!'; or 'Don't ever touch that tremulant; if you do that with the *vox humana* you get a quite impossible noise, it's like a bleating goat.'

Charles, having absorbed the Ireland technique and harmonic idiom, sometimes 'let go' on a Sunday evening in the closing voluntary; this, on one occasion, brought forth from Ireland: 'What were you playing last Sunday? Whatever it was, don't do it, the Archdeacon says it was too pagan.' 'It's your fault, sir', – he almost invariably called him 'sir' – was the reply, 'You taught me those harmonies', and this brought the riposte, 'Don't reharmonize the hymns.' On another Sunday evening, Ireland was waiting, unexpectedly, for Charles Markes to descend from the organ loft; with much foot-tapping he made the laconic observation, 'What do you think you were doing just now? Will you please remember that you have two feet and that the swell pedal is neither a pump nor a foot rest'; then he added, characteristically, that he had come to take him out for a meal at the 'Greyfriars' and that what he had been extemporizing he had been doing very well. Their restaurants were generally the 'Greyfriars', behind South Kensington Station, or 'The Queen's', Sloane Square, at which an extremely good meal could be obtained for two or three shillings, both, also, having the advantage of being within a few minutes' walk of the studio in Gunter Grove, to which they would then return.

Most unhappily this sustained friendship was to come to grief through the break, brought about by an incident in 1920. Charles Markes had been called up in 1918. When demobilized in 1919, he, like so many young men of that age, had to find a job of some sort and to earn a living in the prevailing conditions of uncertainty and unemployment. At a party one evening in 1920 a music hall artist, a light comedian named Alec Regan, wanted someone to accompany him on the piano in a song, and one can savour very well the aplomb with which Charles took the music and said, 'I'll play it for you'; through this incident, Regan found the very pianist he wanted, and so began Charles Markes's career in what he affectionately and familiarly called 'showbiz' – and with a commencing pay packet far in excess of anything he had ever dreamed of. Before long he was at the Palladium, or on tour with a male voice octet called The Rockets. On leaving a rehearsal at the Palladium one afternoon he met Ireland walking in the opposite direction, the latter, no doubt, having been to one of the music publishers in Great Marlborough Street. Ireland looked through him, did not acknowledge him, in fact 'cut' him, and Charles Markes jumped to the conclusion that his disapproval of his having joined 'showbiz' was so great that he was not prepared to recognize him. That was the end of the friendship for many, many years. There was, in fact, a blank, a void from 1920 to 1948.

Charles Markes became entirely involved as a pianist in this very different world of music and recounted to me a touching story of an audition he attended for The Co-Optimists. Here he witnessed a succession of excellent pianists who played ragtime with brilliant technique and complete assurance; when, in due course, his turn came, he sat down at the piano and found his mind a complete blank. What on earth could he play to show off his abilities after the brilliance of the pianists who preceded him? In a daze he sat at the keyboard, fingered the keys for a moment and then burst into 'The Island Spell' from Ireland's suite *Decorations* of 1912–13. The effect was startling, for two of the adjudicators seated in the front row at the Prince of Wales Theatre, the leading pianists Laddy Cliff and Melville Gideon, were beside him on the platform the moment he had finished, saying that he was accepted and 'Would fifteen pounds a week be alright?'; the latter asked for the name of the piece which had been played and whether he could also play ragtime; though Charles Markes did not feel too happy about his abilities in this he again managed to satisfy the judges; as it happened, the vocal highlight of that particular show at that time was *Sea Fever* sung by the tenor, William Senior.

In due course The Co-Optimists went on tour to Hull, Huddersfield, Warrington, Wigan, Hereford, Worcester and Plymouth, and Charles Markes recollected that in the north the West End humour was entirely unappreciated, but that as the show came southwards it began to pick up and was, eventually, highly successful. Shortly after that show Charles Markes left this country through his engagement as pianist for a ten week tour of Australia – Sydney, Melbourne, Perth, Brisbane and Adelaide, and then on to New Zealand. He kept himself to himself, considered very much a loner. But in the interval of a show one day when he was endeavouring to repair some pulled threads in a jumper, his isolation was broken into by a female voice which remarked in his ear, 'I think I could make a better job of that than you are doing, don't you? Let me have it.'

Thus he met Cathy, one of the dancers in the company; she was eighteen and he twenty-four, and in due course they married and returned to London at the end of 1929. Living once again in the Chelsea he and his old friend and teacher, John Ireland, knew so well, Charles was too proud to forget the assumed 'cutting' of him some nine years earlier, but he talked much about him to his sympathetic and understanding wife, and pointed him out to her when they passed in the street or saw him in a restaurant.

Charles and Cathy Markes continued to live in Chelsea and were, with war service breaks, there throughout the Second World War. When Ireland returned to his old home in Gunter Grove in 1948 it was by chance that a local tradesman told Charles Markes of this, and greetings were exchanged between the old friends through the tradesman as an intermediary. So, in due course, Charles, in a state of considerable trepidation, not knowing at all how he would be greeted after such a long separation, called upon Ireland and received a cordial reception with the strange words, as though they had never been apart: 'Oh! there you are Charlie, where have you been all this time? I was just going to advertise for you.'

It was a memorable and moving reunion, and they began to discuss thoughts and ideas as though the gap of so many years had never existed. Night after night they sat up until the early hours of the morning so that both were physically and mentally exhausted; at last Charles felt bound to expostulate that this really had to stop, for he found himself becoming so tired that he could not deal efficiently with his exacting musical duties. Nonetheless, he gladly agreed to help in the correction of the *Satyricon* Overture proofs, for which he was allocated a room with a small upright piano on the top floor, into which room Ireland popped his head every now and then to see how he was getting on. 'I don't know why I have never dedicated anything to you, Charlie', he remarked during this period, 'ought to have done so long ago'; when I questioned Charles Markes on this, he came back with the wry and touching reply that their friendship was too close and too intimate for him to feel any necessity for a dedication.

On another occasion, when they were talking over the long break in their friendship, Ireland asked him how this had come about, what it meant. 'You cut me dead', replied Charles Markes, 'in Argyll Street, near the Palladium, one day in 1920'. Ireland, alas, had no recollection whatever of this and replied quite simply that he was mistaken, that, if it had occurred, it was entirely a misunderstanding, and that he had probably been absorbed in something which had occurred at his publishers. 'But what a lot of time we have wasted, Charlie', he said. 'You could have been an inspiration to me.' And it was in one of these renewed talks that the subject of *Legend* cropped up – as, indeed, it did many times, for both of them knew it to be one of his most significant works. 'That's a work for you and me', Ireland said.

Much as Ireland had enjoyed grappling with the *Satyricon* Overture[7] – and Charles Markes recollected that in writing this in 1946 and in fulfilling the *Overlanders* film music commission (1946–7) Ireland kept himself going on Benzedrine and brandy – he once again made it clear that his strong preference was for smaller works for piano or voice and that he did not like large orchestral works and the scoring troubles that these brought with them, nor did he like commissions, though he was amused to have received one from Lady Wood which, with its obvious references to Ravel, was the piano piece *Columbine* of 1949, revised in 1951. Rather than commissions, Ireland liked to write as a result of stimuli personal to himself, either internally as a result of reading – the tales of Arthur Machen for instance – or externally from the observation of nature and of the Sussex and Guernsey scene in particular.

In 1948 Ireland tried to return to his beloved Guernsey, but it was a failure. He wrote:

> My dear Charlie,
> … everything here is a complete wash-out – and I hope to return on Friday, when I will get into touch with you and can tell you all about it. Meanwhile I understand you have the *Satyricon* proofs and I will be interested to know what they are like when we meet …

But people and, worse, traffic had returned to London with a vengeance, so that what had once been a reasonably quiet home in Gunter Grove became unbearable. Yet, by a strange coincidence, Ireland found at this time a house for sale which he had always coveted, 'Rock Mill' at Washington, Sussex. In a letter to Charles Markes of 25 October 1953 he wrote: 'It would be difficult to describe this place to you. It is wonderful, and absolutely unique and it is a miracle that I have been able to get it. The whole thing came about as if it had been pre-arranged and I seemed to have no choice in the matter.'

In the same letter he wrote of his despair at the noise in Gunter Grove and recalled wistfully the faded beauty and peace of the Chelsea which they used to

---

[7] For Markes's estimate of how many corrections he found, see p. 75.

know; he recorded too his sadness at the absence of his London friends, writing: 'You are one of the very few friends I shall miss – but even so, you have been too busy to come and see me, except very, very seldom, though you were only round the corner, so to speak. And, after all, I am only one-and-half hours' run from Chelsea.'

Although Charles Markes did go down to the Mill from time to time, he never felt that his old master and so-close friend was entirely happy there, as indeed had been the experience of so many town dwellers who have deserted the town for the country. And Ireland was, after all, seventy-four.

The Mill had much to offer, above all else, perhaps, magnificent views of Chanctonbury Ring, a sacred spot for Ireland throughout his life. But, irrespective of its situation and the peace and quiet which this brought with it, the Mill became a practicable proposition because Norah Kirby had abandoned all her own commitments in order to help in the move from London, to run the new home and large garden, and to minister to the aging composer in all his needs; and these needs, it must be remembered, also included the continuation of her secretarial work on his behalf. In the words of Charles Markes, 'She drove herself like a mad thing.'

Charles Markes's observations about the move to the Mill are probably correct – Ireland's letters to him were full of enthusiasm during the summer months, but were tinged with complaints and woes during the winter months. There can be little doubt that he was feeling his increasing years, also suffering from a sense of neglect, for at that time his music was receiving comparatively few performances. But when it was performed, and especially when the larger works were given, the audiences, including those of the younger generation, were enthusiastic; but times and tastes had changed, and indeed there was a lull in the demand for solo piano music and for the intimate type of song of Ireland's maturity.

> Let me advise you, my dear Charlie, not to prolong your life after the age of 70, unless you are able to enjoy a damned miserable rotten life. You will remember, as I often do, the wise words in the burial Service as regards man's allotted span which we often heard, quite unheedingly, in our career as servants to the Muse at St. Luke's Church, Chelsea.
>
> (From Pulborough, 5 September 1951)

And again from Pulborough on 18 August 1952: 'I hope you will be successful in the case of your landlord. As to football pools – I think, somehow, you, like myself, are not born to be lucky in any matters of chance – or, indeed, in anything else. And we have both chosen a rotten profession where success only comes to those who blow their own trumpet, *fff* continuously.'

One remembers with gratitude the tremendous ovation which was given to Ireland on the occasion of his seventy-fifth birthday Promenade concert,[8] when the BBC Symphony Orchestra played, under Sir Malcolm Sargent, the Piano Concerto with Eric Parkin as soloist, and the choral work *These Things Shall Be*. Yet in writing to Charles Markes on the 24th of that month of the pleasure he had experienced in receiving such a large number of birthday telegrams and letters, Ireland underlined his *Weltschmertz* and wrote: 'We old people must die, and

[8] 13 August 1954.

perhaps the most painful part about this will be the pain and trouble we inflict upon others in the process, if this is a gradual one. If sudden, it's better for all concerned.' And some two-and-a-half years later, in January 1957: 'The world of music is no longer any world of mine – my musical days are over – I have no longer any interest in it – can't believe I was once a composer!'

On 13 May 1956 Ireland again wrote, after a prolonged silence from Charles Markes: 'I am very anxious to see you, my very oldest friend, and to know how things are with you.' In fact, Charles Markes's wife had been ailing, whilst his mother was very ill and died towards the end of that year. In his heartfelt letter of 1 January 1957, Ireland expressed his sadness at the grief of his 'very oldest friend' and wrote: 'When my own mother died I was only just 14 (she being only 50) so I was hardly old enough to feel very deeply about it. But if a loved parent has survived until a son has reached your age, then the loss must be very painful.'

Although, owing to his musical commitments, his visits were infrequent and at long intervals, Charles Markes continued to undertake from time to time many small services for his old and now ailing friend, more particularly in setting to rights his beloved grandfather clocks and in other little repairs of a mechanical nature in the house, with which neither Ireland nor Norah Kirby could cope.

Occasionally, a music item cropped up; one reads, for instance, of the organ piece *Meditation on John Keble's Rogationtide Hymn* in a letter dated 4 June 1958:

> I was commissioned to write an organ piece for an American firm, which I have at last. This is only 4½ pages of MS. But I must have two copies made, for which I will pay the proper price. I have to send the piece off fairly soon and could trust no one but yourself to copy it. It is not complicated music, but somewhat musical.

A few days later he again asked for his help, for he was steadily losing his sight, writing:

> It is a slow piece and only five minutes in duration. I would have refused the commission, but was implored for something by the H. W. Gray Co. of New York and they are paying a reasonable sum for the job. However, I had the utmost difficulty in putting the notes in the right places, for I simply cannot see the lines and spaces on a musical stave at all clearly.

The work was done, and Ireland wrote on 30 July:

> My dear Charlie, many thanks for the beautiful copies of that piece. After adding a few dynamic marks, etc. I am posting one off to U.S.A. and as soon as I get paid I shall certainly settle your very modest account. Meanwhile, you have my gratitude, as always.

Once or twice in ensuing years Charles Markes went to the Mill and tended the now very sick man; the last time he saw him alive, as he left the bedroom and was on his way out, he heard his friend call, 'Norah, shall I ever see Charlie ...' The 'again' was unspoken. Some days later Norah Kirby telephoned Charles though, in her grief, she was unable to speak. He soon set off for the Mill, but first of all, as he noted on a copy of the *Chelsea Parish News* which he found in the church: 'Tuesday June 12th 1962. John Ireland died today – I went to St. Luke's for a little while.'

At the Mill Charles, who had done so much so willingly for his master and colleague in his lifetime, did many things for his dear friend in death. There he met the Rev. Kenneth Thompson who acceded to his request that he might be left on his own for a little while with the dead man, from whom he took a lock of hair. The Reverend Thompson, himself a very old friend and from time to time a spiritual adviser of the composer, seemed suddenly to become aware, Charles told me, that there had existed between the two a much deeper relationship and bond than anyone had previously realized; 'He knew', as Charles said.

Charles Markes had just that degree of self-effacement, coupled with a practical and technical knowledge of the subject, which a true mentor needs when associating with a creative genius who is, perhaps, not so decisive or spontaneous in his creativity as a general and less specialized observer might think. Charles has been, virtually, the only person whom I have met – in my search to present a true picture of the musician and of the man – able to provide me with closely experienced first-hand observations from as early as 1908 -1909. Charles Markes really knew Ireland in all his moods throughout what might reasonably be called the great creative period of the piano music, songs and church music up to 1920, the period during which the means and the technique were rationalized in order to produce the music which followed, from 1920 to 1946, the year of the last considerable work, the *Satyricon* Overture. Charles Markes knew him so well that he was one of the very few who were truly aware of his fundamental loneliness and unhappiness. 'John Ireland's disposition', he said, 'is tellingly expressed in the opening words of his song to the poem by Arthur Symons, *The Rat*: "Pain gnaws at my heart like a rat that gnaws at a timber".'

At the back of his mind Ireland had the feeling that there was a non-understanding of his music, despite the world's applause for such works as the Piano Concerto, the cantata *These Things Shall Be*, and the *London Overture*, and a non-recognition of him as a significant composer. He felt deeply that people did not appreciate him as he should have been appreciated. 'People don't like my music', he remarked to Charles on many occasions. He was acutely aware of things himself, and the fact that other people could not understand what he had done and was striving to achieve gave him a feeling of frustration. He wanted to share experiences, as in the poem in *Earth's Call*: 'Come with me and let us lie on the grass'. This mood pushed aside, he would become the dear companion again, the ironic quizzical mentor who could share the dislike of the pupil, 'Charlie', for some of the Beethoven piano sonatas, of the dreaded variation form in them in particular, with 'You and I are not musicians, really, Charlie; we don't like enough music.'

Charles Markes's work for his master and friend continued in his enthusiastic willingness to give of his very self in the editing of some of the earlier scores, such as in his meticulous reconstruction of the two early string quartets, and of *Tritons*, for instance; in fact in any way which would help further music of his former so deeply venerated friend and master. In the light of these observations one does, in fact, rather wonder whether Charles Markes himself truly realized how much he had achieved in helping John Ireland along the creative path which he pursued with relentless searching for the 'right' harmony, for it seems that such were from time to time shown by the pupil to the master.

CHAPTER 13

The John Ireland Charitable Trust

Bruce Phillips

TOWARDS the end of the 1950s two enthusiasts for Ireland's music, Lawrence Norcross and John Steele, formed a John Ireland Society, the object of which was to bring together people interested in attending live performances of what had become rarely heard works.[1] The concerts took place in the drawing room of the Arts Council, then in St James's Square, London and there was at least one tour of venues outside London. The President of the Society was Harold Rutland. One of the great achievements of the Society was the first public performance, on 25 March 1960, of the Sextet for string quartet, clarinet and French horn, one of Ireland's student works from 1898. Ireland was in the audience.[2] That work has now become firmly established in the repertoire.

The Society relied on members' subscriptions and financial support from Mrs Kirby. It seems to have been disbanded some time in the late 1960s. In the 1970s, after her move from Rock Mill to 106 High Street, Steyning, Mrs Kirby set up the John Ireland Charitable Trust with the assistance and advice of Anthony Rubinstein of the law firm Rubinstein, Callingham. The Trustees were Norah Kirby, Eric Parkin, the Revd Kenneth Thompson, George Dannatt, and Peter Taylor. Geoffrey Bush was music adviser. Peter Taylor's wife Margaret was nominated as Curator of the John Ireland House in Steyning, which Mrs Kirby had intended to be kept on after her death as a memorial to John Ireland. Later Trustees were Michael Taylor, Bruce Phillips, Clive Marks, Erwin Mulholland and Fiona Richards. Under the terms of the Trust deed Mrs Kirby assigned three-fifths of all Ireland's royalties to the Trust to support the aims of the Trust and she retained two-fifths for her own needs. Her own estate, including her house in Steyning, was left to Mr and Mrs Taylor for their lifetimes, with the John Ireland Trust as residual legatees.

Not long after the Trust was founded came the hundredth anniversary of Ireland's birth. In August 1979 the Trust mounted an unforgettable week of concerts and a competition in the Wigmore Hall in London. The administrator was the late Gerald Macdonald. The competition was such a success that the Trustees decided to instigate annual John Ireland Competitions at the leading music conservatoires in the United Kingdom, and these continue today. Thus a whole generation of pianists, singers and string players has gained some knowledge of Ireland's music and in many cases gone on to perform his works in public concerts and recordings.

In recent years the Trust has supported Ireland competitions at the University of South Florida at Tampa, where the late Robert Helps, composer, pianist

---

[1] The genesis of the Society is chronicled by John Longmire in his book *John Ireland: Portrait of a Friend*, pp. 152–60.

[2] See Lewis Foreman's reminiscences of the early concerts promoted by the Society, p. xxiv.

Fig. 16 Harold Rutland. Sketch by Juliet Pannett.

and enthusiast for British music, began a tradition of studying and performing Ireland's works and where chamber music competitions are held annually under the patronage of Joan and Daniel Rutenberg.

Norah Kirby died aged eighty-four on 24 November 1982 in an old people's home in Westgate, Kent. She had been in poor health for some time and needed more medical care than could be provided at the home administered by the Musicians Benevolent Fund where she normally spent her summer holidays. Shortly after her death it was revealed that a few days previously she had signed a new will leaving her personal estate to the owners of the Westgate old people's home. At the same time she had authorised them to visit her house in Steyning and transport some of her furniture and belongings to Westgate.

The circumstances in which the final will had been prepared and certain financial transactions made gave rise to very considerable disquiet on the part of the Trustees both of the John Ireland Charitable Trust and of Mrs Kirby's personal estate. Arrangements for her funeral in Margate were immediately halted and a lengthy investigation by the Kent Police led to a court case heard at Maidstone Crown Court in February 1985, at which verdicts of not guilty were returned on all the principal charges.

The Trustees of both trusts involved were thus faced with the prospect of being unable to carry out what they were certain had been Mrs Kirby's intentions until the last few days of her life. After much consultation it was decided to instruct Rubinstein, Callingham to offer the defendant's solicitors a financial inducement to waive any claims arising from the final will. The offer was accepted. Norah's body was finally released from the mortuary for burial shortly afterwards and she was buried in accordance with her frequently expressed wish, in the churchyard at Shipley in Sussex in a plot adjoining John Ireland.

Over the next twenty years the Charitable Trust continued to support a wide range of activities – competitions, recordings, purchase of letters and manuscripts, publications – and preservation of memorabilia and portraits. The house in Steyning was sold – it became a bookshop – and the Trust's office moved to London. Geoffrey Bush served many years as music adviser, after his death followed by Alan Rowlands. Following the sad deaths of the Taylors and of their son Michael, Bruce Phillips was appointed to administer the Trust from his home in Oxford. Most of John Ireland's possessions survive, notably his library and some articles of furniture.[3] All surviving manuscripts and some archival material are in the Music Division of the British Library along with letters and some sound recordings.[4]

The Trust's website is: http://www.musicweb-international.com/ireland/trust.htm. The Trust welcomes enquiries and applications for funding, or information concerning the location of undocumented collections of Ireland letters, manuscripts and other memorabilia. Requests should be sent to the Director of the Trust: brucelphillips@googlemail.com

---

[3] Some key items of Ireland memorabilia were stolen from Mrs Kirby's house in Steyning. These include the bust of Bobby Glassby by his sculptor father which previously had pride of place at Rock Mill (see plate 70) and the little hand-driven organ which Ireland is seen playing in another photograph (see overleaf). The editor and the Ireland Trust would welcome any information from readers as to their present location.

[4] A wide conspectus of the Trust's archive recordings of John Ireland playing the piano may be heard on Dutton CDBP 9799.

Fig. 17 Ireland playing the little hand-driven organ which was subsequently stolen

PART II

The Music of John Ireland

CHAPTER 14

John Ireland: Some Musical Fingerprints

Alan Rowlands

Ireland's Pentatonic Scale

There is a particular five-note grouping that occurs again and again in Ireland's music which has always intrigued me. It is something half-way between a scale and an arpeggio and provides a characteristically Ireland sound. I have not found this form of the pentatonic scale in the work of any other composer, including Debussy and Ravel, and have often wondered how Ireland hit on it. Consider the following examples, all written around 1913, the time when Ireland came to his full creative maturity and established his own individual tone of voice:

Ex. 1 Ireland, 'The Island Spell' (*Decorations*)

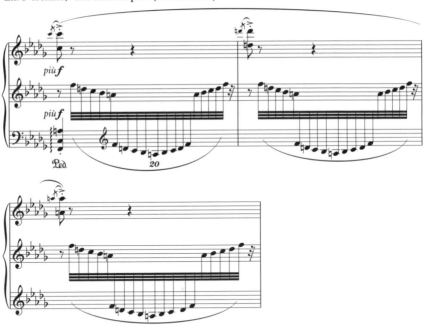

Ex. 2 Ireland, Clarinet Trio

Ex. 3 Ireland, 'Youth's Spring-Tribute' (*Marigold*)

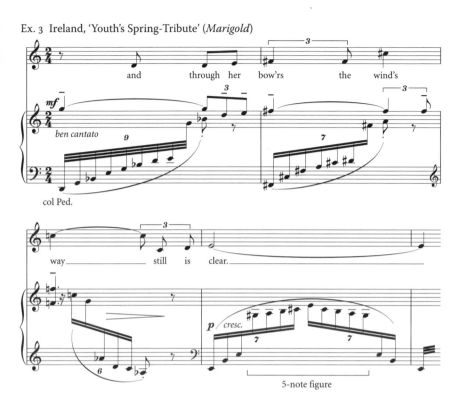

Do you notice something unusual about this grouping? After all, the more common version of the pentatonic scale – that obtained by playing on the black notes of the piano – consists of the first, second, third, fifth and sixth notes of the major diatonic scale, and it can be used melodically (as in much Scottish folk-music) or harmonically, as in these swirls from Ireland's own music:

Ex. 4 Ireland, *Earth's Call*

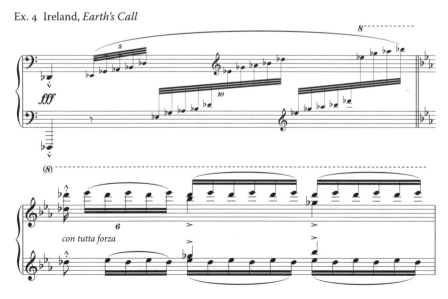

Ex. 5 Ireland, 'Song of the Springtides' (*Sarnia*)

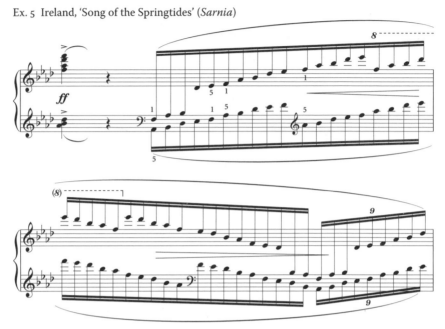

So used, the conventional pentatonic scale is euphonious, even voluptuous, forming a well-recognised added-note harmony. But Ireland's more personal grouping is different. It contains both the third and the fourth of the major scale, thereby embodying a slight semitonal dissonance. Why does this suit Ireland's purpose so well? – one would normally expect the fourth to resolve upon the third, as in a 4–3 suspension. But somehow it works and I sometimes feel his use of this scale suggests a moment of illumination or drawing aside of a veil, as in this extract from the second of the Five Hardy Songs:

Ex. 6 Ireland, 'In my Sage Moments' (*Five Hardy Songs*)

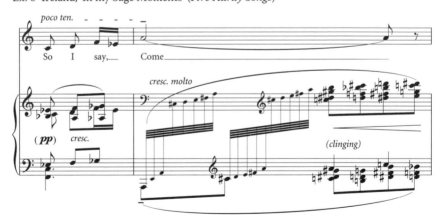

or even more at the quietly ecstatic climax of *The Forgotten Rite* (study score p. 65), perhaps a final vision of the god Pan:

Ex. 7 Ireland, *The Forgotten Rite*

It was only after rehearsing this work in Ireland's piano duet version for the recent (2010) Albion recording that I realised how insistently it is pervaded by this five-note figure. Revealingly, it is first heard on flute as an obvious Pan-pipe motif in bar 13, echoed augmented on horn, then most intensely on trumpets at the first visionary climax (third bar after letter B). In one place it even appears in canon between oboe and bass:

Ex. 8 Ireland, *The Forgotten Rite*

It is interesting that in the duet arrangement the B♮s in the last example do not occur – did Ireland overlook this, or change his mind, thus bringing the figure into exact conformity with the other instances?

Quite magical are the final appearances of the motif on harp and celesta as the vision fades – the harp even sustains the dissonant fourth (though the strings and brass do not), while the celesta slowly picks out the same notes two octaves above:

Ex. 9 Ireland, *The Forgotten Rite*

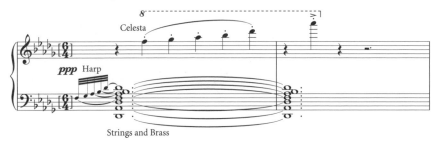

It is worth pointing out that in Ex. 1 above it is important that the demisemiquaver rest at the end of each bar should not sound like a quaver rest – some pianists play the last note of the swirling figure as though it were on the fourth quaver of the bar. I recollect Ireland saying that he only put that rest in so that the player might have a little time before placing the broken octave melody note on the first beat of the next bar.

The Fifth and the Third

One of Ireland's loveliest and most characteristic inspirations is the song *The Adoration*. Here is the opening:

Ex. 10 Ireland, *The Adoration*

This expressive gesture is entirely structured from fifths and thirds – the open fifth and the third contained within it (how effective is the harmony on the third crotchet created by the holding of the top Eb!). Once noticed, this fifth-and-third motif crops up all over the place in Ireland's music, sometimes expressively, as in the Piano Concerto:

Ex. 11 Ireland, Piano Concerto – slow movement

– or more often jovially, or even forcefully:

Ex. 12 Ireland, *Bergomask*

Ex. 13 Ireland, Piano Sonata – first movement

A more vibrant example is the opening of the third piece of *Decorations*:

Ex. 14 Ireland, 'The Scarlet Ceremonies' (*Decorations*)

Does this suggest a musical ancestry? I am irresistibly reminded of the opening of Stravinsky's *Petrouchka*:

Ex. 15 Igor Stravinsky, *Petrouchka*

– and further back, in slower tempo, we have another model in Debussy's *Nuages*:

Ex. 16 Claude Debussy, 'Nuages' (*Nocturnes*)

I feel sure these influences played their part in the formation of the mature style Ireland eventually achieved. England in the first decade of the twentieth century must have been a wonderful place for a budding composer to be alive – you had Elgar and Strauss at the height of their powers, the new works of Debussy and Ravel coming across the channel in successive waves, then from 1911 the visits of the Diaghilev ballet and the impact of Stravinsky. The neo-Brahmsian that Ireland was around 1900 must have revelled in these new sounds. I wonder what Stanford (who once castigated one of Ireland's early works as 'all Brahms and water, me bhoy – and more water than Brahms') made of the direction his pupil eventually took?

It could also be mentioned that the fifth and the third are sometimes sounded together as a chord, giving an ambiguous but expressive substitute for the more expected tonic-in-root-position. This can be seen in the second bars of both Exx. 19 and 20 in my interview (pp. 34 and 35).

I give one more example of the fifth-and-third figure, this time from the Sonatina:

Ex. 17 Ireland, Sonatina – first movement

– chosen because the right hand displays another characteristic Ireland finger-print, leading us directly to a consideration of …

The Four-Note Descending Figure

This consists of four notes descending scale-wise from the tonic, with either sharpened or flattened seventh (both occur in the last example). In the modal form it is often in yearning mood, as in *Month's Mind*:

Ex. 18 Ireland, *Month's Mind*

Very similar examples can again be found in Exx. 19 and 20 of Chapter 3.

In jollier style, though still modal, it can be found in both the first and last movements of the Piano Concerto:

Ex. 19 Ireland, Piano Concerto – first movement

Ex. 20 Ireland, Piano Concerto – last movement

In thoroughly major mode, it is used as a perky counterpoint to the 'Piccadilly' theme of *A London Overture* in two different ways:

Ex. 21 Ireland, *A London Overture*

(a)

(b)

This figure is often used (in slower tempo) as a bass to Ireland's melodies, but to demonstrate that I must digress a little to show a melodic fingerprint that I believe can be derived from the opening of *The Forgotten Rite*, or the similar opening of the third movement of the Piano Sonata:

Ex. 22 (a) Ireland, *The Forgotten Rite*; (b) Ireland, Piano Sonata

(a)   (b)

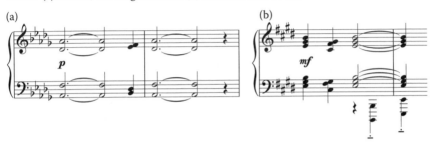

How characteristic is that second chord! But take the melody – a falling and rising third – transpose to C major (for illustrative purposes), introduce a passing-note –

Ex. 23

– and you have a melodic germ-motif that, combined in various rhythms with the four descending bass-notes, gives the opening of many of Ireland's compositions:

Ex. 24

Ex. 25

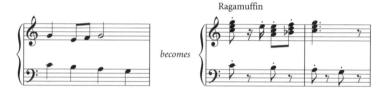

Ex. 26

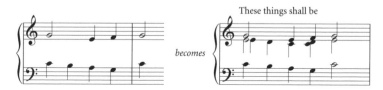

The Passion Motif

We come now to the most important of Ireland's *idées fixes*, and here I use Fiona Richards's aptly coined term, though when I first encountered this gesture my then piano teacher, Angus Morrison, described it as 'an outburst of intense feeling'. This was when I was practising *On a Birthday Morning*, where it occurs as follows, forming an unmistakably climactic moment:

Ex. 27 Ireland, *On a Birthday Morning*

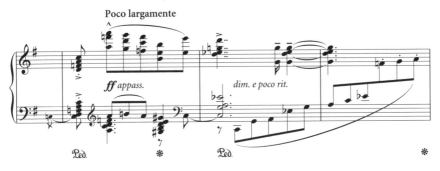

This piece is headed by the words 'Pro amicitia' (for friendship) and followed by the date 'February 22, 1922', evidently someone's birthday, though there is no further indication of the recipient of these friendly feelings. It turns out that it is one of a series of seven works written for this person, and indicated either by an explicit heading at the beginning ('To A.G.M.' or 'To Arthur') or the date 'February 22' at the end. It was of course Arthur Miller, originally one of Ireland's choristers at St Luke's, Chelsea, with whom he developed an ongoing relationship, obviously an intensely important part of his life. The music associated with Arthur is sometimes happily extrovert, as in the above case (also in *Bergomask*, 1925), sometimes idyllically rapturous (*February's Child*, 1929), sometimes sturdily idealistic (the song *Love and Friendship*, 1926), but sometimes touched with a disturbing melancholy (Prelude in E♭, 1924). In the last-mentioned case there are rather tormented references to the opening of *On a Birthday Morning*, but the sense of agonised despair reaches its apogee (or should I say nadir?) in the nevertheless very beautiful song-cycle *We'll to the Woods No More* (1927) with its searingly expressive final piano solo 'Spring Will Not Wait'. In the published version it is simply dedicated 'To Arthur', but in the manuscript this is followed by 'in memory of the darkest days', with some further obliterated words. I was told that in his later years Ireland found this work almost too painful to listen to.

Concerning *February's Child*, I remember Norah Kirby saying several times that although it was dedicated to Arthur Miller (for what would have been his twenty-fourth birthday) it was really about Bobby Glassby, the model for the sculpted boy's head that was always on Ireland's piano, but I do not know (as so often with Norah's pronouncements) of any confirmatory evidence for this.

Perhaps the most touching of the pieces dedicated to Arthur Miller is the song *When I am Dead, My Dearest* (1925). It is writing of the utmost simplicity yet the utmost tenderness, and I remember when we were recording all the Ireland songs how Benjamin Luxon was drawn to this more than any of the others and continually wanted to return to it and sing it again.

One of the unpublished songs that Ireland showed me on some of my later visits to Rock Mill was *If We Must Part*. I did not notice at that time that it bears the words 'for July 25, 1929' at the end, and that the opening represents what one may call a truncated version of the passion motif (retaining the characteristic falling fifth in a dotted rhythm which can be seen in Ex. 27). I now feel, following Fiona Richards, that this song is probably connected in some way with Arthur Miller, though there is no direct evidence. It may be pertinent to mention that Arthur made the first of his two marriages in 1927.

On a Birthday Morning does not represent the first of the seven full appearances of this 'passion motif' in Ireland's works, though it is the only one specifically connected with Arthur Miller. Its first manifestation is in the song *The Trellis* (January, 1920), closely followed by another in *My True Love hath my Heart* (February, 1920). *The Trellis* is considered by Ireland lovers as perhaps his most rapturously beautiful song and repays attention for its autobiographical connotations as well as its outstanding musical quality. The passion motif here occurs as a piano solo just before the idyllic central section:

Ex. 28 Ireland, *The Trellis*

One can see why Ireland was so drawn to this poem of Aldous Huxley when it appeared two years earlier. It touched a psychological nerve and I think it is worth reproducing the words in full:

> Thick-flowered is the trellis
>> That hides our joys
> From prying eyes of malice
>> And all annoys,
>> And we lie rosily bowered.   [passion motif here]

> Through the long afternoons
>> And evenings endlessly
> Drawn out, when summer swoons
>> In perfume windlessly,
>> Sounds our light laughter,

> With whispered words between
>> And silent kisses.
> None but the flowers have seen
>> Our white caresses –
>> Flowers and the bright-eyed birds.

Given the unconventional and necessarily private nature of Ireland's sexuality, it needs no imagination to see why these words must have appealed, the 'trellis' representing the shielding of an idyllic and perhaps forbidden love from the public gaze, and indeed his impassioned setting of them meant so much to him that he quoted from it twice, first in the Cello Sonata (1923) and then in the song *The One*

Hope (1926). The latter, after touching on the subject of 'vain desire' and 'vain regret', has a tender reminiscence of the opening of *The Trellis* leading straight to a despairing but *dolcissimo* rendering of the passion motif. In the Cello Sonata the quotation occurs *tranquillo* just after the first main climax in the first movement; it is also marked by Ireland *secreto* (he should really have written *segreto*), thus helpfully highlighting what for him must have been a very intimate and poignant recollection. All the same, I doubt whether many cellists playing this realise that they are 'secretly' quoting a phrase from a song to which the words are, 'None but the flowers have seen our white caresses'.

The next occurrence of the passion motif is in the song mentioned above, of which the first line is 'My true love hath my heart and I have his'. Ireland certainly considered this a man's song and disliked it sung by a woman. Although it now seems that in Sir Philip Sydney's original *Countess of Pembroke's Arcadia* it is sung by a woman to a man (and it may be that Ireland did not know this, the poem usually appearing in anthology) I remember him telling me something to the effect that it represented the kind of courtly, chivalrous or comradely love that might have been acceptable between men in the Elizabethan era. He certainly would not have allowed any homoerotic implication to arise in the presence of a friend as young and recent as myself – but the music speaks differently. The song opens with the most emphatic of all the statements of the passion motif and develops into one of the most ardent love-songs imaginable, with soaring phrases for the tenor and opulently chromatic piano chords, which are a joy to play (though needing a big hand):

Ex. 29 Ireland, *My True Love Hath my Heart*

I will return to a possible genesis of this figure later. We next find the passion motif in the last song of the Housman cycle *The Land of Lost Content* (1920–21). This is its most serenely happy version and comes in fact in a glowing piano phrase overlapping the words, 'You hearken to the lover's say/And happy is the lover'. Of all Housman's poems, this one – 'You smile upon your friend today' – seems to come closest to a sense of sexual fulfilment, even though it ends with the familiar Housman obsession with death – 'I shall have lived a little while/Before I die for ever'. Ireland's setting matches it perfectly, and to me that central piano phrase (Ex. 30) is one of the most memorable moments in his music. *'And happy is the lover'* – one wonders whether either Ireland or Housman, similar in so many way psychologically and artistically, ever experienced such happiness in their actual lives. The evidence seems to point the other way, but look what riches they have left us ... Strange that the frustrations and fantasies of the human soul could result in such memorable art. After all, even Wagner said that he wrote *Tristan und Isolde* because he had *not* experienced the fullest joys of love.

Ex. 30 Ireland, *The Land of Lost Content* – Epilogue

The next occurrence of the motif is in the first movement of the Piano Concerto, in the orchestral peroration connecting the end of the exposition to the development, four bars before fig. 14. Here it is neither highlighted nor climactic but embedded in a longer passage as follows:

Ex. 31 Ireland, Piano Concerto

Perhaps this more incidental (or accidental?) version is the more appropriate here, as it is the only one to have any connection with a woman – Helen Perkin, who inspired the concerto and with whom he had an intensely affectionate, though almost certainly platonic, relationship.

The final full occurrence of the passion motif comes thirteen years later in the Fantasy Sonata for clarinet and piano (1943). In my view this is Ireland's most perfectly realised chamber work. It was largely inspired by the beautiful clarinet playing of Frederick Thurston (as was the soaring melody of the middle section of *Satyricon* and the idiosyncratic clarinet music accompanying the breaking in of the 'brumbies' in *The Overlanders*). But there are other influences at work, particularly Ireland's thoughts and feelings in relation to the boy Giton in Petronius's *Satyricon*. As he wrote to one friend, with whom he corresponded on these intimate matters, 'He that hath ears to hear, let him hear'. The work is pervaded by an almost new kind of fresh, mellifluous lyricism, with outbursts of impassioned feeling –

Ex. 32 Ireland, *Fantasy Sonata*

– though it might also be considered a summation of everything Ireland had to say. The only factor missing is the tormented chromaticism of some of the anguished works of the 1920s, making this one of the happiest and most rounded and satisfying of all Ireland's works, even the final demonic section having a touch of humour. It will be noticed that this version of the passion motif ends with the emotionally charged falling fifth in dotted rhythm which has not been heard in this context since *On a Birthday Morning* and *If We Must Part*.

I sometimes toy with the idea that the form of the passion motif came about through the influence of Richard Strauss on Ireland. He often talked about Strauss, and once towards the end of his life, when he was saying very little, I remember him beginning a sentence quite emphatically with 'Strauss' – and then tailing off into nothingness. He had been deeply impressed by *Salome* and *Elektra*, and had gone through *Ein Heldenleben*, using score and records, with the young Benjamin Britten. Bruce Phillips has his score of this and at the end Ireland has written, '*Ichabod*' – the glory has departed.

In the part of *Salome* where the young princess begins to declare her amorous feelings for John the Baptist (to the horror of the young Captain) and to praise the whiteness of his body, we find this figure –

Ex. 33 Richard Strauss, *Salome*

– which is used extensively in the later parts of the opera, particularly the gruesome ending. Here we have the three step-wise descending notes in octaves, beginning on the off-beat, which characterise Ireland's passion motif, but here associated with a different kind of forbidden love. A few bars later, there is that typically Straussian gesture of a 6/4 chord approached by auxiliary notes below and above the main note –

Ex. 34 Richard Strauss, *Salome*   [harmonic scheme]

– which I have also applied to a dominant ninth in the key of Ex. 33. Combine the two, and you have something remarkably like the opening of *My True Love Hath my Heart*:

Ex. 35   Ireland, *My True Love Hath my Heart*

I would have ended this article here, but for the late discovery (through another person) that there is yet another reference to the passion motif in Ireland's œuvre. In 1958 the composer was persuaded to accept a commission from a New York firm for an organ piece. In spite of failing eyesight, but with the aid of a powerful magnifying-glass and the assistance of Charles Markes, he was enabled to write down *Meditation on John Keble's Rogationtide Hymn*. It is a retrospective and elegiac piece with several allusions to earlier works, and the central section climaxes with the phrase:

Ex. 36 Ireland, *Meditation on John Keble's Rogationtide Hymn*

Here the rhythmic impulse is different, but the melodic outline is unmistakable, and it is touching to find this reference to Ireland's deepest feelings in this, the last work he ever penned.

CHAPTER 15

John Ireland and the Piano

Eric Parkin

How well I remember first meeting John Ireland. I had written (at the suggestion of Geoffrey Bush – to whom I shall always be grateful) to ask if he would
hear me play *Sarnia*. Realising that he must get many similar requests, I had not
expected to hear anything more. However, I soon received a neatly typed letter
suggesting that I telephone to arrange a time. Standing on the step of 14 Gunter
Grove, Chelsea, my nervousness not helped by a bitterly cold January evening, I
had no idea that this visit would prove a turning point in my career. Looking back
now, I can't help feeling that, without Ireland's generous help and encouragement I
would have remained virtually unknown.

On this first evening I was immediately struck by his friendliness. He had a
sort of old-world charm about him which was tempered with a certain reticence.
I remember thinking at the time that he might be difficult to please. Later I found
this was not so, for he had a way of bringing out the best in my playing by his
criticisms and suggestions. We talked for some minutes and then I played. *Sarnia*
seemed to go quite well and I thought he was encouraging in his remarks. When I
was leaving, he wondered if there were 'any more things' I would like him to hear.

There certainly were! When I saw him again some months later he greeted me
warmly: 'You haven't been to see me for some time!' From then onwards we met
frequently, and during the next few years I had the great privilege of studying the
bulk of his piano music with him. The sessions usually lasted from three to four
hours and were invariably exhausting. On the train journeys home my head was
full of the music, so much so that I was oblivious of everything else. I have so often
wished I had made notes of our conversations, but I am left with only memories.
However, I will try to pass on some of the points he made which helped me to a
deeper understanding and appreciation of his sensitive music.

For a man who spent many years as organist and choirmaster (he got his
FRCO when he was only eighteen), a preoccupation with the piano might seem
surprising. But he was an excellent pianist, and evidently felt that what he had to
say could often be most perfectly expressed on the keyboard. Certainly very few
of his most representative works are without the piano. To my mind, few have
written with more affectionate understanding of the instrument, and certainly no
other Englishman has shown such mastery so consistently.

I remember his telling me how excited he had been when Debussy's First
Book of Preludes appeared in 1910. Nothing like them had been heard before. A
whole new world was opened up by the many possibilities of opposing sonorities,
controlled dissonance, and subtle use of the pedals. Up to this time Ireland had
not published any solo piano music, though he had either rejected or destroyed
a good deal that did not satisfy him. Debussy acted as a catalyst, and the result
was *Decorations* ('The Island Spell', 'Moon-glade', 'The Scarlet Ceremonies',
1912–13).

Far from being mere imitation, the first piece was immediately recognised as an outstanding piece of impressionism and has remained an Ireland best-seller. In it he revealed for the first time how much he could be inspired by particular locations, in this case Jersey. The final page of 'The Island Spell' gave him a lot of trouble. Not until a year later, in the same spot and at a similar time of day was the solution found. By the way, the metronome mark is far too fast. You will be about right if you play it at crotchet = 60, taking care to count in strict time the quaver rests and demisemiquaver swirls which follow on the third page. 'Moon-glade' is also a splendid piece, which makes use of bitonality – rare in Ireland. I have always found 'The Scarlet Ceremonies' a brute to play, but I enjoy its general brilliance. The ending is especially exciting. Underneath the title Ireland added a quotation from *The House of Souls* by Arthur Machen, more of whom later. Though a forceful musical personality with definite views about how (and how not) his music should sound, John Ireland was a man who did not wear his heart on his sleeve. He was shrewd enough to know his own worth without ever courting the publicity that undoubtedly one or two of his colleagues did. He would rarely talk about himself, but I did learn that he had sometimes suffered severe bouts of depression. During one of these, when spending Christmas alone in London, he found solace in the writing of *The Holy Boy*. This lovely carol, with its simple yet moving theme (notice the characteristic drop of a fifth which I have marked × in Ex. 1) was to become the third of four Preludes (1913–15). Repetition might so easily have been wearisome here without the carefully judged key changes. I am especially fond of the first prelude, 'The Undertone', which is built on this two-bar ostinato (see Ex. 2). The remaining two preludes, 'Obsession' and 'Fire of Spring', are very typical. They have been called Schumannesque, though Ireland would hardly have been flattered, for he was not on the whole enthusiastic about Schumann's piano music.

Ex. 1 Ireland, *The Holy Boy*

Andante tranquillo

Ex. 2 Ireland, *The Undertone*

Poco sostenuto

At about this time the first of many songs began to appear, including *Sea Fever* (1913) and *Marigold* ('Youth's Spring-tribute' – 'Penumbra' – 'Spleen', 1913). Ireland came from a literary background (both parents were writers) and his settings reflect this. I shall refer to the later song cycles in another article, for there is marvellous music among them. They should be heard more often, not least for their accompaniments, which often match the quality of Ireland's best piano solos.

Fortunately they are recorded as a boxed set by Benjamin Luxon, John Mitchinson and Alfreda Hodgson with Alan Rowlands.

I have space here only to mention the Rhapsody, a virile piece on the scale of a Chopin Ballade. For publication in 1915 Ireland revised an earlier manuscript which shows a strong Brahms influence. At the end of my copy he pencilled '8m 20s'! no doubt to make sure that I would not take it faster.

The Violin and Piano Sonata no. 1 in D minor had deservedly won a Cobbett First Prize in 1909, so it was to be expected that Ireland would produce more chamber music, His strong lyricism found an ideal outlet in this intimate medium. The masterpiece of these years is undoubtedly the Second Violin and Piano Sonata in A Minor (1915–17). There is an inevitability about this work that Ireland may later have equalled but certainly never surpassed – no wonder the first edition was sold out before it was even printed. There are so many wonderful moments, from the *Deciso* opening bars of the first movement:

Ex. 3 Ireland, Violin Sonata no. 2 – first movement

to the exuberance of this tune in the finale:

Ex. 4 Ireland, Violin Sonata no. 2 – finale

It is all the work of a fine craftsman and will richly repay the closest study.

John Ireland loved London, where he lived for much of the time until traffic noise drove him out in 1953. He captured some of its moods in *London Pieces* ('Chelsea Reach', 'Ragamuffin', 'Soho Forenoons', 1917–21). 'Chelsea Reach', a richly sonorous barcarolle, is the finest of the set. Its thick chord clusters spread themselves over the whole keyboard and need very careful pedalling. He used to shout at me if I hurried the climaxes, missed out any notes or played wrong ones. The other two pieces are attractive in a more percussive vein. 'Ragamuffin' portrays a whistling errand boy, whilst 'Soho Forenoons' gives us a brief glimpse of street musicians long since past.

Ireland's achievements in the 1920s were considerable, and include a splendid collection of short piano pieces. One of these, *February's Child* (1929), was the first piece of his that I learnt. It is a fine example of a heart-easing lyricism which often sounds like an improvisation but, on closer inspection, is seen to be carefully put together. Its very touching coda, marked 'quasi tranquillo' uses added sixth chords, the flattened seventh and pianistic figuration in typical Ireland fashion. (Play the grace notes, whether singly or in groups, *on* the beat with the left-hand chords always: he frequently pencilled these on my copy.) Notice the curve of the melody from which everything grows. He was fond of this shape, as you can see from the two further instances of it that I have added (see Exx. 5–7).

Ex. 5 Ireland, *February's Child*

Ex. 6 Ireland, *Merry Andrew*

Ex. 7 Ireland, *The Darkened Valley*

The Darkened Valley began life in A♭ minor, but Ireland's publisher could not face all those flats, so it came out in the not so rich key of G minor. The more impressionistic *Amberley Wild Brooks* of the same year, with its captivating modulations, and the superb *April* (1925) are marvellous examples of his keyboard writing at this time. More dance-like and down-to-earth are *On a Birthday Morning* (1922) and *Bergomask* (1925) – the companion piece to *April* which is thematically related. *Equinox* (1922) stands out as the most brilliant: its relentless right-hand figure and restless left-hand arpeggios make it a devil to play:

Ex. 8 Ireland, *Equinox*

I once asked Ireland about the origins of his titles, remarking on how attractive they were. He said they were usually just an indication of mood and feeling, and not intended to be descriptive or programmatic. Beyond this he would not be drawn, though he was obviously much moved by natural scenes.

In an interesting interview for the Canadian Broadcasting Corporation with Murray Schafer[1] John Ireland declared that he knew nothing about folk-song, and that all his tunes were his own! In spite of this I have often wondered if there had been even an unconscious influence, especially in the songs – settings of Housman and Hardy, for example. To enhance the natural stress of the words he frequently changes the time signature, so breaking down the shackles of the bar line in a way that suggests folk-song treatment. I certainly detect a flavour in this cadence:

Ex. 9 Ireland, 'In Boyhood' (*We'll to the Woods No More*)

[1] See Chapter 7.

Housman was a favourite author, for he had already set *Hawthorn Time* (1919), *The Heart's Desire* (a little earlier), and in the six songs that make up *The Land of Lost Content* (1920–21) had shown in a masterly way just how he could match this poet's economy of means.

Peter Warlock once remarked on John Ireland's steady development along personal lines. How true this is, for no composer was more consistently himself at this time. Warlock was here referring to the fine Sonatina (1928). This fascinating work defines certain limits of thought; rarely, if ever, was he to write again so disturbingly as in the second movement with its chilling pedal notes. Apart from this, the typical lyricism is present, though tempered now by a sparser than usual texture and more biting use of chromaticism at points of tension. The rhythmic drive of the rondo which follows the second movement without a break is particularly compelling. At one point the hands argue things out like this:

Ex. 10 Ireland, Sonatina

I have played the powerful Piano Sonata in E minor (1918–20) so many times – he felt I came very close to his thoughts here. Partly for this reason I suppose, but also for its associations with Chanctonbury Ring (near to his last home where I visited him frequently) I have a special affection for it. At the same time I must admit that it does not have the more general appeal of, say, the Concerto. Maybe the slow movement is too expansive for some ears today. The late Ralph Hill – always such a strong Ireland advocate – compared it to Liszt's B minor and bemoaned its neglect. Incidentally, it was a pupil of Liszt – Lamond – who gave it its first performance.[2] It was out of print for some time, but I am very glad to report that it is available today.[3]

I cannot leave out the Sonata for Cello and Piano (1923). Here are its opening bars:

Ex. 11 Ireland, Cello Sonata – opening bars

Here again, second and third movements are linked, in this case by a hushed passage for 'cello alone. In music of great beauty, sometimes brooding, sometimes passionate or tensely energetic; Ireland has revealed something of his feelings about the mysteries of our early history. The spiritual home of this sonata is again West Sussex – so much of which has sadly changed since he first used to stay in Ashington. I find it a deeply rewarding work.

[2] For Lamond's account of the Sonata see pp. 359–63.

[3] The Sonata is issued by Stainer & Bell and is in the *Collected Piano Works*, vol. 5.

Like his contemporary, Frank Bridge, John Ireland poured some of his finest inspiration into his chamber music, and I wish there was more. Space will not allow me to talk about the three Trios (1908, 1917 and 1938 based on earlier material, respectively). I believe everything is available. Ireland was not fortunate (or unfortunate, whichever way you view it) in having only one publisher; his music is scattered among a dozen catalogues.

And so I come to the Piano Concerto (1930). I fell in love with this when I first heard it – of all places up in the balcony of the Royal Albert Hall – and remember thinking how much I would give to change places with the soloist that evening. Years later when this very opportunity did come my way, Ireland made sure I knew it inside out. I can hear him now. 'If you don't take a firm hand with these primadonnas' (he meant conductors!) 'then you'll be in trouble.' Sound advice which I have never ceased to be grateful for. I think I learnt more about the art of concerto-playing with Ireland's concerto than at any other time. There is no room for a tug-of-war in this sensitive music; soloist and orchestra must work together perfectly. It was especially exciting for me to record the concerto with Sir Adrian Boult, whose genius with English music of this period will never be equalled.

What a glorious work it is! One would never suspect that the key layout in the recapitulation of the first movement gave him considerable trouble – it all sounds so assured. That curve is evident again in the orchestral opening:

Ex. 12 Ireland, Piano Concerto – opening motif

and is not far away in the second motif which the piano later takes up like this:

Ex. 13 Ireland, Piano Concerto – second motif

Was Ireland ever more magical than in the haunting slow movement? All ears are tuned to the soloist here, but elsewhere there is perfect balance between piano and orchestra. Orchestral players always enjoy their individual touches, though I have sometimes had to get to know the leader before gently pointing out that the reference to the slow movement (just before the last cadenza in the finale) is *my* solo, not his! If you are looking for the essence of John Ireland's piano style, here it is. Tunes to remember (his own tunes!), luscious though never sickly harmony, exquisite arabesque and bravura in plenty, all coupled with a sure instinct for orchestral colour.

John Ireland knew every inch of the West Sussex downlands. Whenever possible he would go down to his rooms at Ashington and, in search of peace and quiet set off on foot for a day's trek to some remote spot. One of his favourite haunts was Harrow Hill, between Storrington and Angmering. It inspired his *Legend* for piano and orchestra (1933) about which there is a story that is appropriate here.

There was once a leper colony at Harrow Hill: the church having a 'squint' through which the poor creatures could observe the service without contaminating the congregation. Ireland was always susceptible to any associations with the distant past. One day, while resting here, he seems to have had some kind of visual extra-sensory experience. When he told me about it he was most emphatic that he had not been dreaming. For a few moments he had a clear picture of children dressed in archaic clothing who were dancing within a few feet of him. When he turned to take a closer look they vanished. He wrote to Arthur Machen whose books about the occult he had long admired – telling him about this strange experience, but the only response was: 'Oh, so you've seen them too.'[4] Ireland recollected the episode in the music of the middle section of *Legend* which was, incidentally, dedicated to Machen.

Possibly because the soloist is given little opportunity for personal display, *Legend* has never enjoyed the success of the Piano Concerto. It is a most impressive piece, however, with a piano part perfectly balanced against full orchestra minus trumpets. We hear first this magical horn solo, written with Aubrey Brain in mind. Both he and Dennis Brain managed it in one breath; lesser mortals come up for air after the tied E♭ in the third bar:

Ex. 14 Ireland, *Legend* for piano and orchestra – opening

Into this expectant atmosphere the pianist enters with leisurely arpeggios and later announces an important idea, accompanied by ominous thundering from the timpani and vicious comments from the brass:

Ex. 15 Ireland, *Legend* for piano and orchestra

[4] See Chapter 26.

This builds up to a shattering climax and then the orchestra introduces the 'children dancing theme':

Ex. 16 Ireland, *Legend* for piano and orchestra – 'children dancing' theme

which is taken up rhapsodically by the soloist. Eventually the mood of the opening returns, this time with the horn theme being commented upon by the piano. Gradually everything dies down, then with one fervent outburst by the piano the work ends on a series of low Ds which the piano accompanies (very tricky indeed).

I have room only to mention the smaller piano pieces of this period, but urge you to look at them if you do not know them. My own favourites include *Greenways* ('The Cherry Tree' – 'Cypress' – 'The Palm and May', 1937). The last piece was dedicated to Harriet Cohen, a pianist celebrated for her interpretations of Arnold Bax. Ireland once said he thought it was a mistake to write for pianists, as they all seemed interested only in first performances, whereas he was far more concerned about what happened afterwards!

Of the songs, I find most attractive the *Five Sixteenth-Century Poems* ('A Thanksgiving' – 'All in a Garden Green' – 'An Aside' – 'A Report Song' – 'The Sweet Season'. 1938.) The fourth song has a delicious accompaniment, which seems to me to be a close relative of *The Palm and May*:

Ex. 17 Ireland, 'A Report Song' (*Five Sixteenth-Century Poems*)

Just before World War II, John Ireland decided to settle in the Channel Islands. The story of his escape from the Germans is well known. It was a very near thing and he used to shudder about it, being quite convinced that, had the Nazis captured him, he would have been shot. He had to leave everything behind, including his car, in order to get on to the last boat. Fortunately he retrieved the unfinished manuscript of *Sarnia: An Island Sequence* ('Le Catioroc' – 'In a May Morning' – 'Song of the Springtides', 1940–41.) The title is the Roman name for Guernsey, so appropriately the first piece is prefaced by a few lines from Pomponius Mela (*c.* AD 50). 'Heavy silence … hidden terror … shrilling of flutes and clashing of cymbals'[5] are all strikingly conveyed in music that makes much

---

[5] Silet per diem universus, nec sine horrore secretus est; lucet nocturnis ignibus, chorus Ægipanum undique personatur: audiuntur et cantus tibiarum et tinnitus cymbalorum per oram maritimam. (Pomponius Mela, *De situ orbis* [AD 50]) Ireland's English translation: 'All day long, heavy silence broods, and a certain hidden terror lurks there. But at nightfall gleams the light of fires; the chorus of

use of low pedal notes and relentless rhythms. The second piece is a lovely addition to Ireland's other memorable movements in the key of Eb. He once said to me: 'I cannot begin to describe what I felt at the time – you must make it all sound as beautiful as you possibly can.' The last piece in the sequence (each is dedicated to an islander)[6] begins quietly enough, but soon works up to a brilliant cadenza. A quieter middle section is followed by a return to the opening ideas. The last two pages are very taxing, as excitement piles on and on. They need plenty of chordal grip and a sure sense of direction – one wrong note can ruin everything. Certain features recur in each movement: for instance, the beautiful drooping fifths and fourths:

Ex. 18 Ireland, 'In a May Morning' (*Sarnia*)

Ex. 19 Ireland, 'In a May Morning' (*Sarnia*)

On paper all these have an Ireland 'look' about them. I vividly recall his playing parts of *Sarnia* to me. He would get impatient with his fingers, but there was no mistaking the affection for what he had written, which I found rather touching.

Two years later, in 1943, he completed the last (and surely one of the finest) of his chamber works – the Fantasy Sonata for clarinet and piano, dedicated to Frederick Thurston. A tribute to an incomparable artist, the result was very much a labour of love and, as it turned out, a splendid addition to the repertoire. When I said how much I wanted to learn it, but had not been able to find a partner, he suggested that Thurston's brilliant young pupil Gervase de Peyer might be interested. Though de Peyer and I did meet at about this time (the early 1950s), it did not prove possible to work together until quite recently, when we recorded the Sonata for Lyrita.

Ægipans resounds on every side: the shrilling of flutes and the clash of cymbals re-echo by the waste shores of the sea.'

[6] The three movements are dedicated to 'Alfred Sebire'; 'Michael in Guernsey' (Michael was Michael Rayson); and 'Mrs Mignot'.

Compare its opening with some of my previous quotations:

Ex. 20 Ireland, Fantasy Sonata – opening bars

And the thumbprints are unmistakable, All this can be played an octave lower, but down there it is far less impressive. The wide range of the clarinet is fully exploited and there are many exciting swoops, like this one:

Ex. 21 Ireland, Fantasy Sonata

The piano part is superb; not a superfluous note anywhere, either in the luxurious solos or in the accompaniment figures. If I had to choose one Ireland score to take to my desert island, then this would be it.

I will end by offering you a selected list of Ireland's piano pieces. I have graded them approximately in order of technical difficulty, as they strike me – beginning around Grade IV and ending at Performer Diploma standard. The bigger works not down here would all come at the end of any similar list, but do not be put off by this. Anybody who has reached Grade VII comfortably will find much to enjoy in these more difficult works. The list includes better known pieces as well as some less familiar. I have marked with an asterisk those suitable for smaller hands, with slight adjustments here and there.

> The Darkened Valley
> * The Towing Path
> The Holy Boy (*Preludes*)
> Cypress (*Green Ways*)
> * Soliloquy
> Moon-glade (*Decorations*)
> * The Cherry Tree (*Green Ways*)
> * Summer Evening
> The Undertone (Preludes)
> Month's Mind
> Prelude in E♭
> February's Child

Fire of Spring (*Preludes*)
Obsession (*Preludes*)
April
On a Birthday Morning
* Sonatina
Bergomask
* Puck's Birthday (*Three Pastels*)
The Island Spell (*Decorations*)
Amberley Wild Brooks
Merry Andrew
Chelsea Reach
Ragamuffin (*London Pieces*)
Soho Forenoons
The Palm and May (*Green Ways*)
Equinox
The Scarlet Ceremonies (*Decorations*)

Ireland was a slow worker and took infinite trouble with his manuscripts, which he would only part with when he was satisfied. He used to say that publishing was such an irrevocable step. Certainly he had a very distinct idea of how each piece should sound. I do not know why – unless it had something to do with my being English and, like Ireland, of north country stock – but I seemed to sense his feelings. After going into details he would invariably say he could leave it all to me to manage in my own way. Naturally it would be difficult to pass such matters on here, though I think they are important. I have seen him physically upset by the 'interpretation' of even a well-known artist, and have more than one letter about this which I would not dare to publish! Ireland is a composer who can so easily be over-interpreted and distorted, so the performer should at least take trouble to play what is there on the page before letting his own personality get the better of things.

I have said earlier that Ireland would get annoyed if passages were hurried or got out of hand. He demanded a steady tempo (always allowing for varying degrees of rubato). He also expected rests to be given their full values, especially in silences. Rhythms had to be taut (*Ragamuffin, Merry Andrew*, for example): arabesques to be sensitive, clear and clean, as in Chopin (*April, Amberley Wild Brooks*, etc.).

He usually indicated phrasing, disliking 'breathiness' or what I call short puffs. I find I can best shape the phrases by just lifting hands from the keyboard whilst at the same time holding with the right pedal. I am thinking here of a piece like *Soliloquy*, but there are many other instances where this procedure seems to work. It is really a case of playing with your ears and listening with your feet!

Ireland's dynamic markings are always relatively precise. He used to mark them up a bit on my copies (*pp* would be altered to *p*, and so on). This was no sign of hard-of-hearing but an attempt to make sure that I would give sufficient emphasis where it was needed. He wanted the melodic line to be always clear and *cantabile*, whether it was on top of the chords, underneath them, or in the middle of the texture. The ability to bring out any one note of a chord is essential, so this technique needs to be practised hard.

Much of the pedalling required is of the *legato* type, so that chords melt into each other clearly. True, this is not usually shown, no doubt because he thought it was obvious: also, the old sign 'Ped.' takes up too much room and is not precise enough. He always indicates special effects which should be observed – the long holds in *The Island Spell* and the use of *una corda* in the Sonata's slow movement are two instances. Sparing use of the feet is always advisable, but in Ireland's piano music the pedalling is often rapid, since this is the only way to preserve the feeling of rich sonority.

As regards fingering, he sometimes suggests this, but not often. Fingering is very much a personal matter. Speed, dynamics, and sheer numbers of notes all affect which finger goes where, and the important thing is to try to decide as soon as possible on a suitable fingering, pencil this in and stick to it. Some of Ireland's spread chords need a firm thumb across two notes in either hand as well as strong wrists.

In my conversations with him he would sometimes fill in a little background for me which helped towards a clearer understanding of what he was getting at. At the same time he would point out that the music itself contained its own emotional meaning and did not require a programme to bring it to life. Whenever I missed a point he would say, 'That doesn't sound quite what I have in mind there, but I'm not sure if I can show you, as I never practise these days.' This was a cue for me to get off the piano stool, because he invariably *could* show me exactly what was wrong!

I do hope that my few remarks may be of some help to those of you who may be playing John Ireland for the first time. There is nothing quite like the excitement of a discovery, and nothing more rewarding than the work needed to perfect its performance. I have so often felt this about John Ireland's piano music – a priceless heritage.

CHAPTER 16

John Ireland in the Concert Hall: Orchestral and Choral-Orchestral Music

Lewis Foreman

JOHN Ireland wrote a large number of songs, and his piano music dominated the repertoire of British music teaching for decades, but there are only a dozen or so works for orchestra. Yet Ireland's orchestral scores have had a profile with audiences, at least in the UK, out of all proportion to their number. In this chapter we survey the music, including vocal and choral music which requires orchestral accompaniment. This is largely intended as an introduction to this area of Ireland's art for the student and music lover, rather than a thorough-going analysis for an academic audience. Later in his career Ireland could be vitriolic about the way his orchestral music was neglected, yet viewing his career over more than half a century, it is clear he achieved a major reputation with a comparatively small catalogue of perfectly finished and highly distinctive orchestral works.

Although Ireland was reticent about revealing his non-musical sources[1] they were gradually built into programme notes and accounts of the music by his friends. This developed a climate for the reception of the music. In a world where the romantic-impressionist scores of Vaughan Williams, Bridge, Holst, Bax and E. J. Moeran were competing for the public's attention, at a time recording was not yet ubiquitous, and broadcasting only just developing, Ireland's small œuvre found its audience by its distinctiveness. With his contemporaries this was music to be played in London's Queen's Hall, and the perfect acoustic and scale of that hall surely defined the orchestral sound of Ireland's music as with that of his contemporaries.

The critic Edwin Evans appended a list of works to his extended critical survey of Ireland's music which he published in 1919,[2] and he then included two overtures, *Midsummer* and *Pelléas et Mélisande*, scores whose whereabouts are now unknown, presumably destroyed by the composer. Craggs[3] also lists a lost overture *The Princess Maleine: Poem for Orchestra*, citing as his source the *Monthly Musical Record* of July 1915. The Belgian playwright Maurice Maeterlinck's five-act symbolist drama *The Princess Maleine* had appeared in an English translation in 1892, and before the First World War it inspired overtures by Cyril Scott and the French composer Pierre de Bréville and an unfinished sketch by Lili Boulanger. Maeterlinck was all the rage with John Ireland's musical contemporaries in the first couple of decades of the twentieth century, the major work for musicians being *Pelléas et Mélisande*. So whether the inspiration was *Pelléas* or *The Princess*

---

[1] See Colin Scott-Sutherland's discussion of various works in Chapters 1 and 10.

[2] *Musical Times* 1919, reprinted here on p. 376–92.

[3] Stewart R. Craggs, ed., *John Ireland: A Catalogue, Discography and Bibliography.* (Oxford: Clarendon Press, 1993; 2nd edition, Aldershot: Ashgate, 2007).

Maleine or both, the music is lost and we merely need to note the composer's artistic sympathy at the time.

Also listed by Evans was an *Orchestral Poem in A minor*, later withdrawn but now recorded, as well as the early orchestral score *Tritons*. The stylistic break-through came with *The Forgotten Rite* in 1913. After the First World War came the tone-poem *Mai-Dun*, the Piano Concerto in 1930, the *London Overture* and *These Things Shall Be* in 1937; all were received as the work of a leading composer and he was regarded thus by a wide musical public.

Other contributors to this *Companion* have summarised his early years, but it is worth emphasising that John Ireland came from a literary Manchester family. He was born in 1879, in Bowdon, Cheshire, which he described as 'a pleasant country place ... south of Manchester'. His father, Alexander Ireland, who was seventy when John was born, was part-owner and editor of *The Manchester Examiner*, that city's second newspaper, and was a well-known literary figure on the Manchester scene. His second wife, John's mother, Annie Ireland, who was nearly thirty years her husband's junior, was an author in her own right. However, *The Examiner* declined as the fortune of the *Manchester Guardian* came to dominate, and during John's childhood his domestic circumstances gradually became more and more Spartan. The future composer was also bullied by his older brothers and sisters. Ireland's memories of his childhood were unhappy, though the cultivated family circle in his parents' lifetimes – and especially his mother's – introduced him to music through the piano.

It was his sister Ethel who first aspired to a professional musical training, going to London and the Royal Academy of Music in 1891. John followed her to London, but to the Royal College of Music, two years later. John's mother suffered from a heart condition and was frail, and she died soon after John entered the Royal College of Music at the age of fourteen. The following year his father followed her, so the young John was an orphan at fourteen, and he had to make his own way. Although Ireland himself could be self-deprecating about his achievement he must have been a brilliant pupil, for he was accepted for the Royal College of Music at an early age with the piano as principal study, becoming a Fellow of the Royal College of Organists at just eighteen.

With the death of his mother, almost immediately the circumstances of his life changed. Money must have become much tighter, but Ireland's life remained focused on London, and he did not leave the RCM until 1901. During this time his allowance was meted out with Victorian frugality by a guardian,[4] but to keep body and soul together he took on a range of paid work: whatever came up – organist, choir master, teacher or accompanist. A typical example of an older contemporary finding him work came when he prepared the piano reduction of Cecil Forsyth's Viola Concerto for publication by Schott in 1904. In those days it was possible to live in central London for comparatively little and Ireland gradually built a career based on a portfolio of freelance activities, which included appearing as a concert recitalist and accompanist. Like so many others, he soon looked to the church for a modest living, and he was organist and choirmaster at St Luke's Church, Chelsea from 1904 to 1926. Later he taught

---

[4] For the terms of Alexander Ireland's will, see p. 4.

composition at the Royal College of Music, numbering Benjamin Britten among his pupils.

In 1897 he had been awarded a scholarship to study composition with Stanford, with whom he remained for four years. As a young man Ireland wrote a variety of works but said that he discarded or destroyed everything he wrote before the age of twenty-seven on the grounds that 'not till then did I feel I had even partially mastered my problems or formed any individual style'. He had some successes with chamber works and piano music, collecting Cobbett Competition prizes for his Phantasie Trio in A minor (second prize in 1908) and [First] Violin Sonata in D minor (first prize, 1909) but it was not until he produced his Violin Sonata no. 2 in 1917 that he suddenly found himself famous, literally overnight.

Among the early works that Ireland had withdrawn but not destroyed, was the glorious Brahmsian Sextet for clarinet, horn and string quartet, written while he had been a student of Stanford. Revived at the end of his lifetime, its late success underlined how, with the changed perspective of over half a century, Ireland's early works were revealed as certainly being worthy of exploration. Ireland himself had already acknowledged this when, in 1944, he took his early Symphonic Prelude *Tritons*, composed in 1899, and made it the basis of his *Maritime Overture* for military band. His next orchestral work, the *Orchestral Poem in A minor* (dated 26 February 1904) certainly leaves us in no doubt as to Ireland's command of the orchestra at the age of twenty-four.

The recent revival (2009)[5] of Vaughan Williams's early (and impressive) *Heroic Elegy and Triumphal Epilogue* reminds one that after a performance of the first part of this long-withdrawn work on 21 March 1901 by the RCM students orchestra conducted by their teacher Stanford, at which Ireland's *Tritons* was also heard, Stanford turned to John Ireland and said: 'That's better than anything you could write, me bhoy.'[6] Vaughan Williams's promise was fully evident in that score, whereas there are only passing portents of Ireland's future orchestral works as he filters the procedures of Brahms through the personality of his teacher, Stanford. Nevertheless, Ireland's ambition is never in doubt. This is still a composer intent on saying big things in his music.

Vexilla Regis (1898)

As we have seen, Ireland withdrew almost all his earlier music. This included *Vexilla Regis*, for chorus accompanied by trumpets, trombones and organ, composed in 1898. This subsequently resurfaced, and when it was recorded by Chandos it revealed a striking score which handles a big sound in a large space with impressive confidence. The nineteen-year-old, still a pupil of Stanford, was assistant organist at Holy Trinity Church, Sloane Square, London, a large and impressive space. Very much under the influence of Parry, this work is nevertheless an imposing and self-assured piece and it is difficult to understand why Ireland should have rejected it. Stanford, for one, was so pleased with the work

[5] Recorded by Dutton Epoch on CDLX 7237, where the BBC Concert Orchestra is conducted by John Wilson.

[6] British Library, Add. MS 60535. See p. 197.

that he persuaded Walter Alcock, Director of Music at Holy Trinity, Sloane Square, to perform it, and Ireland conducted. That was some time in 1899, but it was then withdrawn and was not published until 1963, after Ireland's death.

This Hymn for Passion Sunday sets words by Bishop Venantius Fortunatas (AD 530–609) translated from the Latin by J. M. Neale. Ireland, for all his many years' connection with the Church was curiously ambivalent about his religious beliefs. To his mentor, Father Thompson, Ireland wrote (on 16 July 1936): 'I am a bad sort of (Anglo) Catholic … one's heart must turn towards what represents permanence. I do not wish ever to lose this. I am a Pagan, a Pagan I was born & a Pagan I shall ever remain. That is the foundation of religion.'[7]

Tritons: Symphonic Prelude (1899)

The overbearing influence of Stanford on the personalities of his less self-confident students was considerable, for none more so than John Ireland. The celebrated story of Stanford handing back a manuscript score to another student while passing an undertaker with the words 'better take it in there m'bhoy' was not the act to inspire a young composer's self-confidence. Ireland, one suspects, felt this regime more keenly than many. Resulting from this, as we have seen, Ireland withheld several of his student works, and they were not heard during his life-time. Right at the end of his life Ireland relented and certain scores, particularly the Sextet for Clarinet, Horn and Strings, were allowed to be brought out. I was present at the Arts Council Drawing Room, St James's Square on 25 March 1960 when the Sextet was resurrected and I can remember how positive was the reception it received. It revealed music which should have been performed much earlier.

Another example of this is the symphonic prelude *Tritons*. The work was composed in 1899 and received its only performance in the composer's lifetime at that RCM student concert on 21 March 1901, when it was conducted by Stanford. As a clue to its subject matter the composer quoted the following verse in the programme:

> At high noon, 'neath the sun, the strong surf beats,
> The free exultant sea-wind sweeps the shore;
> And Life, glad, great, tumultuous, with the sea
>   Wildly rejoices.

In the programme for the first performance the composer is described as 'John N. Ireland (Scholar)'.

In 1944 the composer submitted to Ralph Hawkes a short score derived from this work under the title *A Maritime Overture*, in response to a request for a piece to mark the centenary of the first publication of a military band score by Hawkes before they amalgamated to form Boosey & Hawkes. It was scored for military band by Norman Richardson and published in 1946; he subsequently produced a symphonic wind band version including saxophones, published in 1988.

Listening to the fine Chandos recording of the original score conducted by Richard Hickox, one has to say that this is more than merely promising, and at its date was in fact a remarkable achievement. Although Ireland has not yet

[7] For the quotation in full see Jeremy Dibble's chapter, p. 234.

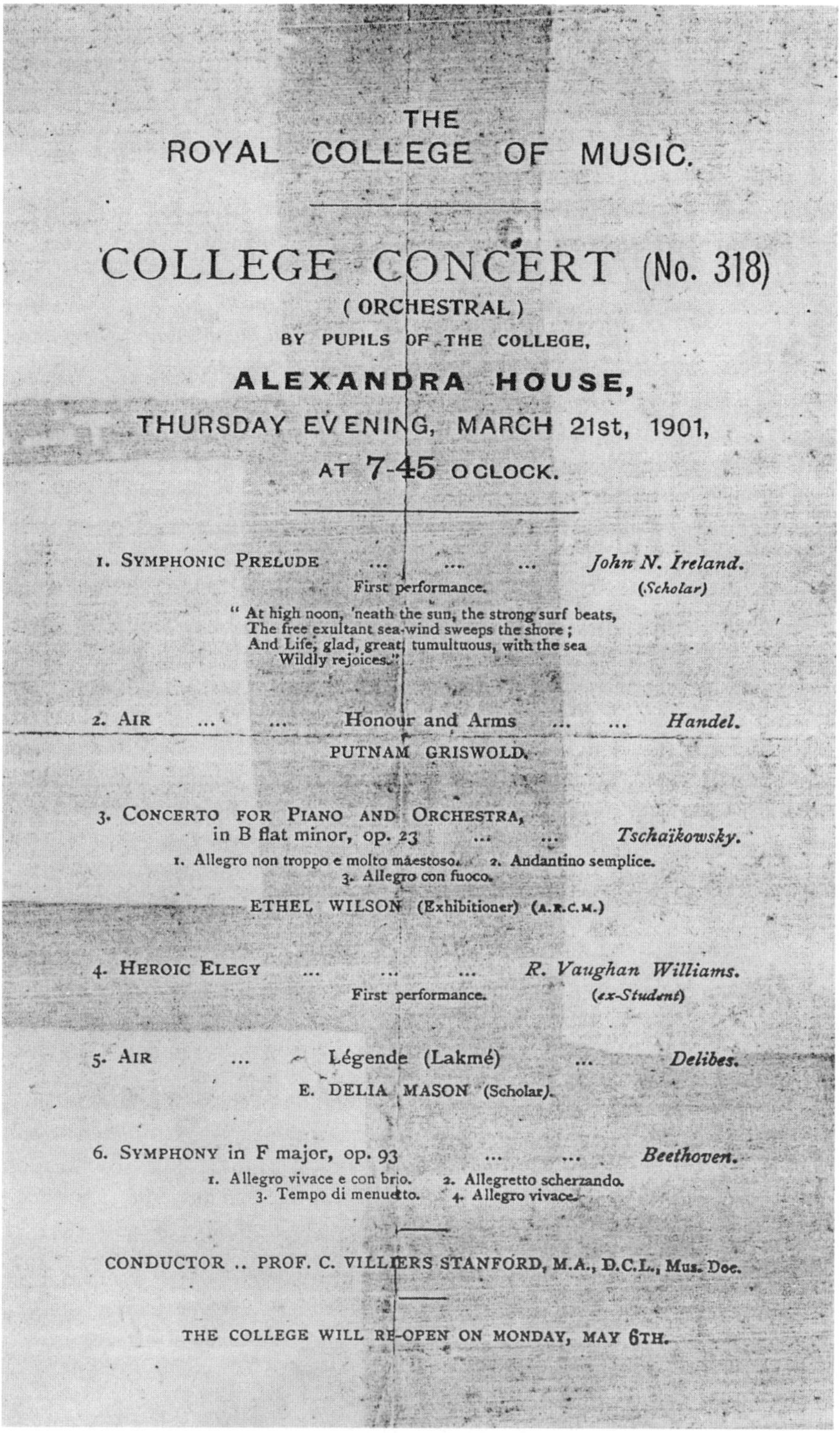

THE
ROYAL COLLEGE OF MUSIC.

COLLEGE CONCERT (No. 318)
(ORCHESTRAL)
BY PUPILS OF THE COLLEGE,

ALEXANDRA HOUSE,

THURSDAY EVENING, MARCH 21st, 1901,

AT 7-45 O'CLOCK.

1. SYMPHONIC PRELUDE   ...   .   *John N. Ireland.*
   First performance.   *(Scholar)*

   " At high noon, 'neath the sun, the strong surf beats,
   The free exultant sea-wind sweeps the shore ;
   And Life, glad, great, tumultuous, with the sea
   Wildly rejoices."

2. AIR   ...   ...   Honour and Arms   ...   ...   *Handel.*

   PUTNAM GRISWOLD.

3. CONCERTO FOR PIANO AND ORCHESTRA,
   in B flat minor, op. 23   ...   ...   *Tschaïkowsky.*
   1. Allegro non troppo e molto maestoso.   2. Andantino semplice.
   3. Allegro con fuoco.

   ETHEL WILSON (Exhibitioner) (A.R.C.M.)

4. HEROIC ELEGY   ...   .   *R. Vaughan Williams.*
   First performance.   *(ex-Student)*

5. AIR   ...   ...   Légende (Lakmé)   ...   ...   *Delibes.*
   E. DELIA MASON (Scholar).

6. SYMPHONY in F major, op. 93   ...   ...   *Beethoven.*
   1. Allegro vivace e con brio.   2. Allegretto scherzando.
   3. Tempo di menuetto.   4. Allegro vivace.

CONDUCTOR .. PROF. C. VILLIERS STANFORD, M.A., D.C.L., Mus. Doc.

THE COLLEGE WILL RE-OPEN ON MONDAY, MAY 6TH.

Fig. 18 The programme for the RCM Concert which included Ireland's *Symphonic Prelude* (later called *Tritons*) and Vaughan Williams's early *Heroic Elegy*

developed his skill in inventing memorable instrumental solos – the feature which makes his later works so personal – the handling of the orchestra is completely assured, the ideas are memorable and the concept arresting.

Orchestral Poem in A minor (1904)

The *Orchestral Poem in A minor* is dated 'London: 26 February 1904' and so doubt-less had occupied him during at least the second half of 1903. This is a substan-tial score, in Richard Hickox's recording[8] running 13½ minutes. Cast in a broadly ternary form – *Andante* – *Andante con molto moderato* – *Allegro giusto* – $\downarrow$ = 48 – in many ways it is a more confident work than *Tritons* of nearly four years before, so why it seems to be a less successful score is difficult to pinpoint. Probably it is because generally the invention is less memorable.

The statement of the two principal subjects constitute the opening two sections of the piece, running nearly five minutes and beginning and ending with a sustained high pedal A on the strings. This leads on to the extended development section, Ireland's barely emergent personality lost in the block scoring of wind and brass. And yet there are many cherishable moments – almost any one-minute extract from the Hickox recording has the listener sitting up and asking to hear more.[9] No performance is documented from Ireland's lifetime, and it seems to have gone unheard. Whether it is, in fact, one of the two 'overtures', *Midsummer* or *Pelléas et Mélisande* or more likely *The Princess Maleine: Poem for Orchestra*, it is impossible to say. One could well imagine, for example, those opening sections evoking the princess in her tower, and the middle section her escape and wandering through an oppressive and frightening forest. But we have no documentary evidence. However it seems likely that a score which must have cost him much effort would still be in his list of works ten years later, and significantly the *Orchestral Poem* as such is nowhere listed, though it was not among the scores he destroyed.

Psalm 42 for SATB soli, SSATB chorus and string orchestra

1. Chorus: 'Like as the hart'; 2. Soprano solo 'The Lord hath granted His loving kindness'; 3. Solo quartet *a cappella* 'My tears have been my meat'; 4. Introduction and fugue for chorus and orchestra 'Why art thou so vexed?'

At a time when 'Doctor of Music' was the aspiration of many British musicians seeking posts in organ loft or administration, composers of the late nineteenth and early twentieth centuries submitted the extended works required as examination scores to crown their academic work – ranging from the tremendous Cambridge D.Mus. exercise that is Vaughan Williams's early *A Cambridge Mass* of 1899 for

---

[8] City of London Sinfonia / Richard Hickox Chandos CHAN 9376 (1995).

[9] For example (timings from the Chandos CD) at 7'48" a momentarily original orchestral texture make us wonder if this is, after all, an immature score by Vaughan Williams, almost immediately followed (at 7'55") by an involving string phrase, but Ireland cannot seize his opportunity, the magic dissolving in uninspired punchy sequences, his short phrases destroying the atmosphere where long lines are required. At another reflective passage (at 9'54") Ireland almost makes it, but again is unable to crown the invention with a mature resolution.

Fig. 19 John Ireland's *Psalm 42*, the second page of the second movement for soprano solo 'The Lord hath granted His loving kindness in the daytime', bars 11–22

SATB soli, double chorus and orchestra, to Dyson's as yet unperformed choral symphony which is also his D.Mus. submission.

Until recently little thought has been given by those researching British music of this period to examining the accumulations of such submissions that are preserved in thesis collections in all the relevant libraries, including Durham, London and Oxford and Cambridge Universities. Most of these have probably never been performed. The first such find to impinge on my own musical activities was Herbert Howells's *Fantasia for Cello and Orchestra*, first performed in January 1982.

By and large there has not been a rush to research such material, and attention only turned to this setting by John Ireland in 2007. It is Ireland's successful submission for the external Durham B.Mus. The music is dated London 28 February 1908, a signed declaration of originality to the university is dated 21 March 1908. Although he was awarded the degree, so far as is known the work went unperformed in Ireland's lifetime – to all intents and purposes it was merely 'paper music'. The first performance took place a century later, at London's Cadogan Hall, at the instigation of the John Ireland Trust, on 25 February 2009 with soloists,[10] the London Chorus and New London Orchestra conducted by Ronald Corp.

One can understand why Ireland was not keen to have the work performed at the time, for the ghost of Mendelssohn certainly hangs over some of the invention. Yet it is only really in the third movement, for four unaccompanied soloists, written thus to meet the requirements of the degree, that the work is in any way inappropriate for concert use, and, indeed, the first and second movements might well be extracted and performed independently as short concert or liturgical pieces in their own right.

Ireland does not set the whole psalm but focuses on one or two verses for each movement, using a wording that is taken, not always in sequence, from the Book of Common Prayer and not entirely reflecting the wording of the King James Bible, with a variety of repetition. In effect each movement is therefore a biblically derived libretto by Ireland himself to suit the purposes of his setting. The first movement sets, *In tempo moderato*, the first two verses. This is a charming, mellifluously flowing setting,[11] certainly Mendelssohnian in its vocal treatment, but more nearly anticipating the later Ireland in the treatment of the string orchestra.

The second movement, *Allegretto*, a soaring soprano solo,[12] setting 'The Lord hath granted his loving kindness', takes words from verse 10 and 11 (8 in The Bible). Here Ireland writes a piece that would not be out of place as a solo during a service, though when the springing accompaniment is played by the string orchestra we are not far away from where Finzi would later set out in *Dies Natalis*. Even twenty years later church composers were finding success with this sort of solo, the example that springs readily to mind being Mabel Fairlie's *Send Out Thy Light* of 1929, and there is no reason why Ireland's piece would not have been widely sung if he had chosen to publish it.

[10] Mary Bevan (soprano); Catherine Hopper (mezzo-soprano); Adrian Ward (tenor); Peter Willcock (baritone).

[11] At the first performance it ran for 4′ 20″.

[12] It ran for 3½ minutes.

The third movement, verses 3–4, is marked *Andantino, ma non troppo lento*, and is for four soloists, SATB, entirely unaccompanied, setting the words 'My tears have been my meat'. Far from being just a contrapuntal academic exercise, this is remarkably effective, but is vocally demanding.

Ireland once remarked that he had never written a fugue. In fact, of course, he had, and it appears in the finale, a bold *Allegro* headed 'Introduction and Fugue'. It sets verses 14 and 15 (11 with elements of 5 in the Bible), with florid concluding Amens. This is the most academic movement, demonstrating Ireland's technical competence in contrapuntal writing. But it is certainly invigorating to sing and one can well imagine choral societies enjoying its muscular part-writing and grand peroration.

Performed without the third movement this would make an enjoyable concert-filler for choral societies, running a little over 12 minutes. The *Psalm*, in all or part, is available for performance, and performing materials can be supplied by the John Ireland Trust.

The Forgotten Rite: Prelude for Orchestra (1913)

The earliest orchestral work which Ireland was willing to acknowledge during his lifetime, this 'Prelude' is in reality an orchestral tone-poem. It dates from August–November 1913,[13] though its first performance took place during the First World War. This was at Queen's Hall in September 1917, Sir Henry Wood conducting. It is a score in which Ireland emerges in command of a vivid orchestral technique informed by the impressionism of Debussy, and is strikingly similar at that stage of his career to some works of his colleague (also a pupil of Stanford) Frank Bridge.

Ireland was particularly attracted to the Channel Islands, both to Guernsey and Jersey, and it is the latter which is reflected in this score, an island rich in pagan and Roman associations. Ireland first found his full voice as a composer when he visited Jersey during the years before the First World War, the piano piece *The Island Spell* being dated 'Le Fauvic, August 1912'. In the programme note for the first performance[14] of *The Forgotten Rite* reference was made to the work evoking the 'mystical aspects' and 'occult forces' of nature. Ireland had a heightened aware-ness of place and captured this in several of his finest works. Racial memory in places of habitation of the remote past would often evoke a special sympathy with his almost psychic sixth sense. He found the books of the writer Arthur Machen particularly revealing in this respect, when he first came across *The House of Souls* in 1906 and in the following year *The Hill of Dreams*. The opening *Poco lento e mistico* gives an immediate feeling for this mystical quality, underlined by the superb and evocative horn writing.[15]

Ireland's friend Julian Herbage, responsible in the 1930s and 40s for programme planning of the Proms, wrote about this work:

It is a compact evocative work which is concerned, not with any sensory

[13] Date given on the last page of the printed full score (London: Augener, 1913).

[14] Queen's Hall Promenade Concert, 13 September 1917.

[15] See Colin Scott-Sutherland's discussion in Chapters 1 and 12, and Exx. 7 and 9 on p. 169 and Ex. 8 on pp. 389–90.

impressionism, but with the illumination of some primitive aspiration, the reawakening of a sense of exaltation long dormant in our benighted civilization. The score is laid out simply, and the atmosphere of the opening (*Poco lento e mistico*) is suggested merely by a soft timpani roll, four part harmony from violins, violas, and cellos, and a repeated note on muted horns. No bar goes by, however, without its full quota of expression marks which lead the music inexorably to its climax, after which the mood of the opening returns, but now marked *Lontano possibile.*[16]

For the first time in an orchestral work John Ireland writes hauntingly and evocatively for horns. The composer in mystical mood finds much of his magic in the 'horns of elfland faintly blowing'. Ireland shows a particular expressive power when writing for solo instruments in an orchestral texture. He often has specific players in mind and fashions themes for them, doubtless having their *sound* in mind. To quote Julian Herbage again:

> For him an instrument's tone has a meaning and a personality, and he has always been avid to learn from the great wind-players of his day. I have before me a score used at a Promenade performance of *The Forgotten Rite* in 1937. At the fourteenth bar is a note in pencil '... Aubrey Brain played this *senza sord.*, conducted by the composer, who said it was better so'. It needs, indeed, a perceptive conductor to re-create John Ireland's music in terms of the orchestral sound conceived by the composer.[17]

Writing at first-hand about the sound which Ireland sought in such scores, here is Julian Herbage again:

> A last word should be written about the orchestral sound envisaged by John Ireland, for orchestral tone has considerably changed during the last thirty years or so. Horn-tone for instance, is an essential colour in Ireland's orchestral palette, though perhaps that metaphor is misleading, for to Ireland the tone quality of instruments represents, not colour, but rather emotional concept. The horn is used to evoke the past, or something as yet dimly perceived. The oboe brings a youthful, spring-like atmosphere to the music, while the clarinet provides a warmer emotion. When Ireland scores for solo instruments he imagines them in terms of the great orchestral players of the last thirty or forty years. The horn tone he requires is not the thick, woolly and coarse sound of the modern German keyed instrument, but the more limpid yet penetrating tone of the narrower-bored French valve-horn. Those who heard Aubrey Brain in his prime will remember the expressive quality he brought to every solo passage, and though his brilliant son Dennis may have excelled him in sheer virtuosity he could never bring tears to the eyes quite as his father did. The woodwind tone which Ireland has in mind is the French and Belgian style, which I believe Sir Henry Wood first introduced orchestrally to this country, and which I first remember hearing in his Queen's Hall Orchestra of the middle 'twenties.[18]

[16] Julian Herbage, 'John Ireland and the Orchestra' *The Listener*, 4 June 1959, p. 1001.

[17] Ibid.

[18] Ibid.

The Holy Boy (1913)

This 'carol of the Nativity' was written as a piano solo on Christmas day 1913, the third of the four Preludes published in 1918. After the First World War he arranged it both for violin or cello and piano and as an organ solo. During the second world war he produced a short choral version setting of Herbert S. Brown's poem 'Lowly, laid in a manger', and a version for string orchestra. As we have seen, there was a real-life 'holy boy', one of Ireland's choristers at St Luke's, Chelsea. He was Robert Glassby, the son of Ireland's sculptor friend who also became his landlord. A cherubic sculptured head of the young boy remained one of Ireland's treasured possessions, even after the boy, by then in his early thirties, had died in tragic circumstances.[19]

Variations on 'Cadet Rousselle' (1918, orch. Goossens, 1930)

At the suggestion of their friend the critic Edwin Evans, four composers published by J. & W. Chester – John Ireland, Frank Bridge, Arnold Bax and Eugene Goossens – jointly produced this miniature set of variations on a French folksong. Initially it was for soprano and piano. In 1930 it was arranged by Eugene Goossens for orchestra without voice. Ireland contributed three variations, only two of which were incorporated in Goossens' final orchestral score.

Mai-Dun: Symphonic Rhapsody (1921).

When *Mai-Dun* was first performed it was simply billed as 'Symphonic Rhapsody'. More atmospheric and evocative non-musical associations became apparent after a few performances. It is worth noting the composer's own programme note, written for the 1922 Leeds Musical Festival, when it was performed by the London Symphony Orchestra conducted by Albert Coates on 7 October 1922. Here John Ireland could not be less colourful in his account of the music.

> This work, which occupies about 12 minutes in performance, was first sketched in October 1920, and completed in November 1921. It was first performed by Goossens, at Queen's Hall, on December 12th, 1921, the second performance being under the direction of Sir Henry Wood, at the Promenade Concerts, on September 27th, 1922. The Rhapsody is, more or less, in sonata form, although there is little, if any, repetition of the material. It opens with a decisively rhythmical subject of a somewhat grim and bleak character, which is developed at some length before the second subject is reached. The latter, which is sustained and melodic, is first heard on the horn, with muted string accompaniment. This material forms the first section. The second section corresponds to the 'development' of a sonata movement. The third and final section is occupied with different treatment of the preceding material, the music becoming brighter and more vivid in colour until the close. The Rhapsody is scored for the usual full orchestra, with the exception of the harp, which is not employed.

[19] See Alan Rowlands' comments in Chapter 3.

The work was first printed as 'Symphonic Rhapsody', this title only becoming subordinate to 'Mai-Dun' as that title came into use. In their first printing the orchestral parts (1923) are headed just 'Symphonic Rhapsody', while the first printed scores have the title *Symphonic Rhapsody: Mai-Dun*. This soon changed to *Mai-Dun: Symphonic Rhapsody*. This history is exemplified by the entry on John Ireland by Edwin Evans in *A Dictionary of Modern Music and Musicians* (1924) where *Mai-Dun* appears in the text, but 'Symphonic Rhapsody' in the catalogue of works.

Later commentators related *Mai-Dun* to Maiden Castle, the enormous early British earthworks near Dorchester. In 1935 John Ireland went to see the opera *Iernin* by the young composer George Lloyd, and in writing to congratulate him, confirmed the source of his imagery concerning *Mai-Dun* as 'my impressions of the hill-fortress of that name'. He added, 'As was said some two thousand years ago, there are two kinds of people – the children of this world, & the children of light.'

'It is a direct representation, rather than an evocation, of the scene conjured up in *The Forgotten Rite*', wrote Julian Herbage. He went on to say: 'Ireland's Symphonic Rhapsody powerfully conveys the struggle inherent in the lives of our primitive ancestors, and its magnificent coda has a strength that has rarely been equalled in British music. The more lyrical sections are perhaps less evocative than those in *The Forgotten Rite*; but the forward urge of the music, particularly towards the close, is enormously compelling.'

Greater love hath no man *(1912, orch. 1924)*

Ireland produced several hymns and church pieces that have become well-known. The best, and the best known, is this motet, a meditation for Passiontide, written in 1912 for Charles Macpherson (then sub-organist at St Paul's) and his choristers at St Paul's Cathedral, and orchestrated in 1924. The words are a patchwork of verses from the New Testament, including John, Peter, I Corinthians and Romans, and opening with words from the Song of Solomon. Despite the fact that it was written two years before the outbreak of the First World War, Ireland's anthem (also known as 'Many waters cannot quench love') has become closely associated with services of remembrance.

Concerto in E♭ major for Piano and Orchestra *(1930)*

When John Ireland indicated he was working on a piano concerto he was seen by many as a miniaturist taking a late significant step forward. The concerto was first heard on 2 October 1930 at a Queen's Hall Promenade Concert, and was soon widely played.

Ireland composed two works for piano and orchestra, both written for his pupil and protégée, the young pianist Helen Perkin (1909–96) who gave their first performances. It was her performance of the Prokofiev Third Piano Concerto at the Royal College of Music, when that work was still new, that drew attention to

Perkin, and Ireland came under the spell of both, and we may note elements of the Prokofiev in his concerto.[20]

Ireland's last companion, Norah Kirby, took it upon herself to destroy any of Ireland's papers which she considered doubtful, and so we may never fully understand his ambivalent sexuality. However, his feelings for his young pianist are germane in the context of the concerto. What we do know is that on 17 December 1926, at the age of forty-seven, Ireland had married another pupil, Dorothy Phillips, when she was seventeen. In retrospect, with more than a tinge of farce, he had immediately regretted it and never consummated the marriage, which was dissolved nine months later. So when little more than a year later he began to be attracted to Helen Perkin, a brilliant nineteen-year-old piano student at the RCM it was not surprising that he wrote the concerto for her. On 4 April 1930 Helen was soloist in a RCM performance of Prokofiev's Third Piano Concerto with Malcolm Sargent conducting, both the soloist and Prokofiev influencing Ireland as far as his forthcoming concerto was concerned. From his position at the RCM, and as a leading composer of the day, he was able to influence the conductor Sir Henry Wood to ensure she was given the premiere at a Queen's Hall Promenade Concert. This was an important event for them both: it literally put them on the map. For a while she was Ireland's companion, and played his music, but she studied in Europe in 1932, and while she gave the first performance of the one-movement *Legend* in January 1934, this was the end of his influence: Ireland was not amused and could be quite catty about her playing.[21]

The concerto, which is in three movements – *In tempo moderato – Lento espressivo – Allegretto giocoso* – seemed to come to Ireland fairly quickly in the spring and summer of 1930. Not least of Ireland's coups in this piece is the way the timpani do not play until towards the end of the slow movement, when they do so with notable effect and lead the music into the finale. At the time much play was made by commentators for Ireland's use of fibre dance band mutes by the trumpets. Were the critics trying to suggest Ireland was another Gershwin? Evan Senior later quoted Ireland's comments to him on the origins of this innovation:

> Few remember nowadays that this concerto marked a departure in music of its type in two ways – first for the use of a new type of mute for brass instruments, and secondly, for unusual writing for tympani. For the Ireland Concerto was the first classical music to go to the dance-band for an idea for its brass.
>
> 'When I was writing the concerto', John Ireland told me, 'I was telephoned one day by an old friend, the then dance-band leader Jack Payne, who told me he'd heard that I was writing a concerto, and asked if I intended using any muted brass in the score. He reminded me that there were many other types of mute used in dance bands, apart from the usual pear-shaped piece of brass, pierced with holes, then in general used in the symphony orchestra as a mute.'
>
> John Ireland went to Jack Payne's studio and spent quite some time

---

[20] For Helen Perkin's identification of elements of the Prokofiev reflected in Ireland's treatment see p. 369.

[21] This is discussed more fully by Fiona Richards in Chapter 11.

listening to effects which were, until that time, quite outside the range of the symphony orchestra. One of the mutes, cone-shaped and made of fibre, seemed to him far more effective than the one then generally used in the symphony orchestra. So in the score he gave directions that this fibre mute should be used. 'I think I was the first composer of serious music to specify this particular type of mute. And at the time I was severely hauled over the coals by the most famous critic of the day for what he called "hob-nobbing with dance band conductors"!' But Ireland's borrowing from the dance band has proved justified – since then fibre mutes have become the standard symphony orchestra usage, and have almost entirely superseded the pear-shaped brass type.[22]

Whatever, it had a considerable following, and for many years it was the paramount British piano concerto. All the leading pianists of the day played it, including notably Moura Lympany and Eileen Joyce. Once or twice it was played by Ireland himself, and other pianists included Gina Bachauer, Clifford Curzon, and Artur Rubinstein. Between 1950 and 1960 it appeared at the Proms every year but one.[23]

Although usually designated in three movements, in fact only two are marked in the score, the music moving straight on from the slow movement into what is *de facto* the high spirited finale, *Allegretto giocoso*. The short orchestral prelude on the strings with which Ireland starts his concerto surely contains the ghost of the plainsong he would have known in church, while the mysterious distant horns at the fourth bar seem to be heralding some far-off world. This forms a sort of motto, becoming the generator of later invention and is assimilated in the first subject that soon follows as a piano solo. In launching his concerto it is typical of Ireland that the piano introduces itself with quiet musings that could easily be the opening of one of his evocative piano miniatures. This is soon over and the music accelerates to the catchy theme first heard on trumpet and clarinets and repeated many times during the movement. This is not a classical opposition between soloist and the orchestra; rather, the latter provides colourful texture to link extended passages of unaccompanied piano. Ireland only uses the full orchestra at the climaxes.

Is the slow movement a love song? Ireland does not tell us, but with its yearning falling sevenths in the strings he surely does not have to. The music which opens the movement is in fact a slow version of the second theme of the first movement, and it is followed, as in the first, by a solo passage of evocative dreaming that could again be one of Ireland's characteristic miniatures. Eventually a side drum tattoo breaks into the reverie and with a miniature cadenza leads into the energetic finale. To a British audience in 1930 the use of Chinese block to tap out the rhythm, in addition to those muted trumpets, must have seemed very modern.

We now reach the slower second subject which is of special interest. It includes a motivic reference, a feature of Ireland's music at this time. In this case we have a motif of four semiquavers which come from his piano prelude 'Spring Will Not Wait' and his song cycle *We'll to the Woods No More*. Both these were dedicated

---

[22] Evan Senior, 'How a Dance Band Helped An English Composer', *Records and Recording*, October 1957, p. 14.

[23] For a list of Prom performances see pp. 111–15.

to his earlier constant companion Arthur Miller. As Ireland reintroduces themes from the earlier movements he underpins them with a regretful countermelody, a reference to a tune from a student string quartet by Helen Perkin.[24] Yet Ireland seems to want this to remain a private allusion and wherever it appears he tries to disguise it.

A London Overture (1936)

This work originated as *A Comedy Overture,* the test piece for the Crystal Palace National Brass Band Contest in 1934. In May 1936 Adrian Boult, then Director of Music at the BBC, suggested to Ireland that he should orchestrate it for that year's Promenade Concerts. It occupied the composer through the whole of the summer, the first performance having to be put back at least once. It was finally heard at Queen's Hall on 23 September. Shortly after completing the full score (which is dated 31 August 1936) Ireland wrote to Boult underlining that 'the piece is now of far greater artistic significance, more complex in detail, technically difficult and subtle in style, than in its original form'.

At first called *In Town,* this title was dropped because it was too similar to a contemporary work of Eric Coates. As *A London Overture* it immediately caught on, and the little figure of four notes heard after the slow introduction was recognised as representing the cry of a London bus conductor: "dilly, Piccadilly!" Though, as the composer remarked: 'Beyond that, the work has little to do with Piccadilly, or at any rate, the Piccadilly of 1938'. Despite its extrovert manner and apparent light-heartedness, at the centre of the music is a tragedy. The clue comes in the dedication: 'In memory of Percy G. Bentham, Sculptor and friend – died June 1936'. The death of Bentham, one of Ireland's closest friends, came about on a hot summer's day as a consequence of his wearing a cheap panama hat in which, unknown to him, the hatband had been treated with a toxic substance and imperfectly washed; the wearer absorbed it, with fatal results, when sweating profusely in the heat. Ireland did not publicise this story, which was recounted to the writer by Ireland's former choirboy Charlie Markes, but once one appreciates this history the slower music that signals the development section takes on a new significance. The beautiful horn solo of the middle section weaves an elegiac strand through the opulent string texture, creating one of the most deeply felt passages in Ireland's music. Unlike horn solos in other orchestral works this is no elegy for long ago, no nostalgic race-dream, but a personal sorrow at sudden and unexpected loss in the capital city of the Empire. The words 'Memento mori' appear in the score and to underline the feeling of remembrance, muted strings outline the melody of Schumann's song *Widmung.* In August 1940 the composer wrote to the conductor Clarence Raybould to thank him for a performance of the work and remarked: 'That section was deeply moving, as I intended it to be'.[25] Between 1917 and 1920 Ireland had composed his three *London Pieces* for piano ('Chelsea Reach', 'Ragamuffin' and 'Soho Forenoons') and he now said his overture should be 'regarded as the fourth, and is in a similar light and unportentous manner'.

---

[24] See Helen Perkin's identification of her theme, p. 369, n. 7.

[25] John Ireland to Clarence Rayboult 12 August 1940; BBC WAC John Ireland file.

CENTRAL HALL, WESTMINSTER

Saturday, 11th October, 1941 at 2.30 p.m.

GOLDSMITHS' CHORAL UNION

AND

LONDON PHILHARMONIC ORCHESTRA

under the patronage of M. Maisky and Mr. Anthony Eden

Anglo-Soviet Concert

PROGRAMME

CHORAL WORKS :		ORCHESTRAL WORKS :		
These Things Shall Be " ...	*Ireland*	Overture - Portsmouth Point	....	*Walton*
Coronation Scene from		Trumpet Voluntary... ...	...	*Purcell*
" Boris Godounov " ...	*Moussorgsky*	Symphony No. 1		*Shostakovitch*
Dance Polovtsienne (Prince Igor)	*Borodin*	Overture - Russlan and Ludmilla ...		*Glinka*

Conductors :

FREDERICK HAGGIS
LESLIE HEWARD

TICKETS : (Reserved) Area 5/-; 3/6.   Balconies 7/6 5/- & 3/6
(Unreserved)- Area 2/6 & 1/6   Balconies 2/6
From **Box Office, Central Hall,** 11 a.m. to 5 p.m. (Sat. 11 a.m. to 1 p.m.) Telephone: WHItehall 7197
and all **Ticket Agencies.**
A Stamped addressed envelope must accompany all applications for tickets by post.

Fig. 20 A wartime Anglo-Soviet concert, 11 October 1941 including *These Things Shall Be*

These Things Shall Be (1937)

Early in 1937 Ireland was approached by the BBC with a commission for a work for the BBC's Coronation Concert to mark the crowning of King George VI which was to take place on 12 May that year. After some initial haggling over fees Ireland quickly responded with a scheme to set eight of the fifteen verses of the idealistic poem 'A Vista', from *Lyrics of Life and Art*, by John Addington Symonds (1840–93), and the sketch was ready during April. Ireland remarked that he felt the words were 'an expression of British national feeling at the present time'. In fact he had earlier made a quite different setting of these words for *The Motherland Song Book* published in 1919. The composer made a few adjustments to the words, most notably where 'Sad heart' becomes 'Say heart' at the beginning, and 'Transcending aught' becomes 'Transcending all' in the last line.

It was delivered bit by bit – the first half of the chorus part on 12 April. Ireland was not a quick worker and sensing that he could not finish it in time he recruited his friend and pupil Alan Bush to assist in preparing the full score. Ireland would indicate the instrumentation he had in mind, and Bush would then prepare the full score following Ireland's instructions. Later Ireland adopted a similar method of working when scoring the film music for *The Overlanders* to a pressing deadline. By 22 April the BBC had the remainder of the chorus part and the first half of the full score. The completed full score, dedicated to Alan Bush, arrived at the BBC only a fortnight before the first performance. After this performance in the BBC's Coronation Concert broadcast on 13 May 1937, Eric Fenby prepared the piano reduction used in the published vocal score. The first public performance followed at Queen's Hall on 1 December that year. Both this and the Coronation Concert were conducted by Sir Adrian Boult.

Rather late in the day Ireland decided to incorporate the *Internationale* into the music, and Alan Bush obliged him by writing it out. Ireland put the tune on the horn after the words 'paradise' at the end of the penultimate stanza. Almost immediately he had cold feet and asked the critic Edwin Evans not to identify the tune in his programme notes. After its first public hearing Ireland wrote a new horn part at this point.

The shadow of the First World War hung long over Ireland, as it did more overtly over the works of many of his contemporaries, and it is not surprising that the motif to which Ireland sets the words 'These things shall be' is also found in several other works, in particular in his setting of Rupert Brooke's *The Soldier* (1917) at the words 'If I should die'.[26]

While *These Things Shall Be* quickly found Ireland an enthusiastic following among choral societies and the wider public, it signalled the low-point of Ireland's relationship with his pupil Benjamin Britten. With its idealistic sentiments Ireland's music was very much of its time and found performance before the outbreak of war in September 1939 in concerts advocating peace, when it was heard alongside music by his pupils Britten and Alan Bush. Britten and his circle listened to the broadcast of the first performance of *These Things Shall Be* on 13 May 1937. Marjorie Fass's description of their reaction, in a letter to Daphne Oliver, underlines how Ireland was then seen by the younger generation:

---

[26] For Alan Rowlands' discussion of the *These Things* motif see p. 174. See also p. 90, n. 15.

It was <u>really</u> a disgrace. John Ireland has indeed sold his birthright for a mess of potage. A vulgar, would-be pretentious popular work, which might do for the mob. With <u>no</u> distinction, and only 1 passage of what even might be called music – indescribably yelling clichés, & a tune that was Elgar at his worst & most sentimental mushy ... Benjy was surprised at <u>our</u> surprise of the vileness of it, because for him Ireland is really bad all through ...[27]

A Downland Suite (1932, orch. 1941, 1978)
I. Prelude; II. Elegy; III. Minuet; IV. Rondo

Written as the test piece for the National Brass Band Championships of Great Britain in 1932, *A Downland Suite* was performed repeatedly by the competitors at that year's festival at Crystal Palace on 1 October. Later Ireland arranged the middle two movements for string orchestra, reversing their order and observing that they were much more effective when heard on the strings. In making this arrangement Ireland shortened the Minuet, but he extended the Elegy, writing a new introductory passage. These two movements were heard in a wartime BBC broadcast on 2 May 1942.

The German invasion of Guernsey in 1940 interrupted Ireland's work on the orchestration of the remaining movements, which he never resumed. It was left to his pupil Geoffrey Bush to complete it, and he was commissioned in 1978 by the John Ireland Trust to orchestrate the opening Prelude and concluding Round. Only then did we have a version of the whole suite for string orchestra. Geoffrey Bush remarked that he had 'followed the composer's example in reconceiving the music as a composition for string orchestra rather than making a literal re-arrangement of the brass band version'.

Legend for piano and orchestra (1933)

In terms of non-musical imagery the *Legend* is the third and last of that group of evocative orchestral scores that included *The Forgotten Rite* and *Mai-Dun*. Ireland's ambition to write a second piano concerto actually came to fruition in this single movement, half the length of the Concerto in E♭. First performed by Helen Perkin in January 1934, it was subsequently played by Harriet Cohen, and Ireland actually played it himself on a couple of occasions, including a Prom in 1935. The reception of the music was informed by Jocelyn Brooke's account of Ireland's mystical experience on the West Sussex Downs which is evoked in the music.[28] Writing before this, just after the Second World War, his friend and pupil Peter Crossley-Holland wrote:[29]

---

[27] *Letters from a Life: The Selected Letters and Diaries of Benjamin Britten, 1913–1976*, vol. 1: *1923–1939*, ed. Donald Mitchell (London: Faber & Faber, 1991), p. 531.

[28] See p. 353–4 for Brooke's complete text.

[29] Peter Crossley-Holland, 'John Ireland', ed. Lewis Foreman, *Manchester Sounds* vol. 7 (2007–8), pp. 16–18.

The gulf of time is also crossed in the *Legend* for piano and orchestra (1933). This work was the result of four months' sojourn in a lonely cottage on the West Sussex Downs. Somewhere there lies hidden an almost inaccessible spot, remote from human ways; human company is rarely to be found there, even at this late day. Becoming increasingly detached from ordinary life, the composer submitted day by day to the influences haunting the place, which could have changed but little since prehistoric times – although the only visible link with those days is a group of tumuli there. Perhaps they communicate something of the life of a tragic figure, whose sole memorial they are. The music opens with the mysterious summons of a horn call. A passage based on this leads later to music associated in some way with the idea of judgement: indeed the *Dies Irae* may be detected as the basis of the melody. As the tension increases there is a sense of penance being undergone: a soul running the gauntlet of the rumbling, groaning, and pounding of drums, horns and plucked strings. After a horrifying climax the music quickly subsides and an effortless ghostly dance takes place. Then, for a moment, there is promise of warmth and beauty 'over the top of the hill'. But soon the music grows cold and desolate, and the little decorative figures of the piano might almost suggest snowflakes falling: all ends in pain. The musical landscape, like the actual one that inspired it, is totally devoid of human life. There is no doubt that for this very reason *Legend* is the least-known of the major works: its message is unmistakable, and yet in an age of preoccupation with noise and the so-called realities of the external world, it speaks to the very few.

Crossley-Holland goes on to compare it with Holst's *Egdon Heath,* that gaunt haunted musical landscape inspired by Hardy's description of haggard Egdon – the stretch of desolate country between Wool and Bere Regis in Dorset described by Hardy in his novel *The Return of the Native.* As we have already seen, seven years before Holst, Ireland had evoked the ancient earthworks of Maiden Castle south-west of Dorchester. Now seven years later the country recalled is 60 miles to the east in Sussex.

Concertino Pastorale (1939)
I. Eclogue; II. Threnody; III. Toccata

In the period immediately before the Second World War the Boyd Neel String Orchestra had a high reputation for virtuosity and tone. They had presented Britten's *Variations on a Theme of Frank Bridge* at the Salzburg Festival in 1937, and it was Boyd Neel who commissioned Ireland's three-movement *Concertino Pastorale* and gave the first performance at Canterbury[30] some ten weeks before the outbreak of war. It was soon being performed by string orchestras in the UK and on the BBC, and was recorded by the Boyd Neel Orchestra in February 1940.

In April 1939 we find Ireland writing to his confidant, the Reverend Kenneth Thompson: 'I am having a hellish time trying to concoct a suite for string orchestra, with no ideas at all ... I do not see how anyone with any sensibility can compose

[30] 14 June 1939.

music in the present world-atmosphere ...' Even if invention came with increasing difficulty for Ireland it was in the context of a superb technique at the peak of his craft, and this is a delightful score, very much a work of its time, and it was widely performed.

The first movement, 'Eclogue', is a large-scale conception running over nine minutes. It opens with a darkening slow introduction perhaps coloured by the world crisis at that time and presaging the approaching storm clouds. One can imagine the composer in the expressive 'Threnody' that follows anxiously contemplating the familiar summer landscape of Sussex and Kent, and wondering what was to come. After the war the 'Threnody' was attached to *Mai-Dun* by the Sadler's Wells ballet and the resulting concoction was danced under the title *The Vagabonds*.

The virtuosic third movement, 'Toccata', contrasts nervous scherzando writing which is extended over many bars, with a lyrical pastoral invention which appears twice in brief lyrical interludes.

Sarnia (An Island Sequence)
(written for solo piano during 1940 and completed in 1941, orchestrated by Martin Yates, 2011)

I. 'Le Catioroc'; II. 'In a May Morning'; III. 'Song of the Springtides'

The piano suite *Sarnia* has been orchestrated by Martin Yates, to a commission from the John Ireland Trust, and recorded for Dutton Epoch by the Royal Scottish National Orchestra conducted by Martin Yates. While a remarkably effective piano suite, once one starts to consider it in orchestral terms one begins to suspect that perhaps Ireland might have imagined orchestral sonorities all the time and just could not face the labour of producing a score. Martin Yates remarked to the present writer: 'Ireland surely had the orchestra in mind when writing this evocative music.'

Treating it orchestrally adds a significant piece to the small corpus of Ireland's orchestral scores. This is a brilliant triptych of orchestral tone poems, evoking Guernsey and exploiting the music's latent colour and resonance, if not quite an English *La Mer* certainly a distinctive score. The first clue comes in 'Le Catioroc', Ireland's evocation of the Le Trépied Dolmen on the crest of 'La Pointe du Mont St. Jean' where the score's prefatory quotation from Pomponius Mela refers to 'shrilling of flutes and clashing of cymbals' (see Chapter 15, n. 5). This is very much music of atmosphere characterised by low pedal notes and with a rhythmic impetus given added colour by the orchestra, evoking the hidden terror lurking there, and reminding us that Ireland is again visiting the pagan ambience of his earlier orchestral scores *The Forgotten Rite* and *Mai-Dun*.

The sunny middle movement, 'In a May Morning', is even more of an Ireland musical bon-bon when heard on the orchestra than as a piano piece, alongside those earlier short Ireland pieces that have been scored by other hands. The finale, 'Song of the Spring Tides', when heard in orchestral dress, takes on a radiant impressionistic colour. Those sparkling climaxes at the brilliant cadenza-like culmination of the opening section and the thrilling closing bars acquire a new excitement in their orchestral dress.

Fig. 21 Martin Yates's orchestration of 'Le Catioroc' from *Sarnia* exploits the music's latent colour and resonance.

Epic March (1942)

At the prompting of the Ministry of Information, Sir Adrian Boult, then still Director of Music at the BBC, wrote to John Ireland a letter dated 28 November 1940. He suggested that Ireland might consider composing a patriotic march, combining the spirit of *A London Overture* and the broad tune of *These Things Shall Be.* By the following spring the matter had not progressed, and in a letter to Sir Adrian, Ireland reported 'I have thought the matter over carefully, and it is certain that I cannot do anything on the lines of "Pomp and Circumstance" no. 1. It is not what I feel appropriate at the present time ... What I have in mind is stern and purposeful rather than jolly or complacent.'

By 5 June Ireland was ready to send Boult a rough sketch (see Fig. 7, p. 96) of the opening of the march for his approval, quoting Winston Churchill's 'grim and gay' as a possible title. Later he wrote to Father Thompson: 'I shall aim at strength and definition ... rather than excessive brilliance ... The BBC wanted something jolly and hearty, but that is not my idea at all. ... There is something rational to be said in a direct and forcible way & I hope I may be given the power to do this work aright. You may specially remember me in this at the Altar, as I know it will help me. Except the Lord build the house ...' In July 1941 the V-Campaign (the Morse for the letter V – dot dot dot dash) became the subject of press comment – and Ireland was quick to point out that the opening theme of his march quite fortuitously adopted this very device.

By 2 September Ireland, to whom the whole thing was not coming easily, wrote to Sir Adrian again, announcing the completion of the first section and discussing whether to use the tune from *These Things shall Be* and whether to have it in triple or duple time. In the end he wrote something new. Ireland briefly considered 'The Liberators' as a title. On the published score he printed the definition of 'Epic' taken from *Nuttall's Standard Dictionary*: 'Concerning some heroic action or series of actions and events of deep and lasting significance in the history of a nation or a race.' The score is dated March 1942,[31] and it was first performed on the opening night of the 1942 Promenade Concerts on 27 June at the Royal Albert Hall, a performance that survives on an acetate disc and has been issued on CD.[32]

Scherzo and Cortège on themes from Julius Caesar *(1942), arranged by Geoffrey Bush*

John Ireland's incidental music to Shakespeare's play was written for a BBC wartime production broadcast in September 1942, and although he referred to it at the time as orchestral music, the score was actually written for a wind band, forces which are almost exactly retained in the concert arrangement by Ireland's pupil Geoffrey Bush. The arranger tells us that the music presented him 'with formidable problems. The score consists (apart from Lucius's song) of 18 instrumental fragments, the biggest of them only four pages long.' Thus the music is framed by

[31] Last page of the published miniature score, Boosey & Hawkes 1942.

[32] *Great Prom Premieres*, BBC MM295. There only half the performance was included. It is complete on a disc issued as a free cover-mounted CD with *BBC Music Magazine*, vol 6 no. 12 (2008).

Caesar's ceremonial trumpets. The opening scherzo presents the music celebrating the feast of Lupercal in Act 1 scene 2, with a motif used in the crowd scenes. The cortège encompasses Ireland's original overture and the various marches for Brutus and Cassius – a short Tragic March and the final Funeral March.

Satyricon (1946)

The overture *Satyricon*, after Petronius, was commissioned by the BBC for the 1946 Promenade Concerts and first played in the Royal Albert Hall on 11 September, when the BBC Symphony Orchestra was conducted by Constant Lambert. It was Ireland's last orchestral work (its composition originating as early as 1944, and overlapping his work on the film music for *The Overlanders* in 1946). It was doubtless commissioned by Julian Herbage at the instigation of Sir Henry Wood who died before it was completed. Herbage was then responsible for planning the Proms and he was soon to be Ireland's neighbour and drinking companion in Sussex. It was dedicated as a wedding present to Anna and Julian Herbage. A vivacious and somewhat Waltonesque score (if innocent, in the light of Fellini's later film) it reflects aspects of Petronius's fragmentary Latin chronicle. 'It was prompted', wrote Ireland, 'by the author's description of some of the vagabond and carefree adventures and escapades of the three Roman youths around which the story revolves.' On the flyleaf of his score he quoted from Burnaby's translation of Petronius: 'I ... am resolved to be as good as my Word, being so met to our Desires; not only to improve our Learning but to be merry, and put life into our Discourse with pleasanter Tales.'

It was completed on 19 August 1946 after considerable effort. The middle section clarinet solo was written with Ireland's friend Frederick Thurston in mind. Thurston, for whom Ireland had also written his Fantasy Sonata, had long been first clarinet of the BBC Symphony Orchestra, though unfortunately he left this post on 27 June 1946 and did not play in the first performance. As with so many of his later orchestral works it seems that Ireland was only able to get things finished when working against a deadline which cost him dear in stress and strain.[33]

The Overlanders (1946)

Written and directed by Harry Watt, produced by Sir Michael Balcon and starring Chips Rafferty, Ealing Studios' 1946 film *The Overlanders* is very much a child of the pre-war documentaries of Cavalcanti and the Post Office Film Unit. Almost a dramatised documentary, with little serious plotting or development of character, and with the use of a narrator to explain the salient points of the story, it has long sequences without music. The music, nevertheless, made a significant contribution both to the pacing of the film and to its success, especially when issued on two sides of a 12-inch 78.

In 1942 the Japanese were driving southwards from Singapore. It seemed inevitable that next into their hands would fall the Northern Territory of Australia, with a million head of cattle and only 5,000 settlers. Scorched earth and space were

---

[33] See Charles Markes' account of correcting errors in the proofs of *Satyricon*, p. 75.

Australia's final weapons, and across Australia moved a tidal wave of animals. This film told the story of the first of these and of the drover whose vision made the impossible possible.

As is so often the case in film music that quickly appeared in concerts and on recordings, the exact extent of the 'suite' was determined by the conductor, initially Muir Mathieson, probably reflecting the performing materials that survived. The orchestral 'suite' generally played (and recorded by Richard Hickox in 1991) was prepared by Sir Charles Mackerras and published in 1971. It was first recorded by Sir Adrian Boult in 1964, and later by David Measham, Richard Hickox and John Wilson. It consists of five movements: March: 'Scorched Earth'; Romance: 'Mary and the Sailor'; Intermezzo: 'Open Country'; Scherzo: 'The Brumbies'; Finale: 'Night Stampede'. The first movement consists of the title and the scorched earth music of the opening, the first two cues in the film. The contrasting Romance that follows comes from later in the film: the shy attraction between Mary and the sailor who hates the sea and joins the drovers as their cook, is very lightly sketched and some commentators have been irritated by what they took as an unnecessary twist to the plot. That brief love scene comes immediately before the night stampede (the fifth movement of the suite) after which the sailor is found lying injured from his untutored efforts to turn the cattle. The opening phrases of the Romance are heard as Mary tends the injured sailor, cutting quickly into the earlier love music.

The great trek sets out with the 'Open Country' music. Ireland's invention for the droving music returns in many guises throughout the film and becomes a sort of leitmotif. It is first heard in the extended open country cue with which the drove begins. The task is to drive 968 head of cattle 1,500 miles to Queensland, and they have fifty-three horses to help them in the task: the contrasted 'Broad and Noble' passage that follows is the backdrop in the film for one of the passages of narration.

After 500 miles disaster strikes when the horses eat poisoned weed and die. To replace them, wild horses called 'brumbies' are caught and broken to saddle. The music in the suite starts with the scene where the horses are driven through a slip-gate into the trap, and then moves on to the more jagged music, evoking the process of breaking them in. The clarinet solo here again embodies Ireland's admiration of the playing of Frederick Thurston, so recently celebrated in the Fantasy Sonata for Clarinet, and in the middle section of *Satyricon*. After many further vicissitudes the herd stampedes at night, a scene strongly evoked in the nocturnal black and white camera work of Osmond Borradaile and excitingly underlined by Ireland's music.

The orchestrations for the film was mostly done by the music director, Ernest Irving, in accordance with the instructions marked on the short score by Ireland. 'The Brumbies' is an exception: Alan Rawsthorne worked on the full score, which was then altered in one important respect by Irving at the recording session. He added a *pizzicato* violin counter-melody above the clarinet solo in order to overcome Harry Watt's objection to the chamber-music texture of the original.

Ireland composed the music for *The Overlanders* during March and April 1946. It was recorded on the soundtrack on 3 May and the film was released in London in October that year to considerable acclaim. A proposal for a second film score for Cavalcanti's *Toilers of the* Sea came to nothing when Cavalcanti left Ealing Studios.

Two Symphonic Studies

These two movements consist of some of the music that Ireland wrote for the film *The Overlanders*: cues that were not incorporated into the concert suites which Muir Mathieson and later Sir Charles Mackerras extracted from the film score. The composer Geoffrey Bush, who arranged these two extended movements, remarked that they should be regarded as 'concert music complete and self-sufficient in its own right' and he felt they were a worthy successor to Ireland's previous orchestral tone poem *Mai-Dun* written twenty-five years earlier.

Short Works

Even in his lifetime a number of John Ireland's short keyboard pieces and songs were orchestrated by others, apparently with the composer's approval. Since his death others have been so arranged including several orchestrated by Martin Yates and Graham Parlett to John Ireland Trust commissions for Dutton Epoch recordings. It is remarkable how effective these have been. While Ireland orchestrated several of his ballads and other songs before the First World War, subsequently a variety of other songs have been similarly arranged. These arrangements are:

ORCHESTRAL PIECES

(A) FOR SMALL ORCHESTRA

The Holy Boy (1913, orch. Ireland 1941), see note above
The Towing Path (1918, orch. Martin Yates 2009)
A Downland Suite (1932, orch. 1941, completed Geoffrey Bush 1978),
　　see note above
Scherzo & Cortège on themes from *Julius Caesar* (1942, arr. Geoffrey Bush),
　　see note above
Elegiac Meditation (1959, orch. Geoffrey Bush, 1982), see note on pp. 257–8
Two Salon Pieces: *Menuetto-Impromptu; Villanella* (1904, orch. Leslie
　　Bridgewater 1931)
Merry Andrew (1919, orch. C. H. Clutsam 1931)

(B) WITH SOLO VIOLIN

Berceuse (1903, orch. Yates 2009)
Cavatina (1904, orch. Graham Parlett 2008)
Bagatelle (1911, orch. Leslie Bridgewater 1924)
Soliloquy (1922, orch. Parlett 2009)

(C) WITH SOLO CELLO

The Holy Boy (1913, orch. Christopher Palmer 1994)

VOICE AND ORCHESTRA

Annabel Lee: recitation with orchestra (1910, orch. Roderick Williams 2009)

In Praise of Neptune (1911, orch. Ireland)

Here's To the Ships (1911, orch. Ireland 1912)

Sea Fever (1913, orch. Ireland; also orch. G. Williams)

When Lights go Rolling Round the Sky (1911, orch. D. Darlow)

Youth's Spring-Tribute (1913, orch. Ireland)

The Holy Boy: a Carol of the Nativity (1913, orch. Ireland 1938)

Hope the Hornblower (1911, orch. Frederick Bye)

If There Were Dreams to Sell (1918, orch. Frederick Bye, also E. Griffiths)

When I Am Dead, My Dearest (1924, orch. Graham Parlett)

Five Songs for Soprano & Orchestra (orch. Graham Parlett 2008):

   Love and Friendship (1926)

   My True Love Hath My Heart (1920)

   The Trellis (1920)

   Adoration (1918)

   I Have Twelve Oxen (1918)

Four Songs for Soprano & Strings (orch. Graham Parlett 2008):

   The Salley Gardens (c. 1931)

   The Heart's Desire (1917)

   Baby (1918)

   Her Song (1925)

CHAPTER 17

The Happy Highways:
John Ireland's Chamber Music

Bruce Phillips

> That is the land of lost content
> I see it shining plain,
> The happy highways where I went
> And cannot come again.[1]

W HEN the fourteen-year-old John Ireland enrolled at the Royal College of Music in 1893 his ambition was to become a concert pianist. He studied the piano and organ, but seems to have begun composing music soon after he arrived in London and before he won the scholarship that enabled him to study composition with Stanford. Very few works from this period survive. Either Ireland disposed of the manuscripts or he withheld them from performance or publication, referring to them as scholarship or studentship pieces. He soon realised that a career as a concert pianist was beyond his pianistic abilities, though he was able to obtain several posts as a church organist and published a handful of organ and church pieces in the early 1900s.

Towards the end of his life he allowed several works dating from his student days to be performed and published: two string quartets, a sextet for clarinet, horn and string quartet, two pieces for piano which made up a work entitled *In Those Days*, and *Vexilla Regis*, a hymn for Passion Sunday scored for soloists, chorus and brass.

John Ireland's first attempts as a student at extended scores were cast as chamber music, and although an early Trio is now lost, in the same year, 1897, he also wrote the two string quartets, dated respectively 6 March and 13 September, which have survived and have been played again and recorded.

String Quartet no. 1 in D minor

The First Quartet is in four movements – 1. *Allegro*, 2. *Scherzo (molto allegro)*, 3. *Andante moderato*, 4. Finale (*vivace*). It was written at the period when he ceased to be a mere student and obtained a scholarship enabling him for the next four years to study composition with Charles Villiers Stanford. Another work that dates from this time is the Sextet for string quartet, clarinet and French horn, discussed below. Stanford appears to have been discouraging. Ireland relates how his teacher dismissed his teenage attempts at composition as 'all Brahms and water and more water than Brahms' and instructed Ireland to take them away, study Dvořák, and bring him music that did not sound like diluted Brahms. However, the head of the RCM at that time, Sir Hubert Parry, was impressed

---

[1] A. E. Housman – XL from *A Shropshire Lad*.

by Ireland's untutored efforts and awarded him the scholarship. For many years these and other student works were unperformed (apart from student concerts at the RCM) and unpublished. Ireland went on to develop a much more individual musical language deriving not only from the German nineteenth-century tradition of Beethoven, Mendelssohn and Brahms but also from the new music of the turn of the twentieth century, notably that of Ravel and Debussy. Another influence was that of English folksong, though he never embraced it as wholeheartedly as his contemporaries Ralph Vaughan Williams and Gustav Holst. The music of his student days was put away in a drawer and had to wait some sixty years until the formation of the John Ireland Society in the late 1950s persuaded him to allow it to be performed and published. Though Ireland's reputation rests in part on his chamber music he never returned to the medium of the string quartet, preferring the piano trio and the sonata for solo instrument and piano.

The D minor quartet bears witness to Ireland's teenage mastery of the form and texture of the string quartet and also of his ability to write striking and memorable tunes. One can see why Stanford complained of the overwhelming influence of Brahms, and at the same time why Parry thought its composer worthy of a composition scholarship. Another influence might be thought to be Elgar, notable in the falling sixth of the main theme of the opening movement were it not for the fact that Ireland's quartet was written two years before the *Enigma Variations*, when comparatively few of Elgar's early works had been heard in London.

Quartet no. 2 in C minor for strings

Even more than his first Quartet, in his Second, completed some six months later, all Ireland's models were classical ones, dominated by Beethoven, and with contemporary music represented by Brahms and Dvořák. From the first it is clear that the composer is no tyro at string quartet writing, although he has not yet found even a shadow of his mature voice. But this is writing on a considerable scale, the first movement complete with exposition repeat followed by a series of varied episodes characterised by an almost Schubertian change of key, the briefest of recapitulations bringing the closing flourish.

Here in the C minor Quartet he has surely matured in the few months since its predecessor. The 53-bar slow movement is really only an interlude, a brief meditation on a wide-spanning warmly Brahmsian theme. In this second movement, an evocative, singing Nocturne, Ireland has his first violin accompanied by muted strings, later taking the mute, and then all the quartet throwing off the mutes for the closing *Più animato*.

The third movement is a thistledown scherzo. The 20-bar exposition is again repeated, with a lyrical 16-bar trio extended *Allegretto* episode effectively forming the trio played twice. Ireland follows with a *da capo* of the first half of the piece.

But perhaps the headlong, singing, finale is the most successful movement, with its ebullient opening theme, its dancing treatment and lyrical second subject. Here in the finale the repetition of sections is used most extensively, and the listener needs to be aware that there are seven such passages.

Sextet for horn, clarinet and string Quartet (1898)

In 1892 and 1895 the celebrated German clarinettist Richard Mühlfeld visited England and gave many performances of the then new Brahms Clarinet Quintet. Ireland seems to have been present at those at St James's Hall in 1895, two years before the clarinettist's death, though Ireland later appears to have been under the impression it had been the first performance.[2] Mühlfeld's playing and tone had a profound effect on many composers who heard him, not least Ireland's teacher, Charles Villiers Stanford, who wrote a concerto that Mühlfeld never played. Ireland had also played the piano part in Brahms's Piano Trio, op. 8, and was fully conversant with the music of the composer who was then regarded as the greatest living. Stanford had also recommended Ireland to study Dvořák, and the blend of these two great masters of the period seems to have inspired Ireland to produce a work that displays a thorough grasp of their music and a strong feeling for melody and form. Stanford criticised the last movement for not being organic.

Despite his lifelong admiration for Stanford as teacher and composer, Ireland did not have enough confidence in his student works to allow them to be performed outside the bounds of the Royal College, or to be published. The manuscripts of the quartets and the sextet were filed away in a drawer, and were not heard again until very near the end of his life. In the case of the sextet the request to permit a performance came from the late Dame Thea King (1925–2007). She was visiting the composer in his converted windmill home under the lee of Chanctonbury Ring in West Sussex to discuss his Fantasy Sonata for clarinet and piano. She asked him if he had written anything else for clarinet, and Ireland produced from a drawer the manuscript of the Sextet. After going through it with her (despite his failing sight he remembered every noteworthy aspect of the work even though he had not heard it for over sixty years) he sanctioned its first public performance at a London concert of the Hampton Music Club in the drawing-room of the Arts Council's London offices, St James's Square on 25th March 1960.[3] Thea King played the clarinet, John Burden the horn, and the quartet was the Pro Musica. Ireland sat in the front row, hearing the work for the first time for sixty-two years.

The work opens with a soft horn-call which brings to mind the opening of Brahms's Second Piano Concerto. The violin answers with the main theme of the movement. The clarinet steals in with two upward arpeggios. The horn announces the second subject, and the two principal themes are developed and decorated until the first subject returns and the movement ends in an emphatic coda. The slow movement is marked *Andante con moto* and Ireland unfolds a songlike melody in D major on the clarinet, supported by the quartet. Later the key changes to C minor and the horn plays a dotted theme in thirds with the clarinet over pizzicato strings. The music rises to a brief climax marked *Appassionato* then subsides back into the A major theme until the end of the movement. Ireland originally called the sextet 'Intermezzo' and this remains as the heading to the third movement, a lilting *Allegretto con grazia* which summons up thoughts of the scherzo of the

---

[2] See Ireland's own account on p. 410

[3] See Plate 71.

Brahms clarinet quintet. Two main themes predominate until the horn announces another horn call over pizzicato strings and the movement ends quietly. The finale, marked *In tempo moderato*, opens with a melody played by the viola, subsequently taken over by the clarinet. Towards the middle of the movement the tempo slows and the horn and quartet adopt a chugging rhythm suggestive of a steam train leaving a station. The music broadens out into a dialogue between clarinet and horn and eventually the opening theme returns on the horn, gathers pace and concludes in a brief *Presto* section in which all the instruments combine to bring the work to an end.

A MONG Ireland's early music there are several violin sonatas, of which we can document an example in G Minor dating from 1905, though it is now lost. For Ireland, recognition as a composer did not come about until 1908–9, when his *Phantasie* for piano trio won second prize in the Cobbett Chamber Music competition and was performed and published. Between then and the 1940s he produced a steady stream of works on which his reputation rests, mainly in the fields of solo piano and chamber music and song. Ireland's suite of three pieces written in 1912–13 under the collective title *Decorations* ('The Island Spell', 'Moon-glade' and 'The Scarlet Ceremonies') reveals the impact made upon him by the new music of Debussy and Ravel. He followed these with the four *Preludes* of 1913–15 and the three *London Pieces* ('Chelsea Reach', 'Ragamuffin', and 'Soho Forenoons') of 1917–20. A major piano piece from this period was the powerful *Rhapsody* of 1915, a work in which Ireland combines sections of dramatic keyboard virtuosity with gentler and more melodically reflective passages.

For unknown reasons Ireland withheld an earlier *Rhapsody* in F♯ minor written in 1905–6. Fortunately a complete autograph manuscript dated London, 16 January 1906 exists in the British Library. We have no information as to whether it was ever performed nor about Ireland's reasons for completely suppressing it. He seems not to have mentioned it to any of the many pianists who played his music whereas he attached particular significance to the later *Rhapsody* and regarded it as one of his major works. Yet Ireland did not destroy the manuscript. As is made clear by Mark Bebbington and John Lenehan in their recordings, the piano writing is passionate, brilliant and virtuosic. The opening statement, marked *allegro appassionato* and very Brahmsian in its directness and ruggedness (compare the *Intermezzo* op. 118, no. 1), also calls to mind Liszt or even Rachmaninov with its octaves in the right hand and surging arpeggios in the left. The vigorous mood slows and Ireland introduces a calmer and gentler theme in G♭ major marked *dolce, cantando*. The remainder of the work consists in the development of this central theme in combination with the opening statement. At around 12½ minutes it is Ireland's longest single work for solo piano, and an important new addition to the annals of British piano music.

Phantasie Trio in A minor

The name of Walter Willson Cobbett (1847–1937) resounds through the annals of chamber music in Britain in the early part of the twentieth century. He was born in Blackheath, London, the son of a businessman with literary and musical interests. After private tuition in England, France and Germany he started work as an underwriter at Lloyds, then became, in his own words, 'an exploiter of certain patents, one of which turned up trumps'. He co-founded the firm of Scandinavian Belting Ltd, a very successful and profitable company manufacturing a new type of woven belting that has now become part of the large aviation company BBA Aviation Ltd. This enabled him to retire at the age of sixty and devote himself to what he considered to be his life's work, the development and promotion of the art of chamber music. Himself an amateur violinist and an enthusiastic string quartet player, he inaugurated in 1905 a series of Cobbett chamber music competitions which were of great significance in the careers of many British composers of that era. He also endowed the Cobbett Medal in 1924, awarded annually by the Worshipful Company of Musicians for services to chamber music, and a series of Cobbett Prizes at the Royal College of Music. His *Cyclopedic Survey of Chamber Music*, published in 1930,[4] encompasses a lifetime's practical experience.

One of Cobbett's aims was to revive and popularise the appreciation of chamber music and to this end he asked that works submitted should consist of a single-movement structure in the manner of the Fancy or Fantasia widely cultivated by such English composers as Orlando Gibbons in the years between the death of Elizabeth I and the early years of Charles II – thus a piece of short duration performed without a break but, if the composer desired, to consist of different sections varying in tempo and meter. The prizes were originally supplemented by generous donations from liverymen of the Worshipful Company of Musicians, a City Guild whose members took a great interest in Cobbett's scheme.

The first competition, in 1905, was for string quartet and attracted sixty-seven entries. It was won by William Hurlstone, with Frank Bridge's Phantasie in F minor placed second.

The second competition in 1907 was for piano trios, this time won by Frank Bridge (born the same year as Ireland) and with John Ireland's Phantasy in A minor placed equal second with James Friskin's Phantasie also in A minor. It was Ireland's first work to bring his name before a wider audience.

The third competition was announced in 1909, for a sonata, not a Phantasy. It attracted 134 submissions, and the first prize was awarded to Ireland in 1910 for his Violin Sonata (no. 1) in D minor, which is discussed below.

Ireland's second venture into the piano trio genre – he had composed one in A minor in 1897 but this was discarded and the manuscript has been lost – was the first chamber music work he allowed to be published. Hitherto he had published only church and organ music and a couple of the short pieces for violin. It remains one of his most immediately attractive and popular compositions, beautifully constructed, its four sections condensing into a single continuous structure, the movements of a work in sonata form, as prescribed by the rules of the competition. It was dedicated to Stanford, and first performed at the Aeolian Hall in London on 26 January 1909 by the London Trio, the first classical piano trio to have been

---

[4] *Cobbett's Cyclopedic Survey of Chamber Music*, 2 vols. (London: Oxford University Press, 1930). The John Ireland entry (vol. 2, pp. 20–4) is by Edwin Evans.

formed (in 1904) in Great Britain (Amina Goodwin, violin; Achille Simonetti, cello; W. E. Whitehouse, piano). The same trio played it at three of the Thomas Dunhill chamber concerts at Steinway Hall in March 1909, and another performance was given in February 1910 by Beatrice Langley, violin; May Mukle, cello; and York Bowen, piano.

Violin Sonata no. 1 in D minor (1908–9)

The third, and this time international, Cobbett competition was for a sonata for violin and piano. It attracted 134 submissions, the initial screening of which took, in Cobbett's words, 'heavy toll of my leisure hours'. Cobbett added a fascinating personal reminiscence about Ireland after the Ireland entry in his *Cyclopedic Survey of Chamber Music*[5] which is relevant here:

> This British composer has expressed himself so generously to me on the subject of the stimulus these competitions afforded him in early days to enter the lists as a composer of chamber music, that I cannot let the occasion pass without my own personal tribute to his genius, and above all to the originality of thought which swayed the judges in 1910 and induced them, after six months of patient plodding through 134 MS. sonatas for piano and violin sent from all parts of the world where music is cultivated, to award him the first prize. The competitive field naturally holds Ireland no longer, and he stands as one of the most prominent British composers of the present day. I may add that Bronislaw Hubermann includes this sonata in his repertory.

The jury pronounced John Ireland's Sonata in D minor the winner, and the sonata was published by Goodwin & Tabb in 1911, dedicated to Cobbett himself, and the first performance was given on 7 March 1913 at a Thomas Dunhill Chamber Concert at Steinway Hall by Marjorie Hayward, violin (the dedicatee of Ireland's short 1911 piece for violin and piano *Bagatelle*) with the composer at the piano. Augener published a revised edition in 1917 in the wake of the success of Ireland's second violin sonata, and then a further revision in 1944.

The work is in three movement: 1. *Allegro leggiadro* – 2. Romance: *in tempo sostenuto, quasi adagio* – 3. Rondo: *allegro sciolto assai*. In his remarkable Internet blog on English music[6] John France quotes from a review of July 1915 in the *Monthly Musical Record*. After a list of works contributed by Ireland himself (of interest in itself since it lists several works of his student period most of which he withdrew) the article quotes from press reviews of some of Ireland's works including the first violin sonata. The critic of the *Star* writes:

> Delicacy, lucidity, and tonal charm are qualities inherent in the music. Coherence of ideas is apparent in the three movements, which are cleverly and definitely contrasted in mood. There is a strong vein of temperament in every one.

This pinpoints the essential features of this most genial and optimistic of Ireland's

---

[5] *Cobbett's Cyclopedic Survey*, vol. 2, p. 24

[6] http://landofllostcontent.blogspot.com

sonatas. Though not a single movement phantasy, there are plenty of motivic inter-connections between the movements, not the least of which is the murmuring piano figure in the opening movement which occurs in modified form in the other two movements and acts as a unifying link.

One of the most striking of Ireland's inventions occurs in the middle movement: the key changes abruptly from B major to D♭ and the tempo slows to *lento*. The pianist plays pianissimo a phrase consisting of block chords in modal harmony which is strikingly similar to the opening of the third song of Vaughan Williams's Housman cycle *On Wenlock Edge*, 'Is my team ploughing?'. This song was first sung in public on 26 January 1909 at a concert sponsored by Gervase Elwes and James Friskin. The complete song cycle was first performed at the Aeolian Hall on 15 November 1909. Ireland's sonata, as we have seen, was submitted for the 1909 Cobbett Prize but not published until 1911 and not performed in public until 1913. But Ireland and Vaughan Williams had been friends and fellow composition students of Stanford at the Royal College of Music and were in the habit of playing through their new compositions to each other.[7] It was only on one of these occasions that they discovered they had independently composed very similar passages but had employed them very differently.

Clarinet Trio in D minor

Ireland's next chamber work involving the clarinet was a Trio for clarinet, cello and piano written between April 1912 and October 1913. It was first performed on 9 June 1914 at Steinway Hall in a Thomas Dunhill Chamber Concert, when the players were Charles Draper, clarinet, May Mukle, cello, and Ireland himself as pianist. Charles Draper (1869–1952), sometimes called the grandfather of English clarinettists, had also heard Mühlfeld play in London and was influenced by his style of playing. He taught many British clarinettists including Ireland's later champion Frederick Thurston. He had given the first performance of Stanford's Clarinet Concerto, of which he was the dedicatee. May Mukle (1880–1963)[8] was a prominent cellist who played in the first performance in England of Ravel's Piano Trio (when Ireland was the pianist).

Ireland withdrew the Trio after a couple of performances and reworked it in a different key and with violin instead of clarinet. This too was withdrawn, and not revived until Ireland again radically reworked some of the material for his Piano Trio no. 3 in 1938 and added a completely new slow movement. The manuscript is incomplete: the missing sections are the last few bars of the first movement, and much of the scherzo, in total amounting to about a quarter of the duration of the piece. One of the original movements, presumably the slow movement, has disappeared altogether. We now know it in the performing edition that has been reconstructed and edited by the Canadian clarinettist and clarinet-maker Stephen Fox, and full details of his edition are to be found on his website.[9] He has rewritten the missing sections by close analogy with the corresponding parts of the 1938 Piano

---

[7] See Ireland's reminiscence of Vaughan Williams, p. 413–14.

[8] Pronounced 'Mooclay'.

[9] http://www.riverdaleensemble.com/Ireland_Trio.html

Trio, and in place of the missing slow movement, probably now lost for ever, he has inserted the *Lento* section from the interim violin version as the optional slow introduction to the third movement.

It is not known why Ireland withdrew the work, nor why he did not allow it to be resurrected with the Sextet in answer to Thea King's plea for more works for clarinet. He may have felt dissatisfied with some of the writing for clarinet, and his reworking of those parts that he did re-use in the 1938 Piano Trio demonstrates how far his style had travelled since the versions produced during the early part of World War I. Nevertheless Stephen Fox's reconstruction, published by Emerson Edition Ltd, has redeemed from unmerited oblivion a work of beauty and craftsmanship and has made an invaluable addition to the repertoire of clarinet trios.

Piano Trio no. 2 in E minor-major (June 1917)

Ireland spent the First World War years living in London, working as organist and choirmaster at St Luke's Church, Chelsea, and writing two major chamber works that clearly reflect his reactions to the war – a mixture of patriotism and anger at the appalling slaughter. A thirty-five-year-old man, and somewhat short in stature, he would not have been an obvious choice for military service.[10]

The crucial year in terms of Ireland's reputation as a composer was 1917. That year saw the performance, in March and June respectively, of his Violin Sonata no. 2 in A minor and his Piano Trio no. 2 in E. The second violin sonata, premiered at the Wigmore Hall by the celebrated violinist Albert Sammons and the Australian pianist William Murdoch, both wearing khaki, made a huge impression on the audience, not least on Frank Bridge. Three months later came the second piano trio, and this too was recognised immediately as expressing in music some of the intense emotions evoked in a composer of great personal sensitivity. Fiona Richards describes it very well:[11]

> This is a work of mixed emotions, contrasting passages of stark textures and caustic harmonies with effusive moments and grim marches. The structure of the work is a succession of episodes exploring different moods, all of which are melodic metamorphoses of the first eighteen bars of the piece.

The critic Edwin Evans remarked that the Trio 'bears the impress of the grim contrast between the season and the wastage of war at the very springtime of life'.[12] The cellist Florence Hooton, who performed Ireland's music a great deal and recorded the three trios with her violinist husband David Martin and the pianist Nigel Coxe, reported that Ireland told her that the section marked *Allegro giusto* evoked 'the boys going over the top of the trenches'.

---

[10] For Ireland's own account see p. 418.

[11] Fiona Richards, *The Music of John Ireland* (Aldershot: Ashgate, 2000), p. 179.

[12] For Evans's complete text see p. 385.

Sonata no. 2 in A minor for violin and piano

Ireland's most successful chamber work, the Second Violin Sonata, is in three movements – 1. *Allegro*, 2. *Poco lento quasi adagio*, 3. *In tempo moderato – con brio*. Ireland started work on his second violin sonata in 1915 and completed it in January 1917. He submitted it for a competition organised by a fund for assisting musicians in wartime (not a Cobbett competition). The jury was made up of the violinist Albert Sammons, the Australian-born pianist William Murdoch and the organist and conductor Percy Pitt. Ireland was awarded the prize of 40 guineas and the first performance was given by Sammons and Murdoch, both privates in the Grenadier Guards and wearing their khaki uniforms, at Aeolian Hall, New Bond Street on 6 March 1917. Many leading musicians were present. Ireland wrote of it:

> For me it was an electrifying occasion. Little of my music had been publicly heard, and I felt that my fate as a composer was to be decided at that particular moment in time, as proved to be the case. … It was probably the first and only occasion when a British composer was lifted from relative obscurity in a single night by a work cast in a chamber-music medium. [13]

The work caused something of a sensation. Reviews were wildly enthusiastic ('a brilliant specimen of his powers' – *Musical Times*) and the music publisher Winthrop Rogers undertook immediate publication, we are told selling out the first printing before publication. Ireland 'woke up to find himself famous', and there were many calls for more performances, including one given by Ireland and the violinist Désiré Defauw[14] at an Anglo-French Concert at the newly reopened and renamed Wigmore Hall (formerly Bechstein Hall). As Robert Matthew-Walker explains[15] Ireland and Catterall recorded on 78s a truncated version of the work on acoustic discs, and then Sammons and the composer the full work in 1930, though the recording was not issued until Dutton Epoch remastered it and issued it in 1999 on a CD which also includes the 1945 Decca recording of the first violin sonata played by Ireland and the violinist Frederick Grinke.[16]

As might be expected, the sonata bears witness to an increasing mastery of structure, and may be said to reflect the impact of the war. Ireland was rejected for military service but along with the whole of sensitive humanity was deeply affected by the slaughter in the trenches. As the choirmaster of St Luke's Church, Chelsea he was acutely aware of the loss of life of young men, and in this sonata he

---

[13] See p. 419.

[14] Defauw was a refugee from Belgium during the First World War, later he became the leading Belgian conductor of his day. References to him as M. Defauw are merely referring to his French-speaking nationality. At the time all French artists tended to be referred to as 'Monsieur xxx' by the British press.

[15] See p. 315.

[16] Dutton Epoch CDLX 7103 – as well as the two violin sonatas with Ireland as pianist, the disc also includes the first recording of the *Phantasie Trio* played by Grinke, Hooton and Kendall Taylor, and *The Holy Boy* in a cello arrangement, played by Florence Hooton accompanied by Lawrence Pratt.

seems to have captured both the anguish and the pity of war (as the poet Wilfred Owen put it) in a way that evoked very strong feelings in those who heard it.

Sonata in G minor for cello and piano

Like his violin sonatas, John Ireland's cello sonata, written in 1923, is in three movements – 1. *Moderato e sostenuto*, 2. *Poco largamente – non troppo lento*, 3. *Con moto e marcato*. It may have been written with the cellist Beatrice Harrison in mind, and was first performed by her at Aeolian Hall on 4th April 1924 with Ireland's RCM friend Evlyn Howard-Jones as pianist. Other works closely connected with her were Delius's cello sonata and his cello concerto and double concerto, and Elgar's cello concerto, of which she made two famous recordings conducted by Elgar himself. At the time she was celebrated for her recording and broadcast of her playing the cello in her garden at Limpsfield accompanied by nightingales. Later in the 1920s Ireland's sonata was discovered by the Spanish cellist Antoni Sala, who gave many performances with the composer and recorded it with him. Ireland broadcast it with several other cellists and subsequently it was championed by Florence Hooton, Karine Georgian and most recently Julian Lloyd Webber, who is on record as saying that in his view it is the finest cello sonata written in the twentieth century.

Like the Second Violin Sonata, the Cello Sonata was also arranged for viola by Lionel Tertis and first performed by him at a National Gallery Concert on 17 October 1941 with the composer at the piano, and they broadcast the work from the BBC's wartime Bedford studios on 14 December 1942. The Sonata is music of deep emotion, passion and intensity, among Ireland's most profoundly expressive utterances. A clue to its private significance can be found in the first movement,

Fig. 22 Antoni Sala. Detail from a cartoon by L. Brunet.

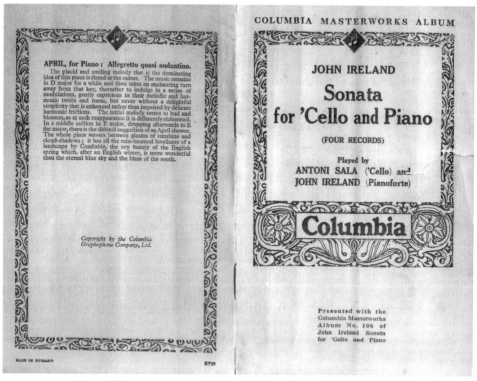

APRIL, for Piano : Allegretto quasi andantino.
The placid and smiling melody that is the dominating idea of this piece is stated at the outset. The music remains in D major for a while and then takes an enchanting turn away from that key, thereafter to indulge in a series of modulations, gently capricious in their melodic and harmonic twists and turns, but never without a delightful simplicity that is enhanced rather than impaired by delicate harmonic frictions. The initial melody seems to bud and blossom, as at each reappearance it is differently elaborated. In a middle section in E major, dropping afterwards to E flat major, there is the distinct suggestion of an April shower. The whole piece wavers between gleams of sunshine and cloud-shadows ; it has all the rain-haunted loveliness of a landscape by Constable, the coy beauty of the English spring which, after an English winter, is more wonderful than the eternal blue sky and the blaze of the south.

Copyright by the Columbia Graphophone Company, Ltd.

MADE IN ENGLAND   K725

JOHN IRELAND

Sonata
for 'Cello and Piano

(FOUR RECORDS)

Played by
ANTONI SALA ('Cello) and
JOHN IRELAND (Pianoforte)

Columbia

Presented with the Columbia Masterworks Album No. 106 of John Ireland Sonata for 'Cello and Piano

Fig. 23 The outer covers of the booklet for Ireland's own recording of his Cello Sonata, coupled with *April* (Columbia, 1929)

in the short section marked *tranquillo* and *secreto*. Here Ireland quotes the music from two lines of his 1918 setting of Aldous Huxley's poem *The Trellis*:

> None but the flowers have seen
> Our white caresses

This almost certainly alludes to his deep affection for Arthur Miller, the son of a Chelsea antiques dealer, and the individual behind the initials AGM which are found on several of Ireland's pieces. Miller had been a member of Ireland's choir at St Luke's, Chelsea, and in 1923 they took a motoring holiday together in Dorset,[17] visiting many of the megalithic remains which so deeply stirred Ireland's imagination in such works as *Mai-Dun*, his orchestral evocation of Maiden Castle near Dorchester.

The slow movement consists of a song-like melody similar in its passionate lyricism to the slow movement of the piano concerto (1930) and the middle piece, 'In a May Morning', of Ireland's *Sarnia* (1940–41), his powerful evocation for piano of his beloved Guernsey.

According to Ireland's friend John Longmire, another inspiration behind the cello sonata, in particular in the third movement with its upward leaps on the cello and the skipping-like piano accompaniment, was another favourite landscape with strong pagan and pre-Christian associations, the South Downs in West Sussex: the

---

[17] See Plate 19.

Devil's Jumps, a set of Bronze Age round barrows on Treyford Hill near Uppark. The writer Jocelyn Brooke (1908–66), an enthusiast for Ireland's music and in later life a friend, was strongly attracted to the cello sonata and writes imaginatively about it in his semi-autobiographical books *A Mine of Serpents* and *The Goose Cathedral*, two of the three volumes that make up his *Orchid Trilogy*.

Piano Trio No. 3 in E minor-major (1938)

Ireland did not return to the piano trio form until the end of the 1930s, twenty years after his previous essay in the medium. In 1938 he completed his Third Piano Trio, also in E, and this time in four movements. Perhaps because of his forebodings of the coming war his thoughts may have turned back to the work he had written just before the outbreak of the First World War. At all events he resurrected the manuscript of his abortive pre-First World war trio and reworked it extensively, drawing on material in the original clarinet version and the revised version for violin and adding a completely new slow movement.[18]

Ireland's Third Piano Trio was dedicated to William Walton, whose first symphony Ireland had greatly admired. The first broadcast performance was in April 1938 by Antonio Brosa, violin, Antoni Sala, cello (the Spanish cellist who had declared Ireland's cello sonata a masterpiece) and Ireland at the piano. The performers in the first London performance in June 1938 were Frederick Grinke, Florence Hooton and Ireland, and the location was the Upper Regent Street music room of the publishers Boosey & Hawkes, the occasion being part of the International Society for Contemporary Music festival.

In the first movement, *Allegro moderato*, Ireland is writing in the spirit of those earlier 'Phantasy' forms; only in the finale does he look to sonata form to shape his thought. The second movement has a jig-like character and with its modal feel one wonders whether Irish folk song may have been a distant influence. Throughout, the material of the first movement informs the remainder of the piece, perhaps most effectively in the *Pochissimo più moto* interlude in the slow movement.

Fantasy Sonata for clarinet and piano (1943)

Ireland had had great success with his first *Phantasie Trio* in A minor of 1908, which, as we have seen, had won second prize in that year's Cobbett Competition. He returned to a single-movement structure for one of his most popular chamber music works, the *Fantasy Sonata* for clarinet and piano. It was written in the period January–June 1943, when Ireland was lodging with the former curate of St Luke's Church, Chelsea, the Rev. Paul Walde and his wife Marjorie in Little Sampford Rectory, Essex. Ireland wrote it for, and dedicated it to, the greatest British clarinettist of his generation, Frederick Thurston (1901–53). Thurston, universally known as Jack, inspired many other British composers to write works for him: Bax, Bliss, Finzi, Howells, Malcolm Arnold, Iain Hamilton, Alan Rawsthorne and Elizabeth Maconchy among others. He married his pupil Thea King in 1953 but

---

[18] For a detailed account of the relationship between the two works see http://www.sfoxclarinets.com/Ireland.html and Fiona Richards's *The Music of John Ireland*.

Fig. 24 Antoni Sala, John Ireland and Antonio Brosa (violin), from an unidentified press cutting, *c.* 1938

died in the same year, as untimely a loss to music in Britain as Dennis Brain and Noel Mewton-Wood.

In this highly concentrated but richly romantic work Ireland gives expression to his love of the clarinet. To him it was the finest of the woodwind instruments, and in his orchestral works he never failed to include the clarinets in some of his most inspired scoring. One thinks for example of the beautiful clarinet tune in the *Andante sostenuto* section of his overture *Satyricon*. The *Sonata* opens in E♭ with a confident and arresting melody for the clarinet underpinned by some characteristic chromaticisms in the piano part. The music moves through a transitional passage for both instruments to a section in A major in which the piano writing mirrors that of another wartime work, *Sarnia*. There follows an episode in A♭ marked *Tranquillo* in which the clarinet meditates on the opening theme while the piano accompaniment ripples along underneath like a stream. The clarinet slows the proceedings down in a short four-bar cadenza leading to a section marked *Più lento*, a modification of the main tune in the piano part with the clarinet as if commenting on it from above. This moment of tranquillity is dispelled by more rippling arpeggios in the piano which then give way to a return to the songlike tranquillity. The tempo broadens, the clarinet plays a rapid downward scale, and we reach the penultimate section marked *Giusto* in which the pianist introduces a series of *marcato* chords in the right hand over a marching bass over which the clarinet plays a rhythmically altered version of the main theme. The suggestion is of horses galloping. A brilliant and dramatic final section propels the work to its stirring conclusion.

Fig. 25 St Luke's Church, Chelsea;
engraving by Thos. Shepherd, published by Jones & Co., 31 January 1828

CHAPTER 18

The Church Music of John Ireland

Jeremy Dibble

J OHN Ireland's contribution to the repertoire of the Anglican Church, though not particularly extensive, nevertheless represents a significant part of his crea-tive personality. This is measured not only by the works he produced in fits and starts throughout his lifetime for use within the Anglican liturgy, but also by his professional activities as an active church musician, and as a man of faith who increasingly grappled with Christian truths. The latter is particularly evident from the noteworthy correspondence between Ireland and the Rev. Kenneth Charles Thompson from 1936 until the composer's death in 1962.[1] Thompson admitted to being a form of private chaplain, even confessor, to Ireland, and besides revealing many personal, indeed more intimate aspects of Ireland's sexuality and emotions, their often lengthy and detailed correspondence includes much discussion of reli-gion and church music. According to Thompson, who first encountered Ireland in or around 1930, while he was priest-in-charge at St Cuthbert's, Kensington, Ireland inclined instinctively towards Anglo-Catholicism and his love of ritual shored up his faith even when, towards the end of his life, he was haunted by uncertainty: 'John was a sincere & faithful Anglican Christian – soon (I think) after his arrival in London he, accidentally as it were, wandered into a very high Anglo-Catholic Church (I believe it was St Mary Magdalen's Paddington) & was henceforth attracted to Anglo-Catholicism.'[2]

Though Ireland was attracted to the historic permanence of the Roman Cath-olic Church and to the multi-layered symbolism of its liturgical practices, he was not persuaded to convert.[3] Apart from Westminster Cathedral, recently completed in 1903, which offered under its Director of Music Richard Runciman Terry a vision of Roman Catholic music not seen since the Reformation, there were few opportunities afforded to an ambitious organist and composer in this tradition in England. The ritual and ceremony of Anglo-Catholicism therefore amply accom-modated Ireland's taste, not least because the musical tradition of Anglicanism, with its infrastructure of liturgy and choirs (and more specifically all-male choirs), provided much more ample musical opportunity for him as an organist, choir director and composer. In particular the Anglican liturgy had sympathetically and malleably evolved since the days of the Anglo-Catholic revival in the nine-teenth century to embrace not only a rich tradition of music for the Communion Service, but also for Matins and Evensong. Moreover, Anglicanism, wishing to take full advantage of the Nonconformist tradition of congregational participation in hymn-singing, had enthusiastically encouraged the composition of hymn tunes

---

[1] See *GB-Lbl*. Add. MSS 60535–6.

[2] Letter from Kenneth Thompson to Colin Scott-Sutherland, 20 September 1976, quoted in F. Richards, *The Music of John Ireland* (Aldershot: Ashgate, 2000), p. 37.

[3] See letter from Ireland to Ethel Ireland, 17 June 1936: *GB-Lbl*.

(as evidenced by the abundant proliferation of hymn-books during the second half of the nineteenth century) and, by the Edwardian era, original carols. Ritualism within the tradition of Anglo-Catholicism was also consistent with Ireland's inclination towards a kind of Romantic Paganism, to the rites of a more deep-seated, primeval existence when religious ceremony was more unbridled, perhaps suggesting that, as Fiona Richards has insinuated, paganism for Ireland implied a 'sense of liberation and loss of control', Nietzsche's Dionysiac categorisation perhaps, whereas Anglican ritual required a more Apollonian deportment of self-control and cerebral aloofness.[4] Ireland did at least attempt to articulate this very personal emotional bifurcation in a letter to Thompson:

> I am a bad sort of (Anglo) Catholic – not a constantly practising one, though it is ever in my heart and mind. It is the only thing which represents and prevents what is permanent – and age-long. As one grows older & ambitious pride & all becomes rather lacking in fire and significance, one's heart must turn towards what represents permanence. I do not wish ever to lose this. I am a Pagan, a Pagan I was born & a Pagan I shall ever remain. That is the foundation of religion. The deepest religious emotions I have ever felt have been at the Ceremonies on the Thursday and Friday before Easter – and what *we* cannot have – the ceremonies on the Saturday before Easter as practised by the Roman Church – something absolutely agelong & from everlasting – the rekindling of Fire – *Lumen Christi*.[5]

As a second-study organist at the Royal College of Music, where he studied under Walter Parratt, Ireland began to undertake services at London churches for small fees.[6] His first significant appointment appears to have been in *c.* 1895 at St Barnabas, South Lambeth, a large neo-Gothic church, where he deputised for six months. (Its principal organist at this time was Vaughan Williams, a fellow RCM student.) In or around 1897 he became deputy organist to Walter Alcock at the Church of Holy Trinity, Sloane Street, in Chelsea.[7] This move in every way brought a more challenging and pleasing environment to Ireland, who later described the church as having a 'reputation of the best musical service in London.'[8] There was a fine four-manual organ built by Walker in 1891, and forty boys' voices drawn from

---

[4] See Richards, *The Music of John Ireland*, p. 63.

[5] Letter from Ireland to Thompson, 16 July 1936: *GB-Lbl*. Add. MSS 65303–6.

[6] M. V. Searle, *John Ireland: The Man and His Music* (Tunbridge Wells: Midas Books, 1979), p. 17.

[7] Ireland arrived at Holy Trinity, Sloane Street at an auspicious time. The church's previous organist, Edwin Lemare, had been principal organist from 1891 and it was he who oversaw the Walker organ. Lemare left Holy Trinity in 1895 before taking up the position of organist at St Margaret's, Westminster in 1897. Alcock was appointed organist in 1895 and held the post until 1902: see Watkins Shaw, *The Succession of Organists* (Oxford: Clarendon Press, 1991), p. 268. Ireland's appointment at Holy Trinity may also have been assisted by the fact that Alcock had been a Professor of the Organ at the RCM since 1893 and was clearly acquainted with Ireland as a student.

[8] Richards, *The Music of John Ireland*, p. 41.

the Holy Trinity Church School and who lived locally.[9] Daily evensongs, with boys' voices only, were complemented by a full choir on Sundays. The building, recently finished and paid for by the 5th Earl Cadogan, was the last to be designed by the architect, John Dando Sedding. It embodied the apotheosis of William Morris's Arts and Crafts Movement, and was richly ornamented with Ruskin-inspired marbles, windows designed by Sir Edward Burne-Jones and William Blake Richmond, and a magnificent set of decorative choir stalls. Ireland was required to play two or three times a week for evensong, for choir practices taken by Alcock, and, during the summer, he was expected to play for Sunday services.[10] When Alcock, much in demand,[11] resigned his position in 1902 in order to take up a position at the Chapels Royal, Ireland had hoped that promotion to the principal organistship might come his way, but he was considered too young for the job (a decision that was latterly thought to be a serious error of judgment).

With Alcock's departure, Ireland found himself playing more at Holy Trinity's sister church at St Jude, Turks Road, Chelsea, a less amenable situation, and so began to look for a new and more promising appointment. This came in 1904 when Everard Hulton, the organist of St Luke's, Sydney Street, Chelsea, resigned after thirty-four years in post. Ireland's appointment, which began in July, was probably facilitated by the rector, the Rev. Henry Bevan, who had hitherto been incumbent at Holy Trinity between 1895 and 1902.[12]

St Luke's, built in the Gothic manner to a lofty design by James Savage, offered new opportunities for Ireland.[13] Consecrated in 1824, it boasted a 142-foot-high tower (an intended spire was never constructed), a noted landmark in Chelsea, and the tallest nave in London. It had also, for many years, enjoyed a fertile musical tradition. At one time John Goss had been organist before his move to St Paul's Cathedral as Thomas Attwood's assistant. With the High Church revival, a paid surpliced choir was introduced in the chancel, and Hulton, who came to St Luke's on the recommendation of John Stainer, oversaw services with orchestra (a style much advocated by Stainer) and encouraged Sunday evening concerts attended by large numbers of people. Markedly less attractive was the Nichols organ originally installed in 1824 (described later by Ireland as 'Heath-Robinsonish'),[14]

---

[9] This appreciable number of boys matched that of St Paul's Cathedral and was no doubt intended to fill the grand scale of Holy Trinity, at the time the widest church in the capital.

[10] *The Music of John Ireland*, p. 41.

[11] While at Holy Trinity, Alcock continued to undertake duties as assistant organist at Westminster Abbey, where he was appointed official assistant organist by the Dean and Chapter in 1896. It is therefore not surprising that Ireland's position as an assistant at Holy Trinity was a highly active one.

[12] Searle asserts (*John Ireland*, p. 23) that Ireland also continued at St Jude's though she does not provide a date when he ceased to play there.

[13] As principal organist at St Luke's, Ireland was responsible for playing the organ and training the choir.

[14] Letter from Ireland to the Rev. Paul Walde (one-time curate at St Luke's), 12 June 1940, quoted in Richards, *The Music of John Ireland*, p. 56. Ireland was, nevertheless, well known for his brilliant organ extemporisations (see Searle, *John Ireland*, p. 35).

and the boys of the choir were not of the quality he had relished at Holy Trinity. Indeed, we know that, on Ireland's arrival, he wasted no time in instituting daily practices and regular attendance at the daily services in order to ameliorate the standard of singing. By all accounts, the effect of the new regime was swift.[15] Yet, even with this noticeable improvement, Ireland could not muster the same enthusiasm for St Luke's. Though the church had, in the nineteenth century, embraced a modest degree of High Church ritualism, its level of ceremony, closer to a more 'Broad Church' practice, was not the equal of Holy Trinity.

Ireland remained at St Luke's for twenty-two years. The level of singing remained consistently high in the years leading up to the war – arguably the zenith of Ireland's career as a church musician – but after war broke out, it was hard to maintain senior choir members who were enlisting for the military services. For Ireland this also meant a waning of a corporate social entity he had enjoyed since his time at Holy Trinity where the relationship between choirmaster, choristers and men, while maintaining a professional distance, encouraged a sense of bonding, sustained by summer holidays to the coast for the boys, community outings and sumptuous annual choir dinners.[16] After the war, choir excursions resumed but there was less of the old social cement and fervour of the pre-war years. In 1925 Ireland spearheaded an initiative to replace the Nichols organ, but this project was not seen to fruition for, under pressure from other work and commitments, Ireland felt the need to resign in October 1926.

Works for Holy Trinity, Sloane Street

Ireland's earliest sacred compositions date from his time at Holy Trinity, Sloane Street. Dedicated to Alcock, *The Office of Holy Communion/with the Benedictus and Agnus Dei set to Music in the Key of A flat for Boys' Voices*, was composed in 1896, published by Houghton in 1902 and explicitly written for the boys for use at weekday services at Holy Trinity (and with the inclusion of the 'Benedictus qui venit' and 'Agnus Dei' reflected its suitability for more high church practice). Though stylistically inchoate, the work, cyclic in design, indicates how much he had already learnt from the example of Stanford's services (though by this time only the communion services in B♭, Op. 10, and A, Op. 12, would have been known to him). The musical idea of the opening 'Response' ('Lord have mercy upon us' – Ex. 1) appears at two important strategic points in the structure of the Credo ('Who for us men, and for our salvation' and 'and I believe in the Holy Ghost') and the larger scheme of the Credo itself is bound together by a rising phrase that is reworked with some vigour and invention. The material for the Benedictus is an inversion of the original 'Response' idea, while the Gloria makes reference to the 'Response' (particularly in the final 'Amen') and the Sanctus. Moreover, Ireland, as a seventeen-year-old, shows some notable harmonic dexterity in the service as a whole. One noteworthy instance is the climax of the Credo where Ireland's harmonic scheme reveals an enviable ingenuity in its strong bass voice-leading. By the deployment of a series of descending dominant pedals, of C, B♭

---

[15] See Richards, *The Music of John Ireland*, p. 44, quoting from *St Luke's* [Parish Magazine], November 1904, 231.

[16] See Searle, *John Ireland*, p. 22.

Ex. 1 Ireland, Office of Holy Communion – 'Response'

and A, where the pinnacle of the vocal line is reached on a top A ('dead'), A major is deftly used as the Neapolitan to return to A♭, providing the last line of the text with even greater force and meaning. The Sanctus, with its unusual tonal obliquity (commencing tangentially on the submediant) and its enhanced, chromatic cycle of fifths progressions, perhaps give a passing hint of Ireland's later harmonic predilections (Ex. 2). Ireland clearly retained an affection for his youthful creation and wondered some years later whether, if the demand was there, it might be republished. But, ultimately nothing came of this proposition.[17]

Two years after completing the Communion Service, his 'Hymn for Passion Sunday', *Vexilla Regis*, was composed under Stanford's tutelage.[18] Showing a considerable leap in terms of scope and ambition, *Vexilla Regis* made such an impression on the Irishman that he persuaded Alcock to perform it at Holy Trinity under Ireland's direction the following year.[19] The sixth-century Latin text of Venantius Fortunatus, Bishop of Poitiers, in a translation by J. M. Neale (a prominent High Anglican Ecclesiologist) was an ideal ritualistic template for the nineteen-year-old Ireland. A sombre, processional hymn, originally written when a relic of the True Cross, sent by Justin II of Byzantium, was carried in great pomp from Tours to the monastery at St Croix at Poitiers, it occurs in the Roman Missal on Good Friday when the Blessed Sacrament is carried from the Repository to the high altar.[20] Ireland's desire to create a sense of solemnity is conveyed by his scoring for organ, two trumpets and three trombones, an instrumentation that is exploited with full gravity in the forty-six bars of the extended prelude, one which is also intensified by the impressive 'self-development' of the quasi-medieval 'hymn' proclaimed

---

[17] See letter of 17 July 1939 to Thompson (*GB-Lbl*. Add. MS 60535); also Stewart R. Craggs, *John Ireland: A Catalogue, Discography, and Bibliography* (Oxford: Clarendon Press, 1993), p. 4.

[18] The extant manuscript (*GB-Lbl*. Add. MS 52894) is dated 'London, 2 December 1898'.

[19] Searle, *John Ireland*, p. 156. Later Ireland dismissed *Vexilla Regis* as no more than an 'RCM Studentship Work' (see Craggs, *John Ireland*, p. 7) and withdrew it. It was not published until after his death, by Galliard (now Stainer & Bell) in 1963.

[20] The plainsong hymn can also be found in the Roman Breviary, where it was sung at Vespers from the Saturday before Passion Sunday until Maundy Thursday of Holy Week.

Ex. 2 Ireland, Office of Holy Communion – Sanctus

by the brass in the opening bars (Ex.3). The rising fourth intervals of this melody are generative of much that follows. The first major choral statement ('The Royal banners forward go'), the C major affirmation ('Fulfill'd is now what David told') and the reprise ('To Thee Eternal Three in One') are all important reworkings of this material, as is the contrasting 'dirge' ('There whilst he hung') based on an inversion of the seminal 'fourth' cell. The paragraph in E major contrasts in the manner of a 'verse' as one might find, for example in the extended anthems of S. S. Wesley or Stainer, and Ireland's harmonic language shares much with this earlier nineteenth-century idiom. Once again, Ireland asserts his 'fourth' cell in the initial strain of the soprano's melody (Ex. 4), to the extent that one senses the influence of the 'Grail' theme from *Parsifal*, an opera of similar ceremonial bent (note especially the choral delivery 'And spoil'd the spoiler of his prey'). Yet, for all his deference to German models and Brahmsian processes of 'developing variation'

Ex. 3 Ireland, *Vexilla Regis*

Ex. 4 Ireland, *Vexilla Regis*

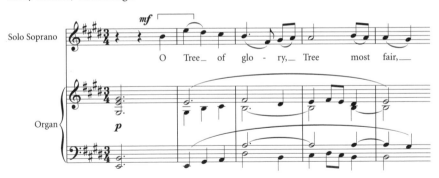

and chromatic harmony (one exploited, incidentally, with notable boldness immediately before the return to C major – Ex. 5), the style of *Vexilla Regis* owes much
more to Ireland's deployment of diatonic, and more specifically, *modal* harmony
which he learned as a student with Stanford. Through the agency of Rockstro, an
incipient specialist at that time on Renaissance modality (*teste* his articles on the
subject in *Grove's Dictionary of Music and Musicians*), Stanford had 'discovered'
the potential of modal progressions as a catalyst for modernism (just as Brahms
had done in the music of Schütz and Hassler) and had sought means of deploying
these harmonic techniques in his *Morning, Communion and Evening Service* in F
(1889) and his oratorio *Eden* (1891). Not only did Stanford understand the worth of
modal harmony as a stricture, but he also realised that it was both a useful teaching
tool and creative resource for his students.[21] We also know that Ireland was made
to work in this idiom while he studied composition under Stanford between 1897
and 1901. More significant, however, is that Ireland himself recognised the value
of such teaching and caused him to assimilate modal processes within his own
compositional style. Admitting to the influence of plainsong, he declared: 'You
see, I was the first pupil to whom Stanford expounded the modal scales. "Your
music is all Brahms and water, my boy," he said. "You'll have to study Dvořák." I
did, but he still wasn't satisfied, so he taught me the modal system, basing it all
upon Palestrina; he kept me at it for a whole year.'[22] *Vexilla Regis* is the first of his
sacred works to essay this harmonic idiom with such self-assurance, and it can be
felt not only in the robust homophonic textures of much of the choral writing but
also in the explicitly arcane counterpoint of the concluding 'Amen'.

[21] Stanford's interest in modal harmony was manifested by his advocacy of modal
progressions in such composers as Palestrina, the opening of whose *Stabat Mater*
has a striking modernity. Moreover, with the opening of Westminster Cathedral
in 1903, Stanford would insist on his pupils attending services to witness the
Renaissance style – what he dubbed 'Palestrina for 3d', referring to the bus fare
from South Kensington to Victoria. Hence the subsequent application of modality
by Charles Wood, Vaughan Williams, Gustav Holst, Herbert Howells as well as
Ireland is testimony to Stanford's pervasive influence.

[22] See 'Dr Ireland reviews his long career', *The Times*, 3 August 1959, reprinted here
on pp. 414–17.

Ex. 5 Ireland, *Vexilla Regis*

The church music written at St Luke's

One of the most important stylistic precedents of *Vexilla Regis*, beyond those already articulated, was the technically accessible nature of the choral writing, clearly intended to be practical for a range of choirs from the cathedral to the smaller but ambitious church. Rarely did he broach the denser chromatic language of his instrumental works, replete with their complex language of higher dissonances, secondary ninths, elevenths and thirteenths, bitonal colourings and involuted chromatic substitutions. Instead he preferred to manipulate the diatonic and modal apparatus so inventively exploited by Stanford and Charles Wood which was more pragmatic for its performers and musical environment. There was, undoubtedly, an element of stylistic compromise here, but Ireland's creative imagination, in many instances, was able to transcend these constraints through his ability to produce memorable thematic material, telling tonal juxtapositions and moments of genuine emotional drama.

The vast majority of Ireland's sacred compositions date from his appointment as organist at St Luke's, Chelsea. Much of it took the form of service music which was performed regularly in the liturgy of the church; there were also a number of hymn tunes, and only one anthem, though the latter proved to be of lasting worth.[23] Though relatively undistinguished, the Magnificat of the early Evening Service in A (1905) retains its effect through the use of a Gregorian intonation (probably a device he gleaned from Stanford's Service in B♭ which makes extensive use of similar Gregorian incipits).[24] The rest of Ireland's service music written for St Luke's was published between 1907 and 1915. Perhaps the best known of this music was the Te Deum in F (1907) which was dedicated to Bevan. The structure of Ireland's canticle clearly demonstrates some compelling connexions with Stanford's setting in B♭ (a work firmly established in the St Luke's repertoire). Ireland's choice of tonal departures is essentially simpler than Stanford's, but it is striking that most of the crucial textual delineations correspond, including the reprise of the tonic key ('Day by day we magnify Thee') and the coda material that follows:

Ireland: Te Deum in F (1907)

Metre/Tempo	Key	Theme	Text
With movement and breadth – 2/2	F major	1	'We praise Thee, O God'
	A major	2	'The glorious company of the Apostles'
A tempo	D minor	3a	'Thou art the King of Glory, O Christ'
		3b	'When Thou tookest upon Thee'
Maestoso	F major	1	'Day by day we magnify Thee'
[Coda]	F major	4 [with 1]	'Vouchsafe, O Lord'

Stanford: Te Deum in B♭ (1879)

Metre/Tempo	Key	Theme	Text
With breadth and not too slow	B♭ major	1	'We praise Thee, O God'
	E♭ major	2	'The glorious company of the Apostles'
	B♭ major		'The Father of an infinite Majesty'
	D♭ major	3a	'Thou art the King of Glory, O Christ'
		3b	'When Thou tookest upon Thee'
	A major	4	'We therefore pray Thee, help Thy servants'
	B♭ major	1	'Day by day we magnify Thee'
[Coda]		5 [with 1]	'Vouchsafe, O Lord'

[23] I have deliberately ignored Ireland's setting of Psalm 42, a cantata for SATB soli, chorus and string orchestra composed in 1908 specifically to comply with the rubric of the Durham University B.Mus. degree (See *GB-Dul*.Music Exercise 278). This is work is perceptibly more neutral in style and is discussed on pp. 198–201.

[24] At the bottom of the first page of the autograph M (*GB-Lbl*. Add. MS 52894), Ireland wrote that 'this melody is based on a well-known Gregorian intonation'. The intonation is, in fact, that used for the plainsong Magnificat in the 2nd and 8th modes.

Ireland's use of a broad, memorable theme at the opening has much in common with Stanford's interpretation. However, for the central portion of the work, Ireland chose to couch almost the entire text in an elegiac D minor, in marked contrast to Stanford whose internal ternary structure is based on a strident D♭ major, inspired largely by its initial trumpet fanfare. This predilection for lyrical contrast, stirred in this instance by contemplation of man's frailty and redemption ('When Thou tookest upon Thee to deliver man'), seems distinctly characteristic of Ireland's more pensive personality.

To the Te Deum in F were added further items in 1914 and 1915. For the Morning Service, settings of the Benedictus, and Jubilate Deo, and the Benedicite for use during Advent, Septuagesima and Lent were written, and a Magnificat and Nunc dimittis for the Evening Service. In accordance with the model of Stanford's services, Ireland's intention was to imbue these additional pieces (save the more plainsong-like Benedicite) with a matrix of cyclic thematic references in which the doxology ('Glory be to the Father'), restating the opening material of the Te Deum, functioned as a concluding statement of 'unity'. Most substantial is the Benedictus where Ireland permits himself to exercise his more symphonic instincts. Here the thematic material is allowed to expand and transform more freely, and the tonal range – which extends as far as B minor – has much more in common with the later, instrumentally-orientated services of Stanford (namely those in G of 1904 and C of 1909), and there is more subtle play on the Service's quintessential *topos* of progressions inclined towards the subdominant (see 'And thou, Child, shalt be called the Prophet of the Highest') established in the first fifteen bars of the Te Deum. By contrast the Evening Service is more conservative, not to say atavistic, in its exploitation of modal harmony, as if Ireland was out to recreate a tangible link with the sixteenth century; moreover, the 'verse' element of the musical structure is suggestive of earlier nineteenth-century designs, namely those of Walmisley, S. S. Wesley and Goss.

In addition to the service music in F, Ireland responded to a call from George Martin (who appears to be have been some form of general editor), the organist of St Paul's Cathedral, to produce a Communion Service for a series published by Novello. At a time when choral services were, to use Martin's term, 'universal', the demand was considerable. Again the brief was to provide music 'within the capabilities of an ordinary choir' without impinging too much on artistic imperatives, a remit with which Ireland certainly did his best to comply. The organ part is well within the capacity of a modestly competent player and the choral writing is almost uniformly homophonic and consonant. Within this stricture, Ireland endeavoured in the larger structures of the Credo and Gloria to create a more telling sense of thematic unity and interaction. In the through-composed Credo, for example, rarely do the full choral sections stray from the rising scalic figure of the opening bars, though monotony is obviated by an interesting tonal schema that fluctuates between C and A♭. The importance of A♭ is established in the paragraph beginning 'And the third day He rose again'. This yields to C major for the cadence ('Whose kingdom shall have no end'), but A♭ reasserts itself with emphasis as an expression of confidence ('And I look for the Resurrection of the dead') shortly before the end, which renders the final statement of the seminal scalic passage in C all the more effective. The lively Gloria is simpler still in both its use of modal harmony and the uncomplicated ternary structure (which accentuates the analogy of a Scherzo). Moreover, the central paragraph, characterised by the exchange between solo quartet and chorus, is once again evocative of earlier verse-anthem models of the eighteenth and nineteenth centuries.

The one significant anthem Ireland produced while at St Luke's was written as a commission in 1912 for Charles Macpherson, the sub-organist of St Paul's Cathedral.[25] Intended as a meditation for Passiontide, *Greater Love Hath no Man* drew its text from a compilation of scriptural passages from *Daily Light on the Daily Path*, a series of booklets containing Bible readings which Ireland used to observe on a regular basis.[26] The anthem rapidly gained currency in cathedrals and church choirs and, with the outbreak of war in 1914, its text acquired a special resonance as the casualties mounted. Indeed, with Alice Meynell's poem 'Summer in England, 1914', which contrasted the slaughter of Flanders' fields with the tranquil, unknowing scenes of England, and the subject of sacrifice emanating from pulpits throughout the land, Ireland unexpectedly found that his anthem had taken on a new, contemporary significance:

> Who said "No man hath greater love than this,
>> To die to serve his friend?
>> To die to serve his friend?"
> So these have loved us all unto the end.
> Chide thou no more, O thou unsacrificed!
> The soldier dying dies upon a kiss,
>> The very kiss of Christ.[27]

In terms of genre, *Greater Love* has a scope and narrative that is redolent of a small cantata, yet, at the same time, the solo material for soprano and bass is, once again, reminiscent of the older style of verse anthem suggested by *Vexilla Regis*, though composed here with a greater sense of continuity and 'dialogue' between soloists and chorus. Indeed, there are moments when the full chorus assumes the role of 'turba' in contrast to its more normal role of reflective commentary. Here Ireland subtly assigns those words of Peter (1 Peter ii:24), presented in the first person plural ('That *we* being dead'), to the chorus, as if they were the people of the church. Similarly, Paul's beseeching words from Romans xii:1, used to encapsulate the anthem's theme of self-sacrifice, are assigned initially to altos and tenors in unison before they are joined by a the 'willing body of believers'. And even when reflective commentary is operative, passages such as the opening twenty bars

---

[25] Ireland produced one other anthem at St Luke's during the war, 'An Island Hymn' for male chorus (TTBB), in June 1915. It was composed as one of twelve anthems published by Stainer & Bell and dedicated 'to all brave Defenders of the Realm of George V, whether on sea, land or in the air, and especially the men's Choir of HMS 'Achilles', somewhere in the North Sea'. Simple and effective, the anthem was intended to be sung not only in church but also 'on deck, in camp or in trench, as occasion may require'. In musical substance it is slight, but it is an interesting example of Ireland's ability and willingness to compose *pièces d'occasion* for the war effort.

[26] See *Daily Light on the Daily Path*, 3 October 1912.

[27] A. Meynell, 'Summer in England, 1914', *The Times*, 10 October 1914 [final stanza].

Ex. 6 Ireland, *Greater Love*

are afforded greater impact by the method of solo voices (tenor) affirmed by full chorus.

Much of the success of *Greater Love* is predicated on its carefully planned textual and tonal scheme, but it is also the result of Ireland's greater confidence in handling his harmonic apparatus. Though still couched in a style aromatic of Parry and Elgar (the three-part counterpoint of the 'turba' is classically Elgarian – Ex. 6), Ireland's language is here virtually devoid of the modality so prevalent in the service music, being replaced by a more overtly late nineteenth-century combination of chromaticism and higher diatonic dissonance.[28] [29] The former is particularly apparent in the first major transition from Ireland's initial A major to the climax on the augmented sixth (an agonised culmination which skilfully accentuates the seminal words 'Greater love' in bar 39), while a second phase of chromatic progressions is deftly employed in the 'verse' for solo treble and bass where F♯ minor yields to G major. By contrast, higher diatonic dissonance is used to underpin musical ideas of a nobler disposition, such as the 'turba' material, the striking cadence at its reprise, and the hushed supplication of the coda. It is, however, in the closing bars of the anthem, with its pensive suspensions and appoggiaturas, that Ireland approaches more closely that melancholy sensibility of his songs and chamber music (Ex. 7).

[28] Ireland's orchestration of 'Greater Love', completed on 16 May 1922, served only to heighten the anthem's romantic sensibilities. This was made for Macpherson who conducted it at the Festival of the Sons of the Clergy in St Paul's Cathedral on 30 May 1922: see Craggs, *John Ireland*, p. 27 (1st edition), p. 32 (2nd edition).

[29] I am grateful to Stephen Lloyd for pointing out that for three or four bars this is strongly reminiscent of the opening chorus of Elgar's *The Apostles*.– EDITOR

Ex. 7 Ireland, *Greater Love*

Hymn tunes

With only one exception – SAMPFORD, which Ireland wrote in 1947 in response to a commission from Sir Sydney Nicholson for the forthcoming *Revised Hymns Ancient & Modern* of 1950 – all Ireland's hymn tunes were composed at St Luke's. Ireland was one of a generation of church musicians whose attitude to the hymn tune was shaped irrevocably by the desire to introduce and nurture 'good taste'. This policy had begun life essentially with the musical board of the 1904 edition of *Hymns Ancient & Modern* (chaired by W. H. Frere, whose music committee consisted of H. Luard Selby (chairman), and among others, Parry, Stanford and Parratt). At the heart of this zeal for reform was the desire to purge modern hymn books of the (so-called) saccharine sentimentality of Victorian hymn writers such as Dykes, Barnby and Stainer and, in particular, eliminate their propensity for chromatic harmony. In place of these tunes, among which, incidentally, were many highly popular with congregations, new, robust melodies would be created supported by 'healthy' diatonic harmony and these would take their place beside folk tunes, plainsong, chorales, old melodies from sixteenth- and seventeenth-century collections, as well as metrical psalm tunes from the Old and New Versions.[30]

This was equally valid as a policy for the *English Hymnal* published in 1906 in which Vaughan Williams was musical editor,[31] and Ireland's one tune written for the edition dutifully conformed. The solemn, chorale-like manner of Ireland's EASTERGATE, commissioned for the *EH*, was clearly intended to suggest an 'old' style, though this impression is undermined by the unusual 8.5.8.3 metre and by the closing, epigrammatic refrain of three syllabic feet which, unusually, takes the tonality to the relative major (B♭). Such artifice in miniature would prove to be typical of Ireland's approach to hymnody in the future.[32]

At Holy Trinity there was a tradition of singing John Leland's 'Lord, keep us safe this night' at evensong. Ireland's setting of these words, to the tune VESPER HYMN, was published in 1911, with the note 'as sung at Holy Trinity, Sloane Square' though it may well have been written during the composer's time at the church. It derives much of its effect from its appoggiaturas, the cumulative force of which climaxes on the double appoggiatura of 'ap-*pears*', emphasising the coming of the morning light, a comfort further accentuated by the dominant ninth and eleventh harmony that follows, and the subtle augmentation of the opening progressions for the 'Amen' (Ex. 8). The prominent chromaticism of this tune tends to suggest a more Victorian sensibility – of Dykes or Stainer – rather than an Edwardian one.

---

[30] The 1904 edition of *Hymns Ancient & Modern* proved to be a major disappointment, with few congregations wishing to adopt it over the popular 1889 supplement. In 1916 Sydney Nicholson was asked to revise the hymn book with the proviso that he return to the 1889 edition as the foundation of the new publication.

[31] See the Preface of *EH*. Ireland was also acknowledged by Vaughan Williams as having given assistance to the preparation of the 1906 edition.

[32] EASTERGATE took its name from the cottage at Eastergate, near Chichester, in Sussex where Ireland holidayed for weekends after 1905 (see Searle, *John Ireland*, p. 28).

Ex. 8 Ireland, *Vesper Hymn* – Amen

After the First World War, Ireland provided tunes for two hymns devoted to the peace across the continents. IRENE, a full-bodied unison melody, was written for Alfred Moss's *Hymns for the Celebration of Peace* in 1918. Implicit in the text and music is a lingering sentiment of patriotism. FRATERNITY, on the other hand, written a year later, explored a very different world. Published in the first volume of the official publication of the League of the Arts for National and Civic Ceremony, *The Motherland Song Book*, the words of this unusual hymn were selected from verses from John Addington Symonds's poem 'A Vista'. There is little or no religious allusion here; instead, the poem – entitled 'These things shall be' (which Ireland would later use for his eponymous choral work in 1937) – expresses those aspirations of a war-torn Britain emerging from an unprecedented world conflagration in which mankind will live 'inarmed ... as comrades free' in search of a better world. They were sentiments of a new democratic order, a new race of men, imbued with a socialist, not to say communist idealism and a renewed sense of

Ex. 9 Ireland, *Fraternity*

pacifism that had been rejected in the years before 1914. Ireland's more consciously modernist setting, strangely listless, is full of unusual modal tensions, essentially created by a homespun dialectic of the tonic Eb and its supertonic F (the dominant, Bb, is subtly bypassed – Ex. 9). Such modernisms, significantly enough, were to be jettisoned in his setting of the same text in *These Things Shall Be* when he, perhaps rejecting the political sentiments of this brave new world (and Ireland himself wholeheartedly discarded Communism),[33] returned to the more familiar diatonic hunting-ground of a former era.

The type of tunes commissioned by Geoffrey Shaw and W. H. Ferguson for the second edition of the *Public School Hymn Book* (1920) were, as the didactic preface enunciates, very much of the same aesthetic bent as for *HA&M* 1904 and the *EH*: 'Not every tune can combine all the most desirable features; but, speaking generally, the tunes in this collection will be found to possess broad melodies, strong harmonies, dignity, vigour, and sincerity. In the choice of tunes a careful attempt has been made to illustrate the distinction between words of a subjective and an objective character. Any tune that savours of weakness or false sentiment has been rigidly banned.'

For MIGHTY FATHER, Ireland returned to the more austere world of EASTERGATE, recreating the idiom of an eighteenth-century chorale melody, but

[33] See John Longmire, *John Ireland: Portrait of a Friend* (London: John Baker, 1969), p. 93.

Ex. 10 Ireland, *Love Unknown*

with a more familiar, periodic 7.7.7.7. double metre. Just as in *EH*, the presence of Bach, and emulations of his style, were a moral imperative. His other tune, LOVE UNKNOWN,[34] on a much favoured Passiontide theme, was, by contrast, much more romantic and melodically imaginative.[35] In fact, it was rapidly to become Ireland's most often sung hymn and one of the nation's favourites. Conforming to the remit of the 'unison' tune (a path already trodden by Parry and Stanford in *HA&M* 1904 and Vaughan Williams among other contemporary native composers in *EH*), and to the symbolic first line of text, Ireland's response to Samuel Crossman's poem was an emotional 'song' in which the enjambments of the eight poetic lines were given a seamless fluidity in the construction of two long, sustained musical phrases.[36] Into these effusions Ireland built a wonderfully flexible interaction of 3/2 and 2/2 bars, through which Crossman's metrical pattern of 6.6.6.6.4.4.4.4, gained impact, especially in the more reflective, questioning second half. Here, after the climax on the top E♭ in line three, Ireland, with masterly adeptness, introduced the D♭

[34] Searle mentions (*John Ireland*, p. 68) that Ireland wrote the tune rapidly on the back of a menu during a lunch with Geoffrey Shaw, though she was clearly confused about the date of composition.

[35] This disparity of styles can also be observed in Henry Ley's tunes SAVILE (free metre) and OTTERY ST MARY (Bachian), both of which appear in the *PSHB*.

[36] This technique of fluctuating metres was one widely practised by English composers in hymn books of the 1920s and 30s. Other illustrative examples may be found in Hugh Allen's MIDIAN, Arthur Warrell's FARMBOROUGH and William Harris's ALBERTA.

triad,[37] as a passing subdominant inflection (and so adroitly placed on the key word of 'O, *who* am I?'), lending an affecting introspection to the melody as it subsides, by degrees, to the cadence (Ex. 10). LOVE UNKNOWN soon found its way into other contemporary hymn books such as *Songs of Praise*, the *Clarendon Hymn Book* and the revised edition of *HA&M*. The tune for C. A. Alington's Easter hymn, CHELSEA, of 1925, had, by comparison, a more chequered career. Written for the 1925 edition of *Songs of Praise*, it was not included by the editors until the enlarged version was published in 1931. Using the same flexible metre as LOVE UNKNOWN, it nevertheless lacked the appeal and melodic immediacy of its counterpart and is now little known.

Nostalgia for the organ loft

After Ireland's resignation from St Luke's in October 1926, he turned his back on the organ and the church for fourteen years. Only one piece from this period, the carol 'New prince, new pomp', was published in 1927 and for this setting of words by Robert Southwell, he returned to the well-trodden path of modality and the effect of a piece in the *stile severo*. Ireland did, however, remain a regular communicant in the Church of England and attended services at St Cuthbert's, Kensington (where he clearly delighted in the high-church ritual) and St Andrew's, Deal in Kent (where he was less impressed). The incumbent at St Cuthbert's at this time was Kenneth Thompson who remained at the church until his move to Lancing College, Sussex in 1936 as chaplain (and the following year as librarian and lecturer for Chichester Theological College). So close, in fact, was Ireland to Thompson that he even considered the notion of moving to the area of Chichester, perhaps in the capacity as organist of the cathedral.[38] Such thoughts indeed reflected Ireland's inner longing to return to the organ loft and a renewed desire to be involved in church music. His hope of some kind of appointment at Chichester may have ended in disappointment, but, on visiting Guernsey in 1939 and 1940 (with the idea of settling permanently on the island) he found himself in the unlikely position – at the age of sixty-one – of taking over as director of music at St Stephen's, St Peter Port.[39] At a church where ritual was central to worship, Ireland's cravings were satisfied. A letter to his old friend, Walde, articulated his deep-set nostalgia:

> For a long time I have felt I would like to play the organ again and to handle a choir, not too strenuously – and I was influenced by the fact that at this Church (St Stephen's), there is a splendid up-to-date 3-manual Walker organ, with all-electric action, which no local organist has ever been able to tackle, except with disastrous results – also, as you know, Popery has always had a

---

[37] This technique had already been practised with similar emotional effect in the second half of Dykes's HORBURY.

[38] Richards, *The Music of John Ireland*, p. 56.

[39] In his introduction to his edition of the *Missa Sancti Stephani*, Geoffrey Bush explains that Ireland's appointment at St Stephen's came about after the widow of a Guernsey rector decided to give an organ to the church in memory of her husband. 'At her request', Bush illuminated, 'Ireland agreed to draw up the specification, but only on condition that he was appointed organist and choirmaster.'

strong appeal for me, and in the morning, services are all thoroughly Popish, with the Mass in most of its glory.[40]

The assiduous attention to detail in the liturgy held a considerable fascination for Ireland and it was evidently a factor which retained his services at St Stephen's even when the standard of singing and musicianship was not of the same level as he had been used to in London. The 'inoffensive' choir (to use Ireland's term)[41] was mixed, an arrangement that was not really amenable to him; 'I don't think I like female voices in church', he declared to Thompson,[42] but the possibilities of an all-male choir of boys and men offered by the urban environment of the metropolis was not open to him. After taking up his post in February 1940, he was able to determine the choir's ability. None was formally trained, and much of the music had to be learned through repetition. Still, in spite of its limitations, Ireland admitted to Thompson that 'the choir is not bad, for a place like this. ... They sing in tune & with fair quality.'[43] At the end of April he took his first Sunday service:

> I took my first Sunday at St Stephen's last Sunday (18th) – the ritual of the Sung Mass at 11 is very dignified and well managed, and the Vicar, Fr Hartly Jackson, is a delightful man. The choir might be worse, but it is very unsatisfactory. There are about 12 boys, 3 young girls, about 6 adult females, and only 3 men. Boys and men are very difficult to get in this island. The ritual of the Mass is about up to the standard of St Cuthbert's except that there are only 2 priests, so they cannot do High Mass.[44]

Contented with his position at St Stephen's, Ireland sketched a mass setting for the choir, in a simple homophonic style commensurate with their ability, using a style heavily influenced by the metrical freedom of plainsong and more modally astringent than ever. By September 1942 Ireland informed Thompson that he had 'practically finished a simple mass',[45] but by this time Ireland was back in England, having been forced to flee from the invading Germans in the previous June. At this stage the work was left incomplete and Ireland consigned his sketches to the shelf after it proved impossible for two years after the allied victory for non-residents of Guernsey to travel there. With Ireland's extended leave of his position as organist, the rector of St Stephen's naturally looked to a local musician to fill his shoes, which, as Bush has conjectured, influenced the composer to put it aside. It was later edited and completed by Geoffrey Bush in 1991.

During the war, with his Chelsea dwelling at Gunter Grove closed down, and under constant threat of destruction by enemy bombing, and there being no possibility of seeking refuge in his Deal accommodation, itself a prime target of German attack, Ireland looked to his friends for temporary lodging. In 1941 he stayed for a

[40] Letter from Ireland to Walde, 12 June 1940: *GB-Lbl.*

[41] See foreword to *Missa Sancti Stephani*, ed. Geoffrey Bush (London: Braydeston Press, 1991).

[42] Letter from Ireland to Thompson, 14 July 1938: *GB-Lbl.* Add. MS 60535.

[43] Letter from Ireland to Thompson, 1 March 1940: *GB-Lbl.* Add.MS 60535.

[44] Letter from Ireland to Thompson, 25 April 1940: *GB-Lbl.* Add.MS 60535.

[45] Letter from Ireland to Thompson, 10 September 1941: *GB-Lbl.* Add. MS 60535.

time in Banbury, where he attended services at Christ Church, South Banbury, as well as at Christ Church Cathedral, Oxford, where he renewed his friendship with Thomas Armstrong. As Armstrong noted:

> I recall particularly an Evensong at Christ Church when we arranged for all the music to be Ireland's. We sang his C major service, the anthem 'Greater Love', and I played organ music by him and extemporized for quite a long time on themes from his music. Balfour [Gardiner] had a too-kind opinion about my extemporization, and stood beside me urging me on to fresh effort. Ireland was very much moved, and wrote me a lovely letter about it ...[46]

At Banbury Ireland commenced work on a number of sacred works. He completed a choral arrangement of his piano piece *The Holy Boy*, now subtitled 'A Carol of the Nativity', in 1941, for Trevor Harvey, assistant chorus master at the BBC and the BBC Singers, to words by Herbert S. Brown ('Lowly, laid in a manger, With oxen brooding nigh'). The same performers also sang *A New Year Carol*, another modal manifestation, for a Home Service broadcast at the BBC's wartime headquarters at Bedford on 29 December 1941. The words, by W. H. Auden, set by his former pupil, Benjamin Britten, had appeared in children's songs *Friday Afternoons*, op. 7, published in 1936, though whether Ireland was aware of this earlier setting is not known. The Morning and Evening Services in C were intended to be companions to the much earlier Communion Service.[47] Though decades lay between the composition of these canticles and those written at St Luke's before the First World War, Ireland was at once able to recapture that once-fluent Edwardian style written during his heyday as a church musician. The Te Deum, the most modally acerbic of the pieces (and which has more in common with the plainsong ethos of the *Missa Sancti Stephani*), reveals an economic yet cohesive symphonic cement, while the other movements such as the Benedictus and Nunc Dimittis hint at the richer diatonicism of *Greater Love*.

After a number of stays at the wonderful Georgian rectory at Little Sampford, near the Essex town of Saffron Walden, where his friend Walde was rector, he moved in more permanently in 1942. Five years later, as a fond tribute to his time there he produced the sturdy Easter hymn, SAMPFORD, to Jane Leeson's 'Christ the Lord is risen to-day!' Included in the revised *HA&M*, commissioned by its editor Sydney Nicholson, it is another masterly example of phraseological suppleness, though this time derived essentially from a more systematic manipulation of the hemiola.

While still at Little Sampford, Ireland responded to another commission from Nicholson, this time for a piece for boys' voices for the Royal School of Church Music's summer school in Durham in 1944. He chose the poem 'It is a thing most wonderful' from *Children's Hymns* (1872) by Bishop William Walsham How, recognised in his time as the 'children's bishop' for his ministry to the young. How's words, a naïve and deeply moving reflection on Christ's passion seen from a child's

---

[46] Searle, *John Ireland*, p. 101.

[47] The MS of the Te Deum (*GB-Lbl* MS 52894) is dated February 1941: see Craggs, *John Ireland*, p. 103 (1st edition). The Morning Service also included his Ninefold Kyrie in A minor.

Ex. 11 Ireland, *Ex Ore Innocentium*

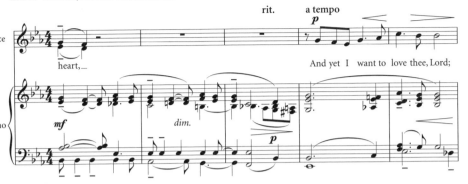

perspective, had been well known as a hymn text. (It was included in the 1903 edition of *Church Hymns*, the *EH*, and Nicholson also incorporated it into the revised edition of *HA&M*.) But Ireland's conception of the poem (omitting verses three and six) was altogether different. *Ex Ore Innocentium* ('Out of the mouths of innocents'), so styled by Ireland, took the form of a through-composed, elegiac song which, on this rare occasion, he chose to couch in the richer harmonic palette of his secular music. The structure of *Ex Ore* also reveals one of balance and beauty. The first verse, in E♭, is given to a solo treble (or semi-chorus), the second to the full chorus of trebles who, in the more melancholic vein of C minor, conclude on a questioning half-cadence. Contemplation of Christ's agony ('I sometimes think about the Cross'), signals a shift to the Neapolitan minor (E minor) and the first of two climactic passages underpinned by the more intense two-part texture of the boys' voices. The first of these climaxes concludes in E major, from which, through Ireland's deft conversion to an augmented sixth, allows the tonality to enter the darker world of D♭ minor ('But even could I see him die'). This, however, is only a momentary shadow, for a series of sequences carries the vocal lines inexorably to a second climax on top A♭ ('which like a *fire*') and the arrival of the dominant of E♭. Ireland's handling of this harmonic 'catastrophe' and its allegiance to How's words is masterly, as is the lamenting air of yearning in the transition to the reprise (Ex. 11), characteristic of so many passages in his piano music and songs. Moreover, his transformation of the opening material, effected through a simple yet powerful change of mode to the minor ('O light a flame within my heart'), injects a thrilling warmth to the final verse which is subtly resolved by the *tierce de Picardie* of the cadence (uncannily reminiscent of *The Holy Boy*) and a final division of the voices. At the first performance of *Ex ore* in Durham Cathedral, Ireland was delighted by the sound of his work as was Nicholson and the boys.[48] It was as if Ireland, having begun his career with a composition for boys' voices, had come full circle, this time with a miniature masterpiece.

Although Ireland considered the idea of returning to his position as organist in Guernsey, this ultimately proved impractical. Thereafter, he abandoned any practical links with church music save for a simple carol setting *Adam Lay Ybounden* (1956), which makes passing reference, ruefully perhaps, to *The Holy Boy* in its

---

[48] Richards, *The Music of John Ireland*, p. 61.

Ex. 12 Ireland, *Adam Lay Ybounden* – reference to 'The Holy Boy'

second line (Ex. 12). In the final years of his life Ireland wrestled with his faith. Around his Sussex home were churches that were too Protestant for his liking, and yet, in spite of his attraction to Romanism, he strongly disapproved of Thompson's dalliance with it in the late 1940s. Such tensions haunted him to the end. Yet, religion for Ireland proved to be a constant draw for much of his life, its weekly service providing a structure for his daily existence, while the need for ritual and mystery, of which music was an intrinsic part, fuelled his desire to be involved both practically and creatively. Ireland's church music, therefore, undoubtedly forms an important part of his output, particularly in what it tells us about the composer and his convictions. With the exception of *Ex ore innocentium* and passages of *Greater Love*, however, the manner of this output represents a quite different aspect of the composer's style where, perhaps sharing the zeal of the nineteenth-century Ecclesiologists for a 'purer', devotional church music, he was happy to embrace a much more conservative language dictated by its environment. Yet, though we may be required to judge the service music and hymns as a discreet part of his productivity, works such as the Te Deum in F and LOVE UNKNOWN remind us that he was able to bring a particular flair and craftsmanship to this traditionally conservative idiom.

There is a curious yet ultimately touching footnote to Ireland's church music – his setting of Psalm 23 written for unaccompanied solo voice and thus a stylistic bridge between his church music and his songs. Written on a single sheet, it survives in the only manuscript, which was attached to a letter dated 22 March 1958 written to his friend and champion, the baritone George Parker. Ireland omits the fifth verse and makes no claim for it as music, describing it in the letter as 'only inflected speech'. Yet as recorded by the baritone Roderick Williams[49] in 2009, possibly its first performance, it has a remarkable eloquence.

---

[49] Dutton Epoch 7246.

1 John Ireland's parents. Lucy Ireland's copy of a photograph by J. Lloyd, Lord Street, Southport, with contemporary handwritten annotation: 'To our dear Lucy. Papa and Mother'. A second annotation reads: 'Taken on Sep 13 1890, their Silver Wedding Day.'

2 'Inglewood', Bowdon, Cheshire

3 John Ireland's dame school, 1887: John Ireland in front row, extreme left

4 John Ireland and his father, 1886

5 John Ireland, aged 15, when a student at the Royal College of Music, 1895

6 Royal College of Music when newly built, without buildings to right or left: contemporary postcard by A. Beagles & Co., postmarked 'Kensington' in November 1904

7 Charles Villiers Stanford:
from a cigarette card

8 Holy Trinity, Sloane Street

9 St Luke's Choir, *c.* 1908. The Rector, the Rev. Henry E. Bevan, is third from the left, second row. John Ireland with Charles Markes and Bobby Glassby, on the extreme right, may be seen more clearly in the enlargement, Plate 13.

10 The west end of St Luke's showing the organ rebuilt in 1932 by John Compton incorporating the original casework and some of the pipes that John Ireland would have known

11 St Luke's Church, Chelsea

12 John Ireland *c.* 1909

13 Charles Markes
and Bobby Glassby,
with John Ireland, *c.* 1908
(Detail from plate 9)

14 John Ireland on the beach: photograph *c.* 1909

15 A stamp commemorating John Ireland, issued by Jersey post office in 1985

16 John Ireland on holiday in Jersey, 1910

17 John Ireland: detail from a photograph taken in Norfolk, 20 August 1922

18 John Ireland driving his Morgan three-wheeler, *c.* 1921, the car probably acquired in the second half of the First World War

19 Arthur G. Miller, in Dorset, 1923, with Ireland's Talbot 8/18 car. The smallest car in the Talbot range, it had entered production in 1922.

20 Maiden Castle – Mai-Dun – 1923

21 Chelsea Reach: water colour

22 14 Gunter Grove, Chelsea

23 Plaque on
14 Gunter Grove,
unveiled in 1896

24 The Studio, 14a Gunter Grove today

25 John Ireland playing the piano at the Studio, 14A Gunter Grove. According to Charles Markes, who originally owned the photograph, it was taken in July 1926

26 Chanctonbury Ring

27 E. J. Moeran and John Ireland, Norfolk, 1923

28 John Ireland, mid-1920s

29 Arthur Miller's parents

30 Helen Perkin, a studio photograph, 1930

32 Sir Henry Wood

31 Bobby Glassby returning from the war –
signed to Ireland February 1920

33 Queen's Hall from the Arena Promenade

34 Thomas F. Dunhill, John Ireland and Lionel Tertis, late 1930s

35 Richard Arnell

36 Alan Bush

37 Geoffrey Bush

38 Edwin Evans by Mary Eristoff, 1916

39 Detail from Thomas Dugdale's painting *Lunch at the Chelsea Arts Club*, 1933. John Ireland and Percy Bentham are shown dining at the table at the rear.

40 The Chelsea Arts Club from the street

41 The dining room at The Chelsea Arts Club today

42 *(top)* Guernsey: view over Le Catioroc at low tide from Le Trépied

43 *(centre)* Guernsey: view over Le Catioroc at high tide from the entrance to Le Trépied

44 *(bottom)* The entrance to Le Trépied

45 St Stephen's Church, Guernsey

47 Bust of John Longmire, artist unknown, in the Longmires' sitting room on Guernsey

46 The organ of St Stephen's Church, Guernsey

48 SS *Antwerp*

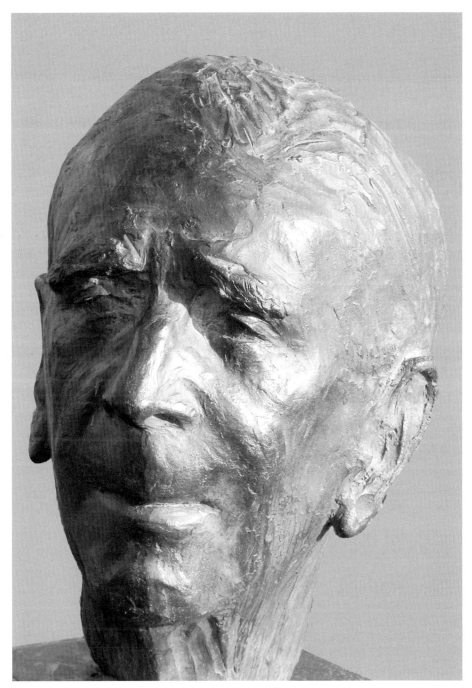

49 Bust of John Ireland by Nigel Konstam, 1960

50 Sir Granville Bantock, Agnes Maisky wife of the Soviet Ambassador Mischa Maisky, Benjamin Britten, John Ireland and Sir Arnold Bax at the British Council, Margaret Street, on 26 August 1942. As part of the cultural diplomacy of the time, Bax is handing Mrs Maisky a letter signed by various British composers sending greetings to their Soviet counterparts.

51 The Rev. Kenneth Thompson, John Ireland and Norah Kirby at Rock Mill, late 1950s

52 Rock Mill

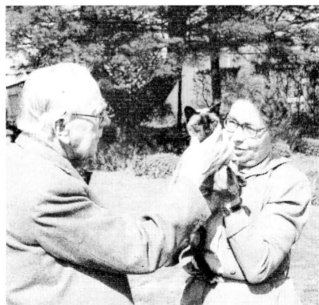

53 John Ireland and
Norah Kirby with 'Smoky'
in the garden at Rock Mill.
'Smoky' was a Seal Point
Siamese.

54 Angus Morrison, 1933

55 Alan Rowlands, 1959

56 Eric Parkin

57 Frederick Thurston

58 Amberley Wild Brooks, photograph by S. & O. Mathews

59 John Ireland at the piano on his 75th birthday, 13 August 1954

60 John Ireland

61 Norah Kirby at Rock Mill

62 Ralph Hill and John Ireland at the BBC, *c.* 1943

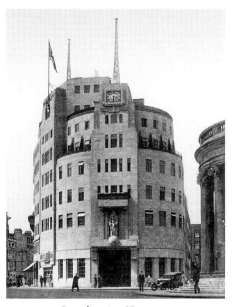

63 Broadcasting House, 1930s

64 Julian Herbage

65 William Murdoch

66 Antoni Sala

67 Albert Sammons in army uniform,
playing in Trafalgar Square, c. 1918

68 The John Ireland Memorial Window in the Musicians' Memorial Chapel at the Church of the Holy Sepulchre, Holborn Viaduct

69 Shipley Church

70 John Ireland at work; in the background the bust of 'The Holy Boy', Bobby Glassby, which, after Ireland's death, was stolen in a burglary in the 1960s

71 After the first performance of John Ireland's early Sextet by the Hampton Music Club at the Arts Council Drawing Room, St James's Square, on 25 March 1960 in the composer's presence. *Left to right:* Ernest Scott (second violin), John Burden (horn), Patrick Halling (first violin), John Ireland, Thea King (clarinet), Peter Halling (cello), Gwynne Edwards (viola). The string players comprised the Quartet Pro Musica.

72 John Ireland with Sir Eugene Goossens, 1960

73 John Ireland. Portrait by Alan Chappelow, 1960

74 John Ireland at Rock Mill

The Organic Music

Stephen Le Prevost

JOHN Ireland's organ music belongs in the main to the early years of his composing career, between 1902 and 1911, when he was organist of St Luke's, Chelsea. However one piece, the *Meditation on John Keble's Rogationtide Hymn*, was written in 1958 and was Ireland's very last composition.

As a young student at the Royal College of Music the organ was Ireland's second study, and his lessons were with Sir Walter Parratt. Ireland spent several years from the age of seventeen, in 1897, as assistant organist to Walter Alcock at Holy Trinity, Sloane Street and gained his FRCO at the age of eighteen, at that time the youngest member of the Royal College of Organists to achieve this distinction. Alcock (later Sir Walter) had succeeded the legendary Edwin Lemare who had been organist at Holy Trinity between 1891 and 1895, and a particularly fine J. W. Walker instrument had been installed in the recently built church in 1891 to Lemare's specification.[1] In old age Ireland often recalled with great affection his days spent at Holy Trinity and its fine four-manual organ.

Ireland was hoping to succeed Alcock when Alcock was appointed assistant organist of Westminster Abbey in 1902, but the job went to an older and more experienced colleague, H. L. Balfour. Nevertheless, Ireland was sufficiently gracious to dedicate his *Capriccio* of 1911 to Balfour. As a consolation Ireland was given the post of organist and choirmaster at the daughter church of St Jude's, Chelsea and then in 1904 St Luke's, the parish church of Chelsea, where he stayed for twenty-two years until 1926. In 1923 Ireland was appointed Professor of Composition at the Royal College of Music.

The organ at St Luke's was always a disappointment after the Holy Trinity instrument and it was not until 1940 when Ireland took on the post 'more or less informally' of Director of Music at St Stephen's, Guernsey that he found an instrument that he could delight in once more. In a letter dated 12 June 1940, Ireland wrote: 'I was influenced by the fact that at this Church (St Stephen's), there is a splendid up to date 3-manual Walker organ, with all-electric action ... It (the high church atmosphere) is a change from the hypocrisy and banality of St Luke's, Chelsea – also from the frantic and 'Heath-Robinsonish' organ I had to play on.'

Sadly, a week after writing this letter, he had to leave Guernsey before the German occupation of the Channel Islands. Ireland had been in post for just three months. It is disappointing that although Ireland spent a great deal of time in the organ-loft during his career, his organ music and music for Church choir represents a very small part of his output.

By far the most outstanding piece that Ireland composed for organ was his earliest, the rich and colourful *Elegiac Romance*, composed in 1902 and published in 1903 (Ex. 1). The ripe harmonic style and warmth is similar to his later piece

[1] For Ireland's reminiscences of Alcock see pp. 404–7.

Ex. 1 Ireland, *Elegiac Romance*

for treble voices and organ *Ex Ore Innocentium* written in June 1944. Ireland was obviously fond of this early work as he reworked the score in 1958 – some 146 bars with a duration of seven and a half minutes. His next work in 1904, *Cavatina*, was an arrangement of a piece for violin and piano, to which he added an inner part, and this was published in 1912. The *Marcia Popolare* was also composed in 1904 and has a broad majestic theme reminding one of the big tunes in the marches of Elgar, to whom he was introduced in 1900.

The *Intrada* and *Menuetto-Impromptu*, both of 1904, were also added to the *Marcia popolare* to form the 'Three Pieces' published in 1912. Ireland subsequently took the *Intrada* and *Menuetto*, added the *Villanella* of 1904 (published by Ascherberg, Hopwood & Crew in 1912) and with some slight revision published these with the title *Miniature Suite for Organ* in 1944, dedicated to John Stuart Archer. These are all tuneful pieces of light music of the kind included in programmes by organists such as Lemare in concert halls, churches and pavilions, and also were arranged for orchestra by various other hands, apparently with Ireland's approval.

The *Capriccio* of 1911 begins in the same feather-light style (Ex. 2). This is a difficult scherzo which builds up to a grand tutti with use of the tuba,[2] and no doubt composed to show off the Holy Trinity organ and its organist H. L. Balfour, to whom the piece is dedicated.

The *Alla Marcia* and *Sursum Corda* of 1911 (both dedicated to Ireland's old teacher Sir Walter Parratt) are more appropriate for use in a church service. The *Alla Marcia* is a fine recessional piece which always works well on a ceremonial

---

[2] A footnote in the score indicates that if there is no tuba, the passages so marked must be played on the Great organ.

Ex. 2 Ireland, *Capriccio*

occasion. The *Sursum Corda* is reflective and suitable as a prelude at the start of a service or during communion (Ex. 3).

Ireland's own arrangement of his piano prelude written at Chelsea on Christmas Day in 1913, *The Holy Boy* subtitled 'A Carol of the Nativity', should be in every organist's repertoire for the Christmas season.

Although Alec Rowley arranged the 'Elegy' from the *Downland Suite* for brass band (1932) for the organ, there is a long gap in years before Ireland's final original work for organ, the *Meditation on John Keble's Rogationtide Hymn*. There had been a sculpture containing a representation of John Keble (1792–1866) carved in oakwood above the choir in Ireland's beloved Holy Trinity Church. Taking as his theme Keble's hymn 'For Rogation: Lord in thy name thy servants plead', Ireland's 'swan-song' was written in May 1958 and contains musical references to orchestral pieces written up to forty years before: the Piano Concerto, the *Concertino Pastorale*, and the orchestral prelude *The Forgotten Rite*. Keble's hymn is usually sung to the tune 'Lincoln' from Thomas Ravenscroft's *The Whole Booke of Psalmes* (1621) but Ireland does not give us variations on the tune but seems to be concentrating on the words.

> Lord, in thy name thy servants plead,
> And thou hast sworn to hear;
> Thine is the harvest, thine the seed,
> The fresh and fading year.

Ex. 3 Ireland, *Sursum Corda*

Our hope, when autumn winds blew wild,
    We trusted, Lord, with thee;
And still, now spring has on us smiled,
    We wait on thy decree.

The former and the latter rain,
    The summer sun and air,
The green ear, and the golden grain,
    Are given us by thy care.

Thine too by right, and ours by grace,
    The wondrous growth unseen,
The hopes that soothe, the fears that brace,
    The love that shines serene.

So grant the precious things brought forth
    By sun and moon below,
That thee in thy new heaven and earth
    We never may forgo.

This has been explored by Fiona Richards, who concludes:

> The piece is a meditation in several senses: on Keble's verses, on the observance and customs of Rogationtide and on Ireland's own life. The choice of Keble was surely a nostalgic backward glance both at Holy Trinity Church, with its statue of Keble dominating the choir stalls and at St Luke's, a church much influenced by the Oxford Movement.[3]

The Tractorian/High Church inclination of Keble (as a leader of the Anglo-Catholic revival) clearly appealed strongly to Ireland.

As this was Ireland's very last work, he seems to be looking back on his life as a musician and chooses the medium of the organ to do this, just as Brahms had done with his final Chorale Preludes, op. 122. Later his pupil Geoffrey Bush scored it for string orchestra as *Elegiac Meditation*, in which form the references to earlier works, occasionally obscure in organ registrations, become more immediately apparent. Geoffrey Bush underlined this aspect of the music by heading his score with a quotation from J. B. Priestley's play *The Linden Tree*:

> Listen – he's remembering the earlier themes now . . . and saying goodbye to them. Wandering through the darkening house of life – touching all the things he loved – crying Farewell – for ever – for ever.

And indeed, Ireland's last notes in this music take us back to his first visionary success with the opening evocation of *The Forgotten Rite* written forty-five years before (Ex. 4). Ireland's richly evocative piece runs to ninety-one bars and lasts for some seven minutes.

Robert Gower's excellent edition of *Organ Music of John Ireland* is published by Novello. Produced with financial assistance from the John Ireland Trust, it

---

[3] Fiona Richards, *The Music of John Ireland* (Aldershot: Ashgate, 2000), p. 242.

Ex. 4 Ireland, *Meditation on John Keble's Rogationtide Hymn*

conveniently provides the musical text for the *Elegiac Romance, Intrada, Menuetto Impromptu, Villanella, Capriccio, Sursum Corda, Alla Marcia, The Holy Boy,* and *Meditation on John Keble's Rogationtide Hymn*. Gower recorded *Alla Marcia, Capriccio, Elegiac Romance* and the *Meditation on John Keble's Rogationtide Hymn* on the organ of Holy Trinity, Sloane Street in September 1979,[4] and all of Ireland's works playable on the organ have been recorded by Stefan Kagl on the organ of Herforder Münster.

[4] Issued on LP on Wealden ws 179.

CHAPTER 20

The Songs of John Ireland

Charles Markes

This article was written in 1973, but is published here for the first time.

I T has been said that 'Thought is deeper than all speech – feeling, deeper than all thought.' John Ireland carried this idea to the ultimate in the *Rhapsody* for piano, where, at the *Tranquillo*, just before the final onrush to the end, we find the additional words 'with innermost feeling'. The capacity for feeling is a prerequisite to any understanding of Ireland's music, and nowhere is it more necessary than in contemplation of his songs, which were engendered by deep feeling, and must be approached with a like mind and heart in order fully to appreciate them.

When a poem aroused an emotional response in him, Ireland would read and reread it, become immersed in it and ultimately, it would seem, assume the identity of the poet or of the characters in the poem; in this sense he became a participant, seldom a spectator, such was his dedication to his art.

Ireland's harmony is unique, and is the key which unlocks the door to that private garden in which he found his own especial flowers, from the earliest buds of spring, to the winter holly. If you are sensitive to his harmony you will find that he will wreak emotional havoc upon you – if not, then indeed you may be found among those 'Cold Hearts, counted cast away'.

Ireland derived his inspiration from many sources – the beauty of nature in all its aspects, the idealization of youth, poetry, the aura of remote places, and the idea of perfect friendship, which was synonymous with love. He was uncompromising with himself: a thing was either right or wrong, and he would wait until exactly the right sound came to him which would accurately express the emotion he was feeling at the time – maybe just one note in a chord, which had to be exactly in the right place. If you doubt this, try altering some of his harmony and you will speedily find out how wrong you are, and how absolutely right he is. (I say *IS* because, for me, his music lives, as no other does.)

Songs of a Wayfarer

1 Memory

There is no introduction to this song, just an accented octave A for the right hand – the dominant, which seems to be a command for quiet, during which the poet, William Blake, summons up his memories. The accompaniment flows along as gently as the stream in which he sees, mirrored, the reflections of his own imaginings. There are flashes of harmonic colour here and there along the way, and the trill which illustrates the linnet's song. The day passes dreamlike, until, over the last six bars the shadows fall. The piano sounds its final chord two bars from the end, D major, played *ppp*, suspended under the voice, which finishes the song alone, leaving us with a feeling of indefinable melancholy.

2 *When Daffodils Begin to Peer*

The short, gay introduction sets the mood of this song, which is virile and robust. One senses the restless urge of the countryman to be up and doing. It is spring, the sap is rising, and everything is on the move. One can imagine the frolics in the hay, and the over-brimming mug of ale held aloft as in a toast, with the fanfare-like accompaniment underneath. The whole accompaniment is a joy to play, something to get your teeth into, and let fly here and there. The countryman is quite sure where he is going as he merrily grasps the stile and continues on his way with a rather pitying contempt for the laggard, as he increases his own pace over the last five bars, surefooted, emphatic.

3 *English May*

This lovely setting of Dante Gabriel Rossetti's poem is Ireland at his best, every nuance of the poem is illuminated by the accompaniment. The poet is despairing of the health of his loved one who is apathetic in the dull English spring which is lagging behind. He would willingly give his own life, full of Italian sunshine, that she might be restored to full beauty; he would then be at peace.

During the first sixteen bars we feel this fervent wish, after which the accompaniment becomes tentative as the poet reflects upon the lateness of spring in May time. At the end of this section there are three bars on the piano, increasing in intensity over the last two, leading to an impassioned plea that the poet might give the strength of his own life to the loved one. Ireland felt 'Would God that I might yield it all to you!' so strongly that he repeats the words, making the second time higher and more emphatic than the first. This accomplished, the poet relaxes, and the song ends quietly on the mediant with magical effect.

4 *I Was Not Sorrowful*

It was Ireland's intention to end the cycle with this song, but at the request of the publisher, he reluctantly provided a further song 'I will Walk on the Earth', which had the hearty ending fashionable at the time. Ernest Dowson was a tragic figure – almost inarticulate, apart from some gems of poetry, hopelessly in love with the wrong person.

Arthur Symons says of this woman in his memoir prefacing the *Poems of Ernest Dowson* dated 1900: 'Did it ever mean very much to her to have made and to have killed a poet?' Ireland establishes this mood of tragic despair in the first bar of the introduction, with the dissonant note in the right hand chords and the drooping accompaniment in the left hand. The music continues in this vein over the first two stanzas, and the mood of monotonous resignation is well set. There is then an upward modulation over two bars to a key a major third higher, which increases the emotional tensions although marked *pp*. After two bars of the third stanza, the right hand takes over the drooping figures, prefacing an ascending melodic phrase played by the left hand, marked *caldamente*. After seven bars this melody appears again, and yet again seven bars later, each time a semitone higher, thus magically increasing the emotional effect. The third time this phrase is marked *piangente*, and one has certainly been led to breaking point over the fourth, fifth and sixth stanzas. After this, the accompaniment subsides, and one feels that both the poet and the composer are emotionally exhausted, and the song ends as it began, with the introduction repeated, and an ascending passage spread over three bars, fading away into the silent distance.

Marigold

These three songs are about love: the first, 'Youth's Spring-Tribute' is the only happy one, but for each one, the composer has provided a perfect setting.

1 Youth's Spring-Tribute

The introduction is a gentle invitation, a caressing love-call, – never have perfect fourths plus Ireland's individual harmony been more expertly employed in creating an atmosphere of youthful desire. The first two pages in E♭ set the scene for that which is to follow: at the key change to C the music becomes hesitant though anticipatory – spring is still not quite with us. After seven bars in this vein, things start to happen. Under the words 'and through her bow'rs the wind's way still is clear', the accompaniment starts to move – on the word 'clear' there commences surging passage-work of increasing amplitude, spread over four bars back into E♭, where the music becomes ecstatic as the sun bursts through, and the moment of fulfilment draws near.

At the words 'So shut your eyes' marked *pp tranquillo* we have those caressing perfect fourths again, and then the piano starts an undulatory movement, creeping upwards in exact parallel with the words until the climax is reached on the word 'lips'. The next bar marked *rit. molto* is a reference point in Ireland's music, he often used it with slight differences in similar emotional situations in other works. The last eight bars of the song are a dedication to the cause of love, note the lovely ascending passage under the words 'with whom cold hearts' and the regretful chord for those 'counted cast away'.

The song finishes with those enticing perfect fourths fading away into recollection.

2 Penumbra

This is a poem of frustration – the poet feels unable to reveal his love by sight, touch, sound or a sharing of mutual happiness. He comments on this in parenthesis, and then gives the reasons why he is unable to communicate. The last verse sums up the hopeless futility of their relationship – there is nothing left but memory.

The song commences with an introduction of one short, spaced, musical phrase, and the voice starts *parlante*. The harmony becomes colourful almost immediately, until a bitter accented chord is reached at the first 'reason' – 'Because they should not gaze rebuke' etc. There is a flowing passage of four bars into the second verse. The voice part is almost the same, the accompaniment slightly enriched. We reach that bitter chord again at the second 'reason' – 'Because it should not prove a flake', etc., less ample because of the scale leading up to it.

This time, the tune linking the passage into the third verse is played in octaves, the left hand travelling in the reverse direction until the fourth bar which finishes with an extended arpeggio distributed over both hands up to an A *in altissimo.* In the third verse, under the words 'listen to her voice', left and right hands play the vocal line one and two octaves higher respectively. The harmony is increasingly embellished and there is an ecstatic two bars under 'All might rejoice in listening'; note the different chord used after the word 'cling', from the chord used after the words 'rebuke' and 'flake' in the first and second verses respectively, it gives an entirely different colour. The linking passage this time is mysterious, reminiscent of the piano piece 'Moon-glade' from *Decorations*, commencing *pp* and finishing *fff.*

The fourth verse is entirely different, becoming gradually more impassioned up to the words 'wept to her' where everything stops, and we feel the poet's immobility at the words 'and yet I did not speak nor stir'. After four mysterious quiet chords ('Moon-glade' again), the piano embarks upon a surging link into the last verse. In this linking passage, note that where the tune starts at the third bar, it is the first half of the tune used in the previous links, with the note values doubled, enabling it to be spread over four bars, establishing the broad expanse of a wind-capped sea.

From here onwards the song rushes to an impassioned climax of tragic despair. Note the composer's insistence on C♯ or D♭ as the bass note, which started at the commencement of the final link and gives this feeling of thudding desperation. This bass note does not change until the word 'drowned', when it becomes E, but this partial brightness lasts for only two bars, because on the word 'cry' bitterness is back, the dissonant F♮ having terrific impact.

Under the words 'bewail one hour the more' we have the 'link' tune. At the 3/4 *più moto*, note the bleakness obtained in the triplets by omitting the third of the chord. At 3/2 on the word 'memory', the accompaniment, with its restless major thirds in the right hand and arpeggio-like left hand, gives the effect of wind and sea combined. This gradually diminishes to *pp*, where C♯ minor is heard in the bass, and two lone major thirds, like a distant cry, are repeated against the lingering harmony. C♯ minor is heard again an octave lower, and the song ends with the two major thirds played *ppp*, lingering on, and finally carried away on the last wisp of wind.

3 *Spleen*

The poem is by Ernest Dowson, similar in mood to 'I was not sorrowful'. The introduction starts with a melancholy tune in single notes, falling a major third in the third bar, like a sigh. This is repeated an octave higher, this time harmonized finishing with an upward modulation to E major. Against the lingering harmony two notes are heard an octave higher – a perfect fourth downwards carrying an entirely different meaning from the all-pervading fourths found in 'Youth's Spring-Tribute'.

The voice starts with a tune of almost despairing apathy, with a falling cadence at the end of each phrase. The accompaniment in the left hand ignores the first beat of the bar, whilst the right hand plays a figure which is derived from the first bar of the plaintive tune of the introduction. The combination of the two establishes a gentle, lilting rhythm. The harmony is entrancing.

At the end of the first couplet, we hear a subtly altered version of the introduction as a link to the second couplet, where, for the first time, the poet speaks to her of love. The second link, marked *poco agitato*, is gently syncopated, the left hand now playing the first beat of every bar. There is no link between the third and fourth couplets, the music gradually becomes more intense by upward modulation, reaching its climax under the words 'some lamentable flight from Thee'. There is then a dramatic bass note F, which, although marked only *mf*, has the impact of a gong; before it has died away we hear again the tune of the introduction with its falling cadence at the end. From here onwards, the tendency is all downwards; the composer is still using the same figures, this time in two-bar phrases, and at the end of each is this gong-like bass note.

One feels the poet's emotional exhaustion at 'of all the endless country ways'. The accompaniment to these words is the sad tune of the introduction now over a low sustained E♭, which is the last of the gong-like bass notes. The composer emphasizes the effect of the falling cadence by repeating it twice more, at tenor pitch and at bass pitch, and the last notes of all three are sustained with a pause while the repeats go on underneath.

There is a burst of passion in the accompaniment to the words 'of everything alas' – the song subsides, the key changes to D♭ at the word 'thee' which is sung on A♭, sustained over four bars. The piano part finishes the song with a development of the introduction to 'Youth's Spring-Tribute' marked *pp come prima*, which is an echo of the bygone ecstasy of springtime. The last we hear, is those endearing perfect fourths, wistful, unresolved.

Five Poems by Thomas Hardy

These inspired settings reveal John Ireland at the summit of his power – so highly concentrated are they, that they become, as it were, a distilled essence of his thoughts and feelings on the subject of the 'ONENESS' of Poetry and Music. As has been remarked before, these settings are a supreme example of his complete absorption by the poem, and his absolute identification with the person speaking. His voice, speaking from within, illumines every word, every emotional nuance – nothing escapes him and for lovers of John Ireland's music, every bar has something to offer – something delightfully new, of a familiar echo of something gone before. For instance, on the word 'come' in 'Beckon to me to come', and again in no. 5 'Dear, think not they will forget you' – after the big build-up to the three sustained chords on the word 'shrine', the following bar starts with arpeggio-like passages, each commencing with the first five notes of the flute entry in *The Forgotten Rite* at the bar before and the first horn echoing it a bar later.

There are many subtle instances, but no space to go into them here, but for those who have 'ears to hear', there can be no more rewarding experience than these songs. I say 'experience' deliberately, as they go far beyond just 'hearing' and 'listening' – to participate in them is an Emotional Experience.

1 Beckon to me to Come

There is a wistful uncertainty pervading this song – He is by no means certain that she *will* come – there is nothing between them but 'Two fields, a wood, and a tree' – Should she give the sign, any sort of sign, nothing will keep him from her, be it parental opposition, or the marshalled forces of nature – he is eager, poised, waiting.

There is a two-bar introduction, the first, two perfect fourths in the right hand, the left hand gently moving downwards – the effect of this bar is to say 'Please come' – the second bar has a little figure which is, in effect, a coquettish toss of the head, tantalizing – as if to say 'maybe'. There are moments of passion in the song, albeit bittersweet – but we always come back to the tentative motif of the first two bars, which also end the song over the last five bars on the piano. These five bars have a touch of Ireland magic in completely altering the harmony to take on a greyish tint of uncertainty – the little figure – the toss of the head, ends the song, low down in the bass in A major, the original key not quite knowing how we get there. It's all been going down – to dejection.

2 *In my Sage Moments*

This is a song wherein the intensity of love overcomes reason. In a moment of clear-headedness, he realizes that he can only have peace of mind if she is far away – but he cannot endure the separation, and begs her to return, knowing that the ecstasy of reunion will be beyond his strength and can only result in pain even unto death – 'A phantom past all trace'.

The accompaniment opens thoughtfully, forebodingly, but under the man's reasoning we sense the inevitable Tragedy. On the words 'so that a mind may grow again serene and clear', Ireland establishes 'clarity' by dispensing with a true bass, just playing the descending melody of the right hand an octave lower with the left – in fact these three bars could all be played by the right hand alone.

Then come the foreboding bars of the introduction again into the second verse where at the words 'But the thought withers' an air of defiance creeps in. The music gradually increases in emotional intensity and on the words 'Old fires new burn me, and lastly maybe, tear and overturn me' – the music is agonising and overpowering – the effect of the chord on the word 'tear' is excruciating – one literally feels torn apart. There are two more foreboding bars, hesitant – then Love overcomes Reason as the poet says 'So I say Come' – on this word you will hear, in an arpeggio, the five significant notes of *The Forgotten Rite*, then an ascending passage of harmonized major sevenths which you will also find in the *Ballade* at an equally agonising place.

After this climax comes emotional reaction and acceptance of the inevitable – at the words 'From that sweet fire' notice the exquisite effect of the chord on the word 'sweet', and the ensuing downward passage to those chords of foreboding which presage the end. The tragedy is played out over the last five bars which are marked 'estinto', which is, in effect 'fainting' – the left hand is slowly descending – the final word 'trace' is left to the voice alone, then we hear a quiet chord of D♭ major – a quaver rest follows, and then a lone chord of D♮ minor even quieter, which is quite unrelated to that which has gone before. The deliberate isolation of this lone chord of D minor, emphasised by the quaver rest preceding it, is a touch of sheer inspiration – as it fades into silence, comes the moment of dissolution – there is no trace – only a phantom is left.

3 *It was What you Bore with you, Woman*

It was the intangible extrovert qualities of this woman (the poet says they were not 'inly') – her aura, carriage, personality – that enslaved this man, and, for him, enthroned her above all others – her errant freshness penetrated to the very depths of his being – his soul. Unfortunately, for him, she does worse than ignore him – she is unaware of him – not even for 'two moments' do her thoughts dwell on him. The third verse of this poem is an allegory upon this emotional status quo. His thoughts and feelings are as good as dead before they leave him – since they are unable to reach the woman he idolizes – for her, they are of no more importance than chaff blown before the wind.

The music starts with rippling semiquavers, groups of six in the right hand, four in the left – in fact the semiquavers never stop throughout this work – one feels all the time the waywardness of this woman, and the breeze blowing, sometimes gently, but towards the end, fiercely, indeed. The first climax starts on the word 'Fair', almost immediately into, as it says, a 'rather more tranquil' second verse. The harmony at this point is of Ireland's intriguing subtlety; listen to it as you play it, and savour it. Almost immediately, the music starts to expand, which it does right to the final emphatic chord. The harmony under the words 'and out from his spirit flew death' has a cutting edge to it, and on the word 'ban' the wind starts to blow with increasing intensity – There is a terrific gust on the word 'cornchaff' and a gale on 'winnowing fan', which is unrelenting to the end.

4 *The Tragedy of that Moment*

Strange it is not, that the melodic setting of the words 'The tragedy of that moment was deeper than the sea' should be exactly the same as the tune of 'It's pleasant in Holy Mary by San Marie Lagoon'. The time signature and all else is different of course, but the tune is the same. It demonstrates what the touch of genius can do in creating two songs, at opposite ends of the emotional scale, from the same basic ingredients.

This man appears to be pacing slowly from room to room, intent upon his grief – on entering a room he encounters the crystallization of his thoughts and feelings in the form of an apparition – the woman he loves, who speaks to him.

His sanity tells him that this cannot be – yet he is seeing it. The rest is oblivion – blotted out. The music accompanying this tragedy consists of slow, spaced chords, some of which are entirely unrelated to the ones preceding them. Each new sound is like a separate stab of pain – there are only two passing notes in the whole work – and the all-pervading feeling is of that numbness which is deeper than grief.

5 *Dear, Think not they will Forget you*

This is the simple story of a man – forgotten – 'None now knows his name' – the operative word is HIS – who knows that he will lose his identity in focusing all attention upon the woman he loves, by building a temple, and enshrining her therein. He is determined that she shall be remembered in perpetuity – as for him, he doesn't really care. Here, we have come full-circle – the introduction to this song is, melodically, the same as that of the first song – but there is one very significant embellishment. A Rite is about to be performed – that of building and enshrining – therefore it is not strange to discover that, in the left hand, the last half beat of the first bar, four hemidemisemiquavers, followed by the first beat of the second bar, comprise the first five notes of the flute entry in *The Forgotten Rite* mentioned previously.

There is always more about John Ireland than appears on the surface; in fact, if you stay on the surface, you will not discover anything at all about him. The voice entry 'Dear, think not they will forget you:' implies his intention (notice the colon, it is important) – the idea takes shape over the next two bars on the piano, and then Ireland starts to build, and how marvellously, expanding all the time until the words 'and set you therein' are reached. The chords under these words, pace by pace, enact the slow dignified approach to the altar or dais – the actual act of enthronement takes place on the word 'Shrine' – three slow, elevated, colourful chords, punctuated by three gong-like perfect fifths low down in the bass (fundamental harmonies). Then follow arpeggio passages entirely compounded of those same five notes of *The Forgotten Rite* – the Rite is accomplished. The rest is soliloquy – notice the harmony under the words 'O, so sweet was her fame' – a little slower – bitter-sweet nostalgia, it is all retrospective to the end – the music gradually subsides to the final *ppp* chord denoting quiet, calm, resignation. John Ireland must have suffered with all these people as he wrote – otherwise, he would not have written these wonderful songs.

Three Songs

The underlying significance of these three songs – settings of poems by Emily Brontë, an anonymous poet, and Dante Gabriel Rossetti respectively – is epitomised in Shakespeare Sonnet 116, the one that begins 'Let me not to the marriage of true minds admit impediments'. To Ireland 'Love and Friendship' are synonymous, but, having to make a choice, it would be on the side of 'Friendship', which, to him, was all-important – an ideal relationship. 'Love' can be momentarily ecstatic, but transitory – 'Friendship', embodying enduring 'Love', permanent, indestructible.

1 Love and Friendship

The composer set this poem to music as it seemed to him a mirror, in which he found, reflected, his own ideas of the respective values of 'Love' and 'Friendship'. 'Love – the wild Rose-briar' is emblematic of that springtime burgeoning which cannot survive the darker days – 'Holly' unobtrusive, like 'Friendship' is always there when you most need it, and is unaffected by the winter of adversity, or old age. Therefore, we are urged to embrace it. Emily Brontë abjures Love in favour of Friendship, and Ireland endorses this view point emphatically in the music.

The accompaniment moves along in a ruminatory manner throughout, the high-spots of this dialogue of comparison being given very definite musical emphasis. The first, on the word 'Spring' is an almost note-for-note quotation from *The Merry Month of May*. Six bars later, the composer transposes the main theme of the accompaniment one tone downwards under the words 'Yet wait till Winter comes again', and we feel the imminence of darker days. After this, the argument is decided as the music rises to a climax on the word 'scorn' and 'Rose-wreath' appears silly, as the 'Holly', signifying 'Friendship', comes into its own in dignified fashion. After this, the music subsides, contemplating the reasoning again, and Ireland feels the importance of this decision in favour of 'Friendship', by repeating, twice, the words 'He still may leave thy garland green.' The piano ends the song by repeating the main theme – the tune of the introduction.

2   *Friendship in Misfortune*

Ireland chose this poem as a corollary of 'Love and Friendship' – it is a sublimation of that 'Friendship' which is unwavering to that highest pinnacle of 'Love' with which it is synonymous. Db was chosen as the key, because it is a 'warm' key, and all the markings point to this one thing – 'with warm tone', 'sustained and fervent'. The piano is quietly assured, singing a tune of its own, gently balanced against the voice – there are long melodic phrases in the accompaniment, and a wonderfully harmonized succession of chords with a melody on top, surging upwards to the words 'Give me that fond confiding Love' under which the harmony is exquisite.

This beauty is momentarily interrupted by a bleak chord on the word 'Blight', followed by three bars of slightly dissonant modulations conveying the feeling of going upwards, until the original key of Db bursts upon us on the word 'Burns', with the intensity of a flame blazing into light. This is the climax of the song, which ends upon a note of quiet assurance, which the piano affirms.

3   *The One Hope*

The poet muses upon whether, in death, his soul may attain that peace which has eluded him in life – he prays that memories may be washed away, and that, having passed through this spiritual purification, he may be permitted to grasp the amulet of peace which comes from the ability to forget – a 'gift of grace' unknown to him in life. To this end, he prays that no other thoughts will obtrude upon his only desire for 'Hope' – in fact it is 'The One Hope.'

The music starts in sombre vein, each chord accented – with that bitterness which only Ireland knew how to impart. The bass interjects with remorseless, painful blows, underlining each agonizing thought. This unrelenting bass goes on and on, as the Poet asks himself these questions through a mind clouded by the pain of recollecting all the things which have proved vain. On the words 'or may the soul at once in a green plain' – the poet thinks, for the first time, that there may be 'Hope', and on the word 'green' the music undergoes a metamorphosis of wondrous change – an upward modulation of exquisitely harmonized chords, to the chord of Eb major on the word 'Stoop' the first definite key, and the first glimmer of light upon what has been, heretofore, a desolate scene.

The next interesting thing is the upward arpeggio on the word 'Fountain' wherein will be found, twice, the five notes of *The Forgotten Rite*. Probably the most important word is 'Amulet', which, in this context, bears the significance of the Holy Grail. On this word, a long quotation from 'The Trellis' commences – this is especially poignant as, at the very moment the poet is holding out his hands grasping at the Amulet of Peace, the composer evokes the memory of that sun-drenched afternoon in the secret bower, with none but the birds watching – an idyllic moment which has ended in 'Vain regret' and 'Unforgotten pain'. Notice the sad tune the piano sings under the words 'Ah, whom the wan soul' – one feels the wanness, and the poet's pale hopelessness in searching for 'The Gift of Grace unknown'. Then one hears two bars of dissonant chords in contrary motion, leading upwards to an anguished, imploring cry on the words 'Ah! – Let none other alien spell so-e'er' – the harmony under these words is that of exquisite pain.

After this, only 'Hope' is left – the one thought – the poet's one desire, and Ireland underlines this singleness of purpose, by leaving the last words to the voice alone, it is utterly concentrated. The song ends on the piano, with the same three bars that have ended no. 2. There is a subtle re-arrangement of the notes, but in essence, they are the same. No. 2 ends on the word 'bright' – and after all 'Hope' is the one thing that remains perpetually 'bright'. As we have remarked before, there is more to Ireland than meets the ear.

We'll to the Woods No More
Two Songs and a Piano Solo

1 *We'll to the Woods No More*

In seeking the deeper implications of this poem by Housman, one feels an intruder, prying into a deeply intimate, personal and private grief. Something has happened which has brought to an irrevocable end a relationship which was wonderful while it lasted. There is a tragic finality about it – the night is falling, the trees are bare, the laurels are out, and 'The Bowers are bare that once the muses wore' – maybe one of these was the bower in 'The Trellis', wherein, in happier days, such wonderful ideas were exchanged. Ireland is at one with the poet, it could be himself saying in music what the poet says in words.

In the piano interlude before the words 'Oh, we'll to the woods no more – no more' – these first two bars are those of the main theme of the second movement of the Sonatina – a movement which the composer described to me as 'dark, abstruse', his own words.

In the following four bars (the second two under the voice) one feels that the composer is weeping, I know I did when I first penetrated to the meaning underneath the written notes, which are, after all, only dots on paper. You have to go deeper, and if you do, and are sensitive, the effect is emotionally devastating. Under the words 'to the high wild woods' notice the bass creeping upwards, anticipating the main pulse of the three chords above. One climbs a hill to these high trees – it is only momentary however, and the song ends, on the piano, in typical Ireland phrases, veiled references to things we have heard before, and are to hear again – in implied D minor, lapsing unresolved into an infinity of sorrow.

2 *In Boyhood*

Here we meet a boy, fired by the ideals, the enthusiasms of youth, who would if necessary die for his friends – (I wonder if he had read 'Greater Love'). Alas, as time goes on, comes the Great War, and it is his friends who go overseas, and eventually die for him. A simple story apparently, but not so for Ireland, who in 1921 wrote a piano piece entitled *For Remembrance*, some of the features of which are ascending passages for the left hand, sometimes in triplets – here, in this poem, under the word 'Young' we find these ascending triplets. The implications are obvious – the war had not been over very long, Ireland loathed the idea of war, and the involvement of his friends in this holocaust, devastated him. Just after the words 'I sought them far' the music, marked *cresc. ed incalzando*, starts to build, gently with restrained nostalgia – to the words 'The souls I could not save', which commences a descending passage of great poignancy. The song ends quietly as he thinks of the death of his friends. The last word 'me' being the ultimate irony, whereon his ideals are thrust back at him, and it is left to the voice alone – it is the focal point. The piano adds a final comment – again in D minor – with the last three notes in the bass adding an air of bereavement and finality.

3 Spring will not Wait

This piece is prefaced by the words of Housman's poem 'Spring will not wait the loiterer's time who keeps so long away'. If we make one small adjustment, we find that the first two bars of the melody of this piece, constitute a setting of these very words, namely:

Ex. 1 Ireland, 'Spring will not Wait' (*We'll to the Woods No More*)

Spring will not wait   the loit - rer's time who keeps   so   long__ a - way.

Underneath a great deal of Ireland's music is a poem lurking somewhere – in fact Poetry and Music were to him indissoluble. He says of this piece that 'It must be considered as a completion of the two previous numbers' – and one can easily understand why, as it contains so many quotations from the first song. Notice the anticipatory, climbing bass used at bar 29 in this piece, and the harmony of bars 30 and 31 – they are almost identical to what happens under the words 'High wild woods of laurel, and the bow'rs of Bay' in the song.

The ending of this piece which is marked *poco più lento*, is practically the same as the ending to the song – a two bar phrase, repeated a major third lower. The last chords we hear of the piece are a combination of the endings of both songs; the piece has the three bass notes repeated. Song no. 2 uses them once, Song no. 1 not at all – but the harmony of all three is, in essence, the same. Overall this composite work is a wonderful idea, carried to a perfect conclusion.

Two Poems of Rupert Brooke

Ireland was psychic in some things. He felt the imminence of war long before 1914. He even foreshadows it in the First Violin Sonata at the *Lento* eighteen bars before letter D. When war finally came, it dealt him a bitter blow, as it struck at one of the main sources of his inspiration, 'Youth'.

Thereafter the thought of war haunted him. In the middle of the slow movement of the Piano Sonata, notice the sombre chords and the menacing bass punctuating them, marked *ppp una corda*, and, many years later in the Piano Concerto, the foreboding passage towards the end of the slow movement commencing four bars before 39 which links it with the *giocoso* last movement.

1 *The Soldier*

For those who have copies of the original printing of this song, I should like to draw attention to an error in notation in the voice part. In the ninth bar, the notes on the word 'Richer' should be crotchets, not quavers.

The soldier tells us, if he dies, to regard his body, wherever it happens to be, as an indivisible part of England. The inference is, not to think of sad things, but only of things of which to be proud: thoughts emanating from and returning to – England. The introduction is a quiet meditative tune, immediately taken up by the voice. There is, however, a burst of pride in the accompaniment, at the first mention of 'England'. The piano part is never static, and, by its movement, seems to echo the rhythm of marching feet. The song is mainly contemplative, but always conveys that feeling of intense pride whenever the word 'England' is about to be mentioned, particularly the last time, where the composer uses the tune of the introduction, up a major third, marked *f*, with great effect. After this, the mood becomes contemplative again, moving gently to the end, the piano finishing the song with that same tune. It is marked *pp* but the composer has subtly emphasised it by making the accompaniment sparse. Notice how this tune has been used throughout the song, in various keys, and at different pitches, to illustrate the words.

2 *Blow out, you Bugles*

There is not a hint of sorrow here as such – only a fierce pride in the men who have died, and, in dying, sacrificed so much, and gave so much back of inestimable spiritual value, and moral integrity.

Blow bugles, Blow! And how they do, in this so splendid song. It is interesting that the first few notes are those of 'Chelsea Reach' and a decorous version of the 'cocky' tune of 'Ragamuffin'.

The song starts in stately fashion; again, in the bass, we hear the marching feet. On the word 'gold' the accompaniment shows us a 'ragamuffin' who has become a man. This tune is used again and again throughout the accompaniment and on the words 'poured out the red sweet wine of youth' becomes transfigured and poignant. Six bars later, on the word 'age', the piano starts to build up to the word 'sons', where the bugles start to blow, heralding the ultimate sacrifice – 'their immortality'. On this word, the composer transposes upwards, heightening the effect, and the bugles are blowing madly.

At this point, the composer makes an inspired decision – to detach the words 'Blow Bugles, Blow! from being the start of the second verse, to becoming the corollary of the first – in effect, a salute to the final sacrifice just made.

Two Songs

By his settings of these two poems by Arthur Symons and Dante Gabriel Rossetti respectively, John Ireland has created two of his most lovely songs – less well known than some, even to the elect. They remain, for me, two of his most imperishable.

1 *Tryst*

How lovely Fountain Court must have been in the old days – Arthur Symons outlined it for us in the poem, and John Ireland fills in all the colours by his own unmistakable methods. The first four bars of the introduction are four sustained chords, each punctuated by the three bass notes we have met before, which are such a feature of the composer's comment. The repose of these chords establishes a feeling of external peace, but the harmonic colour of them indicates an inner feeling, latent – at the moment. None knew better than Ireland how to impart the right atmosphere in music. There is then a quiet, ascending passage of seven quavers, single notes, which lead to a harmonized tune of two bars and ushers in the murmuring of the fountain in a gentle undulation, almost somnolent. Underneath this murmuring there is a tune for the left hand which must be brought out. There are other examples of this momentary counterpoint in the left hand, and important single notes which must be heard (e.g. in the chord on the word 'light' at the beginning of the phrase 'The light of June'). The C♭, played by the thumb of the left hand, is the most important note – it is the source of that 'light' which has emanated from that chord, by the impact of the key-change on this word.

There is a linking passage to the second verse, punctuated by those brooding bass notes. At this point, the composer detaches the first two lines of the second verse from the remainder – making of them a separate thought – 'A waiting ghost, in the blue sky, the white curved moon'. He starts by saying *on the piano* 'A waiting ghost' by means of four accented single notes, which are immediately echoed by the voice, an octave higher, as the piano waits on a single note – C, which is suspended to the next bar, and is the start of a short duet between the voice and single notes on the piano – one gets the effect of the moon hovering, and waiting to come into its own as the light fades.

The piano interlude which follows is a recapitulation of part of the introduction, subsiding into that murmuring fountain once again, expanding over the last bar into the climax of the song. Up to this point we have been waiting in hushed expectancy – now the poet, with the composer, says 'Come' – it is a 'Come' of combined urgency and pleading that an end may be put to his waiting all through the afternoon. Notice the lovely ascending chords under the words 'Soon, Love – Come'. The last word 'Soon' is left to the voice alone on the first beat. On the second beat is one chord with those three bass notes underneath. The last two bars on the piano start with a crotchet rest, then there is harmony and a bass note marked *pp* sustained by the pedal, in the middle of which is a despondent little tune marked *p*. The harmony stops at the last bar, and the tune finishes with two single notes, a falling cadence of a major sixth. These two notes are slurred, and the last one permitted to drift away into silence. These last two bars seem to say 'Ah well – there's nothing to do, but wait'.

2 *During Music*

To this man there is no respite from pain and frustration – joy can be only imagined and dreamed about. He looks at the music, it is as inscrutable as the pyramids – but he is aware that from the keys of the piano, sometimes equally mute, she is conjuring up a glory of sound that shakes him to the depths of his being. From the soft rise and fall of her breast he knows that she is unperturbed, and completely unaware of the emotional turmoil she is engendering in him. This accompaniment is beautiful, it is elusive, subtle, and of that yearning bitter-sweetness which is Ireland's especial language. There are gently moving figures in the right hand with an upward feel – the left hand is eloquent, providing essential harmony, and singing tunes of its own. Over these places, the composer has provided phrase markings and accents. On the words 'dark to me as hieroglyph' – the left hand takes over the figures previously played by the right hand, two octaves lower, culminating in mysterious brooding chords punctuated by ominous bass interjections – on, and following the word 'Egyptian'. After this momentary reflection on the shrouded past, we are brought back, immediately, to the present, as the poet compares that past glory to the glory of the sounds now enveloping him in emotional turmoil.

Under these thoughts, Ireland has been building up to the climax of the song, which occurs on the words 'O Swift – O Swift'. The following two bars under the words 'As in melodious haste, float o'er the keys' – took me back immediately to the mood of 'Obsession', no. 2 of the Preludes for Piano. From here to the end of the song, the music is elusive, and indicative of the remoteness of this woman. Just as the Past is unaware of the Present – so is she unaware of his feelings for her? He notes with sadness that 'the shade within her breast is but gently stirred' – This sadness is underlined by the three despondent chords under the words 'rise and fall' – This is the whole poignant point of the song – her indifference. The final word 'breast' is unaccompanied, but the piano establishes a mood of quiet acceptance of the situation over the last three bars, by resolving to the original key of E by the movement of the thumb of the left hand from A♭ to G – and the last note of all E♭ – in the bass.

Songs Sacred and Profane

In these six poems, two by Alice Meynell, three by Sylvia Townsend Warner, and one by W. B. Yeats, John Ireland found a vast field in which to evidence his genius for expressing the particular significance of each poem and fire his inspiration. These poems, in turn, express devout observation and contemplation, the certainty that the qualities which have inspired 'love' can only survive in that love's eternity, love lost, an illusion created by the intensity of love, and an ironic observation of hypocrisy at work. Ireland points an unerring finger at the salient aspects of each work.

1 *The Advent*

As the Latin subtitle assures us – the dew falling upon the earth in the form of rain renews it, and brings forth the buds of spring and, in turn, the seasonal changes of the year – so by this renewal of nature's bounty in 'slow nature's days' – was Our Lord, Jesus Christ nourished, and so came He into Being. The music expresses this in slow measured chords – reverence for the approaching Divine event, but with an undertone of sadness – a veiled apprehension of what the future held. The actual 'Advent' in the winter is hailed by a majestic climax of three bars, followed by two bars which are a quotation from the Piano Sonata (first movement, top of

p. 15) then subsiding over the next three to an important comma – indicative of that latent period between winter and spring. After this comma, the music climbs by four expanding chords to a spread chord of the major thirteenth, very carefully marked ($\downarrow$= 60) which is slightly faster, and illustrates the gradual unfolding of the buds of spring: it is underlined by a rhythmic pattern played by the left hand based upon the rest of the chord of C. This removal accomplished, there is a keychange to D major, the song enumerates those essentials which have been reborn and sustain the Holy Child, and ends with the sun shining and the calmness of a summer day.

2 *Hymn for a Child*

The Gospel of St. Luke, chapter 2, verse 40 reads: 'and the Child grew, and waxed strong, filled with wisdom and the Grace of God was upon Him'. At the time of the episode narrated in this poem, Jesus was twelve years old, and had been in the Temple for three days. The voice of God speaking through Him had been expounding knowledge and answering questions with an erudition beyond their comprehension, and nullified argument. When Joseph and Mary found him at last, and Mary reproached him, Jesus uttered a gentle reproof, saying 'Wist yet not that I must be about my Father's business', but went with them with instant humility and obedience. Nobody understood the Divinity which lay behind it all, and the pathetic irony lay in the fact that they only thought of Him as a 'nicely brought-up child'. As an onlooker remarks in the last verse 'that my elders be always pleased with me'. That it was God who needed to be pleased was a thought that never entered their heads.

The music portrays the movement in and about the Temple. The first momentary climax occurs on the words 'eloquence' and then resumes the gentle level of speech. In passing it may be noted that the music indicates that two bites and a snap of the jaws were enough for the dogs to dispose of Jezebel. We now come to the words 'Just as He disposes of the Law and Moses'. Here 'disposes' does not mean 'to get rid of' but 'to place in the right order' Mosaism and the laws of man. While this discussion is going on, Mary comes upon the scene, and the music takes on a certain urgency as she reproaches Jesus, followed instantly by His quiet obedience. For the rest of the song, Ireland, in the accompaniment, remains in the background, letting the vocal line of the multitude speak for itself in the 'nicely brought up child'. Following this, the introduction is repeated, just two bars of movement, and then the postscript, the last verse ending 'that my elders be always pleased with me'. The composer places an accent on the word 'pleased' and a tenuto sign. It is the elders who must be 'pleased' – doubtless God is looking on, shaking His head as Dr Ireland does in the last two bars of the four which close the song.

3 *My Fair*

In this poem the lover is permitted only occasional glimpses of the qualities which, combined, make up the overall beauty of the beloved – the fitful smiles – the sweet words, the laughter – all will die unless –. He pleads that all these, which she is unwilling to lose, may be hidden in his heart, where they will be cherished in the eternity of his love, and not lost amid the wide waters of anonymity.

Ireland's reaction to this poem was immediate – he felt an emotion of such intensity, that when he translates it into terms of music, it bursts upon us with almost overwhelming force. There is no 'getting into' this song, you must be prepared for it, because you are in it from the first note of the introduction, which is an impassioned cry: 'My Fair!' The music throughout is intensely concentrated, the harmony complex but exquisite – there is often more than one voice singing in the accompaniment, and all these inner parts *must be* brought out, as they are of the utmost significance. There are little trilling figures in either the left or right hand, which emphasise the qualities which must cease to be – the 'sweet words' – the 'laughter'.

In the first part of the song the bass is often climbing upwards, giving a sense of urgency. The seven bars following the words 'except the few that sing to me', constitute one of the most poignant, impassioned utterances that Ireland ever made – you cannot describe it in words – you can only feel it. After these seven bars, the music calms, but is, none the less, emotionally intense. There is a final climax on the words 'my cupful'. The lover is determined that what she may give shall not be lost, and the song ends on this note of firm but tranquil assurance. To sum it up, this is a stupendous song, it envelops, leaves one breathless, and near to tears.

4 *The Salley Gardens*

In this poem impetuosity has lost this boy his love – her restrained hand on his 'leaning shoulder' was not enough. He realizes the extent of his foolishness, does not fully understand how this has come about, but is bereft, and 'full of tears'. There is a short, sad little introduction which seems to ask a question, and the voice proceeds in retrospect – the boy speaking his thoughts aloud. Under this, the accompaniment moves in quiet sympathy and simple sorrow, only coming to the surface twice, with a little tune of its own, picturing the growing of the leaves, and the grass on the weirs. The question asked in the introduction is not answered until the final chord of the song, where this little tune, instead of finishing upwards, falls a minor sixth to E minor – 'Tears'.

5 *The Soldier's Return*

It was Dr Ireland's opinion that the soldier in this poem is dead. This interpretation was endorsed by Miss Townsend Warner when she visited him later. The girl is running to meet her man – 'Jump through the hedge lass!' 'Run down the lane' – the sunset is in her eyes, and at his back, and all she sees is a vague, black outline – an apparition. She is told not to fear: 'He will speak better when the sun's gone down' – or, in other words, will take on definition as the light fades.

The two-bar introduction establishes the rhythm of the marching feet, and is given a sense of urgency by the use of ascending triplets in an inner part. The accompaniment moves along until the words 'Coming over the hills with the sunset at his back' are reached, where rhythm stops in the right hand, giving place to legato chords: there is just a hint of rhythm in the left hand, more implied than expressed. On the word 'back', the right hand is immobile, harmony suspended from the previous bar. However, there are four ghostly beats in the bass, and this is the moment when she realizes that it is an apparition confronting her. She is told immediately 'Never be feared, lass' – From here onwards the harmony takes on a macabre bitter acridity, only enlivened by the 'Leaping over the water-course' – a short, trilly figure. The bitter harmony then continues on its rhythmic way – upwards for 2½ bars, then downwards for a further 2½, until the implied 'walking from the town' ends. The last words heard in the voice are a sardonic comment 'He will speak better when the sun's gone down' – it is cold comfort, and the accompaniment marches away into the distance, gradually diminishing, but still emphatic.

6 *The Scapegoat*

In the ancient Jewish ritual, a goat, on which the chief priest on the Day of Atonement symbolically laid the sins of the people. The goat was then driven into the wilderness. (Leviticus 16.) The song is an ironic comment on hypocrisy – the poor beast, unaware of the human burden laid upon it, dances on and on – with more than one step it may be noted, as the music of this carefree dance is sometimes in two, sometimes in three – sardonic quaver-chords all, and acridity is applied to the harmony of these chords by the use of appoggiatura, which also emphasises the rhythm of the dance. When we move to the town scene, the music slows to the parody of a waltz – the hypocrites can afford to relax and make merry. This mocking waltz ends abruptly after seven bars, and we switch back to the scapegoat, still dancing on his lonely purposeless way. The music ends in a frenzy of abandonment *ffz*, and accelerating to *presto*. Norah Kirby told me that when Dr Ireland played this accompaniment at a recital he had the audience rippling with laughter, as he skipped from one end of the piano to the other, and finished with that well marked flourish, and all the force at his command. This is a song cycle of infinite variety covering, as it does, the gamut of human experience.

Five Sixteenth-Century Poems

Every aspect of nature's loveliness evoked a response from John Ireland, but particularly did he love spring and early summer, and in these poems, except no. 3, 'An Aside', which comments on the vagaries of woman, he found an appreciation of the various qualities of the 'Sweet Season' which fired his imagination and inspiration.

1 *A Thanksgiving*

In this the poet thanks God for nature's bounty, and the joy to eye and ear occasioned by this annual renewal of spring's loveliness. The music marked *'with impulse and warmth'* is just that – an instant response – an outpouring of joy, expressed in the composer's spring-time harmonies, which are exquisite and full of light. John Ireland repeats the words 'Pleasure it is to hear, iwis, The birdès sing', and sings the song on the piano, with arpeggio passages evolved from his individual harmony. Under the words 'God's purveyance' and those following, the music takes on an atmosphere of warm devout praise, and the song ends with a further repetition of the words 'Pleasure it is to hear, iwis, The birdès sing', the piano having the last word, singing over the last three bars an enlargement of the main theme into an outpouring of joyous sincerity, and belief in the goodness of God.

2 *All in a Garden Green*

The poet avers that of all nature's beauties which come to fruition in the early part of the year, nothing can compare with the beauty of the red rose which blooms in June. The music moves in easy contrast to the voice, singing its own tune of quiet appreciation of *all* beauty – the harmony is again delightful, moving smoothly all the time from one entrancing sound to another, coming to a gentle climax under the words 'Of all the pleasant flowers in June'. The voice ends on the tonic at the word 'peer', conveying quiet belief in its own observation. The piano ends by repeating the introduction, this time ending on the dominant – the next most important note – quiet affirmation.

3 *An Aside*

The poet takes a quizzical look at women, observes all their capriciousness, thinks that possibly you can make something of the best of them, but dares not express his thoughts aloud. The music flits about in gay humorous manner, adding pungent comment here and there, but, like women, moving from one dimension to another, without the slightest warning. The last four bars are marked *Vivo* – on the final words 'But I will not say so', then he takes to his heels, and runs. You could put words to the last two bars: 'But I daren't stay here longer'. It is all a very pertinent observation of the female sex in words and music.

4 *A Report Song*

In this, the poet dreams of all the pleasant things one can do in time of spring, each verse an idyllic concept of one particular aspect of Love. Unfortunately, he wakens and the dream is ended. This accompaniment is derived entirely from the dance subject in 'The Palm and May' from the *Green Ways* piano suite, written a year earlier than these songs, in 1937 – and, like the songs, written in Deal. It should be noted that the inspiration for 'The Palm and May' stems from a quotation from another sixteenth-century poet, Thomas Nash. In the piano suite, this subject becomes more and more ecstatic. Here, it is gentle, relaxed and lilting from start to finish, except for one bar, on the words 'waked' where there are just two quiet chords. On the word 'done', the music dances away into the distance, diminishing, but with an air of finality. These last three bars for the piano are marked *senza ped.* (without pedal). This enables the differing harmony of each group to take crystal clarity.

5 *The Sweet Season*

This poem extols the outstanding joys of the month of May. In the first half of the poem, each separate line paints a picture of May's effect on Man and Nature. The last half of the poem enjoins us to 'Rejoice in May', while it is with us – tardiness is fatal and June, too late to enjoy the best that the 'Sweet Season' has to offer. As the poem passes, line by line, from one cheerful simile to another, so does the music underline each passing thought with gay but controlled movement. It is like a spring-time breeze blowing through the countryside. Although the overall design of the accompaniment is the same for all three verses, there are often subtle differences in treatment of recurring phrases, adding colour and variation to the music as it unfolds – never stopping until the words 'While May doth last – when May is gone' are reached in the last verse. At this point, to the end of the song, some of the movement subsides, but not all – the word 'gone' is given much greater duration by the composer, and at the end of it, falls a minor sixth, and the music stops, momentarily, indicating the last words 'Of all the year the pleasant time is past', under which the music is sparse, with only a hint of movement. Six bars on the piano close the song; they are an attenuated and thinned out version of the interlude between the verses. This is a song cycle of great contrasts, and is a joy to play.

When Lights Go Rolling Round The Sky

Writing out the words of this song, one finds that they conform to the pattern, chorus – verse, chorus – verse, chorus. Within these confines Dr Ireland has created a delightful song of the ballad type popular in those days – 1911.

The story is simple: two friends and their wives wake to the sunshine of a summer day, enjoy the day – and, under the 'light' of the moon, meet together in 'sequestered willow shade' to enjoy that quiet communion of kindred spirits. There is no room for melancholy in this happy rural setting. The accompaniment is delightful to play, of perfect craftsmanship, leaving the voice free to pursue its own joyous way. To remind us that it is John Ireland we are hearing, discerning listeners will be able to detect veiled references to the last movement of the First Violin Sonata, which came earlier, and for good measure, the first movement of the Second Violin Sonata almost ends with an upward scale and an emphatic chord as does this song.

Hope the Hornblower

The sentiment of the words of this poem of three verses indicates another ballad-type setting, this time: first verse – major; second verse – major; third verse – minor-major. The link into the third verse where the composer changes to the minor mode, and the first few lines of his last verse, are a veiled hint that the chase may have a more sinister meaning, and that the quarry may be human, not animal. The idea of killing anything was repugnant to John Ireland; what would appeal to him is the drive and energy – the urgency, and the freshness of the day. These aspects of the poem he has translated into terms of music with infallible touch. Again, there is no getting into the song, the spirit of it all must be established in the mind before starting, as one is driven along from start to finish. There are characteristic John Ireland touches throughout the accompaniment, particularly the perfect fifths in the left hand which he uses in many works with individual effect, and if one looks at the last page of the First Violin Sonata where it is marked *prestissimo*, it will be found that the same left hand device is employed, which is used three times in this accompaniment. This is a great song, of impelling drive and energy.

Sea Fever

This song, written in 1913, speedily became Ireland's best-known song. Its appeal is universal, speaking as it does of practically every Englishman's love of the sea, and all that appertains to it. The accompaniment, in the main, consists of spaced crotchet chords, each chord a differing harmony, but proceeding logically from that which has preceded it. There are only two quaver passing notes in the whole work.

I was in almost daily contact with Dr Ireland during its composition, and, as it is so well known, can only add one or two personal recollections of its performance by the composer himself. For the most part, the voice has to sing three notes to the piano's one, so plenty of time must be given for diction and clear enunciation; also, the composer wanted plenty of time for each successive change of harmony to be heard effectively, therefore the performance must not be too fast. Dr Ireland played it very carefully himself, slightly stressing those chords which he considered of especial importance in the harmonic scheme. These are all marked. He used to instruct me to sing the last verse, while he played the descending chords which are its feature. We would do this two or three times, as he had not written anything like it before, and enjoyed the effect. When we got to the end of the song, a warning finger would be held up, and I dare not come down to the last note until he gave the signal. This satisfactorily accomplished, he would play his last note, very carefully, in the bass. Here, singer and pianist must be in absolute rapport – the suspension must be given its full value, and the last few bars in perfect proportion.

If There were Dreams to Sell

The poet's dream-choice of a cottage in the country 'lone and still' needs no explanation. The music is an example of how to achieve great effect by simple means. The song is melodic throughout with a hint of wistful longing. The accompaniment as unobtrusive as it can possibly be, but the composer's delicacy of touch and feeling are always apparent. Under the words 'and the crier rang the bell', the bell-like effect of the three chords is obtained by the simple means of leaving out the third of the chord. There is a very gentle climax under the words 'were dreams to have at will, this best would heal my ill' – and the song closes equally gently, but with firm assurance 'this, this would I buy' – altogether a sincere and appealing song.

I Have Twelve Oxen

In this early English poem of four verses, the poet tells of a man who has great pride in his herd of beautiful oxen, twelve of each, of four colours, brown, white, black and red. He seems to have been making a tour of inspection and appreciation, as he knows where each group is grazing. Contemplating their beauty as he goes upon his way, he meets a small boy whom he greets in pleased surprise: 'With hey! With ho!', noticing also that the boy is '*pretty*'. He tells the boy of these oxen and asks has he seen them. In the last verse, which tells of the 'red' ones, it seems of increasing importance that the boy should see them, as it were. Beauty should meet and appreciate Beauty. The music is gay, and utterly delightful, obviously it is a summer day, the grass is lush, and the cattle browsing contentedly.

The vocal line is the same for each verse, the harmony the same in its implications, but not in its development, which enlarges verse by verse, by its colourful treatment and increasing amplitude. Each 'colour' has a different and slightly larger chord. This climax of colour and chord occurs when the man speaks of his oxen which are 'red'. Ireland makes a climax to the song by repeating the words 'Sawest not *you* mine oxen, you little pretty boy?' Under the repeat of these words the music takes on a gay ecstasy and there is a very important accent over the chord under the word 'you'. When the composer played this to me during the course of its composition, he enlarged the feeling of this phrase to all-embracing proportions – it was of paramount importance that this lovely boy *should* see the equally lovely oxen. The accompaniment then rushes joyously to its headlong conclusion. This song is an imperishable gem full of the composer's rare, uninhibited gaiety.

Spring Sorrow

Ireland was bound to react to this poem by Rupert Brooke, as it so faithfully portrays his own feelings – that seemingly interminable wait through the winter months, when everything appears to be dead, and that forlorn, but hopeful, looking around every morning to glimpse the first buds of spring. This song is of imperishable beauty, its very simplicity and perfection almost defy adequate performance – there is always something just around the corner – something just out of reach – something you wish you could do a little better. It is a supreme example of how the quality of musical thought outstrips mortality. Even when the sound has ceased, it is still there, in the mind, and in the heart, and you cannot touch it. The music eludes you. The written notes tell you that, for the most part, it is in the major, but the poignant quality of the harmony tells you something entirely different. This is the illusion, and the composer's genius.

The Bells of San Marie

This song, published in 1919, has many points of reference to *Sea Fever* published six years earlier. It has the same poet, John Masefield, three verses, the same basic rhythm, although the time signatures differ. This song is written in 6/8, *Sea Fever* is written in 4/4 though the vocal line is, in effect 12/8. Also, like *Sea Fever* the melody is the same for each of the three verses. In this song, however, the subject matter is not a yearning for the sea itself, but quiet enjoyment of the bells, and contemplation of the happy-go-lucky seamen who come in to ring them. The treatment of the poem is different; Ireland repeats the last couplet of each verse, underlining that particular thought. The harmony, basically the same throughout, is structurally enlarged in each verse, building, in some way, nearly all the time. We feel the bells swaying with every increasing clamour, and each verse has its own individual imitation of this – the most striking example being the first half of the last verse, where the bells clang upwards for two bars, and then downwards throughout the whole range of the accompaniment. From this point, the clamour subsides, and you could be sitting on the harbour wall day-long listening, to the end. This song is another Ireland paradox, although it is written in the minor, the effect is one of rugged gaiety, which could be easily reversed – if you look over your shoulder, you will see the sea, which is not always kind.

The Journey

In this poem of two verses by Ernest Blake, we travel along a winding road which descends into autumnal shade over-topped by craggy pine trees, past the rivers where the tall reeds whisper of seasonal change, emerging into the sunlight again 'a-top the hill at the far end of the journey', accompanied all the way by the jingling of the bells on the horse's harness. In this accompaniment, the jingling of the bells is portrayed by little rippling figures, which cease at once as we pass through the deepest shade: they become audible again *pp* on the word 'gloom' and from here there is a gradual crescendo to the end of the song, as we realize 'the shadows are but shadows', and that there is full sunlight on top of the hill, at the end of the road. This crescendo is a gradual modulation in subtle, typical Ireland language, and the tonic is not fully established again until the final note of the voice on the word 'hill', where the piano closes the song over four bars, triumphantly in the major, and it is a burst of sunshine.

The Merry Month of May

This poem by the sixteenth-century poet Thomas Dekker tells of two lovers in an atmosphere of pastoral gaiety. It is May, and all nature conspires to provide lush beauty in everything – the nightingale sings entreatingly, and the cuckoo mocks, but it is a perfect summer day, and the sun is shining throughout. The music reveals the composer in his most happy mood – it is all compounded of his 'springtime' sounds: the edgy freshness of the harmony, the perfect fifths in the left hand dancing along, which we have met before in the Second Violin Sonata (last movement, p. 46, *molto più moto*), and a delightful descending modulation under the words 'true love say', which occurs in each of the four verses at the same place in the music. This modulation has its counterpart in 'Fire of Spring' (*Preludes* no. 4, p. 16). The accompaniment is virtually the same for all four verses, the only difference being those occasioned by the requirements of the words. The fourth verse is a reprise of the first, but this time ends upon the tonic as 'sweet Peg' finally becomes 'summer's Queen' and the song dances to its close in unrestrained gaiety.

Vagabond

In this poem by John Masefield, we meet a wanderer who translates all the complicated things of Life and Death into the simple terms his simple mind can understand. His rugged philosophy takes comfort from the warmth of a gypsy fire, a lonely Inn – and then it's the dusty road again. The composer sets this as if it were a poem of two verses, establishing continuity of thought by joining the second to the first and the fourth to the third. The harmony is as simple and rugged as the vagabond himself. After the opening chord, the voice is free to roam, and the music unobtrusive, but strong, and often with that touch of wistful sadness that the composer understood so well. The song reaches its climax, after its questing progress, when the wanderer speaks of the things he does understand, 'the gipsy fires', the 'lonely inns' and 'jest the dusty road'. The piano ends the song with the same simple chord with which it began.

When I am Dead, my Dearest

In this poem by Christina Rossetti, the lover speaks of death, and desires that only the simple things of nature shall mark the passing – 'The green grass' – 'the showers' and 'the dewdrops' – memory on either side, if it survives at all, will be purely fortuitous.

The accompaniment to this sad poem is one of Ireland's most simple poignant settings. The piano commences by speaking the first words 'When I am dead' in four notes accented with quiet but firm deliberation, the voice following immediately, and continuing its sad meditation upon the inevitable parting, and the gentle requests stemming from it. The music flows in sustained, simple chords, from one sound to another, in penetrating sensitivity. In the falling phrase under the words 'I shall not see the shadows', notice the tearful effect of the B♮. No other way of harmonizing this phrase would have comparable emotional impact. It is the most poignant appeal in the whole song.

Basically, the voice is the same for each verse, but the adjustments that are made show perfect insight and depth of feeling for the words. The last two bars of the song are marked *estinto* and resolve into D minor, but as the chord is in its first inversion, we are left with that feeling of resigned sadness which permeates the whole work.

Santa Chiara
(Palm Sunday – Naples)

Santa Chiara is a monastery on a small island about 10 miles from Naples which takes its name from a local woman named Chiara, who was canonized, thus becoming Santa Chiara. In this place, on Palm Sunday, will be re-enacted the pageant of Christ's entry into Jerusalem, with a villager playing the part of Christ. This is a story of a man who has almost lost his faith and, as a result, has become disillusioned and tired of everything he sees. He feels that he has no place in Santa Chiara on Palm Sunday; 'any other day', but that a remnant of faith left to him prompts the feeling that he could not withstand a spiritual confrontation in person, but must be at least represented – so he asks his friend to carry a palm for him.

The introduction has the dignity of a slow procession, and sets the background to the song by painting a picture of Palm Sunday in Santa Chiara. The voice starts with a simple request – 'Because it is the day of Palms, carry a Palm for me', followed by one bar on the piano which is an allusion to the procession which is in the forefront of his mind. All the things of which he has become tired are perfectly illustrated in the music, the undulatory accompaniment to the words 'The sea is blue from here to Sorrento' and the Italian feel to the melody of those words. The music then climbs with the 'sea wind' to the 'white clouds', flowing with increasing amplitude and colour, subsiding gently as he observes, for the second time, 'the dark sail lean upon the sea' – and the undulations stop. The music then becomes dark and brooding, with a downward-going inner melody of its own, which continues under the voice as he says he has 'grown tired' and asks 'what is left for me'. The piano then plays the one bar which hints of the impending procession which has come back into his mind, followed by an anguished chord.

This chord is an impassioned outcry of mental agony, and the music sustains this pain under the words 'I have no place in Santa Chiara – there is no peace upon the sea', reaching its climax at the words 'but carry a palm' – this time, the words are not a polite request, but an imploring cry, and this continues to the end of the song, where the music reiterates the processional theme of the introduction, finishing this time in the major – one heavily accented chord, which seems an affirmation of faith.

Mrs Norah Kirby told me recently that the monastery at Santa Chiara was destroyed by a bomb during the last war, a grievous event which affected Dr Ireland very deeply.

Great Things

This poem of four verses by Thomas Hardy has none of the bitter-sweet character of the other Hardy poems – it is a countryman's tale of the simple, basic things which give him greatest pleasure – the cider at the inn – the dance-revelry and the secret love-interlude by night. Even when called to account at the last, these things, remembered, will always have been his greatest joys.

The music is a ballad-type setting with four verses – major, major, major, minor– major, that typifies exuberant rustic gaiety almost throughout. Between the first and second verses there is a seven bar link, and on the last four of these, the left hand plays a country-style rhythm, and prepares the way for the dance, which occupies the whole of the second verse, except for the 'going home' phrase towards the end, where there are descending chords, *legato*. Gaiety is then resumed in the link to the third verse, in which is pictured love-by-night. The music dances as 'a figure flits like one a-wing' and underneath it all is the joy of this secret meeting. There is a similar gay link into the last verse, then straight into the minor, as the man reflects 'will these be always great things' when he is called to account – 'soul, I have need of thee'. Under this, there are quiet chords, but as the harmony is the same as that of the dancing second verse, we never quite lose the feeling of joy behind the momentary shadow.

The question asked: 'What then?' is answered immediately in the major, as the gay dancing music returns on the words 'joy jaunts, impassioned flings', and continues irrepressibly to the end of the song – the piano having the last word with three accented chords over a rhythmic left hand, an emphatic bass, and a final full chord for each hand. The piano part is a joy to play – tremendously exhilarating.

If We Must Part

This poem by Ernest Dowson expresses the intense anguish of parting – if parting has to be – feelings are too deep for words, and more than a hand's touch unendurable. The music is of bitter-sweet poignancy throughout and, after a short introduction of two bars, rises to a momentary climax of recollected ecstasy under the words 'anguish of a kiss'; and so it continues, the accompaniment proceeding from one exquisite harmony to another, above which the voice sings its lone tune of pain. At the words 'let silence speak', the piano stops and the voice continues its solitary way with the words 'life is a little while' and we feel sheer emotional desolation. The words 'and love is long' are echoed by the piano on its re-entry in single notes, leading to a bleak climax on the word 'long', and this heightened emotional intensity is sustained to the word 'sleep'. The last words of the poem 'but words are weak' have but one sad chord under them on 'words' and we feel then the poet is spent, and can say no more. The piano closes the song, by repeating the poignant introduction, subsiding into a final dark chord.

Tutto è sciolto

In this poem by James Joyce, it is one of those quiet, breathless evenings, when even the very silence seems suspended – there is endless space pierced by the light of one lone star, as into the poet's mind come pictures of 'the youthful beauty of that love long past' – love, however, was but loosely held, elusive at the last, and the poet realizes the futility of regret, remembering only the sweetness of that love so nearly achieved.

There are only 27 bars of music, no introduction, just one lone third, and the piano, an octave lower than the voice, sings with it 'a birdless heaven'. The voice continues over an accompaniment gently moving downwards to a chord, rather sultry, and of hushed expectancy, and we feel that a climax must come soon, which it does, on the word 'rememberest'. The voice continues picturing the beauty of that youthful love – 'the clear young eyes – soft look' etc. The accompaniment is equally clear, quiet chords descend to the words 'dusk of the air'.

There are then two bars on the piano, expectant, emotionally held back, but leading upwards to an emotional climax on the words 'why then' continuing with restrained passion under the words 'remembering those shy sweet lures'. The harmony throughout is of penetrating bitter-sweet nostalgia, and so continues to the end of the song in sad reminiscence, as the past accepts the futility of regret. Under the last words of the song 'was all but thine' the piano moves to a quiet close, repeating twice, the melody first heard at the beginning of the song, under the words 'a birdless heaven'. This song is a gem; it is 27 bars of the most deeply felt music, its complete emotional insight belies its apparent simplicity, and a hovering pendulous atmosphere is all-pervading.

CHAPTER 21

Songs of Innocence:
The Part-Songs of John Ireland

Philip Lancaster

I T is not often that one is presented with a part-song in the contemporary concert hall. It is a medium that seems to have fallen out of favour, whether through the trends of current programming or because of the low esteem of the works themselves, this is not the place upon which to expound. Such an unfavourable view of the part-song is nothing new, as is shown by an unsigned article on 'The Modern Partsong' that appeared in *The Times* in August 1910:

> Not so very long ago the part-song was a thing usually dreaded by musical people, who regarded it as the last word of ineptitude, a form of music in which success of a kind was so easily won as not to be worth having. The hearts of critics fell as they gazed on the pile of foolish tunes and dreary harmonies, for the part-song was a kind of outlet in secular music, a refuge for those organists whose inspiration might possibly last them through the course of a single [psalm] chant, but could not be trusted to carry them further.[1]

However, as the tone of the opening suggests, the writer goes on to suggest that a number of recent publications heralded a new age in the genre. He attributed such a change of fortune to the revival of the polyphonic style of the Elizabethan composers; a revival of interest in the arts of the heyday of English arts in the sixteenth century that had been fuelled by the work of Runciman Terry at Westminster Cathedral and others, the integration of which is exemplified by Vaughan Williams's monumental *Fantasia on a Theme by Thomas Tallis*, premiered in the year in which the article was published.

This move to create an English music through rediscovery of our heritage, devoid of the Teutonic influences that had been seen to have thwarted the development of a national art, had a monumental effect upon all composers in the early twentieth century. The revival of the madrigal and Elizabethan consort music encouraged the exploration of such ensembles and forms in the contemporary setting. Instrumentally this manifested itself in the Cobbett prize for chamber music, reviving the 'fantasy' form, in which in 1908 John Ireland was awarded second place for his *Phantasie Trio*. As a nation of choral singers, established through the growth in the nineteenth century of 'Bach Choirs' and the various choral festivals, the oratorio had prominence, but in these groups and a number of smaller choirs there was an avenue also for madrigalia and, following a slightly more modest Viennese model, perhaps, the part-song. As is often cited, Parry advised Vaughan Williams to 'write choral music as befits an Englishman and a democrat', and this democratic aspect led to the desire – notably by George Dyson,

---

[1] *The Times*, 5 August 1910.

but also in Parry, Holst, Vaughan Williams and others – to write choral works that were, fundamentally, accessible and enjoyable, but being so without compromising their artistic merit.

Ironically for the part-song, it could have been its Elizabethan progenitors that brought the genre into disrepute in the first place, the regular fare of the growing number of madrigal and glee clubs in the early nineteenth century perhaps giving off too heavy a whiff of lowbrow triviality for the serious composer to want to contribute to the genre. However, the new contributions of the early twentieth century lifted the part-song beyond the harmonised song tune into a genre of life and integrity. Prior to 1914, part-songs by composers such as Granville Bantock and Edward Elgar buoyed up the repertoire that was in great demand in competitive choral competitions, which were rife in the pre-war period, and for which Ireland could later be seen to adjudicate on occasion.[2] Publishers such as Novello & Co., Edward Arnold and The Year Book Press were rapidly expanding their series of unison and two-part songs, supporting a growth in school singing, the repertoire for which also included the folksong arrangements of Cecil Sharp.

The *Times* article of 1910 speaks principally of a set of six part-songs by Hubert Parry and several part-songs by Elgar, published in the preceding months by Novello. Towards the end of the piece is mentioned a setting of Shakespeare's *Full Fathom Five* by John Ireland, which had been published in 1908, and which with its bell-like ostinato accompaniment and largely imitative vocal writing certainly merits its description as 'musically interesting'.[3] Ireland was at this time still an emerging composer, for although he had already had works published in 1902 and 1903 (the earliest of which, a Communion Service in A♭, was later withdrawn) he had not yet developed, notably, the harmonic style of his maturity which makes his work so distinctive.

Full Fathom Five was published alongside a second part-song, a setting of Richard Alison, *There is a Garden in her Face*, both of which were issued in Novello's *Collection of Two Part Songs* [with piano], nos. 150 and 151, probably commissioned by the publisher for their catalogue of songs for the schools market.

These were not the first part-songs to be written by Ireland. His earliest is a setting for four-part, SATB choir of Thomas Campion's *The Peaceful Western Wind*, dating from sometime during the 1890s. It is one of his earliest works, Ireland only just embarking upon his musical career, joining the Royal College of Music in 1893 as a student pianist and organist. (He was not to persuade Stanford to allow him to become a composition scholar until 1896.) It is a piece of its time: cloyingly Victorian in its manner and sentimentality, both melodically and harmonically, with ever-present sevenths and occasional (and essentially pointless) chromatic auxiliary notes. But it is not without skill: its essential ternary form shows a little development of texture in the recapitulation, rather than being a direct repetition, whilst the central section in some part grows out of the material of the first. In fact there are some nice touches, notably in the delayed cadence to the dominant

[2] Ireland recollected to Charles Markes that he had adjudicated at the Blackpool Competition Festival in about 1930, quoted in Muriel V. Searle, *John Ireland – The Man and his Music* (Tunbridge Wells: Midas Books, 1979), p. 142.

[3] *The Times*, 5 August 1910.

half-way through the outer verses, and in a cheeky ninth in the first line of the same. *The Peaceful Western Wind* was brought to publication only in 1994, and it seems that Ireland had regarded the work as immature, this setting being super-seded in 1912 by a second setting of the same words as a two-part song with piano written under a title deriving from the second verse of Campion's poem *See How the Morning Smiles.*

Ireland's sympathy with the prevalent interest amongst his contemporaries in the Elizabethan poets is confirmed in his subsequent works: settings of Thomas Nashe's *Spring, the Sweet Spring* and John Dowland's *Weep you no more, sad fountains* for SATB choir, composed in 1906, a unison setting of an anonymous sixteenth century text, *The Frog and the Crab*, and a two-part setting of Thomas Morley's *In Praise of May*, both published in 1909. The first of the 1906 settings could have been written to commission, dedicated 'To Lionel Benson Esq., and the Members of the Magpie Madrigal Society', perhaps being written to commemo-rate the twenty-first anniversary of the founding of the group, which changed its name in 1911 to the Elizabethan Madrigal Society. The Dowland setting was given a more personal dedication much later, in December 1932, when he presented the unpublished (and perhaps unperformed) score to Percy Bentham, a friend and sculptor whom Ireland had come to know following his move to his flat and studio in Gunter Grove, Chelsea, and to whose memory *A London Overture* was written in 1936. *Spring, the Sweet Spring* is a lively, playful setting that gives us our first glimpse in the genre of Ireland's emerging interest in harmonic colour. At the opening of each verse he delights in a major seventh paired with an added fourth in the tenor resulting in a juicy tritone, and as we approach the chorus we find a wonderfully chromatic phrase, presaging the voice of the mature Ireland, heralding the entry of the bird-songs played out in the text: the calls of cuckoo, nightingale, lapwing and owl. The cuckoo here is played out with its traditional minor third. In the cuckoo's later appearance in Ireland's work, in the solo song *Earth's Call* (1918), it becomes a more melancholically imbued major third.

Birdsong and the seasons are recurrent themes in Ireland's work, the most dominant season being Spring – a season depicted in music by a number of composers of the early twentieth century, most infamously by Stravinsky in *Le Sacre du printemps*, but also in works such as the colourful orchestral tone poem, *Enter Spring*, by Ireland's direct contemporary, Frank Bridge. Ireland's represen-tations are more understated, the season making numerous appearances in his settings for both solo voice and choirs, and in his instrumental works also. A number of piano works bear titles or prefatory quotations relating to the season: *In Green Ways*, the outer movements of which quote A. E. Housman and Thomas Nashe's 'Spring'; his 'Island Sequence', *Sarnia*, includes a movement titled 'Song of the Springtides'. It is depicted in both its 'joyous celebratory romp'[4] and in more melancholic mode, as found in the Rupert Brooke setting 'Spring Sorrow' and in the valedictory movement for solo piano in the short song cycle to words by Housman, *We'll to the Woods No More* (1927), musical embodiments of unfulfilled potential. It is a season whose imagery can be seen as directly representative but

[4] Fiona Richards, writing on 'The Sweet Season' from *Five Sixteenth Century Songs*, in F. Richards, *The Music of John Ireland* (Aldershot: Ashgate, 2000), p. 105.

which can also double as metaphors relating to sexual experience, either real or imagined.

Sometime before 1905 Ireland had begun his first song cycle for solo voice and piano, *Songs of a Wayfarer*. It predates all but the first of Ireland's part-songs, but it gives a strong indication of some of Ireland's literary preferences. One of those represented is William Blake, to whose *Songs of Innocence* and other miscellaneous poems Ireland turned for five choral settings between 1910 and 1913 (no further settings for solo voice followed), and whose words preface the piano work *The Darkened Valley* (1920). The four-part settings of *Laughing Song* and *Cupid* (1910) are light madrigalian affairs, whilst in the 1912 setting of *A Cradle Song* ('Sleep, sleep, beauty bright') the lower vocal parts set up an ostinato accompaniment over which the melody is sung in the soprano part, later developed with some rather nice chromatic descendings in the accompaniment, similar to those seen briefly in *Spring, the Sweet Spring*, which lift the work slightly out of the ordinary.

A setting of *The Echoing Green* – a two-part song with piano composed in September 1913 – is dedicated to 'To Gwennie, in Jersey'. The Channel Islands had increasingly fascinated Ireland since his first visit to Jersey at the turn of the century as a chaperone to the choristers of St Jude's Church, Chelsea. From 1907 Ireland would return to Jersey or Guernsey regularly on holiday, and would spend a year on Guernsey, eventually leaving in the face of the imminent Nazi invasion of the islands in June 1940.

Perhaps the most interesting of Ireland's William Blake choral songs is the second setting of 1913: a unison song, *Nurses' Song*, published in 1914 by The Year-book Press as 'Sunset Play', alongside a counterpart *Child's Song* – a setting of a poem by Thomas Moore also written in 1913. Like *A Cradle Song* it is a work of great simplicity, which is based predominantly on another ostinato (this time in the piano). However, the simple beauty of *Nurses' Song* is in its melody, which is in the Lydian mode – F major but with B naturals – although the song finally resolves onto C major. Although Ireland was never influenced by the folk song revival, which is sometimes associated with the resurgence of modality in English music at this time, Fiona Richards asserts that it was the 'introduction to and emphasis on the modal system of Palestrina' and the modal scales first expounded, as Ireland recalled, by Charles Stanford, that 'led Ireland to his own brand of modality'.[5] It is this 'brand' of modality, in his harmony more than the overriding tonality that makes Ireland's musical voice so unique. Whilst *Nurses' Song* is limited in its harmonic exploration, the melodic line has the same beauty, almost hypnotic in effect, as that achieved by the use of the same mode (although transposed and starting on a different degree of the mode) in Ireland's popular *The Holy Boy*, written in the December of that same year.

The cycle of *Songs of a Wayfarer* was only brought to completion in 1911 with the addition of its final song, 'I will Walk on the Earth'; a setting by a now unknown American poet, theologian and Illinois Unitarian minister, James Vila Blake (1842–1925). J. V. Blake must have been a great discovery for Ireland at this time, for in 1911–12 he was to complete nine settings of his poetry: four for solo voice (one, unusually, with optional organ obbligato, and another, *Hillo, my Bonny*, written

[5] *Ibid.*, p. 16.

under the pseudonym 'Turlay Royce'), three unison songs, and three two-part songs for female voices. Two of the solo songs took their words from Blake's 1902 collection of *Songs*,[6] whilst all the unison and part-songs are settings of poems from a series of translations from the German in his 1887 collection of *Poems*.[7] Most of those translations used by Ireland are either anonymous in their original German or just unacknowledged; one, *Evening Song*, is a translation of a poem by Friedrich Rückert.

In keeping with the words' origins, Ireland's settings are very Viennese in manner: *At Early Dawn* is in the manner of a German *ländler*, with a brief flutter of interest at 'The birds but twitter in a dream', where a recurrent appoggiatura at the top of the piano echoes the birds' song. As with this song, the vocal parts of the pastoral *Evening Song* are largely in thirds, in a bucolic 6/8 setting, which opens once more with an open fifth pedal. Such writing in thirds is not unique to these songs, being also the essential means in the 1908 song *There is a Garden in her Face*, for example, which alternates passages in thirds with short imitative phrases passed between the voice parts. The unison *Slumber Song* is a simple, strophic song in an easy triple time given over a simple repeated piano figure similar in shape to the setting of J. V. Blake's *Spring*: another pastoral song, that tells of an Alpine setting with sheep bells and shepherds piping – the latter depicted in the running quaver figure that accompanies the last verse of the song. The repeat of the last line at the end of each verse of *Spring*, in both manner and melodic shape, is redolent of the song setting of Henry Newbolt's *Hope the Hornblower*, composed in the same year as the Blake setting. There is some similarity also in the manner of the accompaniment, although *Hope the Hornblower* contrives to be more rumbustiously English, and for that matter becoming more typically John Ireland, than this Alpine fancy. This leads one to wonder whether these were therefore consciously written in the German manner; an exercise in fulfilling a need for practical balladry and earning a living rather than being an outlet for musical originality. Muriel Searle, in her biography of Ireland, speaks at length of the Blake *Alpine Song*, which she describes as being 'melodic enough to remain staple school-choir fare, yet demonstrates the sense of space between the piano's bottom and top registers that also so gloriously characterises his best orchestral music. Who, remembering *Alpine Song* from schooldays, can forget how words and music leap up an E♭ arpeggio like a Swiss goatherd after his flock.'[8] Whether the assertion about the piano's range can be said to be true (perhaps in the song's coda), or particularly unique to this song is questionable, but her comments exemplify the market which Ireland was endeavouring to satisfy: young singers in schools and singing competitions, who it would appear responded to this song and others like it, although few, if any, will have sung such songs in recent times, at school or elsewhere. Such a market would not be able to cope with any great strides forward into modernism, desiring more straightforward traditional pieces that are readily teachable to the young amateur singer. This said, of all of the J. V. Blake choral settings, the unison *Alpine Song* is

[6] James Vila Blake, *Songs* (Boston, MA: J. H. West & Co., 1902).

[7] James Vila Blake, *Poems* (Chicago: C. H. Kerr & Co.; Boston, MA: G. H. Ellis, 1887).

[8] Muriel Searle, *John Ireland: The Man and his Music* (Tunbridge Wells: Midas Books, 1979), p. 32.

the least like a pastiche, with moments of more Ireland-like chromaticism in the accompaniment; and with its more angular melody it could have been aimed at the more experienced school singers.

Although the part-song and unison settings of 1911–13 are predominantly of J. V. Blake, other poets were not excluded: he turned to Robert Louis Stevenson's *A Child's Garden of Verses* for a short unison song, *Bed in Summer*; a setting of Sydney Dobell's *Aubade*, for two-part female voices, like the Blake settings, was reviewed in the *Musical Times* in June 1913: 'Mr John Ireland has made a deservedly high reputation as [a] composer of graceful vocal music, which he is able to adorn with a beautiful accompaniment. 'Aubade' is a good specimen of his refined and artistic style.'[9]

As mentioned above, at this time Ireland also returned to Campion's *The Peaceful Western Wind*, in 1912, in a two-part accompanied setting dominated by quaver quasi-trills in the piano, depicting Campion's winds. The two voices again sing largely in imitation or in thirds; the melody's opening six notes covering a tenth, in an almost fanfare-like manner, which tune finds its climax with the first voice leaping to the minor seventh at the words 'would *fain* bedeck'd with flow'rs'. And in the second verse, where we have mention of the 'music-loving birds', Ireland once again adorns the melody, this time with acciaccaturas rising to the inverted pedal.

In the preceding year Ireland had set another Campion poem, *In Praise of Neptune*; this proved successful enough for him to arrange the unison song for four-part choir and piano, and for four-part choir and orchestra. It was very successfully recorded by Roderick Williams[10] as a solo baritone song with orchestra. Another work to receive such repeated treatment is one of the icons of Ireland's œuvre: *Sea Fever*. This solo song-setting of John Masefield proved so popular that it was arranged variously for orchestra, military band, bass solo, chorus and orchestra, and was also used as a unison song.

During the First World War Ireland turned to other genres in his composition. Most notably, in 1916 the procession of solo songs began: the beginning of a repertoire of song which is amongst the most individual in the genre. In some ways one might argue that particularly the numerous unison and two-part songs Ireland had composed up until this point had served as his apprenticeship in word-setting. 1918 in particular saw a great concentration on song, with the composition of four of his most enduring settings, as well as other single songs and his Christina Rossetti cycle, *Mother and Child*. Rossetti was a poet to whom Ireland, amongst other composers, became increasingly drawn, owing to the directness of her poetic language, her simple rhyme schemes, so suitable for musical setting, and, for Ireland, her frequent 'images of domesticity which pepper her poetry, the antithetical representations of control and passion and the frequently dreamy tone.'[11] This year saw the composition also of one unison song, for which he turned for the last time to the work of

[9] *Musical Times*, vol. 54 (June 1913), p. 387.

[10] With the BBC Concert Orchestra conducted by Martin Yates on Dutton Epoch CDLX 7246.

[11] Richards, *The Music of John Ireland*, p. 146.

James Vila Blake: *A Song of March*. The poem was taken from Blake's sequence, *The Months*, published in 1907;[12] a series of prose pieces and poems arranged month by month, starting with the high Spring of April and running through to March, that month 'soothsaying the spring mid wintry dearth', as Blake writes in his introduction. Spring once more; a setting perhaps symbolic of the end of the war and the opportunity for life to return once more, without the wintry pall of death that had cast its shadow over the previous four years.

The song is comparable to the 1917 Housman setting, *The Heart's Desire*, in its easy 3/4 Allegretto, and the wonderfully effective use of the flattened seventh, transforming the words 'heaven's bright arch' in the first verse – a hint of modality which makes this song uniquely Ireland. Once again, the birds of the second verse are illustrated with acciaccaturas, as well as a trill. It is a song of optimism and one which could work well sung by a solo baritone; a bridge between the unison and solo repertories.

With the new found affinity with the solo song, the writing of part-songs was undertaken with less frequency than before the war. When he did turn to them during 1919 and 1920, it was again on the subject of Spring and the month of May. In January 1919 he turned again to Christina Rossetti, setting her poem *May Flowers* in memory of Lillian Dunhill, the niece of composer Thomas Dunhill (himself the dedicatee of the 1912 *A Cradle Song*), who had recently died of pneumonia at the age of twelve: a Spring setting belonging to those melancholic works that tell of the unfulfilled promise of youth. In the following year, Ireland composed a substantial SATB part-song setting of words by the sixteenth-century poet Richard Edwardes, *When May is in his Prime*. May was indeed in his prime at this time, for Ireland turned again to the subject in his solo song setting of Thomas Dekker's *The Merry Month of May*. The lively Edwardes setting was reviewed in the *Musical Times*, alongside a second work published at the same time, a setting of Tobias Hume's *Fain would I Change that Note*.

> Two part-songs for S.A.T.B. by John Ireland will appeal to those with a palate for the slightly tart rather than the sweet. *When May is in his prime* abounds in roughnesses of the bracing, tonic kind. In a curious way, too, modern as it is, it reproduces admirably the spirit of the 16th century words. The polyphony is free and the harmony mainly diatonic. This part-song is a good example of choral music that should not be judged from a 'try over' on the pianoforte. Only when sung, and sung at the right animated pace, does its fine quality show itself. *Fain would I change that note* is more suave, partly because it has a more immediately attractive treble part. In every respect a delightful part-song, it reminds us of the best work of Stanford in this field. No higher praise can be given.[13]

No higher praise indeed. While *When May is in his Prime* is rather direct and principally diatonic in its means, *Fain would I Change that Note* does take a big leap towards greater originality, and is an interesting and worthwhile song which

---

[12] Blake, James Vila, *The Months: A Book of Those Handsome Kin, for Love of them All, and of Life, and of the Earth* (Boston, MA: J. H. West Company, 1907).

[13] 'H.G.', 'Part Songs', *Musical Times*, 62 (October 1921), p. 703.

shows more fully some of Ireland's own musical character than has been seen before in this repertoire. The move into the central section of this ternary song is particularly telling, the assured F major close of the first verse being immediately dispelled with an immediate launch into a passing C minor ('O Love! they wrong thee'). The setting of *When May is in his Prime* seems to have left Ireland dissatisfied, perhaps fulfilling a purpose but not necessarily satisfying his envisioning of the text, for in 1938 he returned to the poem, setting it as the last of his *Five Sixteenth Century Songs* for solo baritone, 'Sweet Season'. This later setting is much more measured in both its tempo and its 'roughness', with the piano taking the principal part in setting the late-spring scene. The work has a far greater harmonic fluidity than the choral setting, as one might expect to be possible with the piano, giving the later setting of the poem a very different atmosphere.

At around the time of *Fain would I Change that Note*, Ireland composed a further Christina Rossetti setting, a simple unison school song built over a repeated falling four-note scale in the bass, *The Ferry*, with its catchy quasi-refrain of 'Do, boatman, do'; and a year later, in 1922, there followed another, for SATB choir, *Twilight Night* – a work that was twice performed at the Queen's Hall Promenade Concerts, in 1930 and 1937, something unimaginable in modern Prom programming, but testament to the popularity of this part-song at the time.

That this should be the case is understandable, for *Twilight Night* stands out from Ireland's part-song repertoire as being by far the most original of all of his short choral works hitherto, building on the step towards a more serious approach to the form as seen in *Fain would I Change that Note*. We obviously find Ireland writing for his own pleasure, rather than to any prescribed demands, in a song that tells of the loss of love or friendship: a parting of company which is deeply regretted, but which it is hoped might be renewed, 'If we should meet one day'. It is essentially strophic in form, with its repeat of the same music in the two halves of the work – the first verse telling of the loss, the second of the hope – but the rhythm of the second verse has been skilfully altered in entirety to accommodate the text, with only minor alteration to the melody, also being foreshortened by a line of music making it sound fresh to the ear. It is imbued with deeply melancholic harmonies, which rarely settle, the subtly shifting colours being redolent of some of his piano works, such as the epilogue to the Housman song cycle, *We'll to the Woods No More*. These are typified in the moment of parting 'We parted face from face' illustrated in Fig. 26. *Twilight Night* is the work of a great musical craftsman, and is fully deserving of a return as a regular repertoire piece.

During the 1920s Ireland's productivity waned. Following *Mai-Dun* he composed a number of solo songs and a little chamber and piano music, but little else. One occasional piece was a unison *Graduation Song*, a setting of words by John Drinkwater, written for, and apparently sung by, the 1926 graduands of London University on the occasion of their graduation, which ceremony took place at the Royal Albert Hall on 12 May. Aside from a four-part carol, *New Prince, New Pomp* (1927), the only choral work is a four-part setting for men's voices of William Cory's *Heraclitus*, a poem also set as a part-song by Stanford in 1908. Ireland's *Heraclitus*, written in 1924 for the De Reszke Singers and dedicated to the Irish composer and arranger of folksong, Herbert Hughes, is a beautiful setting (requiring some good high tenors!) which continues in the vein of *Twilight Night* in

Fig. 26 Ireland's partsong *Twilight Night* – a page from the published vocal score

its originality and colour. The melody and modality of the closing lines of the solo songs 'The Salley Gardens' (*Songs Sacred and Profane*, 1929–30) and 'The Tragedy of that Moment' (*Five Poems by Thomas Hardy*, 1926), are highly redolent of the closing lines of each verse of *Heraclitus*. It is a melody that appears to have gained some significance, representing the disconsolation of loss. At the end of the first verse of *Heraclitus*, leading up to and including this last line, the poet tells us why:

> I wept as I remember'd
> How often you and I
> Had tired the sun with talking,
> And sent him down the sky.

In 'The Salley Gardens' the singer concludes, 'And now am full of tears'; and similarly, 'The Tragedy of that moment' laments the knowledge 'that you were not.'

The few pieces composed by Ireland during the 1930s are predominantly large-scale offerings, including two major works for piano and orchestra – a concerto (1929–30) and *Legend* (1933) – and substantial works for the National Brass Band competitions of 1932 and 1934. In 1936 and 1937 he was at work on a major piece for chorus and orchestra, *These Things Shall Be*, commissioned by the BBC to commemorate the accession and coronation of King George VI. Being short of time to work on the piece, Ireland commandeered his pupil, Alan Bush, to assist with its preparation. Bush was a Communist, and perhaps it was at his suggestion that Ireland included the tune of *L'Internationale* in the commission – the anthem of international socialism, although it was later excised from the work. Whether such political activism or sympathies were in Ireland's make-up I cannot determine, but at the time he was working on *These Things Shall Be*, he was commissioned by the British National Committee of the International Peace Campaign to write a song to support their work. The organisation was set up in 1936 following the Peace Ballot of 1935, campaigning for arms reduction and a peaceful resolution of conflict. Ironically, the Campaign was wound up in 1941 owing to the difficulties in sustaining its activities following the outbreak of war and the German invasion of Russia. The 'anthem' arising from the 1936 commission, *Ways of Peace*, set words by an English poet who had joined the Communist Party of Great Britain in 1934, and whose poetry at this time principally supported the Communist interests, Randall Swingler. It was perhaps mediated by Bush, who in 1938 would collaborate with Swingler in the compilation of *The Left Songbook*.

Ways of Peace is a stout, quasi-marching hymn, written in such a manner as to be able to be sung as a unison accompanied song or by an unaccompanied four-part choir. With its startlingly Soviet-style cover, it serves its purpose well, written in C minor, lending gravitas to the cause, with a brief ray of light with a turn into G major at the mention of the 'hope of youth's career', which has been blighted by the shadow of death that hangs over society, at which moment the melody breaks out briefly from its limited, octave range.

In the early 1940s, following his evacuation from Guernsey, Ireland developed a renewed interest in the choral song, inspired by the discovery of a volume of children's poetry by Eleanor Farjeon published in 1933, *Over the Garden Wall*. He wrote a series of unison song settings from this collection: *Boys' Names*, *The Boy*, *Looking On*, *Joseph fell A-Dreaming*, *The Bell in the Leaves* and *Autumn Crocus* – the last of which is now lost. The titles of some of these works alone betray Ireland's interest in some of the many boy choristers whom he had befriended and encouraged during his years as an organist and choirmaster. But these works may also find Ireland, now in his sixties, wanting to look back and rediscover his own youth. There are subtle recurrences of such boyish themes throughout his career, many of his choristers being immortalised in his work's dedications, but there is a curious concentration at this time, particularly seen alongside the set of *Three Pastels* for piano of 1941, the movements of which are titled 'A Grecian Lad', 'The Boy Bishop' (a tradition played out in church choirs), and 'Puck's Birthday'. The first of these betrays a homoerotic overtone, which may have been present at a distance, but which was essentially directed in an admiration of, and longing to regain, perhaps in part through association with, the innocence of youth.

Boys' Names is dedicated to one of Ireland's most recent choristers, Peter Lihou, whom he had met during his brief tenure as organist of a church on Guernsey. This song, like the others, is a playful children's song, although it is lifted by some nice modal touches and its wonderfully contrived procession of modulations.

One advantage of Ireland's enforced removal from the Channel Islands to Oxfordshire came in the renewal of old friendships. One curious unison song arose from an evening's pursuit on 6 February 1941 in which Ireland, Thomas Dunhill and two local organists set about the task of each composing a setting of the nursery rhyme, *Ride a Cock-Horse to Banbury Cross*.[14]

After the promising individuality of *Twilight Night*, Ireland's two last secular part-songs, for SATB choir, to some extent revert to the Stanfordian mould. The first, *Immortality* (1942) was written for, and dedicated to Leslie Woodgate and the BBC Chorus, which Woodgate directed – for whom Ireland would in 1947 also write a choral song with brass accompaniment dedicated to the mineworkers of Britain, *Man in his Labour Rejoiceth*. *Immortality* was published in Winthrop Rogers' edition of Choral Music for Festivals, and was reviewed in the *Musical Times* in 1943:

> Ireland's *Immortality* (unaccompanied S.A.T.B.) sets a poem by H. P. Compton about the compulsion which the simple devotion of the long-dead peasant lays upon us to plough our furrows straight. The setting has all the easy diatonic strength we know, the occasional unison bit, the occasional seven-part chord, the climactic rise – the craft of the old hand, enjoying writing the sort of thing that sensible singers enjoy getting at the heart of. Nothing is here for tears, or tuning-forks.[15]

This is not to say that it is devoid of interest: just lacking some of Ireland's musical individuality which shows itself so distinctly elsewhere.

The last work was Ireland's contribution to what was the final flowering of the part-song genre: a set of part-songs by ten composers and poets written to celebrate the coronation of Elizabeth II in 1953, *A Garland for the Queen*, devised and convened by John Denison under the auspices of the Arts Council. It was sung

---

[14] Recounted in Searle, *John Ireland*, p. 101.

[15] W. R. Anderson, 'New Music: Choral Music', *Musical Times*, 84 (October 1943), p. 310.

and recorded by the Cambridge University Madrigal Society directed by Boris Ord for issue on Coronation Day. Such a compilation echoed a similar collection written to celebrate the work of the first Queen Elizabeth, towards the end of her reign, *The Triumphs of Oriana*, which similarly became one of the last flowerings in the genre at that time. With Vaughan Williams and Arnold Bax, Ireland was one of the senior contributors to the *Garland*, and whilst his chordal setting of a poem by James Kirkup, *The Hills*, which speaks of constancy of the hills, 'the earth's enduring thrones' – a metaphor for the stable bedrock of the monarchy – is charming and effective, receiving polite mention in the ensuing reviews, it paled into relative insignificance against the works of the younger composers, such as Arthur Bliss and Michael Tippett.

Before concluding, mention should be made of Ireland's final choral work: a setting of the fifteenth-century carol *Adam Lay Ybounden*, written in 1956, to which Jeremy Dibble makes reference in his chapter on Ireland's church music, where the work most properly belongs. However, carols, like some part-songs, can bridge the divide between the sacred and the secular, as exemplified in Parry's *Songs of Farewell* of 1918, which figure in the programming of both concert hall and church service. Ireland's *The Holy Boy* is perhaps an exception owing to its music being abstracted as instrumental music, but in considering the programming of Ireland's part-songs, these carols should not be overlooked. *Adam lay ybounden*, Dibble observes, perhaps apes *The Holy Boy* to some degree, but it is a setting that deserves attention both for its beauty, its simple directness, and in its embodiment of Ireland's style. The modality of the carol is immediately identifiable as Ireland, as is the shape of the melodies. In this, as in many of those songs aimed at school singing, Ireland is hugely successful at portraying innocence, imbued with a unique melancholy. Many of his two-part songs are functional, accessible balladry, serving a purpose, as is the case with some of the music written for the church, but at a time when efforts are well underway to reverse a decline in singing in schools, these songs are waiting to be reclaimed and enjoyed, as once they were by many. One or two of the unison songs, such as *A Song of March*, could be introduced into solo recital programmes; and of those purely secular choral works, *Fain would I Change that Note*, *Heraclitus* and, most notably, *Twilight Night* should be taken eagerly back into the regular choral repertoire.

CHAPTER 22

John Ireland and Poetry: A Singer's Experience

Roderick Williams

JOHN Ireland has several different approaches to composing songs. There are the blustery ones, like *Hope the Hornblower*, ballads, that are not highly emotional but with more of the feel of a community song, songs that perhaps in yesteryear could have been sung by the sixth form, bowling along. Then there are the songs that are passionate and expressive, and almost experimental. I am thinking of those songs like the *Marigold* trio – 'Youth's Spring-Tribute' and 'Spleen' – songs that are harmonically very adventurous.

The other vein is the recitative song, almost like a heightened recitation of the poem in which one needs to do little more than declaim the poem as honestly as one can. If one looks at the most famous example, *Sea Fever*, one has a real case in point. The first two verses use the same accompanying harmonies in the piano and all the singer needs to do is to read the text. In the third verse the power of new, richer harmony is very interesting, and it opens up a completely new dimension, because the melody remains the same. My personal response to it is heightened by the harmony becoming more complex, with wonderfully descending chromatic chords. For me the power of this famous song is in two parts – the simplicity of the vocal line with Masefield's words and the undercurrent of adventurous harmony, particularly in the last verse.

Another example, full of emotion, is 'We'll to the Woods No More' and its partner 'In Boyhood'. Again, on the page they appear extremely bare, simple settings. But the harmony is hugely adventurous: the augmented intervals make it sound something like Debussy, and the vocal phrases seem to go somewhere but then evaporate. This is very different from my first memories of Ireland's music, singing his anthems in church. The vocal line here is simpler, which looks easy to sing but this actually allows one to be very expressive, especially when the melody goes to the top of the voice. The vocal part of these two Housman songs sits mostly D to D, right in the middle of a baritone's range, but at the climaxes they reach a top F which gives one a chance to access something quite impassioned.

I have found, in performance, 'In Boyhood' can be deceptively hard to sing. It is only three pages long, it may only be 40 bars, but in those bars the power of the poem is really accentuated by the rich harmony combined with simple chordal accompaniments, hardly any counterpoint. This allows the sentiment of the last lines in particular to creep up on me and it's then hard to finish the song with a lump in the throat!

> They braced their belts about them,
> They crossed in ships the sea,
> They sought and found six feet of ground,
> And there they died for me.[1]

---

[1] 'In Boyhood', the second half of the second and final verse.

This taps into one aspect of A. E. Housman's poetry that I find particularly interesting and which suits recital programmes dealing with the subject of war and its consequences; there is a strong sense of sacrifice, of others going to die for me while I am left behind. All I can do is watch them go.

The words are clearly very important to Ireland. You could contrast, say, the Housman settings of Bax or Moeran and find examples where the words have inspired such composers into real flights of fancy, especially in the piano parts, trying to evoke the spirit of the poem or the essence of Housman's landscape. For me, though, Ireland shares with Finzi a knack of setting a poem that feels ultimately as though this is simply the way that they would have read it out loud. There is often very little melisma, very little rearticulation of words, very little repetition; it just comes across as a poetry reading. Take 'In Boyhood' again:

> When I would muse in boyhood
> The wild green woods among

I say it aloud without any music and find that that is the exact rhythm he has written for me. It has that almost improvisatory feel. You can also hear straight away in the opening of this song one of Ireland's trademarks – the low, minor chords in the piano part, with an off-beat fifth to the tonic in the bass.

Ex. 1 Ireland, 'In Boyhood' (*We'll to the Woods No More*)

It reminds me of the opening bar of *Sea Fever*, and both have that sort of announcement, that sense of something serious, almost grim, but resolute in a typically understated, English way. Later in the song 'In Boyhood' there is a wonderful example of his free, rhapsodic way of writing melody (Ex. 2). I have always enjoyed that quarter bar here. It is there because Ireland is following the recitation of the poem and has tried to find a way to write the bars to reflect the spoken stresses. He could have barred it in many different ways to make the metre more uniform, but he is more concerned about the natural flow of the words than he is about making the music look simple. (In contrast, Vaughan Williams would put his songs regularly in, say 3/4, which is what makes RVW so difficult to memorise, because although in regular time signatures, the metre is constantly broken up by the will of the vocal line; in Ireland all seems to fall very naturally.)

I think there is a perception that a lot of English song in the first half of the twentieth century can be charming yet harmless, nice to listen to but avoiding any real depth in sentiment or compositional techniques. It is one thing to be

Ex. 2 Ireland, 'In Boyhood' (*We'll to the Woods No More*)

charming, in the mould of, say Roger Quilter, but to try to express anything more profound is somehow not done. Which is why I love programming Ireland's songs dedicated to Arthur Miller; there is so much more subtext expressed in the music and its effect is quite striking:

> *When I am Dead, My Dearest* (June 1925)
> 'Love and Friendship' (22 February 1926)
> 'We'll to the Woods No More' (1927)
> 'In Boyhood' (1927)
> 'Spring will not Wait' [piano epilogue] (1927)

Particularly the interlude in 'We'll to the Woods No More', where the thirds in the piano part meander towards an incredible chord at the beginning of the second line, with a muted horn-like chord. I love the harmonies here and the sense of distance; it is a very unusual song.

Ex. 3 Ireland, *We'll to the Woods No More*

Which prompts me, at the top of my voice, to sing:

> Oh we'll to the woods no more, no more
> To the leafy woods away,

It is very rewarding to sing, and highly emotional.

I think the end of the First World War saw an incredible loss of innocence in music and poetry. Talking about programming Ireland's war songs, I was hugely affected when I was first introduced to two settings of Eric Thirkell Cooper. 'Blind' is again an essay in under-statement – it is what he does not say but what he only alludes to. In this song 'Blind'

> Help me through the heavy hours
> When I think what others see.
> God who took my sight away,
> Help me do without it, pray.

I love the thud of the last line in that poem. Again, Ireland sets it in a very simple, hymn-like, chordal way. But then, you turn the page and there is 'The Cost' and the thundering piano part in the bass. It comes from nowhere in a succession of upbeats. I thought it was just fabulous, a real heart-on-sleeve number, with that wonderful refrain:

> O God, O God,
> O God, if miracles can be,
> May he be given back to me.

Unlike Housman's poems there appears to be no attempt to hide the homo-eroticism either in the poem or in the heartfelt setting of it. The harmonies, particularly in the second refrain, are almost painful. The way the song then ends on a minor chord with an added major sixth is really open-ended.

Ex. 4 Ireland, *The Cost*

It is dated 'Chelsea, November 1916'. I like to imagine at a performance of those songs there would have been a stunned silence, and people would have looked at each other and thought 'Is this entirely proper?' Contrast that with Somervell's setting of 'The Street Sounds to the Soldier's Tread'. Do the right thing, brace your belt about you, and off to war you go. Or compare it with the empty bravado of Elgar's *A War Song*: 'Glory or death for true hearts and brave'. To hear the unbuttoning of Englishness in the Ireland songs is to say 'actually we do feel, we do bleed'. It is fantastic; the words themselves are very bold and Ireland's setting is remarkable.

Looking at the two Rupert Brooke songs, 'The Soldier' and 'Blow Out, You Bugles', I feel a certain insincerity on Ireland's part. Certainly, this could just be my own reaction to it, and it is of course subjective – but a song like 'The Cost' speaks to me directly, and these two Brooke songs so much less so. In 'The Soldier', in particular, I feel Ireland has done the job, written the song but that is all. The song is perhaps intended for that unison singing I was talking about earlier – for me it hasn't that immediacy of Ireland's best settings.

Talking about the honesty of his songs, Ireland's *Vagabond* – words by John Masefield – is another song that has always worked well for me in concerts. Audiences really seem to appreciate the directness of that poem. It shares something with Robert Louis Stevenson's 'Vagabond' as set by Vaughan Williams, which is admittedly a fairly romantic notion of 'wayfaring'. Yet there is something about John Ireland's simple response to Masefield's words that helps you picture clearly someone out on the road with the practical philosophy of survival. Today they would have a stack of *Big Issue*s under arm, or be sitting in a doorway somewhere. Neither the song nor the poem seeks to judge this character, but in the end he comes across as someone very noble. There is a great deal of honesty about it which I find incredibly appealing.

I think, to a certain extent, I do see Ireland's piano parts as his confessional and his songs as being a very personal expression of his thought and character. In his choice of poems, he presents us with *his* selection of words. He also reveals himself in the layers of ambiguity of the settings and his way of using a musical language that is not necessarily the English archetype one might expect, including shades of foreign harmony and texture. Some of his songs seem deliberately and ostentatiously adventurous. In *Marigold*, a set of three songs, he experiments with whole-tone scales, thematic cross-references and striking textures. I like to compare 'Youth's Spring-Tribute' with Vaughan Williams's setting of 'Silent Noon', both pretty much versions of the same poem by Rossetti but Ireland chooses to give us an X-rated version; it's incredibly graphic. Take the end, for example:

> So shut your eyes upturn'd
> and feel my kiss creep,
> as the Spring now thrills
> through ev'ry spray,

The piano part is working itself up into a lather as the vocal part rushes on, breathlessly, almost falling over itself:

> Up your warm throat
> to your warm lips

At which point there is a wonderful Technicolor explosion in the piano part with *Rosenkavalier*-like bells in the right hand (Ex. 5). I don't think there is any doubt in his mind what has occurred there. Throughout the other two songs as well, he makes reference to those textures, certain harmonies and an *idée fixe* as well, which comes back at the end of 'Spleen'. It is very deliberate. But just looking at the songs we can see the textures. For example, the scattering of accidentals in the bass part: he is being very deliberately experimental there.

Ex. 5 Ireland, 'Youth's Spring-Tribute' (*Marigold*)

In *During Music*, we have two songs setting poems by Arthur Symons and D. G. Rossetti, 'Tryst' and 'During Music'. In the former again we have a wonderfully ambiguous open-ended poem.

> June, hushed and breathless,
> waits, and I wait too with June;
> Come, come, through the lingering afternoon,
> Soon, love, come soon.

There are incredible shifts in harmony. It feels as though he is pushing his own whole-tone harmony as far as he dare. I compare this with the deft chromaticism of Peter Warlock songs and feel that Warlock's clever harmonic twists are not used so much to access the darker places that Ireland is exploring here. I feel that a work like *Marigold* demonstrates Ireland's desire to push boundaries in his songs and for the English art song to be taken seriously alongside European models.

There are nine Ireland settings of Thomas Hardy – the *Five Poems*, the *Three Songs* and *Great Things*. I find this serious intent also in the group of five Hardy settings. I am not sure all of these are fully successful, but I am very fond of programming 'The Tragedy of that Moment'; it strikes a particularly grim note. The song has an incredibly bleak opening with minor harmony that soon shifts to a tritone, the note A insisting on the dissonance to an almost Mahlerian rhythm. The song ends with the same incredible unresolved chord in the depth of the piano and I cannot think of a more desolate song in the English language. It was only really in recording all five with Iain Burnside that I discovered them as a set; they are again very experimental, impressionistic, with big washes of colour. Each of the five is self-consciously craftsman-like – not just harmonically but also in terms of the textures.

In contrast, *Great Things* is a tremendous breath of fresh air among Ireland's setting of Thomas Hardy. In 'Summer Schemes', the first of the *Three Songs to Poems by Thomas Hardy*, I enjoy how easily Ireland's meandering harmonies shift so that the second verse is in a different key to the first by a semitone but the transition does not sound at all forced.

I spoke earlier about the perceived charm of the English song, perhaps a remembrance of the pleasing parlour song from the previous century. Ireland is, of course, well able to write these too; take, for example, *I Have Twelve Oxen*. It is charming, a real audience-pleaser, a wonderful song with which to end an Ireland group or to produce as an encore. I feel it has all the wit and charm of a Quilter song with all the harmonic variety of Warlock or Moeran. Similarly, I have frequently sung *If There Were Dreams to Sell* as an encore. This is a sweet Thomas Lovell Beddoes poem set with complete effortlessness.

Here's a bit of an oddity – almost Ireland's last song, *Tutto è sciolto*, to words by James Joyce. This is a strange song to match a strange poem – an experimental setting which I still don't know if I understand. He wrote it for *The Joyce Book* in 1932, beautifully printed and published in a limited edition, and perhaps in 1932 he might have been self-conscious of the occasion. But overall, I wonder if it sounds a little manufactured. If it had been unsigned one would have been hard pressed to identify it as being by Ireland.

Although I have recorded programmes of Ireland songs, with piano and with orchestra, I realise there are many of his songs I have not sung and still do not know. I remember listening to the first edits of my Ireland recordings, a while after the sessions, once all the singing work has been done and forgotten, and being quite overwhelmed by the power and beauty of the music. I feel there are some fantastic art-songs that people – including a lot of singers – just do not know. Reviewing Ireland's as presented in the five-volume 'Complete Works for Voice and Piano', I find some remarkable art-songs, and many songs I have yet to discover. I cannot emphasise enough how important it is for any singer to be able to express themselves in their own language. It seems so obvious for English singers to start with songs in English. Given that Ireland's vocal style is so closely wedded to the words and his melodies are lyrical and accessible, I can think of few better places to start for a singer interested in the English song repertoire.

CHAPTER 23

John Ireland on Record:
The Composer and the Growth
of the Gramophone

Robert Matthew-Walker

I N the broader world, the very earliest years of the twentieth century saw the development of inventions destined to revolutionise communication, some still in their infancy: the telegraph, telephone, radio, moving pictures, the motor-car, air travel – and in London the Underground network – as well as gramophone recordings, the success of the last ensured by the voice of Enrico Caruso, the first artist to sell one million copies of a single record, whose singing was first captured for all time by Fred Gaisberg in Milan in 1902.

It would take several decades before the more tangible fruits of these developments could be harvested, but in 1901, a young British composer could face the future with no little confidence. The Cheshire-born John Ireland, then twenty-one years old, had graduated that year from the Royal College of Music as a pupil of Stanford before successfully entering for the Durham University external Mus.Bac. with his *Psalm 42*.[1] Ireland, having just reached his majority, was by now set on his course as a composer and executant musician – for, apart from being naturally drawn towards composition, he was a very gifted pianist, as we may hear in the commercial recordings of his own music he was later to make; he was also by all accounts an accomplished organist, as befitted someone who was sub-organist at Holy Trinity Sloane Street, London SW1, and who later became organist and choirmaster at St Luke's Church, Chelsea.

The basis of what follows is not a critique of every important recording of Ireland's music to have been issued commercially during the last one hundred years, but an attempt to trace the more significant achievements of the gramophone in making his art available to the interested music-lover against the background of such technological developments as took place during that period, alongside the general critical reception of his music, concentrating upon the earliest (and therefore the most immediately significant) recordings in so far as they contributed to the wider appreciation of his music.

From the distance of one hundred years, and by consulting Stephen Lloyd's detailed discography elsewhere in this book (to which we shall occasionally direct the reader), we see that virtually all of Ireland's music (alongside that of countless composers) has been issued on commercial recordings for the listener to study at their own pace. But it is not so generally understood that in the early years of the gramophone – even in the acoustic era, that is to say, up until about April 1925 – what may appear as a rather surprisingly representative repertoire had been recorded and issued on 78 rpm discs.

---

[1] For *Psalm 42* see pp. 198–201.

Commercial recordings had been on sale throughout the world for more than twenty-five years before the first magazine devoted to assessing them critically was launched in April 1923. This was *The Gramophone*, founded by Compton Mackenzie, which, over many years, became for its readers the world's authority on classical recordings, the archives of which largely trace the history of Ireland's discography. When confronted by the evidence of these archives, one can state confidently that the relatively constant stream of new recordings of Ireland's music on 78 rpm discs meant that his work had not been neglected by the record companies. This may have naturally reflected several characteristics of his work in general and, more importantly perhaps, of the esteem in which it was held by his contemporaries. In considering such matters, we should not forget the economic and practical factors constraining the record companies' investments, and the fact that Ireland's output was never that of a prolific composer. None the less, it is clear that the appeal of Ireland's music, as reflected in those early recordings, and despite including a handful of relatively larger works, rested upon his songs and chamber music especially. Equally, however, his music was more frequently heard in concert and recital programmes, from the early 1920s until the late 1950s, than it is today.

Of course, the vagaries of fashion will always be felt, but the music undoubtedly remains the same: it is often considered to be merely the reaction of audiences to works that are infrequently performed (if at all), but audiences can hardly be expected to express opinions on music with which they are never given the opportunity of coming into contact. In that regard, it is the selectiveness, or perhaps downright ignorance, of individual artists and the media reaction to their programmes, that drives opinion; if Ireland's music is not so often heard today as it was, say, sixty to eighty years ago, a glance at the current record catalogues shows that virtually all of his life's work as a composer is available to the enquiring music-lover.

Early Works

Clearly, the availability of such a wide range of his music ensures that we are in a better position to evaluate his stature than ever before, and such evaluation is now predicated upon a number of what Ireland claimed were 'discarded works 1895–1906' in a brief appreciation of him, published in the *Monthly Musical Record* July 1, 1915, most of which have now been recorded. There are nineteen such works listed, including three orchestral pieces, a Piano Trio, a Sextet for strings and wind, two String Quartets, two Violin Sonatas, a setting of Psalm 42 for chorus and orchestra, a Piano Sonata in C minor and three sets of variations for solo piano.

In recent years, both String Quartets have been recorded by the Holywell and Maggini Quartets – enabling this music to be heard for the first time for over a century. These works date from 1897, in August of which year Ireland turned eighteen. Both are positively conceived in terms of the medium, and are of a quality with which the more mature composer would surely not have felt ashamed, for he did not destroy them (as he appears to have done with many of his student compositions). Stanford, his Royal College of Music teacher, was apparently somewhat scathing of these quartets (as was his wont) – but not Parry, who was encouraging. Both Quartets are confident and assured in the composer's handling of his material. Neither comes across as so-called 'student' works, nor are they 'modern' for their time; they are full of genuine music with an admirable sense of inner momentum. The attractive First Quartet and the more seriously probing Second deserve to take their places in the English quartet repertoire. Any ensemble looking for British works to include in programmes alongside Brahms and Dvořák need look no further: either would fit ideally in such company.

The Second Quartet is more overly serious and possibly more 'Brahmsian', but only in inflexion, although Ireland's invention in the Scherzo's Trio fades somewhat, leading to a curious ending to the movement following the recapitulation. The finale, a large-scale set of variations, is most adventurous, wherein the scurrying fugal coda brings the Quartet to an exciting conclusion. As with the almost contemporaneous chamber music of Vaughan Williams (another Stanford pupil), which has also recently been recorded, one is led to two conclusions: the first is that Stanford must have been a teacher of considerable strength of character, and, second, that composers are not always the best or final judges of their own work. In 1960, two years before his death, Ireland allowed the first movement of another of those 'discarded works', a three-movement suite for solo piano, *Sea Idyll*, to be published.

This suite, together with an even more recently released early solo piano work, a first *Rhapsody* in F♯ minor, has been recorded by Mark Bebbington for the Somm label, part of what is planned to be a four-CD collection of Ireland's complete solo piano music (Bebbington has also recorded for the company Ireland's Concerto and Legend for piano and orchestra). Bebbington's discs will constitute the most complete integral recording of Ireland's piano music (solo and concerted) ever issued, but from the earliest days of electrical recording, examples from this part of Ireland's repertoire have been made available, indicative of the wide appeal of his music to his contemporaries.

The string quartets and the various solo piano pieces from this by no means insubstantial body of work by the young (one hesitates to use the word 'student') composer demonstrate Ireland's burgeoning creativity. In the light of his later compositions perhaps a greater interest attends the two orchestral works from this period which have been admirably recorded on the Chandos label by the City of London Sinfonia conducted by Richard Hickox. We know that later in life Ireland would give titles to his works after he had written them, but the appellation 'Orchestral Poem' to this (almost) 15-minute single movement piece implies an underlying programme which will – it seems – forever remain unknown. What cannot be denied is the young composer's assured handling of the orchestra, in this, only his second or third essay in the medium. By the age of twenty-four, Ireland had attended many orchestral concerts (and doubtless College rehearsals) and had studied many scores – in this work, there are no miscalculations at all, to the point where one wishes to investigate his other pieces from these early years and perhaps have this work enter the Ireland repertoire on its own merits and not as some kind of youthful curio. In the light of Ireland's mature 'orchestral poems' – *The Forgotten Rite* (1913) and *Mai-Dun* (1920–21) especially – there might appear to be some reflection of natural phenomena here, rather than dramatic narrative, and we must admire the commitment of Hickox and his orchestra for revealing the qualities of this score – almost without parallel in English music of the time.

With recordings of these three major scores from Ireland's own list of 'juvenilia'– the noun is misleading, as we have demonstrated – alongside shorter vocal and sacred pieces, we enter the composer's self-admitted maturity. In the following parts of our discussion, we shall take the order as set out (and followed by many discographers since) in the first edition of *The Record Guide* (1950) by Edward Sackville-West and Desmond Shawe-Taylor: first, instrumental works, from the largest number of performances to solo musicians, and secondly vocal works, similarly decreasing in number.

Music for Orchestra

Ireland's largest orchestral concert work is his Piano Concerto in E♭ major, completed in 1930 and first performed at a Henry Wood Promenade Concert on 2 October that year. It created an immediate and lasting impression and was – uniquely up to that time for a British piano concerto – an international 'hit' with pianists such as Gina Bachauer and Arthur Rubinstein taking it up (indeed, Rubinstein confessed to the present writer that it was one of his greatest regrets that he was never able to persuade his American record company RCA to record it, although the second recording of the work was made by an American company, in Germany).

The correspondence columns of *The Gramophone* often contained repertoire suggestions for record companies. By November 1932, that is to say a little over two years after the Concerto's premiere by Helen Perkin, one correspondent, putting in a plea for more recordings of British music, ends by claiming that: 'enthusiasts have strange fancies, but do we really prefer Prokofiev and Poulenc to Bliss and Arnold Bax? Would we really buy records of the Stravinsky *Capriccio* and neglect the John Ireland Pianoforte Concerto?'

In the light of the later fate of recordings of this work the correspondent's final comment is peculiarly apt. None the less, collectors had to wait a further ten years before the first commercial recording of the Concerto was made – by English Columbia, with the Australian-born Eileen Joyce as soloist and the Hallé Orchestra under Leslie Heward. This remains a landmark recording of the work – and, interestingly, was the first of four consecutive recordings of Ireland's music to be made by the Hallé (the last three for HMV, sponsored by the British Council).

This premiere recording has not entirely been rendered redundant[2] by later versions (of which there have been almost a dozen in all), for there is a welcome freshness about Joyce's playing, allied to the mastery of Heward's conducting, which in purely interpretative terms would be hard to equal in any circumstances. It is the one work of Ireland which, in discographical terms, bears out the

---

[2] Eileen Joyce's performance has been reissued on the CD given away with the 2007–8 issue (Volume 7) of the journal *Manchester Sounds* (still available in 2011 from the Manchester Musical Heritage Trust).

international appeal the work had from its early years, with later recordings having been made with orchestras in Scandinavia, Australia and in Germany.

The last-cited was in fact the second recording the Concerto received, by the American pianist Sondra Bianca with the 'Philharmonia of Hamburg' conducted by Hans-Jurgen Walther. This was for the American MGM company in 1956, one of a series of concerto recordings made for the label. It was coupled with the first recording of Britten's Suite for solo piano, *Holiday Diary*, op. 5, clearly with an eye to the British market, although a review of the LP in the American trade newspaper *Billboard* for 24 November 1956 was relatively non-committal, speaking of an 'Interesting set of modern compositions, for the first time on disks. Both sides have picturesque British quality mixed with the school of Paris. The Concerto is often impressive, and the Britten piano pieces are delightful. Neither side is difficult to swallow, tho' the market is as limited as the public's interest in rarely heard contemporary music.'

In 1956 the label was handled in the UK by EMI, who reserved the 'MGM' name for pop music, including soundtrack recordings; the few classical issues that EMI issued from MGM were released on the Parlophone label, selected by (later Sir) George Martin, whose experience as a classical record producer (six years before he signed the Beatles to the label) had led him to issue two of Ms Bianca's Hamburg-made MGM LPs, concertos by Tchaikovsky, Grieg and Gershwin. It may be that Martin had played this recording to various British music critics, one of whose opinions was unfavourable. Equally, at that time, Martin would doubtless have known of HMV's plans to record the Concerto with Colin Horsley as soloist and Basil Cameron conducting the Royal Philharmonic Orchestra, although that (third) recording was not released until 1958.

Oblique reference to Sondra Bianca's recording was made in *The Gramophone* review of the Colin Horsley LP when Alec Robertson wrote:

> It is extraordinary that we have had to wait so long for a recording of John Ireland's Piano Concerto on LP. It is a work popular enough to be placed, and not for the first time, in the programme for the last night of this season's 'Proms' … there are few, if any, modern piano concertos to equal it for sustained lyrical beauty and intimacy of expression. It is also the work of a composer who loves the piano and has notably enriched its repertoire.
>
> Colin Horsley and Basil Cameron, who have been chosen to restore the concerto to the catalogues, have long been associated with it, and will indeed be performing it on the occasion mentioned above. This is wise casting, for it is by no means a concerto that more or less plays itself; and how astray pianist and conductor can go was shown on an LP of the work issued some time ago in America. At first hearing I thought there was a little dawdling in the first movement; but after listening again that feeling was replaced by one that the right tempo had been chosen and the right amount of give and take applied.

Robertson's reference to the version 'issued some time ago in America' implies that he had heard it, but Sondra Bianca's playing is really very good – perhaps the unfamiliarity of the orchestra (and conductor) with the work tells against the overall conception, and the rather odd coupling (by no means unusual for MGM recordings of the era) will have added to the negative appraisal by Robertson, but his further references to the popularity of the Concerto, its inclusion in the Proms of 1958 (the work once an annual feature of those concerts), reinforces his surprise at the record-buying public having to wait so long for a new recording.

Yet Robertson missed a trick here: the coupling of Horsley's Ireland Concerto was Stravinsky's *Capriccio* – the work mentioned by *The Gramophone* correspondent in November 1932 in his plea for a recording of the Ireland. For some commentators at the time (1958) the Stravinsky was as odd a coupling as Britten's *Holiday Diary* had been for Bianca, but the conductor may have swayed matters in this instance. Cameron was a lifelong Stravinsky admirer – as 'Basil Hindenburg' (his real name) he had conducted the British premiere of Stravinsky's Symphony in Eb, op. 1, with the Torquay Municipal Orchestra early in 1914, and he went on to select the *Symphony of Psalms* for his eightieth birthday concert (another Prom) on being given a free hand by Proms director William Glock in 1964.

Another trick had also been missed: Horsley's recording (as was Bianca's) seems not to have been made in stereo but in mono only, which – combined with the Stravinsky coupling – led to the appeal of the record being considerably restricted. (The first stereo LPs had been issued some months before Horsley's disc was released.) Horsley's performance is a fine one, and the single-channel recording is one of EMI's best of its day; in addition, Sir Thomas Beecham's Royal Philharmonic Orchestra was then renowned for its woodwind and string sections (by no means inferior to those of the contemporaneous Philharmonia Orchestra). The conception by soloist and conductor may have been different to the Joyce/Heward version, but was one which – as with Bianca – demonstrated that the work could certainly make an impact through more than one interpretation.

Despite the continuing popularity of Ireland's Concerto, a further decade elapsed before the first stereo recording of the work was made. For many listeners, the fourth recording, by Eric Parkin with the London Philharmonic under Sir Adrian Boult, became first choice, not least because of Parkin's close association with the composer. (The similarity of the surnames 'Perkin' and 'Parkin' led some commentators to confuse the pianists, despite their gender differences.)

Parkin has recorded Ireland's Concerto commercially twice; two recordings (albeit not necessarily commercially made) each by Eileen Joyce and Kathryn Stott have been issued, but Parkin is the only pianist to have done so under studio conditions. His second recording was for Chandos, also with the London Philharmonic, under Bryden Thomson, in 1985. As may be expected, his interpretation has changed little – if at all – but one must welcome the improvement in recording techniques that the digital system brought; the finely judged details of Ireland's orchestration are beautifully caught. Yet another feature unites both of Parkin's recordings – both discs include Ireland's second work for piano and orchestra, *Legend*, first performed also by Helen Perkin, with the BBC Symphony Orchestra conducted by Adrian Boult, in January 1934.

Parkin's pioneering Lyrita LP of the Concerto included the first recording of *Legend*, thus bringing the work to the attention of music lovers for the first time in many years. (Interestingly, Alec Robertson's review of the Horsley version included a plea for a recording of 'Legende', as he termed it.) After Parkin's first recording almost all succeeding versions have included the later work with the Concerto. The result has been that *Legend* is now well known to Ireland admirers, as indeed its musical merits demand that it should be. It is now generally accepted that it began as a Second Piano Concerto, but ended as a single-movement piece, at 15 minutes (the timing marked on the score, although every recorded version comes in under that). Seemingly too short to be called Concerto no. 2, by 1934 there were works by other composers of similar duration which warranted the 'concerto' title – Prokofiev no. 1, Milhaud no. 1, Tcherepnin no. 2, and Roussel's and Rimsky-Korsakov's Concertos. It may well have been that had Ireland termed the 'Legend' his Concerto no. 2 it would have received greater attention, following the successful earlier work.

In addition, pianists who have studied *Legend* have a high opinion of the music – many rate it above the Concerto itself, yet the thematic attraction of the Concerto cannot be gainsaid: as we might expect, the solo part is superbly written for the instrument, and the balance with the orchestra is masterfully handled. But it is not an 'easy' work to balance: such a superficial approach sets a trap for the unwary conductor. Ireland's Concerto has been fortunate in its subsequent recordings, although one cannot deny the additional sense of character that comes from soloists who have recorded other music by the composer. In this regard, Eric Parkin and Mark Bebbington share a greater empathy with the solo parts of both Concerto and *Legend*.

After the Piano Concerto and *Legend*, the symphonic rhapsody *Mai-Dun* is Ireland's biggest orchestral score. While it is signed 'J.I. 1920–1921', it had to wait until 1949 for its first recording (prompting the rueful quip from the composer 'May not be done!'), the third of Sir John Barbirolli's HMV recordings with the Hallé Orchestra of an Ireland work. This was in the series made 'under the auspices of the British Council' (promoting British music, 'under the auspices' being a euphemism for the Council meeting the entire cost of the recording sessions, including interval drinks and food for the engineers). Perhaps the contemporaneous Festival of Britain prompted the decision to release *Mai-Dun* eventually in 1951,[3] it being one of the first Hallé/Barbirolli 78 rpm recordings seeing orchestra and conductor 'promoted' from the cheaper plum-label C and B series to the highest-price DB and DA red-labels.

Although long-playing (LP) 33⅓ rpm vinyl records were introduced in Britain in June 1950 by the Decca Company (two years after their successful launch in the USA by Columbia Records) it was not until October 1952 that EMI first issued LP records. EMI included HMV and Parlophone among their labels, as well as Columbia – but the last, despite the similar name, was not the same company as the American Columbia Records.

The result of EMI's delay in embracing LPs meant their new recordings, for almost two and a half years, were issued only on 78 rpm discs. Even after the EMI launch in 1952, by no means all of their recent recordings were released in the new

---

[3] Researching in the EMI archives some years ago I remember seeing an internal memo written by John Whittle, Classical Sales Manager, in which he asked his colleagues about Barbirolli's Ireland recordings before they were issued: 'Does anyone want this sort of thing?' – EDITOR.

format. The Hallé/Barbirolli *Mai-Dun* was eventually reissued almost thirty years later (!) on LP, with the result that the impact this fine account and excellent technical recording of a major Ireland work could and should have made was considerably reduced. It was reduced further by the recording being made available only to 'special order' in automatic couplings – it could not be bought in the usual way through stock held in record shops. Despite these self-defeating EMI decisions, in terms of placing obstacles in the way of the interested purchaser, Lionel Salter, writing in *The Gramophone* in October 1951, could hardly have given the records a warmer welcome:

> *Mai-Dun* is one of those works in which he [Ireland] muses over some legend or relic of early times, evoking a powerful pagan spirit of nature-worship and mystery: such also are the piano pieces 'Le Catioroc' (in *Sarnia*), 'The Island Spell' and 'Scarlet Ceremonies'. The subject of this ruggedly austere rhapsody is the enormous Iron Age hill-fort earthwork known as Maiden Castle, whose great brooding presence is referred to by Hardy in his Wessex tales and poems: there is an elemental, primitive quality about the music which worthily matches the grandeur of the subject.

Of Ireland's works, *Mai-Dun* is the one which most closely approximates to what one might term the Baxian mould – the Bax of *Tintagel*, which 'influence' is often cited by thoughtless commentators unfamiliar with the facts: although *Tintagel* was composed in 1917, it was not orchestrated until two years later, and not first performed publicly until two years after that in October 1921, by which time Ireland had completed *Mai-Dun*.

However strong the connections between these contemporaneous works are, they are surely coincidental. What cannot be denied is Ireland's total command of the orchestra – there is an impressive surety in his instrumentation which does not show uncertainty or miscalculation. It is a fine challenge for conductor and orchestra, to which Barbirolli responds admirably; *Mai-Dun* is by no means an easy work to conduct, but – not for the only time in our survey – it is to Barbirolli's performance that we should return to experience the work's full impact, despite the excellence of Sir Adrian Boult's later Lyrita version or Bryden Thomson's Chandos recording.

From his earliest years Ireland was totally assured in his use of the orchestra, to a degree that we may regret his relatively small overall output, even when considering that one or other of those works began life in a different form. Nowhere is this more clearly seen than in *A London Overture* of 1936, which began life originally several years earlier as the *Comedy Overture* for brass band, in which form it has been recorded several times.

As *A London Overture*, its first recording was with Malcolm Sargent conducting the Liverpool Philharmonic. Despite shortcomings surrounding earlier microphone techniques (although in 1945 Paul Kidman in *The Gramophone* reported that it was 'a new recording of exceptional brilliance'), there is a sense of genuine life in the performance no other version quite possesses, until the arrival of the latest (at the time of writing, 2011), by the Hallé Orchestra under John Wilson, part of an all-Ireland disc on the orchestra's own label.

It is clear that in its orchestral reincarnation, Ireland's *London Overture* needs some care on the part of the conductor: this is no breezy affair, a latter-day *Cockaigne*, but a tone-poem that – as a 'comedy overture' in its original version – is rather light on 'comedy' of the rib-tickling kind. The main attraction of the work is the (once) famous 'Dilly, Piccadilly' tune on the violins, suggested when Ireland, riding on the top deck of a No. 9 bus *en route* to the Royal Albert Hall, heard the conductor call out the next stop. Up to that point in the work, the music can appear somewhat non-committal, unless the (orchestral!) conductor keeps an underlying sense of forward momentum towards the delightful first appearance of the *Allegro brioso* 'Dilly' theme. It is interesting to note the number of affectionate tributes to the capital made by English composers who were not themselves London-born – Elgar, Holst, Vaughan Williams, Dyson, Ireland, Walton and Malcolm Arnold among them.[4]

Ireland's other overture, *Satyricon*, composed between 1944 and 1946, proved to be his last major orchestral work, although he lived another sixteen years. It seems that the commission came from Henry Wood, his death later in August 1944 meaning that Ireland's work was premiered under Constant Lamber at a Promenade concert in September 1946. Since that first performance, *Satyricon* has been less frequently heard and recorded, and it may be that the composer's heart was not as fully engaged as it had been in *A London Overture*. Boult's recording for Lyrita in the mid-1960s is perhaps more fully convincing than Hickox's Chandos recording of twenty or so years later, which does not entirely find this excellent conductor on top form, although the superiority of the Chandos digital sound cannot be denied.

Perhaps it was the rather lukewarm fate of *Satyricon* that caused Ireland to abandon orchestral composition almost entirely, although the impact of the *Epic March* – a brilliantly positive reaction in 1942 to the War – must have given the composer much satisfaction. Once again, Ireland in *Satyricon* appears to have been poorly served by the record companies: it is an impressive and somewhat surprisingly concentrated piece of no little impact. If anything tells against the work, it is perhaps the title, but the genre of overtures appears to have disappeared from many orchestral programmes, across the world, by the dawn of the second decade of the twenty-first century.

So, too, has much music for string orchestra, to which British composers have, for over 100 years, made arguably the most significant contribution to the repertoire than any group of composers from any nation. Ireland's contribution is one of the finest – his *Concertino Pastorale*, dating from 1939. The work was soon recorded, by the Boyd Neel String Orchestra, on three Decca 12-inch 78s in February 1940, a performance – especially in the conductor's control of the ebullient finale – that has in some respects never been surpassed. In this work, Ireland is entirely himself, showing no 'influence' (a euphemism for plagiarism) in any part. Surprisingly, this endearing score had to wait in its country of origin for a quarter of a century before a second recording, in Boult's Lyrita LP series, was

---

[4] For an extended list of music about London see 'Musical Compositions Evoking London', in *London: A Musical Gazetteer* by Lewis Foreman and Susan Foreman. Yale University Press, 2005, pp. 338–44.

issued – although, somewhat intriguingly, it was the American MGM company once more that made the second recording of this music, by what was billed as the MGM Studio Orchestra (drawn from the Los Angeles Philharmonic) under Izler Solomon, a fine recording on its own terms which underlines the international appeal Ireland's music often had up to the time of his death. The coupling was Britten's *Simple Symphony*: MGM's second Ireland-Britten LP. This was never issued in the UK.

Mention of Boult's pioneering Lyrita recordings of the orchestral works reminds us of the importance of Richard Itter's championship of Ireland with his Lyrita Recorded Edition, starting with the first complete (albeit mono) survey of the piano music in Alan Rowlands' cherishable readings which had the composer's approval. Later, too, on Lyrita came surveys of the songs with the leading singers of the day and the chamber music. These are now reissued on CD in boxed collections and as such are major cornerstones of the Ireland discography.

Since Boult's recording, Ireland's *Concertino Pastorale* has appeared intermittently on disc – rather more frequently, one might suppose, than it has in concert programmes; of later issues, that by George Hurst and the Bournemouth Sinfonietta (long since disbanded) is probably the best. Each recording the work has had has been of high class – but the continuing absence from concert programmes of this music remains a standing reproach to those who should know better.

One might make a similar case for the string orchestra version of Ireland's *A Downland Suite*, a rewriting of the Brass Band Championship Test Piece from the early 1930s, which is similarly neglected, although the Minuet movement managed to secure a toe-hold in discographical terms – it was for some years in the 1950s the only 'orchestral' piece by Ireland available on LP. Half a century and more later, there have been several recordings of the string orchestral arrangement, but many more of the original brass version, of which that conducted by Ifor James has a sense of character that few rival versions share.

Other of Ireland's works for brass have been recorded from time to time, so his contribution to that genre has rarely been neglected by the record companies, but the remaining main orchestral music by Ireland is his score for the Ealing Studios film *The Overlanders* in 1946, the story of a Second World War journey of stockmen droving a cattle herd 1600 miles across Australia. Ireland delivered a magnificent score, but it was his only music for films. A suite was extracted by Sir Charles Mackerras after Ireland's death, and two separate movements, *Two Symphonic Studies* (the title attesting to the quality of Ireland's music), were put together by Geoffrey Bush.

The music, in whichever format, has not lacked representation on disc. Excerpts were issued on a Decca 78 rpm disc by the London Symphony Orchestra under Muir Mathieson in 1947,[5] although it is odd that Mackerras was never asked to record the suite, thus rescuing the music from oblivion. It was due to Sir Adrian Boult's pioneering Lyrita recording in 1970s that this splendid music was brought again to the public's attention, away from the black-and-white film it first accompanied.

---

[5] A CD reissue is on Dutton CDEA 6146.

Chamber Music

Earlier in our survey, we commented upon Ireland's 'student' string quartets, regretting the composer's decision not to include them among his mature list of works. Our regret is based upon the belief that composition cannot really be taught in the conservatoire room, and that Ireland – as with all genuine composers – was, before he was twenty-one, fully cognisant of the challenges he was either set or chose to accept to the point where his decisions regarding those earlier works deprived generations of music-lovers (and performing musicians) the opportunities of hearing such generally fine works.

One such work, similarly withdrawn by the composer, is Ireland's Sextet for clarinet, horn and string quartet. Because of its unusual instrumental make-up, the work is – as one would expect – almost never heard in concert, its instrumental requirements being virtually unique in the history of music. In such instances, the gramophone can play its most important role, and in this, Ireland's earliest surviving chamber work, from 1898, has done so. The Sextet is an exceptionally well imagined composition for such a combination and although it had to wait until 1960 before it was publicly heard, and until 1970 before it was recorded by Lyrita, the worth of the music – which has (perhaps unfairly) been described as 'Brahmsian' (not so much as a criticism of the piece, more in describing its 'genial' character) – is such that it has received two further recordings since then, all three being played by some of the finest chamber musicians in Britain.

It may be significant that the first piece listed in Ireland's 'discarded works' is a Piano Trio in A minor, clearly written around 1895 (when he was sixteen). The significance is that the first 'adult' (after his 'apprenticeship' period) work of his is the *Phantasie* Piano Trio, also in A minor. Ireland went on to write two more piano trios, so clearly this genre appealed to him from the very beginning of his composing life. It should be clear to even the most cursory observer that with the Sextet and the two string quartets, alongside those early orchestral pieces, by 1907 Ireland had achieved his full maturity as a composer, and almost as homage to his teacher Stanford, he dedicated one of the first of his own acknowledged 'mature' works, that selfsame *Phantasie* Trio in A minor, to the Irishman. The circumstances surrounding the rules governing the successive W. W. Cobbett chamber music competitions are well enough known not to need repeating here; Ireland's work, whilst not taking the top prize in the 1907 competition (which was won by Frank Bridge's Piano Quartet), none the less made a very strong impression in coming second – and on its public premiere in January 1909. It later went on to make a more immediate impression on disc, when it was first recorded in 1938. Bridge's fine Piano Quartet had to wait many more years for its first recording.

The original Decca artists in Ireland's *Phantasie* Trio were Frederick Grinke, Florence Hooton and Kendall Taylor; the second recording of the work, on the low-priced Saga LP label, came twenty-six years later – also with cellist Florence Hooton; her participation in the second recording adds a strain of authenticity, for Ireland attended the original Decca sessions and would have discussed the music with all three artists then; at that time, Ireland himself was no stranger to the recording studio.

Since that pioneering 78 rpm Decca set, the artists soon returned to the company's studio for Ireland's latest piano trio, no. 3 in E major, dedicated to another composer, William Walton, in 1938. It may well be that Walton had expressed his admiration for Ireland's *These Things Shall Be*, which was (as we shall comment upon later) a 1937 Coronation commission from the BBC (as was Walton's *Crown Imperial* march), scored for male soloist, chorus and orchestra (as was, of course, *Belshazzar's Feast*); at that time, Decca was also recording much of Walton's music.

The 78 rpm set of Ireland's Third Trio was soon issued by Decca, but in some ways it is a pity that an integral recording of all three works was not completed by these artists, for the Second Trio is fully the equal of the others and is arguably the finest of them all. Once again, we might ask why these works are virtually ignored by ensembles today, especially those specialising in British music, for there is nothing to touch them in the national repertoire, with the possible exception of the two trios by Edmund Rubbra.

All of Ireland's trios were, however, brought together in the early 1960s by Saga, on the LP mentioned earlier (Florence Hooton being the cellist in that ensemble). Since that pioneering Saga disc, these works have made fairly regular appearance as a set in the record catalogues, in inverse proportion to their appearance in recital programmes. It may be felt that the recording costs of chamber music, being less than those for orchestral music, would naturally lead to greater representation of a composer's work in that field.

In some respects, that is probably true, and in Ireland's case the appearance on disc of his three Trios alongside early LP recordings of other of his chamber works would indicate the continuing interest in, and admiration for, his music, an admiration initially brought about by the astonishing success of his Second Violin Sonata, following its triumphant premiere in 1917 at the then newly renamed Wigmore Hall by Albert Sammons and William Murdoch. As an indication of the impact the work made, here is part of a letter sent to Ireland by Frank Bridge:

> Until I have sent you a line or two I shall not be able to get your new work out of my head. Not that I shall ever lose the impression – that's impossible – but while the recollection is so vivid I feel I must write and tell you how overjoyed I am with the Sonata … Its power is tremendous. I have the greatest faith in its future. … I am convinced it is not only a landmark in your own history but also in that of contemporary music … I feel proud that any one of us has produced such a work.

For many people, including the present writer, Ireland's Second Violin Sonata is arguably the greatest such work by a British composer: today, almost one hundred years after the event, it remains so, and was so admired following its first appearance that it became the earliest of Ireland's chamber works to be recorded on 78 rpm discs, within months of that premiere, by Arthur Catterall and William Murdoch (it may be that Sammons, then serving in the British Army, could not get leave to make these first records himself), although the work (as was often the case in those days) had to be abridged to accommodate it on two 12-inch discs.

This first recording was in the acoustic process, of course, and it is interesting to note that in a very early issue of *The Gramophone* (for July 1924), in a little feature 'On making good programmes' concerning contemporary composers, Ireland's

Second Violin Sonata was joined with Scriabin's *Poem of Ecstasy* and Elgar's Violin Concerto (also not then recorded complete) to make an attractive evening's listening at home (this was, of course, before national broadcasting had properly got under way). The appeal of the work had not waned five years later, for in a National Gramophonic Society list of compositions to be recorded (now in the electrical process and without abridgement), approved by the Society's advisory committee, we find Ireland's A minor Violin Sonata alongside music by Brahms, Haydn, Mozart, Schumann and Sibelius.

The NGS request was met the following year by Albert Sammons and Ireland himself, though it was not issued at the time. This magnificent composition has had a long and distinguished career on disc – from acoustic 78s to digital CDs – and has never had less than a very good performance on record from a wide spectrum of illustrious violinists, although it similarly remains a comparative rarity in recital programmes today.

The earlier D minor Violin Sonata also appeared first on 78s – from Decca, following the end of the Second World War, in a distinguished performance by Frederick Grinke, with Ireland as his partner[6] – and that work, by no means a wholly inferior precursor to the A minor, has similarly enjoyed myriad representation by the gramophone companies over the years. It has often been coupled with its successor and on CD with other works as well. Some idea of the quality of the D minor Sonata can be gauged from the fact that it was the winner out of 134 entries for another W. W. Cobbett chamber music competition. It was revised in 1917, around the time of the appearance of the Second Sonata.

In recent years, the appearance of a reconstruction by the Canadian clarinettist and clarinet maker Stephen Fox of Ireland's Trio of 1912–14, which was itself reworked by the composer, has widened our knowledge of Ireland's creative procedures. Fox naturally made the first recording of this reconstruction, and a second recording forms part of the excellent and immensely valuable series of Ireland's complete chamber music by Naxos.

Although Naxos has included every known chamber music work by Ireland in their series, including several brief salon-type pieces, earlier Chandos recordings of Ireland's major compositions in this field, themselves following previous Lyrita LPs (which featured Yfrah Neaman (violin), Julian Lloyd Webber (cello) and Eric Parkin (piano) in much of this repertoire) have been distinguished by some of the finest chamber musicians of the day: Lydia Mordkovitch (violin), Gervase de Peyer (clarinet), Ian Brown (piano) and Karine Georgian (cello) – and one may be sure that the evident success of the newer digital CD issues from Chandos (in reissued form, no fewer than eight works accommodated on just two discs) proved a spur for the later Naxos recordings by artists of a younger generation.

Such concentration by international labels such as Chandos and Naxos has led naturally to a revived interest in Ireland's other duo sonatas – those for clarinet and piano and for cello and piano, and the seeker after musical truth, exemplified by composers' own recordings of their music, will wish to investigate the premiere 78 rpm sets of these works which feature Ireland as pianist, with Frederick (Jack)

---

[6] Reissued with the Second Sonata played by Sammons and Ireland and the first recording of the Phantasie Trio by Dutton Epoch on CDLX 7103.

Fig. 27 Ireland's recording of the Cello Sonata, 1929

Thurston and Antoni Sala, clarinettist and cellist respectively,[7] and a curious aspect of recording history had the admirable clarinettist Thea King – Thurston's wife – make the second recording of the Fantasy Sonata for clarinet and piano, the first to be issued commercially, also by Saga, in 1963.

The first Cello Sonata recording with Antoni Sala and John Ireland at the piano, dating from October 1928, was made relatively soon after the work's premiere. So far as major record companies were concerned, of whom Columbia was certainly one, Ireland's music in the earlier decades of the gramophone was a safe commercial bet, more so, perhaps, with the cachet of the composer participating in the performance.

If later generations have shared that confidence, we should note that almost from the first appearance of Ireland's major chamber music compositions, their representation on disc has been remarkably consistent, alongside the release of some of the composer's miniature offerings, and is itself surely an indication of the inherent consistent quality of his music.

---

[7] The recordings of the Cello Sonata and Fantasy Sonata with Ireland at the piano, along with other recordings with Ireland as pianist are on Dutton CDBP 9799.

Solo Piano Music

Our discussion of Ireland's chamber music on disc has naturally referred to those recordings in which the composer participated. They stand as living testaments to his prowess as a pianist – a prowess more widely spread than is generally recognised. For example, in 1944 Ireland was the soloist in a performance of his *Legend* for piano and orchestra in Cambridge, conducted by Basil Cameron. Ireland was clearly an artist who was exceptional among composers in that discipline, and when we turn to his extensive output for solo piano we come to arguably the finest body of music for the instrument by any British composer.

The attraction of this music for the pianist is that Ireland's own mastery of the keyboard ensures that the music naturally falls under the hands – it is outstandingly well written for the piano. It has always been so considered. Ralph Hill, writing of Ireland's Piano Sonata in 1946, had this to say:

> This remarkable work, which is so full of intensity of expression, would appear to have been generated by deeply felt experiences; nowhere are Ireland's keen melodic style and his apt and expressive use of harmonic colour shown to greater effect. I hold that this Sonata is not only one of the greatest written by a British composer, but one of the finest and most important since Liszt's in B minor. It ought to have been in the repertoire of every virtuoso pianist, but unfortunately virtuosity and artistic discernment are rarely combined in one pianist.

Having noted the early representation and success on disc of Ireland's chamber music, it remains an extraordinarily inexplicable aspect of gramophone history that his piano music – so widely admired, almost from the word 'Go!' – was infrequently encountered on commercial records. Indeed, as will be seen from Stephen Lloyd's discography, it was not until 1953 that the Sonata was first recorded, thirty-three years after it was written. Up to that time very few of Ireland's piano works, of any significance, had been issued on records. The first recording of the Sonata was on the Argo label, then a small independent company (it was later acquired by the Decca Group), which two years earlier had issued their first John Ireland LP of solo piano music, played by Graham Mitchell. It has to be said that at that time the sound quality of very early LPs, especially in solo piano music, was often a hit-and-miss affair. The Mitchell LP fell into the 'Miss' column, but if Argo were soon to dispense with their pianist, they did not abandon Ireland's music, for – as we have noted – two years later they began again with Eric Parkin, including the much admired E major Sonata.

Another pianist, a contemporary of Parkin's, was also closely connected with Ireland's music through the gramophone for a similar length of time. This was Alan Rowlands; yet it was the development of post-war tape recording and the 33⅓ rpm LP record that brought about the discovery of Ireland's piano music to the wider record-buying public, beginning with those pioneering Argo discs, to the point where today, in the second decade of the twenty-first century, we have had many fine recordings of Ireland's output for the instrument from which to choose. Rowlands' pioneering piano cycle was for Lyrita but just predated the widespread establishment of stereo and therefore are all mono recordings.

Thereafter, Parkin was for many years the gramophone's first choice as an Ireland pianist, and it is a fascinating journey to trace his discography of the composer's music over more than four decades. In that regard, we owe Eric Parkin – who had the inestimable advantage of having studied Ireland's music with him (the recording claimed to have been made 'under the personal supervision of the composer') – a great deal; in the course of his long and distinguished career he recorded virtually all of Ireland's piano music, almost all of it more than once, for both the Lyrita and Chandos companies.

There remains one oddity in the Ireland piano discography – among the earliest recordings of his music is one by the composer himself, made on a piano roll. The piece was 'Amberley Wild Brooks', and a further curiosity of gramophone history is that Ireland himself recorded his delightful miniature 'April' twice for what became the EMI conglomerate: for Columbia in 1928 and for HMV in 1951– the latter version occupying the final side of the Barbirolli/Hallé Orchestra recording of *Mai-Dun*. Lionel Salter, writing in *The Gramophone* of this later recording, was not impressed by Ireland's pianism – '... rather untidy, and by no means a perfect performance ...', at the same time acknowledging the historic nature of the performance itself.

Choral Music, Secular and Sacred; Organ Music

In Ireland's list of works *These Things Shall Be* stands high in his achievements. The cantata takes on a genre which was largely invented by English composers (Berlioz's Requiem and Te Deum always excepted), that of solo male voice, chorus and orchestra. Within this English tradition – Delius's *Sea Drift* and Walton's *Belshazzar's Feast* being prime exemplars – *These Things Shall Be* contributes mightily to it. It is an inspired and inspiring work, commissioned (as we noted earlier) by the BBC to mark the Coronation of King George VI and Queen Elizabeth in May 1937. For some commentators, the composer appeared to be an odd choice for this commission: surely no previous work by Ireland suggested he could satisfactorily fulfil such a request, although the other BBC request for the occasion, Walton's Coronation march *Crown Imperial*, was an equal commitment of faith on the Corporation's part – by that time Walton had not yet assumed the mantle of public celebration bequeathed by Elgar.

In the event, both BBC choices were inspired: the text of Ireland's cantata, by John Addington Symonds, may, in the light of soon-to-occur later events, seem somewhat utopian or paradisiacal to more cynical minds, but it is surely no more than what Elgar attempted to do (and succeeded in doing) in his First Symphony; the work, as he said, expressing 'a massive hope for the future'. An aspect of Ireland's score that is not often remarked upon concerns his original use of voices in the 'whispered' passage; not a semi-chorus, but – dramatically – the full choir, as manifest of the individual, suddenly, almost conspiratorially, asking again the question: 'Say, heart, what will the future bring?'

The work has had but four commercially issued recordings in the seventy-five years of its existence, but as with so many pioneering issues of twentieth-century scores, there appears to be a sense of discovery and of enlightenment in the first recorded performances that are not always replicated subsequently. This is surely due to the impact the individual work has made on those musicians commissioned to make the relevant first recording: if the music is any good, it will of its essence contain features which set it apart from other compositions, and artists who are given the opportunity to make the first recording will want to demonstrate those features, if not to the exclusion of others, yet in a manner which highlights them, that moves towards them with a certain alacrity.

Barbirolli's British Council-sponsored recording from 1948 has, as a performance, never been equalled, let alone surpassed. The text of course looks to the future, far-seeing in many ways, but Symonds's verses also imply a forward momentum of thought, word and deed, which are surely echoed in the forward thrust of Ireland's music. This was nothing new in Ireland's music up to that time, but in this big choral work we find a response by the composer which took many people by surprise. In its unerring consistency of style, inspired melodic expression, dramatic impact and quite thrilling solo and choral writing, it is an unqualified success. Of the later recordings, none quite achieves the sense of inspired exhilaration that marks out many passages in the choral writing and in the three orchestral interludes, or that simple yet deeply moving account of the solo part as sung by Parry Jones in Barbirolli's recording: Bryn Terfel, in the Chandos recording under Richard Hickox, delivers a far too 'operatic' treatment of the noble theme, unsuitably exaggerating the text, and Hickox himself holds back at certain climactic moments when the music should surely move forward.[8]

Ireland doubtless knew what he had achieved. The music publisher and author Robert Elkin told a story surrounding the first performance at Queen's Hall, when he, Ireland and one or two others had been drinking during the interval in 'the gluepot' (as Henry Wood dubbed it) bar of The George public house close to the old artists' entrance. (The tiny road leading to the entrance and a fragment of the Hall are extant.) The party arrived back at the Hall almost as the second half (and Ireland's piece) was to begin and were barred by the doorman from entering. Ireland, so Elkin recounted, proceeded to berate the doorman in no uncertain terms until the man asked: 'Who do you think you are, Sir?' 'I'm the composer, I wrote the bloody thing!' Ireland shouted, at which point the group was allowed to retake their seats and hear the work for the first time – in the nick of time.

No other choral work in Ireland's output approaches the structural and expressive mastery of *These Things Shall Be*, a statement which, thanks to the breadth of repertoire now available on commercial recordings, is demonstrably true, but none the less we should be grateful particularly to the Chandos company for their support of Ireland's choral music, which support includes first recordings of several of Ireland's lesser-known but eminently worthwhile shorter works, notably the setting of 'Greater love hath no man than this'. Whatever comparative shortcomings one might level at Hickox's recording of the cantata, none can be made of his performances of Ireland's other choral works, demonstrating the influence of this sadly missed conductor's early musical provenance as organist and choirmaster.

Ireland himself of course was organist and choirmaster of St Luke's, Chelsea, for a quarter of a century and he left a body of church and organ music that has

[8] See p. 90, n. 15.

rightly taken its place among the best examples of that English tradition. As with other composers, very few commercial recordings of such repertoire were issued on 78 rpm discs, although the music was heard every week in cathedrals and churches across the nation.

Once more, it is only in recent years that record collectors have been able to supplement their knowledge of Ireland's contribution to the field of English church music, especially his early but exciting setting of the Te Deum in F major. Despite the lack of representation of Ireland's sacred music in what one might term the pre-digital era, the growth of the CD medium has led to a vast selection of his church and other choral music being made available since the mid-1980s; a further consultation of Stephen Lloyd's discography will trace the quite remarkable growth of the commercial interest in this area of Ireland's output, an area related to his organ music in terms of the provenance of its inspiration.

We have earlier mentioned the international appeal of Ireland's music, in so far as recordings of it have emanated from the United States, Canada, Scandinavia and Australia, in addition to those mainly from the British Isles, and in 2009 the appearance on CD of Ireland's complete music for organ occasioned surprise in that it was played by a German organist, Stefan Kagl, on the instrument in Herforder Münster, issued on the German CPO label. Although this was the first complete disc of Ireland's organ music, parts of this repertoire had not been entirely overlooked by British companies before, and there are a number of fine performances by native organists in the catalogues.

Solo Songs

If Ireland's piano music was considered by Ralph Hill to be 'without equal in English piano music', his songs were equally, indeed more popularly and much more widely, admired. Perhaps one should qualify this by adding 'one song in particular' – namely *Sea Fever*, a setting of John Masefield's poem. This quite masterly song did more to spread Ireland's name among the music-loving public as well as the wider radio listening public from the 1920s to the 1950s, than any other single work of his. Ballad singers of all description took *Sea Fever* to their hearts, and in the 78 rpm era it was by far the most frequently recorded of the composer's songs. So popular was it that Roy Henderson recorded it twice on 78s – for Columbia and for Decca – and Paul Robeson's version was but one of no fewer than five separate recordings by various artists listed in the HMV catalogue alone, evidence of the high regard in which this haunting ballad was held. Indeed, whilst we have not necessarily checked every record catalogue since 1919 (when *Sea Fever* was first recorded) it is surely the case that a commercial recording of this song has been available continuously until the present day.

The Ireland discography by Stephen Lloyd reveals not only the extent of the commercially issued recordings in the early 78 rpm era, especially of *Sea Fever*, but also the number of great internationally admired singers who recorded Ireland's vocal music – too many even to list here, as the discography shows. In the long list of important achievements by the gramophone in bringing Ireland's music before the public, the commitment to Ireland's song output first by Lyrita and later by the Hyperion company has been wholly exceptional. Chief in the hundreds of recordings of Ireland's songs, the Lyrita set which first appeared in the 1970s offers Benjamin Luxon, John Mitchinson and Alfreda Hodgson, all in their prime, with Alan Rowlands the totally sympathetic pianist, a total of 80 tracks now they are gathered as a CD three-disc set. The Hyperion CD set, released in 1999, contains sixty-nine individual songs, uniformly splendidly performed by three fine English singers, Lisa Milne, John Mark Ainsley and Christopher Maltman, partnered by Graham Johnson. The presentations from Lyrita and Hyperion are a further example of what music and music-lovers owe to the gramophone.

The Composer and the Gramophone

Our survey has been of the music of one composer and the relationship of his art to the public as exemplified through recordings of the last hundred years. Although Ireland died in 1962 and his music is now widely available through whichever medium currently delivers it, in the course of our observations we have mentioned the output of mainly British recording companies, but the vicissitudes of commerce have played their part: some of those record labels no longer exist, and newer ones have arisen, yet behind all of this activity the music remains constant.

It is no little achievement, stemming from the ethos of classical recordings, that the cachet of a first recording of previously unknown music by a significant composer can still excite the imagination. In recent years two British record companies have contributed significantly to our understanding of Ireland's art. The Somm label has undertaken the first entirely complete recording of Ireland's music for piano and for piano and orchestra, played by Mark Bebbington throughout; this is a fine achievement by all concerned, not least by the pianist himself. The second company is Dutton Epoch, dedicated to the release of new recordings of British music, almost all of it new to the catalogues, and particularly exploring orchestrations of Ireland's shorter instrumental pieces and the songs marvellously sung by baritone Roderick Williams and soprano Susan Gritton.

Such enterprise is admirable, and although the Ireland discography may not yet contain every work to have come from the composer's pen, a recent Dutton issue includes his final vocal piece – an unaccompanied setting of Psalm 23, written in 1958, finely performed by Roderick Williams. This may be a convenient moment to bring our discussions to an end, in so far as new recordings are ever complete, but we should perhaps add a postscript concerning arrangements of Ireland's music by the composer and others, for there are several unique transcriptions on that self-same Dutton CD, including one by Ireland himself of a gem which has long since rivalled *Sea Fever* in popularity, and in some respects exceeds it.

The third of Four Preludes for piano, 'The Holy Boy', has received literally dozens of recordings over the years in a variety of transcriptions and arrangements (ranging from unaccompanied viola to violin and orchestra). When one considers the public demand for this haunting piece, and the practical responses of the composer to that demand, it must be quite clear that, alongside his other qualities, we are led to the inescapable conclusion that Ireland, in many ways a shy and retiring man, was the complete musician in almost every regard.

PART III

Ireland's Pupils on their Teacher

CHAPTER 24

John Ireland: A Personal Impression

Geoffrey Bush

First published in Left, Right and Centre: Reflections on Composers and Composing *(London: Thames Publishing, 1983), pp. 100–12.*

I. The man

That autumn a new assistant chaplain arrived at the school.[1] This event, commonplace in itself – in those days chaplains appeared and disappeared almost unnoticed – gained great significance from the fact that this particular priest came from Chelsea, home of none other than John Ireland the composer. When he discovered that my heart was in the composing of sonatas rather than Latin proses, he promptly wrote to his famous parishioner about me. The reply was astonishing: 'Send me everything that boy has written.'

Little did John Ireland know what he was bargaining for. Nowadays I often spend hours sniffing cautiously round a single bar, like a dog encountering a suspicious lamppost; but then I used to pour the stuff on paper with reckless abandon, disregarding every consideration except that of adding one more to a Bradman-like total of opus numbers. Even ruthless pruning could not prevent the parcel being a formidable one. There followed (not surprisingly) several weeks' delay: then at last a letter in a strange handwriting (which later I got to know so well), postmarked Chelsea.

I searched in vain for any sentence that could remotely be construed as 'Hats off, gentlemen, a genius.'[2] Instead, there was a great deal of kindly but sober advice:

> I see you are at present much in love with what I must call, for want of a better word, dissonance – the kind of dissonance, I mean, which has been in vogue mainly during the last 10 or 15 years. This is an extremely difficult medium to handle in a convincing way, and to do so (if one admits the works of Schönberg and Bartók and Hindemith to be convincing) implies, at any rate as a basis, a thorough and efficient working knowledge of harmony and counterpoint in the accepted sense. All the composers I have mentioned (and of course one could add Stravinsky) have undoubtedly been through a protracted and severe course of this kind of training before blossoming out into what may at first sight appear to be without rhyme or reason.

After recommending a study of classical styles and strict counterpoint as a preliminary to 'sailing the uncharted seas which I see appeal so strongly to

---

[1] The school was Lancing College and the new Assistant Chaplain Kenneth Thompson.

[2] Schumann's celebrated tribute to Chopin. He is also reputed similarly to have greeted the young Sterndale Bennett.

you just now', he added the warning 'but all this involves time and labour, and, in fact, musical composition is a whole-time job. This will all sound very prosy and old-fogey-ish to you, I fear, but then there is no short cut.' (Hard work and old-fogeydom are two themes which are constantly recapitulated in later letters: 'When I was your age I was considered a dangerous innovator – now you know what they think of me – a bloody old fogey. What does it matter? You should write to please yourself. But don't be too easily pleased.')

Came the holidays – and with them an invitation to visit him at his Chelsea studio. Everything about the first visit was exciting – the trip on the No. 11 bus to that romantically named fare-stage 'The World's End'; the vast studio seemingly empty save for a grand-piano and a fiercely-burning stove, and John Ireland himself, to uninformed eyes a prosaic and even insignificant-looking person, but to me the composer of the Piano Concerto and of two pieces rather more within my limited pianistic reach (*The Darkened Valley* and *The Holy Boy*) and therefore the greatest man I had met or was ever likely to meet.

I returned home in a daze; such a daze, in fact, that I took the wrong train at Victoria and landed myself in some benighted suburb which neither I nor anyone I asked had ever heard of. Which somehow made the day even more magical than ever.

A visit to John Ireland became a regular feature of the school holiday after that, and I never lost the thrill of it. I would bring him my latest composition, and he would turn the manuscript over in an abstracted sort of way, before eventually opening it somewhere in the middle. Invariably he chanced on the very page where there was some weak passage or other which had gone in at that point because I had been unable to think of anything better. I never understood how, even before he spoke, he was able to make me realise my shortcomings, until I came across the phrase (in Thomas Mann's *Doctor Faustus*) 'the teacher is the personified conscience of the pupil'. Passages which seemed tolerable when looked at through my eyes immediately became intolerable when looked at through his – because in my heart of hearts I had really known they were intolerable from the word go.

John Ireland never gave me any formal instruction, but the help I received from these unofficial sessions was incalculable. He was always friendly, extremely patient, often encouraging and invariably critical. One page once made him declare that the very sight of it made him need seven beers. In his outspoken denunciation of anything he disliked he followed the example of his own teacher, Stanford, whose toughness he found as valuable as it was disagreeable. 'Vaughan Williams, Holst and myself', he once wrote to me, 'owe much to that great man, Stanford.'

Meanwhile at school I was being coached for a classical scholarship, and there seemed little prospect of my ever becoming a professional musician. Then, one day, John Ireland told me that he had heard of a composition scholarship being offered at Balliol, which he thought was just up my street. (He had in fact heard of it from one of his own pupils, who in Ireland's opinion was more of an organist than a composer: the accuracy of his assessment was borne out by the fact that as soon as the examiners heard his pupil play they offered him the organ scholarship on the spot.) Winning this composition scholarship, besides saving me from almost certain failure in the classical one, was the turning point in my life; from this time onwards – although the college made me continue with Latin and Greek – music was officially recognised as my main interest.

About this time I wrote a clarinet *Rhapsody* which was an improvement on my previous efforts, and John Ireland came up to Oxford for the first performance. The players and I took him for dinner to the George, and I think he thoroughly enjoyed being made a fuss of by the younger generation. Possibly this is why he retained a strong affection for this *Rhapsody*. Later on he tried to interest a London publisher in it, and took up the cudgels on my behalf when the BBC wrote to inform me that their reading panel considered it unsuitable for broadcasting. Unfortunately for the BBC, John Ireland was at this time chairman of their reading panel, and was therefore in a position to know that he and his colleagues had, in fact, unanimously recommended it. On hearing that I had been told the opposite, Ireland lodged an immediate and furious protest, an act requiring more courage than the layman might realise; since the BBC is the composer's chief, indeed perhaps only, employer nowadays, it takes a bit of nerve to risk antagonising those in charge of it. I never received any apology or explanation; but I got the broadcast.

Years later I asked him if I might show my thanks for all he had done for me by dedicating a piece of mine to him. He expressed a preference for the *Rhapsody*, but since this was already occupied, so to speak, by the clarinettist for whom I had written it, I proposed my new Violin Sonata, which I proceeded to play through to him for his approval. After listening in silence for about a quarter-of-an-hour, he suddenly interrupted:

'This is rather long for a first movement, isn't it?'

"There is only one movement.'

(Short pause)

'Good'.

Before the war John Ireland was for many years organist of St Luke's, Chelsea, and when the post fell vacant again after the war he recommended me for the job. I wasn't much of a success. The war had decimated the considerable musical establishment, and besides a handful of untrained boys, only a tenor aged sixty-eight and a bass aged eighty-six remained. More alarming – to an organist like myself, who needs constant reassurance that all is well before proceeding from one note to the next – was the timelag caused by siting the organ console and its elaborate pipe-cum-electronic apparatus at opposite ends of the church. Moreover, the Vicar tended to base his musical opinions on the reaction of the congregation, and he placed particular reliance on one whose authority he considered unimpeachable for the curious reason that he was an Admiral.

My year there was chiefly memorable in that it enabled me to see quite a lot of John Ireland at a time when he was composing the *Satyricon Overture* and the music to the film *The Overlanders*. Both these works gave him a lot of trouble, the latter owing to the producer, who knew nothing of musical technique but had a very decided idea of what he wanted written. I remember at one recording session he complained that the music Ireland had composed for the taming of the wild horses, a wonderful jagged clarinet solo accompanied by pizzicato lower strings, sounded like a Sunday afternoon chamber concert. Only the ingenuity of the musical director, who devised a countermelody prominent enough to deceive the producer but not so prominent as to obscure Ireland's original conception, saved the situation.

As early as 1943 Ireland had thought of writing a choral work based on the *Satyricon*, a novel written during the reign of Nero by the Latin author Petronius, which attracted him by reason of 'its general atmosphere of roguery and vagabondage'. He was hindered by the fact that some of the text was at that time untranslated and considered untranslatable (though nowadays it would hardly cause the raising of an eyebrow). In 1944 the receipt of a commission for a purely orchestral work in honour of Sir Henry Wood's Jubilee Season at the Proms caused him to change his mind. He composed the opening of the overture there and then, but was forced by shortage of time to abandon it. In 1946 he resumed work, again for the Proms and again at short notice ('I was a fool to undertake it in the time available'); but on this occasion he carried it through successfully, though not without some misgivings about some unusual elements in the structure:

> I have got it sketched out, but would like six months to think about it. For one thing, I have made an experiment in the form, and am not yet sure if it is satisfactory. I have not made any recapitulation of the first subject until the Coda – so the form stands:
>
> A. 1st subject, etc.
>
> B. 2nd subj., etc.
>
> C. Development section which contains a new theme.

This joins up to the section of A which leads to the 2nd subject (B) then the Coda, which is short, and based on the 1st subj., (A). It is an unusual way of treating the form. And the main sequence of keys is also unusual – not taking account of intermediate and modulatory passages the key centres are: A E flat G C D flat F and back to A for the Coda.

Lack of time to think things over always bothered Ireland – in fact he altogether hated working at pressure to meet a deadline. During the war he composed incidental music for a BBC production of *Julius Caesar*, using the 'nice clear-cut sound' of eight wind, eleven brass, percussion and three double basses. For this task he was allowed a fortnight, which meant that he 'had to put everything else on one side and just stick at it all day every day and a good part of the night as well.' In my innocence I had written to him that I had enjoyed a holiday writing music, and he replied 'Well, well. Compared with writing the music for *Julius Caesar*, penal servitude would have been a recreation.'

Ireland's letters were always forthright, and never more so than when he was discussing his fellow-musicians. He could be generous, but compliments had to be earned. No living composer (not even himself) had, in his opinion, the right to the adjective 'great', with the possible exception of Sibelius; for him few, if any, modern works could stand comparison with Debussy's 'ravishingly beautiful and satisfying pieces' *Nuages* and *Fêtes*. But he admired Vaughan Williams's Fifth Symphony (though that composer's music was largely antipathetic to him) for its 'sincerity and reticence', and he expressed great enthusiasm for the virtuosity of Britten's *The Turn of the Screw* and for the austerity of Alan Bush's Symphony no. 1

in C major. He described the latter as 'very original, virile and well-made – clearly a work of considerable importance, written with no regard to the mob, the box-office or the publisher', and added 'I am anxious to hear it again.'

He listened carefully and critically to performances of his own work; he spoke unprintable things about one conductor who took his *London Overture* so fast that it was listed in the returns of the Performing Right Society not as a complete performance but as a 'short selection'. The best performance he ever heard of *Mai-Dun* was given, so he told me, by Rudolf Schwarz: this at a time when that fine conductor was a favourite victim of London's hatchet-men.

He was always stimulating to talk to, and though he was famous for his pessimism, a touch of wry humour could be discerned even in his most pessimistic utterances. The last time I saw him, in the converted windmill facing Chanctonbury Ring to which he had moved after leaving Chelsea, we were discussing the changes of fashion which had led the BBC – for the first time I could remember – to discard his music from the Proms. (He didn't live long enough to hear it restored the following year: an episode wholly characteristic of English musical history.) I comforted him with the assurance that the pendulum was bound to swing back again, adding that in artistic matters there were inevitably some ups and downs. 'Yes', he replied darkly, 'but more downs.'

II. *The musician*

The outbreak of war brought my regular visits to John Ireland to an untimely end. But there was compensation in the form of a series of letters written to me, first from Banbury and later from the little Essex village where Ireland had taken refuge with friends after escaping from the Channel Islands a few hours before they were invaded by the Germans. In the course of our correspondence a dispute arose over neoclassicism. Despite his admiration for Stravinsky's early works, Ireland had not cared for the Symphony in C, which he had heard on the radio in 1943, and feared (correctly) that I was longing to jump on that particular band-wagon. 'Don't you think that you should avoid that method, if you can think of any other? It is so easy to write in the style of Bach or Mozart or Gluck or Handel, sprinkled with a few wrong notes and some jazzy rhythmic perversions.' Being an opinionated young man of twenty-odd, I objected that the methods of many another great composer could be reduced to absurdity in this way; to which he replied 'Delius had a style of his own, and so has Vaughan Williams – though both are easy to imitate, as you point out. I note that (out of politeness – double question-mark) you have refrained from giving the simple recipe for *my* formula – if it is a formula – I am not aware that it is.'

I never replied to this at the time; but now, as an opinionated man of fifty-odd, I feel like having a try. Before starting, however, the point should be made that Ireland's musical preoccupations were not solely creative. Like practically every composer one can think of, Ireland in his time played many parts. He was a notable organist, choirmaster, composition teacher and pianist; in fact, when he came south on his fourteenth birthday to study at the Royal College of Music, he was enrolled as a piano pupil. (It wasn't long before he conceived a passionate ambition to study composition with Stanford; this ambition was realised when Parry heard a student performance of his First String Quartet and awarded him a scholarship on the spot.)

His first professional job was as assistant organist and choirmaster at Holy Trinity, Sloane Street, for which he was chosen by Walter Alcock from a long list of more experienced applicants, although he was only 17 years old.[3] Nearly 30 years service followed in various organ lofts, principally that of St Luke's, Chelsea – a vast neo-Gothic pile just behind the old theatre in the King's Road. He appeared regularly as pianist in public performances of his own compositions, though he didn't have as much time to play the instrument as he would have wished. (He used to say that he practised either too little or – when a concert was approaching – too much.)

One of the occupations which reduced the amount of time available was teaching at his old college. His most notable achievement there was taking up the cudgels on behalf of a young scholarship candidate from Suffolk who for some unknown reason – possibly he was too brilliant – had aroused the antagonism of the other examiners. Ireland dealt with the situation in characteristic fashion: 'Either the boy is awarded a scholarship or I resign.' The boy in question was, of course, Benjamin Britten; and at the request of Frank Bridge, to whom he had already been going for lessons during the school holidays, he was enrolled as Ireland's composition student. Britten felt frustrated at the college because there were so few opportunities for trying out his compositions in performance; but during his time with Ireland he wrote several works of astonishing promise, including the String Quartet in D of 1931 and the choral variations *A Boy Was Born*.

To return to John Ireland's challenge: obviously there is no question here of giving a formula or recipe, let alone a simple one. Ireland was a complex musical personality and, as I hope to show, his character was formed by many different interests and influences. Merely to catalogue a handful of mannerisms would be as misleading as it would be superficial. Most composers tend to respond to an emotional situation which they have met before with the sort of music they have written before; and there are some turns of phrase, some harmonic progressions, some keyboard textures of which Ireland was particularly fond. In actual fact there are not all that many of these recurring fingerprints, nor are they of any great importance. What *does* distinguish Ireland's music from that of his contemporaries is his entirely personal reaction to the problem which faced all of them at that particular moment in our musical history: how to recover a sense of identity in a country that had forgotten that such a thing as an English musical tradition had ever existed.

John Ireland was born into a century which had been dominated first of all by Mendelssohn and then by Brahms. It is easy to understand the reasons for this. As Nicholas Temperley has pointed out, the German style 'was central to European music at the time'; moreover, Germany was the only place where English

---

[3] For Ireland's account of Alcock see pp. 404–7. Ireland liked to recall that his youthfulness proved his undoing on one occasion; at choir practice he was too inexperienced (to prevent the boys marching round and round the church bawling the principal motif of Stanford in B♭ to the words of a popular song of the day: 'Army duff, army duff.'

composers could get a hearing. It was in Leipzig that Sterndale Bennett received an ovation for his Third Piano Concerto, in Hamburg that Henry Hugo Pierson made his reputation with his music for the second part of Goethe's *Faust,* in Hanover that Stanford's first opera, *The Veiled Prophet,* was staged, and at Dusseldorf that *The Dream of Gerontius* was rehabilitated after the Birmingham fiasco. It is not surprising that John Ireland arrived in his teens at the Royal College of Music so thoroughly Germanised that Stanford declared his compositions to be 'all Brahms and water' and made him write music in the style of Palestrina for the whole of his first year. The spirit of Brahms had not been completely exorcised by the time Ireland came to write the Sextet for clarinet, horn and string quartet in 1898. The first three movements are technically faultless and in their conventional way delightful to listen to; the finale, however, marks a milestone in Ireland's development, for in it we can hear for the first time intimations of the composer's own authentic voice. Stanford strongly disapproved of this movement, and in one sense he was right. Since it was Ireland's first exploratory step into a new world, it was a clumsy, hesitating step. In another sense he was quite wrong – indeed, there could be no better illustration of Hans Keller's thesis that the successes of a student composer ought to be blue-pencilled, whereas the failures (because these are alone his own unaided work) should be encouraged.

For Holst and Vaughan Williams the path to freedom from German musical domination lay through folksong. Ireland felt not the slightest inclination to follow their example, though he did acknowledge the immense importance of the rediscovery of our heritage of Tudor choral music. The *chief* liberating factor, however, was the discovery that Germany did not have the monopoly of the mainstream of European music. Two other countries had things of equal importance to contribute and to which he could instantly respond. The first of these was Russia. Ireland heard the first performance in this country[4] of Tchaikovsky's Sixth Symphony, and as he said himself in an interview 'we all, students and teachers alike, went mad about it'. Several years later came *The Rite of Spring*; Stravinsky's immensely powerful evocation of a remote and sinister past moved Ireland deeply. But though he admired the clear, hard outlines and the driving rhythms of Stravinsky's music, you will look in vain for any obvious traces of the Russian master's style in Ireland's work. Composers like Stravinsky were not influences in the sense of being models to be imitated, but beacons to illuminate the path along which his own true direction lay. Nonetheless, the kinship can be clearly heard in the pithy motives and nervous rhythms with which Ireland's overture *Satyricon* begins.

Another work inspired by Petronius' Latin novel is the one-movement *Fantasy Sonata* for clarinet and piano; in its quieter and more meditative passages this lovely piece shows Ireland's affinity with the music of French Impressionism, the second of the two counter-influences which helped to free him from the Brahmsian strait-jacket. Of all his French contemporaries Ireland preferred Ravel, and always spoke of his music with deep understanding and affection. Ireland, incidentally, was the pianist in the first English performance of Ravel's Trio; to make sure that the occasion should be worthy of the work, Ireland insisted – so the players subsequently calculated – on 35 rehearsals. (It is as well to remember that Ravel was

---

[4] For Ireland's own account see pp. 410–11.

not an actual Impressionist; like Ireland himself, he was a classicist using Impressionist techniques.)

Next to Ravel, John Ireland held Debussy in the highest esteem. In 1941 he wrote to me about the first performance of a violin concerto by a British composer, sympathising with him because Debussy's *Nocturnes* had been played immediately before the premiere of the new piece: '… hardly a good choice to precede a new work – few, if any, modern works could have stood up to them.' Exciting though these new musical experiences, Russian and French, were to Ireland, and helpful as signposts directing him along his own individual path, the composer never fell into the trap of cutting himself off from his roots. In particular, he never forgot the lessons learnt during his student days at the Royal College. 'Stanford could be severely critical, almost cruel at times', Ireland once told an interviewer. (A characteristic verdict on an apprentice quartet was 'dull as ditchwater, my boy'.) 'His best quality as a teacher was that he made you feel that nothing but the best would do.' Such was the impression Stanford made on Ireland as teacher and composer, that he kept his photograph by him for the rest of his life.

So much for the make-up of Ireland's musical language; to what purpose was it put? And what were the non-musical sources of Ireland's inspiration? These latter were many and various: English poetry; a feeling for place, or rather places; and that very rare thing, a sense of the immanence of the past – in other words a past so close to the present as to be immediately perceptible by any sensitive person on the lookout for it. It was this quality which he recognised and responded to in Stravinsky's *Rite of Spring*, and he also found it one memorable day in 1906 at Charing Cross [actually Penrith, see p. 126]], when he bought from the station bookstall a copy of Arthur Machen's *The House of Souls*. Machen is a writer seldom read nowadays – except perhaps by enthusiasts for John Ireland's music; but his tales of other worlds and other days are filled with so powerful a sense of the supernatural that an impressionable reader like myself is frequently reduced to terror or, in the more emotional stories, to tears. Ireland's *Legend* for piano and orchestra is perhaps the finest, certainly the most extended, work written under Machen's influence, and it is dedicated to the author. The central section embodies a strange Machen-like experience: in Julian Herbage's words, 'the composer had taken a picnic lunch to a favourite spot on the Downs, but had scarcely unpacked it before he was conscious of some children dancing in front of him. He at first thought they were real, but then he noticed their archaic clothing. He glanced away for an instant, and when he looked back the children had vanished.'

So far as I know Ireland never set any of Machen's words to music, though he used them as an epigraph for his piano piece *The Scarlet Ceremonies*. Of the many poets to whom Ireland went for his song texts, the one with whom he was most in sympathy was A. E. Housman. There are fine settings of Housman by other composers – Vaughan Williams' cycle *On Wenlock Edge* is, deservedly, the most familiar; but in none of them can one find that total identification of poet and musician which is the hallmark of Ireland's work. The gritty, grimly humorous, pessimistic and cantankerous Housman spoke straight to the composer's heart, and he responded with two masterpieces, *The Land of Lost Content* and *We'll to the Woods No More*. The first of these two cycles is the better known, thanks to a splendid recording made by Peter Pears and Benjamin Britten, but the second is even more remarkable. There are only three movements, the third of which, astonishingly, is for piano alone. The title-song is so tense and emotional – an emotion all the more poignant because expressed with the utmost concision and restraint – that Ireland himself in later years could scarcely bring himself to listen to it. When I wanted to include it in a broadcast he urged me to use the second song, 'In Boyhood', instead. Not, he hastened to add, that he regarded it as inferior: 'I consider *In Boyhood* a very fair song, and fully expressive of the essential Housman, as far as is possible in such a short space.' Two interesting cross-references are to be found in the first song: to the slow movement of the Piano Sonatina and (in anticipation) to the finale of the Piano Concerto.

For the text of another major work, the *Five Songs* for baritone and piano, Ireland turned to the poems of Thomas Hardy, in which he also found a resignation to fate but considered more profoundly than in Housman's poetry; and it was of course Hardy country which inspired the symphonic rhapsody for orchestra, *Mai-Dun*. But despite the attraction of Dorset's ancient history, three other places had a more lasting effect on John Ireland's music: the Channel Islands, Sussex and London.

A glance through the solo piano music[5] immediately shows this three-fold influence at work. To Jersey we owe *The Island Spell*, a piece which exultantly celebrates the composer's emancipation from the grip of German music, and to nearby Guernsey the magnificent three-movement cycle *Sarnia*. Sussex was a particularly happy place for Ireland; after the war he lived in retirement there in a converted windmill facing Chanctonbury Ring, and during his creative years he drew inspiration from the Downs for *Equinox, Amberley Wild Brooks* and the massive Piano Sonata. It may seem surprising that such a lover of the country could respond equally readily to the moods of a big city. (His pupil Britten could not endure London after East Anglia.) Ireland's long residence in Chelsea, however, had taught him to appreciate the strange fascination and curiously beautiful ugliness of the city scene. One consequence was the *Ballade of London Nights*, a work put aside for revision and never published during the composer's lifetime, which has since been posthumously edited by one of his most sympathetic interpreters, Alan Rowlands. Fine though it is, it cannot compare with the *London Pieces*, which were completed in 1920. The three movements are, in reverse order, an atmospheric evocation of *Soho Forenoons; Ragamuffin*, perhaps a portrait of one of the local boys – 'grubby but beautiful' as Ireland put it – who belonged to his church choir; and a barcarolle, *Chelsea Reach*. This, with its haunting melody, perpetually shifting piano textures and impressive command of large-scale musical design, is unquestionably a masterpiece.

John Ireland made an outstanding contribution to English music in three media in particular: songs, piano and chamber music. In this respect he reminds one of Fauré, and indeed he is to be spoken of in the same terms as the great French master. Like Fauré he wrote comparatively seldom for larger forces, but with great effect whenever he did so; Fauré's gentle *Requiem* is matched by Ireland's incisive *These Things Shall Be*. Unlike the Frenchman, Ireland wrote nothing for the theatre;

---

[5] The collected piano music had recently been published in five volumes by Stainer & Bell.

he did, however, write incidental music for a radio production of *Julius Caesar* and for the film *The Overlanders*, scores which have recently been arranged in a form which makes them suitable for concert performance.

The pride and joy of all who love Ireland's music, however, is the Piano Concerto, written in 1930. This shows many facets of the composer's art that I have not yet touched on: his skill at motivic development – all the passionate outpourings of the opening movement derive from the first five simple crotchets; the incisiveness of his orchestration; and his marvellous economy and sense of timing. What other composer, having created the great arch of melody that begins the slow movement, could have refrained from repeating it later once or even twice in its entirety? Ireland is content merely to recall half-a-dozen bars. And when, reluctantly, we are awakened from the dream world of the slow movement by the entry of the timpani – the drums have been silent up to now, held in reserve for this special purpose – there is compensation in the shape of one of Ireland's happiest melodic inventions. (This has a tick-tock accompaniment marvellously evocative of the spirit of Joseph Haydn – himself a Londoner by adoption.) The personal and the popular are so well blended in this concerto that it would not be out of place to apply to it Mozart's own self-analysis: 'There are passages here and there from which connoisseurs alone can derive satisfaction; but these passages are written in such a way that the less learned cannot fail to be pleased, though without knowing why.'

In 1958, after hearing the first LP recording of the concerto, with Colin Horsley as the soloist, I wrote to John Ireland to express (not for the first time) my enthusiasm for the work. His reply shows the concern which most composers feel about changing public attitudes to their music:

> My dear Geoffrey,
>
> So many thanks for your kind, generous letter. I value very highly your appreciation of my concerto. Coming from a musician of your generation and high standing it is indeed heartening and encouraging to one whose music is not in the current fashion. Some writer in *The Times* said it was like very sweet marsala as compared with the 'dry Burgundy' quality of Stravinsky's *Capriccio*, which occupies the other side of the record. In the 1940s the late James Agate found it so dissonant and ugly that he almost refused to speak to me again! He regarded it as a personal insult …
>
> Your old friend
> John Ireland

He need not have worried about the shifts in musical taste where his concerto was concerned. If there is ever going to be any future at all for British music, Ireland's concerto will (without any doubt whatever) be part of it.

CHAPTER 25

Ireland's Pupils on their Teacher

Richard Arnell, Alan Bush, Benjamin Britten,
E. J. Moeran & Humphrey Searle

1. Richard Arnell

This account is taken from a talk recorded for the Canadian Broadcasting Corporation's programme, 'Music Diary', subsequently printed in Tempo *no. 61–2 (Spring–Summer 1962), pp. 39–40.*

JOHN Ireland, one of our most distinguished Grand Old Men of music, died on 12 June, at the age of eighty-two. His contemporaries were Vaughan Williams, Bax, Gordon Jacob, the neglected Cyril Scott, and Havergal Brian, whose *Gothic Symphony* was given its premiere here recently, some forty years after it was written! England is not an easy country to be born into as a composer, and Ireland had a hard struggle to support himself. He went to the Royal College of Music on a scholarship at the age of fourteen, and kept himself alive by playing at Smoking Concerts (he was a fine pianist), teaching and coaching.

Ireland's composition teacher was Stanford. As a pupil of Ireland's myself, I heard a great deal about Stanford's 'method' – or, rather, his deliberate lack of it. Both of them disliked standard textbooks but had a great reverence for James Higgs, on fugue, and [Sir Frederick] Bridge, on counterpoint. I don't believe Ireland ever wrote a fugue[1] after he had left college, and he rather heartily disliked contrapuntal music; he had a respect for its intellectuality though, I suppose. Our lesson, which was of indeterminate length, often consisted of discussions which had little to do with the miserable piece of work which I might have brought with me. He had a very lively, well-read mind and knew exactly how to bring out the best in a student by indirect means. He was fond of the poet A. E. Housman's work, for example, and by talking about him would somehow challenge one's own beliefs.

The lessons were given in a large, dark studio in the garden of his large, dark Chelsea house. In a sort of yellowish light from the skylight (there were no windows), not much could be seen but a huge piano, given him by some now vanished piano company. The keys were thick with dust and cigarette ash, and I am sure the instrument was never tuned. We would both sit at this monster, sometimes for two hours or more (the lesson was theoretically for an hour), while he stared absentmindedly at my music, making a few extremely telling comments, then digressing everywhere. He had a wonderful eye for a weakness and would spot it immediately. He believed that everything should 'sound' or work properly, and had no patience with passages put in for effect or to add to the general confusion. In this, he was a craftsman of the French school, meticulously studying the inflexion and meaning of the word in a song, or the exact phrasing in a piano piece. He had the same attitude towards accurate notation (the composer's bugbear) and

[1] He did in Psalm 42.

towards orchestration. Once we spent most of one lesson discussing the virtues of a particular tuba passage in his *London Overture*. He preferred to work in smaller forms, and, I think, disliked symphonies and string quartets. He stressed economy of means and believed simplicity was the hardest thing to achieve.

Most of his music was written before the Second World War, in the 1920s and 30s, and he was really very progressive in using so many contemporary poets – Yeats, Rupert Brooke, Rossetti, Masefield and Ernest Dowson. Many of his works indeed have literary or other associations. Ireland's important orchestral works, *Mai-Dun*, *The Forgotten Rite*, and *Legend* for piano and orchestra, are tokens of his sympathy for old, forgotten Celtic religions. He was, in fact, very much of a Pagan himself, although the very opposite in his personal behaviour of the Bohemianism the word Pagan wrongly suggests. In the hills of Kent, near Deal, where he often stayed, prehistoric man made huge drawings on the hills by removing the grass and exposing the brilliant white chalk beneath. Archaeologists, discovering one of these hill carvings, laboriously uncovered it. The local authorities decided it was obscene and it was carefully covered over again. Ireland was pleased, and cynically amused, by this very British behaviour!

Unfortunately, very little of his music is now available on discs. Most of it was recorded at the height of his fame in the 1930s. These recordings are now either unobtainable or not up to present-day technical standards. In recent years, the record companies have been increasingly unwilling to record British or any other contemporary music.[2] This is due to rising costs, to the increase of 'pop' music, which overloads their facilities, and to public apathy. To offset this, the British Council has subsidised recordings; but Ireland, already so well-known at that time, was not, perhaps, the sort of composer the Council wished to help, believing that those who had *never* been recorded should have priority. I myself believe that quality is better than quantity or good intentions. On the other hand Ireland has been well and truly published. Almost everything he wrote has been printed.

Like all of us, the man had his weaknesses. The particular cross he, and his friends, had to bear was his belief that he was being terribly neglected. This was perhaps true in very recent years, when the serialists were trying to sweep us all into the dustbin, but certainly was untrue for the greater part of his career.

'Nobody plays my music', he used to complain only too frequently. One of his friends was forced to exclaim, 'But John, your piano concerto was done at the Proms this week, and has had a broadcast; and isn't there a performance abroad?' After a short silence, Ireland replied, 'Oh, so they're trying to play it to death!'

As a personality, he was a little bit aloof, but not at all a member of the Establishment. There was a good deal of old-world courtesy about him, though, and he was always rather formally dressed.

During the years in which I studied with him, he never unbent very much; he called me Mr Arnell, but did once ask me to dinner – very different from the far more casual teaching methods today, when everyone is Jack and Jill.

[2] Arnell is writing in 1962, soon after the establishment of the Lyrita Recorded Edition by Richard Itter, and before he started orchestral recordings – the first two of which were Ireland's orchestral music – and long before the establishment of other independent record labels that would develop this repertoire.

He wrote music of many kinds, mostly songs and piano works, but in addition many excellent sonatas and other chamber works, two overtures, a choral work *These Things Shall Be* and a film score for *The Overlanders*. There are no operas – he found them pretentious – and no symphonies.

Without a trace of condescension, one might say that John Ireland was a minor master, comparable some people might think, with Fauré or Grieg: his was not a negligible achievement.

2. *Alan Bush*

Script for a BBC John Ireland Centenary Programme, October 1979.

FROM 1918 to 1922 I was a student at the Royal Academy of Music. One of my piano professors was Miss Lily West, who had performed some of John Ireland's piano music in public. I studied his *London Pieces*, composed in 1917–20, and his Sonata, composed in 1918–20. Miss Lily West introduced me to him personally in 1921, when I played his Sonata to him. Subsequently, I played this Sonata in the Wigmore Hall in 1929 and also in Berlin in 1931.

I left the Royal Academy of Music in July 1922 and started my five years of composition studies with John Ireland in September of that year.

John Ireland's methods of teaching composition followed those which he had himself undergone twenty years before as a student of Charles Villiers Stanford at the Royal College of Music. For my first year, I studied the idiom and contrapuntal technique of Palestrina and was introduced to English, Irish and Scottish folk music. I then proceeded to actual composition, and wrote a *Fantasy Sonata* for violin and piano, op. 3, a String Quartet in A minor, op. 4, a Quartet for piano, violin, viola and cello, op. 5, songs, a *Symphonic Impression* for orchestra, op. 8, and lastly, a Prelude and Fugue for piano, op. 9.

John Ireland was an exacting teacher. A student of his had to produce work of consistently high quality, though voluminous quantity was not expected. During my period with him I was also appearing as a concert pianist. In 1928, I went abroad to study with Artur Schnabel, and, entering Berlin University, I studied the elements of philosophy and musicology systematically. I returned to Great Britain in 1931 and continued to see John Ireland quite frequently.

In 1936, he was invited by the B.B.C. to compose a work which was to celebrate the accession to the throne of King George VI. As there was little time, he asked me to do the orchestration for him. He would indicate the instrumentation he had in mind. This work I did and he dedicated the piece to me. It is the choral work, *These Things Shall Be*.

In assessing his contribution to musical art in Great Britain, one should remember that except for some compositions by Elgar, such as the Violin Concerto and the first part of *The Dream* of *Gerontius*, the general level of professional musical life was poor.[3] Yet in John Ireland's contributions to music are to be found his thirty-nine solo piano works and his sixty-eight songs for voice and piano, which are musical works of such quantity and quality that he was unrivalled

---

[3] We cannot explain Bush's assessment of musical life, nor his preference for the first part of *Gerontius* over the second.

in both these genres during the first half of the twentieth century by any British composer and by very few composers of any nationality during this period.

In his mature works, the basis is an English melodic style, absorbed during his study with Stanford. At first he combined this with a harmonic vocabulary, derived either from nineteenth-century Germany chromaticism or from French twentieth-century Impressionism; but later his harmony was developed in an English idiom, personal to himself, which overcame the eclecticism which colours his earlier mature works.

3. Benjamin Britten

During his time as a student of Ireland at the Royal College of Music, Britten frequently mentions Ireland and his music in his diaries and letters. The following extracts arranged in chronological order document Britten's encounters with Ireland and his music between 1930 and 1936 as they were recorded in his diary.[4]

Thursday 25 September 1930 (p. 54)
Am at College from 10–1. Waiting for J. Ireland for 1½ (10–11.30), & he eventually doesn't turn up.

Friday 26 September 1930 (p. 54)
Practice 9.30–10.30, then go to Coll. & have ½ hr (waiting ½ hr outside his door) lesson with Ireland. Very nice, but he is even more critical than Bridge – no that's not possible – anyhow he's very good.

Thursday 2 October 1930 (p. 54)
I go to College for lesson with Ireland, but he doesn't turn up (rehearsal); & I walk back to Prince's Sq. ... Go ... to Queen's Hall & prom. – ... J. Ireland Pft Concerto (very beautiful, interesting & excellently played) ...

Thursday 9 October 1930 (p. 54)
Have 1 hrs. lesson with John Ireland (after waiting ¾ hr): very nice tho' very subduing! He's going to take me thro' a course of Palestrina; tho' to reassure me he tells me that every musician, worth his salt has done this.

Thursday 16 October 1930 (p. 55)
I go to College in morning & have a topping lesson with John Ireland for nearly 2 hrs. 10.15 or less – 12.0 He is <u>terribly</u> critical and enough to take the heart out of any one! ...

Tuesday 21 October 1930 (p. 55)
... leave at 3.45 to return to write the Mass in the style of Palestrina for Ireland. I spend most of after tea & after dinner doing it (in Henderson's room): this strict counterpoint does take ages to write! [The Mass, dated 'Oct 4th 1930–Jan 16th 1931' survives in the Britten Archive but appears never to have been performed.]

---

[4] *Journeying Boy: The Diaries of the Young Benjamin Britten, 1928–1938*, ed. John Evans (London: Faber & Faber, 2009, 2010), page numbers as cited throughout.

Thursday 30 October 1930 (p. 56)
Go to College at 10:0 for lesson with Ireland (He arrives 10.30!). V. fierce! I had done rather a bad bit of pt. writing in the mass – those consecutive 5^{ths} always escape my notice ...

Thursday 4 December 1930 (p. 57)
I go to College at 10.0 & have v. nice lesson with Ireland – he is quite pleased with my Credo ...

Friday 5 December 1930 (p. 58)
... I go after dinner to a concert at the R.C.M. (1st Orchestra). Cockaigne (Elgar) J. Ireland pft. concerto (which I like better each time – Helen Perkin plays it beautifully) ...

Thursday 22 January 1931 (p. 61)
I go to John Ireland's studio for my lesson at 10.0. Have a very instructive one, if not very encouraging! Certainly I seem to be doing nothing right or worth doing nowadays. ...

Thursday 12 February 1931 (p. 64)
Go to Ireland's Studio at 10.0. He is quite pleased with my work (more or less i.e.) except for numerous consecutive fifths. Walk back ...

Thursday 19 February 1931 (p. 64)
I go to Ireland's Studio for my composition Lesson. It is, I suppose a very good one, but certainly not a cheering one! I am now "getting it" for variety of styles in my carol – it is quite right, but that doesn't make it any the more pleasant! ...

Thursday 26 February 1931 (p. 65)
Composition lesson at 10.0 Ireland is quite pleased with my latest carol. ... Go to Chamber Concert at R.C.M. 8.15. In a long programme Helen Perkin (Ireland's star & best comp. pupil) plays her own Ballade for pft. V. competent with only about 1 bit of original work. Too long, I thought, for material ...

Tuesday 17 March 1931 (p. 67)
Go to John Ireland's via the college at 10.30. Have v. good lesson. I think he quite likes "Preparations". ...

Thursday 19 March 1931 (p. 67)
Quite good lesson with Ireland in Chelsea at 10.0. ...

Friday 8 May 1931 (p. 72)
... 1st Comp. lesson with Ireland. He is quite pleased with My fugues, more especially with the last ...

Thursday 4 June 1931 (p. 75)
Lesson with Ireland 10.0–11.30; quite helpful. He likes my second slow. Mov. Better than the 1st one ...

Thursday 18 June 1931 (p. 77)
Go to Ireland for good comp. lesson at 10.0. ...

Wednesday 15 July 1931 (p. 78)
I go for a lesson to Chelsea with Ireland at 10.30. He is quite pleased with my Psalm so far. ...

Thursday 8 October 1931 (p. 85)
John Ireland cannot have me at 10.0, which I find when I arrive at his studio at this hour, but I have a lesson at 8.45 in evening, being back at 11.30, Mostly talk, – his opinions of various contemporary composers! ...

30 October 1931 (p. 87)
Lesson with Ireland at Coll. At 11.10. V. good; on orch. of ballet ...

4 December 1931 (p. 91)
No lesson with Ireland again which I find out after tramping to the R.C.M. ...

Friday 11 December 1931 (p. 92)
... Lesson with Ireland nominally beginning at 11.10 actually past 11.45 as he was rehearsing a trio of his ...

22 January 1932 (p. 97)
Have about ¼ hrs. lesson with Ireland at (nominally) 10.35 – 11.50. He spends the rest of the time telephoning, finishing someone else's lesson & talking about his concerto. ...

Wed 10 Feb 1932 (pp. 98–9)
Listen to Ireland's Pft. Conc. from Bournemouth before tea [when Helen Perkin was the soloist] ... Go to B.B.C. concert Queen's Hall ... Ireland's magnificent Mai-Dun – quite well played for the B.B.C. orch.

Tuesday 1 March 1932 (p. 101)
Lesson with Ireland at 10.55: have nothing to show him, except orchestration of Psalms ...

27 May 1932 (p. 105)
Lesson with Ireland in morning at 10.37 & investigate about coming Mendelssohn schol ...

Tuesday 12 July 1932 (p. 110)
Still very hot – R.C.M. for lesson with Ireland. He's very pleased with my Sinfonietta ...

11 October 1932 (p. 117)
... a Concert of the Music Club: – Mangeot's International St. Quart. (pretty poor) play ... with B.B.C. wind a long, meandering Pastoral Phantasy by Helen Perkin who plays Ireland's fine Sonatina rather poorly ...

Thursday 5 January 1933 (p. 127)
... There is some doubt as to whether I shall continue with Ireland at the R.C.M. Pop wrote to him, & he replies very agitatedly[5] + a telegram (& he also rings up F.B. [i.e. Frank Bridge])

[5] Ireland's letter to Mr Britten is dated 4 January 1933 and is written from Ivy Cottage, Ashington, Sussex. He writes: 'I very much regret it if anything has occurred to lead

Friday 27 January 1933 (p. 129)
V. good lesson with Ireland in morning. Write letters & rewrite end of Var. IV in aft. ...

Tuesday 18 April 1933 (p. 138)
... listen to Chamber Concert ... Ireland's 1st Vln Sonata (himself & that superb Brosa). Fine material but over long. ...

Friday 26 May 1933 (p. 141)
Bit of copying before lesson with Ireland at 10.35. We play my Oboe Quart. To him ...

Thursday 9 November 1933 (p. 153)
... I go to Ireland's Studio at 5.0 for lesson. But the dear man doesn't turn up. So far in 8 weeks I have had 4 (so-called) lessons from him ...

Friday 12 January 1934 [Lowestoft] (p. 196)
... Listen to last Brit. Music Concts inc J. Irelands new Legend for Pft (Helen Perkin – inadequate) & Orch. Seemed unsatisfactory & meandering – & rather reminiscent – tho' some nice things in it ...

Sunday 22 April 1934 (p. 209)
... Listen to an Ansermet Concert from the BBC at 9.5. H. Perkin plays Ireland's 'Legend' with orch. – an attractive idea, but he hasn't the creative power or technique to do it – tho' there is fine atmosphere in parts of it. ...

Saturday 29 September 1934 (p. 226)
... Berlioz' interesting Corsair Ov. & Irelands meandering Pft concerto. The form is so loose & it really is only cheap ballade music (attractive in its way) touched up. Helen Perkin doesn't make it sound as effective or snappy as she might.

Tuesday 1 September 1936 (p. 369)
... Meet Boyd Neel for a meal & then we go to Prom together to hear Rubensten [*sic*] play Ireland's piano concerto. Of course he plays it brilliantly, although last movement didn't go well – lack of rehearsal. But the work wears terribly thin – bad scoring & construction; & all the lush beauty of the 1890 Ballades dressed in modern clichés. ...

Although Ireland could make acid remarks about Britten during and after the war – indeed, it seems almost to have been expected from him by a close group of friends and colleague – his appreciation of Britten's achievement certainly seemed

yourself or your son Benjamin to feel (however mistakenly) that I do not take the keenest interest in his work or musical affairs. It was a most unfortunate thing that I was prevented from giving him his last lesson last term, & I fully intended this should be made up at my Studio with a really long time working together. However, at mid day on that Friday, my Sister was taken seriously ill, & the whole of my time and thought was taken up with that matter for some days. I was also sorry that I did not see Benjamin, at the time, to congratulate him on his fine Quintet, a work of which he knows I hold the very highest opinion – as, indeed of all he has done of late with me ...' (Britten-Pears Library).

to grow, a regard reinforced by the warmth of his appreciation of Britten and Pears singing his songs. For example, writing to Peter Pears on 11 December 1947 he was notably enthusiastic:

> I can find no words adequate to express gratitude and appreciation of your wonderful performance of my Songs last Monday.[6] Such a performance was a unique experience for the composer. Both the musicians present (Clark & Bush) were deeply moved. Scott Goddard listened in, & wrote me:–
>
> 'That sounded very lovely last night – a rare treat. To my thinking P.P. sang them with great expressiveness and sympathy. Listening, I felt: How strange – they might have been written for him!'
>
> I shall see you on Monday as I am coming to Searle's broadcast. There I hope to hear if there is any hope of a recording.
>
> Meanwhile, a thousand thanks to a truly great artist.

Ireland and Pears performed Ireland's songs at the Wigmore Hall on 14 May 1951, when Britten insisted on turning pages for Ireland.[7] Ireland's companion Norah Kirby wrote, 'I was most impressed with Britten's attitude towards John. He asked whether he might turn pages and John was rather reluctant. Britten, however, persuaded him to agree and really his behaviour was surprisingly nice. He treated John rather as boy would have treated a much revered master. He kept in the background so far as the audience was concerned and was most deferential without putting on any act. He really seemed sincerely proud of his old master.' On 17 May Ireland wrote to Pears:

> A thousand thanks for your <u>superb</u> presentation of my songs on Monday, and for giving me so much of your time & energy at rehearsals, in a period when you were overworked and none too well.
>
> It was a memorable occasion, and made a deep impression – even Mann[8], of the Times, seemed moved by it, if one can judge by his sympathetic notice.
>
> And I was happy that Ben honoured me by his presence on the platform – even though this made me extra conscious of my pianistic deficiencies!
>
> My love – and thanks – to you both.
>
> Yours gratefully
>
> John Ireland

Later Ireland wrote very cordially to Britten about his operas *Billy Budd*, *Gloriana* and *The Turn of the Screw*. After the first performance of *Billy Budd* at Covent Garden[9] he delayed his congratulations to Britten, finally writing on Christmas Eve 1951:

> My dear B.B.,
>
> Thinking you would be overwhelmed with a deluge of letters about "Billy Budd", I have delayed writing to tell you I was present at the first performance

[6] 8 December 1947.

[7] The concert was broadcast and Ireland had it recorded off-air, now issued for the first time on a Dutton compact disc CDBP 9799.

[8] William Mann (1924–89).

[9] 1 December 1951.

at Covent Garden. Melville's story was well known to me, and I was deeply moved by your splendid musical expression of the profound emotion of it all. Your opera is indeed a masterpiece, and embodies music which is entirely characteristic of your own genius, not a phrase or even a <u>bar</u> of which could have been written by any other composer.

The clarity, the economy of means – the invariable certainty of touch – the spontaneity, the invention – all constituted a perfect joy to me.

I believe I recognised the unique quality of your gifts when you came up for your scholarship at the R.C.M. If only Frank Bridge could have heard "Billy Budd". He too would have rejoiced, as I do. Need I, can I say more –

"What were praise left to say
Have not been said by me?"

Yours in affection and admiration

J.I.

But perhaps the most interesting positive reaction by Ireland was to Britten's opera based on Henry James's ghost story *The Turn of the Screw*. Ireland first responded to Britten about it after Britten had sent him greetings for his seventy-fifth birthday. Ireland wrote from Rock Mill, in a letter dated 26 August 1954:

My dear B.B.

I was delighted to get your letter and birthday greetings and wish I had seen you and Peter personally on 13th – but you are both <u>ever</u> in my affectionate thoughts. I knew from Leslie Boosey that you were terribly busy with the new opera, so I will refrain from harassing you with a long letter.

I wish you every success in this stupendous venture, and am all agog to learn how you have managed to handle (in your own inimitable way) the terrific problems presented by Henry James's famous story. You are at any rate the only composer in the world who could adequately approach it, and I am sure it will constitute another of your many triumphs.

Having left London after living there for 60 years I now go there as little as possible – but if there is a chance of seeing you and Peter in October I will make a special effort.

You know well, my dear, dear Ben, the deep regard and admiration I have felt for you and your work ever since I first met you when you were still in your 'teens – you know also, I hope, that Europe holds no more loyal and constant supporter of you in the maze of jealousy your well-deserved success has aroused in the world of pygmies, who – well – I need say no more!

My love to you and to Peter, and again, warmest thanks for your kind thoughts and remembrance of your old friend,

John

P.S. When you and Peter came to Lancing for 'St. Nicholas' you were within a few miles of Rock Mill – a lovely place which will delight you. You must visit the next time you are this way.

Ireland listened to Britten's opera on the radio and was certainly impressed with the technical command, writing in a letter dated 4 June 1955:

For a long time I have meant to tell you how immensely I was impressed by 'The Turn of the Screw' of which I heard the two broadcasts (from Venice and London). It is a wonderful piece of imaginative musical expression. What you have achieved with that small number of instruments and the normal tonality is nothing short of miraculous. Much more could be said (and no doubt has been) but at any rate your music held me spellbound from the first note to the last.

Benjamin Britten and Peter Pears performed Ireland's song cycle *The Land of Lost Content* at the Aldeburgh Festival on 22 June 1959, on which occasion Britten contributed the following programme note.

John Ireland will be eighty years of age this August, and so we are giving this Cycle tonight as a tribute to a composer of strong personal gifts and real single-mindedness of purpose. Ireland is best known for his songs and chamber music, and rightly so, because they form the bulk of his output and contain his most individual thoughts. His first great impact on the public was with his Second Violin Sonata (1917) written under the terrible shadow of the First World War.

This Cycle, perhaps his most personal, certainly his most famous, was published in 1921. There have been many English composers to set Housman's poems, and none, to my mind, more sympathetically successful than Ireland; there is much in common between Ireland and Housman, who 'in his strange, magical, musical, and at times sentimental way ... seems to say good-bye to the vanishing peacefulness of the country, and to the freshness and innocence of its young men'. These words come from a recent broadcast by William Plomer on the centenary of the birth of the poet. It is good that we can also pay tribute to Housman by including these settings of some of his most succinct and characteristic poems.

The six songs are: 1 *Lent Lily*, typical of Ireland's rhythmic suppleness; 2 *Ladslove*, a crystalline setting of the Narcissus legend; 3 *Goal and Wicket*, tough and bitter; 4 *The Vain Desire*, very personal tonal ambiguity; 5 *The Encounter*, strong and rhythmic with a fine tritonic bass; 6 *Epilogue*, in which is embedded a quotation from his setting of 'My true love hath my heart' – a phrase with great significance for the composer.

4. Ernest J. Moeran

This first appeared as 'John Ireland as Teacher', Monthly Musical Record, March 1931, pp. 67–8.

I LIVED and worked for a time in a Kentish village. One day I was feeling very pleased with myself; having composed a pianoforte piece which I liked. I was playing it over when my landlord, the village grocer, looked in on me. 'You made that all up yourself, did you?' he asked, and added rather sorrowfully, 'Ah, I wish I could do that; but then you see, I never had the education.'

I should mention that my good friend's knowledge of music amounted to precisely NIL. He was one of those who even had to be told when the National

Anthem was being played. It is undoubtedly a fact that there are some people who imagine that musical composition can be taught, even in the same way that a knowledge of languages, chemistry, mathematics, hairdressing, horse-coping and countless other subjects can be hammered into the receptive brain of any willing pupil by a skilled teacher. Also there are many who believe that, given enthusiasm and a first-rate professor of composition, any intelligent musician may become a composer if he works sufficiently hard. Hence, unfortunately, the existence of so much of that type of music which is known as 'Kapellmeister' music.

In this sense, John Ireland, in spite of the title of this essay, is not a teacher of composition. This at once is his virtue. He is a very wise adviser and an astute critic, both of his own work and of that of others, and he succeeds in instilling into his pupils that blessed principle of self-criticism. Moreover, he possesses an uncanny knack of immediately and accurately probing the aesthetic content of what is put before him, thus arriving at the state of mind which gave it birth, and understanding its underlying mood and aims. It is here that his sympathy is aroused, for he has the faculty of feeling the music from the pupil's point of view, and his wide experience then steps in to suggest the solution of difficulties, and not only the technical ones.

These are not the qualities of an academic teacher of composition, who is accustomed to dole out weekly lessons of forty minutes' duration to all sorts and conditions of students. Ireland is not a mere machine whose brain may be purchased at so much an hour. I recollect one session – this is a better word than 'lesson' in his case – which lasted for about an hour, and continued for another half-hour after tea. At this point Ireland advised me to go home and work at the problem concerned while our discussion was still fresh in my mind, and to bring it back to him later in the evening for a final talk.

Ireland does not believe that any standardized technique can be taught. 'Every composer must make his own technique', is his dictum. At the same time he is a firm believer in the value of the study of strict counterpoint, and, much to my surprise and sorrow, I found myself expected to spend many weary hours struggling with *cantus firmus,* and its embellishments in all the species. I state emphatically that I am glad of this today, for I have come to realize that only by this means can a subconscious sense of harmony, melody, and rhythm be acquired.

Genuine harmony arises out of counterpoint, for it implies contrary motion among the parts; otherwise it is no longer harmony, but faux-bourdon. Moreover, there can be no rhythm without melody; otherwise it descends to mere metre, which is not music. On the other hand, melody, divorced from harmony and rhythm, degenerates into a meandering succession of fragmentary ideas, bearing little relationship one to another, and totally lacking organic unity. Thus it is that the greatest music, from Palestrina and Vittoria down through Beethoven to Wagner and the present day, has been polyphonic. For without polyphony nothing can be complete, and any attempt to break away from it has invariably ended in a blind alley.

I confessed just now that first of all I was surprised at Ireland's insistence on counterpoint, but I hope I have grown a little wiser than I was just over eleven years ago when I commenced work with him, and I feel unbounded gratitude for having been encouraged to do the drudgery. I deliberately use the word 'encouraged', for Ireland has no interest in work done which is not worthwhile, and it is by the lucidity of his argument that he expounds to his pupils the logic of doing something which hitherto may have seemed futile, and the task, distasteful as it may appear at the time, is undertaken with the sure sense that there is a real reason for doing it, and doing it to the best of one's ability. Personally, I have always been so lazy that it would have been nearly impossible to induce me to go to the trouble of working a single counterpoint exercise, had I not been encouraged to believe in some very definite value in so doing.

Ireland's remarkable individuality in his own work does not hinder him from observing and fostering unity of style in the work of his pupils, even though it may be very different from his own. He will not tolerate the slightest falling off or failing in continuity. He has no use for padding in any form, and he does not consider a piece of work done with until the minutest detail has been scrutinized again, down to the last semiquaver rest and the smallest mark of phrasing or dynamics. 'What about that *sforzando*?' he will ask. 'Have you thought carefully about it?'

His own mastery of form has been evolved in the wake of some hard thinking and deep experience, the results of which, apart from his creative work, bear fruit in the guidance which he is able to give to those who study with him. For him, form does not necessarily imply a dry-as-dust formula of first and second subjects, double-bars and so on. He enjoins his pupils to look ahead and plan.

I took him one day the exposition of a movement in sonata form. 'This is most exciting', he said. 'But the question is, will you be able to go one better before the end? Otherwise, you will have an anticlimax.' Here again, Ireland is emphasizing one of the *raisons d'être* of the heritage which has come down to us from the old masters. All the music which has escaped consignment to the shelf has been inherently logical. Music, without logical continuity and shape, is lifeless from its inception.

As for instrumentation, Ireland holds that the true principles thereof are not necessarily to be found in text-books, but that they eventually come about in relation to the music ('Every composer must make his own technique'). It is essential, however, to understand the true nature and character of each individual instrument, apart from its compass and its technical resources. This is knowledge which can only be gained by listening to concerted music, but it is when the beginner sets forth on his own first full score that the experienced adventurer is able to guide his faltering steps. It is here that Ireland's psychological sense, in getting to the rock-bottom of what the pupil is making for, enables him to put his finger on the weaknesses and, by means of his considered suggestion, to point out the right road to take to overcome them.

I have tried here to show that John Ireland is an exceptional counsellor for those who are fortunate enough to work under his teaching. When all is said and done, it is the fact that he is the very antithesis of the so-called teacher of composition: that is the secret of his success. He gives unstintingly of his very best to those who come under him, and behind that keen intelligence which he brings to bear on their work and its many aspects and problems, his pupils soon discover a very human personality and a warm friend.

5. Humphrey Searle

This account is taken from Chapter 5 of Humphrey Searle's autobiography
Quadrille With a Raven, *published on the MusicWeb International website*
(www.musicweb-international.com/searle/london.htm).

FOR my composition lessons at the college Walton had suggested that I should
study with John Ireland. Ireland was chiefly known for his impressionist piano
music – he was an excellent pianist – and songs, particularly his sensitive and
lyrical settings of Housman and Hardy, apart of course from the famous *Sea Fever*.
The College compiled an official time-table of pupils for him, but he refused to
teach in the building itself, and we all had to go to his studio in Gunter Grove,
Chelsea. As I was a latecomer in the College term I was his last pupil of the day;
when I arrived there were usually four or five of his other pupils in the studio,
none of whom had had much in the way of a lesson. Ireland used to walk round
and round the room, and as he passed one of his pupil's MS on the piano he would
throw out remarks such as 'Y'know, I am the only person who was a pupil of Elgar',
and he said to me: 'Don't use your trombones on the fourth beat of the bar; don't
use your trombones on the fourth beat of the bar!' He would also make uncompli-
mentary comments on his colleagues, such as: 'That man Williams, gallivanting
about all over America when he should be staying at home thinking about death.'
'Walton, coining money hand over fist.' And 'Master Britten, always having something to show in the shop window – if he farts they'll record it.' (Britten had been
a pupil of his at the College, and I gather they did not get on too well.)[10] But most
of this prickliness was in fact assumed, and really he was a very endearing character. My short period of lessons with him led to a friendship lasting many years
up to the time when he retired to the country towards the end of his life. He would
sometimes take me out to supper at the Queen's Restaurant, Sloane Square, and
we would have long discussions on music and many other subjects.

Ireland was very interested in primitive ritual and magic, an element which
may be felt in some of his works such as *The Forgotten Rite* and *Mai-Dun* (an
evocation of the ruined Maiden Castle in Dorset). He was impressed by Arthur
Machen who had written several books on these subjects ('He only lives in two
rooms in Amersham, but he's got the works'). He also referred half humorously to
what he considered the neglect of his music ('Mai Dun may not be done', 'nobody
loves me, nobody plays my music'). When Julian Herbage of the BBC pointed out
to him that three major works of his were being broadcast within a few days, be
countered with: 'Hm – I suppose they want to kill it by overplaying it.' But he had
a good sense of humour and I enjoyed my time with him. Among my fellow pupils
were Richard Arnell, Peter Crossley-Holland, Patricia Morgan and Peter Pope.

[10] But see pp. 337–43.

PART IV

Notable Articles on Ireland
and his Music

CHAPTER 26

John Ireland: Two Reminiscences

Jocelyn Brooke

(1) *From* London Magazine, *April 1965, pp. 75–80*

I HAD better begin by saying that I am not competent to assess the merits or the status of Ireland as a composer, and these random notes are purely personal. Well – perhaps not 'purely', for I had known and loved Ireland's music, in an uninstructed way, for nearly forty years before I met him, and I cannot wholly dissociate the man from the music,

Let us begin with the music. In my first or second term at Bedales[1] (I had just turned fourteen), my music mistress, a middle-aged lady called Miss Turner, used to gather her pupils together, every so often, for classes of 'musical appreciation'. She was a good pianist, but her tastes in music might well have made her superiors on the music staff raise their eyebrows. At least one of these sessions was devoted entirely to the music of John Ireland, for which Miss Turner had a passion; she rated Ireland high above all modern composers and (I suspect) above most composers of any other age. After playing half a dozen of his pieces, she turned to her audience and said: 'Now tell me *quite honestly* – what did you think of them?'

Being a dishonest and pretentious child, I think I said I liked them; I wanted to please Miss Turner, and already had slight ambitions to be a highbrow (chiefly, no doubt, because I was quite hopeless at all sports and games). Most of the other children were more honest, saying that they thought the pieces 'discordant', and full of 'wrong notes'. (It seems strange, at this date, that Ireland's music should have seemed so defiantly 'modern' – even to children – some forty-odd years ago; but Ireland, I suppose, was almost the only composer later than Brahms whose music I – and probably the other children – had ever heard.) Secretly, I agreed with my fellow pupils; but I dared not go back on my original judgment. I decided, in fact, there and then, that I would like John Ireland; perhaps some quality in the music had – in spite of the 'wrong notes' – genuinely appealed to me, though I think it more likely that the attraction lay in Ireland's evocative titles: *The Island Spell, The Towing Path, Chelsea Reach*. This latter piece was a special favourite with Miss Turner, and I did in time honestly come to like it: it had a fine, flowing tune, some juicy chords, and not too many dissonances.

I suppose I must have heard a certain amount of Ireland's music during my later schooldays, though at Bedales our musical training tended to concentrate, austerely, upon the three Bs (with Chopin as occasional light relief). After a year or so Miss Turner, regrettably, left the school; perhaps she wasn't really a very good teacher, for her music-lessons were too often devoted, either to impromptu recitals of John Ireland, or to long and fascinating discussions on spiritualism, to which she was also addicted. But before she left she told me a rather touching little story: she had been to a concert in London at which John Ireland was actually performing; he was her hero, the occasion was plainly a major event in her

---

[1] Bedales, the progressive co-educational boarding school near Petersfield, Hampshire.

Fig. 28 Jocelyn Brooke.
Sketch by Juliet Pannett.

life, and goodness knows what romantic and fascinating figure she had expected – perhaps a glamorous combination of Chopin and Paganini.

'But d'you know', she confessed to me, almost tearfully, 'he turned out to be just a rather *grubby* little man.'

Now the lighting of concert halls is sometimes defective, and performers do not always appear, in the matter of looks, at their best. Yet I find it difficult to believe that John Ireland ever looked 'grubby'; and I wish that Miss Turner could have met him, as I did, in his last years, when he was the very pattern of the exquisitely mannered, well-dressed and (it must be emphasized) scrupulously clean old gentleman.

It wasn't till after I left school that I really became addicted (and I think this the right word in the context) to John Ireland's music. I began to seek it out: listening to any performances of his works on the wireless, and even buying some of his easier piano pieces, a few of which I managed to muddle through in a ham-handed and incompetent way. My musical tastes ran mainly to Debussy, Ravel and Delius, though later I developed a liking for Erik Satie and Les Six – particularly Poulenc. Being an intellectual snob, I enjoyed extolling the merits of these composers to such friends of mine (and I had several) to whom any music later than Beethoven was anathema. But about Ireland I kept rather quiet. He remained separated from my other musical enjoyments, the pleasure he gave me was perhaps not purely musical, but rather 'literary', consisting as it largely did of vague and 'poetic' associations. My musical friends, if I did happen to mention him, tended to write him off as a minor composer: 'Oh yes, of course, his second Violin and Piano sonata was pretty good, but ...'

Perhaps the 'but' was in some sense justified; Ireland was admittedly a minia-turist, he never wrote a symphony, and apart from his Piano Concerto his works are all conceived on a relatively small scale. Nonetheless, his music continued to haunt me, particularly the Cello Sonata, *The Forgotten Rite* and the piano pieces. These works *said* something to me; and I gather from other of his admirers that they have shared my own experience. Ireland's music, in fact, has the quality of a personal communication which, if one happens to be, so to speak, on the right 'wave-length', seems to be addressed to oneself alone. Most people, I have found (whether professional musicians or mere music-lovers), have no such feeling about Ireland, even though they may admire his technical dexterity as a composer. But for the minority who are in sympathy with the spirit of his work (and this category, again, includes both professionals and amateurs), much of his music corresponds almost uncannily with certain moods and emotions which one recognizes as being part of one's own experience, associated in the main with the English countryside and with the tutelary genius of particular places: the sense of

> old, forgotten far-off things
> And battles long ago.

I can think of no other composer with whom I have (and had for many years before I met Ireland himself) this sense of personal relationship; and incidentally, his evocations of country scenes are for me far more vivid and profound than the more calculated, folk-song-based rusticity of Vaughan Williams. It is worth noting, by the way, that Ireland never wrote a note which was derived from folk-music, though he admitted to being influenced by plainsong. Nor did he rely for his effects upon musical 'impressionism'; he was very little affected, for that matter, by Debussy and his other near-contemporaries in France, and I can only think of one work, the piano piece *April* (with its suggestion of an April shower), which can fairly be called impressionist. Much of his inspiration was confessedly literary (many of his works have suggestive quotations appended); among poets he had a special affinity with Housman (his song-settings of whom are surely unrivalled), and his favourite modern prose-writer was Arthur Machen, whose deep interest in the occult he shared, though he was notably unwilling to discuss the subject.

In a semi-autobiographical book of mine I once tried to convey (in purely literary terms, needless to say) my feeling about Ireland's music at its most charac-teristic, and I think I cannot do better than quote part of the passage here:

> The dominant image evoked is of a wooded and remote countryside, silent and frost-bound in the early twilight of a winter's evening. It is the dead season, yet there is a subtle, half-realized feeling of spring in the air: a stirring of bird-life in the woods, the catkins lengthening upon the hazels, the first celandine, perhaps, gleaming precociously in the sheltered hedgerow. After a day of rain and unbroken cloud, the western sky is suddenly clear, a broad rift of brightness palely green over the humped outline of the woods: the days are 'drawing out', and the land itself seems to extend with the length-ening days, one is suddenly aware of far, illimitable distances. The dimension of Time, also, is extended in this country of the mind, Uricon or Camelot lie beyond those further woods; and on the beech-crowned hill, where the

cromlech rises stark against the rainy sunset, the ancient and bloody rites are celebrated anew, and the beacon fires are lit for Beltane or Samhain.

Now this, as I very well know, represents the sort of subjective and literary attitude to music which is guaranteed to make any genuine musician heave. But strangely enough John Ireland himself who happened to come across the book some time before I met him – didn't heave at all. On the contrary, he showed the passage to Norah Kirby, the saintly woman who so devotedly cared for him in his last years, and said 'No *music critic*' (enunciating the phrase with a devastating contempt) 'has ever understood my music as well as *that* man.'

This, of course, sounds abominably conceited on my part, and will suggest that I am making special claims for my intuitive judgment as a non-musician. But I am honestly doing no such thing, and when Mrs Kirby first told me the story, I could only suppose that Ireland, perhaps from a natural vanity, had grossly exaggerated the value of what I had written. After all, most of us like a bit of praise, even from the wrong quarter, and John Ireland, who had suffered a longish period of comparative neglect, was probably quite pleased to get a write-up, even by somebody so dim and unmusical as myself. He was also by this time very old, and was disposed to be hostile to the contemporary breed of music-critics. On the other hand, one should recall that Ireland was, after all, an old-fashioned romantic composer: he felt that his music 'expressed' something, and Stravinsky's bleak assertion (in his autobiography) that music expressed nothing, seemed to John Ireland sheer nonsense. Later, I was convinced that John had really meant what he said: lengthy conversations with him persuaded me that a certain 'country of the mind', roughly adumbrated in the piece I had written about him, was a territory which we genuinely shared in common.

In the late 1920s and early '30s I had several friends who frequented the pubs of Chelsea, and who claimed to be acquainted with John Ireland. I longed to meet him, but I was shy of chasing celebrities; I wouldn't even seek a casual introduction, still less would I have dared to write a fan-letter to anybody so much older than myself, and so eminent.

It was not, in fact, till some thirty years later that we did at last meet. Our encounter was mainly due to the passage in the book of mine from which I have quoted. It turned out that Ireland, after reading the book, had expressed a desire to meet me, though like myself thirty years before he was far too shy to write and suggest a meeting. It was a curious reversal of rôles, to say the least. A year or two passed; a composer friend of mine who had been his pupil did suggest taking me down to see him, but the plan came to nothing. Perhaps John was afraid I should bring my wife: he was not particularly keen on the female sex, and much as he enjoyed meeting younger composers and writers, he dreaded meeting their wives. As it happened, I was not married, and at long last an old friend and admirer of John's (having managed to persuade him, presumably, that I was a bachelor and likely to remain one) took me down to the converted windmill in Sussex where the composer was then living.

Far from being the 'grubby little man' who had so disillusioned Miss Turner in the early 1920s, John Ireland was one of the most distinguished-looking men I have ever met: like Yeats, he looked (and was) one of nature's aristocrats. He was by now nearing eighty, and was indeed becoming senile; his memory had begun to fail, and his conversation was apt to be repetitive. He had composed nothing for years, and for a considerable time had not even played the piano; yet, most touchingly, he had that very morning been practising *Month's Mind* and *The Holy Boy*, which he knew to be two of my favourite pieces; and he played them to me that afternoon.

His talk was always rather grave and carefully pondered. Though I came to know him very well, he always kept what Cyril Connolly, writing of Desmond MacCarthy, called 'a certain Johnsonian distance' between himself and even his more intimate friends. He was a Victorian, and something of a Puritan, yet he would discuss any subject under the sun, however scabrous – but always (and again I am reminded of MacCarthy) in strictly impersonal terms. He also enjoyed making malicious remarks – in a poker-faced, *pince-sans-rire* manner – about his fellow-composers: a taste which he shared with that *éminence grise* of early twentieth century French music, Erik Satie.

Thus, I once happened to say of an eminent contemporary musician, 'He had a bad accident recently, didn't he?' To which John replied drily: 'Not *bad enough*.'

He was also a considerable raconteur, and many of his anecdotes had the same quality of dead-pan malice. There was the story, for instance, of his meeting with the celebrated composer X. John was bemoaning the fact that, nowadays, his works were so seldom performed on the wireless. 'Oh *really?*' said X. 'Why, I spend half my time trying to *prevent* the BBC performing mine.' 'Oh, do you?', said John, in his slow, considering drawl; then added, after a long pause: 'Well, you seem to be *singularly* unsuccessful in your efforts.'

There was also a story about a female composer of whom John was not over-fond.[2] One night, soon after the last war, he met her in a London pub. As he entered, she bawled at him, convivially: 'There'll *always be* an Ireland', a sally which fell a trifle flat owing to the intervention of a very genteel lady seated at the bar. 'You mean *England*, don't you, dear?' Doubtless John felt that the oblique and unintended snub was deserved.

In the latter period of our acquaintance he talked a good deal less; his health had grown worse, and he was liable to fall into a doze after tea. From one such doze he awoke, when I was sitting with him, and suddenly remarked: 'You know ...' (There was a long pause.) 'You know, I don't really *like* music.' (Another, yet longer pause.) 'Mind you ... I like my *own*.'

As I have said, his music was being performed, at this time, less frequently than formerly, and this he undoubtedly found discouraging. His fine orchestral piece *Mai-Dun* seemed to him particularly neglected (as indeed I think it was, and is). Whenever there was talk of a possible performance, on the wireless or elsewhere, John would mutter to himself: 'H'm *Mai-Dun* ... may *not* be done.'

I hope I have not given the impression that John Ireland was by nature ill-disposed towards his fellow-men. On the contrary, he was the soul of generosity and kindness. The malice was a surface affair: he liked to amuse his friends by such tetchy little digs as I have quoted. I think the fact that he was never awarded any public honour was probably a source of sorrow to him: he would never admit to

---

[2] Brooke is probably referring to Freda Swain. For her account see pp. 123–5.

such feelings, but I suspect they were there all the same, and that he would have been gratified by a knighthood – which was surely the least he deserved.

Today, he is unfashionable, and apt to be dismissed as 'minor': a fate which overtakes most artists in the period immediately following their deaths. I am not, as I have emphasized, competent to judge him on his merits as a composer; but quite apart from my purely subjective feelings about his music, John Ireland, when I met him, struck me as having, quite unmistakably, the quality of greatness. Fashions in music, as in all the arts, have been known to change almost overnight; and perhaps the recent foundation of a 'John Ireland Society', dedicated to the live performance as well as to the recording of his works, may be some indication as to which way the wind is blowing.

(2) *From* The Birth of a Legend: A Reminiscence of Arthur Machen and John Ireland *(London: Bertram Rota, 1964)*

T HAT composers should often have drawn their inspiration from the works of poets or prose-writers seems to us, today, a normal enough state of affairs; yet this debt which music owes to literature is, in fact, of comparatively recent origin, and – apart, of course, from song-settings – can hardly be traced back further than the early nineteenth century, when musicians, no less than writers and painters, felt the first impact of the Romantic Revival. From Beethoven onwards, music became progressively less 'pure', and more closely allied to the other arts; by the end of the century these affinities had become obvious: a good example is Debussy, who was strongly influenced by the poetry of Verlaine and Mallarmé, and even more by Impressionist painting.

Less obvious but no less close, and perhaps indeed more intimate and personal, is the link between the music of John Ireland and the writings of Arthur Machen. In this case it is not a question, merely, of two artists working in different media but inspired by the same aesthetic principles or by some current trend or movement. Not only were Ireland and Machen widely separated in age (Machen was a generation older than his comparatively young admirer), but both were, as artists, notably independent of contemporary fashion. They were also, by temperament, in many ways opposed, and if Ireland admired the work of the elder man, Machen – who had no taste for modern music – did not return the compliment. Yet the two men had much in common, more especially in their approach to what, for want of a better word, must be called the 'supernatural'. Both were Anglicans by upbringing, but both, at one time or another, were interested in those shadowy beliefs and practices comprised under the elastic title of 'occultism'. More particularly, both Machen and Ireland possessed a profound feeling for the *genius loci*, and for those 'old unhappy far-off things', pagan rites and Druidic sacrifices, whose memory seems still to haunt certain remote and unfrequented places in the English countryside.

I knew John Ireland well during his last years, and he often spoke of Machen, who, he would declare, was his favourite modern prose-writer. He had discovered Machen's work comparatively early in life, and quite by accident: the title of a book on a railway bookstall happened to rouse his curiosity, and he bought it. The book was *The House of Souls,* and Ireland at once recognized the deep affinity between himself and the author. I do not know the exact date when this chance discovery occurred, but it was certainly not later than 1913, for in this year Ireland wrote the piano piece 'The Scarlet Ceremonies', which takes its title from a mysterious passage in Machen's story *The White People*. In the same year Ireland composed the well-known orchestral work *The Forgotten Rite*, which, both in title and mood, also suggests the Machen influence. Another, later orchestral composition, *Mai-Dun*, is also an evocation of ancient pagan ceremonies; and a similar spirit pervades many of the piano pieces and much of the chamber music (notably, I would say, the Sonata for Cello and Piano).

John Ireland was of a shy and retiring disposition, and though he would have much liked to know Machen personally, he did not for many years take any steps to make his acquaintance. Eventually, however, the two men did meet: probably in the late twenties or early thirties, about twenty years after Ireland's discovery of the author who was to mean so much to him. What was discussed at that first meeting we do not know; but it appears that Machen was inclined to be reticent, both on the subject of his work and of his dealings with the occult. The acquaintance never ripened into a close friendship.

At about this time Ireland was at work upon his *Legend* for Piano and Orchestra, which was first performed in 1934. The composer was staying, as he often did, in West Sussex, and one day took a picnic lunch to a remote spot on the downs which had for him a peculiar and inexpressible attraction. Soon after he had sat down and unpacked his sandwiches, he was suddenly aware that a number of children had invaded the open space in front of the bank on which he was sitting. His first feeling was one of annoyance at being thus unexpectedly disturbed in so lonely a place. A moment later he realized that the children were in fact no ordinary children: they played and danced together on the downland turf, but in complete silence; and they were dressed in white garments of a curious and archaic pattern. Ireland watched them for some time: that they were 'real' enough he had, at first, no doubt whatsoever. Then reason reasserted itself: *could* they be real – these silent, dancing children in their strange white raiment? The composer glanced away for an instant, then looked up again: the 'children' had vanished.[3]

Later he wrote a full account of the experience to Machen, hoping, no doubt, that the writer who had so often described similar occurrences would proffer some explanation of the mysterious children on the downs. But Machen was not to be drawn: his reply came on a postcard, offhand and laconic: 'Oh, so *you've* seen them too, have you?'

Appropriately enough, the *Legend* for Piano and Orchestra, when completed, was dedicated to – Arthur Machen.

---

[3] EDITOR'S NOTE: One is struck by the parallel between Ireland's account and Robert Louis Stevenson's similar experience reported in *Travels with a Donkey in the Cévennes* (1879). Stevenson was lost on a path between Fouzilhac and Fouzilhie, and at nightfall on the marches he reported the following eerie sight: 'As I came out on the skirts of the woods, I saw near upon a dozen cows – perhaps as many more black figures, which I conjectured to be children, although the mist had almost unrecognisably exaggerated their forms. These were all silently following each other round in a circle, now taking hands, now breaking up with chains and reverences ...'

CHAPTER 27

Appreciation and Biographical Sketch

Norah Kirby

This account first appeared in John Ireland: A Catalogue of Published Words and Recordings, compiled by Ernest Chapman ... and an Appreciation and Biographical Sketch by Norah Kirby *(London: Selling Agents Boosey & Hawkes Ltd, 1968).*

JOHN Ireland was born at Bowdon, Cheshire, on 13th August 1879. Both his parents were writers and were visited by many of the eminent writers and musicians of their day. Indeed, Ireland had a childhood recollection of dropping a handful of daisies into an upturned top hat which he saw in the hall of the family home one day: it belonged to Emerson.

At the age of fourteen Ireland went to London, where he lived for the next sixty years, mostly in Chelsea. He was a piano student at the Royal College of Music from 1893 to 1897, and from then until 1901 continued at the College as a composition scholar under Sir Charles Villiers Stanford. At the age of sixteen he was the youngest student ever to have been awarded a fellowship of the Royal College of Organists, the organ having been his second subject at the R.C.M. under Sir Walter Parratt.

When he was seventeen Walter Alcock chose him from among many, very much older, applicants to become assistant organist and choirmaster at Holy Trinity Church, Sloane Street. It was a bitter blow to his youthful ambition when he was considered too young to succeed Alcock at Holy Trinity, but as a consolation he was given the post of organist and choirmaster of its daughter church, St. Jude's, Chelsea. From 1904 to 1926 he was organist and choirmaster at St. Luke's, the parish church of Chelsea, and during those many years he worked quietly and steadily in his nearby studio in Gunter Grove – to the late Sir Eugene Goossens, 'the quiet haven of a few intimate friends'. Goossens also wrote that 'a life-long friendship with him has been a rewarding experience. If the humility and artistic sincerity of a modest artist find their best expression in that artist's work then John Ireland's contains the deepest known to me.'

During Ireland's connection with Holy Trinity it was customary for the organist and the curate to take the younger choristers for a seaside holiday to such places as Deal, Herne Bay and Worthing. For this purpose a suitable school premises was rented for a fortnight, during the summer holidays. The boys were encouraged to go bathing, swimming and walking, with occasional drives in a char-a-banc into the surrounding countryside. In 1900 the curate was a native of the Channel Islands, and the annual holiday was arranged to be taken in Jersey. Thus began the long association with the Channel Islands which attracted the composer and stimulated his musical ideas and imagination.

Always moved by remote places with prehistoric associations, he returned alone to the Islands (Guernsey in particular) during many subsequent years.

In 1912 the idea for his best known piano piece *The Island Spell* came to him whilst bathing one hot sunny day in Jersey, but when he returned to London to write it down he could not find a satisfactory ending. Exactly a year later he returned to bathe in the same cove at the same time of day – and then thought of the perfect conclusion. In his book *A Hundred Years of Music* Dr. Gerald Abraham[1] has written: 'It would be difficult to find a better example of pure pianistic impressionism than John Ireland's *Island Spell* (1913)'; and of the slow movement of the Pianoforte Sonata Dr. Abraham says: 'it is profoundly true to the character of a nation that has produced a Milton and a Wordsworth'.

At a slightly later date Ireland was so greatly attracted to the quiet little town of Deal (chiefly frequented in those days by anglers and a few holiday makers) that he rented the top floor of one of the most beautiful old houses in the High Street. This he furnished and converted into a self-contained flat, using it as a refuge from the noise of London until it was destroyed by a bomb during one of the zeppelin raids of the First World War.

After the war, in 1920, he was taken by his friend Christopher à Becket Williams to Chanctonbury Ring and the South Downs. The influence of Jersey had inspired the orchestral prelude *The Forgotten Rite* as well as the *Island Spell*; but West Sussex and the Downs captivated him and he took permanent lodgings in a cottage in Ashington within sight of Chanctonbury Ring. At this time, too, he bought his much loved and never forgotten Talbot '10'[2] in which he frequently motored from London to Ashington for long visits during which he explored, and came to know intimately, the Downs from Steyning to Amberley. The tumuli and 'barrows' fascinated him and during early morning walks the ideas for a considerable amount of his best known and most significant music came to him, to be written down in his Chelsea studio on his return to London. Thus originated the Sonata, *Rhapsody*, *Equinox* and *Amberley Wild Brooks* for piano solo and the Concerto and *Legend* for piano and orchestra, the inspiration for which last the late Jocelyn Brooke wrote about at length in his book *The Birth of a Legend*.[3]

A significant development resulted from Ireland's frequent sojourns in Deal. Waiting one day on the platform at Charing Cross Station [in fact Penrith Station, see p. 126], the title of a book on the bookstall attracted him and he bought it: *The House of Souls* by Arthur Machen. Ireland was at once conscious of a deep affinity between himself and the author and he afterwards bought and read every book Machen had written. *Legend* is dedicated to Arthur Machen, under whose influence was also composed *The Scarlet Ceremonies* for pianoforte (1913). This takes its title from a mysterious passage in Machen's story *The White People*, and together with *The Island Spell* and the harmonically daring but most beautiful and effective *Moon-glade*, was published in 1913 under the collective title of *Decorations*.

In 1917 Ireland 'awoke one morning to find himself famous' with a publisher waiting on his doorstep before breakfast. This was after the first performance of his Violin Sonata No. 2 in A minor, given the previous evening by the (then) khaki-clad Albert Sammons and William Murdoch, who had obtained special leave for

[1] Gerald Abraham, *A Hundred Years of Music* (London: Duckworth, 1938).

[2] See plate 19, actually model 8/18.

[3] See pp. 353–4.

the occasion. To quote from a programme note by Harold Rutland: 'the power and beauty of the music were instantly recognised as giving poetical expression to the feelings of many people at that time of the first world war. Orders came in for the whole of the first edition before it was even printed. Never, in fact, had a chamber work by an English composer received such acclaim.' A later chamber work, the Fantasy Sonata for clarinet and piano was, like the Overture *Satyricon,* inspired by the *Satyricon* of T. Petronius Arbiter (Burnaby's translation of 1694.) Another source of inspiration was A. E. Housman's *A Shropshire Lad,* many poems from which were set by the composer.

In 1932 an honorary doctorate of music was conferred on Ireland by the University of Durham. A little earlier, the widow of a Guernsey rector had decided to give to her late husband's church an organ in his memory. She asked Ireland to draw up the specification and this he agreed to do on condition that he should be the organist and choirmaster. The instrument was built to the same specification as the fine one he had loved so much, as the youthful organist of Holy Trinity, Sloane Street. He took up the Guernsey position shortly before the Second World War. Thus, the outbreak of hostilities found him there and in danger of imprisonment in a concentration camp, for after the German invasion and occupation of the Channel Islands in 1941, all males between the ages of sixteen and sixty who were not native-born Islanders were deported to Germany.

Ireland managed to escape on the last boat sailing for the mainland. This necessitated leaving behind all his possessions, including his car. The crossing was on a boat built to carry five hundred people but with 1,500 aboard. Water was unobtainable, food scarce, and an enemy submarine shadowed them most of the way. The only thing he brought back with him, apart from the clothes he was wearing, was the sketch for *Sarnia,* one of his most important piano works. He finished this in Banbury, Oxfordshire, where he stayed with a former curate of St. Luke's, Chelsea, who had a living there.

In 1946 Ireland returned to his house and studio in Gunter Grove, Chelsea, but in 1953 he left London to live in a converted windmill in the West Sussex Downs facing Chanctonbury Ring. He had known 'the Mill' by sight, and had desired it, for nearly thirty years. Here he lived his last and happiest period.

It is no small tribute to the composer that in honour of his eightieth birthday, a group of young students formed the John Ireland Society. So enthusiastic and immediate was the response from lovers of his music, who considered it to be in danger of neglect, that an inaugural concert was given a few months later. Continued and increasing support enabled the Society to give twelve concerts in the first two years of its existence – five of them in London.

Ireland's music does not rely for its effect upon superficial decoration but upon its rich and colourful content and its combination of poetry and ruggedness. Owing nothing to folksong, it is as essentially English as are the Thames or the West Sussex Downs. His music has that rare quality of revealing fresh secrets with each hearing, which amply reward the listener who needs more emotional and sensitive satisfaction than that derived from mere spectacular virtuosity.

Himself his severest critic, Ireland was a composer of the highest integrity and one of the greatest in his understanding of the pianoforte, whether used by itself or in association with the orchestra, other instruments, or the voice. His idealism and faith in mankind expresses itself in his great choral work *These Things Shall Be*, commissioned by the British Broadcasting Corporation for the coronation of George VI in 1937. Its qualities of 'broad sympathy and great-hearted fervour that inform both text and music' (to quote a review in *The Times*) have made their mark in countless performances in many lands. His motet *Greater Love hath no Man* is sung in cathedrals and churches throughout the English speaking world on Armistice Sunday. His Services in F and C are universally known and sung, as is his hymn *My Song is Love Unknown*. The practical side of his musicianship was also demonstrated in his brilliant abilities as a composition teacher. For many years he taught both at the Royal College of Music and privately, and among his pupils may be counted talents as diverse as those of Richard Arnell, Benjamin Britten, Alan Bush, E. J. Moeran and Humphrey Searle.

The late Ralph Hill summed up Ireland's music 'as one of the greatest contributions to the renaissance of English music that began with Elgar and Delius. It is not music for those who think and feel only in terms of the grandiose and spectacular. His music appeals strongly to the sensitive, romantic listener who knows that music in which the emotion is controlled by fastidious craftsmanship and exquisite taste can often be, through its subtle implications, more poignant or exhilarating than music that is obviously and directly sensuous.'

John Ireland's gentle and retiring disposition made him a less spectacular figure than might otherwise have been the case. But it has been truly said that his music 'has that rare quality which inspires feelings akin to personal affection'.

CHAPTER 28

The First Performance of the Piano Sonata

Frederic Lamond & Marion M. Scott

Some Remarks on John Ireland's New Sonata

FREDERIC LAMOND

First published in Monthly Musical Record, *August 1920.*

O NE rainy, murky, Sunday evening, last November, I found myself in a dingy Hammersmith theatre, studying the programme of a concert consisting of works by British composers, on which stood the name of John Ireland.

A small number of people were assembled in the badly-lit theatre, and all had that half-bored, half-interested expression peculiar to a London audience brought together to listen to British music; faces that looked unutterable things and seemed about to say: 'We might tell you what we think about Debussy and Scriabin, but we won't.'

Suddenly, faint applause, and I turned to the stage, and saw from the programme that a trio by Ireland was about to commence, with the composer at the piano. After listening for a few minutes I found myself following the composer's trend of thought with increasing interest and sympathy, and very soon came to the conclusion, 'Here is a man who has not only something to say, but who says that something in his own way.' The clearness of outline; the ease with which knotty harmonic problems were solved; the unusual technical facility surprised and delighted me; and after the performance, which by the way seemed after all to impress the audience, I was anxious to learn more of a composer of whom I had hitherto heard comparatively little.

The Sonata in E minor, on which the following remarks may be of interest, is a work of extraordinary power, and I have no hesitation in proclaiming this Opus as being one of the best of its kind the last years have produced.

Underneath the plain exterior of its diction there is a warm, pulsating life, a plaintive tenderness and depth of feeling, an artless charm, genuine and sincere, which reveals the true artist.

I.

The principal theme of the first movement is as follows: [Ex. 1].

Witness the subsidiary themes Ex. 2, 3, and 4.

The short but masterly development which follows is built principally on theme No. 1, and is distinguished by some novel pianistic effects. Then follows the 'Recapitulation', somewhat shortened. The *coda* is full of vigour and life, and a few characteristic sharp chords end the first movement.

Ex. 1 Ireland, Piano Sonata – first movement

Ex. 2 Ireland, Piano Sonata

Ex. 3 Ireland, Piano Sonata

Ex. 4 Ireland, Piano Sonata

II.

The second movement, *non troppo lento,* opens with a melody which is full of nobility and dignity, and has something of the character of an improvisation.

Ex. 5 Ireland, Piano Sonata – slow movement

Then comes a theme replete with the atmosphere of mystic self-communion in some gigantic cathedral.

Ex. 6 Ireland, Piano Sonata – slow movement

This increases to *fortissimo,* then subsides. The passionate middle section which succeeds, is a welcome contrast to the solemnity of theme No. 2.

Ex. 7 Ireland, Piano Sonata – slow movement

After increasing in volume and intensity it gradually dies away, and theme No. 1 reappears in a slightly different form. A *coda* of great beauty follows, and a few quiet chords reminiscent of theme No. 2, with some deep notes in the lowest register, like distant bells, bring the second movement to an impressive close.

III.

The principal theme of the last movement has a stately dignity about it:

Ex. 8 Ireland, Piano Sonata – Finale

And alternates with the following:

Ex. 9 Ireland, Piano Sonata – Finale

A climax, with the repetition of theme No. 1, leads to A major, and is succeeded by the following themes: [Ex. 10, 11].

Themes Nos. 1 and 2, interlaced with each other and finishing in a passage of almost cataclysmic power, conclude the first half of the last movement. The 'Recapitulation', much abbreviated, follows, and after a short *coda* of exceptional brilliancy the work comes to a triumphant end.

Ex. 10 Ireland, Piano Sonata – Finale

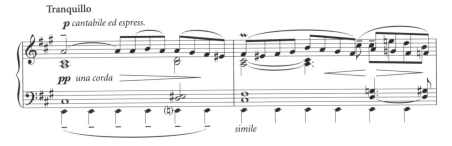

Ex. 11 Ireland, Piano Sonata – Finale

Concert Review: John Ireland, Piano Sonata

MARION M. SCOTT

First published in Christian Science Monitor, *Saturday 24 July 1920. This article appears here with the kind permission of Pamela Blevins.*

T HE production of a large new work by John Ireland could not fail to arouse attention, since he is now regarded as one of the most individual and progressive members of the young British school. The actual event, so far as London was concerned, took place on June 12, Lamond producing Ireland's sonata for piano at his recital at Wigmore Hall, though it is understood that he had played it in Bournemouth a week earlier.

It was placed centrally in Lamond's programme, preceded by Beethoven's 32 Variations in C minor, and followed by a long group of miscellaneous solos. There is no need to dwell specifically upon these. Lamond's Beethoven playing was as powerful and intellectual as usual; his Chopin over-robust and devoid of idealism; his Liszt of an amazing virtuosity.

This new sonata is undoubtedly a big work, and like most of Ireland's things, has evidently been written with deliberation and fixity of purpose, companioning his thoughts for many months, since the score bears the date 'Chelsea: October 1918 to January 1920'.

The sonata is cast in three movements: (a) *allegro moderato*, (2) *non troppo lento*, (3) *con moto moderato*, and is described as being in E minor. Analysts, however, who may wish to trace the old, obvious key centres and relationships in this work, will find they have a difficult task. Not that the sonata is devoid of key; far from it. Ireland has his centres of harmonic interest, he balances his progressions with as complete a personal awareness of his intentions as an architect brings to a building, and his work is never loose-flung nor carelessly finished. But the sonata is difficult to follow in virtue of the extremely close chain of reasoning which governs its structure, and the marked individualism of its style.

The first movement of the sonata contains much that is striking, and the form (a refinement upon the classical sonata form) is as interesting to a composer as the brilliant passages are effective for a pianist; yet in some ways it is the least satisfactory movement of the three, for in it Ireland is closest to what he has done before and there are moments which recall his 'Ragamuffin' or the Violin Sonata in A minor. But in the second and third movements he seems to have got clear of his earlier works and to be speaking directly from his present experience, revealing John Ireland as a man who has progressed.

The second movement is in B flat major, this unexpected juxtaposition of keys having been already foreshadowed by the first movement. Melodic beauty, harmonic colour, breadth of design, together with much introspection, are the characteristics which appear upon a first hearing. Probably the movement does not give up all its secrets at once.

The finale (E major) begins with spacious dignity, and, gradually gathering momentum as it proceeds, seems impelled by some terrific energy to a tremendous end. It forms a fine close to a powerful work.

Lamond played it with immense conviction, a strong man interpreting the work of a strong man, his flowing tone, great striding passages and thunderous chords suiting the titanic mood of much of the music. But there were also delicate half-shades and fantasies which he missed, and therefore the performance did not stand as perfectly balanced. The Sonata, however, made an instant impression, and both Lamond and Ireland were called to the platform at the close to bow their acknowledgments.

Fig. 29 Frederic Lamond. Photograph from a concert programme, May 1923.

CHAPTER 29

Discovering John Ireland

Kenneth A. Wright

This account is an extract from a letter of 17 October 1962 from 77 Ashworth Mansions, London W9 to John Longmire, previously unpublished.

M Y first meeting with John was in, I think, 1924. Percy Scholes, then Music Critic of the BBC, and of *The Observer*, was editing the Duo Art Rolls for the Aeolian Vocalion Company, and he asked me if I would annotate John's *London Pieces*. So, greatly daring (for John's reputation was curiously exaggerated – he was said to be egotistic, overbearing, rude, contemptuous of orthodoxy and even 'regulations') I rang him up and he immediately asked me to spend an evening with him. It was a memorable one for me. His attitude was of appreciation of the fact that I turned to him, the authority, for my information; he said that so many critics and writers were too lazy – or conceited – and he actually seemed grateful that I had asked him himself. To me it had been the obvious thing to do.

He played his pieces, talked about them; played other things of his own, put on a record of Strauss's *Don Juan* which obviously gave him an enormous pleasure every time he heard it; discussed the latest books he had read, and fired off a few of his famous jibes at certain composers who seemed to be anxious to be up-to-date at all costs. We became friends on the spot, and that meeting was the forerunner of many more pleasant evenings in the Chelsea Studio. Nothing ever happened to change that. I remember he was worried by his small returns from the then new PRS. So I looked into them myself[1] with the friendly help of R. J. F. Howgill, then looking after copyright matters for the BBC. (He had come out of the Forces, a well qualified musician, and went as a clerk to Novello's; it was they who recommended him to us.) Howgill spent the whole of his BBC life in Administration – he had that sort of mind, but inside he loved music more than anything – and he later became chief admin. officer to the Entertainment Division of the BBC, then its Controller. When Sir Steuart Wilson left the Corporation the Music Dept. was made into a Division and Howgill moved over to be its first Controller. He made many superb arrangements of orchestral works for the equally superb BBC Military Band. I mention this because he was one of the nicest people, and the best qualified professional musicians, in the BBC, and he *loved* John's music, although like me he realised a great deal of it was too subtle to be appreciated by the general public.

John affected to hate being known as the composer of *Sea Fever*, but as I told him at the time he owed a debt to Betty Chester who sang it hundreds of times in The Cooptimists in London and on tour.[2] (My own initiation was through

---

[1] See my chapter on Ireland and the BBC, pp. 77–115.

[2] Betty Chester recorded it with Melville Gideon at the piano on 23 November 1922, issued on HMV B 1445. See accompanying CD, track 15.

Fraser Gange's HMV record[3] while I was still an engineering student in Sheffield University.) The days of radio's paramount influence in promoting 'pops' had yet to come. Even then (*c.* 1924) *Sea Fever* had become so popular, that 'listeners-in' voted it the most popular of all British songs; a rather ironical fact, for several London publishers had turned it down before it finally got into the hands of Willy Strecker of Schotts, who published it with the firm of Augener in 1915. Jersey had been its inspiration. I wonder how many know of its association with 'The Holiday Isle'.

Incidentally I was astonished how out-of-tune his piano was; and the tone was hard – those hammers hadn't been pricked for years. How I wondered could he realise those subtle, melting, complex harmonies on such an instrument? Obviously, the sour tuning did not worry him in the least. I have since noticed the same phenomenon in the homes of other distinguished composers, who shall be nameless.

On one occasion Ireland rang me at my Savoy Hill office and said he must see me urgently; would I dine with him that night at the Queen's in Sloane Square? I thought that his secrecy might mean that he had totted up his recent performances and found that the P.R.S. cheque didn't tally – he had a curiously suspicious nature in some matters, in contrast to his generosity in others. At dinner at his favourite restaurant he was chatty – alternately wise and amusingly sarcastic – but still evaded the main subject of his almost peremptory telephone call.

Later in his studio, out came the whisky bottle, and – a ten-inch plum-labelled record. So *that* was the secret! 'Listen!' said he. And on the turntable of the rather groany old-fashioned gramophone he started the mysterious disc … It was Gershwin's famous song, *The Man I Love*. The composer's *Rhapsody in Blue*[4] we already knew – the BBC had relayed the first London performance from the Savoy Hotel some time before. When the record had finished, Ireland put the needle back to the beginning, and while it played he kept walking back and forth, his hands behind his back, pausing now and again to sip the whisky. The music was haunting in its nostalgic way; logical in its harmonic and melodic sequences. I liked it, but still could not divine whether Ireland was about to conduct a case of plagiarism, or censorship, or what. Three times we heard the record. Then he stopped the machine and turned to me.

'Well?' he said, in a fierce query. 'What about *that*?' He stopped in front of the little stove and wagged a finger at me. 'That, my boy, is a masterpiece – a *masterpiece*, do you hear? This man Gershwin beats the lot of us. He sits down and composes one of the most original, most perfect, songs of our century. Symphonies, Concertos? Bah!' (A lovely Ireland snort). 'Who wants another symphony if he can write a song like that? Perfect my boy, perfect. This is the music of America, it will live as long as a Schubert *Lied*, and a Brahms *waltz*. Listen to it again, and tell me I am right!' So we had it again – and yet again. He *was* right. And I for one have never tired of it.

[3] The baritone Fraser Gange's recording is not listed in WERM. He recorded it for HMV on 3 July 1919, issued on E 3. See accompanying CD, track 14.

[4] *Rhapsody in Blue* had been first played by the composer with the Savoy Orpheans and the Savoy Havana Band from the Savoy Hotel, 15 June 1925.

Sammons[5] and Murdoch's truncated recording of the D minor sonata [actually no. 2] thrilled me; my then fiancée's playing of pieces like the *Decorations*, 'The Island Spell' etc. and songs in visiting recitalists' programmes like *Twelve Oxen*, all built up in me a keen appreciation of John's very personal idiom and his deep beauty inherent in the simplest song or piece, and in the bigger things too. Herbert Heyner was one who showed me other songs; Frank Laffitte the *Rhapsody* and that great little piece, *Equinox* which many big pianists should play – but how many of them have even heard of it? Ansermet loved *The Forgotten Rite* – it was after his performance at Queen's Hall that John sent me the original Score as a gift – also *Mai-Dun.*

His enthusiasm for another composer's craft was exemplified in the early '30s when he accompanied me to the Queen's Hall to hear a Hamilton Harty concert. As *Ein Heldenleben* approached, out came a miniature score. Every time another daring contrapuntal passage came, Ireland enthusiastically pointed to it in the score and his eyes glistened with enthusiasm. When finally the four great themes came together he bashed the score with his hand (it was on that red plush edge to the balcony) and shouted: 'What about *that*, my boy?' so that the shocked audience around us cried, not for the first time, SSH!! almost louder than the orchestral fortissimo – which implies an out-size SSH! After the concert, in Pagani's round the corner, he gave me a most interesting lecture on Strauss and his techniques, his orchestration, and his 'free counterpoint', to which most of the other diners had to listen, whether they wanted to or not.

One other occasion I would like to quote. In 1930 I had my tonsils removed, and under the anaesthetic had a wonderful dream, which, although it soon faded left me with the conviction that I had been privileged to see, stretched before me as it were, the Secret of Life. I have since been told that all I had experienced was the ebb and flow of the stages in returning consciousness, but I still believe in my vision, and in fact have twice experienced it again under similar circumstances. Ireland was most interested in my story and shortly afterwards extended one of those urgent invitations to spend an evening with him. He had just read Aldous Huxley's *Eyeless in Gaza*,[6] certain closing pages of which Ireland felt had a bearing on my experience. He too was fascinated by such questions – you know his interest in Arthur Machen's books – which linked up in his mind with emotions stimulated, obviously, by the atmosphere persisting in ancient sites like Druidical meeting places and Roman forts; evidence, he felt, of the continuity of life. The outcome of this and similar discussions was the gift, not only of a copy of Huxley's book, but of the much-treasured original MS score of *The Forgotten Rite.* That followed a memorable performance of the work at Queen's Hall by Ansermet, who was particularly drawn to it. Ansermet later discussed the work with Edward Clark and me but in such complicated terms, and such strange mixture of French and tortured English, that his philosophy was far too deep for me.

Helen Perkin was an excellent interpreter of John's music; including the Concerto, but of course when Edward Clark – ever a great supporter of

---

[5] Wright's memory has failed him here; in fact the acoustic recording of the Sonata on four sides was played by Arthur Catterall and William Murdoch.

[6] Aldous Huxley, *Eyeless in Gaza* (London: Chatto & Windus, 1936).

John's – managed to get Rubinstein to play it, it became a true virtuoso piece – and incidentally ran 3 minutes shorter![7] Laffitte played the Sonata well too, with tuition from John (he teaches at the Guildhall), but I don't think the later style of the Sonatina appealed to him as it did to Helen. John was always afraid his 'These Things Shall Be' must sound to the musician like a hymn tune – but at the end it carries one up to divine heights of sound – heavenly sound, in fact – like the passages in Holst's *Hymn of Jesus*.

[7] In a letter from Australia dated 25 October 1962 Helen Perkin wrote to John Longmire, then writing his book on Ireland:

I was interested in Wright's piece about Rubinstein. I remember his performance regularly, and of course he played it magnificently, but the fact that he shortened the timing by 3 mins would not have endeared him to John. I'm sure you'll agree. One thing he could not bear was to have his music played too fast, & several of his later letters to me, referring to coming broadcasts, urged me not to hurry his music.

If you look up the following passages in the Ireland & the Prokofiev [No. 3] you will see the marked similarities in the passage work.

1 { Prokofiev p. 10 No. 18 onwards
{ Ireland p. 16 before 23

2 { Prokofiev p. 20 No. 41
{ Ireland p. 21 No. 29

3 { Prokofiev p. 70 149 to the end
{ Ireland p. 47 74 to end.

The reference to a theme in my String Quartet is more a reminiscence than a direct quotation. My melody is a follows

& in the 1st movement of the Ireland you will see soon after the piano opening

It is perhaps rather too vague to mention. He has even reversed the 1st bar as you see, but I remember him telling me what he had done.

CHAPTER 30

John Ireland

E. J. Moeran

This article was originally published as 'Introductions: X. John Ireland'
The Music Bulletin, *vol. 5 no. 10 (October 1923), pp. 300–3.*

W E live in an age of ephemeral reputations, easily gained and quickly obliter-ated. Artists proclaimed as men of genius by the Press tread fast upon each other's heels, with the result that, as Mr. Heseltine has recently pointed out in his book on Delius, genius is undervalued, while mere talent is over-praised. It would be very difficult, if not actually impossible to formulate an abstract definition of the qualities that go to the making of a musician of genius; but it is not really so difficult to recognize the work of genius, when it appears, as the present-day writers of promiscuous panegyrics would, all unconsciously, persuade us by their uncritical laudation of any and every moderate talent. One result of their activi-ties, at any rate, is to make the more cautious appraiser of contemporary music at once suspicious when he reads about the work of a young composer, whose works, already, perhaps, as numerous, as the years he has spent in this world, are heralded as manifestations of a significant and mature mind. It is true that both Mozart and Schubert wrote lovely things before they had emerged from their teens; but these two illustrious precedents do not by any means give the average, moderately gifted youth of to-day the right to claim as great a share of our attention as a man who, having worked hard in his youth, has decided to leave his early indiscretions on the shelf, reserving for the public eye and ear only those works in which he feels he has achieved a mature and adequate expression of his personality.

It is, after all, not the bulk of a man's work that counts, but its quality. Some of the Elizabethans left no more than a handful of songs behind them – and the reputation of Beethoven himself would be no whit the less if several hundred pages of his work were to disappear for ever. But, when one sees a large body of work from the pen of one whose severe method, of self-criticism have suppressed all the merely experimental or imitative work (of which every musician that ever lived has had necessarily to write a fair number in his early years), one is bound to admit that its composer has made his mark in the musical world of his time. He is entitled to more serious and detailed consideration than the authors of those unconsidered trifles which provide so much better copy for the newspaper man.

No one who has made a careful study of his recent work could deny that John Ireland is one of the most completely original, as well as one of the most serious, composers of the present day. These two adjectives are employed with deliberate intention – for originality and seriousness are qualities which, though praised in the abstract, do not make for immediate and widespread popularity when they appear in contemporary music. The cult of the clique has put strongly marked individuality at a discount while the vogue for parody and an embittered vein of cynical gibing in music have caused seriousness to be accounted the distinctly *démodé* prerogative of nineteenth century German romanticism.

Ireland's style is by no means easy to assimilate after a few casual hearings of his work. A definite intellectual effort is needed if the full purport of his music is to be properly understood. This is not equivalent to saying that his methods are obscure, revolutionary, or unduly complicated; rather the reverse. The so-called revolutionary in music generally achieves his effects by means of some extremely simple, perhaps almost childish, device, which demands for its appreciation a complete surrender of the intellect and a total dismissal from the mind of all thought of tradition and all one's preconceived nations of how music should be made. But Ireland's very personal technique (and it is a very considerable one) is so intimately associated with traditional forms that, unless these latter be familiarly borne in mind, the full and deliberate significance of its points of divergence from tradition will be lost. His methods are the reverse of impressionistic. Everything that he writes, whether it be a short piano piece or an elaborately worked sonata, exists, so to speak, as a definitely organized emotional whole, before it is actually expressed in musical terms. The result is that the final structure is governed by vital rather than formal considerations, but, at the same time, none of the logical shape of classical form is lost, but rather developed.

A casual glance at a characteristic page of Ireland's work might lead one to think that his chief strength lay in the richness and variety of his harmonic texture. But harmonic texture without line and form is like flesh without a skeleton, and yet so rarely is complete mastery in these respects to be observed in any composer's work that at first sight Ireland's harmonic elaboration is a little baffling. For it is not enough to grasp merely the big lines of a work of his. Every bar, every note has its precise significance in relation to the whole, and although none of his bigger works are over-long, they are all more richly loaded with vital matter than the average work cast in traditional form. The argument never flags in this music; it is concise and closely reasoned, and there is neither repetition for formality's sake, nor redundant padding and perfunctory working-out. It is this combination of meticulous attention to detail, and a spacious vision in which the whole work is continually held throughout the process of its composition, that allows Ireland to succeed equally well as a writer in small or extended forms. There is certainly no other living composer of pianoforte music who has contrived to say so much within the limits of a short piece of three or four pages, and to say it with such precision and fine finish of craftsmanship. One feels in such pieces as *Soliloquy On a Birthday Morning* and *For Remembrance* a particularized inspiration, as though the composer were recording some definite occasion or emotional experience. This kind of work is as far removed from the crude programme-music in which an attempt is made to describe things unmusical in themselves as it is from the mere music-making, figure-patterning, or sound for sound's own sake, which seems to be the ideal of the extremists in both the academic and revolutionary camps.

This particularizatian of mood is also noticeable in some of the songs; the best of them bear the imprint of intense personal experience. They are like pages from a diary in which every fine shade of emotion is expressed with the most acute analytical accuracy. Ireland very rarely seems to be attracted by the rhythm or the shape of a poem; it is nearly always the underlying emotion rather than the mere words which he has clothed with music; though he leaves nothing to be desired on the score of just declamation. But a song is for him first and foremost a musical form. He never indulges in those line-by-line illustrative settings which invariably result in an amorphous kind of accompanied recitative. Sometimes, as in that very happy inspiration, *I have twelve oxen*, the emotion of the poem lies more in its form than in its words. Sometimes, as in *Spring Sorrow* of Rupert Brooke, an apparently artless stanza enshrines a poignant emotion with subtle simplicity. Both these poems have been treated by Ireland with great mastery, and it would be hard to find in the whole range of modern British songs two better examples of ideal correlation between words and music.

In passing from Ireland's piano works to his chamber music mention must not be omitted of the very remarkable sonata for pianoforte. This work is, perhaps, the most characteristic example in extended form of Ireland's maturity. Unfortunately, up to the present, it has not had the recognition it deserves. This is possibly because of the complexity of the harmonic texture referred to earlier and an elaboration which had not become developed to such a vital extent in the earlier violin sonatas and trios; possibly because of its concision, for there is not a redundant note in it from beginning to end and there is the minimum of repetition. But whether it be in the first movement with its rugged energy, the heroic middle movement, or the finale with its bold contours so redolent of the lofty uplands of the South Country, the whole work, as indeed does so much of Ireland's music, seems to breathe the spirit of the English countryside experienced by a mind capable of the most keen human sensibility.

The published chamber-music consists of two violin sonatas and two pianoforte trios. Ireland, it may be mentioned here, studied composition at the Royal College of Music under Sir Charles Stanford. For seven years, after his studentship came to an end in 1901, he produced nothing which he considers representative of himself. The turning point came in 1908 with the A minor Phantasie trio, which was awarded a prize in a Cobbett Competition and subsequently published. Even by this time he had been unable to throw off entirely the squareness and pomposity induced by his early associations, although this work reveals a certain transition in style. It was soon followed by the violin sonata in D minor; this work contains many glimpses of the later Ireland, and fourteen years have done nothing to impair its freshness and directness of aim. It would be superfluous here to repeat the history of the second violin sonata in A minor. By this time Ireland had entirely found his own means of personal expression. Perhaps more than any other musical work belonging to the period of the Great War, it was representative of the times that produced it, and it at once revealed its composer as a man who felt deeply, even angrily, but not with the sickly despondency so dangerously prevalent in those days. The second trio in E minor dates from 1917 and, no less than the second sonata, it bears the grim seal of the times. This work, curiously enough, did not make the immediate impression of the sonata, but it is now coming into its own, as one may note from the increasing frequency of its performance.

The culminating point, up to the present, of Ireland's maturity is to be found in the Symphonic Rhapsody [i.e. *Mai-Dun*] for orchestra. This work may be said to be the result of recent association with the Wessex of Thomas Hardy, its villages and Roman camps. Again, here is the work of a man whose spiritual outlook is engirt, so to speak, with the influences engendered by nature, susceptible to the irony as well as the beauties of existence. The whole of Ireland's larger works, up to date, have shown a consistent advance, not only in mastery of means, but in intensity of feeling. It, therefore, does not seem too much to hope that this advance may be continued and that the next few years may bring forth worthy successors to the *Rhapsody* and the later chamber works. We must now look forward with keen anticipation to the sonata for violoncello and piano which, it is good to hear, is rapidly nearing completion.

CHAPTER 31

John Ireland the Man

C. B. Rees[1]

This article first appeared in Radio Times, *6 April 1945, p. 5.*[2]

An original. It does not take long to discover that. The eyes are kindly, quizzing, shrewd. John Ireland is philosopher as well as composer. There is a brooding quality about him. You catch him listening to the overtones of life, and I sometimes have had the feeling on greeting him that I was interrupting a process of thought begun long before the encounter.

Short, stocky, slow-moving, pipe in mouth, a cap – quite often a cap – on his head, he has that unhurrying habit so many of us envy, without being able to emulate, in these days when most things travel and few arrive.

In John Ireland a southern charm does not too much soften his northern burr – he was born in Cheshire, nearly sixty-six years ago. The first time I met him I was struck by his wary geniality. After a time the inner watchful eye closes and you are aware that the sentry is off duty. He is really a shy man – men of powerful creative gifts often are. But he is not a self-effacer, oozing mock-modesty. He rumbles – with a slight glint of mischief in the eye – now and then about the so-called neglect of his music, especially in the presence of those who may have some concern in the matter. You point out to him (also with a sly, understanding smile) that between one date and another he has had several performances of this or that work. He grunts into the throttle of his pipe and reaches for his glass of beer, knowing that he has said exactly what the admiring company of his friends expected him to say.

To his friends he is a lovable legend. In his absence we regale ourselves with the saga of John Ireland.

He has a caustic tongue and a beautifully sensitive pen. There is a gargoyle naughtiness in his humour at times and a profound capacity in his nature for the appreciation of the works of others. The mystical exercises a big influence on him – but that is his affair. He dreams dreams and often has the abstracted look of the dreamer, but it would be a waste of time to try seriously to fool him.

John – he is John to the large company of his intimates – has long since established himself as a character, quite apart from his music. His range of interests is wide: literature, poetry, the countryside, people, the human comedy and tragedy. His tempo is of the countryside. He works slowly, self-critically, and will not be rushed. He likes success but is not prepared to pay any price for it. He knows he has written fine things and does not embarrass you with phoney self-depreciation.

---

[1] Clifford Burwyn Rees, always known by his initials.

[2] I am grateful to Sally Hulke of Comarques, Deal (see p. 116) for drawing my attention to this short article, and to Alan Rowlands for pointing out that this is possibly the most accurate and balanced of the many pen-portraits of the John Ireland he knew, one that, were it not reprinted here, could easily be forgotten.

I cannot imagine him tearing his thick, grey hair in a frenzy of work because a publisher is sitting on the doorstep.

He is a good mixer, without the least acrobaticism in achieving it. He listens well, and talks well, and has a salty style in debunking. Many stories gather round his name, but they are best remembered, not written. There is on him also a kind of unspoiled innocence and a still wide-eyed wonder. I know tough people who feel rather tenderly about him. He is so engaging. He makes friendships grow and deepen. Scores of times I have heard the eager announcement, 'Here comes John', and the obvious pleasure and expectancy of the party brighten and sharpen into a quick welcome, and will unconsciously assume an attitude of affectionate deference, even when we are rewarded, for the first moment or two, with 'Well, you lot of rascals ...'

It is a privilege as well as a delight to know him. A big man, and so much nicer than many big men have time to be. And he still seems rather surprised about it all. 'You're pulling my leg,' he says, not quite sure. But we are quite sure about John Ireland.

CHAPTER 32

Modern British Composers: John Ireland

Edwin Evans

Immediately after the First World War the critic Edwin Evans was a major musical influence of his time, a champion of the new who simultaneously had the ear of Diaghilev, most of the music publishers and journal editors of the day, as well as all the leading composers British, French and Russian. He published extensively, assessing and promoting the younger composers and conductors of his day. He wrote several major articles on John Ireland and as such provided a view of Ireland when he was almost entirely known for chamber music, songs and piano music. This example from the Musical Times *in August and September 1919 probably achieved the widest circulation of any, and was a major factor in the promotion of Ireland, then aged forty, as a leading younger composer of the day.*

O NE of the most remarkable features in modern British music is that its creators do not group themselves into anything resembling a school or even a party-system. In Russia the dividing line between nationalists and eclectics is still discernible, though it has become less sharply defined. In France all music that is not purely academic, and much that is, can be referred back to the Franckist movement on the one side, or to the Impressionist movement on the other. Here in England it is only the composers who do not matter that can be grouped into a school. Take, for instance, the many musicians who have graduated at the Royal College of Music. Where is the common denominator between Vaughan Williams and Frank Bridge, or between Holst and John Ireland, or between Goossens and Herbert Howells? It is only among those whose timidity keeps them within the narrow path of Brahmsian virtue that one can find the elements of a school. The others can at best be classified by technical distinctions, such as, for example, the respect they do or do not pay to those great diatonic principles which continue their authority as robustly as ever, refusing to give place to modern chromaticism. But there is no real antagonism between parties thus divided, for each has a full right to independent existence which neither wishes to impugn. There is nowhere any sign of such exclusiveness as prevails, for example, at the Schola Cantorum in Paris, where even social intercourse with heretics was at one time discouraged. On the contrary, within recent years there has grown up among our composers a feeling of kinship that seems likely to put an end to the old reproach that the art of sweet concord was productive of more personal discord than of any other practised by man. Nowadays, even critics agree to differ with mutual esteem and cordiality.

The foregoing remarks may seem irrelevant to the consideration of John Ireland as a composer, but in reality they indicate the background against which such individualities as his detach themselves with more or less rapidity and precision, according to their dominant traits. It is impossible to deal adequately with any of the composers of his generation, that is to say those born, roughly speaking, between 1870 and 1885, without bearing in mind that they belong to a phase of British music in which the stage was full, and perhaps even overcrowded. Such conditions are conducive to a kind of feverish activity constantly threatened with the dangers of over-production. Looking back from our present point of vantage, we are sometimes driven to the conclusion that the coming of age of those composers might have had even better results for us if the activity had been less, or if music paper had been rationed. But the end of our musical stagnation was so welcome to us, that ever we were only too ready to accept as achievement compositions showing no more than promise that has in some cases remained unfulfilled. Our attitude of friendly expectancy was almost bound to weaken the disciplinary self-criticism of the composers concerned. The fault was ours rather than theirs, and the best we can say for it is that it was a fault on the right side; but it is precisely this that places the personality of John Ireland in high relief, for, if he was long in attaining that eminence which commands the respect of his fellow-musicians, it was chiefly because in him his faculty of self-criticism was unusually robust. So far from there being any danger of his succumbing to the prevailing tendency towards too facile production, there was even a risk of his self-judgment making him almost inarticulate. It has often been stated that he now rejects as immature all that he wrote prior to 1908, but it would be more correct to date the rejection back for he passed this verdict upon each work in turn almost as soon as it was written. Yet the only difference between these early compositions and the contemporary output of his peers is that he was conscious of the difficulties before him, while they, in many instances, came to realise them later.

To understand those difficulties it is necessary once more to touch upon contemporary musical evolution. Ireland had to solve the eternal equation between the old and the new, and he was retarded by an austere conscience that set him firmly against either compromise or self-delusion. He could not emulate the Tory undergraduate who proclaims himself a socialist and really believes he is one! Not only were the principles bequeathed from the 16th century sacred to him as such, but they were part of his very nature, and it was as difficult for him to disguise them with modern elaboration as it would have been to sin against them. But to breathe into them the spirit of the times, without resorting to artifice, is no easy matter. He was not content to erect a diatonic structure and surround it with a cloud of notes. The result would have been too flimsy for his rigid taste. In addition to this, the character of his melodic invention had a sturdiness that confirmed him in his rejection of mere expediency. There was thus at the outset an acute divergence between the texture and the pattern of his music, for his modern ear demanded a richness that seemed for a long time to be foreign to his musical thought. The contradiction was however only apparent, as he himself was well aware, and the task before him was in the main one of reconciliation without compromise. The measure of his present success is that he has completely reconciled matter with manner, and has not compromised with principles. How much is implied by that only the closest observers of modern music can tell.

The conscientiousness with which he engaged in this struggle towards a definite end is the key-note of his character as a musician. His probity is practically unrivalled. He remains as alert as ever for the detection of any hiatus in his style, and more than one manuscript is even now detained on suspicion. Such honesty as this, in the ordinary ways of life, is accompanied with a manner which leads to frequent association with the adjective 'rugged'. Its appositeness in the musical field is equally happy. There is in much of Ireland's writing, a certain ruggedness, of thought rather than expression, that plays an important part in giving it its individual character, which is so pronounced that the mere statement of one of his themes would generally suffice to indicate the author. Almost invariably the dominant impression they leave is that whatever distinction they have is the reward, in the first place, of sincerity, to which mere proficiency is no more than incidental.

John Ireland was born August 13, 1879, at Inglewood, Bowdon, Cheshire. His father, whose family hailed from Fifeshire, was a writer, and for some time edited the *Manchester Examiner and Times*. He included among his friends many eminent authors of the day, notably Carlyle, Leigh Hunt, and Emerson. The composer's mother belonged to a Cumberland family, so that his heredity is Northern on both sides, which may perhaps account for some traits in his personality. He studied at the Royal College of Music, and was a pupil of Sir Charles Stanford for composition. His studentship came to an end in 1901, and from then to 1908, the date of his Phantasie Trio, he was forming his style by means of works which he no longer considers representative.

The more important of these early works[1] will be found included in the list of John Ireland's compositions which will appear at the end of the second portion of this article. It is essential that they should be placed on record, lest anyone should be led to believe, for instance, that *The Forgotten Rite* represents an isolated experiment in orchestral writing, or that the Violin Sonata in D minor, which now stands as No. 1, had no predecessors in this form. Mr. Ireland's judgment of all this music means neither more nor less than that he does not invite performances of it, because the incomplete impression they would give of his work as a whole might affect the prospects of those compositions to which he attaches importance. It does not mean that it contains no redeeming elements. Far from that being the case, I can speak with some knowledge of its excellence, for I saw a number of his manuscripts about fifteen years ago, and my recollection of them is, with certain reservations, entirely in their favour. What those reservations are may be deduced from what I have said concerning the special difficulties which the composer had to overcome before he could express himself with freedom. I use the word 'freedom' here advisedly, as conveying something radically different from fluency or facility, which John Ireland has never possessed and has no ambition to acquire. His whole temperament is imbued with suspicion of the facile, and it needs no great stretch of the imagination to picture him unjustly rejecting material to which he ascribed little value for no better reason than that it shaped itself too plausibly. There were also among those early works a few small things which owed their existence more or less to the difficult circumstances in which a rising composer is placed, especially in this country. Access to publishers is only too often purchased, in the first place, by conforming to certain of their commercial requirements, and there is probably no composer, however eminent, who has not some reason to sympathise

---

[1] Including the overtures *Midsummer* and *Pelléas et Mélisande*, neither of which have come down to us.

with Elgar's feelings on becoming known through the medium of *Salut d'amour*. So far as I am aware, nothing that John Ireland considered at the time to be a pot-boiler has become famous, but if he did on occasion write such pieces, the main responsibility for them rests elsewhere. In any case they have no more relation to the serious works he wrote at this time than they have to those by which he has since become known.

This early period came to an end in 1908 with the Phantasie in A minor for pianoforte, violin, and 'cello, which, in its revised form, may be regarded as the starting point of the new. Although not representative, there is much in the writing of it that is characteristic. The feeling is classical throughout, and unity is secured not so much by the derivation of the thematic material, which is a familiar device in cyclic works, as by a less obvious affinity of themes which maintain their independence. The use of themes which are homogeneous without being positively related often produces the better result, and the cohesion of this attractive trio is not the least of its many qualities.

From this point onwards the choice lies before us of dealing with John Ireland's works chronologically, or according to the usual subdivisions. He has written since then one orchestral work, *The Forgotten Rite*, two Violin Sonatas, two Trios, a number of songs, and some pianoforte works.

It was in 1913 that he reverted to the pianoforte for which he had written several works in his immature period. In the meantime his style had passed through an important transformation, and when *Three Decorations* made their appearance there were many who considered that he had joined the ranks of the Impressionists and even a few who charged him with a French allegiance. Both were wrong, and the collective title of these three pieces is a more reliable clue to their significance. Incidentally, it should be noted here that the separate titles – 'The Island Spell', 'Moon-glade', and 'The Scarlet Ceremonies' – as well as the quotations from Arthur Symons and Arthur Machen which appear below them, were selected after the music was written, and are therefore to be considered as kindred suggestions and not as subjects to be illustrated musically. The first of the pieces has attained to a certain measure of popularity on account of its delicate, evanescent charm which calls for the utmost refinement in performance. 'Moon-glade' is harmonically characteristic, and the third piece has at least one subject which is thematically so: [Ex. 1]. All three seem to have an inherent relation to the literary movement of the later 'nineties, though it would be quite wrong to regard them as literary music.

The next pianoforte work was the *Rhapsody*, which dates from 1915. I quote the following from an article which I contributed to the American *Musical Quarterly* for April of this year:

> The 'Rhapsody', an uncompromising piece of work in which the 'rugged honesty' of John Ireland's lyricism is perhaps more completely expressed than elsewhere, has, perhaps for that very reason, had to wait out of its turn for full recognition. Austerity is a quality that does not meet with quick appreciation from recital audiences – or, indeed, from pianists – unless it happens to be signed with a magic name that begins with B. But 'airs and graces' would have been lamentably out of place in it. In fact they would sit ill upon most of John Ireland's work.

Ex. 1 Ireland, 'The Scarlet Ceremonies' (*Decorations*)

Appended are two characteristic examples from this work; the first comprising the opening bars and the second an important theme:

Ex. 2 Ireland, *Rhapsody*

(a)

(b)

The next important work for pianoforte consists of *Four Preludes*, written at various dates and collected in 1917. From the same article I quote concerning them, and the *London Pieces* which appeared soon afterwards, as follows:

> The first Prelude, which is dated January, 1914, is entitled 'The Undertone', and consists of a two-bar phrase treated as an 'ostinato' with great harmonic variety, but consistently in one definite mood. In its way it is a miniature *tour de force*. The second, 'Obsession', might have been suggested by Edgar Allan Poe, or by the counsels of a witch's familiar. The mood it expresses is an evil one which most people prefer to fight or to throw off. One way of getting rid of it is to express it, just as one can be rid of an unwelcome train of thought by committing it to paper. That is what Ireland has done with singular felicity, if the word may be used in this connection. The third, dated Christmas, 1913, bears for title 'The Holy Boy', and is almost like a carol in its naive and simple charm, which is akin to that of some of the more direct songs, *Sea Fever* or *Heart's Desire.* The fourth Prelude, 'Fire of Spring', is a rhapsodical outburst the motive of which is sufficiently explained in the title. Then followed the two[2] *London Pieces*, labelled 'Chelsea Reach' and 'Ragamuffin'. These might be variously described as Cockney grave and gay, or excursions into the vernacular. The first is not a picture, but a reverie in which the sentimental side of the Londoner – the side that takes 'ballads' seriously – comes uppermost. This somewhat ingenuous sentiment being thoroughly honest in its unsophisticated way, deserves to be treated kindly and without irony, for the sake of its sincerity, and where the inevitable sugar seemed excessive the composer has used his harmonic skill to preserve the real flavour. It is a paradox in musical psychology, and an engrossing one. The 'Ragamuffin', with his blatant animal spirits, is a welcome counter-irritant, and the two pieces should invariably be played together, lest the sentiment of the first should be taken too literally.

It is natural, in dealing with John Ireland, to pass direct from his pianoforte works to his chamber music, as – except two string Quartets and a Sextet for strings, clarinet, and horn belonging to his immature period – all his chamber music is associated with the pianoforte. It is difficult to believe that the possibilities of the string quartet can have lost their attraction for a composer so staunch to the tradition in which it is an element. We must therefore conclude that the successes of the change that has taken place in his method found in the pianoforte a more favourable 'culture-medium', and that, these processes having run their course, his return to that form will not be long delayed. It is certainly not claiming too much to say that no news would arouse more interest amongst the devotees of chamber music at this moment than the announcement of a new string quartet from the pen of John Ireland. There is something about his present method that points to his finding in it a mode of expression at least as fertile as any he has attempted in the past ten years, and probably more so. When a composer combines elaborate

[2] The first two *London Pieces* had been played by Ireland at the Aeolian Hall on 7 June 1918. The third of the *London Pieces*, 'Soho Forenoons' was published in 1920 and first heard at Wigmore Hall on 10 June 1920 when it was played by a now forgotten pianist, Violet Clarence.

imaginings with an austere simplicity of structure, the string quartet offers a prospect of virtue rewarded.

I have already referred to the Phantasie Trio in A minor which ushers in the later manner of John Ireland's writing. It dates from 1908, and is followed a year later by the Sonata in D minor which now ranks as No. 1, although it had two predecessors, both since discarded.[3] It is in three movements – an *Allegro* in conventional form, a 'Romance', and a *Rondo*. The quality of the music is intimate and unassertive, little calculated to make an immediate sensation, as did its better-known successor. This is by no means a disadvantage, as it has caused the work to maintain its freshness unimpaired, whilst gradually extending its circle of friends. In course of time a second edition became necessary, and the composer took advantage of the opportunity for a revision which has enhanced its effectiveness. A desire to revise is, in fact, characteristic of him; for although, as I have said elsewhere, he is a deliberate worker who takes elaborate pains to give every bar the character of finality, that very trait constantly leaves him to dream of further improvement. Many of his works have been subjected to this kind of revision, and none who have followed his development will be surprised if every subsequent reprint continues to show divergences from the original edition. The Sonata in D minor, however, does seem at present to have reached its final form.[4] The idiom in which it is written is not that in which John Ireland writes to-day, and the temptation to 'bring it up to date' is not one to which he is at all likely to succumb. It could only end in failure, and the work is an attractive one as it stands. I could well understand some musicians – not necessarily of conservative hue – even preferring it to its more exciting successor. It is not old-fashioned to take musical pleasure quietly.

Between 1909 and 1913 there occurred a break in the composer's output for which no explanation is forthcoming. A holiday spent in Jersey in 1912 seems to have supplied the incentive to at least two of the works that appeared in the latter year: the *Decorations*, for pianoforte, and an orchestral Prelude, *The Forgotten Rite*, and it is unlikely that the new impetus spent its force in one year, though what one may term its topographical form disappeared almost as quickly as it came. There is no 'Island Spell' about the Trio in E minor, in three movements, which made its appearance in 1914, but has remained unpublished. This work, which is not to be confused with the later Trio in the same key but in one movement, has a somewhat transitional character, not unlike that of the *Phantasy* Trio, but representing a later stage of transition. It seems to face both ways, 'for it has phases that might serve as connecting-links with his period of struggle for freedom in self-expression, and others which predict the complete emancipation of the later Sonata. Through its three movements runs a vein of connected inspiration which seems to reach its loftiest point in the introduction to the Finale.'[5] This work maintains a strong hold

---

[3] Craggs lists a Sonata in C minor dated 1898 and another in G minor from 1905, neither of which appears to have survived. – EDITOR

[4] Ireland did, in fact, produce a third edition of the Sonata in 1944. – EDITOR

[5] EVANS' NOTE: This quotation from the paper I contributed to the *American Musical Quarterly* for April 1919. Where I still feel I have earnestly expressed my attitude towards a certain work, I do not consider it necessary to paraphrase what I have once written.

upon the composer's affection, possibly because of memories which correspond to its transitional character, for in the case of John Ireland a transition in style is never merely technical. It invariably represents the passage to a new point of view, and, in a mind so scrupulous, such passages are apt to be stormy. The American who wrote 'God will look you over for scars, not for medals', cannot have been concerned solely with ethics. The struggle of a creative artist towards expression is no less strenuous than the struggle for life.

Soon afterwards another struggle – a world struggle – was to fill the minds of all thinking men. Already in 1915 a small group of songs, consisting chiefly of the two which are bracketed under one title, *The Cost*, had made their appearance as an outward indication – or rather an indication prompted from without – that the events of these stirring times were clamouring for musical expression, not indeed in their external aspect, but through the channel of those deeper, as yet scarcely avowed emotions which they have aroused in the more sentient of our people. Is it going too far to look upon the Violin Sonata in A minor as an expression of these emotions? That is as it may be, but it is at this date the most consummate work John Ireland has given us, and if the much maligned British public rose to the occasion, as it did beyond all question, it is at least permissible to believe that the music struck some latent chord of sentiment that had been waiting for the sympathetic voice to make it articulate. Never in the recent annals of British chamber-music has success been so immediate. The press was practically unanimous, and within a short time violinists, who as a rule do not fly to new works, found that this Sonata, for their credit's sake, must be included in their repertoire. One feature of this success must be mentioned: a British work was actually included in our programmes not as a make-weight or as a duty-task, but as the chief attraction from the box-office point of view, a position hitherto reserved for standard classics. It is indeed an excellent omen for the future. The Sonata is in three movements which one might term respectively dramatic, lyrical, and a relaxation of the prevailing tension. The first section, with its rugged vigour, strikes a serious note, but its gravity is strikingly free from elements of questioning or of even momentary despondency, and if one quality more than others accounts for the spontaneously receptive attitude of the musical public from the first note, it is confidence. It is the music of a man who feels deeply but who is sustained by confidence, not necessarily in the outward shapings of destiny, but in that ultimate faithfulness of events which is the creed of men of good understanding. The slow movement, which maintains the same high level of sane idealism, is concerned with lyrical solace. 'Even the humour of the last section gathers a flavour of the heroic from the context, much as the fun of our soldiers gathers it from their hardships.'[6] The Sonata is, in short, a worthy expression of the times that gave it birth, and one of the few great works of art hitherto resulting from the underlying impulses of to-day.

The first movement is a rugged *Allegro*, the formal freedom of which is more apparent than real, for its sternness admits of no laxity. Its character is fully expressed in the opening phrase entrusted to the pianoforte. Some contrast is afforded by the first subsidiary, which makes an unusually early appearance:

[6] *Pall Mall Gazette*, 7 March 1917.

Ex. 3 Ireland, Violin Sonata no. 2 – first subsidiary

The *Lento* is entirely lyrical. After a page of introductory matter, the theme of which recurs during the movement, we have a suave melody of classic purity. It is repeated in dialogue and followed by a brief reference to the opening theme leading to:

Ex. 4 Ireland, Violin Sonata no. 2 –*Lento*

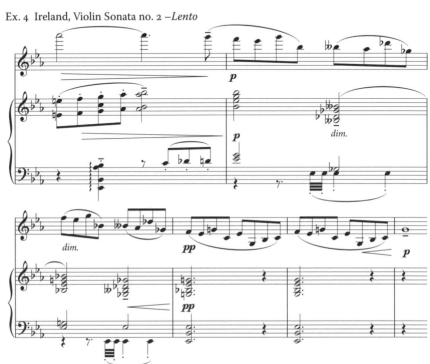

An episode in 12/8 time forms the middle section of the movement.

The Finale is almost entirely based upon a boisterous theme of unaffectedly popular type.

Another almost equally important contribution to recent chamber music is the one-movement Trio in E minor for pianoforte, violin and 'cello, not to be confused with the earlier, more extended work in the same key. It was written in the spring of 1917, and bears the impress of the grim contrast between the season and the wastage of life at the very springtime of life. Here the atmosphere is more martial, and one might suspect a glorification of the 'panache' did not a touch of bitter emphasis remind one of the tragic futility that has overtaken the glitter of the armies of the past. One feels an element of rancour in the psychology of the work, yet it is not the morbid resentment of the weak, but the angry impatience that every one must feel who has not despaired of civilization. It is a poem of mixed emotions inspired by an attitude more critical than that of the Sonata and expressing itself with more directness, though in terms into which one may read a note of sarcasm if one likes. The form is simple: a strain of thematic material progressively metamorphosed in the manner of free variations.

As examples we quote the opening bars:

Ex. 5 Ireland, Piano Trio no. 2 – opening

Ex. 5 continued overleaf

Ex. 5 *continued*

and a characteristic passage from the *Andante* section:

Ex. 6 Ireland, Piano Trio no. 2 – *Andante*

John Ireland's contributions to the art of song are scarcely second in importance to his chamber music, and, in one respect at least, they offer a key to some apparent contradictions in his larger works. In the latter the two strands which run through his musical texture are inevitably interwoven. In the songs he may place his trust in one or the other according to the poetic intention, but there is seldom scope for both. It thus becomes possible to study them separately. I wrote 'two strands' advisedly. Although I am well aware that among his songs are to be found some intermediate types, it is significant that none of these attains to the high artistic value of *Sea Fever* or *Earth's Call*, which are definitely characteristic of the two contrasted styles.

To describe them is more difficult than it would appear from the current generalisation of 'art-song' and 'folk-song'. The designation 'art-song' is in any case a hateful one, and it has the additional drawback of being meaningless, for any good song is surely a work of art, and certainly not less so if it can be traced to a man of the people, as is claimed by folk-song enthusiasts. It is also misleading to lay stress on the melodic character of one style and the harmonic character of the other, for there is often quite as much harmonic richness in his treatment of a simple tune as in the more elaborate method, and quite as much melodic interest in the latter as in the most tuneful of his less sophisticated songs.

Perhaps the true solution lies not so much in the divergence of the two types as in their one common denominator, which is a close communion with nature. This has been evident in some of the works we have passed in review, such as the 'Island Spell' and 'Moon-glade', and it is still more prominent in the orchestral prelude *The Forgotten Rite*. It is so strong that on one winter's day the composer assured me he would be unable to set a certain poem until the summer brought the right mood for it. If we now examine the two songs I selected as typical, we find that in *Sea Fever* the human interest is placed in relief against a natural background, in this case a seascape, whilst in *Earth's Call* it is Nature herself who provides the chief interest, the human element being merely incidental. In the same way *The Heart's Desire*, which is a setting of the 'March' poem in A. E. Housman's *A Shropshire Lad*, has the human interest which attaches to the whole of that wonderful collection of lyrics. This may partake of a mere coincidence, and I do not put it forward as an explanation, especially as it would ill fit *Marigold*, but I venture to suggest that it affords a clue to the two different attitudes the composer assumes alternately towards the musical treatment of a lyric poem, the direct approach by means of a metrical melody, and the enveloping movement of a method that is often symphonic. The subject of *Earth's Call* plainly called for symphonic treatment.

The songs of John Ireland's mature period open in 1910 with a cycle, *Songs of a Wayfarer*, which is of unequal merit, but deserves to survive if only for the sake of one song. The year 1913 established the differentiation described above, on the one hand, with the setting of John Masefield's *Sea Fever*, which continues to be the most frequently heard of John Ireland's compositions, and, on the other, with the song cycle *Marigold*, which belongs to the rich vein leading to *Earth's Call*. It comprises three songs: two settings of Rossetti, 'Youth's Spring-Tribute' and 'Penumbra', and one of Ernest Dowson's translations of Verlaine's 'Spleen'. The last is woven round a phrase so characteristic that, but for its unusually disturbed tonality, it might almost serve as a *motto* to Ireland's collected works:

Ex. 7 Ireland, *Spleen*

As a whole, the cycle is one of his most remarkable works, though it may perhaps be slower to attain to general acceptance than the songs whose appeal is more primitive.

In 1915 the war-songs referred to in the course of this article commenced to make their appearance with a version of Rupert Brooke's famous sonnet 'The Soldier', in which he has not overcome the special difficulties inseparable from the shape of the poem. 'He relies upon the intensity of meaning, expressed in the simplest of terms, rather than upon the actual form of the sonnet, deeming the soldier-poet's message of greater importance than the literary rôle of the sestet, for which he is content to draw upon the musical phrases of the octave. A setting that adhered more faithfully to the form might have missed the substance.' Then followed two songs from Eric Cooper's *Soliloquies of a Subaltern*.[7] In the first of these, 'Blind', the composer has reached a degree of poignancy that is almost painful. One has to go back to Moussorgsky to find anything equally magnetic. In 'Savichna' and in some songs dealing with the peasant, the Russian composer, though hampered by technical shortcomings, attained to a tragic grandeur that has rightly been regarded as his loftiest vein. Here we have its English counter-part. Truthful, unadorned, and thus the more touching, is this simple, irresistibly appealing version of Eric Cooper's poem. In comparison the second song, with an unavoidable note of melodrama, is almost an anti-climax – but one not unneeded to relieve the emotional tension.

Of the songs which follow the most important are, in the direct vein, that exquisite lyric 'The Heart's Desire', a setting of John Masefield's 'The Bells of San Marie', and a very charming excursion into the folk-song idiom, *I Have Twelve Oxen*. An intermediate position might be allotted to the *Mother and Child* cycle, consisting of nursery rhymes from Christina Rossetti's *Sing-Song*,[8] in a happy musical garb. The other method reaches the fullest

[7] Eric Thirkell Cooper, *Soliloquies of a Subaltern Somewhere in France* (London: Burns & Oates, 1915).

[8] Christina G. Rossetti, *Sing-Song: A Nursery-Rhyme Book. With one hundred and twenty illustrations by Arthur Hughes, engraved by the brothers Dalziel* (London: George Routledge, 1872), and later enlarged editions.

development in *Earth's Call*, a sylvan rhapsody for contralto and pianoforte which is too ambitious in design to be adequately described as a song, although its text, like that of many of John Ireland's songs, is a sonnet, this time of Harold Monro. It is in the composer's naturalistic mood, directly assertive, and demands great powers of interpretation on behalf of the singer, for it is music writ large, but although not easy of access the reward is correspondingly great. There is a dearth in the repertoire of compositions ranging in length and calibre between the ordinary song and the dramatic scena. Apart from its great merits, here is another reason for welcoming it. Of less ample dimensions, but too important to be over-looked, is another recent song *The Sacred Flame*, and no survey would be complete that omitted the setting of Rupert Brooke's *Blow Out, You Bugles*, which is far superior to that of *The Soldier*, and has the special merit that the composer has succeeded in the difficult task of preserving his mystic fanfare from the perils of fussy realism.

The one orchestral work which calls for notice is the prelude *The Forgotten Rite*, to which more than one reference has been made in the course of this article. It dates from 1913, the year following the Jersey holiday, and in it he first reveals the naturalistic tendency which is 'far removed from the realism of composers who wax lyrical over the coming of spring. It is the message of a man who feels nature too deeply to 'make a song of it', and yet sings in a subtle idiom that is, as it were, esoterically lyrical. It is the mood that returns in *Earth's Call*. We quote a fragment from the arrangement for pianoforte, four hands:

Ex. 8 Ireland, *The Forgotten Rite*

Ex. 8 continued overleaf

Ex. 8 *continued*

Thus ends our survey of the output of John Ireland's maturity. It should be noted that although the importance of the compositions has varied, their honesty of purpose has not, for there is not one in this comprehensive list that is not the outcome of the need of the artist to express himself – not one that is either a concession to a taste less cultivated than his own, or an attempt to set commercial before artistic considerations. The probity of musicians and their sense of responsibility towards the art they serve has seldom been so completely proof against temptation to 'make an effect', or to secure an easy material benefit. This probity is associated in John Ireland with a genial sincerity and love of artistic truth that will tolerate no meretricious blandishments, and a scrupulousness that rejects anything that is arbitrary or fortuitous. Thoroughly English in his outlook and in the directness of his method, he has one point of contact with the French, and one only, in the meticulous care which he devotes to detail. His is no feverish productivity. He never will be, as many composers have been, the victim of a fatal facility.

He is content to spend days on a single passage so that he gives it the one ultimate form which afterwards proves to be the inevitable form it should take. Yet this constant preoccupation with precision in detail has nowhere resulted in laboured writing. His harmonic texture may be complex or simple, suave or acid, smooth, or, as it is more often, rugged or sharply defined, but it is constantly adjusted to the needs of the composition, and, although he is not given to finicalities, his taste in these matters is no less acute than that of those who trade in them – over all of which, rightly understood, it is in the end one quality that predominates: sincerity.

LIST OF COMPOSITIONS

Unpublished

FULL ORCHESTRA

Midsummer. (Overture)
Tritons. (Symphonic Prelude)
Orchestral Poem, in A minor
Pelléas et Mélisande (Overture)

CHORAL

Mass in the Dorian Mode, for four voices
'Vexilla Regis', for chorus, soli, brass instruments, and organ
Psalm 42, for chorus, soli, and orchestra

CHAMBER MUSIC

Quartet, for strings, in D minor
Quartet, for strings, in C minor
Sextet, for strings, clarinet, and horn
Trio, for pianoforte, clarinet, and violoncello, in D minor.
Trio, for pianoforte, violin, and violoncello, in E minor
Sonata, for violin and pianoforte, in C minor
Sonata, in one movement, for violin and pianoforte, in G minor

PIANOFORTE MUSIC

Sonata, in C minor
Sea Idyll. (Three movements)
Rhapsody
Three Pieces
(Also shorter pieces and songs)

Published

FULL ORCHESTRA

The Forgotten Rite. Prelude (Augener)

CHAMBER MUSIC

Phantasie, in A minor, for violin, violoncello, and pianoforte (Augener)
Trio No. 2, in one movement, for violin, violoncello, and pianoforte (Augener)
Sonata No. 1, in D minor, for violin and pianoforte (Augener)
Sonata No. 2, in A minor, for violin and pianoforte (Winthrop Rogers)

PIANOFORTE MUSIC.

Decorations (1. The Island Spell; 2. Moon-glade; 3. The Scarlet Ceremonies)
(Augener)

Rhapsody (Winthrop Rogers)

Preludes (The Undertone; Obsession; The Holy Boy; Fire of Spring.)
(Winthrop Rogers)

London Pieces – I. Chelsea Reach. II. Ragamuffin (Augener)

The Towing-Path (in the press) (Augener)

Leaves from a Child's Sketch Book (Winthrop Rogers)

SONGS

Sea Fever (Augener)

The Bells of San Marie (Augener)

Hope, the Hornblower (Boosey)

Songs of a Wayfarer (Boosey.)

Marigold, Impression for voice and pianoforte (1. Youth's Spring-Tribute:
2. Penumbra; 3. Spleen) (Winthrop Rogers)

I was not sorrowful (Boosey)

The Cost (1. Blind; 2. The Cost) (Winthrop Rogers)

The Soldier (Winthrop Rogers)

Blow out, you bugles (Winthrop Rogers)

The Heart's Desire (Winthrop Rogers)

Earth's Call (Rhapsody for voice and pianoforte) (Winthrop Rogers)

Spring Sorrow (Winthrop Roger)

I have twelve oxen (Winthrop Rogers)

The Sacred Flame (Winthrop Rogers)

Bed in Summer (Curwen)

The Rat (in the press) (Chester)

The Adoration (in the press) (Chester)

There were three Ravens (folk-song setting) (Winthrop Rogers)

VARIOUS

Bagatelle, for violin and pianoforte (Novello)

Elegiac Romance, for organ (Novello)

Sursum Corda, and Alla Marcia, for organ (Novello)

Morning, Communion and Evening Service (Novello)

Greater Love hath no Man. Anthem (Stainer & Bell)

TWO-PART SONGS

There is a garden (Novello)

Full fathom five (Novello)

Aubade (Novello)

Evening Song (Novello)

The echoing green (Curwen)

May Flowers (Arnold)

PART V

*John Ireland's Writings on
Music and Musicians*

CHAPTER 33

John Ireland's Writings on Music

Personal Anecdotes

Undated typescript: John Ireland Trust

W HEN I was about 16 I had to devise every possible way of raising enough money to meet my modest daily needs. I heard of a post as Church organist, but was warned by my friends that I looked too young to be entrusted with such a position. To remedy this they suggested the expedient of wearing a false moustache. So on the day I went to the church to be tried out, I visited Clarkson's, who supplied and fitted me with what seemed necessary. The musical part of my trial went well, but after this I had to be interviewed by the Vicar. I thought he gave me some rather curious looks, and, needless to say, I did not obtain the appointment.

Another source of fees amounting to a few shillings was to act as accompanist at 'smoking concerts', and I well remember having to play for the late Charles Coborn, that famous comedian, at the Holborn Restaurant in some of his songs. Most of these began with a sort of 'rum-tum' of chords, on the piano, marked 'Till Ready' – meaning that one had to go on repeating these till the comedian elected to start.

Beethoven: A Speech for the Opposition

Music & Letters, vol. 3 no.2 (April 1927), pp. 109–10

T HE opinion has been expressed by some people that Beethoven's music is beginning to lose its hold on the public in general and on musicians in particular. Does the C minor Symphony sound so thrilling as it did thirty years ago? Does the Choral Symphony hold one spellbound, from first note to last, as it did, say, in the 'nineties? Do the *Waldstein*, the *Appassionata*, the *Hammerklavier*, the best of the earlier and later chamber music, transport us into another world with such certainty as they used to do? The answer is for the individual. Speaking personally, the works of Beethoven which I have always loved best still appeal to me with their original thrill.

But there must be some reason for the alleged decline in Beethoven's popularity. It may be that the times in which he lived imbued his work with a quality which is antipathetic to some of us who live in such a totally different age, when every manifestation in art is expected to be built on trope and ellipsis. I will try to enter into some of the more obvious reasons why Beethoven's work as a whole does not make such a forcible appeal as its deep humanity, its greatness of outlook, and marvellous technical invention would seem to command.

It is not because the idiom of Beethoven is outworn. The modern mind can turn with joy to Palestrina or the more daring Byrd, Haydn and Mozart still delight us, and the amazing variety of Bach perhaps counts for more with the public, at present, than the music of any of the earlier composers. Harmonic idiom is not the point in question.

Probably the crux of the matter, as regards Beethoven, is his extreme subjectiveness and seriousness, coupled sometimes with a certain triteness of material which is so often relentlessly developed to its utmost logical conclusion. His endless repetitions in form, his inexorable insistence on cadential points, his long development sections and codas often seem to detract from the effect of even his greatest works. He is so intent on the music itself that a sense of sound, for its own sake and as an aural experience, is generally lacking, and this deficiency is often productive of unpleasant sensations to modern ears. One might say that as the outstanding musical figure of the century he influenced the course of music towards an unduly logical classicism of form and expression which is the very reverse of all modern ideals in art.

The formalism of Mozart is a convention so transparent as not to obscure the innate grace and beauty of his ideas, and his work, so much slighter than Beethoven's, is often more acceptable, partly on account of his unfailing sense of sound as sound, and his love for a translucent, flexible texture, wherein every note is in its right place – a quality which Ravel shares with Mozart.

The greatness of Beethoven can never be in question, but whether his music as a whole will continue to command the unquestioning idolatry, accorded to it as a matter of course until recently, may be doubted. It seems unlikely that modern taste can return whole-heartedly to anything, however great, which is open to criticism on the grounds of formality or portentousness.

The tendency nowadays is towards brevity of statement, flexibility and conciseness of form, clarity of texture, and attention to sound as an experience for the ear. The works of Debussy, Ravel, and Stravinsky display these qualities, and form a natural continuation of the pre-Beethoven period – a period in music more in accord with present-day taste than the Beethoven-Brahms epoch, which includes not only some of the greatest things in music, which are obviously for all time, but also, if one may say so without treason, a good deal which now seems to many people dull and faded.

Alan Bush: The Student

From *A Tribute to Alan Bush on his Fiftieth Birthday* (London: Workers' Music Association, 1950), pp. 15–16

I T has been suggested that I should add a few words to this symposium which celebrates the fiftieth birthday of one of our leading and most active musicians.

My first meeting with Alan Bush took place nearly thirty years ago when he, still in his early twenties, approached me with a view of continuing his studies in composition. I use the word continuing, because he had already completed his course at the Royal Academy of Music. While there, he had been a pupil of Frederick Corder, who had to his credit as pupils such men as Bax, Benjamin Dale, Bantock, Holbrooke, and others who have since achieved their place in the story of British music. Corder, in fact, was for the R.A.M. what his opposite number, Stanford, was to the R.C.M. – the professor most eagerly sought after by the students who wished to make composition their main study.

I can well remember my impression of Alan Bush when he came to interview me at my Chelsea studio – a tall, distinguished-looking young man, dark, clean-shaven, whose face showed energy and character, intellect and imagination. Beneath his amiability and charm of manner one felt he had ideals and purposes already well in the course of formation. Here, I said to myself, is one who is likely to reach achievement in what he undertakes. And time has proved that my surmise was not incorrect.

He had brought with him various compositions in manuscript representing work done during the period of his studentship at the R.A.M. Our first few sessions were occupied in going through these manuscripts, which we discussed in detail and in all their various aspects. I gave him my opinions with complete frankness, and he was equally frank in agreeing or disagreeing with my comments. After we had thrashed the whole thing out thoroughly we found ourselves in agreement that whatever the merit and promise of these works they failed to express the real Alan Bush and his personal mode of musical thought. The task before us was to clear the ground and prepare a way by which he could build for himself a style adapted to the expression of his own musical ideas. How we set about this Bush himself may remember better than I can. To cut a long story short, Bush gradually but surely evolved a style of his own, which has steadily and consistently developed in the series of mature and significant works by which he has become known to the public and won the respect of the inner circle of musicians – works distinguished by sincerity, singleness of purpose and complete musical integrity.

In addition to his achievement as a composer, Alan Bush's musical activities are wide and far-reaching in their scope and influence, whether as organiser, conductor, trainer of choirs and orchestras, or teacher and inspirer of the younger generation of students. On his fiftieth birthday his many friends unite in congratulating him on what he has already accomplished, thanking him for the manly and stimulating message embodied in his music and wishing him every happiness and success in his future career.

My Introduction to Beethoven

BBC broadcast on 16 December 1945, first published in *Music Magazine* edited by Anna Instone and Julian Herbage. Rockliffe, 1953 pp. 26–31[1]

TODAY we celebrate the 175th anniversary of the birth of the greatest figure in music – that giant, Ludwig van Beethoven. No other composer has inspired such universal reverence and affection, not only during his lifetime, but in the long period since his death, a stretch of time now getting on for 120 years. A stretch of time into which have been crowded more radical changes in the modes of man's life and trend of thought than can have been manifest during many preceding centuries. Yet there has been no time when the glory of Beethoven's work and fame has suffered any lapse in radiance. Indeed, the stormy world-period from 1914 till now, embodying two world wars with their incalculable and unending consequences, has only served to establish Beethoven more firmly than ever before in the hearts of his hearers as their true prophet and spokesman, and an ever-living force in music, so long as music, in the form we have known it, remains.

[1] Ireland's broadcast is on the accompanying compact disc, track 2.

To say anything fresh about the Master would be an impossible task for me. Every aspect of his life and work has been copiously written about, and I am quite incompetent to add anything to the mountains of laudation, comment and analysis that have been heaped and heaped on the tomb of the Master. From those sublime regions we will now descend to some ordinary, practical, probably quite commonplace considerations.

It must have occurred to all of us that anyone remotely or even unwillingly concerned with the practical side of music cannot escape from contact with the music of Beethoven. The unwilling schoolboy, who has to learn something about piano-playing as a task, early encounters the difficulties to be struggled with, poor little wretch. Then, the music of Beethoven is the test and touchstone for every examination candidate, and for every would-be solo pianist. Every orchestral conductor, great or small, must be able to persuade his audience and the critics that his readings (oh, those readings!) of Beethoven Symphonies are well up to standard – or at any rate better than So-and-So's. Then where would the concert violinist be who cannot muster at least a *commendable* performance of the Violin Concerto? No – we cannot escape our Beethoven. ...

It seems to me that our outlook on Beethoven's music, as on Shakespeare and the Bible, must be greatly affected by our earliest contacts with it. In the days of good Queen Victoria, when children were to be seen and not heard, child psychology, so far as I remember, and the question of forming complexes and inhibitions at an early age did not figure very prominently in the methods of school-ma'ams and those ambiguous ladies known as 'governesses'. As an infant of six or seven, my innocent life was blighted, yes, positively blighted, by the simplest little piece of music Beethoven ever wrote – namely his Sonatina in G. There were certain bits in it which my infantile fingers could not cope with, and every time these bits were reached, down came a sharp rap on my knuckles with a round, black and quite hefty ruler, wielded by the worthy governess who was then in charge of all my studies, music included. Did the said difficulties vanish in consequence of the ruler treatment? No, they did not, but my terror and incompetence increased. A year or two later I was advanced to the 'Easy Sonata' in G, this time by another governess, who was an even more vigorous exponent of the ruler system of piano teaching.

Thus between the ages of six and ten I learned to associate the name of Beethoven and his music with punishment and physical suffering. Nor did I feel I was suffering in a good cause, as I simply loathed and detested these trite little pieces, both of which were in the key of G. Later on when I began studying the piano seriously, I was put to learn the charming but not so easy Sonata, Opus 14, No. 2, also, be it noted, in G. When my technical development had advanced somewhat from the flabbiest stage in which he found it, my excellent master, the late Frederic Cliffe, plunged me into the formidable task of studying the Sonata, Opus 31, No. 1. Another one in G, I thought. This story of my approach to Beethoven through punishment and the key of G is not complete unless I relate the crowning catastrophe.

I must explain that when I came to London to study at the Royal College of Music, then, as now, close to the Albert Hall, I was domiciled in rooms at the far end of Broadhurst Gardens in West Hampstead. The nearest Underground station

Fig. 30 Frederic Cliffe by 'H.B.'.
Cutting from *The London Figaro*

in those days was Finchley Road. The trains were run by steam, not electricity, and such buses as there were, were drawn by ordinary horses. To get from my lodgings to the Royal College of Music was quite an undertaking. The dear old Underground was slow, though famous for the properties of its sulphurous vapours. Early one November afternoon I arrived in Mr Cliffe's room at the College for a lesson on the last movement of the Sonata in G, Opus 31, No. 1, a very tricky and difficult piece for a poor technician. In those days the custom was for three pupils to attend at the same time, each receiving twenty minutes to himself, and listening (with profit, it was hoped) for the remaining forty minutes. On this occasion, I was to be the third victim, and had ample time to perceive that my worthy master, efficient but always exacting, was in no mood to put up with any nonsense in the way of shoddily prepared work.

At last my turn came. I sat down, shaking inwardly, and made some feeble, half-hearted attempt at the difficult Finale of the Sonata. I felt, rather than saw, that the Professor was rapidly losing his temper. The climax came when I reached a passage I simply could not play, and there was a complete breakdown. Here the storm burst. 'Where do you live?' thundered Mr Cliffe. 'West Hampstead, Sir', said I, in a breaking voice. 'Go home at once', said he, 'practise this passage for three hours, then come straight back here.' And in those days, that is to say, in the early 'nineties, discipline was so strong, that I did not dream of doing other than I was told … Students of the present age of freedom, see what you have escaped … or, maybe, missed.

But the first shattering revelation to my adolescent mind of the real Beethoven came about in this way. The students' orchestra at the R.C.M. in those early days used to be rehearsed by Stanford in the concert-hall attached to the old building beside the Albert Hall, now the Royal College of Organists. We students were encouraged to attend these rehearsals. On some dreary winter afternoon in 1893 or 1894 I wandered in there, not taking much note of what was going on, when suddenly a piece of orchestral music began, quite unlike anything I had heard before. It was compelling, wild, free, full of a divine mirth, a new experience. I listened entranced, excited, led into a world new to me – a world of fauns, glancing sunlight, godlike mischief and joy. To a lad puritanically brought up in those Calvinistic days this music seemed almost wicked – at any rate quite opposed to the sombre, sober ideals I had been led to associate with great music. What I heard was the Finale of Beethoven's Eighth Symphony. And today, fifty years later, I still think that Symphony (what the Master called his 'Little' Symphony) gives me more unalloyed pleasure than any other piece of music.

The Dionysian No. 7 is, perhaps, more exciting. Also it embodies that strange, unearthly movement in A minor – that unique piece of musical expression which is said to have caused Schubert to faint on first hearing it. No other movement in music bears any resemblance to it, and it is impossible to convey in words the impression it makes on one. Such words as 'foreboding', 'mysterious' and any kindred words one could find scarcely touch the fringe of what this music conveys to the mind. Beethoven, the prophet, the seer: could he be confronted with the world as it is now – and as *he* would see it; could he be inspired to make any more fitting and significant musical comment than that movement, composed in 1812?

Sir Charles Villiers Stanford (1)

BBC broadcast on 24 March 1949[2]

CHARLES Villiers Stanford, Irishman to the marrow, was the foremost of a trio of eminent native composers whose pioneer work as composers and musical leaders prepared the ground and laid the foundations for the revival of British music witnessed in our time. The others were the Englishman Hubert Parry and the Scotsman Alexander Mackenzie. All three were outstanding Victorian figures, men of great personality, wide culture and social distinction. Not one of them ever played to the gallery or lowered their standards for the sake of money, publicity or cheap popularity.

Born at Dublin in 1852, son of a Dublin legal official who himself was a distinguished amateur musician, Stanford grew up in a stimulating musical and literary atmosphere, and shewed signs of genius in early childhood. At the age of 18 he went to Cambridge, where he remained for 23 years. His activities there as organist of Trinity and conductor of the Musical Society made Cambridge an important musical centre. He visited Germany at intervals, where in his more impressionable years he came under the influence and enjoyed the friendship of such men as Joachim, Von Bulow and Brahms – influences which may have tended to overshadow his native genius – but, as Scott Goddard truly says: 'His Irish blood may be said to have saved him from complete Teutonicising.' When the Royal College of Music opened in 1893, Stanford became Professor of Composition and conductor of the orchestra and the operatic class, and came to live in London. He had begun to achieve distinction as a composer in 1876, and from then onwards until the end of his life a stream of symphonies and other orchestral works, operas,

² Ireland's broadcast is on the accompanying compact disc, track 1.

cantatas, choral and chamber works, church music and songs, flowed from his fertile, imaginative brain. All this concurrently with his other musical activities, which, in themselves would have absorbed the entire energies of any lesser man.

He was, as I have said, a prolific composer yet few of his larger works are heard at all nowadays. I hope to say something about these later on, but even Stanford's most hostile critics do not deny the inspiration and great lyrical beauty displayed in his songs. Listen to this one:

'Loughareema' – 'The Faery Lough' [from *An Irish Idyll*, Op 77]

I knew Stanford, for I was a pupil of his from 1897 to 1901. He was then about 45, and at the height of his powers. To look at he was tall and loosely built. He had a commanding presence and an alert challenging face, which generally wore an expression of humour tinged with irony, quickly warming to kindly quizzical interest.

At my first lesson, after looking over the MSS I had brought, he turned to me and said – 'All Brahms and water, me boy and more water than Brahms.' After a pause – 'Study some Dvořák for a bit, and bring me something that isn't like Brahms.' I followed his instructions, and wrote him as time went on two sets of piano variations and a Sextet in 4 movements for clarinet horn and string quartet. Stanford had this tried over. It sounded well, and when I occasionally look at the score I feel rather a nostalgic affection for the piece.[3] But the Master was not satisfied. He said, 'The last movement is not organic, me boy.' After one or two further tentative experiments on me he said, one day, 'I shall have to try another way with you, me boy, but ye'll find it a hard one.' He then started me on an exhaustive study of the modes, and modal counterpoint, based on Palestrina. He kept me at this for a whole year, not allowing me to write a bar of music, even secretly, except in this strict style. Stern discipline indeed – but I have since had every reason to bless him for it. I believe I was the first pupil to whom he applied this modal treatment, at any rate in such a drastic way.

As to orchestration, Stanford's plan with me was to let one find out by hearing one's mistakes, however glaring. He would let one's score progress, week by week, with practically no comments. When it was finished he would say: 'Now, me boy, go home and copy out the parts and we'll try it over.' In due course one's piece *was* tried over by the orchestra. One stood beside Stanford on the rostrum while he conducted it – When the more or less appalling sounds had subsided, the Master would close the score, hand it to one with a grin, and say: 'Well, me boy, you see it won't do – you'll have to find some other way.' That was that, and one just HAD to 'find some other way'. Such, at any rate, was my experience.

I think his real success as a teacher came from his masterful personality that we came into contact with, week in, week out – a personality which seemed to implant in one's subconscious self his own unswerving conviction that only the best would do and that nothing slipshod or equivocal could pass muster …

Contemporaries of mine in Stanford's class were Holst, Vaughan Williams, George Dyson, Frank Bridge – to mention only a few at random. Before my time

[3] Ireland was writing this long before the successful modern premiere of the piece at the Art's Council Drawing Room at St. James's Square on 25 March 1960. It was warmly received and published in 1961.

were Charles Wood, Walthew, Hurlstone, Walford Davies and Coleridge-Taylor. After me came Herbert Howells, Gordon Jacob, Arthur Bliss, Moeran and Eugene Goossens. An incomplete list, but surely a remarkable testimony to Stanford as teacher.

Returning to Stanford's more extended works, which nowadays are practically unperformed, it may be that his symphonies would fail to gratify the taste of present-day audiences, whose musical palate has been sharpened with more exciting and highly-spiced dishes. But some of his shorter orchestral works are inspired and characteristic, for instance, the beautiful 'Ulster' Rhapsody *What the Fisherman Saw*. This is sheer magic, Stanford at his best, and deserves a regular place in the orchestral repertory. His treatment of the orchestra is always masterly in its clarity and spacing, its sense of instrumental colour and suitability, and its freedom from both the thick muddiness and the blatant over-brilliance which disfigure many a more modern score.

Passing over the large output of Chamber music, some of which certainly deserves to be heard – why not in the Third Programme? – mention must be made of Stanford's operas. It was to this branch of composition that he most pinned his faith, which led him to write nine operas, though only one of these, *Shamus O'Brien* met with any real success in his lifetime. But recently there has been a revival at Oxford of *Much Ado About Nothing*, first produced in 1901. This is a delightful work, full of charm, humour, and where needed, deep feeling. I shall always remember the lovely 5/4 theme he uses in the Lament for Hero, in the third act – let me play you a few bars of it.

A musician friend of mine whose opinion is authoritative wrote to me as follows: *Much Ado* at Oxford lately was, even in an undergraduate performance, a revelation. That opera ought to be given at once in town. It would go like anything.' Perhaps those responsible at Covent Garden will seriously consider this suggestion.

My time is nearly ended, and since the gramophone companies have neglected to make available any recordings of Stanford's larger works as a tribute to his memory – lying as he does in Westminster Abbey, next to his great fore-runner, Purcell – we will close with one of his most beautiful and moving partsongs – 'Heraclitus' –

> 'They told me, Heraclitus
> They told me you were dead'

Stanford (2)

Undated typescript: John Ireland Trust

SIR Charles Villiers Stanford had a facile and masterly technique, founded on classical models, and in everything he wrote there is something of his own strongly marked individuality, which, I think, is most fully expressed in his songs and shorter works. As a teacher, his personality and influence counted for more than his methods. His contempt for 'padding', or for anything shoddy, carelessly made or over-emphasised insensibly impressed itself on his pupils. His love of order, form and efficiency was the motive of the advice he gave to those who were privileged to study with him.

In spite of his prejudices, his frequent cynicism, and intolerance for any point of view not coincident with his own, he is to be remembered as a great man and a great musician, who often inspired affection as well as admiration.

Elgar (1)

Undated typescript: John Ireland Trust

I WAS introduced to Elgar about the year 1900 at the house of friend B.G.N., who forms the subject of one of the *Enigma Variations*. It was about the time when Elgar's *Sea Pictures* were being made known by Clara Butt. Elgar said to me: 'Young man, so you intend to become a composer?' On my timidly assenting, the great man said: 'For God's sake, let it alone! Look at me – I have been composing for many years, yet no-one in England took any notice of me till a *German* said my music was good.' (The German was, of course, Richard Strauss.)

Many years later, it happened that an orchestral work of mine was given at a Queen's Hall concert, where Elgar was conducting his Second Symphony. He listened to my piece and spoke to me kindly about it. I asked if he would let me show him my score, and he at once arranged for me to take my work to him the next morning. At his chamber in St. James's Street we spent a couple of hours over my piece, in the course of which he gave me many valuable hints on orchestration, embodying fundamental points which I have never seen mentioned in any text book. This interview was the finest lesson I ever had.

Elgar (2)

Undated typescript: John Ireland Trust

S O much has been written about Elgar by musicologists, critics and personal friends that little of consequence seems left to add. Over the years, the genius, originality and greatness of stature evident in all his finest works [was] to become ever more firmly ~~recognised~~ [Ireland's deletion] established.

During my studentship at the R.C.M. Stanford gave a concert performance of the *Sea Pictures*, the singer being, I think, Muriel Foster. Shortly after this, I was introduced to the Master at the Chelsea house of B.G.N. (of the *Enigma Variations*). Elgar said to me: 'Young man, are you endeavouring to become a composer?' On my timidly assenting, he replied: 'For God's sake leave it alone. Look at me! No-one in England took any notice of my music until a German said it was good.' At a later date I heard his First Symphony under the inspired direction of Nikisch – an unforgettable experience.

When his three chamber works were first performed at the house of his friend Frank Schuster, I was among those invited. During the playing of these Elgar walked up and down, smoking a pipe. At the subsequent supper party I found myself seated on his right. When presently he turned to me I ventured to ask him if he smoked when he was working. 'Working? Working?' he exclaimed, 'I'm afraid I don't understand you, Mr Ireland.'

But on occasion he could be kindness itself, as when, at his own suggestion, I showed him a MS score of mine. Going through it carefully, he made clear to me several ...

Listen to the Bands!

Daily Mirror, 29 September 1934, p. 12

Listen to the Bands!
Great National Musical Festival
Today at the Crystal Palace
By JOHN IRELAND
the Well-Known Composer, Who Has Written the
Championship Test Piece for the Occasion

N O fewer than 190 brass bands, representing over 4,500 players from all parts
of England and Scotland, will be heard to-day in the National Band Festival
at the Crystal Palace, London, by an audience expected to number 50,000. Thirty-
four years ago, few people in the south of England had ever seen a brass band.
Now there are about 6,400 brass bands in Great Britain. Mr John Henry Iles, who
as usual will conduct the massed bands at the Crystal Palace to-day, arranged the
first National Band Festival in 1900, with the personal help of Sir Arthur Sullivan.
On this occasion only twenty-nine bands competed, the players numbering only
600. A comparison between these figures and those I have just mentioned gives
a graphic impression of the extremely rapid growth of the British brass band
movement. Brass bands are a very old institution in the north of England. The
Manchester contest, which is held annually at Belle Vue, has been running for
eighty-two years. Then why, it may be asked, have brass bands been so slow in
attaining popularity in the south of England ?

Effect of Radio

This, it must be confessed, is a psychological puzzle. There is no doubt that, generally speaking, young people, say in London and most of the towns in the south,
enjoy comparatively better opportunities for expressing themselves musically. But
there are many thousands of young men, particularly in Lancashire and the north-
east, who, apart from choral work, have very scanty facilities for developing any
latent musical talent except by means of a local brass band, which, more often
than not, is run in connection with their place of employment.

I often hear people say that radio, the gramophone and the mechanisation of
music we have witnessed in recent years have led to a decline in personal playing.
However true this may be in other directions, it is certainly incorrect so far as
brass bands are concerned. Far from the radio having an adverse effect, I think that
the ever-growing popularity of brass bands can be attributed to a large extent to
the interest created by radio, for in my opinion brass bands are conveyed specially
well over the wireless medium.

One matter, however, has seriously retarded the development of brass bands
– the lack of suitable music written specially for them. In fact, until Mr Iles organised the National Band Festival, the repertoire of most brass bands consisted
almost entirely of music written for other combinations. There was then no significant music at all written specially for brass bands by serious composers.

Yet, so far has interest in brass bands now developed, that music for the National
Band Festival has been written in recent years by such eminent composers as the

late Sir Edward Elgar, Sir Granville Bantock, Gustav Holst, Herbert Howells and many others.

Test Piece

For many years I have been impressed by the virility of the brass band movement, but my actual introduction to it came about quite by chance. At a dinner of the Worshipful Company of Musicians, when I had the honour of being presented with the Cobbett Gold Medal, of which only a few have been awarded, I happened to sit next to Mr Iles, and in the course of the evening he invited me to compose the test piece for the 1932 Festival. This year I have dedicated my 'Comedy' overture to Mr Iles, who has done yeoman work in furthering the brass band movement in Great Britain.

It is a happy coincidence that my Concerto in E flat, for piano and orchestra, is also being broadcast today, as it will be played by Helen Perkin in the Promenade Concert conducted by Sir Henry Wood to be given at the Queen's Hall, London.

Strong Force in British Music

I will admit that, even to-day, brass bands do not yet interest a large number of composers of note, and this is no doubt because of the comparatively limited range of tone colour available. On the other hand, until the National Band Festival was inaugurated and began to gather its present momentum, it cannot be said there was much incentive to any composer to turn his attention to the enormous possibilities of brass band music.

The limitations I have mentioned, from the composer's point of view, arise from the unescapable fact that the cornet, baritone, euphonium and brass all are instruments more or less of the same type, and the only instruments of contrasting type in a brass band are the trombones. I have often thought that it might be a decided improvement if trumpets were added, but whether this is practical at the present time is debatable.

A composer for brass bands is also limited in the use of compass by the cornet, the top note of which, for practical purposes, is about the B flat above the treble stave. But in a military band a much greater range is possible, while in the symphonic orchestra the composer has another two octaves at his disposal.

Notwithstanding these inherent disabilities, brass bands must undoubtedly be recognised as one of the strong forces in British music today. It is especially notable that they have been built up usually from humble beginnings, with no adventure of professionalism, the only motive of the players being a sheer love of music.

Sir Walter Alcock

Undated typescript: John Ireland Trust

WHILE it is nowadays the recognised procedure to decry the work of any generally admitted great artist, almost before his mortal remains have grown cold, it is the practice as regards the rather lesser lights in the arts, that on their demise, a lukewarm obituary notice appears in *The Times*, followed perhaps by an appreciative letter from some friend, perhaps not. A noteworthy example is Arthur

Machen, whose posthumous press has not begun to do justice to his personal and unique contribution to literature.

In the world of music, Church music in particular, the late Sir Walter Alcock is another personality whose achievements have not met with the immediate posthumous recognition so obviously merited. Or at any rate, that is the opinion of one who had the privilege of being associated with him during his prime, when he was organist and choirmaster at the Church of Holy Trinity, Sloane Street, where he succeeded the great Edwin H. Lemare, who in his day was a 'star' organist and choir trainer.

At that time, in 1896 or thereabouts, Holy Trinity Sloane Street was a fashionable church, and had the reputation of the best musical service in London. The Rector, Canon Fyton, a famous and successful preacher, was appointed Canon of Westminster and incumbent of St. Margaret's Westminster. At short notice another Rector and another organist had to be appointed. Canon Fyton took with him to St. Margaret's not only Lemare but the most efficient section of the choir, both boys and men. It was put up to the then Dr Alcock to make up all these deficiencies at the very shortest notice, as best he could.

Early in the year 1897, when I was a pupil of Stanford and Parratt at the Royal College of Music, I received a letter from Dr Alcock offering me the job of assistant organist at Holy Trinity. At the time, I was on holiday with my sister in the Isle of Wight, but I felt the matter sufficiently important to curtail my holiday and come to London. Alcock asked me to me to meet him at Holy Trinity after Evensong on Easter Eve. I attended Evensong at 6 o'clock, and was immensely impressed with the splendid choir of forty first-class boys and twelve men singers of the finest sort. The acoustics of the Church lent an extraordinary atmosphere to everything sung and played, and when the time came for me to interview Dr Alcock I could scarcely pull myself together for what then seemed a real ordeal, at any rate to a shy boy under eighteen years of age.

Alcock was kindness itself, and showing me into the loft of the fine 4-manual Walker organ said, 'Now will you please extemporise', he himself retiring into nave of the Church. Embarrassed with four manuals, and infinitely more stop-knobs than I had ever had to deal with, I cannot remember what sort of a show I managed to put up. A poor one, I expect. However, Alcock seemed fairly satisfied and appointed me on the spot, and said, 'Now I shall expect so-and so, and your duties will be such-and-such – you will not be able to have any summer holidays as you will have to take all the Sunday Services during August and September.' Naturally I made no demur, being deliriously excited at the mere prospect of being allowed to spread my half-grown wings in such wonderful surroundings.

At that time there was daily Evensong at 6 with the choir of boys only, followed by the boys' practice, which at that time was always taken by Dr Alcock. At first I was allowed to play for Evensong two or three nights a week, Dr Alcock having the habit of coming in before the end to see what I was doing. One slip on the pedals was enough for him to read a sharp lecture not without threats. The books on the organ music desk must be left in a certain exact position. If one of these happened to be an inch out of the prescribed position Alcock would say 'Now Ireland, this will not do. If you cannot leave the books in their right places I must find another assistant.'

It was a part of my duties to attend the choir rehearsals, from which I learnt much. Alcock had an extraordinarily easy way of getting the best results from the boys. He always began with a series of vocal exercises, followed by attention to chanting and hymn-singing, before he attacked the elaborate work which had to be done. Indiscipline was unheard of; the boys loved him and did their utmost always, and the men responded unfailingly to his fine instinctive musical influence, which resulted in splendid performances.

It must be noted there was no choir school, all the boys being selected from the Holy Trinity Church School, but in those days they were mostly the sons of servants of the gentry who at that time lived in the neighbourhood, and consequently well-fed, well-groomed, well-clothed, and of a type not to be found in these days. Moreover, every year the Church provided them with a seaside holiday of a fortnight, some of the Church officials and clergy being in charge, which laid the foundations for a fine esprit-de-corps which led to the happiest co-operation in the choir work of the Church, and the kindliest relations between all concerned. I myself was always invited to join these pleasant vacations, and they were delightful times I shall never forget.

These were Alcock's surroundings in his work at Holy Trinity, which must be considered as the finest period of his work as a Church musician. But in the ultimate estimate of Alcock much has so far been overlooked. He was a composer mainly if not entirely of Church music. This, perhaps, cannot be considered of the first value, musically. It was somewhat academic and stilted in expression, although every now and then there are moments of inspiration, as perhaps in the quartet 'We therefore pray Thee' in the Te Deum in B flat. But actually, Alcock's musical soul was outpoured in his extemporisations before and after the Services. I have listened to many, perhaps hundreds of these. No organist has ever so beautifully expressed the mood of the moment, of the Church's season, of what was 'in the air' on that particular day – and how many of those days there were – and it is sad to know that all this spontaneous music-making can be no more for us.

In his extemporisations – preludes and postludes to quiet, unassuming services – Alcock was at his very best. His sense of the quieter tone colours of the organ, of moving contrasted partwriting, of subtle, expressive harmony and flexible building of small forms, was such as many a composer might well envy. And all was controlled by the most exquisite and unfailing taste and musical sensitiveness. It is sad to think of the impermanence of this side of Alcock's art.

He was meticulous in the extreme (and rightly so) about part-playing. If in a 4-part chant or hymn one played the treble part on a solo stop he always insisted that the two inner parts should be played by the left hand exactly as they were written. No mere 'filling-up' for him. Which reminds me of a favourite quip on the part of Sir Walter Parratt – 'Why is the Parish Church Organist like a muffin?'

It would be almost superfluous to say anything of Alcock as a solo organist. Up to the end of his life an organ recital by him was something for a musician to listen to. Other organists have technique, but Alcock's control of rhythm, phrasing, manipulation, and playing the work as a whole creation, on this most obstinate and unresponsive of instruments – most ruthless in showing the player's faults – was something absolutely unique and personal to himself, which gave unrestricted joy to his discerning listeners.

This truly fine musician, who never condescended to blow his own trumpet, which is now the universal fashion, will live in the memory of' those who knew his work as a Master whose contribution to the temple of Art is of real and lasting significance.

Ravel at a Party

Undated typescript

ROUND about the 1920s I was asked to a party where Ravel was present. There were many guests, and in the course of the evening the drinks flowed pretty freely. As a climax, Ravel was induced to play his Sonatine to the assembly. He very reluctantly sat down at the piano, but it soon became evident that the Master had lost the control of his fingers necessary for a clear rendering of this difficult piece. In fact, I could scarcely believe my ears as the slips and wrong notes poured from the instrument. However, a conclusion was reached and a storm of applause followed.

My friend Frank Bridge was at the same party, but neither of us spoke French well enough to convince the Master of our great reverence and admiration. Bridge described Ravel as having a 'sparky' look, which well expresses the bird-like impression he gave one.

Challenges

Introduction to Ralph Hill, *Challenges: A Series of Controversial Essays on Music* (London: Joseph Williams, 1943). Dated January, 1943, John Ireland's Introduction to his friend Ralph Hill's slim wartime book of musical essays is prefaced by three quotations from the book.

> Music is an art to be enjoyed like good cooking or a vintage wine, or to be contemplated like fine poetry.

> … the most deplorable characteristic of British musical life is the indifference that is shown towards the fortunes and achievements of our own composers.

> When people talk about the universality of music, and the sanctity of internationalism they mean really the universality of German music and the sanctity of Teutonism.

THERE is a refreshing candour and directness about these statements, typical of many in these pages and characteristic of the forthright personality of the author—music critic, historian, and in his spare time, wrestler. A big, genial, forceful figure of a man, he flings out his challenges in the way you would expect – certainly *fortiter in re* if not always *suaviter in modo*. Controversial essays he calls them, and controversial in the main they admittedly are. If your views or proclivities force you into the position of opponent to this wrestling essayist, you are likely to find yourself thrown (if that is the correct term), at any rate for the moment, by the burly vigour of his arguments and assertions. Conversely if by luck you happen to find yourself at one with the challenger, you will be fortified in your opinions by the reassuring feeling that this formidable fellow is fighting for the cause you have always cherished but has been too weakly modest to argue about or too timid to stand up for. But whether you see things from Ralph Hill's standpoint or not (and I for one do not always find myself in alignment) you will not fail to be impressed by his sincerity and singlemindedness even though you may sometimes feel tempted to accuse him of bias.

As a whole and in its several parts this book so teems with ideas that it is not possible, within the limited space here, to do more than touch upon a few of the features which most readily strike the reader. The two most elaborate and extended essays in the series, while dealing with some general aspects and principles of musical criticism, are incidentally occupied in refuting opinions expressed in the writings of a veteran colleague of the author. For the opposition he marshals clear and spirited arguments of his own and calls to his support other shining lights in the hierarchy of writers on this subject. These two essays, 'Some Reflections on Musical Criticism' and 'The Apotheosis of the Plain Man' are in themselves characteristic and significant – and not to be confused with the ever-growing mass of dialectic which, like a sandstorm, tends to envelop the subject in a dark and gritty mystery. Probably the 'plain man' or average reader may find easier going and lighter entertainment in the next essay, 'Composers as Critics'. Here amongst other comments we are given Tchaikovsky's views on some of the music of Brahms and Debussy's reactions after hearing the *Ring of the Nibelung* at Covent Garden in 1903. Though our author holds a poor opinion of the composer as critic one cannot help feeling (even with regret) that there may be more than a modicum of truth in Tchaikovsky's strictures on Brahms, and only the die-hard Wagnerian could fail to register some response to Debussy's rather mordant raillery at the expense of that almost painfully monumental masterpiece, the *Ring*.

On every page one finds evidence of the wide scope of the author's knowledge of his subject and the breadth of his sympathies. In 'Gold and Coal Dust', where he compares the so-called Golden Age of English music with the nineteenth and twentieth centuries, and traces the influence of social conditions and certain economic factors, such as the growth of industrialism, we find the following sentences:

> ... owing to the development of the orchestra during the nineteenth century and the decline of singing during the twentieth century the ears of the public have become so saturated with and used to great masses of sound and gorgeous instrumental colouring that the purer and more subtle forms of music have lost their appeal and popularity. The orchestra and its prima-donna conductor have become almost the *raison d'être* for the art of music.

And one might add, almost the sole concern of the would-be-successful composer.

More controversial in tone is 'The Cult of Academicism', where the author refers to 'diploma-ridden teachers' ... 'these poor misguided creatures, who would be better employed in domestic service or behind shop-counters.' This seems rather a sweeping statement. Again, it may be very well to quote the gibes of Chopin, Joachim and Clara Schumann at the attitude of the English towards music (when they visited this country about the middle of last century), but these art-for-art's-sake foreign artists have always been ready and even eager to come here and pocket the substantial and often fabulous fees the unmusical English were prepared to pay them. The essay closes with an unexpected but welcome appreciation of the outstanding qualities of Parry and Stanford.

After calling in question the value of nationalism generally and folk song in particular as a basis for the formation of style in musical composition (see 'The Folk-Song Bubble') the author proceeds to stress the apathy and mental indolence of listeners and the concert-going public in 'Music of Our Time', where he tells us '... the public thinks of music in the terms of Bach, Beethoven and Brahms: to offer a programme of Bax, Bridge and Britten would be an insult to the hallowed names of the three Bs'. Or for that matter, of Bliss, Bantock and Bush, as we British are well supplied with composers whose names begin with B!

The reader will find the remaining essays fully as thought-provoking and enjoyable as the preceding, whether the author is dealing with the fallacy that foreign performers and conductors are incapable of presenting British music as it should be presented, or infecting us with his admiration for the clarity and conciseness of French music – ('I believe', he says, 'that far too much importance is attached to size and length in music') – giving us his views on the effect of broadcasting on the musical situation, and finally, defending his beloved Brahms from what he regards as unjust attack.

Combative in tone, these essays are essentially constructive because they not only emphasise the author's intolerance of shams and what he sees as falsity of outlook, but embody positively his love of beauty and truth as these qualities reveal themselves to his selective and analytical mind. And so we come to the end of Ralph Hill's *Challenges*, a little breathless, perhaps, but with a desire for more of these fascinating studies from his agile pen, the pen of a ready writer.

Memorable First Nights

Broadcast on the Home Service, Sunday 23 August 1942

John Ireland recalls with gramophone records three memorable first performances in this country. [Brahms' Clarinet Quintet; Tchaikovsky's Sixth Symphony and Stravinsky's Rite of Spring.]

I WANT to tell you today about two or three of my most interesting musical experiences. Perhaps you think this would have been meeting famous composers or conductors, or maybe hearing great performers or singers – but the most exciting thing to me has always been, and still is, hearing a piece of music for the first time.

Now some people enjoy most of all listening to something they know (and are fond of) over and over again – and there's a great deal to be said for this – because every time one hears it one finds some fresh beauty, or notices some fresh point. I feel like that too, but hearing a piece of music I haven't heard before is like making a journey into some undiscovered country – or setting out on a holiday full of adventures and new impressions.

I thought you might like to hear about three first performances which stand out in my mind as great occasions which attracted the whole of musical

London -- occasions when works which have become well-known were heard here for the first time.

For the first of these I am going back a long way – to the time when, as a boy, I first came to London to study music. That was in the 'nineties, when Brahms was the greatest living figure in music, and every new work of his was a great event. I think he was regarded with more reverence than any composer since that time. In those days we had a regular series of splendid concerts of chamber music, the Monday and Saturday 'Pops', which were in the old St. James's Hall. It was at one of these we first heard the now famous Clarinet Quintet. The quartet of strings was led by the great violinist Joachim, an intimate friend of Brahms. The clarinet part was taken by Mühlfeld, whose playing inspired Brahms to write several works for this instrument. The clarinet, in Mühlfeld's hands, was like something we had never heard before. I think it is fairly safe to say that he was the first solo player on a wind instrument whose style and finish reached the artistic standard of the great string players.[4]

So on this occasion there was not only the thrill of a new and splendid work from the pen of the greatest living composer, but the revelation of Mühlfeld's clarinet playing. Let's listen to part of the first movement of this Quintet, and try to imagine what it must have sounded like to the London audience who heard it for the first time.

RECORD

The next occasion I am going to tell you about was quite different. This time there was colour and glamour, from the orchestra. Nowadays you can hear the orchestra on your own wireless set or gramophone, but in the 'nineties there was nothing of that sort. If you wanted to hear the orchestra you had to go to a concert-hall – the orchestra did not come to you. So perhaps as one had to take a good deal more trouble to hear it, an orchestral concert seemed a more important event than it does today.

At that time very little was known of Tchaikovsky's music here, except perhaps to a few people. But for some reason when the Royal Philharmonic Society announced the first performance in London of Tchaikovsky's Sixth Symphony, the 'Pathetic', the rumour got about that we were going to hear something very unusual and sensational. And so it proved. The work, now so famous and popular, was first heard[5] in Queen's Hall, and the Philharmonic Orchestra was directed

---

[4] In fact Ireland is unlikely to have heard Mühlfeld play the actual *first* London performance of the Brahms Clarinet Quintet or the Joachim Quartet with Joachim himself leading. The first performance of the Quintet at St James's Hall was on 28 March 1892, before Ireland came to London. It was repeated there on 2 and again on 4 April, and played yet again when Mühlfeld returned to London in December 1892 when it received a further three performances. But Ireland almost certainly heard it in 1895 when Mühlfeld was the clarinettist but Norman Neruda – Lady Hallé – led the quartet, which tended to be flexible in its London concerts that late in Joachim's career. They played it at St James's Hall on 2 February 1895 and repeated it on 4 February. Ireland could well have attended both performances as ticket prices were low.

[5] 28 February 1894, repeated on 14 March by popular demand.

by the late Sir Alexander Mackenzie, who was then the Principal of the Royal Academy of Music. (I remember he conducted the Symphony seated in a chair placed on the rostrum which in those days was nothing unusual.) The work made an immediate impression, and was followed by a scene of enthusiasm which left no doubt about the success of the Symphony – in fact, it's difficult to realise now, how very novel and arresting it sounded in 1894. It was full of striking rhythms – who has ever heard of a complete movement in 5–4 time? – and a *Symphony*, too! Perhaps above all one was carried away by its tremendous gamut of tempestuous emotion, expressed with such force and freedom. It was repeated by general request at the next Philharmonic concert, and was performed by Manns at the Crystal Palace concerts, and by Richter in Manchester at the Hallé concerts. I heard it under Richter, and what a performance it was! One thing I particularly remember about Richter's interpretation. When he came to the third movement – the one in common time with the march tune in the middle – he just started the orchestra and then laid down his baton on the desk in front of him, leaving the orchestra to itself, for the rest of the movement.

The Symphony is now so familiar to you all that there is no need for me to say anything more about it. Let some of the music speak for itself in the record you are about to hear.

RECORDS

We now pass over a good many years, and come to the rather queer, uneasy period leading up to the last war. In artistic and musical circles there was a feeling of searching for something new – and *different* – yes, we all wanted something different and how soon we were to have it! There were all sorts of *ISMS* in the air – Futurism, Cubism, Atonalism, and so on. Interest in the Russian Ballet of Diaghileff[6] was at its height, and that brings me to the work with which I shall end this programme – the *Rite of Spring*, by Stravinsky.

The first London performance of this was given by the Russian Ballet in 1913.[7] the theatre was packed, and it was what could be called a brilliant occasion. As people settled down in their seats one could feel the air electric with a sense of intense expectation. The conductor was in his place and the huge orchestra ready to begin. Out of this breathless silence there emerged a single sustained note – a kind of note we had never heard before – it was the top C on the bassoon, which opens the unaccompanied melodic phrase beginning the music. To place this strange, ancient-sounding phrase in the very top register of the bassoon gave exactly the remote, pre-historic atmosphere which is the prevailing note of the whole work. It was the inspiration of a master – a stroke of genius.

RECORD

It would take too long to describe one's impressions on first hearing this astonishing piece of music. Most people were puzzled – some were furious. When the music ended with the really terrifying Sacrificial Dance, the foyer was soon filled with groups of excited people, heatedly arguing about what they had heard …

This was a long time ago – nearly 30 years –. The *Rite of Spring* is still

[6] Ireland prefers 'Diaghileff' to the 'Diaghilev' we should use today.

[7] Theatre Royal, Drury Lane, 11 July 1913, conducted by Pierre Monteux.

occasionally performed, and some people seem able to hear it without turning a hair. I must confess *I* am not one of these. The work was given a concert performance by Goossens at Queen's Hall in 1921, and on that occasion[8] it created even more of a sensation than at its first performance as a ballet. Personally I think it is a mistake to try to associate this music with any definite happenings, real or imaginary – but I always feel that the musical sounds Stravinsky makes in this work seem to have the power of calling up something from the subconscious mind – some racial memories, perhaps, of things long hidden, and belonging to a remote and forgotten past.

RECORD

Albert Sammons: A Tribute

Musical Times, October 1957, p. 548

M Y personal association with Albert Sammons began during the first World War, when he had already achieved a considerable, even unique, reputation as the finest English exponent of his instrument. Naturally his playing was known to me, and I particularly remember superb performances given by him of the solo part in the concertos of Elgar and Delius. His qualities as a violinist were personal, and entirely different from those of any British or foreign performer of his time. He had a steadiness of sustained, singing tone, under perfect control, which I have never heard except in the playing of Ysaÿe. His bowing and left-hand technique reached such a degree of co-ordination and perfection that one was unconscious of them as such. When he played a work, whether chamber music or in conjunction with the orchestra, one was conscious only of the music, to which he gave sensitive and completely satisfying expression. As a personality, like all great artists, he was essentially modest, humble, and ever open to learn.

I first came to know him soon after my Second Sonata for violin and piano was completed. It was decided that he and William Murdoch should give this work its first public performance, which took place in the Aeolian Hall in March 1917 before an audience in which many leading musicians were present. At that time Sammons and Murdoch were serving in the Grenadier Guards, and were, of course, in their khaki uniforms; both of them young and boyish-looking, radiating youth and energy.

For me it was an electrifying occasion. Little of my music had been publicly heard, and I felt that my fate as a composer was to be decided at that particular moment in time, as proved to be the case. On that I need not enlarge. It was probably the first and only occasion when a British composer was lifted from relative obscurity in a single night by a work cast in a chamber-music form.

Following the results of this recital, after which Sammons and Murdoch played my A minor Sonata many times, I became musically associated with the two,

---

[8] 7 June 1921. *The Forgotten Rite* was also given in this concert, but Ireland was completely overshadowed. The Stravinsky was in the second half, with Stravinsky, Diaghilev and Massine creating a stir by arriving at the last minute before the music was due to start.

and later they gave the first performance of my Trio No. 2 in one movement, in conjunction, I think, with Warwick Evans.[9]

At a somewhat later date Columbia, then a separate company, recorded the Sonata with Sammons, the piano part played by myself; but this recording of which I still possess a copy, was never issued.[10] Naturally the preparation of this recording brought me into closer personal contact with Sammons, and for some years we met from time to time. He always impressed me as a true artist, selfless and of deep integrity, a man whose mind, personality and consummate art commanded one's unqualified respect and admiration. And it is in this light that he will ever be remembered by all who heard him and knew him; while his great qualities as an artist and teacher will, one feels sure, be passed on through a younger and rising generation.

He had a hard life, and the disabilities which attacked him in later years were a cause of great grief to those who had been privileged to know him and to profit spiritually by his wonderful art, and his pure, gentle but great personality. In these ways his name will always shine as one of the really great men in British music.

A Tribute to Vaughan Williams

Musical Times, October 1958, pp. 535–6

I N the concluding years of the 'nineties Vaughan Williams was a student with Stanford during the period when I also had that privilege. Among our fellow-students were Holst and Dunhill, and a little group or coterie resulted, which included the pianist Evlyn Howard-Jones, also a student. We were much together, attending regularly Stanford's bi-weekly orchestral rehearsals with the R.C.M. Orchestra, led at that time by Sam Grimson of the distinguished Grimson family. In those days we could attend comparatively few orchestral concerts, and there were no gramophone records.

Our group were together frequently and discussed music voraciously. We showed each other our compositions with much mutual criticism. We used to frequent a teashop in High Street, Kensington, then known as Wilkins', where we could sit for hours in animated discussions. At that time, though Vaughan Williams was by some years the eldest of us, he had not developed his later love of paradox;[11] he was, in fact, just 'one of us' as the saying goes. There was no question among us of which was the greatest. We were all humble-minded students eager to learn from Stanford and from each other. We formed a debating society with regular meetings when one or other of us would read a prepared discourse followed by mutual arguments. These were not confined to music. I recollect that Vaughan Williams delivered a discourse on Hardy's *Jude the Obscure*, at that time considered rather a daring, if not shocking, work. On one of these occasions I

---

[9] According to Craggs, John Ireland was the pianist in this performance.

[10] Now issued on CD by Dutton Vocalion on CDLX 7103.

[11] On the typescript of this article Ireland originally wrote: 'he had not developed his later habit of ex-cathedra assertions ...'

animadverted on Schopenhauer, some of whose less extended works were known to us all.[12]

When V.W. first married and went to Germany to study with Max Bruch, he was organist of the Church of St. Barnabas, South Lambeth. He persuaded me at the time to undertake his work there for the period of his six months' projected absence. Even in those early days his activities were prodigious, for, in addition to the normal work of a church organist and choirmaster, he ran a choral society and an orchestral society in connection with the church. He instructed me to prepare and produce performances of Mendelssohn's *Lauda Sion* and Stanford's *Revenge*. This was no easy task for a lad still in his 'teens and quite inexperienced.

On his return from Germany, V.W. bought or leased what he described as 'a small, cheap house' on Chelsea Embankment. The house, a beautiful one, was at the eastern corner of the fine terrace of houses, one of which, Queen's House, was at one time the residence of D. G. Rossetti, the great pre-Raphaelite painter and poet. The house, always painted white, still stands where it did, though the principal books I have read on Chelsea do not disclose the fact that it was once the residence of England's great and famous composer. For many years during Vaughan Williams's subsequent life in Chelsea, he and I remained friends, and continued our musical companionship and mutual advice and criticism.

In conclusion I have an anecdote which perhaps throws some light on the character of this great figure. In 1908, when I was writing my first Sonata for violin and piano, I showed him the slow movement, then in manuscript. When we reached the central theme in E flat minor (in Dorian mode dress) he stopped me and was silent for a minute or two. Then he said, 'Play that theme again'. After another pause he said, 'Well, that's odd. I have used practically the same theme in a song.' I was rather taken aback and asked him what we should do about this curious coincidence of a musical idea. After a moment's thought V.W. said, 'Well, we must both have cribbed it from something else, so we had better both leave it as it is – nobody will notice it'; And so far as I know, nobody ever has!

Dr Ireland Reviews his Long Career

The Times, 3 August 1959, p. 10 [signed 'From our Special Correspondent']

I T is easy to think of Dr John Ireland, who celebrates his eightieth birthday on August 13, as one whose career spans a great creative period of English music. To sit recently in his music room looking across to Chanctonbury Ring and listen to his memories of his childhood near Manchester, where Sir Charles Hallé was a visitor to his home (as were Ford Maddox Brown and Emerson), of his first meeting with Elgar, his memories of first English performances of works by Brahms and Tchaikovsky, of the musician friends who sat with him at the first performance in London of *The Rite of Spring* unable to identify the bassoon that opens the work in

---

[12] Ireland deleted the following anecdote from his published text: 'Vaughan Williams, who even then we called V.W. had a somewhat naïve sense of humour, his favourite tale or joke was: "Why does an oratorio remind you of an elderly Conservative?" Answer being *Judas Maccabaeus*. The interpretation being "Hoary Tory, O, you just mak' a bee-us (bee-house)."'

its highest register and his immediate recognition of Mr Britten's tremendous gifts when the younger composer was a candidate for a Royal College of Music scholarship, as well as his tribute to Sir Charles Stanford's greatness as a teacher, was to become aware of that period's history with all the flesh and blood excitement it brought to those who, like Dr Ireland, helped to make it.

Dr Ireland's personality has so impressed itself upon us through the certainty of aim we know in his own work – a love of nature, a spontaneous lyrical response to emotion, a swift apprehension of poetry and scenes – that it was almost surprising to listen to the range of his enthusiasms and his alert awareness of current musical activity; he spoke with lively affection of the works of Cyril Scott, Tchaikovsky, Richard Strauss, Debussy, Ravel and the Stravinsky of the early ballets and *The Symphonies of Wind Instruments* – 'So different', he said, 'from *The Rite of Spring*, but you'd know it was the same composer. You can tell Stravinsky always.'

'When I went to the Royal College of Music', Dr Ireland said. 'I was there for four years before I was able to study with Stanford in 1897; I was eight years at the college altogether. When I was a student, Brahms was still alive, the basis of Stanford's teaching and accepted as the greatest living composer. You must remember that there is a very complex musical situation nowadays, but all the time I was Stanford's pupil I heard no Debussy, no modern French music at all. Stanford knew the works of Richard Strauss; he didn't like them, but he said: "Oh well, he knows his Mozart, my boy." That was about *Till Eulenspiegel.*

'One could write a lot about Stanford; we all owe a lot to him. There was Coleridge-Taylor, who died young; then Vaughan Williams, who was about seven years my senior, Holst, myself, Sir George Dyson, Dunhill, and Dr Howells. If you take it chronologically, he was in his forties, his best period, when we all went to him, but he deplored the turn music had taken even then.

'It's difficult to analyse why he was a great teacher. I've thought, and Vaughan Williams thought, that it was because he would never accept anything but the best; he wouldn't accept work done in pencil, for instance; he would say you had no respect for your own work if you did it like that. He could be cruel, but he had no hard and fast rule; he adapted his ideas to each pupil. For example, folk-song influenced Vaughan Williams, but I have been more influenced by plainsong. You see, I was the first pupil to whom Stanford expounded the modal scales. "Your music is all Brahms and water, my boy", he said. "You'll have to study Dvořák." I did, but he still wasn't satisfied, so he taught me the modal system, basing it all upon Palestrina; he kept me at it for a whole year.'

Dr Ireland had much to say of Elgar, whose sympathy and kindness he praised. 'I met Elgar', he told me, 'when I was about nineteen, in the house of one of his Variations – B. G. N., Basil Nevinson, who used to play the cello. Elgar was in his forties; he had written the Variations and Clara Butt was singing the *Sea Pictures*, which were becoming very popular. He said to me: "Young man, are you thinking of becoming a composer?" I hesitantly told him that I hoped to do so. "For God's sake don't", he said. "Look at me. No one in this country took any notice of my music until a German told them it was good." Of course, he was referring to Strauss's praise of his work.

'I met him again four or five years before his death. Elgar was conducting at the Queen's Hall – I think it was his Second Symphony – and my *Mai-Dun* was in the same programme. Elgar told me that he was interested in the work, and I asked him if I might show him the manuscript. He told me where I could find him the next morning, and, of course, I went along with the manuscript. He didn't criticize the composition, but he impressed certain details of orchestration upon me; I've never forgotten them. He altered a few details – for example, leaving out occasional notes in some of the subsidiary parts. "I think it would be better like that", he would say. "More comfortable to play." Of course, Elgar played every instrument in the orchestra to some extent. I remember a famous bass tuba player named Barlow[13] telling me that he was giving lessons to Elgar. "He's not completely satisfied with his handling of the bass tuba", Barlow said.

'It's a curious thing that Elgar should have said to me that no one noticed his music until a German praised it, for it was a German who first published my music. I suppose my most famous and popular song is *Sea Fever*. It was refused by all the publishers in London until Wilhelm Strecker saw it in 1915 and had it published. It took the song another three years to become known. Strecker also published my piano pieces, *Decorations*; the first of these, 'The Island Spell', has become very well known. It was a best-seller among that kind of thing in the days when people still bought music.'

The music Dr Ireland composed before 1908 is not known, for much of it was destroyed and Dr Ireland told me that he had not wished to publish such pieces as he had preserved. When I asked him about these works, he said, 'I did not feel that I had found my feet when I wrote them. I wrote several orchestral pieces for Stanford – not symphonies, but fairly extended movements.'

From the first performances of Brahms's later works and the introduction of Tchaikovsky's *Pathetic* Symphony to England by Sir Alexander Mackenzie, Dr Ireland turned to historic occasions in English music, like the first performance, under Sir Adrian Boult, of Gustav Holst's *The Planets*, and the deep impression made upon him by the mastery of its orchestration. 'There is a funny story about Holst that Balfour Gardiner used to tell', he said. 'Holst used to compose only in the summer holidays at St Paul's Girls' School in Hammersmith. He had a small room with a gas fire, which he always lit. "There sits Holst", said Balfour Gardiner, "and the room gets hotter and hotter whilst the music gets colder and colder."'

Turning to modern conditions, Dr Ireland talked about the changes in the actual sound of music that have come about in more or less recent times; to him they indicate a sacrifice of richness to efficiency. 'The use of wire strings has altered string tone very much', he said. 'The oboe has altered considerably – it's much milder than it used to be; the clarinet is losing robustness – there are very few players now who play like Frederick Thurston. The bassoon has become much more gentlemanly. You remember the four descending notes in the bassoon that leave it exposed at the end of the exposition in Tchaikovsky's Sixth. Symphony?' Dr Ireland hummed the phrase to remind me. 'In the early days the bassoon couldn't be trusted with them and they had to be played by the bass clarinet. We don't have the noble E and F trumpets now, and the bassoon is less sonorous. Nowadays,

[13] Mr H. Barlow played in the first performance of *The Apostles* at Birmingham in 1903.

when I'm listening to a string quartet, the two violins sound sharp and wiry against the mellow viola and cello; they don't seem to blend so well.

'I had a curious experience of the change in the orchestra a little time ago', Dr Ireland continued. 'When I was at the Royal College and Stanford was in charge of the orchestra, he was very fond of Dvořák's overture *In der Natur* and he often used to play it in rehearsal, so I got to know it very well. It was played again at a concert in the Royal College not very long ago, and I heard *In der Natur* again in the same hall, with the same acoustic conditions, and the sounds were quite different.'

Dr Ireland rarely comes to London nowadays, partly, he suggested, because London has a special atmosphere, compounded of petrol and diesel fumes, which begin at Leatherhead, but he intends to be present at a concert to be given in the autumn in celebration of his birthday.

JOHN IRELAND'S PROGRAMME NOTES FOR HIS OWN MUSIC

Ireland only left notes for a small selection of his works, not all of them published in his lifetime. Among them he included one actually written by the baritone George Parker, which we have included here for its authentic first-hand history of the song.

Sea Fever: A Note by George Parker

Undated typescript: John Ireland Trust

'SEA Fever' was composed in Chelsea in October 1913. I saw the MSS immediately after it was composed and like it very much. It was given a first performance by another singer who did not think a great deal of it. I had the second performance with John Ireland at the pianoforte at the Three Arts Club in Marylebone Road. This was from the MSS. Before it was ever published I sang it a great deal particularly to the soldiers in the 1914–1918 war in France and England. It was always received well. In 1914 with John Ireland I sang it to Mr Leslie Boosey at their Regent Street premises with a view to Booseys publishing it. Mr Boosey liked it but John Masefield having given the right of setting the poem to music to Geoffrey Morland, nobody knew where to look for him and get the necessary release of this right. Incidentally, some years afterwards, when I was speaking to the professional Manager of Booseys, I told him (the song then having a very big and successful sale) what a chance they had missed. He replied that they had just at that time published a song about the sea which was not a success, so they did not much wish to publish another. (This song was 'The Sea Road'[14] by Haydn Wood.)

Soon after this Boosey audition John Ireland and I went to Augeners. The principal director Dr Strecker said at once that he would publish it in 1915 and the

---

[14] One of *Three Sea Songs* with words by P. J. O'Reilly first published in 1910 and separately in 1911. Soon after, Ireland would set words by O'Reilly in his *Here's to the Ships!* and *Song from Over the Hill*.

Manager Mr Volkert, some years afterwards, said it was selling 10,000 a year and it would sell at this rate for 20 years.

Some years after all this I sang the song at a lecture in Folkestone where John Masefield was speaking and reading some of his poems. It was the first time he had heard the setting. He told me that the music did not agree at all with his meaning of the poem.[15] I have in my possession two original MSS of the setting.[16]

Sonata no. 2 in A minor for Violin and Piano

Undated typescript: John Ireland Trust

I WAS born at Bowdon in Cheshire, a pleasant country place about ten miles south of the town of Manchester. Both my parents were distinguished in the literary world, and when I was a child our home was the rendezvous of many famous authors, poets, painters and some musicians. My mother was a good amateur musician who played the piano and sang well. At that time Manchester was a great place for the cultivation of music, because many German men of business had made their home there, and besides meetings for performance of Chamber Music there was the still famous Hallé Orchestra, conducted by its founder, the late Sir Charles Hallé. Artists of world-wide reputation visited Manchester, and I remember that as a child I first heard Paderewski, who was then a young man with a great shock of red hair.

When I was about six years old, I had my first music lessons from my mother. Later on at school I was taught the piano and the violin, thus learning something about stringed instruments. Before I was 14 I had quite made up my mind that I wished to become a musician. At that time my sister was studying music in London, and in 1893 I joined her and entered the Royal College of Music. For four years I took the piano as my principal study, learning also the organ and submitting to a very thorough, and indeed severe course of training in harmony, counterpoint, form, and general musical subjects such as history and the technique of the orchestra. I was able to attend many concerts, both chamber and orchestral. There were the Monday and Saturday 'Pops' at the old St James's Hall where one constantly heard Chamber Music under such exponents as the Joachim Quartet, and so one became familiar with the classics, and the works of Brahms, who was still the greatest living composer. Also I attended the bi-weekly rehearsals of the R.C.M. orchestra, which familiarised me with many works. Meanwhile I had made various efforts at composition, and in 1897 I was awarded a scholarship for that subject, and became a pupil of the late Sir Charles Stanford, with whom I remained for 4 years. He was a severe master but a great teacher, though his sympathies were with the classics and he was somewhat suspicious of modern developments in music, that is to say, anything later than Brahms.

By this time, both my parents had died, and when my studies were ended, and even before then, I was faced with the problem of making my living, by taking whatever musical work I could find. I took a post as organist of a church where

[15] Masefield subsequently authorised several settings but none of them achieved the celebrity of John Ireland's song.

[16] Now in British Library Add. MS 71543.

I had to train the choir and conduct a choral society. I also took pupils in piano, organ and composition, and did accompanying, and any odd jobs I could find. Meanwhile I was able to devote much time to composition. Naturally, during my student days, and afterwards, I composed many works of various kinds, but I discarded or destroyed everything I wrote before I was 27. Not till then did I feel I had even partially mastered my problems or formed any individual style. My first Violin Sonata in D minor was completed in 1908, the one you are about to hear, No. 2 in A minor, was finished in 1916. This was written during the First World War, and the music displays the influence of those strenuous days. Why was I not in the British Army fighting for my country? My health and physique failed to reach the standard required, and after several medical examinations I was rejected for any form of military service. I was able, however, to undertake civilian work in connection with the War and this left me enough time to continue my composition, in the intervals of other duties.

I am not one of those composers who feels anxious, or, indeed, able to talk about his own music. Whatever I have to say is said in the music, and if this does not speak for itself, then I have failed. All I can say is that as it was written 34 years ago[17] it does not show the influence of any modern fashion, such as atonality. The work was first played in public at the Aeolian Hall, London, in March 1917,[18] by Albert Sammons (violin) and William Murdoch (piano) who were at that time the foremost English performers on their respective instruments. On this occasion the *élite* of musical London were present and the work, by a practically unknown composer, made a deep and immediate impression, in fact it was said at the time that it scored a *succès fou*, and almost at once put the composer's name 'on the map', so to speak.

I may say this was the first and only time any work of mine has met with such an unmistakably enthusiastic reception on its first performance. It would seem that this sonata appeared at just the right, the psychological moment, and that it expressed in music something which everybody was feeling, which, up to that moment, had not been embodied in musical sound by an English composer. This is not to say the work itself is either good or bad – only the test of time can decide that – but that is what actually happened in 1917. So it came about that the sonata was played nine times in London during that first season, and all the copies of the first edition were bought or ordered before it was actually printed. In fact, the very next morning after the performance a music publisher called on me before I had breakfasted and practically tore the MS out of my hands! This was a strange experience in those days, when music publishers were very unwilling to take the risk of publishing a work of this sort, especially in the case of a little-known composer. Now, in 1950, *nous avons changé tout cela*!! It is in three movements, and follows a more or less classical form in its construction.

Mai-Dun: Symphonic Rhapsody

Ireland's note from the Leeds Festival on 7 October 1922 appears on p. 203.

[17] Ireland wrote this note in 1950.
[18] 6 March 1917.

Piano Concerto in E♭

Typescript: John Ireland Trust

T HE work was begun in 1929 and completed in 1930. It was not 'commissioned' or written for any special occasion. Though some of the work was composed in Sussex and some in London, the music is not influenced by either locality. Having written a good deal of piano music it happened that at the time I decided my next work should be for piano and orchestra in concerto form. Not primarily for display of virtuosity but treated in such a way that the solo part and the orchestra are of equal importance and not independent in the presentation of the musical ideas which are comprised in the work.

At the time I was writing the Concerto I was rung up by Jack Payne. He said he had heard I was at work on this and asked me if I intended to use any muted brass in my score. At that time the mute in general use was a pear-shaped piece of brass, pierced with holes, which was inserted in the bell of the trumpets, trombones, and occasionally in the tubas. Payne asked me if I was aware that in dance bands several other types of mutes were used, and offered to let me hear the effect of these. I paid a visit to a studio to hear his band, when he let me listen to the results of the four or five types of mutes he had referred to. After listening carefully to these, I decided that one type of mute, a cone-shaped mute made of fibre, was far more effective than the one type then used in symphony orchestras. In my score I gave directions that the fibre mute should be used. I believe I was the first composer of serious music to specify this special type of mute, and I was hauled over the coals by the most famous critic of that day for 'hob-nobbing with dance band conductors'. Since then the fibre mute (first used in British symphonic music by me), has become standard and entirely superseded the pear-shaped brass mute referred to above.

Another unusual point in my orchestral treatment in this concerto has been entirely overlooked by all critics. The timpani being an integral part of the full orchestra have been used, at several other places, in all orchestral movements. It occurred to me ~~that~~ in orchestrating the concerto that a special effect would be obtained by omitting the timpani entirely in my first movement, and reserving their entry till the soloist's closing bars of the slow movement, where they are heard for the first time, played softly, in a rhythmic figure characteristic of these instruments.

A London Overture

Programme note by John Ireland for the Queen's Hall Promenade Concert on 23 September 1936 when the BBC Symphony Orchestra was conducted by Sir Henry Wood. It is described as 'first orchestral performance'.

T HIS Overture in its original state was written in 1934 as the Test Piece for the Championship Bands in connection with the National Brass Band Contest at the Crystal Palace. Recently it was suggested to the composer that the piece should be made available for a symphonic orchestra, and it has now been re-written for this medium.

In course of this process the music has had to be entirely re-cast, the original material forming only a basis, so that it is virtually a new work.

The Overture is in normal classical form. A slow Introduction presents the material from which the two main subjects of the succeeding *Allegro* arise. It has been stated that the first four notes of the principal theme were based on the word 'Piccadilly' as called out by a bus conductor. The fragment on which this theme is built certainly follows the rhythm and inflection of the word. The second principal theme is a tune of some length first heard on the oboe with accompaniment of muted strings. The middle section, after reaching a climax, embodies a contrasting period in slower time, where a solo horn is prominent. There is a condensed recapitulation and a short *coda*.

The composer wishes this Overture to be regarded as No. 4 of his *London Pieces*, the first three, 'Chelsea Reach', 'Ragamuffin', and 'Soho Forenoons', having been written for piano in 1917 and 1918.

Concertino Pastorale

IN reply to your letter[19] re my 'Concertino Pastorale' for String Orchestra, this was composed during the early months of 1939. At the time, I was living partly in Deal, Kent, though domiciled, as always, in Chelsea.

The work was NOT commissioned, but I was asked to write a work for this occasion, and felt disposed to do so at the time, though I am not partial to 'commissions', and have very seldom accepted them.[20] But it happened, at the time, that I felt like writing something for this medium.

Whatever I had in mind is expressed in the music, and cannot be put into words. At that particular time, the menace of Hitler hung rather heavily on any thinking person, and it is to be noticed, perhaps, that the first movement opens with a distorted and 'nightmarish' treatment of the spring-like theme which is the real basis of the movement. The Threnody perhaps expresses in some way the transitoriness and poignancy of the beautiful. After the seriousness of the two preceding movements, the Toccata gives some sense of liberation, and musically is a change in texture and form from the closely-packed Eclogue and the emotion of the Threnody. A heavy, substantial movement would, in my opinion, have been out of place, though I have been criticised for its not being substantial enough. You will note that the Toccata really has only one theme, the quieter middle section being a melodic version of what at first appears as mainly a rhythmic motif involving the notes A, C, D, G. The repeat indicated should always be played, but the second time more softly than the first.

Curiously enough, though this work was written for small string orchestra, it really 'comes off' much better when given by a large body of strings – superb performances have been given by Boult and Cameron with the B.B.C. orchestra and the L.P.O. respectively – the former in 1940, the latter in 1950. Such is the fate of works by British composers who do not cultivate the gentle art of Publicity for most of their time.

---

[19] In fact a letter to Harold Rawlinson dated 9 June 1951.

[20] Ireland fails to acknowledge that all his later orchestral works were commissions.

I may say the first movement is often taken too fast for the harmonic structure to be taken in by the listener – and the Threnody, if *too* slow, becomes a bore. The Toccata should *not* be taken at virtuoso speed – [i.e. as fast as the players can move their bows.] It should give a sense of movement of a bustling kind but not a terrible rush. It has an underlying humour which is often absent in performance, owing to breathless hurry.

You can make whatever use you like of the above, but please do not indicate that any of it comes from myself! Please on no account 'acknowledge' any of it to me, except the bare facts about date and place of composition.

As to 'years to come', you are indeed an optimist. No one can tell whether any composition from the living British writers will have any existence at all in 50 or 30 or even 20 years hence.

In this piece I did my best to express something I had felt myself, pretty keenly, and in a way which would be grateful to those musicians who did me the honour to perform it.

There are in existence three other of my pieces (of a similar kind) for string orchestra – namely – ELEGY and Minuet, and making an arrangement of my tune 'the Holy Boy', all published by Boosey and Hawkes. The two former are free arrangement from a suite I wrote for brass band, but are very much more effective on string orchestra. All three are practically unknown and unperformed.

Sarnia

From a letter to Edwin Evans dated 1 December 1941

I N reference to your sympathetic note on 'Sarnia' in the B. & H. programme,[21] the dates I have placed after Nos. 1 & 2 actually refer to the inception of these pieces, not their completion, and 'April 1940 – March 1941' really is meant to cover the whole period from the time when I first thought of this work till it was actually finished.

You may like to know that my association with the Channel Islands began in 1908. In that year, and in every succeeding year till and including 1914 I spent 7 or 8 weeks there, also I was in Guernsey from June 1939 till June 22, 1940. The Germans bombed the Island on June 28 and occupied it on June 30 (1940). The British Government de-militarised the Channel Islands on Wednesday June 19th, and within 24 hours every soldier, every gun and every aeroplane had vanished as if by magic, the harbour and the large aerodrome being left intact for the Germans to use (Guernsey) …

By the way, I prefaced the 2nd number of 'Sarnia' with the Victor Hugo passage[22] after I had finished the piece – it is not intended to describe the music,

---

[21] First performance by Clifford Curzon, Wigmore Hall, 29 November 1941.

[22] Victor Hugo, *Les Travailleurs de la mer*, chap. 5, 'The Great Tomb': 'C'était un de ces jours printaniers où mai se dépense tout entier. Sous toutes les rumeurs, de la forêt comme du village, de la vague comme de l'atmosphère, il y avait un roucoulement. Les premiers papillons se posaient sur les premières roses. La profonde chanson des arbres était chantée par des oiseaux nés d'hier. Ils chantaient leur premier chant, ils volaient leur premier vol. Le printemps jetait tout son argent et tout

which contains some element of regret or wistfulness, but rather the unalloyed beauty to which the music is my reaction. On the other hand, the Latin quotation from Pomponius Mela[23] does embody what I have tried to express in 'Le Catioroc'. Your suggestion that this piece is in some sense related to 'the Forgotten Rite' is true, though the latter is concerned with a less sinister or 'whiter' side of these things – and you might with justice have added that my little-known 'Legend' for piano and orchestra comes within the same category, as perhaps also do 'Mai-Dun' and the finale of my piano sonata.

I don't mean to bore you with all this, but you must be aware that you are the only music critic who has the insight and sympathy to know or care what I or any of us are about.

Satyricon

T HIS overture, which lasts about eight minutes, is not programme-music, though its mood is based on some aspects of the 'Satyricon' of Petronius, which the composer knows principally from Burnaby's quaint translation of the Latin text.

The music describes no particular scenes or episodes, but was prompted by the author's description of some of the vagabond and carefree adventures and escapades of the three Roman youths around which the story revolves – Encolpius, the narrator of the story, his friend Ascyltus, and their attendant, Gito.

The form and musical material of the overture are straightforward and call for no special comment. An orchestra of moderate size is employed. The work is dedicated to Julian Herbage and Anna Instone and was completed in August 1946.[24]

son or dans l'immense panier percé des bois. Les pousses nouvelles étaient toutes fraîches vertes. Partout une divine plénitude et un gonflement mystérieux faisaient deviner l'effort panique et sacré de la sève en travail. Qui brillait, brillait plus; qui aimait, aimait mieux ...'

(THE TOILERS OF THE SEA: It was one of those days of spring when May unleashes her full force. Amid the many murmurs of forest and village, the sound of cooing could be heard. The first butterflies were resting on the first roses. The profound song of the trees was sung by birds born yesterday. They sang their first song, they flew their first flight. The spring set out all its silver and all its gold in the great basket of the woods. The new shoots were all green and fresh with sap. All round a divine plenitude and a mysterious growth signalled the hallowed power of the rising sap. What shone, shone brighter; who loved, loved more.) [EDITOR'S LITERAL TRANSLATION]

[23] Quoted as a footnote on pp. 188–9.

[24] From the programme of the first performance on 11 September 1946, when the BBC Symphony Orchestra was conducted by Constant Lambert.

Fig. 31 John Ireland. Pen and ink drawing by W. Powys Evans, 1932.

John Ireland's Addresses

'Inglewood', St Margaret's Road, Bowdon, Cheshire

Chichester Street, Paddington

Broadhurst Gardens, West Hampstead

10 Sunningdale Gardens, Stratford Road, Kensington

46 Winchendon Road, Fulham

43 Markham Square, Chelsea

62 Limerston Street, Chelsea

54 Elm Park Mansions, Park Walk, Chelsea SW [1904–15]

The Studio, 14A Gunter Grove, Chelsea, London SW10

14 Gunter Grove, Chelsea, London SW10

16 Middle Street, Deal, Kent

'Comarques', 122 High Street, Deal, Kent

'Woodside', Blanches-Pierres Lane, St Martin's, Guernsey, Channel Islands

Fort Saumarez, L'Érée, Guernsey, Channel Islands

Birnam Court Hotel, St Peter Port, Guernsey, Channel Islands [April–June 1940]

'Clifton', 3 Loom Lane, Radlett, Herts [Alan Bush's mother's house]

25 Christchurch Crescent, Radlett, Herts [Alan Bush's house]

15 Calthorpe Road, Banbury, Oxon

The Rectory, Little Sampford, Saffron Walden, Essex

The White House, Great Sampford, Saffron Walden, Essex

Chelsea Arts Club, 143 Church Street, London SW3

Old Rectory, Ashington, Sussex

Meiros Farm, Ashington, Pulborough, Sussex

Rock Mill, Washington, Pulborough, Sussex [October 1953–1962]

A Note on John Ireland's Handwriting

J OHN Ireland's handwriting is generally small and can be difficult to decipher. The two examples reproduced here for comparative purposes date from the early days of the war and from 1953. The writing in the latter period is generally more legible than the former. Ireland's writing is notable for the idiosyncratic formation of capital I in mid-sentence, contraction of words such as should (sh^{ld}) and would (w^{ld}), the abbreviation of various words replacing the missing letters with a colon (:) such as wh: instead of which.

The first (Fig. 31) is the first page of a multi-page letter in which John Ireland tries to persuade his friend Thomas F. Dunhill to join him on Guernsey. In the second (Fig. 32) Ireland writes a letter of condolence to Arnold Bax's Storrington companion Mary Gleaves after the death of Bax.

TRANSCRIPT OF FIG. 31

Sept: 21, 1939

My dear Tom

Many thanks for your letter wh: I received today. The mails leave Southampton on Monday, Wednesday & Friday nights only, so you must have caught Wednesday's mail.

I sh^{ld} think it is a great deal better here, in many ways, than in most parts of England. We have A.R.P. & a strict "blackout", & there are a few warplanes at the aerodrome, but all this is only precautionary, there is no industry here except tomato growing, & it seems to me while England is such an obvious target for attack, anything of the sort here is very unlikely – some stray enemy planes might get here if beaten off Southampton or Weymouth – but if you look at a map & see the great distances from Guernsey (to return to its base) involving flight over France, you will agree it is very improbable. Food is plentiful, & rationing has not begun yet. I am saying all this to see if I can persuade you to come to Guernsey. The Longmire's would be delighted to see you, & needless to say I should welcome a kindred spirit & an old friend, & should be much happier if you were here. I feel very isolated, & altho' Longmire is quite a good chap in his way & means very well, too much of him gets on my nerves. You could be accommodated with a bed here, but you w^{ld} be more comfortable in a seaside hotel, or rooms – there are plenty of both, and at very moderate rates, especially as all the visitors …

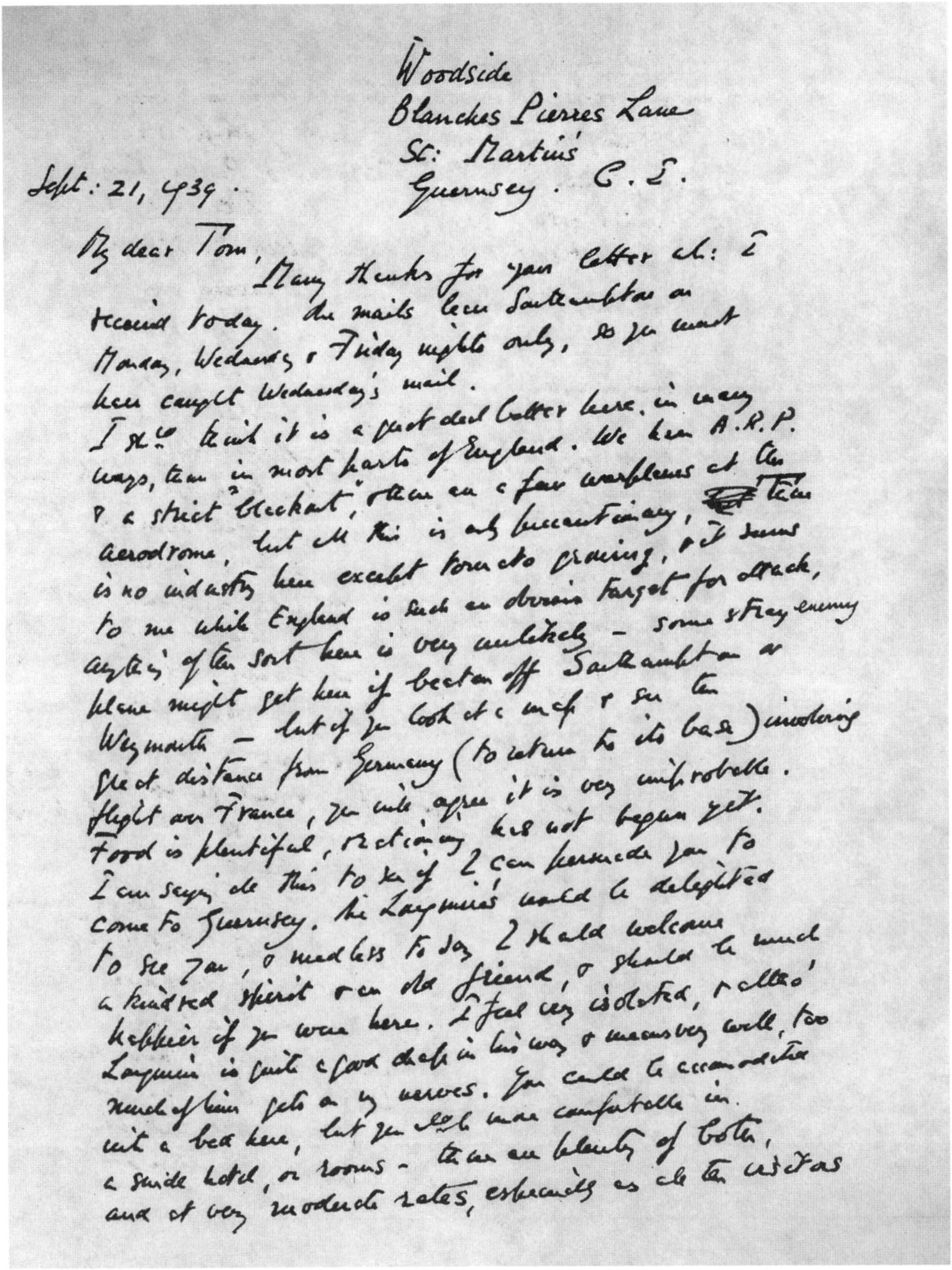

Fig. 32 Ireland's handwriting in September 1939: a letter to the composer Thomas F. Dunhill

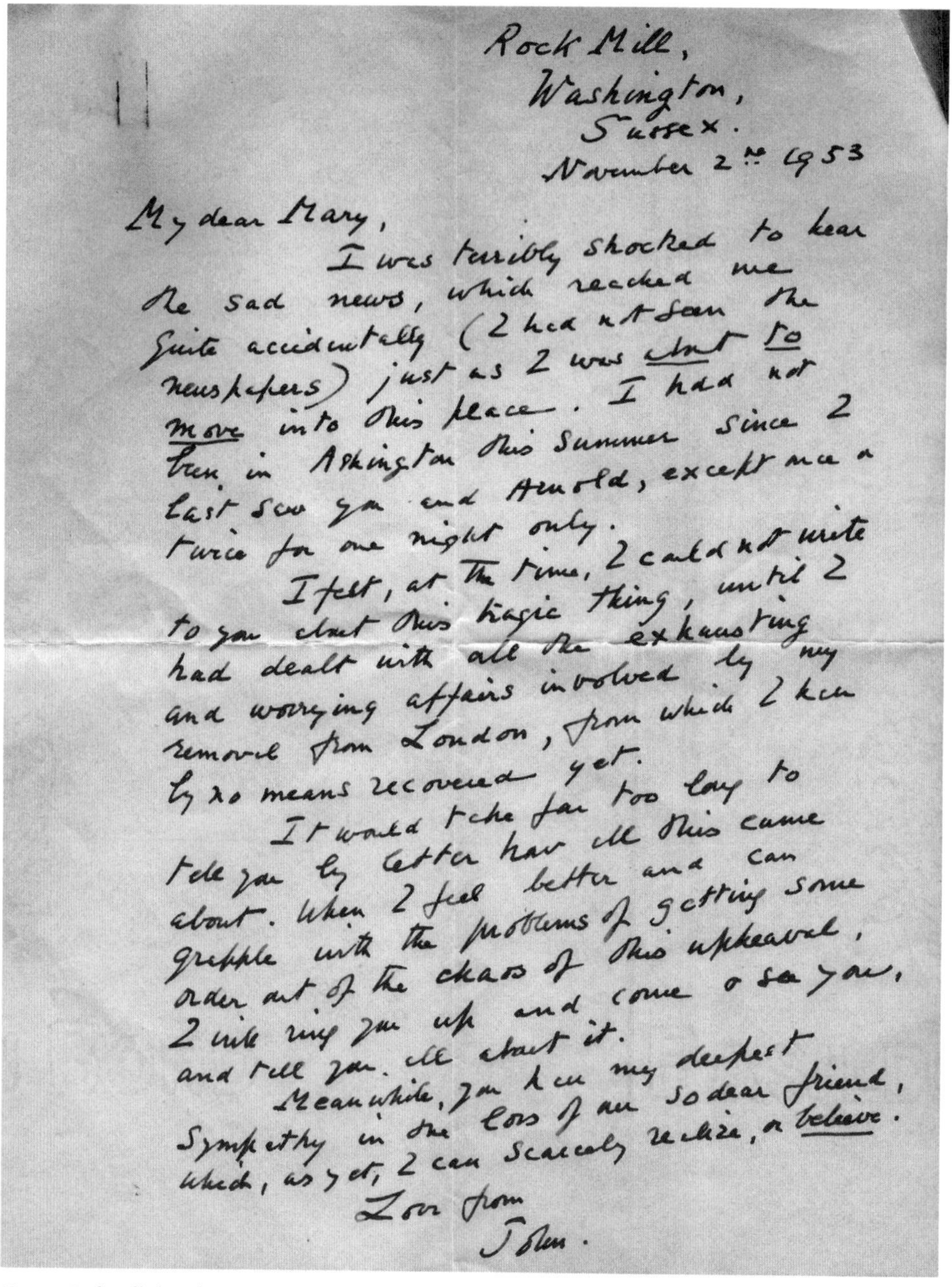

Rock Mill,
Washington,
Sussex.
November 2ⁿᵈ 1953

My dear Mary,

I was terribly shocked to hear the sad news, which reached me quite accidentally (I had not seen the newspapers) just as I was about to move into this place. I had not been in Ashington this Summer since I last saw you and Arnold, except me a twice for one night only.

I felt, at the time, I could not write to you about this tragic thing, until I had dealt with all the exhausting and worrying affairs involved by my removal from London, from which I have by no means recovered yet.

It would take far too long to tell you by letter how all this came about. When I feel better and can grapple with the problems of getting some order out of the chaos of this upheaval, I will ring you up and come o see you, and tell you all about it.

Meanwhile, you have my deepest sympathy in the loss of so dear a friend, which, as yet, I can scarcely realize, or believe.

Love from
John.

Fig. 33 Ireland's handwriting in November 1953: a letter of condolence to Arnold Bax's companion Mary Gleaves

Catalogue of John Ireland's Works

I N this catalogue Ireland's music is listed by genre and then alphabetically. This compilation is primarily intended to aid performers and students, giving the forces required and the source of the music. For a full historical listing the reader is referred to Stewart Craggs' authoritative catalogue.[1] Four popular ballads Ireland published under the pseudonym of 'Turlay Royce' are here listed in the main sequence of songs. For the location of Ireland scores in major libraries, and full bibliographic details of those copies, search Copac on the Internet (Copac.ac.uk). Ireland's published music is widely available from public libraries and where not in local stock via inter-library loan. Many second hand copies can be located by searching ABEbooks.com or other web bookseller co-operatives online. Owing to take-overs Ascherberg, Hopwood & Crew became Chappell (later Warner-Chappell); Augener, Galliard and Joseph Williams are now Stainer & Bell; Boosey, Hawkes and Winthrop Rogers are now Boosey & Hawkes, and are generally cited thus; Novello, J. & W. Chester and Edwin Ashdown are now Music Sales but retain their own imprints.

ORCHESTRAL AND BAND

The forces required by each work are given in the customary shorthand, the instruments listed in the order: flute (piccolo), oboe (cor anglais), clarinet (bass clarinet), bassoon (contra-bassoon) – horn, trumpet (cornet), trombones, tuba – harp, timpani, percussion, strings. Thus 2222 4231 hp timp 2perc org strings would mean two each of the woodwind (flute, oboe, clarinet, bassoon), 4 horns 2 trumpets, 3 trombones and 1 tuba, harp, timpani, percussion for two players, organ, strings (violins 1 and 2, viola, cello and double basses). If one of the players doubles on another instrument that will be in parentheses; if an additional player is required it will be indicated by a + sign. Thus 2(1) 2(1) 2(1) 2(1) in the woodwind line means two flutes one doubling piccolo, two oboes, one doubling cor anglais, 2 clarinets one doubling bass clarinet, 2 bassoons, one doubling contra-bassoon. 2+1 2+1 2+1 2+1 would mean an extra player would be required for each of the additional instruments. 'Ad lib' (e.g. in the case of the organ) means that instrument is optional.

Publishers (in a few cases individuals) are given from which orchestral materials may be hired or otherwise obtained. Amateur and student performing groups may wish to note that sets of printed parts of nine of Ireland's orchestral works which were once on sale are available from public library collections via interlibrary loan at nominal cost. A full listing of these with locations of sets can be found in the Encore! Database[2] on the IAML (UK&Irl) website. They include *Concertino Pastorale*; *A Downland Suite* (band version and the 'Minuet and Elegy' scored for strings); *The Forgotten Rite*; *The Holy Boy*; *Mai-Dun*; the *Orchestral*

---

[1] Stewart R. Craggs, *John Ireland: A Catalogue, Discography and Bibliography*, 2nd edn (Aldershot: Ashgate, 2007).

[2] ENCORE! The British Union Catalogue of Performing Music Sets (www.iaml.info/iaml-uk-irl/projects/encore.html or select from the IAML-UK front page (iaml-uk-irl.org).

Poem; *Villanella*, *A Maritime Overture* (for band). There are also twelve similar screens of locations for choral music by Ireland. Those thus available are noted below.

The following listing includes works initially written as instrumental solos that have been orchestrated by hands other than Ireland, and vocal works with orchestral accompaniment.

ANNABEL LEE (1910; orch. Roderick Williams, 2010)
  (Stainer & Bell: 2222 2000 timp perc hp strings)

BAGATELLE (1911; orch. Leslie Bridgewater 1916)
  (Novello/Music Sales: 1121 21cnt10 timp perc strings)
  ⁎ arr. military band, C. F. Smyly
  orchestration of *Bagatelle* for violin and piano, *q.v.*

BERCEUSE (1903; orch. Martin Yates 2009)
  (Stainer & Bell: solo violin, 2122 2000 timp perc hp celesta strings)
  orchestration of *Berceuse* for violin and piano, *q.v.*

CAVATINA (1904; orch. Graham Parlett 2008)
  (solo violin, strings; available from John Ireland Trust)
  orchestration of *Cavatina* for violin and piano, *q.v.*

COMEDY OVERTURE for brass band
  (R. Smith & Co., 1934)
  ⁎ arr. wind band, R. Steadman-Allen (R. Smith & Co., 1987)
  later reworked as the orchestral *A London Overture*, *q.v.*

CONCERTINO PASTORALE for strings
  (Boosey & Hawkes: there are many locations for sets of parts on Encore)

A DOWNLAND SUITE for brass band
  1. Prelude 2. Elegy 3. Minuet 4. Rondo
  (R. Smith & Co., 1933)
  ⁎ arr. strings: nos. 2 & 3, composer; nos. 1 & 4, Geoffrey Bush
  nos. 2 & 3 (Boosey & Hawkes: there are locations for sets of parts on Encore)
  ⁎ arr. winds, R. Steadman-Allen (R. Smith & Co., 1985)
  ⁎ nos. 2 & 3 arr. piano, composer (Edwin Ashdown, 1933), *Vol. 6*
  ⁎ no.2 arr. organ, Alec Rowley (Edwin Ashdown, 1940)

ELEGIAC MEDITATION for strings (1959; orch. Geoffrey Bush 1982)
  (Novello, 1982)
  orchestration of the *Meditation on John Keble's Rogation Hymn* for organ (1958), *q.v.*

EPIC MARCH (1942)
  (Boosey & Hawkes: 2+1 222 4231 timp 2perc org ad lib strings)
  ⁎ arr. symphonic wind band, Geoffrey Brand, 1989
  (R. Smith & Co, 1990: 2+1 2 3+5 0 4sax 42+2 30 euph timp perc double basses)
  ⁎ arr. piano, composer (Boosey & Hawkes, 1942)
  ⁎ arr. organ, Robert Gower 1988 (Boosey & Hawkes, 1988)

THE FORGOTTEN RITE: Prelude for Orchestra
(Stainer & Bell: 3+1 2+1 2+1 2 4230 timp celesta hp strings; also available via
Encore)
% arr. piano duet (Augener, 1918)

**GREATER LOVE HATH NO MAN: A Motet for Passiontide and Other
Seasons** ('Many Waters Cannot Quench Love') (1912; orch. 1922)
(Stainer & Bell: bar and treble soli, SATB 2222 4331 timp organ strings;
locations for sets of vocal scores on Encore)

THE HOLY BOY for strings (1913; orch. composer 1941)
(Boosey & Hawkes)
% arr. cello and strings, orch. Christopher Palmer 1994
% arr. violin and strings, Graham Parlett 2008

IN PRAISE OF NEPTUNE: SATB and orchestra, or baritone and orchestra
(Chappell: 2222 2200 timp 2perc strings. Locations for sets of the two-part
version on Encore. See below for the unison song version with piano and the
version for SATB and piano.)

IN SUMMER WOODS (arr. SATB and orch., T. Widicombe)
(BBC Music Library: 1121 2000 perc strings)
arr. of original version for SA and piano, *q.v.*

LEGEND for piano and orchestra
(Schott: solo piano 22+1 22 4020 timp 2perc strings)
% arr. two pianos (Schott, 1932)

A LONDON OVERTURE
(Boosey & Hawkes: 2+1 222 4321 timp 3perc strings)
reworking of *A Comedy Overture* for orchestra, *q.v.*

MAI-DUN: Symphonic Rhapsody
(Stainer & Bell: 3+1 2+1 2+1 2 4331 timp 3perc strings; also available via Encore)
% arr. piano duet (Augener, 1931)

MARITIME OVERTURE (arr. from *Tritons*)
% for military band by Norman Richardson
(Boosey & Hawkes, 1946: 2(1) 2 3+1 2 3 sax 42+3cnt 30 euph percussion double
basses)
% arr. symphonic wind band, Norman Richardson
(Boosey & Hawkes, 1988: 2+1 2 3+3 4 2+3cnt 30 euph timp perc double basses)

MERRY ANDREW (1919; orch. C. H. Clutsam 1931)
(Chappell: 1121 2210 timp perc hp strings)
% orch. James Brash 1934
(score John Ireland Trust, no parts: 111+1 alto & tenor sax 1 2011 timp strings)

O HAPPY LAND (unison chorus and strings)
(Boosey & Hawkes, 1941)

ORCHESTRAL POEM in A minor
(On sale from Da Capo Music Ltd, 26 Stanway Road, Whitefield, Manchester M45 8EG or loan via Encore or from John Ireland Trust: 2(1) 222 4231 timp 1perc strings)

THE OVERLANDERS, Film Music
※ Incidental music arr. Mathieson
※ [Prelude only arr. Mathieson]
※ Orchestral Suite (arr. Mackerras)
(Boosey & Hawkes: 2+1 2+1 22 43+1 31 timp 3perc hp strings)
※ Two Symphonic Studies (arr. Geoffrey Bush)
(Boosey & Hawkes: 2222 4331 timp 2perc strings)

PIANO CONCERTO in E♭
(J. & W. Chester [Music Sales]: Solo piano 2+1 222 4231 timp 2perc strings)
※ arr. two pianos, composer (J. & W. Chester, 1932)

SARNIA: AN ISLAND SEQUENCE (1940–1; orch. Martin Yates 2011)
(Boosey & Hawkes: 3(1) 2+1 2+1 2+1 4331 timp perc bells hp celesta strings)
orchestration of *Sarnia: An Island Sequence* for piano, *q.v.*

SATYRICON OVERTURE
(Stainer & Bell: 2+1 222 422+1 1 timp 2perc hp strings)

SCHERZO AND CORTEGE (from *Julius Caesar*, arr. Geoffrey Bush)
(Boosey & Hawkes: 2+1 2+1 2+1 2 3231 timp 2perc no upper strings double basses only)

SOLILOQUY (1922; orch. Graham Parlett 2009)
(Stainer & Bell: solo violin, strings)
arr. of *Soliloquy* for piano, *q.v.*

SONGS WITH ORCHESTRA

Annabel Lee: recitation with orchestra (1910; orch. Roderick Williams 2009)
(Stainer & Bell/BBC Music Library: 2222 2000 timp hp perc strings)

Five Songs for soprano & orchestra (orch. Graham Parlett, 2008)
Note: 'Five Songs' is not the composer's usage, but reflects their grouping on Dutton Epoch's recording CDLX 7228.

Love and Friendship (Emily Brontë, 1926)
(Stainer & Bell: 21+1 22 2000 perc strings)

My True Love Hath My Heart (Sir Philip Sydney, 1920)
(Stainer & Bell: 2222 2120 timp strings)

The Trellis (Aldous Huxley, 1920)
(Stainer & Bell: 2222 2000 timp strings)

Adoration (Arthur Symons, 1918)
(Chester/Novello: 1122 2000 strings)

I Have Twelve Oxen (Anon., 1918)
(Boosey & Hawkes: 2222 2000 perc strings)

Four Songs for soprano & strings (orch. Graham Parlett, 2008)
Note: 'Four Songs' is not the composer's usage, but reflects their grouping on Dutton Epoch's recording CDLX 7228.

The Salley Gardens (William Butler Yeats, *c.* 1931)
(Schott)

The Heart's Desire (A. E. Housman, 1917)
(Boosey & Hawkes)

Baby (Christina Rossetti, 1918)
(Boosey & Hawkes)

Her Song (Thomas Hardy, 1925)
(Cramer)

Here's To the Ships (1911; orch. composer 1912)
(John Ireland Trust: 2222 2220 timp perc strings)

The Holy Boy: A Carol of the Nativity (Herbert S. Brown)
(Boosey & Hawkes: strings)

Hope the Hornblower (Sir Henry Newbolt) – orch. Frederick Bye
(Boosey & Hawkes: 1121 2000 hp strings)

If There Were Dreams to Sell (Thomas Lovell Beddoes) – orch. E. Griffiths
(Boosey & Hawkes 2222 4230 timp perc hp strings)
(BBC: orch. Frederick Bye, 0000 0000 hp strings)

In Praise of Neptune (1911, orch. composer)
(Chappell: 2222 2200 timp perc strings)

Sea Fever (John Masefield), bar, chorus (ad lib) and orchestra
(Stainer & Bell: 1121 2330 timp perc strings)

When I Am Dead, My Dearest (Christina Rossetti)
(John Ireland Trust: strings)

When Lights Go Rolling Round the Sky (James Vila Blake) (1911, orch. D. Darlow)
(Boosey & Hawkes 3+1 222 4231 timp perc hp strings)

Youth's Spring-Tribute (Dante Gabriel Rossetti) (orch. composer, completed Graham Parlett)
(3+1 2+1 2+1 2 4000 timp celesta hp strings)

THESE THINGS SHALL BE for baritone, chorus and orchestra (John Addington Symonds) (1937)
(Boosey & Hawkes: 3 2+1 2+1 2+1 4331 timp 4perc celesta organ strings; locations for sets of vocal scores on Encore)

THE TOWING PATH (1918; orch. Martin Yates 2009)
(Stainer & Bell: 2 1+1 22 2200 timp glock hp celesta strings)
orchestration of *The Towing Path* for piano

TRITONS: Symphonic Prelude (1899)
    (Boosey & Hawkes: 2+1 2 2+1 2 4231 timp 2perc strings)
    later arr. as *A Maritime Overture* for military band, *q.v.*

TWO SALON PIECES (1904; orch. Leslie Bridgewater 1931)
    1. Menuet Impromptu; 2. Villanella
    (Chappell: 1. 1121 2200 perc strings; 2. 2222 2230 timp perc hp strings)

VARIATIONS ON 'CADET ROUSSELLE' [with Bridge, Bax and Goossens]
    (J. & W. Chester/Music Sales: 2121 2100 timp perc hp strings)
    ℀ for voice and piano (J. & W. Chester, 1920)

VEXILLA REGIS: A Hymn for Passion Sunday for SATB soli, SATB chorus, brass and organ
    (Galliard, now Stainer & Bell, 1963: locations for sets of vocal scores on Encore)

CHAMBER & INSTRUMENTAL

BAGATELLE for violin and piano (1911)
    (Novello, 1913)
    ℀ orch. Leslie Bridgewater 1916
    ℀ arr. military band, C. F. Smyly

BERCEUSE for violin and piano (1903)
    (Augener, 1903)
    ℀ orch. Martin Yates 2009

CAVATINA for violin and piano (1904)
    (Ascherberg, Hopwood & crew, 1911)
    ℀ arr. organ, composer
    ℀ orch. Graham Parlett 2008

CELLO SONATA in G minor (1923)
    (Augener, 1924)
    ℀ arr. viola, Lionel Tertis

CLARINET TRIO in D minor (1913, rev. 1914; ed. and reconstructed Stephen Fox 2009)
    (Emerson Edition, 2009)

FANTASY SONATA for clarinet and piano (1943)
    (Boosey & Hawkes, 1945)

THE HOLY BOY: various instrumental arrangements of piano original
    ℀ arr. string quartet, composer (Boosey & Hawkes, 1941)
    ℀ arr. brass ensemble, Robert Stepp (Boosey & Hawkes, 1950)
    ℀ arr. violin and piano (Winthrop Rogers, 1919)
    ℀ arr. solo viola, Lionel Tertis, 1925 (unpublished)
    ℀ arr. cello and piano (Winthrop Rogers, 1919)

※ arr. flute and piano, James Galway (Boosey & Hawkes, 1987)

※ arr. recorder(s) and piano, Geoffrey Russell-Smith (Boosey & Hawkes, 1970)

PHANTASIE TRIO [no. 1] in A minor (1908)
(Augener, 1908)

PIANO TRIO no. 2 in E (1917)
(Augener, 1918)

PIANO TRIO no. 3 in E (1938)
(Boosey & Hawkes, 1938)
See p. 65 for Ireland's reaction to Frank Bridge identifying this trio as a
reworking of a withdrawn Trio of 1915, itself a version of the Clarinet Trio of
1912.

SEXTET for clarinet, horn and string quartet (1898)
(Augener, 1961)

STRING QUARTET no. 1 in D minor (1897)
(Boosey & Hawkes, 1973)

STRING QUARTET no. 2 in C minor (1897)
(Boosey & Hawkes, 1973)

VIOLIN SONATA no. 1 in D minor (1908, rev. 1917, rev. 1944)
(Goodwin & Tabb, 1911; Augener 1917; Augener 1944)

VIOLIN SONATA no. 2 in A minor (1917)
(Boosey, 1917)
※ arr. viola, Lionel Tertis

SOLO PIANO

John Ireland's collected piano works are published by Stainer & Bell in five
volumes (1976), the respective volume being indicated below for each work as the
easiest available source. A sixth volume is in preparation as this book goes to press;
the contents are indicated below as *Vol. 6*. Bibliographical details are only given
for those not included. Many of the original individual printings will be found in
libraries and in the second-hand trade.

THE ALMOND TREES (1913), *Vol. 1*

BALLADE (1929), *Vol. 3*

A BALLADE OF LONDON NIGHTS (1930), *Vol. 3*

THE CHERRY TREE (1937), *Vol. 4*
= the title for a reworking of INDIAN SUMMER, *q.v.*

COLUMBINE (1949), *Vol. 4*
※ original version as *Impromptu* (MS British Library)

THE DARKENED VALLEY (1920), *Vol. 2*

DECORATIONS (1912–13), *Vol. 1*
1. The Island Spell; 2. Moon-glade; 3. The Scarlet Ceremonies

EPIC MARCH (arr. composer)
(Boosey & Hawkes, 1942), Vol. 6
arr. of *Epic March* for orchestra, *q.v.*

EQUINOX (1922), *Vol. 2*

GREEN WAYS: Three Lyric Pieces (1937), *Vol. 4*
1. The Cherry Tree; 2. Cypress; 3. The Palm and May
No. 2 was originally called 'The Intruder'

INDIAN SUMMER (1932), *Vol. 6*
Published in the Danish journal *Pro-Musica* (Wilhelm Hansen), 1932
Early version of *The Cherry Tree*

IN THOSE DAYS (1895, rev. 1941), *Vol. 1*
1. Daydream; 2. Meridian

LEAVES FROM A CHILD'S SKETCHBOOK (1918), *Vol. 2*
1. By the Mere; 2. In the Meadow; 3. The Hunt's Up

LONDON PIECES (1917–20), *Vol. 2*
1. Chelsea Reach; 2. Ragamuffin; 3. Soho Forenoons

MEINE SEELE ERHEBT DEN HERRN, BWV648 (J. S. Bach), *Vol. 6*
chorale prelude 'My soul doth magnify the Lord' arranged for *A Bach Book for Harriet Cohen* (Oxford University Press, 1932)

MENUET AND ELEGY from A Downland Suite (1933), *Vol. 6*
Ireland's transcription for piano

MERRY ANDREW (1918), *Vol. 2*
⌘ orch. C. H. Clutsam 1931
⌘ orch. James Brash 1934

MONTH'S MIND (1933), *Vol. 4*

ON A BIRTHDAY MORNING (1922), *Vol. 2*

PASTORAL (1896), *Vol. 6*
MS in RCM

PENUMBRA
= original title of PRELUDE IN E♭, *q.v.*

PIANO SONATA in E minor (1920), *Vol. 5*

PRELUDE in E♭ (1924), *Vol. 3*
Originally called *Penumbra*

PRELUDES (1915), *Vol. 1*
Originally called 'Obsession'; 'Spleen'; 'Carol'; and 'Rosebud' in the sequence 2, 1, 3, 4.
1. The Undertone (1914); 2. Obsession (1915); 3. The Holy Boy (1913); 4. Fire of Spring
% *The Holy Boy*, arr. strings, composer
% *The Holy Boy*, arr. brass, Robert Stepp
% *The Holy Boy*, arr. voice and piano, organ or strings, composer
% *The Holy Boy*, arr. unacc. mixed chorus, composer
% *The Holy Boy*, arr. cello and piano
% *The Holy Boy*, arr. viola, Lionel Tertis
% *The Holy Boy*, arr. violin and piano, composer
% *The Holy Boy*, orch. Christopher Palmer
% *The Holy Boy*, arr. organ, composer
% *The Holy Boy*, arr. clarinet

[FIRST] RHAPSODY in F♯ minor (1906), *Vol. 6*
MS in British Library

RHAPSODY (1915), *Vol. 1*

RONDO (1927)
(Oxford University Press, 1928)
Third movement of Sonatina published separately as the test piece for the *Daily Express* National Piano Playing Contest

SARNIA: AN ISLAND SEQUENCE (1940–1), *Vol. 4*
1. Le Catioroc; 2. In a May Morning; 3. Song of the Springtides
orch. Martin Yates 2011

SEA IDYLL (1899)
1. Poco andante; 2. Allegro appassionata; 3. Andante mesto
No. 1, *Vol. 1*
Complete, *Vol. 6*
No. 1 was first published as a MS facsimile in a 1960 Chester centenary volume and then in type by Chester, then licensed by Stainer & Bell in *Vol. 1*. Complete with nos. 2 and 3 it appears in *Vol. 6* for the first time.

SOLILOQUY (1922), *Vol. 2*
% orch. Graham Parlett 2009, violin and orchestra

SONATINA (1927), *Vol. 3*

SPRING WILL NOT WAIT
= no. 3 of *We'll to the Woods No More, q.v.*

SUMMER EVENING (1919), *Vol. 2*

THEME AND VARIATIONS [theme only] (1897)
unpublished MS in British Library

THREE [RUSTIC] DANCES (1913), *Vol. 1*
   1. Gypsy Dance; 2. Country Dance; 3. Reapers' Dance

THREE PASTELS (1941), *Vol. 4*
   1. A Grecian Lad; 2. The Boy Bishop; 3. Puck's Birthday

THE TOWING PATH (1918), *Vol. 2*
   ℀ orch. Martin Yates 2009

TWO PIECES (1921), *Vol. 2*
   1. For Remembrance; 2. Amberley Wild Brooks

TWO PIECES (1925), *Vol. 3*
   1. April; 2. Bergomask

TWO PIECES (1929), *Vol. 3*
   1. February's Child; 2. Aubade

VILLANELLA: freely transcribed by the composer for piano (1904, arr. 1912, rev. 1950), *Vol. 6*
   (Ascherberg, Hopwood & Crew, 1950)

ORGAN

Most of Ireland's organ works will be found in *The Organ Music of John Ireland*, ed. Robert Gower (Novello, 1983).

ALLA MARCIA (1911)
   (Novello, 1911)

CAPRICCIO for organ (1911)
   (Stainer & Bell, 1911)

CAVATINA (1904)
   (Ascherberg, Hopwood & Crew, 1911)
   composer's arr. of *Cavatina* for violin and piano, *q.v.*

ELEGIAC ROMANCE (1902, rev. 1958)
   (R. Cocks & Co., 1903; rev. composer: Novello, 1958)
   ℀ orch. Geoffrey Bush

ELEGY (1933, arr. organ, Alec Rowley 1950) *added DR*
   (Ashdown, 1950)
   arr. of no. 2 of *A Downland Suite*

EPIC MARCH (1942; arr. organ, Robert Gower 1988)
   (Boosey & Hawkes, 1988)
   arr. of *Epic March* for orchestra, *q.v.*

THE HOLY BOY (1913; arr. organ, composer)
   (Winthrop Rogers, 1919)

HYMN TO LIGHT for voice and organ (James Vila Blake, 1911)
   (Chappell, 1911)

MARCIA POPOLARE (1904)
(Ascherberg, Hopwood & Crew, 1912)

MEDITATION ON JOHN KEBLE'S ROGATIONTIDE HYMN (1958)
(Feldman, 1959)
※ arr. string orchestra, Geoffrey Bush, as *Elegiac Meditation* (1982), *q.v.*

MINIATURE SUITE (1904)
1. Intrada; 2. Villanella; 3. Menuetto-Impromptu
(Ascherberg, Hopwood & Crew, 1912)
※ Villanella arr. piano, composer
※ Villanella and Menuetto-Impromptu orch. Leslie Bridgewater, as *Two Salon Pieces* (1931), *q.v.*

SURSUM CORDA (1911)
(Novello, 1911)

SONGS

Most of Ireland's songs have been published in five volumes by Stainer & Bell, and this constitutes the simplest way of obtaining them. The volume numbers are given where appropriate below. Bibliographical details or sources are given for those not thus collected. The four published songs by 'Turlay Royce' are *Billie Bowline*; *Hillo, My Bonny*; *Love's Wisdom* and *Porto Rico*. This listing does not indicate where a given song is available in several keys.

ANNABEL LEE: Recitation with Piano (Edgar Allan Poe, 1910)
(Stainer & Bell, 1998)
※ orch. Roderick Williams 2009: see above under Orchestral

BED IN SUMMER (Robert Louis Stevenson, 1913), *Vol. 5*

THE BELLS OF SAN MARIE (John Masefield, 1918), *Vol. 2*

BILLIE BOWLINE (F. E. Weatherly, 1911), ballad by 'Turlay Royce'
(Chappell, 1911)

THE COST: Songs of a Great War (Eric Thirkell Cooper, 1916), *Vol. 5*
1. Blind; 2. The Cost

EARTH'S CALL: A Sylvan Rhapsody (Harold Monro), *Vol. 4*

THE EAST RIDING (Eric Chilman, 1920), *Vol. 1*

FIVE SIXTEENTH-CENTURY POEMS (William Cornysh, Thomas Howell, Anon., Nicholas Breton, Richard Edwardes, 1938), *Vol. 3*
1. A Thanksgiving; 2. All in a Garden Green; 3. An Aside; 4. A Report Song; 5. The Sweet Season

FIVE SONGS SET TO POEMS BY THOMAS HARDY (1926), *Vol. 3*
1. Beckon to me to Come; 2. In my Sage Moments; 3. It was What you Bore with you, Woman; 4. The Tragedy of that Moment; 5. Dear, Think not that they will Forget you

A GARRISON CHURCHYARD (Eric Thirkell Cooper, 1916)
(Stainer & Bell, 1998)

GREAT THINGS (Thomas Hardy, 1915), *Vol. 3*

HAWTHORN TIME (A. E. Housman, 1919), *Vol. 2*

THE HEART'S DESIRE (A. E. Housman, 1917), *Vol. 1*
  ℀ orch. Graham Parlett

HERE'S TO THE SHIPS (P. J. O'Reilly, 1911)
(Boosey & Co., 1912)
  ℀ orch. composer (1912)

HILLO, MY BONNY (James Vila Blake, 1911), ballad by 'Turlay Royce'
(Chappell, 1913)

THE HOLY BOY: A Carol of the Nativity (Herbert S. Brown, 1938)
(Boosey & Hawkes, 1941)
  ℀ accompaniment for strings
(Boosey & Hawkes, 1941)

HOPE THE HORNBLOWER (Henry Newbolt, 1911), *Vol. 5*
  ℀ orch. Frederick Bye

HYMN TO LIGHT for voice and organ (James Vila Blake, 1911)
(Chappell, 1911)

IF THERE WERE DREAMS TO SELL (Thomas Lovell Beddoes, 1918),
  Vol. 5
  ℀ orch. E. Griffiths (in F major)
  ℀ orch. (harp and strings) Frederick Bye (in F and D♭)

IF WE MUST PART (Ernest Dowson, 1929), *Vol. 5*

I HAVE TWELVE OXEN (early English, 1918), *Vol. 5*
  ℀ orch. Graham Parlett
  ℀ version in French as 'J'ai Douze Boeufs'
(Winthrop Rogers, 1919)

THE JOURNEY (Ernest Blake, 1920), *Vol. 5*

THE LAND OF LOST CONTENT (A. E. Housman, 1921), *Vol. 1*
  1. The Lent Lily; 2. Ladslove; 3. Goal and Wicket; 4. The Vain Desire; 5. The
  Encounter; 6. Epilogue ('You smile upon your friend today')

LOVE IS A SICKNESS FULL OF WOES (Samuel Daniel, 1921), *Vol. 1*
  version for solo piano by Robert Helps (available from John Ireland Trust)

LOVE'S WINDOW (H. D. Banning, 1911), ballad by 'Turlay Royce'
(Chappell, 1911)

MARIGOLD: Impression for voice and pianoforte (Dante Gabriel Rossetti, Ernest Dowson, 1913), *Vol. 4*
1. Youth's Spring-Tribute; 2. Penumbra; 3. Spleen
⁂ with orch. [no. 1 only]

THE MERRY MONTH OF MAY (Thomas Dekker, 1921), *Vol. 5*

MOTHER AND CHILD (Christina Rossetti, 1918), *Vol. 2*
1. Newborn; 2. The Only Child; 3. Hope; 4. Skylark and Nightingale; 5. The Blind Boy; 6. Baby; 7. Death-Parting; 8. The Garland
⁂ [no. 6 only] orch. Graham Parlett
No. 1 also published as Your Brother Has a Falcon (Winthrop Rogers, 1918)

O HAPPY LAND (W. J. Linton, 1941)
(Winthrop Rogers, 1941)

PENUMBRA, *see* MARIGOLD

PORTO RICO (F. E. Weatherly, 1913), ballad by 'Turlay Royce'
(Chappell, 1913)

REMEMBER (Mary Coleridge, 1918), *Vol. 1*

THE SACRED FLAME (Mary Coleridge, 1918), *Vol. 1*

SANTA CHIARA (Arthur Symons, 1925), *Vol. 2*

SEA FEVER (John Masefield, 1913), *Vol. 2*
⁂ with orch.
⁂ arr. voice and military band
⁂ arr. solo voice and male chorus, Mansel Thomas

A SONG FROM O'ER THE HILL (P. J. O'Reilly, 1913), *Vol. 5*

SONGS OF A WAYFARER (William Blake, William Shakespeare, Dante Gabriel Rossetti, Ernest Dowson, James Vila Blake), *Vol. 4*
1. Memory; 2. When Daffodils Begin to Peer; 3. English May; 4. I was not Sorrowful (Spleen); 5. I will Walk on the Earth

SONGS SACRED AND PROFANE (Alice Meynell, Sylvia Townsend Warner, W. B. Yeats, 1931), *Vol. 1*
1. The Advent; 2. Hymn for a Child; 3. My Fair; 4. The Salley Gardens; 5. The Soldier's Return; 6. The Scapegoat

SPRING SORROW (Rupert Brooke, 1918), *Vol. 4*

THE THREE RAVENS (trad., 1920), *Vol. 5*

THREE SONGS (Arthur Symons, 1919), *Vol. 3*
1. The Adoration; 2. The Rat; 3. Rest

THREE SONGS TO POEMS BY THOMAS HARDY (1925), *Vol. 3*
1. Summer Schemes; 2. Her Song; 3. Weathers
⁂ [2 only] orch. Graham Parlett

THREE SONGS (Emily Brontë, Anon., Dante Gabriel Rossetti, 1926), *Vol. 5*
    1. Love and Friendship; 2. Friendship in Misfortune; 3. The One Hope
    ※ [1] orch. Graham Parlett

TUTTO È SCIOLTO (James Joyce, 1932), *Vol. 5*
    Written for *The Joyce Book* (Limited edition, Sylvan Press, 1932)

TWO SONGS (Eric Thirkell Cooper, 1916), *Vol. 5*
    1. Blind; 2. The Cost

TWO SONGS (Aldous Huxley, Sir Philip Sydney, 1920), *Vol. 1*
    1. The Trellis; 2. My True Love Hath my Heart
    ※ orch. Graham Parlett

TWO SONGS (Arthur Symons, Dante Gabriel Rossetti, 1928), *Vol. 2*
    1. Tryst ('In Fountain Court'); 2. During Music

TWO SONGS (Rupert Brooke, 1917, 1918), *Vol. 4*
    1. The Soldier; 2. Blow Out, you Bugles

TWO SONGS AND A MELODRAMA (Erik Thirkell Cooper, Ernest
    Dowson, Edgar Allan Poe, 1916, 1920, 1910)
    (Stainer & Bell, 1998)
    The songs are 'When I am Old' and 'A Garrison Churchyard'; the melodrama is
    Annabel Lee.

VAGABOND (John Masefield, 1922), *Vol. 2*

VARIATIONS ON 'CADET ROUSSELLE' for voice and piano [with
    Bridge, Bax and Goossens]
    (J. & W. Chester, 1920)

**WE'LL TO THE WOODS NO MORE: THREE SONGS TO POEMS
    BY HOUSMAN** (1927), *Vol. 3*
    1. We'll to the Woods No More; 2. In Boyhood; 3. Spring Will Not Wait (piano
    solo)

WHAT ART THOU THINKING OF? (Christina Rossetti, 1924), *Vol. 2*

WHEN I AM DEAD, MY DEAREST (Christina Rossetti, 1924), *Vol. 2*
    ※ with orch.

WHEN I AM OLD, in *Two Songs and a Melodrama*, *q.v.*

WHEN LIGHTS GO ROLLING ROUND THE SKY (James Vila Blake,
    1911), *Vol. 5*
    ※ with orch.

CHORAL AND CHURCH

Choirs may wish to note that sets of choral parts of some 92 of Ireland's choral and church music are available from public library collections via interlibrary loan at nominal cost. A full listing of these with locations of sets can be found in the Encore! Database. Items which appear in these are noted against the appropriate entries below.

ADAM LAY YBOUNDEN, SATB (15th century, 1956)
(E. H. Freeman, 1956)

ALPINE SONG, unison with piano (James Vila Blake, 1911)
(Curwen, 1911: locations for sets of vocal scores on Encore)

AT EARLY DAWN, SA and piano (James Vila Blake)
(Curwen, 1911: locations for sets of vocal scores on Encore)

AUBADE, SA and piano (Sydney Dobell, 1912)
(Novello, 1912: locations for sets of vocal scores on Encore)

BED IN SUMMER, equal voices and piano (Robert Louis Stevenson, 1912)
(Curwen, 1915)

THE BELL IN THE LEAVES, equal voices and piano (Eleanor Farjeon, 1942)
(Winthrop Rogers, 1942)

BENEDICITE in F, SATB and piano (1919)
(Novello, 1942)

BENEDICTUS in F, SATB and organ (1912)
(Novello, 1912)

THE BOY, unison with piano (Eleanor Farjeon, 1942)
(Curwen, 1942)

BOYS' NAMES, equal voices and piano (Eleanor Farjeon, 1941)
(Curwen, 1942)

CHELSEA, hymn tune, SATB and organ (C. A. Alington, 1924)
(*Enlarged Songs of Praise*, 1931)

CHILD'S SONG, equal voices and piano (Thomas Moore, 1913)
(Yearbook Press, 1914)

COMMUNION SERVICE in Ab, treble voices organ (1896)
(Houghton & Co., 1902)
withdrawn by the composer but available from John Ireland Trust

COMMUNION SERVICE in C, SATB and organ (1913)
(Novello 1911: Locations for sets of vocal scores on Encore)

A CRADLE SONG, unacc. SATB (William Blake, 1912)
(Stainer & Bell, 1914. Locations for sets of vocal scores on Encore)

CUPID, SATB (William Blake, 1909)
(Augener, 1961)

EASTERGATE, hymn tune, SATB and organ (Isabella Stevenson, 1905)
(*The English Hymnal* or *Methodist Hymn Book*)

THE ECHOING GREEN, SS and piano (William Blake, 1913)
(Curwen, 1914: locations on Encore)

EVENING SERVICE in A, SATB and organ (1905)
(unpublished, MS British Library)

EVENING SERVICE in C, SATB and organ (1941)
(Novello, 1941)

EVENING SERVICE in F, SATB and organ (1915)

EVENING SONG, SA and piano (James Vila Blake after Friedrich Rückert)
(Novello, 1912: locations on Encore)

EX ORE INNOCENTIUM ('It is a thing Most Wonderful'), anthem, SA and
piano/organ (William Walsham How, 1944)
(Winthrop Rogers, 1944)

FAIN WOULD I CHANGE THAT NOTE, SATB
(Novello, 1921: locations for sets of vocal scores on Encore)

THE FERRY, unison song with piano (Christina Rossetti)
(Edward Arnold, 1921: locations on Encore)

FRATERNITY, hymn tune, SATB and organ (John Addington Symonds)

THE FROG AND THE CRAB

FULL FATHOM FIVE, SA and piano (Shakespeare)
(Novello, 1908: locations for sets of vocal scores on Encore)

A GRADUATION SONG, unison with piano (John Drinkwater)
(Curwen, 1926)

**GREATER LOVE HATH NO MAN: A Motet for Passiontide and Other
Seasons** ('Many Waters Cannot Quench Love'), baritone and treble soli, SATB
and organ
(Stainer & Bell, 1912. locations for sets of vocal scores on Encore)
See above for orchestral version.

HERE'S TO THE SHIPS (P. J. O'Reilly)
orch. composer
(Boosey, 1912)

THE HILLS, SATB (James Kirkup)
(Stainer & Bell, 1953: location on Encore)

THE HOLY BOY: A Carol of the Nativity, SATB (Herbert S. Brown)
(Boosey & Hawkes, 1941: locations on Encore)

HYMN TUNES: *see* Chelsea; Eastergate; Fraternity; A Graduation Song; Irene;
Love Unknown; Mighty Father; New Prince, New Pomp; Sampford; Vesper
Hymn

IMMORTALITY (Henry P. Crompton)
(Winthrop Rogers, 1942)

THE PEACEFUL WESTERN WIND (Thomas Campion, 1890s)
(unpublished, MS in British Library)

IN PRAISE OF MAY, SA and piano (Thomas Morley)
(Novello, 1909: locations for sets of vocal scores on Encore)

IN PRAISE OF NEPTUNE, unison song with piano (Thomas Campion)
※ versions for SATB and piano; SATB and orchestra
(Can also be sung as a solo song with orchestra, see above. Locations for sets
of the two-part version on Encore)

IN SUMMER WOODS, SA and piano (James Vila Blake, from the German)
(Curwen, 1911: locations for sets of vocal scores on Encore)
※ arr. SATB and orch., T. Widicombe, 1957. See above.

IRENE, hymn tune, see Three Hymns for the Celebration of Peace

AN ISLAND HYMN, anthem, unacc. TTBB (Isaiah)
(Stainer & Bell, 1915)

ISLAND PRAISE
Revised version of AN ISLAND HYMN, *q.v.*

IT IS A THING MOST WONDERFUL, see EX ORE INNOCENTIUM

JOSEPH FELL A-DREAMING, unison song with piano (Eleanor Farjeon)
(Curwen, 1949: locations for sets of vocal scores on Encore)

JUBILATE in F (1914)

JUBILATE DEO

A LAUGHING SONG, SATB
(unpublished MS British Library)

LOOKING ON, unison song with piano (Eleanor Farjeon)
(Curwen, 1949: locations for sets of vocal scores on Encore)

LOVE UNKNOWN, hymn tune, SATB and organ (Samuel Crossman)
(*Public School Hymn Book*, 1920; *Songs of Praise*, 1925)
※ version with orchestral accompaniment
※ version for bell ringers (St Louis: Concordia, 1989)

THE LORD'S PRAYER (Pater Noster)

MAGNIFICAT & NUNC DIMITTIS (Evening Service in C)
(Novello, 1941: locations for sets of vocal scores on Encore)

MAGNIFICAT & NUNC DIMITTIS (Evening Service in F)
(Novello, 1915: locations for sets of vocal scores on Encore)

MAN IN HIS LABOUR REJOICETH (Robert Bridges), SATB and brass
band (Joseph Williams, 1947)

MASS IN THE DORIAN MODE

MAY FLOWERS, SS and piano (Christina Rossetti)
(Edward Arnold, 1919: locations for sets of vocal scores on Encore)

MIGHTY FATHER, hymn tune

MISSA BREVIS
See also MISSA SANCTI STEPHANI

MISSA SANCTI STEPHANI

MORNING SERVICE in C (1941)

MY SONG IS LOVE UNKNOWN
✠ arr. Christian Forshaw / James Pearson

NEW PRINCE, NEW POMP, carol

A NEW YEAR CAROL, SATB and piano (1941)
(Boosey & Hawkes, 1942: location on Encore)

NINEFOLD KYRIE IN A MINOR

NURSE'S SONG, unison song with piano (William Blake, 1914)
(Yearbook Press, 1914)
Later issued as SUNSET PLAY

O HAPPY LAND, unison song (W. J. Linton)
(Winthrop Rogers, 1941)

PATER NOSTER (The Lord's Prayer)
(Novello, 1913)

THE PEACEFUL WESTERN WIND, SATB (Thomas Campion, *c.* 1895)
(unpublished: MS British Library)

PSALM 23, unaccompanied solo voice
(unpublished: MS John Ireland Trust)

PSALM 42 ('Like as the hart'), SATB soli, SATB and string orchestra (1908)
(John Ireland Trust: score and parts. Ireland's composition exercise for the
University of Durham external Mus.Bac.)

PSALM CHANT
(unpublished: MS British Library)

RIDE A COCK-HORSE
(unpublished: MS British Library)

SAMPFORD, hymn tune

SEA FEVER, unison voices with piano (John Masefield)
(Stainer & Bell 1929: locations for sets of vocal scores on Encore)
✠ version for baritone solo, men's voice and piano arr. Mansel Thomas (Stainer
& Bell, 1989)
See above for version for baritone, chorus and orchestra.

SEE HOW THE MORNING SMILES, SA and piano (Thomas Campion)
(Stainer & Bell, 1912: locations for sets of vocal scores on Encore)
Same words as *The Peaceful Western Wind* now issued by Banks of York

SLUMBER SONG (James Vila Blake, from the German)
(Novello, 1911: locations for sets of vocal scores on Encore)

A SONG OF MARCH, unison with piano (James Vila Blake, 1918)
(Edward Arnold, 1918: location on Encore)

SPRING, unison song with piano (James Vila Blake, from the German)
(Novello, 1911: locations for sets of vocal scores on Encore)

SPRING, THE SWEET SPRING, unacc. SATB (Thomas Nashe)
(Laudy & Co., 1908)

SUNSET PLAY
NURSE'S SONG under a new title

TE DEUM LAUDAMUS in F major, SATB and organ (1907)
(Novello, 1907: locations for sets of vocal scores on Encore)

THERE IS A GARDEN IN HER FACE, SA and piano (Richard Alison)
(Novello, 1908: locations for sets of vocal scores on Encore)

THESE THINGS SHALL BE, baritone, chorus and orchestra (John
Addington Symonds 1937)
(Boosey & Hawkes vocal score by Eric Fenby, see above for orchestral details;
locations for sets of vocal scores on Encore)

THEY TOLD ME, HERACLITUS, unacc. TTBB (William Cory, 1924)
(Boosey, 1924)

THREE HYMNS FOR THE CELEBRATION OF PEACE: No. 2 IRENE
('God of Nations', 1918)
Nos. 1 and 3 by Sir Frederick Bridge and Alfred Moss
(Hunter & Longhurst, 1918)

TWILIGHT NIGHT (Christina Rossetti, SATB)
(Novello, 1923: locations for sets of vocal scores on Encore)

VESPER HYMN ('O Lord, keep us safe'), SATB and organ
(Novello, 1911)

VEXILLA REGIS: A Hymn for Passion Sunday, SATB soli or semi-chorus,
SATB, brass [2 trumpets, 3 trombones] and organ (Venatius Fortunatus, trans.
J. M. Neale)
(Galliard, vocal score by Alan Rowlands, 1963)

WAYS OF PEACE, SATB (Randall Swingler)
(Published by the Music Sub-Committee of the British National Committee of
the International Peace Campaign.)

WEEP YOU NO MORE, SAD FOUNTAINS, SATB (John Dowland)
(unpublished; MS sold by Christies, 22 November 1902, lot 23; now John
Ireland Trust)

WHEN MAY IS IN HIS PRIME, unacc. SATB (Richard Edwardes, 1920)
(Novello, 1920: locations for sets of vocal scores on Encore)

Fig. 34 John Ireland at the keyboard. Sketch by Juliet Pannett.

John Ireland Discography

Stephen Lloyd

THE compiler wishes to acknowledge Eric Hughes' John Ireland discography in *Recorded Sound*, The Journal of the British Institute of Recorded Sound, January 1974, pp. 258–62, and Stewart R. Craggs' *John Ireland: A Catalogue, Discography and Bibliography* (Oxford: Clarendon Press, 1993) and its revised edition (Aldershot: Ashgate, 2007), both of which have been invaluable in the compilation of this discography.

An asterisk (*) denotes a 78 rpm recording; cassette recordings are in italics; compact discs in bold. In multiple sets, the number of discs is inside the square brackets. Wherever possible, the date of the recording has been given and (in parentheses) the month of a *Gramophone* review. Recordings of particular interest held in the National Sound Archive at the British Library or other archives have also been included, their catalogue number being in square brackets. When any of these recordings have also been issued commercially, the NSA reference has not been included.

While this discography cannot claim to be exhaustive, it is hoped that all significant recordings have been included. However, a number of hymn tunes and anthems may have eluded the discographer as these have not always been individually entered in catalogues, reviews, etc.

ORCHESTRAL

COMEDY OVERTURE

Foden's Motor Works Band, Rex Mortimer   BBC 6 April 1965   [NSA M327W SC]
Foden's Motor Works Band, Fred Mortimer   [BBC trans 25922/4]
Fairey Band, Leonard Lamb   (1/69)   Paxton LPT1026
Black Dykes Mill Band, Mortimer   Jamco BD1206–7 *
Virtuoso Brass Band, Eric Ball   (6/74)   Virtuoso VR7303
                                                                                KRCD1025–26
GUS (Kettering) Band, Geoffrey Brand   r. March 1976 (9/76)   EMI TWOX1053
                                    (2/94)   EMI **CDM764716–2**
Grimethorpe Colliery Band, Elgar Howarth
    r. June 1976 (5/77)   Decca SXL6820 *KSXC6820*
              (3/86)   Decca 414 644–1DW *414 644–4DW*
                                                                            Decca **470195–2**
                                                                      DOYCD160 DOYCD181
London Collegiate Brass, James Stobart   r. June 1985 (3/86)   Crd CRD1134 *CRDC4134*
              (9/86)   Crd **CRD3434**
                                                                            Crd **CRD2415** [2]
London Brass Virtuosi, David Honeyball   r. Sept. 1987 (11/88)   Hyperion **CDH88013**
                                                           Hyperion *KH88013* **CDH55070**

℀ arr. wind band, R. Steadman-Allen
City of London Wind Ensemble, Geoffrey Brand
    r. July 1989 (3/90)   Gamut **LDRCD1012** *LDRZC1012*

449

CONCERTINO PASTORALE
1. Eclogue; 2. Threnody; 3. Toccata

Boyd Neel String Orchestra, Boyd Neel r. Feb. 1940 (5/40)	Decca AX253–5 *
Riddick String Orchestra, Kathleen Riddick 21 July 1965	[NSA 30B4849]
MGM String Orchestra, Izler Solomon	MGM E3074
London Philharmonic Orchestra, Adrian Boult	
r. Dec. 1965 (9/66)	Lyrita RCS31 SRCS31
	Musical Heritage Society 1498
(1/08)	Lyrita **SRCD242**
Bournemouth Sinfonietta, George Hurst r. Jan. 1977 (9/77)	RCA RL25071
(7/84)	CBR1020 *CBT1020*
(8/85)	Chandos **CHAN8375**
Westminster Cathedral String Orchestra, Colin Mawby	
r. May 1978 (3/80)	Unicorn UNS260
City of London Sinfonia, Richard Hickox r. Oct. 1994 (11/95)	Chandos **CHAN9376**
English Sinfonia, John Farrer r. July 1996 (11/97)	Carlton **30366 0060–2**
[no. 2 only]	
London Concertante	CMG **CMG017**

CONCERTO FOR PIANO

Kendall Taylor, London Chamber Players, Anthony Bernard	[NSA M615W]
Eileen Joyce, Hallé, Leslie Heward r. Jan. 1942 (3/42)	Columbia CDX1072–4 *
	Columbia DX8178–80 * Auto
(5/93)	Dutton **CDAX8001**
(8/85)	EMI EM290462–3 [2]
	EMI EM290462–5 [2]
Eileen Joyce, London Philharmonic Orchestra, Adrian Boult	
Birthday Prom 10 Sept. 1949 (12/09)	LPO **LPO0041**
Sondra Bianca, Hamburg Philharmonia Orchestra, Hans-Jürgen Walther	MGM E3366
Colin Horsley, RPO, Basil Cameron r. Nov. 1957 (8/58)	HMV CLP1182
(12/65)	HMV HQM1007
	Capitol G7183 SG7183
(6/77)	EMI SLS5080
(2/94)	EMI **CDM764716–2**
	EMI **352279–2** [2]
Eric Parkin, London Philharmonic Orchestra, Adrian Boult	
r. Nov. 1967 (10/68)	Lyrita SRCS36
	Musical Heritage Society 1429
(6/07)	Lyrita **SRCD241**
Eric Parkin, London Philharmonic Orchestra, Bryden Thomson	
r. Dec. 1985 (9/86)	Chandos ABRD1174 *ABTD1174*
(1/87)	Chandos **CHAN8461**
Geoffrey Tozer, Melbourne Symphony Orchestra, David Measham	
r. Feb 1985 (1/87)	Unicorn DKP9056 *DKPC9056*
	Unicorn **DKPCD9056**
Kathryn Stott, RPO, Vernon Handley r. July 1989 (1/90)	Conifer **CDCF175** *MCFC175*
	Dutton **CDLX7223**
Kathryn Stott, BBCSO, Andrew Davies	
Prom 22 August 1993 [2008]	BBC Music Magazine **BBCMM295**
Piers Lane, Ulster Orchestra, David Lloyd-Jones	
r. March 2005 (2/06)	Hyperion **CDA67296**

David Strong, Aalborg Symphony Orchestra, Douglas Bostock
  r. June 2006 (9/07)   Classico **CLASSCD704**
Mark Bebbington, Orchestra of the Swan, David Curtis
  r. April 2009 (12/09)   **SOMMCD242**
John Lenehan, Royal Liverpool Philhamonic, John Wilson   r. Feb 2011   Naxos **8.572598**

A DOWNLAND SUITE
1. Prelude; 2. Elegy; 3. Minuet; 4. Rondo
Foden's Motor Works Band, Fred Mortimer   r. 1932 (12/32)   Zonophone 6228–9 *
                                  (11/93)   Beulah **IPD2**
                                         Choice **CD2 BM2**

  [no. 2 only]
Yorkshire Imperial Metals Band, Trevor Walmsley   (6/67)   CBS CBS62937
CWS (Manchester) Band, Alex Mortimer   (8/68)   Fontana STL5466 TL5466
GUS (Kettering) Band, Geoffrey Brand   r. March 1976 (9/76)   HMV TWOX1053
Besses o' th' Barn Band, Ifor Jones   (1/77)   Pye TB3012
                                         Pye *ZCTPB3012*
London Collegiate Brass, James Stobart   r. June 1985 (9/87)   Crd **CRD3444** *CRDC4144*
Black Dyke Mills Band, Peter Parkes   r. May 1987   Chandos **CHAN4516**
London Brass Virtuosi, David Honeyball
  r. Sept. 1987 (11/88)   Hyperion **CDH88013** *KH88013*
                                   Hyperion **CDH55070**
Brigghouse & Rastrick Band, Geoffrey Brand   Harlequin HAR1122CC
European Winds, Geoffrey Brand   r. Nov. 1993   Albany **TROY120–2**

  [no. 2 only] arr. organ, Alec Rowley
Philip Rushforth   r. May 1994   OxRecs **OXCD59; OXCD103**
Stefan Kagl   r. Herford Minster, May 2008   CPO **777481–2**
Miles Hartley (Manchester College)   Priory **PRCD 1054**

✵ arr. strings: nos. 2 & 3, composer; nos. 1 & 4, Geoffrey Bush
  [no. 3 only]
Boyd Neel String Orchestra, Boyd Neel   r. Feb. 1940 (5/40)   Decca X255 *
                                (3/55)   Decca LW5149
                                      London LD9170
                               (5/69)   Decca ACL316
                               (9/72)   Decca ECS648
                                      Decca SDD2195

  [nos. 3 & 2 only]
LPO, Adrian Boult   r. Dec. 1965 (9/66)   Lyrita RCS31 SRCS31
                             Musical Heritage Society 1498
                        (1/08)   Lyrita **SRCD242**

  [no. 2 only]
Leicestershire Schools Orchestra, André Previn   r. Aug. 1970 (4/71)   Argo ZRG685
English Chamber Orchestra, David Garforth
  r. Dec. 1983 (12/84)   Chandos ABRD1112 *ABTD1112*
              (5/87)   Chandos **CHAN8390**

  [no. 3 only]
Guildhall String Ensemble, Robert Salter   (9/88)   RCA RL87761
                                 RCA **RD87761** *RK87761*

[no. 3 only]
English String Orchestra, William Boughton   r. 1991   Nimbus **NI7020**
                                                                    in Nimbus **NI5450/3** [4]
City of London Sinfonia, Richard Hickox   r. Oct. 1994 (11/95)   Chandos **CHAN9376**

[nos. 3 & 2 only]
English Sinfonia, John Farrer   r. July 1996 (11/97)   Carlton **30366 0060–2**
Royal Ballet Sinfonia, Gavin Sutherland   r. Sept. 2002   Naxos 8.**557752**

✾ arr. R. Steadman-Allen
European Winds, Geoffrey Brand   r. 1993   Albany **TROY120–2**

✾ arr. piano, composer

[nos. 2 & 3 only]
Mark Bebbington   r. Jan. 2008 (11/09)   **SOMM088**

EPIC MARCH
London Philharmonic Orchestra, Henry Wood
    f.p. RAH Prom 27 June 1942 (last half only, 4′30″) (10/95)   BBC **PC98SE**
    (complete, with announcement) [2008]   BBC Music Magazine **BBCMM295**
New Concert Orchestra, Stanford Robinson   Boosey & Hawkes OT2081 *
London Philharmonic Orchestra, Adrian Boult
    r. Dec. 1965 (9/66)   Lyrita RCS31 SRCS31
        (5/07)   Lyrita **SRCD240**
                                                           Musical Heritage Society 1498
West Australian SO, David Measham   r. March 1979 (11/80)   Unicorn KP8001
                                                                 Unicorn **UKCD2062**
LSO, Richard Hickox   r. April 1990   Chandos **CHAN8879** *ABTD1492*
                                                           Chandos **CHAN10110**
        (3/98)   Chandos **CHAN7074**
Cincinnati Pops, Erich Kunzel   Telarc **CD80122**
Hallé Orchestra, John Wilson   r. March 2007 (12/09)   Hallé **CDHLL7523**

✾ arr. organ, Robert Gower
Stefan Kagl   r. Herford Minster, May 2008   CPO **777481–2**
Miles Hartley (Manchester College)   Priory **PRCD 1054**

THE FORGOTTEN RITE
BBC Symphony Orchestra, John Ireland   BBC 10 Jan. 1935 [?]   [NSA T11461W1]
Hallé, John Barbirolli   r. May 1949 (8/49)   HMV C3894 *
        (9/84)   EMI EX290107–3 [2]
                                                           EMI *EX290107–5*
        (4/92)   EMI CDH763910–2
        (4/02)   Dutton **CDSJB1022** [2]
London Philharmonic Orchestra, Adrian Boult
    Birthday Prom 10 Sept. 1949 (12/09)   LPO **LPO0041**
Philharmonia Orchestra, Adrian Boult   [BBC Trans. 11118]
London Philharmonic Orchestra, Adrian Boult
    r. March 1963   BBC Radio Classics **BBCRD9127**
London Philharmonic Orchestra, Adrian Boult
    r. Dec. 1965 (9/66)   Lyrita RCS32 SRCS32
                                                           Musical Heritage Society 1317
        (5/07)   Lyrita **SRCD240**
                                                           in Lyrita **SRCD2337** [4]

LSO, Richard Hickox r. April 1991 (2/92)	Chandos **CHAN8994**
Hallé Orchestra, John Wilson r. March 2007 (12/09)	Hallé **CDHLL7523**

⁄⁄ arr. piano duet, composer
Alan Rowlands and Adrian Sims   (12/10)   Albion **ALBCD011**

LEGEND for piano and orchestra
Kendall Taylor, London Chamber Orchestra, Anthony Bernard
    4 Feb. 1951   [NSA M615W]
Eric Parkin, BBC Symphony Orchestra, Rudolf Schwarz
    13 April 1957   [NSA T10870WR]
Eric Parkin, London Philharmonic Orchestra, Adrian Boult
    r. Dec. 1965 (9/66)   Lyrita RCS32 SRCS32
                                            Musical Heritage Society 1317
            (6/07)   Lyrita **SRCD241**
Eric Parkin, London Philharmonic Orchestra, Bryden Thomson
    r. Dec. 1985 (9/86)   Chandos ABRD1174
                                                        Chandos *ABTD1174*
            (1/87)   Chandos **CHAN8461**
Jane Coop, CBC Vancouver Orchestra, Mario Bernardi   r. 2001   CBC **SMCD5208**
Piers Lane, Ulster Orchestra, David Lloyd-Jones
    r. March 2005 (2/06)   Hyperion **CDA67296**
Mark Bebbington, Orchestra of the Swan, David Curtis
    r. April 2009 (12/09)   **SOMMCD242**
John Lenehan, Royal Liverpool Philhamonic, John Wilson   r. Feb 2011   Naxos **8.572598**

A LONDON OVERTURE
Liverpool Philharmonic Orchestra, Malcolm Sargent
    r. 1944 (6/44)   Columbia DX1155–6 *
            (5/95)   Dutton **CDAX8012**
BBC Symphony Orchestra, Malcolm Sargent   BBC 10 March 1947   [NSA BBCX174346]
Yorkshire Symphony Orchestra, Maurice Miles   BBC 10 Feb. 1949   [NSA T1193W2/4]
London Phiharmonic Orchestra, Adrian Boult
    Birthday Prom 10 Sept. 1949 (12/09)   LPO **LPO0041**
London Philharmonic Orchestra, Basil Cameron
    [Prom 26 August 1950 ?]   [NSA 30B4863}
London Philharmonic Orchestra, Adrian Boult
    r. Dec. 1965 (9/66)   Lyrita RCS31 SRCS31
                                            Musical Heritage Society 1498
            (5/07)   Lyrita **SRCD240**
London Symphony Orchestra, John Barbirolli
    r. Dec. 1965 (2/67)   HMV ALP2305 ASD2305
                                                        Angel 36415 S36415
            (8/80)   HMV ESD7092 *TCESD7092*
            (9/84)   HMV EX290107–3 [2]
                                                        HMV *EX290107–5*
            (12/88)   EMI **CDC747984–2**
            (2/94)   EMI **CDM764716–2**
            (8/94)   EMI **CDM565109–2**
                                                        EMI **568469–2**
                                                        EMI **575790–2** [13]
                                                        EMI **379983–2**
                                            in EMI **4577672–4** [10]

London Symphony Orchestra, Richard Hickox
   r. April 1990   Chandos **CHAN8879** *ABTD1492*
   (3/98)   Chandos **CHAN7074**
                                               Chandos **CHAN10110**
Philharmonia Orchestra, Owain Arwyl Hughes · r. Dec. 1988 (7/89)   ASV DCA634
                                             ASV *ZCDCA634*
                              (7/89)   ASV **CDDCA634**
                                             ASV **CDQS6123**
Hallé Orchestra, John Wilson   r. March 2007 (12/09)   Hallé **CDHLL7523**

※ arr. brass band
Black Dyke Mills Band, Alec Mortimer   Jamco BD 1206/7*

MAI-DUN Symphonic Rhapsody
Hallé, Barbirolli   r. May 1949 (10/51)   HMV DB9651–2 * auto only
                               HMV DB21232–3 * (not used)
          (9/84)   EMI EX290107–3 [2]
                                 EMI *EX290107–5*
          (2/94)   EMI **CDM764716–2**
          (4/02)   Dutton **CDSJB1022** [2]
London Philharmonic Orchestra, Adrian Boult
   r. Dec. 1965 (9/66)   Lyrita RCS32 SRCS32
                         Musical Heritage Society 1317
          (5/07)   Lyrita **SRCD240**
London Philharmonic Orchestra, Bryden Thomson
   r. Dec. 1985 (9/86)   Chandos ABRD1174 *ABTD1174*
          (1/87)   Chandos **CHAN8461**
Hallé Orchestra, John Wilson   r. March 2007 (12/09)   Hallé **CDHLL7523**

※ arr. piano duet, composer
Alan Rowlands and Adrian Sims   (12/10)   Albion **ALBCD011**

MARITIME OVERTURE
※ for military band
Royal Artillery Band, Woolwich, R. Quinn   [NSA M1763W]

※ arr. symphonic wind band, Norman Richardson
City of London Wind Ensemble, Geoffrey Brand
   r. 1988 (7/89)   Gamut **LDRCD1001** *LRDC1001*

ORCHESTRAL POEM
City of London Sinfonia, Richard Hickox
   r. Oct/Nov 1994 (11/95)   Chandos **CHAN9376**

THE OVERLANDERS, Film Music
※ Complete film
Philharmonia Orchestra, Ernest Irving   Optimum Classics OPTD1509 (DVD)

※ Incidental music
London Symphony Orchestra, Muir Mathieson   r. May 1947 (8/47)   Decca K1602 *
                                              Pearl **GEM0100**
                                          London T5055 *
                                      in London LA48 *
                                          CDEA6146

※ Orchestral suite, arr. Mackerras
London Philharmonic Orchestra, Adrian Boult   r. Jan. 1970 (2/71)   Lyrita SRCS45
                                                      Musical Heritage Society 1481
                                                (5/07)   Lyrita **SRCD240**
West Australian SO, David Measham   r. March 1979 (11/80)   Unicorn KP8001
                                                      Unicorn **UKCD2062**

London Symphony Orchestra, Richard Hickox
   r. April 1991 (2/92)   Chandos **CHAN8994**

   [Scorched Earth only]   in Chandos **CHAN241-12** [2]

   [Romance and Intermezzo only]
City of Birmingham Symphony Orchestra, Marcus Dods   (12/79)   HMV ASD3797
                                                            HMV *TCASD3797*
                                                (10/84)   EMI ED290109–1
                                                            EMI *ED290109–4*
Hallé Orchestra, John Wilson   r. March 2007 (12/09)   Hallé **CDHLL7523**

※ Two Symphonic Studies, arr. Geoffrey Bush
London Philharmonic Orchestra, Adrian Boult   r. Jan. 1970 (2/71)   Lyrita SRCS45
                                                      Musical Heritage Society 1481
                                                (6/07)   Lyrita **SRCD241**

City of London Sinfonia, Richard Hickox
   r. Oct./Nov. 1994 (11/95)   Chandos **CHAN9376**

   [No. 2]
Royal Ballet Sinfonia, Kenneth Alwyn   r. Jan. 1997 (7/97)   **FILMCD 177**

SATYRICON Overture
BBC Symphony Orchestra, Malcolm Sargent   Prom 2 August 1949   [NSA 30B653–4 *]
BBC Symphony Orchestra, Adrian Boult   [NSA tape M567W]
London Philharmonic Orchestra, Adrian Boult
   r. Dec. 1965 (9/66)   Lyrita RCS32 SRCS32
                                                    Musical Heritage Society 1317
        (6/07)   Lyrita **SRCD241**
LSO, Richard Hickox   r. April 1990 (2/92)   Chandos **CHAN8994**
Hallé Orchestra, John Wilson   r. March 2007 (12/09)   Hallé **CDHLL7523**

SCHERZO AND CORTEGE (from *Julius Caesar*, arr. Geoffrey Bush)
London Philharmonic Orchestra, Adrian Boult   r. Feb. 1970 (2/71)   Lyrita SRCS45
                                                      Musical Heritage Society 1481
                                                (5/07)   Lyrita **SRCD240**
LSO, Richard Hickox   r. April 1991 (2/92)   Chandos **CHAN8994**

TRITONS: Symphonic Prelude
London Philharmonic Orchestra, Adrian Boult   r. Jan. 1970 (2/71)   Lyrita SRCS45
                                                      Musical Heritage Society 1481
                                                (5/07)   Lyrita **SRCD240**
LSO, Richard Hickox   r. April 1991 (2/92)   Chandos **CHAN8994**

VARIATIONS ON 'CADET ROUSSELLE' [with Bridge, Bax and Goossens]
※ for voice and piano
Ian and Jennifer Partridge   [NSA M4674W]

℀ orch. Eugène Goossens
Royal Scottish National Orchestra, Martin Yates   r. Jun/Aug 2008   Dutton **CDLX7215**

CHAMBER MUSIC

BAGATELLE for violin and piano

Marjorie Hayward and pno.   (9/28)   HMV **B2648** *
Michael Davis, Nelson Harper   r. Aug. 1993   Vienna Modern Masters **VMM2009**
Paul Barritt, Catherine Edwards   r. Dec. 1995 (11/96)   Hyperion **CDA66853**
Lucy Gould, Benjamin Frith   r. June 2008 (8/09)   Naxos **8.570507**

℀ orch. Leslie Bridgewater
Lorraine McAslan, Royal Scottish National Orchestra, Martin Yates   Dutton **CDLX7215**

BERCEUSE for violin and piano

Paul Barritt, Catherine Edwards   r. Dec. 1995 (11/96)   Hyperion **CDA66853**
    Hyperion **CDH55164**
Lucy Gould, Benjamin Frith   r. June 2008 (8/09)   Naxos **8.570507**

℀ orch. Martin Yates
Charles Mutter, BBC Concert Orchestra, Martin Yates
    r. Nov. 2009   Dutton **CDLX7246**

CAVATINA for violin and piano

Paul Barritt, Catherine Edwards   r. Dec. 1995 (11/96)   Hyperion **CDA66853**
    Hyperion **CDH55164**
Lucy Gould, Benjamin Frith   r. June 2008 (8/09)   Naxos **8.570507**

℀ arr. organ, composer
Stefan Kagl   r. Herford Minster, May 2008   CPO **777481–2**
Miles Hartley (Manchester College)   Priory **PRCD 1054**

℀ orch. Graham Parlett
Justine Watts, Royal Scottish National Orchestra, Martin Yates
    r. Jun/Aug 2008   Dutton **CDLX7215**

CELLO SONATA

Antoni Sala, John Ireland   r. Oct. 1928 (9/29)   Columbia **L2314/7** *
    Dutton **CDBP9799**
Anthony Pini, John Ireland   BBC r. March 1949   [NSA **B7602/12**]
Derek Simpson, Leonard Cassini   (4/65)   Summit **LSU3081**
    (12/70)   Revolution **RCB5**
André Navarra, Eric Parkin   r. May/Oct. 1971 (5/72)   Lyrita **SRCS59**
    Heritage Musical Society **1610**
    Lyrita **SRCD2271** [3]
Julian Lloyd Webber, John McCabe   r. Aug. 1979 (5/81)   ASV ACA1001 *ZCACA1001*
    (2/93)   ASV **CDDCA807**
    ASV **GLD4009**
Karine Georgian, Ian Brown   r. Dec. 1993 (12/95)   Chandos **CHAN9377/8** [2]
    Chandos **CHAN241-40** [2]
Raphael Wallfisch, John York   r. 1994 (8/95)   Marco Polo **8.223718**
Alice Neary, Benjamin Frith   r. Oct. 2009 (Awards 2010)   Naxos **8.572497**
Parry Karp, Howard Karp   Univ. of Wisconsin Madison   **913956907** [2]
Emma Ferrand, Jeremy Young   r. Jan. 2008 (6/09)   Meridian **CDE84565**

℀ arr. viola, Lionel Tertis

Martin Outram, Julian Rolton r. Oct. 2009 (6/10)	Naxos **8.572208**
Roger Chase, Michiko Otaki r. May 2009 (10/10)	Dutton **CDLX7250**

CLARINET TRIO ed. and reconstructed by Stephen Fox

Stephen Fox, Laura Jones, Ellen Meyer	
r. Sept. 2005	Chestnut Hall Music **CHM080930**
Robert Plane, Alice Neary, Sophia Rahman	
r. April 2008 (6/09)	Naxos **8.570550**

FANTASY SONATA for clarinet and piano

Frederick Thurston, Kendall Taylor	[BBC trans. 32994–7 *]
Frederick Thurston, John Ireland r. 8 Jan. 48	Dutton **CDBP9799**
	Symposium **1259**
Thea King, Alan Rowlands (2/63)	Saga XIP7008
(2/63)	Saga XID5206
John Denman, Hazel Vivienne (1/72)	Revolution RCF009
John Denman, Paula Fan	British Music Label **BML009**
Gervase de Peyer, Eric Parkin r. May/Oct. 1971 (5/72)	Lyrita SRCS59
	Heritage Musical Society 1610
	Lyrita **SRCD2271** [3]
Gervase de Peyer, Gwenneth Pryor r. 1982/3 (11/87)	Chandos ABRD1237 *ABTD1237*
(11/87)	Chandos **CHAN8549**
(12/95)	Chandos **CHAN9377/8** [2]
	Chandos **CHAN241-40** [2]
Murray Khouri, Peter Pettinger r. June 1991 (6/92)	Continuum **CCD1038**
Nicholas Carpenter, David McArthur r. 1992 (10/92)	Herald **HAVP152**
Emma Johnson, Malcolm Martineau r. May 1993 (7/94)	ASV **CDDCA891**;
	ZCDCA891
	ASV **CDRSB506** [5]
Peter Nichols, Margaret Ozanne (Holywell Ensemble)	
r. Aug. 1994	British Music Label **BML010**
Victoria Soames, John Flinders r. 1998 (6/00)	Clarinet Classics **CC0025**
Robert Plane, Sophia Rahman r. April 2008 (6/09)	Naxos **8.570550**
Victoria Soames Samek, John Flinders	Clarinet Classics **CC025**

PHANTASIE TRIO no. 1 in A minor

Frederick Grinke, Florence Hooton, Kendall Taylor	
r. Nov. 1938 (3/39)	Decca K899–900 *
(3/00)	Dutton **CDLX7103**
David Martin, Florence Hooton, Nigel Coxe (2/65)	Saga XID5230
Yfrah Neaman, Julian Lloyd Webber, Eric Parkin r. July 1976 (3/79)	Lyrita SRCS98
	Lyrita **SRCD2271** [3]
Sophie Barber, Robert Max, Rebecca Holt (Barbican Piano Trio) (7/89) ASV DCA646	
ASV *ZCDCA646*, **CDDCA646**	
Jaqueline Hartley, Lionel Handy, Caroline Clemmow (Hartley Trio) Gamut **GAMCD518**	
Heritage **HTGCD 218**	
Lydia Mordkovitch, Karine Georgian, Ian Brown	
r. 1993 (12/95)	Chandos **CHAN9377/8** [2]
	Chandos **CHAN241-40** [2]
Kate Bailey, Spike Wilson, Margaret Ozanne (Holywell Ensemble)	
r. Aug. 1994	British Music Label **BML010**

Cantamen Trio   r. March 1996   British Music Society **BMS418CD**
Kiera Lyness, Spike Wilson, Margaret Ozanne (Holywell Ensemble)
   r. March 1997 (2/98)   ASV **CDDCA1016**
Sara Trubäck, Claes Gunnarsson, Per Lundberg   (3/07)   DAPHNE1026
Gould Piano Trio   r. June 2008 (8/09)   Naxos **8.570507**

PIANO TRIO no. 2 in E minor
David Martin, Florence Hooton, Nigel Coxe   (2/65)   Saga XID5230
Yfrah Neaman, Julian Lloyd Webber, Eric Parkin   r. July 1976 (3/79)   Lyrita SRCS98
                                                                Lyrita **SRCD2271** [3]
Lydia Mordkovitch, Karine Georgian, Ian Brown
   r. 1993 (12/95)   Chandos **CHAN9377/8** [2]
                                                          Chandos **CHAN241-40** [2]
Kiera Lyness, Spike Wilson, Margaret Ozanne (Holywell Ensemble)
   r. March 1997 (2/98)   ASV **CDDCA1016**
Daniel Hope, Julian Lloyd Webber, John McCabe   r. Dec. 2003 (1/05)   ASV **GLD4009**
Gould Piano Trio   r. June 2008 (8/09)   Naxos **8.570507**

PIANO TRIO no. 3 in E
Frederick Grinke, Florence Hooton, Kendall Taylor
   (9/39)   Decca DX242–4 * Z799–801 *
David Martin, Florence Hooton, Nigel Coxe   (2/65)   Saga XID5230
Yfrah Neaman, Julian Lloyd Webber, Eric Parkin   r. July 1976 (3/79)   Lyrita SRCS98
                                                                Lyrita **SRCD2271** [3]
Lydia Mordkovitch, Karine Georgian, Ian Brown
   r. 1993 (12/95)   Chandos **CHAN9377/8** [2]
                                                          Chandos **CHAN241-40** [2]
Kiera Lyness, Spike Wilson, Margaret Ozanne (Holywell Ensemble)
   r. March 1997 (2/98)   ASV **CDDCA1016**
Gould Piano Trio   r. June 2008 (8/09)   Naxos **8.570507**

SEXTET for clarinet, horn and string quartet
Gervase de Peyer, Neill Sanders, members of Melos Ensemble
   r. May/Oct. 1971 (5/72)   Lyrita SRCS59
                                                          Heritage Musical Society1610
                                                                Lyrita **SRCD2271** [3]
Holywell Ensemble   r. 1997 (2/98)   ASV **CDDCA1016**
Robert Plane, David Pyatt, Maggini Quartet   r. April 2008 (6/09)   Naxos **8.570550**

STRING QUARTET no. 1 in D minor
Martin String Quartet   15 June 63   [NSA 30B4841]
Holywell Ensemble   r. March 1997 (6/99)   ASV **CDDCA1017**
Maggini Quartet   r. Jan. 2004 (8/06)   Naxos **8.557777**

STRING QUARTET no. 2 in C minor
Holywell Ensemble   r. March 1997 (6/99)   ASV **CDDCA1017**
Maggini Quartet   r. Jan. 2004 (8/06)   Naxos **8.557777**

VIOLIN SONATA no. 1
Frederick Grinke, John Ireland   r. Nov. 1945 (5/48)   Decca K1400–3 * AK1400–3 * Auto
                                    (3/00)   Dutton **CDLX7103**
Alan Loveday, Leonard Cassini   (4/65)   Summit LSU3081
                                    (12/70)   Revolution RCB5

Yfrah Neaman, Eric Parkin r. June 1972 (10/72)	Lyrita SRCS64
	Lyrita **SRCD2271** [3]
Lydia Mordkovitch, Ian Brown r. Dec. 1993 (12/95)	Chandos **CHAN9377/8** [2]
	Chandos **CHAN241-40** [2]
Michael Davis, Nelson Harper r. Aug. 1993	Vienna Modern Masters **VMM2009**
Paul Barritt, Catherine Edwards r. Dec. 1995 (11/96)	Hyperion **CDA66853**
	Hyperion **CDH55164**
Daniel Hope, John McCabe r. Dec. 2003 (1/05)	ASV **GLD4009**
Lucy Gould, Benjamin Frith r. Oct. 2009 (Awards 2010)	Naxos **8.572497**

VIOLIN SONATA no. 2

Arthur Catterall, William Murdoch (abridged) r. 1919	Columbia L1322–3 *
Albert Sammons, John Ireland r. Oct. 1930 (3/00)	Dutton **CDLX7103**
Albert Sammons, William Murdoch r. 1935	[unissued]
Eda Kersey, Kathleen Long r. 1944	[BBC trans. 18202–8]
Tessa Robbins, Alan Rowlands (2/63)	Saga XIP7008
	Saga XID5206
Yfrah Neaman, Eric Parkin r. June 1972 (10/72)	Lyrita SRCS64
	Lyrita **SRCD2271** [3]
Lydia Mordkovitch, Ian Brown r. Dec. 1993 (12/95)	Chandos **CHAN9377/8** [2]
	Chandos **CHAN241-40** [2]
Michael Davis, Nelson Harper r. Aug. 1993	Vienna Modern Masters **VMM2009**
Paul Barritt, Catherine Edwards r. Dec. 1995 (11/96)	Hyperion **CDA66853**
	Hyperion **CDH55164**
Oliver Lewis, Jeremy Filsell r. Jan. 1996 (8/96)	Guild **GMCD7120**
Buckhard Hofmann, Alan Newcombe r. 2003/4	Australian Eloquence **476 6884**
Lucy Gould, Benjamin Frith r. Oct. 2009 (Awards 2010)	Naxos **8.572497**

※ arr. viola, Lionel Tertis

Roger Chase, Michiko Otaki r. May 2009 (10/10)	Dutton **CDLX7250**

PIANO WORKS

THE ALMOND TREES

Alan Rowlands (7/70)	Lyrita RCS28
(10/08)	Lyrita **REAM3112** [3]
Eric Parkin r. Jan. 1975 (4/77)	Lyrita SRCS88
	Lyrita **SRCD2277** [3]
Daniel Adni r. 1978 (7/79)	HMV HQS1414
	EMI **352279–2** [2]
Eric Parkin r. June 1982 (9/83)	Chandos DBRD2006 *DBTD2006*
Eric Parkin r. Nov. 1991 (8/92)	Chandos **CHAN9056**
John Lenehan r. March 2007 (10/08)	Naxos **8.570461**
Mark Bebbington r. Jan. 2008 (Awards 2010)	**SOMM099**
Robin Zebaida	Regent **REGCD218**

AMBERLEY WILD BROOKS – see TWO PIECES

APRIL – see TWO PIECES

AUBADE – see TWO PIECES

BALLADE

Alan Rowlands (8/63)	Lyrita RCS23
(10/08)	Lyrita **REAM3112** [3]
	Musical Heritage Society 7001
Eric Parkin r. 1978 (6/78)	Lyrita SRCS89
	Lyrita **SRCD2277** [3]
Eric Parkin r. Aug. 1992 (6/93)	Chandos **CHAN9140**
John Lenehan r. April 1995 (3/98)	Naxos **8.553700**
Mark Bebbington r. Aug 2007 (10/08)	**SOMMCD074**

BALLADE OF LONDON NIGHTS

Alan Rowlands BBC Third Programme 3 July 1965	[NSA 471W]
Alan Rowlands (7/70)	Lyrita RCS29
(10/08)	Lyrita **REAM3112** [3]
Eric Parkin r. June 1982 (9/83)	Chandos DBRD2006 *DBTD2006*
Anthony Goldstone r. March 1991 (3/92)	Gamut Classics **GAMCD526**
(Awards 2006)	Diversions **24118**
Eric Parkin r. May 1993 (1/95)	Chandos **CHAN9250**
John Lenehan r. March 2007 (10/08)	Naxos **8.570461**
Mark Bebbington r. Jan. 2008 (Awards 2010)	**SOMM099**

BERGOMASK – see TWO PIECES

COLUMBINE

※ original version
Alan Bush (who introduces it)   BBC 11 Nov. 1979   [NSA 1LP0203157]

※ published version	
Alan Rowlands (7/70)	Lyrita RCS29
(10/08)	Lyrita **REAM3112** [3]
Daniel Adni r. 1978 (7/79)	HMV HQS1414
	EMI **352279–2** [2]
Eric Parkin r. June 1982 (9/83)	Chandos DBRD2006 *DBTD2006*
Eric Parkin r. May 1993 (1/95)	Chandos **CHAN9250**
John Lenehan r. April 1995 (3/98)	Naxos **8.553700**

THE DARKENED VALLEY

Alan Rowlands (10/64)	Lyrita RCS24
(10/08)	Lyrita **REAM3112** [3]
Eric Parkin r. 1977 (4/77)	Lyrita SRCS88
	Lyrita **SRCD2277** [3]
Eric Parkin r. Aug. 1992 (6/93)	Chandos **CHAN9140**
Desmond Wright r. Sept. 1992 & Oct. 1994 (4/96)	Classics for Pleasure **CDCFP4674**
	Classics for Pleasure *TC-CFP4674*
	EMI **352279–2** [2]
John Lenehan r. Sept. 1996 (10/99)	Naxos **8.553889**
Robert Helps	Naxos **8.559199**
Mark Bebbington r. Jan. 2008 (11/09)	**SOMM088**

DECORATIONS

1. The Island Spell; 2. Moon-glade; 3. The Scarlet Ceremonies

[no. 1 only]
Persis Cox   Welte-Mignon piano roll 6804

Anderson Tyrer r. 192?	Edison Bell Velvet Face 1138*
Eric Parkin (recorded under supervision of the composer) (6/53)	Argo 1004 RG4
Alan Rowlands (2/63)	Saga XIP7008
	Saga XID5206
Alan Rowlands (7/70)	Lyrita RCS28
(10/08)	Lyrita **REAM3112** [3]
Eric Parkin r. Jan. 1975 (12/75)	Lyrita SRCS87
	Lyrita **SRCD2277** [3]
Daniel Adni r. 1978 (7/79)	HMV HQS1414
	EMI **352279–2** [2]
Eric Parkin r. Nov. 1991 (8/92)	Chandos **CHAN9056**
[no. 1 only]	
Keith Swallow	Cameo CAMEO2044
John Lenehan r. Sept. 1996 (10/99)	Naxos **8.553889**
[no. 1 only]	
Christopher Headington r. Nov. 1989 (11/90)	Kingdom **KCLCD2017**
	Kingdom *CKCL2017*
Mark Bebbington r. Aug 2007 (10/08)	**SOMMCD074**
[no. 1 only]	
Daniel Berman r. live Aug. 1988 (10/10)	**DACOCD299** [2]
[no. 1 only]	
Alan Rowlands r. Spring 2000	**WS&SS¹**

EQUINOX

Frank Laffitte	Duo-Art piano roll
Alan Rowlands (10/60)	Lyrita RCS15
(10/08)	Lyrita **REAM3112** [3]
	Musical Heritage Society 7002
Eric Parkin r. 1977 (4/77)	Lyrita SRCS88
	Lyrita **SRCD2277** [3]
Eric Parkin r. Aug. 1992 (6/93)	Chandos **CHAN9140**
John Lenehan r. March 2007 (10/08)	Naxos **8.570461**

FEBRUARY'S CHILD – see TWO PIECES

FIRST RHAPSODY

Mark Bebbington r. Jan. 2008 (Awards 2010)	**SOMM099**
John Lenehan r. March 2011	Naxos **8.572598**

FOR REMEMBRANCE – see TWO PIECES

GREEN WAYS: Three Lyric Pieces
1. The Cherry Tree; 2. Cypress; 3. The Palm and May

Ross Pratt BBC 4 Sept/ 1950	[NSA M616W]
Alan Rowlands (10/60)	Lyrita RCS15
(10/08)	Lyrita **REAM3112** [3]
	Heritage Musical Society 7002
Eric Parkin r. 1978 (6/78)	Lyrita SRCS89

¹ WS&SS denotes a non-commercial CD, *While Spring & Summer sang*, of works by
  Delius arr. Rowlands and Ireland.

Eric Parkin   r. Aug. 1992 (6/93)
John Lenehan   r. March 2007 (10/08)
Desmond Wright   r. Sept. 1992 & Oct. 1994 (4/96)

Lyrita **SRCD2277** [3]
Chandos **CHAN9140**
Naxos **8.570461**
Classics for Pleasure **CDCFP4674**
Classics for Pleasure *TC-CFP4674*
EMI **352279–2** [2]

Alan Rowlands   r. Spring 2000
Mark Bebbington   r. Jan. 2008 (11/09)

WS&SS
SOMM088

IN THOSE DAYS
1. The Daydream; 2. Meridian
Alan Rowlands   (7/70)
            (10/08)
Eric Parkin   r. Aug. 1992 (6/93)
Desmond Wright   r. Sept. 1992 & Oct. 1994 (4/96)

Lyrita RCS28
Lyrita **REAM3112** [3]
Chandos **CHAN9140**
Classics for Pleasure **CDCFP4674**
Classics for Pleasure *TC-CFP4674*
EMI **352279–2** [2]

John Lenehan   r. April 1995 (3/98)

Naxos **8.553700**

INDIAN SUMMER
John Lenehan   r. March 2011

Naxos **8.572598**

LEAVES FROM A CHILD'S SKETCHBOOK
1. By the Mere; 2. In the Meadow; 3. The Hunt's Up
Eric Parkin   r. Aug. 1992 (6/93)
John Lenehan   r. Sept. 1996 (10/99)

Chandos **CHAN9140**
Naxos **8.553889**

LONDON PIECES
1. Chelsea Reach; 2. Ragamuffin; 3. Soho Forenoons
John Ireland   r. 28 May 1948

[NSA ICD0313831]

[nos. 2 & 3 only]
John Ireland   r. 25 May 1949

Dutton **CDBP9799**

[no. 2 only]
Graham Mitchell   (9/51)
Eric Parkin   (recorded under supervision of the composer) (6/53)
Alan Rowlands   (10/60)
            (10/08)

Argo U1004 *
Argo 1004 RG4
Lyrita RCS15
Lyrita **REAM3112** [3]
Heritage Musical Society 7002

Eric Parkin   r. Jan. 1975 (12/75)

Lyrita SRCS87
Lyrita **SRCD2277** [3]

Eric Parkin   r. Aug. 1992 (6/93)
Desmond Wright   r. Sept. 1992 & Oct. 1994 (4/96)

Chandos **CHAN9140**
Classics for Pleasure **CDCFP4674**
Classics for Pleasure *TC-CFP4674*
EMI **352279–2** [2]

John Lenehan   r. April 1995 (3/98)
[no. 1 only]
Mark Bebbington   r. Aug. 2007 (10/08)

Naxos **8.553700**
Naxos **8.572098–99** [2]
SOMMCD074

MERRY ANDREW
York Bowen
Alan Rowlands   (7/70)
            (10/08)

[NSA LP25575]
Lyrita RCS29
Lyrita **REAM3112** [3]

Eric Parkin   r. Jan. 1975 (12/75)   Lyrita SRCS87
                                                                          Lyrita **SRCD2277** [3]
Eric Parkin   r. Nov. 1991 (8/92)   Chandos **CHAN9056**
John Lenehan   r. Sept. 1996 (10/99)   Naxos **8.553889**

⅍ orch. C. H. Clutsam
Royal Scottish National Orchestra, Martin Yates   r. Jun/Aug 2008   Dutton **CDLX7215**

MONTH'S MIND
Alan Rowlands   (10/64)   Lyrita RCS24
                 (10/08)   Lyrita **REAM3112** [3]
Eric Parkin   r. 1978 (6/78)   Lyrita SRCS89
                                                                          Lyrita **SRCD2277** [3]
Eric Parkin   r. May 1993 (1/95)   Chandos **CHAN9250**
John Lenehan   r. April 1995 (3/98)   Naxos **8.553700**
Alan Rowlands   r. Spring 2000   **WS&SS**

ON A BIRTHDAY MORNING
Alan Rowlands   (10/60)   Lyrita RCS15
                 (10/08)   Lyrita **REAM3112** [3]
                                                         Heritage Musical Society 7002
Eric Parkin   r. 1977 (4/77)   Lyrita SRCS88
                                                                          Lyrita **SRCD2277** [3]
Eric Parkin   r. May 1993 (1/95)   Chandos **CHAN9250**
John Lenehan   r. March 2007 (10/08)   Naxos **8.570461**

PASTORAL
John Lenehan   r. March 2011   Naxos **8.572598**

PIANO SONATA in E minor
Kendall Taylor   BBC 25 April 1950   [NSA T10878WR]
Eric Parkin (recorded under supervision of the composer)   (6/53)   Argo 1004 RG4
Frank Merrick   (5/64)   Frank Merrick Society FMS8
Alan Rowlands   (10/64)   Lyrita RCS24
                 (10/08)   Lyrita **REAM3112** [3]
Eric Parkin   r. 1977 (4/77)   Lyrita SRCS88
                                                                          Lyrita **SRCD2277** [3]
Eric Parkin   r. Nov. 1991 (8/92)   Chandos **CHAN9056**
John Lenehan   r. March 2007 (10/08)   Naxos **8.570461**
Malcolm Binns   r. 2007 (3/08)   British Music Society **BMS434/5** [2]
Mark Bebbington   r. Aug 2007 (10/08)   **SOMMCD074**

PRELUDE in E♭
Eric Parkin   Argo RG28
Alan Rowlands   (7/70)   Lyrita RCS28
                 (10/08)   Lyrita **REAM3112** [3]
Eric Parkin   r. Jan. 1975 (12/75)   Lyrita SRCS87
                                                                          Lyrita **SRCD2277** [3]
Eric Parkin   r. Aug. 1992 (6/93)   Chandos **CHAN9140**
John Lenehan   r. April 1995 (3/98)   Naxos **8.553700**
Mark Bebbington   r. Jan. 2008 (Awards 2010)   **SOMM099**

PRELUDES
1. The Undertone; 2. Obsession; 3. The Holy Boy; 4. Fire of Spring

[no. 3 only]
Boris Hambourg   HMV B3302 *

[no. 1 only]
John Ireland   r. 7 Nov. 1946   Dutton **CDBP9799**

[no. 1 only]
John Ireland   BBC recording 28 March 1947   [NSA B7602/04]

[no. 3 only]
Alan Rowlands   (2/63)   Saga XIP7008
                                                        Saga XID5206
Alan Rowlands   (7/70)   Lyrita RCS28
                (10/08)   Lyrita **REAM3112** [3]

[no. 1 only]
Frank Merrick   Frank Merrick Society FMS3

[no. 1 only]
Frank Merrick   (1/73)   SRRE129

[no. 3 only]
John Ogdon   r. April 1972 (8/73)   HMV HQS1287
                                            Classics for Pleasure CfP4514
                                            Classics for Pleasure *TC-CfP4514*

Eric Parkin   r. Jan. 1975 (12/75)   Lyrita SRCS87
                                                       Lyrita **SRCD2277** [3]

[no. 3 only]
Daniel Adni   r. 1978 (7/79)   HMV HQS1414
                                                       EMI **352279–2** [2]

Eric Parkin   r. Nov. 1991 (8/92)   Chandos **CHAN9056**
John Lenehan   r. March 2007 (10/08)   Naxos **8.570461**
Desmond Wright   r. Sept. 1992 & Oct. 1994 (4/96)   Classics for Pleasure **CDCFP4674**
                                            Classics for Pleasure *TC-CFP4674*

[nos. 1, 2 & 4 only]

                                                       EMI **352279–2** [2]

[no. 3 only]
Mark Bebbington   r. Jan. 2008 (Awards 2010)   **SOMM099**
                  (11/03)   Testament **SBT1288**

[no. 3 only]
Alan Rowlands   r. Spring 2000   **WS&SS**

※ *The Holy Boy* arr. strings, composer
Boyd Neel Orchestra, Boyd Neel   r. Jan. 1945   Decca M595 *
London Philharmonic Orchestra, Adrian Boult
   r. Dec. 1965 (9/66)   Lyrita RCS31 SRCS31
                                            Musical Heritage Society 1498
                  (1/08)   Lyrita **SRCD242**
English Sinfonia, Neville Dilkes   r. June 1971 (4/72) HMV CSD3705
                  (2/81)   HMV ESD7101 HMV *TC-ESD7101*
                                                       EMI **567431–2**

String Orchestra, Jay Wilbur   Boosey & Hawkes ST2009 *

English Chamber Orchestra, David Garforth
   r. Dec. 1983 (12/84)   Chandos ABRD1112 *ABTD1112*
          (5/87)   Chandos **CHAN8390**
Royal Philharmonic Orchestra, David Willcocks
   r. March 1986 (12/86)   Unicorn **DKPCD9057**
                                           Unicorn DKP9057 *DKPC9057*
LSO, Richard Hickox   r. April 1990   Chandos **CHAN8879** *ABTD1492*
                                           Chandos **CHANBM2**
    (3/98)   Chandos **CHAN7074**
                                           Chandos **CHAN10110**
                                           Chandos **CHAN241-16**
                                       Chandos **CHAN241-28** [2]
English Sinfonia, John Farrer   (11/97)   Carlton **30366 0060–2**
English Northern Philharmonic, David Lloyd-Jones   r. 2000   Naxos **8.55068**
                                         Naxos **8.57057374** [2]
Royal Ballet Sinfonia, Gavin Sutherland   r. March 2008   Dutton **CDLX7246**
Maggini Quartet   r. Jan. 2004 (8/06)   Naxos **8.557777**

※ *The Holy Boy* arr. voice(s) & piano, organ or strings or unacc., composer
Clifford Hughes (ten.), George Blackmore (org.)   Pilgrim **KLP35**
Chichester Cathedral Choir, John Birch   Abbey **MVP786**
Worcester Cathedral Choir, Donald Hunt   (6/79)   Abbey **LPB803**
Paul Dutton, Leeds Parish Church Choir, Donald Hunt   1972   Abbey **LPB728**
The Scholars   (12/74)   Unicorn **RHS318**
Norwich Cathedral Choir, Michael Nicholas   (11/79)   Vista **VPS1084**
Neil Mackie, Paisley Abbey Choir, George McPhee   (12/87)   Alpha **APS356**
Stephen Ryde-Weller, Nicholas Richardson (trebles), Bournemouth
   Symphony Orchestra, David Hill   r. Jan. 1994   Decca **444130**
                                           Decca **470195–2**
Coventry Cathedral Choir and Girls' Choir, David Poulter   Lammas **LAMM88**
James Rainbird (treble), Michael Stuckey (pno.)   Priory **5005**
Jeffrey Benton (bar.), Keith Orrell (keyboards)   Symposium **SYMCD1086**
Oliver Lepage-Dean, St John's College Choir, Christopher Robinson
   (4/03)   Naxos **8.557129**
Wells Cathedral Girl Choristers, Rupert Gough   r. Nov. 2004   Herald **HAVP307**
St Bride's Church, Fleet Street, Robert Jones   Regent **REGCD133**
Paul Dutton   Griffin **GCCD4065**
Roderick Williams, BBC Concert Orchestra, Martin Yates   (3/08)   Dutton **CDLX7199**

※ *The Holy Boy* arr. brass, Robert Stepp
London Brass Virtuosi, David Honeyball   r. Sept. 1987 (11/88)   Hyperion **CDH88013**
                                         Hyperion *KH88013*
                                         Hyperion **CDH55070**

※ arr. Peter Cameron
Brass, Tim Hawes   Guild **GMCD7218**

※ arr. Steve Robson
Brass   DOYCD207

※ *The Holy Boy* arr. cello and piano
Boris Hambourg, Gerald Moore   r. Oct. 1929   HMV **B3302** *
Florence Hooton, Ross Pratt   r. Nov. 1938 (3/39)   in Decca **DK899–900** [2] *
           (3/00)   Dutton **CDLX7103**

Julian Lloyd Webber, John Lenehan	Philips **442530–2**
Julian Lloyd Webber, John McCabe r. Feb. 1987 (1/88)	ASV DCA592
	ASV *ZCDCA592*
(9/98)	ASV **CDDCA592**
	ASV CDQS6116
(1/05)	ASV **GLD4009**
Karine Georgian, Ian Brown r. 1993 (12/95)	Chandos **CHAN9377/8** [2]
Holywell Ensemble r. March 1997 (6/99)	ASV **CDDCA1017**
Paul Barritt, Catherine Edwards	Hyperion **CDH55164**
Emma Ferrand, Jeremy Young r. Jan. 2008 (6/09)	Meridian **CDE84565**

※ *The Holy Boy* transcr. Christopher Palmer for cello and orchestra
Julian Lloyd Webber, Academy of St Martin, Neville Marriner
   r. Jan. 1994 (12/94)

Philips **442 530–2**
Eloquence **ELQ4428415**

※ *The Holy Boy* arr. clarinet (after Lionel Tertis)
Robert Plane, Sophia Rahman   r. April 2008 (6/09)

Naxos **8.570550**

※ *The Holy Boy* arr. flute, James Galway
James Galway, Royal Philharmonic Orchestra

RCA **09026 61233–2**

※ *The Holy Boy* arr. organ, composer

Jonathan Bielby Rochdale Town Hall (5/91)	Priory **PRCD298**
John Scott Whiteley York Minster (12/91)	York CD846 *MC846*
Roger Judd r. St George's, Windsor, May 1998 (12/99)	Herald **HAVP225**
Stephen Farr r. Guildford Cathedral, June 2005	Herald **HAVP315**
Philip Smith Lincoln College, Oxford	Guild **GMCD7226**
Douglas Paine Trinity College, Cambridge	GMN **GMNC0118**
Stefan Kagl r. Herford Minster, May 2008	CPO **777481–2**
Thomas Laing-Reilly St Cuthbert's, Edinburgh	Delphian **34077**
Daniel Hyde King's College, Cambridge	Priory **PRCD884**
Thomas Trotter Royal Albert Hall, London	Regent **REGCD322**
Philip Brunelle (organ)	Virgin VC791088–2 *VC791088–4*
Miles Hartley (Manchester College)	Priory **PRCD 1054**

※ *The Holy Boy* arr. viola, Lionel Tertis
Lionel Tertis (unaccompanied)   (3/25)

Vocalion K05144 *
(Awards 2006)   in Biddulph **80218–2** [4]

※ *The Holy Boy* arr. violin and piano, composer

Paul Barritt, Catherine Edwards r. Dec. 1995 (11/96)	Hyperion **CDA66853**
Richard Howarth, Keith Swallow r. Aug. 2002 (Awards 2003)	Cameo **CAMEO2026**
Lucy Gould, Benjamin Frith r. June 2008 (8/09)	Naxos **8.570507**
Angèle Dubeau with string orchestra	Analekta **AN28730**

※ *The Holy Boy* arr. violin and orch., Christopher Palmer
Lorraine McAslam, Royal Scottish National Orchestra, Martin Yates
   r. Jun/Aug 2008

Dutton **CDLX7215**

RHAPSODY

Eric Parkin	Argo RG28
Alan Rowlands (10/64)	Lyrita RCS24
(10/08)	Lyrita **REAM3112** [3]
Eric Parkin r. Jan. 1975 (12/75)	Lyrita SRCS87
	Lyrita **SRCD2277** [3]

Eric Parkin   r. Nov. 1991 (8/92)   Chandos **CHAN9056**
Margaret Ozanne   r. Aug. 1994   British Music Label **BML010**
John Lenehan   r. Sept. 1996 (10/99)   Naxos **8.553889**
Mark Bebbington   r. Jan. 2008   (Awards 2010)   **SOMM099**

SARNIA (AN ISLAND SEQUENCE)
1. Le Catioroc; 2. In a May Morning; 3. Song of the Springtides

John Ireland   broadcast 9 Dec 1945 incomplete recording   [NSA 2CDR0006182]
Graham Mitchell   (9/51)   Argo AU1001–3 [3] *
Eric Parkin   Argo RG28
Alan Rowlands   (8/63)   Lyrita RCS23
                 (10/08)   Lyrita **REAM3112** [3]
                                           Musical Heritage Society 7001
Eric Parkin   r. 1978 (6/78)   Lyrita SRCS89
                                                   Lyrita **SRCD2277** [3]
Daniel Adni   r. 1978 (7/79)   HMV HQS1414
                                                       EMI **352279–2** [2]
Eric Parkin   r. May 1993 (1/95)   Chandos **CHAN9250**
John Lenehan   r. April 1995 (3/98)   Naxos **8.553700**
Oliver Williams   (7/98)   **FAND101**
Mark Bebbington   r. Jan. 2008 (11/09)   **SOMM088**

% orch. Martin Yates
Royal Scottish National Orchestra/Yates   Dutton Epoch **CDLX 7281**

SEA IDYLL
1. Poco andante; 2. Allegro appassionato; 3. Andante mesto

Alan Rowlands   (7/70)   Lyrita RCS29
                 (10/08)   Lyrita **REAM3112** [3]

[no. 1 only]
Eric Parkin   r. May 1993 (1/95)   Chandos **CHAN9250**

[no. 1 only]
Desmond Wright   r. Sept. 1992 & Oct. 1994 (4/96)   Classics for Pleasure **CDCFP4674**
                                           Classics for Pleasure *TC-CFP4674*
                                                       EMI **352279–2** [2]

[no. 1 only]
Mark Bebbington   r. Jan. 2008 (11/09)   **SOMM088**
John Lenehan   r. March 2011   Naxos **8.572598**

SOLILOQUY
Graham Mitchell   (9/51)   Argo U 1004 *
Alan Rowlands   (10/60)   Lyrita RCS15
                 (10/08)   Lyrita **REAM3112** [3]
                                                       HMV HMS 7002
Eric Parkin   r. 1977 (4/77)   Lyrita SRCS88
                                                   Lyrita **SRCD2277** [3]
Eric Parkin   r. May 1993 (1/95)   Chandos **CHAN9250**
John Lenehan   r. March 2007 (10/08)   Naxos **8.570461**

% orch. Graham Parlett
Charles Mutter (vln), BBC Concert Orchestra, Martin Yates
    r. Nov. 2009   Dutton **CDLX7246**

SONATINA
[3rd mvt., Rondo only]
William Murdoch   HMV C4944 *

[complete]
Helen Perkin   BBC 19 June 1951   [NSA 30B4854]
Alan Rowlands   (10/60)   Lyrita RCS15
                 (10/08)   Lyrita **REAM3112** [3]
                                                  Heritage Musical Society 7002
John McCabe   r. 1972 (12/74)   Decca SDD444
      (10/09)   British Music Society BMS103CDH
Eric Parkin   r. 1978 (6/78)   Lyrita SRCS89
                                                                  Lyrita **SRCD2277** [3]
Eric Parkin   r. Aug. 1992 (6/93)   Chandos **CHAN9140**
John Lenehan   r. Sept. 1996 (10/99)   Naxos **8.553889**
Mark Bebbington   r. Aug 2007 (10/08)   **SOMMCD074**

SPRING WILL NOT WAIT – see THREE POEMS BY HOUSMAN

SUMMER EVENING
Alan Rowlands   (7/70)   Lyrita RCS28
Eric Parkin   r. 1977 (4/77)   Lyrita SRCS88
                                                                  Lyrita **SRCD2277** [3]
Eric Parkin   r. Nov. 1991 (8/92)   Chandos **CHAN9056**
Desmond Wright   r. Sept. 1992 & Oct. 1994 (4/96)   Classics for Pleasure **CDCFP4674**
                                                     Classics for Pleasure *TC-CFP4674*
                                                                  EMI **352279–2** [2]
John Lenehan   r. Sept. 1996 (10/99)   Naxos **8.553889**
Alan Rowlands   r. Spring 2000   **WS&SS**

THREE DANCES
1. Gypsy Dance; 2. Country Dance; 3. Reapers' Dance
Daniel Adni   r. 1978 (7/79)   HMV HQS1414
                                                                  EMI **352279–2** [2]
Mark Bebbington   r. Jan. 2008 (Awards 2010)   **SOMM099**
John Lenehan   r. March 2011   Naxos **8.572598**

THREE PASTELS
1. A Grecian Lad; 2. The Boy Bishop; 3. Puck's Birthday
Alan Rowlands   (7/70)   Lyrita RCS29
                 (10/08)   Lyrita **REAM3112** [3]
Eric Parkin   r. June 1982 (9/83)   Chandos DBRD2006 *DBTD2006*
Eric Parkin   r. May 1993 (1/95)   Chandos **CHAN9250**
Desmond Wright   r. Sept. 1992 & Oct. 1994 (4/96)   Classics for Pleasure **CDCFP4674**
                                                     Classics for Pleasure *TC-CFP4674*
                                                                  EMI **352279–2** [2]
John Lenehan   r. Sept. 1996 (10/99)   Naxos **8.553889**

THE TOWING PATH
John Ireland   r. 28 May 1948   [NSA M613R]
Graham Mitchell   (9/51)   Argo U1005 *
Alan Rowlands   (10/64)   Lyrita RCS24
                 (10/08)   Lyrita **REAM3112** [3]

Eric Parkin r. Jan. 1975 (12/75)	Lyrita SRCS87
	Lyrita **SRCD2277** [3]
Eric Parkin r. Nov. 1991 (8/92)	Chandos **CHAN9056**
Desmond Wright r. Sept. 1992 & Oct. 1994 (4/96)	Classics for Pleasure **CDCFP4674**
	Classics for Pleasure *TC-CFP4674*
	EMI **352279–2** [2]
John Lenehan r. Sept. 1996 (10/99)	Naxos **8.553889**
Alan Rowlands r. Spring 2000	**WS&SS**
⅍ orch. Martin Yates	
BBC Concert Orchestra, Martin Yates r. Oct. 2009	Dutton **CDLX7246**

TWO PIECES
1. For Remembrance; 2. Amberley Wild Brooks

[no. 2 only]	
John Ireland Piano roll (11/05)	Duo-Art piano roll 0211
	DSPRCD010[1]
[no. 2 only]	
John Ireland BBC recording 28 May 1948	Dutton **CDBP9799**
[no. 2 only]	
Graham Mitchell (9/51)	Argo U1005 *
[no. 2 only]	
Eric Parkin	Argo RG28
John Clegg	Alpha DB148C
[no. 1 only]	
Alan Rowlands (8/63)	Lyrita RCS23
(10/08)	Lyrita **REAM3112** [3]
	Musical Heritage Society 7001
[no. 2 only]	
Alan Rowlands (7/70)	Lyrita RCS29
(10/08)	Lyrita **REAM3112** [3]
Eric Parkin r. 1977 (4/77)	Lyrita SRCS88
	Lyrita **SRCD2277** [3]
Eric Parkin r. Aug. 1992 (6/93)	Chandos **CHAN9140**
John Lenehan r. March 2007 (10/08)	Naxos **8.570461**
Mark Bebbington r. Jan. 2008 (11/09)	**SOMM088**

TWO PIECES
1. February's Child; 2. Aubade

Alan Rowlands (8/63)	Lyrita RCS23
(10/08)	Lyrita **REAM3112** [3]
	Musical Heritage Society 7001
[2]	
Richard Deering (5/77)	Saga 5445
Eric Parkin r. 1978 (6/78)	Lyrita SRCS89
	Lyrita **SRCD2277** [3]
Eric Parkin r. May 1993 (1/95)	Chandos **CHAN9250**

[1] *Amberley Wild Brooks* is wrongly identified as *Ragamuffin* on both the original piano roll and this CD of piano rolls.

John Lenehan   r. Sept. 1996 (10/99)   Naxos **8.553889**
Mark Bebbington   r. Jan. 2008 (Awards 2010)   **SOMM099**

TWO PIECES
1. April; 2. Bergomask

[no. 1 only]
John Ireland   r. Feb. 1929 (9/29)   Columbia L2317 *

[no. 1 only]
John Ireland   BBC recording 28 May 1948   [NSA B7602/5]

[no. 1 only]
John Ireland   r. Abbey Road March 1950 (10/51)   in HMV DB9651 [2] *
                                              (4/92)   EMI **CDH763910–2**
                                                                         EMI **352279–2** [2]
Alan Rowlands   (7/70)   Lyrita RCS28
                 (10/08)   Lyrita **REAM3112** [3]

[no. 1 only]
John Ogdon   r. April 1972 (8/73)   HMV HQS1287
                                                      Classics for Pleasure CfP41514
                                                      Classics for Pleasure *TC-CfP41514*
                          (11/03)   Testament **SBT1288**
Eric Parkin   r. 1977 (4/77)   Lyrita SRCS88
                                                                         Lyrita **SRCD2277** [3]
Daniel Adni   r. 1978 (7/79)   HMV HQS1414
                                                                         EMI **352279–2** [2]
Eric Parkin   r. May 1993 (1/95)   Chandos **CHAN9250**

[no. 1 only]
Desmond Wright   r. Sept. 1992 & Oct. 1994 (4/96)   Classics for Pleasure **CDCFP4674**
                                                      Classics for Pleasure *TC-CFP4674*
John Lenehan   r. Sept. 1996 (10/99)   Naxos **8.553889**

[no. 1 only]
Alan Rowlands   r. Spring 2000   **WS&SS**
Mark Bebbington   r. Jan. 2008 (Awards 2010)   **SOMM099**

VILLANELLA
John Lenehan   r. March 2011   Naxos **8.572598**

ARRANGEMENTS

MEINE SEELE ERHEBT DEN HERREN, BWV648, Bach arr. John Ireland
Jonathan Plowright   Hyperion **CDA67767**
Angela Hewitt   Hyperion **CDA67309**

ORGAN WORKS

ALLA MARCIA
Robert Gower   Holy Trinity, Sloane St., London   (9/79)   Wealdon WS179
Jonathan Bielby   Rochdale Town Hall   (5/91)   Priory **PRCD298**
Stefan Kagl   r. Herford Minster, May 2008   CPO **777481–2**

Miles Hartley (Manchester College)	Priory **PRCD 1054**

CAPRICCIO

John Robinson Carlisle Cathedral	Priory **PRCD885**
Robert Gower Holy Trinity, Sloane St., London (9/79)	Wealdon WS179
Jonathan Bielby Rochdale Town Hall (5/91)	Priory **PRCD298**
Peter King Bath Abbey	Priory **PRCD335**
Huw Williams St Paul's Cathedral (1/07)	Guild **GMCD7304**
Stefan Kagl r. Herford Minster, May 2008	CPO 777481–2
Thomas Trotter Royal Albert Hall, London	Regent **REGCD322**
Miles Hartley (Manchester College)	Priory **PRCD 1054**

ELEGIAC ROMANCE

Robert Gower Holy Trinity, Sloane St., London (9/79)	Wealdon WS179
Jonathan Bielby Rochdale Town Hall (5/91)	Priory **PRCD298**
Peter King Bath Abbey	Priory **PRCD335**
Paul Plummer Eton College	OxRecs **OXCD65** *OXCA65*
Jane Parker-Smith St Marien Basilika, Kevelaer, Germany (12/07)	Avie **AV2144**
Andrew Bryden Ripon Cathedral	Regent **REGCD224**
Stefan Kagl r. Herford Minster, May 2008	CPO 777481–2
Miles Hartley (Manchester College)	Priory **PRCD 1054**

MARCIA POPOLARE

Stefan Kagl r. Herford Minster, May 2008	CPO 777481–2

MEDITATION ON JOHN KEBLE'S ROGATIONTIDE HYMN

Robert Gower Holy Trinity, Sloane St., London (9/79)	Wealdon WS179
Jonathan Bielby Rochdale Town Hall (5/91)	Priory **PRCD298**
Andrew Sievewright	Alpha APS319 *CAPS319*
Stefan Kagl r. Herford Minster, May 2008	CPO 777481–2
Miles Hartley (Manchester College)	Priory **PRCD 1054**

※ arr. string orchestra, Geoffrey Bush
English Chamber Orchestra, David Garforth

r. Dec. 1983 (12/84)	Chandos ABRD1112 *ABTD1112*
(5/87)	Chandos **CHAN8390**
Royal Scottish National Orchestra, Martin Yates	Dutton **CDLX7215**

MINIATURE SUITE
1. Intrada; 2. Villanella; 3. Menuetto-Impromptu

[no. 2 only]

R. Goss-Custard r. Queen's Hall, 1927 (4/28)	HMV C1466 *
	Amphion PHICD133

[no. 2 only]

Frederick Jackson	Amphion **PHICD193**

[no. 2 only]

Paul Morgan Exeter Cathedral	Priory **PRCD431** *PRC431*

[no. 2 only]

Frederick Bayco	HMV CLP1777
	HMV CSD1539
Jonathan Bielby Rochdale Town Hall (5/91)	Priory **PRCD298**
Andrew Sievewright	Alpha APS319
	Alpha CAPS319

[no. 2 only]

Thomas Trotter Birmingham Town Hall (12/07)	Regent **REGCD265**
Stefan Kagl r. Herford Minster, May 2008	CPO **777481–2**
Miles Hartley (Manchester College)	Priory **PRCD 1054**

※ arr. piano, composer
[no. 2 only]

Mark Bebbington r. Jan. 2008 (11/09)	**SOMM088**

※ orch. Leslie Bridgewater
[nos. 2 & 3 only]

Royal Scottish National Orchestra, Martin Yates r. Jun/Aug 2008	Dutton **CDLX7215**

SURSUM CORDA

Jonathan Bielby Rochdale Town Hall (5/91)	Priory **PRCD298**
Derek Longman Haileybury Chapel	Regent **REGCD139**
Stefan Kagl r. Herford Minster, May 2008	CPO **777481–2**
Miles Hartley (Manchester College)	Priory **PRCD 1054**

VOCAL

ANNABEL LEE for reciter and piano

Richard Baker, Keith Swallow	Cameo CAMEO2044
Richard Baker (narrator), Raphael Terroni	*UKC7015*
	KPM7015

※ orch. Roderick Williams

Roderick Williams, BBC Concert Orchestra, Martin Yates	
r. Oct. 2009	Dutton **CDLX7246**

BED IN SUMMER

Alfreda Hodgson, Alan Rowlands r. Aug. 1978 (11/79)	Lyrita SRCS118
	Lyrita **SRCD2261** [3]
Rachel Ann Morgan, Tan Crone	Etcetera **KTC1128**
Lisa Milne, Graham Johnson r. Sept. 1998 (8/99)	Hyperion **CDA67261/2** [2]

THE BELLS OF SAN MARIE

Hubert Eisdel, piano quintet r. 1919	Columbia 1333 *
Benjamin Luxon, Alan Rowlands r. 1973 (7/75)	Lyrita SRCS66
	Lyrita **SRCD2261** [3]
Rachel Ann Morgan, Tan Crone	Etcetera **KTC1128**
Bryn Terfel, Malcolm Martineau r. 1995 (8/95)	DG **445946–2GH**
	in DG **4778167** [55]
	Decca **470195–2**
Christopher Maltman, Graham Johnson	
r. Sept. 1998 (8/99)	Hyperion **CDA67261/2** [2]
Teddy Tahu Rhodes, Sharolyn Kimmorley r. Aug. 2002	ABC **4767175**
Roderick Williams, Iain Burnside r. July 2007 (9/08)	Naxos **8.570467**

EARTH'S CALL

Alfreda Hodgson, Alan Rowlands r. Aug. 1978 (11/79)	Lyrita SRCS118
	Lyrita **SRCD2261** [3]
Lisa Milne, Graham Johnson r. Sept. 1998 (8/99)	Hyperion **CDA67261/2** [2]
Ellen Frohnmayer, Logan Skelton (11/90)	Centaur **CRC2075**

THE EAST RIDING
John Mitchinson, Alan Rowlands   r. Aug. 1978 (11/79)   Lyrita SRCS118
Lyrita **SRCD2261** [3]

FIVE SIXTEENTH-CENTURY POEMS
1. A Thanksgiving; 2. All in a garden green; 3. An Aside; 4. A Report Song;
5. The Sweet Season

[no. 1 only]
Janet Baker, Martin Isepp   (2/64)   Saga XIP7013
(8/66)   Saga STXID5213; XID5213
CA5213 8T5213
Saga **ECD3360**
(3/82)   Saga **SCD9012**
Regis **RRC1265**
Benjamin Luxon, Alan Rowlands   r. 1973 (7/75)   Lyrita SRCS66
Lyrita **SRCD2261** [3]

Christopher Maltman, Graham Johnson
r. Sept. 1998 (8/99)   Hyperion **CDA67261/2** [2]

FIVE POEMS BY THOMAS HARDY
1. Beckon to me to come; 2. In my sage moments; 3. It was what you bore with you,
woman; 4. The tragedy of that moment; 5. Dear, think not that they will forget you
John Shirley-Quirk, Eric Parkin   (5/64)   Saga XID5207; STXID5207
Saga XIP7015
Benjamin Luxon, Alan Rowlands   r. 1972/3 (5/75)   Lyrita SRCS65
Lyrita **SRCD2261** [3]

Christopher Maltman, Graham Johnson
r. Sept. 1998 (8/99)   Hyperion **CDA67261/2** [2]
Roderick Williams, Iain Burnside   r. July 2007 (9/08)   Naxos **8.570467**

GREAT THINGS
John Shirley-Quirk, Eric Parkin   (5/64)   Saga XID5207; STXID5207
Saga XID7015
Benjamin Luxon, Alan Rowlands   r. 1973 (7/75)   Lyrita SRCS66
Lyrita **SRCD2261** [3]

Christopher Maltman, Graham Johnson
r. Sept. 1998 (8/99)   Hyperion **CDA67261/2** [2]
Paul Whelan, David Harper   r. 1999 (5/00)   Trust **MMT2023**
Roderick Williams, Iain Burnside   r. July 2007 (9/08)   Naxos **8.570467**

HAWTHORN TIME
Peter Pears, John Ireland   BBC 8 Dec. 47   Dutton **CDBP9799**
Peter Pears, John Ireland   r. 1949   [NSA T10871R2]
Peter Pears, John Ireland   Wigmore Hall 14 May 1951   [NSA B7602/08]
John Mitchinson, Alan Rowlands   r. Aug. 1978 (11/79)   Lyrita SRCS118
Lyrita **SRCD2261** [3]

Anthony Rolfe Johnson, Graham Johnson
r. Sept. 1998 (8/99)   Hyperion **CDA67261/2** [2]
Hyperion **CDD22044** [2]

THE HEART'S DESIRE

John Shirley-Quirk, Eric Parkin (5/64)	Saga XID5207; STXID5207
	Saga XIP7015
John Mitchinson, Alan Rowlands r. Aug. 1978 (11/79)	Lyrita SRCS118
	Lyrita **SRCD2261** [3]
Graham Trew, Roger Vignoles r. Aug. 1979 (4/80)	Meridian E77031/2 [2]
Anthony Rolfe Johnson, Graham Johnson (8/95)	Hyperion **CDA66471/2**
	Hyperion **CDD22044** [2]
John Mark Ainsley, Graham Johnson r. Sept. 1998 (8/99)	Hyperion **CDA67261/2** [2]

❧ orch. Graham Parlett
Susan Gritton, strings of BBC Concert Orchestra, Martyn Brabbins
  r. Jan. 2009 (1/10)   Dutton **CDLX7228**

HERE'S TO THE SHIPS

❧ orch. composer
Roderick Williams, BBC Concert Orchestra, Martin Yates
  r. Oct. 2009   Dutton **CDLX7246**

HOPE THE HORNBLOWER

Peter Dawson r. May 1920	HMV B1137 *
Harold Williams (2/25)	Edison Bell VF1118 *
Benjamin Luxon, Alan Rowlands r. 1972/3 (5/75)	Lyrita SRCS65
	Lyrita **SRCD2261** [3]
Lisa Milne, Graham Johnson r. Sept. 1998 (8/99)	Hyperion **CDA67261/2** [2]

❧ arr. with orch., Frederick Bye
Thomas Case, orchestra   Parlophone R 552 *
Stephen Varcoe, City of London Sinfonia, Richard Hickox
  (1/90)   Chandos ABRD1382 *ABTD1382*
  (1/90)   Chandos **CHAN8743**
Roderick Williams, BBC Concert Orchestra, Martin Yates   (3/08)   Dutton **CDLX7199**

IF THERE WERE DREAMS TO SELL

George Baker, Mme Adami r. April 1924 (7/24)	HMV B1816 *
(1/87)	EMI EX290911–3
	EMI *EX290911–5*
Master Frederick Firth r. Sept 1928	Brunswick BA 347 *
	Amphion **PHI CD 158**
Benjamin Luxon, Alan Rowlands r. 1973 (7/75)	Lyrita SRCS66
	Lyrita **SRCD2261** [3]
Sarah Walker, Roger Vignoles r. July 1990 (10/92)	Crd **CRD3473**
Rachel Ann Morgan, Tan Crone	Etcetera **KTC1128**
Lisa Milne, Graham Johnson r. Sept. 1998 (8/99)	Hyperion **CDA67261/2** [2]
Roderick Williams, Iain Burnside r. July 2007 (9/08)	Naxos **8.570467**

❧ arr. with orch., Frederick Bye
Roderick Williams, BBC Concert Orchestra, Martin Yates   (3/08)   Dutton **CDLX7199**
Stephen Varcoe, City of London Sinfonia, Richard Hickox
  (1/90)   Chandos ABRD1382 *ABTD1382*
  (1/90)   Chandos **CHAN8743**

IF WE MUST PART
Benjamin Luxon, Alan Rowlands   r. 1973 (7/75)

Rachel Ann Morgan, Tan Crone
Christopher Maltman, Graham Johnson
   r. Sept. 1998 (8/99)
Mark Stone, Stephen Barlow

Lyrita SRCS66
Lyrita **SRCD2261** [3]
Etcetera **KTC1128**

Hyperion **CDA67261/2** [2]
Stone Records **5060192780000**

I HAVE TWELVE OXEN
Peter Dawson   r. March 1920
   (9/83)

Norman Williams   (2/25)
Stuart Robertson
Peter Pears, John Ireland   BBC 8 Dec. 1947
Peter Pears, John Ireland   r. 1949
Peter Pears, John Ireland   Wigmore Hall 14 May 1951
Peter Pears, Benjamin Britten
   (6/56)
   (6/70)
John Shirley-Quirk, Eric Parkin   (5/64)

            (11/80)
Benjamin Luxon, Alan Rowlands   r. 1973 (7/75)

Rachel Ann Morgan, Tan Crone
Lisa Milne, Graham Johnson   r. Sept. 1998 (8/99)

Felicity Lott, Graham Johnson   (9/04)
Roderick Williams, Iain Burnside   r. July 2007 (9/08)
Albert Pengelly, Ivy Mason Whipp
Lois Marshall

HMV B1137 *
HMV RLS1077053
HMV *TC-RLS 1077059*
Velvet Face 1120 *
HMV B3411 *
Dutton **CDBP9799**
[NSA T10871R2]
[NSA B7602/09]

LW5241
ECS545
Saga XID5207; STXID5207
Saga XIP7015
Saga 5473
Lyrita SRCS66
Lyrita **SRCD2261** [3]
Etcetera **KTC1128**
Hyperion **CDA67261/2** [2]
HYP30
ASV **GLD4003**
Naxos **8.570467**
Pengelly AJP2
USSR DO11577

℁ orch. Graham Parlett
Susan Gritton, BBC Concert Orchestra, Martyn Brabbins
   r. Jan. 2009 (1/10)

Dutton **CDLX7228**

THE JOURNEY
Benjamin Luxon, Alan Rowlands   r. 1973 (7/75)

Lisa Milne, Graham Johnson   r. Sept. 1998 (8/99)

Lyrita SRCS66
Lyrita **SRCD2261** [3]
Hyperion **CDA67261/2** [2]

THE LAND OF LOST CONTENT
1. The Lent Lily; 2. Ladslove; 3. Goal and Wicket; 4. The Vain Desire;
5. The Encounter; 6. Epilogue (You smile upon your friend today)

Peter Pears, John Ireland   r. ca. 1949
Peter Pears, John Ireland   Wigmore Hall 14 May 1951
Peter Pears, Benjamin Britten   (11/64)

Peter Pears, Benjamin Britten   Maltings, Snape 1972
Anthony Rolfe Johnson, David Willison   (1/76)

[NSA T10871R2–3]
Dutton **CDBP9799**
Argo ZRG5418; RG418
Belart **461 550–2**
in Decca **4782345** [6]
[BBC trans. 101167]
Polydor **2460 258** [2]
EMI **CZS574785** [2]

John Mitchinson, Alan Rowlands r. Aug. 1978 (11/79)	Lyrita SRCS118
	Lyrita **SRCD2261** [3]
[no. 5 only]	
Gordon Pullin, Charles Macdonald r. Nov 1998	Hubert Foss **HJF 001CD**
[nos. 1, 3, 4, 5 & 6]	
Anthony Rolfe Johnson, Graham Johnson (8/95)	Hyperion **CDA66471/2**
	Hyperion **CDD22044** [2]
Anthony Rolfe Johnson, Graham Johnson	**675795–2** [9]
[no. 2 only]	
John Mark Ainsley, Graham Johnson r. Sept. 1998 (8/99)	Hyperion **CDA67261/2** [2]
Nathan Vale, Paul Plummer	**SOMMCD063**

LOVE IS A SICKNESS FULL OF WOES

John Mitchinson, Alan Rowlands (8/79)	Argo ZRG898 *4KZRC898*
John Mitchinson, Alan Rowlands r. Aug. 1978 (11/79)	Lyrita SRCS118
	Lyrita **SRCD2261** [3]
John Mark Ainsley, Graham Johnson r. Sept. 1998 (8/99)	Hyperion **CDA67261/2** [2]
Mark Stone, Stephen Barlow	Stone Records **5060192780000**

※ transcr. for piano Robert Helps

Mark Bebbington r. Jan. 2008 (11/09)	**SOMM088**

MARIGOLD Impression for Voice and Pianoforte

1. Youth's Spring-Tribute; 2. Penumbra; 3. Spleen

Benjamin Luxon, Alan Rowlands r. 1972/3 (5/75)	Lyrita SRCS65
	Lyrita **SRCD2261** [3]

[3]

Christopher Maltman, Graham Johnson	
r. Sept. 1998 (8/99)	Hyperion **CDA67261/2** [2]
Roderick Williams, Iain Burnside r. July 2007 (9/08)	Naxos **8.570467**

※ orch. composer

[1]

Roderick Williams, BBC Concert Orchestra, Martin Yates (3/08)	Dutton **CDLX7199**

THE MERRY MONTH OF MAY

John Shirley-Quirk, Eric Parkin (5/64)	Saga XID5207; STXID5207
	Saga XID7015
Benjamin Luxon, Alan Rowlands r. 1973 (7/75)	Lyrita SRCS66
	Lyrita **SRCD2261** [3]

MOTHER AND CHILD (Nursery Rhymes from SING SONG)

1. Newborn; 2. The Only Child; 3. Hope; 4. Skylark and Nightingale; 5. The Blind Boy; 6. Baby; 7. Death-Parting; 8. The Garland

Alfreda Hodgson, Alan Rowlands r. Aug. 1978 (11/79)	Lyrita SRCS118
	Lyrita **SRCD2261** [3]
Rachel Ann Morgan, Tan Crone	Etcetera **KTC1128**
Lisa Milne, Graham Johnson r. Sept. 1998 (8/99)	Hyperion **CDA67261/2** [2]

[no. 6 only] orch. Graham Parlett

Susan Gritton, strings of BBC Concert Orchestra, Martyn Brabbins

r. Jan. 2009 (1/10)	Dutton **CDLX7228**

REMEMBER

John Mitchinson, Alan Rowlands   r. Aug. 1978 (11/79)

Lyrita SRCS118
Lyrita **SRCD2261** [3]

John Mark Ainsley, Graham Johnson   r. Sept. 1998 (8/99)   Hyperion **CDA67261/2** [2]

THE SACRED FLAME

John Shirley-Quirk, Eric Parkin   (5/64)

Saga XID5207; STXID5207
Saga XID7015

John Mitchinson, Alan Rowlands   r. Aug. 1978 (11/79)

Lyrita SRCS118
Lyrita **SRCD2261** [3]

John Mark Ainsley, Graham Johnson   r. Sept. 1998 (8/99)   Hyperion **CDA67261/2** [2]

SANTA CHIARA

John Shirley-Quirk, Eric Parkin   (5/64)

Saga XID5207; STXID5207
Saga XID7015

Benjamin Luxon, Alan Rowlands   r. 1973 (7/75)

Lyrita SRCS66
Lyrita **SRCD2261** [3]

Rachel Ann Morgan, Tan Crone
Christopher Maltman, Graham Johnson

Etcetera **KTC1128**

   r. Sept. 1998 (8/99)   Hyperion **CDA67261/2** [2]
Jonathan Lemalu, Malcolm Martineau   (12/05)   EMI **558050–2**
Roderick Williams, Iain Burnside   r. July 2007 (9/08)   Naxos **8.570467**

SEA FEVER

Fraser Gange r. July 1919	HMV E3 *
Betty Chester, Melville Gideon r. Nov. 1922	HMV B1445 *
Norman Williams (2/25)	VF1118 *
Kennerley Rumford (1/26)	D1532 *
Edgar Coyle (9/27)	Columbia C4385 *
Stuart Robertson, Gerald Moore (12/27)	HMV B2594 *
Jack Collinge	Decca F2243 *
Roy Henderson r. 1928	Columbia C5395 *
	HMV HLM7009
(10/99)	Dutton **CDLX7038**
Roy Henderson, Ivor Newton (2/43)	Decca M526 *
John Brownlee r. June 1929 (5/30)	HMV E553 *
Conrad Thibault	Victor V1583 * DA1296 *
Paul Robeson, Laurence Brown (2/42)	HMV B9257 *
	JO157 *
	EMI **15586** [7]
	Past 7009
	ASV **AJS244**
	BYD77055
	B9073 *
Robert Irwin, Gerald Moore r. 1940 (9/40)	
(1/87)	EMI EX290911–3 *EX290911–5*
John Shirley-Quirk, Viola Tunnard	
(9/63)	Saga XIP7011
(4/66)	Saga XID5211 STXID5211
	Saga *CA5211 8T5211*
(11/80)	Saga 5473
Kenneth McKellar, Denis Woolford (5/65)	Decca LK4663 SKL4663
(8/75)	Decca SPA396

Benjamin Luxon, David Willison   (4/73)   Abbey LPB689
Benjamin Luxon, Alan Rowlands   r. 1972/3 (5/75)   Lyrita SRCS65
                                                                   Lyrita **SRCD2261** [3]
Norman Bailey, Geoffrey Parsons   (5/77)   L'Oiseau-Lyre DSL020
Thomas Allen, Roger Vignoles   (10/85)   Hyperion **CDA66165**
                                                                   Hyperion **HYP30**
Robert Lloyd, Nina Walker   r. Sept. 1977 (9/78)   HMV ASD3545
                                       (2/94)   EMI **CDM764716–2**
Bryn Terfel, Annette Bryn Parri   r. 1989   Sain 9099
Raimund Herincx, John Constable   (1/90)   *NVLC107* **NVLCD107**
Raimund Herincx, John Constable   Gamut GAMCD506
Bryn Terfel, Malcolm Martineau   r. 1995 (8/95)   DG **445946–2GH**
                                                                   in DG **4778167** [55]
                                                                   Decca **470195–2**
                                                         in Universal **4765296** [2]

Christopher Maltman, Graham Johnson
   r. Sept. 1998 (8/99)   Hyperion **CDA67261/2** [2]
Paul Whelan, David Harper   r. 1999 (5/00)   Trust **MMT2023**
Jonathan Lemalu, Roger Vignoles   (8/02)   EMI **CDZ575203–2**
                                                                   EMI **575926–2** [2]
Teddy Tahu Rhodes, Sharolyn Kimmorley   r. Aug. 2002   ABC **4767175**
Roderick Williams, Iain Burnside   r. July 2007 (9/08)   Naxos **8.570467**
R. Bolton, R. Yaro   Silhouette SLP17
Richard Standen, Frederick Stone   Westminster WLE103
                                                                   Westminster WXN18710

✻ orch. composer
Stuart Robertson, Mackenzie-Rogan Symphony Orchestra   1926   Duophone B5098 *
Frederick Harvey with orch.   HMV B10233 *
   (11/58)   in HMV 7EG8370
Roderick Williams, BBC Concert Orchestra, Martin Yates   (3/08)   Dutton **CDLX7199**

✻ arr. voice and military band
Michael Burchill, Band of Royal Corps of Signals, Major K. R. R. Boulding
   (9/73)   Indigo GOLP7003
John Lawrenson, Band of Royal Marines, Capt. J. R. Mason   (12/73)   Polydor 2383 231

✻ arr. solo voice and male chorus, Mansel Thomas
Ivor Lewis, Brymbo Male Choir, Glyn Hughes   Qualiton SQUAD 109

A SONG FROM O'ER THE HILL
Rachel Ann Morgan, Tan Crone   Etcetera **KTC1128**

SONGS OF A WAYFARER
1. Memory; 2. When daffodils begin to peer; 3. English May; 4. I was not sorrowful
(Spleen); 5. I will walk on the earth
Benjamin Luxon, Alan Rowlands   r. 1972/3 (5/75)   Lyrita SRCS65
                                                                   Lyrita **SRCD2261** [3]
Christopher Maltman, Graham Johnson
   r. Sept. 1998 (8/99)   Hyperion **CDA67261/2** [2]
   [no. 2 only]
Anthony Rolfe Johnson, Graham Johnson   Hyperion **CDA66480**

SONGS SACRED AND PROFANE
1. The Advent; 2. Hymn for a Child; 3. My Fair; 4. The Salley Gardens;
5. The Soldier's Return; 6. The Scapegoat

Peter Pears, John Ireland r. 1949 [?]	[NSA T10871R2–3]
Peter Pears, John Ireland Wigmore Hall 14 May 1951	Dutton **CDBP9799**

[no. 2 only]

BBC Music Magazine **BBCMM206**

John Shirley-Quirk, Eric Parkin (5/64)	Saga XID5207; STXID5207
	Saga XID7015

[no. 4 only]

Janet Baker, Gerald Moore r. Feb. 1967 (7/67)	HMV HQS1091
(2/74)	ASD2929 *TCASD2929*
	Angel S36456
(6/83)	HMV ESD 100642–1
	HMV *TC-ESD 100642–4*
(11/83)	HMV ESD 1024391
	HMV *TC-ESD 1024394*
(2/94)	EMI **CDM764716–2**
	EMI **CDM565009–2**
	EMI **575926–2** [2]
Benjamin Luxon, Alan Rowlands r. 1973 (7/75)	Lyrita SRCS66
	Lyrita **SRCD2261** [3]

[nos. 3 & 4 only]

Benjamin Luxon, Alan Rowlands (11/80)	Saga 5473
Rachel Ann Morgan, Tan Crone	Etcetera **KTC1128**

[no. 4 only]

Sarah Leonard, Malcolm Martineau (3/95)	Cala **CD88016**
	Cala **CD88088**
John Mark Ainsley, Graham Johnson r. Sept. 1998 (8/99)	Hyperion **CDA67261/2** [2]

[nos. 1 & 2 only]

Georgina Colwell, Nigel Foster (10/05)	Dune **DRD0237**

✻ no. 4 only orch. Graham Parlett
Susan Gritton, strings of BBC Concert Orchestra, Martyn Brabbins

r. Jan. 2009 (1/10)	Dutton **CDLX7228**

SPRING SORROW

Stuart Robertson	HMV B3411 *
John Shirley-Quirk, Eric Parkin (5/64)	Saga XID5207; STXID5207
	Saga XIP7015
Benjamin Luxon, Alan Rowlands r. 1973 (7/75)	Lyrita SRCS66
	Lyrita **SRCD2261** [3]
Rachel Ann Morgan, Tan Crone	Etcetera **KTC1128**
Valerie Baulard, Simon Wright	Max Sound *MSCB12/13*
Christopher Maltman, Graham Johnson	
r. Sept. 1998 (8/99)	Hyperion **CDA67261/2** [2]
[played as piano solo] Alan Rowlands r. Spring 2000	**WS&SS**

THE THREE RAVENS

Alfreda Hodgson, Alan Rowlands   r. Aug. 1978 (11/79)   Lyrita SRCS118
                                                                          Lyrita **SRCD2261** [3]
Rachel Ann Morgan, Tan Crone   Etcetera **KTC1128**
Alfreda Hodgson, Alan Rowlands   (4/80)   6570044 *7310044*
Nathan Vale, Paul Plummer   **SOMMCD063**

THREE SONGS (Arthur Symons)
1. The Adoration; 2. The Rat; 3. Rest

Alfreda Johnson, Alan Rowlands   r. Aug. 1978 (11/79)   Lyrita SRCS118
                                                                          Lyrita **SRCD2261** [3]
Lisa Milne, Graham Johnson   r. Sept. 1998 (8/99)   Hyperion **CDA67261/2** [2]

   [no. 1 only] orch. Graham Parlett
Susan Gritton, BBC Concert Orchestra, Martyn Brabbins
   r. Jan. 2009 (1/10)   Dutton **CDLX7228**

THREE SONGS TO POEMS BY THOMAS HARDY
1. Summer Schemes; 2. Her Song; 3. Weathers

   [no. 2 only]
Janet Baker, Martin Isepp   r. 1962 (2/64)   Saga XIP7013
                             (8/66)   Saga STXID5213; XID5213
                                                                      CA5213 8T5213
                                                             Classics Club X541
                                                                       Saga 5313
                                                                     ECD3360
                             (3/82)   **SCD9012**
                                                                 Regis **RRC1265**

   [no. 2 only]
Sarah Leonard, Malcolm Martineau   (3/95)   Cala **CD88016**

   [no. 2 only]
Valerie Baulard, Simon Wright   Max Sound *MSCB12/13*
Alfreda Hodgson, Alan Rowlands   r. Aug. 1978 (11/79)   Lyrita SRCS118
                                                                      Lyrita **SRCD2261** [3]
Rachel Ann Morgan, Tan Crone   Etcetera **KTC1128**

   [nos. 1 & 3 only]
Christopher Maltman, Graham Johnson
   r. Sept. 1998 (8/99)   Hyperion **CDA67261/2** [2]

   [no. 2 only]
Lisa Milne, Graham Johnson   r. Sept. 1998 (8/99)   Hyperion **CDA67261/2** [2]
Sarah Connolly, Eugene Asti   r. Oct. 2005 (5/06)   Sigmum **SIGCD072**
Roderick Williams, Iain Burnside   r. July 2007 (9/08)   Naxos **8.570467**

   [no. 2 only] orch. Graham Parlett
Susan Gritton, strings of BBC Concert Orchestra, Martyn Brabbins
   r. Jan. 2009 (1/10)   Dutton **CDLX7228**

THREE SONGS
1. Love and Friendship; 2. Friendship in Misfortune; 3. The One Hope

   [nos. 1 & 2 only]
Peter Pears, John Ireland   r. 1949   [NSA T10871R2]

[nos. 1 & 2 only]
Peter Pears, John Ireland　Wigmore Hall 14 May 1951　　　　　　　[NSAB7602/10]

[nos. 1 & 2 only]
John Shirley-Quirk, Eric Parkin　(5/64)　　　　　　Saga XID5207; STXID5207
Sag XIP7015

Peter Pears, Benjamin Britten　(11/64)　　　　　　　Argo ZRG5418 RG418
Belart 461 550–2
in Decca **4782345** [6]

Benjamin Luxon, Alan Rowlands　r. 1972/3 (5/75)　　　　　Lyrita SRCS65
Lyrita **SRCD2261** [3]

[no. 1 only]
Rachel Ann Morgan, Tan Crone　　　　　　　　　　Etcetera **KTC1128**

[no. 1 only]
Lisa Milne, Graham Johnson　r. Sept. 1998 (8/99)　　　Hyperion **CDA67261/2** [2]

[nos. 2 & 3 only]
Christopher Maltman, Graham Johnson
r. Sept. 1998 (8/99)　　　　　　　　　　　　Hyperion **CDA67261/2** [2]

[no. 1 only]
Georgina Colwell, Nigel Foster　(10/05)　　　　　　　　Dune **DRD0237**

[no. 2 only]
Nathan Vale, Paul Plummer　　　　　　　　　　　　**SOMMCD063**

[no. 1 only] orch. Graham Parlett
Susan Gritton, BBC Concert Orchestra, Martyn Brabbins
r. Jan. 2009 (1/10)　　　　　　　　　　　　Dutton **CDLX7228**

TUTTO È SCIOLTO
Benjamin Luxon, Alan Rowlands　r. 1973 (7/75)　　　　　Lyrita SRCS66
Lyrita **SRCD2261** [3]

Christopher Maltman, Graham Johnson
r. Sept. 1998 (8/99)　　　　　　　　　　　Hyperion **CDA67261/2** [2]
Roderick Williams, Iain Burnside　r. July 2007 (9/08)　　　Naxos **8.570467**
Ailish Tynan, Iain Burnside　　　　　　　　　　　Signum **SIGCG 239**

TWO SONGS
1. The Trellis; 2. My true love hath my heart

[nos. 1 & 2 only]
Peter Pears, John Ireland　r. 1949　　　　　　　　[NSA T10871R2]

[no. 1 only]
Peter Pears, John Ireland　BBC 8 Dec. 1947　　　　　Dutton **CDBP9799**

[no. 1 only]
Peter Pears, John Ireland　Wigmore Hall 14 May 1951　　　[NSA B7602/10]

[no. 1 only]
Peter Pears, Benjamin Britten　(11/64)　　　　　　　Argo ZRG5418; RG418
Belart 461 550–2
in Decca **4782345** [6]

[no. 1 only]
Peter Pears, Benjamin Britten   Maltings, Snape 1972
John Mitchinson, Alan Rowlands   r. Aug. 1978 (11/79)   Lyrita SRCS118
                                                            Lyrita **SRCD2261** [3]
Sarah Leonard, Malcolm Martineau   (3/95)   Cala **CD88016**
John Mark Ainsley, Graham Johnson   r. Sept. 1998 (8/99)   Hyperion **CDA67261/2** [2]
   [no. 1 only]
Felicity Lott, Graham Johnson   (8/04)   DV-VTFL-EUR [DVD]
                              (9/04)   ASV **GLD4003**
                                                         Champs Hill **CHRCD 008**

   [no. 2 only]
Lesley-Jane Rogers, Christopher Ross   r. Dec. 2002   **PCHN2402**
   [no. 1 only]
Nathan Vale, Paul Plummer   **SOMMCD063**
   [nos. 1 & 2] orch. Graham Parlett
Susan Gritton, BBC Concert Orchestra, Martyn Brabbins
   r. Jan. 2009 (1/10)   Dutton **CDLX7228**

TWO SONGS
1. Tryst (In Fountain Court); 2. During Music
Benjamin Luxon, Alan Rowlands   r. 1973 (7/75)   Lyrita SRCS66
                                                            Lyrita **SRCD2261** [3]
Rachel Ann Morgan, Tan Crone   Etcetera **KTC1128**
Christopher Maltman, Graham Johnson
   r. Sept. 1998 (8/99)   Hyperion **CDA67261/2** [2]

TWO SONGS
1. The Soldier; 2. Blow out, you bugles
   [no. 1 only]
Roy Henderson, Ivor Newton   r. 1943   Decca M526 *
   [no. 1 only]
L. Watts, N. Newby   Argo R1007 *
   [no. 2 only]
Benjamin Luxon, Alan Rowlands   r. 1973 (7/75)   Lyrita SRCS66
                                                            Lyrita **SRCD2261** [3]
⅏ orch. by Tom Higgins
Roderick Williams, Guildford Philharmonic Orchestra, Higgins   (1/10)   **SOMMCD243**

TWO SONGS
1. Blind; 2. The Cost
Philip Frohnmayer, Logan Skelton   (11/90)   Centaur **CRC2075**

VAGABOND
Harry Brindle, Mme Adama   r. May 1923   [cat. no. not found]
Benjamin Luxon, Alan Rowlands   r. 1973 (7/75)   Lyrita SRCS66
                                                            Lyrita **SRCD2261** [3]
Bryn Terfel, Malcolm Martineau   r. 1995 (8/95)   DG **445946–2GH**
                                                          in DG **4778167** [55]
                                                            Decca 470195–2

Christopher Maltman, Graham Johnson
  r. Sept. 1998 (8/99)   Hyperion **CDA67261/2** [2]
Roderick Williams, Iain Burnside   r. July 2007 (9/08)   Naxos **8.570467**
Teddy Tahu Rhodes, Sharolyn Kimmorley   r. Aug. 2002   ABC **4767175**

WE'LL TO THE WOODS NO MORE

1. We'll to the woods no more; 2. In Boyhood; 3. Spring will not wait (piano only)

[no. 3 only]
Alan Rowlands (7/70)   Lyrita RCS29
          (10/08)   Lyrita **REAM3112** [3]
Benjamin Luxon, Alan Rowlands   r. 1972/3 (5/75)   Lyrita SRCS65
                                 Lyrita **SRCD2261** [3]

[no. 3 only]
Eric Parkin   r. May 1993 (1/95)   Chandos **CHAN9250**
John Mark Ainsley, Graham Johnson   r. Sept. 1998 (8/99)   Hyperion **CDA67261/2** [2]
Brett Polegate, Iain Burnside   r. 1999 (7/01)   **MVCD1134**

[no. 3 only]
Alan Rowlands   r. Spring 2000   **WS&SS**

[no. 3 only]
John Lenehan   r. March 2007 (10/08)   Naxos **8.570461**
Roderick Williams, Iain Burnside   r. July 2007 (9/08)   Naxos **8.570467**

WHAT ARE THOU THINKING OF?
Alfreda Hodgson, Alan Rowlands   r. Aug. 1978 (11/79)   Lyrita SRCS118
                                 Lyrita **SRCD2261** [3]
Rachel Ann Morgan, Tan Crone   Etcetera **KTC1128**
Lisa Milne, Graham Johnson   r. Sept. 1998 (8/99)   Hyperion **CDA67261/2** [2]

WHEN I AM DEAD, MY DEAREST
Benjamin Luxon, Alan Rowlands   r. 1973 (7/75)   Lyrita SRCS66
                                 Lyrita **SRCD2261** [3]
Rachel Ann Morgan, Tan Crone   Etcetera **KTC1128**
Lisa Milne, Graham Johnson   r. Sept. 1998 (8/99)   Hyperion **CDA67261/2** [2]
Felicity Lott, Graham Johnson   (9/04)   ASV **GLD4003**
Roderick Williams, Iain Burnside   r. July 2007 (9/08)   Naxos **8.570467**

※ with orch.
Roderick Williams, BBC Concert Orchestra, Martin Yates (3/08)   Dutton **CDLX7199**
                                 Dutton **CDSPA2008**

WHEN I AM OLD
Christopher Maltman, Graham Johnson
  r. Sept. 1998 (8/99)   Hyperion **CDA67261/2** [2]

WHEN LIGHTS GO ROLLING ROUND THE SKY
Peter Dawson, Madam Amani   r. Jan. 1922   HMV B1337 *
Stuart Robertson, Gerald Moore   r. Feb. 1929 (8/29)   HMV B3042 *
                      (1/87)   EMI EX290911–3
                                 EMI *EX290911–5*
Frederick Harvey, Gerald Moore (1/67)   HMV CLP3587 CSD3587

Benjamin Luxon, Alan Rowlands   r. 1972/3(5/75)   Lyrita SRCS65
   Lyrita **SRCD2261** [3]
Christopher Maltman, Graham Johnson
   r. Sept. 1998 (8/99)   Hyperion **CDA67261/2** [2]
Paul Whelan, David Harper   r. 1999 (5/00)   Trust MMT2023
Jonathan Lemalu, Malcolm Martineau   (12/05)   EMI **558050–2**

※ with orch.
Roderick Williams, BBC Concert Orchestra, Martin Yates (3/08)   Dutton **CDLX7199**

CHORAL AND CHURCH

ADAM LAY YBOUNDEN
Worcester Cathedral Choir, Donald Hunt   (6/79)   Abbey LPB803
Christ College School, Brecon, Chapel Choir, Jonathan Leonard   Alpha *CAPS407*
St Edmundsbury Cathedral Choir, Paul Trepte   (12/87)   Abbey ACA560
Leicester Cathedral Choir, Peter White   Wealdon WS171

BENEDICTUS
Lincoln Cathedral Choir, Colin Walsh   Priory **PRCD478** *PRC478*
   Priory **PRCD5028**

COMMUNION SERVICE in C
Wakefield Cathedral Choir, Jonathan Bielby   r. June 1990   Priory **PRCD341**
   Priory PRCD5030

A CRADLE SONG (unacc. SATB)
St Martin's Chamber Choir, Timothy Krueger   **Cygnus 002**

EX ORE INNOCENTIUM Anthem
Paul Dutton (treble), Leeds Parish Church Choir, Donald Hunt
   (3/69)   Morgan MR113P
York Minster Choir, Francis Jackson   (6/78)   Abbey LPB695
   Abbey E7620
Worcester Cathedral Choir, Donald Hunt   (6/79)   Abbey LPB803
St Mary and St Anne Choir, Abbotts Bromley, Llywela Harris   (1/75)   Argo ZRG785
   (11/86)   Alpha APS366
Norwich Cathedral Choir, Michael Nicholas   (11/79)   Vista VPS1084
New College Oxford Choir, Edward Higginbottom   Novum **NCR1380**
St Mary's Girls' Choir, Warwick, Simon Lole   r. 1994   Regent **REGCD112**
Lichfield Cathedral Choristers, Andrew Lumsden   r. 1998   Lammas **LAMM107**
Roger Drabble, Malcolm Archer (organ)   r. April/May 1998   Lammas **LAMM105**
Norwich Cathedral Girls' Choir, Katherine Dienes   r. Sept. 1999   Herald **HAVP250**
Manchester Cathedral Choir, Christopher Stokes   (6/02)   Naxos **8.557025**
Winchester Cathedral Choir, Sarah Baldock   r. Feb. 2002 (11/02)   Herald **HAVP275**
Tewkesbury Abbey Choir, Andrew Sackett   **GCCD4033**
Southwell Minster Choir, Paul Hale   Lammas **LAMM141**
Worcester College Choir, Oxford, Judy Martin   OxRecs **OXCD97**
Wells Cathedral Boy Choristers, Malcolm Archer   Lammas **LAMM171**
Arundel Cathedral Choir, Elizabeth Stratford   r. 2004   Herald **HAVP314**
Boys of King's College Choir, Stephen Cleobury   (11/04)   EMI **557896–2**
   EMI **640443–2** [2]
   EMI **557812–2**

Choristers of New College, Oxford, Edward Higginbottom	Novum **NCR1380**
Winchester Cathedral Choir, David Hill	Herald 275
Tenebrae, Michael Short (11/06)	Signum **CD085**
Salisbury Cathedral Choir, David Halls r. May 2007	Priory **PRCD890**
St Alban Cathedral Choir, Barry Rose	Lammas **LAMM95**
Trinity College of Music Chamber Choir, Stephen Jackson r. 2008	Herald **HAVP349**
Coventry Cathedral Choir, Paul Leddington Wright	Regent **REGCD109**
Bath Abbey Girls' Choir, Peter King	Regent **REGCD229**
Metropolitan Cathedral of Christ the King, Liverpool, Mervyn Cousins	
	Cantoris **CRCD6027**
Peterborough Cathedral Choir, Christopher Gower	Abbey **CDCA969**

FAIN WOULD I CHANGE THAT NOTE

St Cecilia Singers, Andrew Millington	Abbey ACA514

GREATER LOVE HATH NO MAN

Choir of St John's Cathedral, Wilmington, Herbert Tinney	Vogt CSRV2614
Choir of Holy Trinity Cathedral, Auckland, Anthony Jennings	Pacific SLD60
Kilgare Presbyterian Church Choir and Austin College Choir, Bedford	Aeolian 310
Carlisle Cathedral Choir, Andrew Sievewright	Alpha APS318 *CAPS318*
Hurstpierpoint College Choir, Nicholas Searls	Wealdon WS138
St Matthew's Church Choir, Northampton, Michael Nicholas	Abbey LPB655
Magdalen College Choir, Oxford, John Harper	Abbey ACA547
(11/91)	Abbey **CDCA914** *CACA914*
St John's College Cambridge Choir, George Guest (3/63)	Argo ZRG5340 RG340
(11/78)	d112d3 [3]
Chichester Cathedral Choir, John Birch r. June 1966 (12/66)	HMV CLP3588 CSD3588
(9/75)	HMV HQS1350
(2/94)	EMI **CDM764716–2**
Exeter Cathedral Choir, Lucien Nethsingha (9/76)	EXCATH 3
	EAS19
Exeter Cathedral Choir, Lucien Nethsingha pp. 1976	EAS26
Worcester Cathedral Choir, Donald Hunt (6/79)	Abbey LPB803
Norwich Cathedral Choir, Michael Nicholas (11/79)	Vista VPS1084
Trinity College Choir, Richard Marlow r. Nov. 1984	**Griffin 4045**
Canterbury Cathedral Choir, Allan Wicks (8/84)	Argo 411714–1ZH
	Argo *411714–4ZH*
St Clement Danes, Martindale Sidwell r. Nov. 1985	**Saydisc SDL356** *CSDL356*
Peterborough Cathedral Choir, Christopher Gower r. 1986	Abbey ACA557
	Priory **PRAB108**
Lichfield Cathedral Choir, Jonathan Rees-Williams r. 1988	Abbey ACA 577
	Priory **PRAB107**
Guildford Cathedral Choir, Andrew Millington (5/89)	Priory *PRC257*, **PRCD257**
St Edmundsbury Cathedral Choir, Mervyn Cousin (5/89)	Priory *PRC270* **PRCD270**
Choir of St Luke's, Chelsea, Ann Elise Smoot r. Sept. 1999	Herald **HAVP241**
St Paul's Cathedral Choir, John Scott (9/90)	Hyperion **CDA66374** *KA66374*
Vasari Singers, Jeremy Backhouse (11/90)	EMX **CDEMX2161**
	EMX *TC-EMX2161*
King's College Chapel Choir, Stephen Cleobury r. Dec. 1991	EMI **CDC754418–2**
	EMI **2289440** [2]
St Bride's Choir, Fleet Street, Robert Jones r. 1991	Regent **REGCD703** *REG703*

St John's Episcopal Cathedral Choirs (Denver, Colorado), Donald Pearson
  (10/92)   Delos **DE3125**
Choir of St Thomas on the Bourne, Surrey, David Swinson
  r. Oct. 1995   Herald **HAVP188**
Total Aberdeen Youth Choir, Christopher Bell   r. 1996   Divine Art **CD25004**
Ryde School Choir, Sinn Marriott   r. 1996   Regent **REGCD119**
Wells Cathedral Choir, Rupert Gough   r. 1998   Cantoris **CRCD6028**
Waltham Abbey Choir, Jamie Hitel   r. 1998   Lammas **LAMM113**
Winchester Cathedral Choir, David Hill   r. Feb. 2002   Herald **HAVP275**
King's College Chapel Choir, Stephen Cleobury   (8/02)   Opus Arte 834 (Video)
                                                           Opus Arte 835 (DVD)
St Paul's Cathedral Choir, John Scott [different performance]
  (12/03)   Hyperion **CDA67398**
Eltham College Choir, Tim Johnson   r. Sept. 2006   Herald **HAVP323**
Guildford Cathedral Choir, Katherine Deine-Williams   r. Aug. 2009   Herald **HAVP352**
                                                                       RRC2031
Giggleswick School Choir, Peter Read   Abbey **CDCA922** *CACA922*
Durham School Chapel Choir, Jonathan Newell   Abbey **CDCA929**
Winchester College Choir, Malcolm Archer   Regent **REGCD290**
Royal Hospital, Chelsea Chapel Choir, Ian Currer   Guild **GMCD7146**
Liverpool Metropolitan Cathedral Choir, Mervyn Cousins   Priory **PRCD798**
All Saints' Church Choir, Northampton, Simon Johnson   Lammas **LAMM120**
All Saints' Episcopal Church Choir Beverly Hills, Dale Adelmann   Gothic **49251**
Choirs of St Paul's Episcopal Church, Akron, Ohio, USA, Jamie Hitel
                                                        Lammas **LAMM144**
Bath Abbey Choir, Peter King   Priory **PRCD421**
                                                        Priory **PRCD5039**
Paisley Abbey Choir, George McPhee   Abbey **CDCA949**
East Carolina University Chamber Singers, Daniel Bara   Gothic **G49256**
Christ's Hospital School, Horsham, Peter Allwood   Carlton **3036600532**

❧ arr. treble and baritone soli, mixed chorus and orchestra, composer
Paula Bott, Bryn Terfel, London Symphony Chorus, LSO, Richard Hickox
  r. April 1990   Chandos **CHAN8879** *ABTD1492*
  (3/98)   Chandos **CHAN7074**
                                                   Chandos **CHAN10110**
                                          in Chandos CHAN 241-17 [2]

THE HILLS
Cambridge University Madrigal Society, Boris Ord   (11/53)   Columbia 33CX1063
Exultate Singers, Garrett O'Brien   (6/77)   RCA GL25062
                                                             RCA *GK25062*
East London Chorus, Michael Kibblewhite   Koch **312662**
Finzi Singers, Paul Spicer   (9/91)   Chandos **CHAN8936**
Cambridge University Chamber Choir, Timothy Brown   (4/92)   Gamut **GAMCD529**
Bristol Bach Choir, Glyn Jenkins   Priory **PRCD352**
Queens' College, Cambridge Choir, Samuel Hayes   Guild **GMCD7287**
Cambridge University Chamber Choir   Heritage **HTGCD213**
St Cecilia Singers, Andrew Millington   Abbey **ACA514**
Hallé Choir, Mark Elder   (12/06)   Hallé **CDHLL7512**

IMMORTALITY
Louis Halsey Singers   [BBC LP33249]

IN PRAISE OF NEPTUNE (unison song with piano arr. for solo voice and
    orchestra)
Roderick Williams, BBC Concert Orchestra, Martin Yates
    r. Oct. 2009   Dutton **CDLX7246**

AN ISLAND HYMN
St Martin's Chamber Choir, Timothy Krueger   **Cygnus 006**

JUBILATE in F
Rochester Cathedral Choir, Barry Ferguson   r. 1992   Priory **PRCD433**
                                   in Priory **PRCD934** [4]
St Alban Cathedral, Barry Rose   Lammas **LAMM95**

MAGNIFICAT & NUNC DIMITTIS
Memorial University of Newfoundland Chamber Choir, Donald Cook
                              Waterloo Music WR 8027
Worcester Cathedral Choir, Donald Hunt   (6/79)   Abbey LPB803
Ripon Cathedral Choir, Kerry Beaumont   Priory **PRCD555**
                                   Cantoris **CRCD6039**

MAN IN HIS LABOUR REJOICETH
Choir and organ   [BBC Sound Archive 13403]

(MY SONG IS) LOVE UNKNOWN
London Recital Group, Richard Sinton   (9/64)   Herald LLR533
Royal School of Church Music Choir   1965   RM1/2 RS1/2
Royal Hospital, Chelsea Chapel Choir, Ian Currer   Guild **GMCD7146**
Paisley Abbey Choir, George McPhee   Abbey **ACA578**
CBSO Chorus, Simon Halsey   Conifer **CDCF502**
Worcester Cathedral Choir   Abbey MVP808
Worcester Festival Choral Society, Donald Hunt   (6/79)   Abbey LPB803
Norwich Cathedral Choir, Michael Nicholas   (11/79)   Vista VPS1084
Guildford Cathedral Choir, Andrew Millington   **WSTCD9705**
Rodney Christian Fellowship Choir, Ronald Smith-Bishton   HMV CLP3638 CSD3638
Arundel & Brighton Diocesan Pilgrimage to Lourdes   r. Sept. 1992   Herald **HAVP160**
Aberdeen Youth Choir, Christopher Bell   r. 1996   Divine Art **CD25004**
Wells Cathedral Choir, Malcolm Archer   r. 1999 (1/00)   Hyperion **CDP12101**
King's College Choir, Stephen Cleobury   r. 2000 (5/01)   EMI **557026–2** [2]
Truro Cathedral Choir, Andrew Nethsingha   (5/03)   Priory **PRCD710**
St John's College Choir, Elora, Noel Edison   (9/04)   Naxos **8.557037**
                              in Naxos **8.578196-7** [2]
Tewkesbury Abbey Choir, Andrew Sackett   **GCCD4033**
St Mary's Episcopal Cathedral Choir, Dennis Townhill   Priory **PRCD376**
New College Choir, David Lumsden   Abbey **LPB725**
St John's Cathedral Choir, David Whitehead   Abbey **LPB767**
St George's Chapel Choir, Windsor, Tim Byram-Wigfield   Naxos **8.557578**
Harvey Brink (treble), Martin Neary (piano)   r. April 1999   Herald **HAVP206**
Chester Cathedral Choir   International Christian Communications **CC0947D** [4]
St Paul's Cathedral Choir, Melbourne, Lance Hardy   RM212
Roberts Weslyan College Chorale   Roberts Weslyan College **RWC1044**

※ arr. with saxophone, James Pearson
Christian Forshaw (saxophone), Choir of King's College, London,
    David Trendell   2004   Integra **ING1004**

※ arr. brass, Steve Robson
Bactiguard Wire Brass   2005   **DOYCD207**

※ arr. flute
David Fitzgerald and ensemble   International Christian Communications **ICC0949D** [4]

NEW PRINCE, NEW POMP
Grailville College Singers   Audio Fidelity AFLP 1820

A NEW YEAR CAROL
Worcester Cathedral Choir, Donald Hunt   (6/79)   Abbey LPB803
Gloucester Cathedral Choir, John Sanders   Abbey CACA917
                                                                         Griffin **GCCD 4066**

PSALM 23
Roderick Williams (a cappella)   r. Oct. 2009   Dutton **CDLX7246**

TE DEUM in F
Norwich Cathedral Choir, Michael Nicholas   (11/79)   Vista VPS1084
Worcester Cathedral Choir, Donald Hunt   (6/79)   Abbey LPB803
Portsmouth Cathedral Choir, Anthony Froggat
    r. July 1984   Guild GRSP7021 *GRSC7021*
                                                                         Guild **GMCD7271**
Lincoln Cathedral Choir, Colin Walsh   r. 1993   Priory **PRCD478**
                                                                        Priory **PRCD5028**
Rochester Cathedral Choir, Barry Ferguson   r. 1992   Priory **PRCD433**
                                                                   in Priory **PRCD934** [4]
Exeter Cathedral Choir, Lucien Nethsingha   Abbey **CDCA590**
Gray's Inn chapel choir, Christopher Bowers-Broadbent   Priory **PRCD744**

THESE THINGS SHALL BE
Unidentified, Ireland conducting [?] (incompl. acetetates)   [NSAT11461W2]
René Soames, BBCSO, Adrian Boult   [BBC Trans. 40980/5]
Redvers Llewellyn, Luton Choral Society, LPO, Adrian Boult
    Birthday Prom 10 Sept. 49 (12/09)   LPO **LPO0041**
Parry Jones, Hallé Choir, Hallé, Barbirolli   r. 1 May 1948 (2/49)   HMV C3826–7 *
                                          (9/84)   HMV EX290107–3 [2]
                                                              HMV *EX290107–5*
                                          (4/92)   EMI **CDH763910–2**
                                          (4/02)   Dutton **SJB1022** [2]
Carol Case, London Philharmonic Choir, LPO, Adrian Boult
    r. Nov. 1967 (10/68)   Lyrita SRCS36
                                                      Musical Heritage Society 1429
                          (6/07)   Lyrita **SRCD241**
Bryn Terfel, London Symphony Chorus, LSO, Richard Hickox
    r. April 1990   Chandos **CHAN8879** *ABTD1492*
                          (3/98)   Chandos **CHAN7074**
                                                         Chandos **CHAN10110**

VEXILLA REGIS
Worcester Festival Choral Society, Worcester Sinfonia Brass, Donald Hunt
  (6/79)   Abbey LPB803
London Symphony Chorus, LSO brass, Roderick Elms (org.), Richard Hickox
  r. April 1990   Chandos **CHAN8879** *ABTD1492*
Chandos **CHAN7074**
Chandos **CHANX10110**

TALKS
'My introduction to Beethoven'[1]
  BBC *Music Magazine*, 16 Dec. 1945   [NSA B7602/03]
'Recollections of Stanford'[2]
  BBC *Music Magazine*, 24 March 1949   [NSA B7602/11]
Interview with Julian Herbage
  BBC *Music Magazine*, 9 Oct. 1954   [BBC SA LP38127]
Interview with Joseph Cooper
  BBC *The Composer Speaks*, 28 July 1957   [NSA 9340BW/05]
Interview
  BBC *Town and Country*, 15 July 1958   [BBC SA LP/24590]
Interview with Arthur Jacobs
  11 Aug. 1959   [NSA B7602/01]

[1] See accompanying CD, track 2.
[2] See accompanying CD, track 1.

Select Bibliography

Items which are reprinted or updated in this volume are not listed here. The following is intended to be a complete listing of books, pamphlets and theses on Ireland, but only the most important articles.

Books & Pamphlets

CHAPMAN, Ernest. *John Ireland – A Catalogue of Published Works and Recordings*. London: Boosey & Hawkes (for The John Ireland Trust), 1968.

CRAGGS, Stewart R. *John Ireland: A Catalogue, Discography and Bibliography*. Oxford: Clarendon Press, 1993. A second enlarged edition, completely reset: Aldershot: Ashgate, 2007.

HARDY, Lisa. *The British Piano Sonata, 1870–1945*. Woodbridge: Boydell Press, 2001.

LONGMIRE, John. *John Ireland – Portrait of a Friend*. London: John Baker, 1969.

MINIATURE ESSAYS. *John Ireland* [in English and French]. London: J. & W. Chester, 1923.

O'HIGGINS, Rachel, ed. *The Correspondence of Alan Bush and John Ireland, 1927–1961*. Aldershot: Ashgate, 2006.

RICHARDS, Fiona. *The Music of John Ireland*. Aldershot: Ashgate, 2000.

RUTLAND, Harold. *John Ireland – A Biographical Sketch with Analytical Notes on Two of his Piano Pieces 'The Island Spell' and 'Ragamuffin'*. London: Galliard, 1965.

SCOTT-SUTHERLAND, Colin. *Edward Thomas and John Ireland*. British Music Society (British Music Society Monograph 2), 1993.

SEARLE, Muriel V. *John Ireland – The Man and his Music*. Tunbridge Wells: Midas Books, 1979.

Theses and Dissertations about John Ireland

ANDERS, Mark. *Der Komponist John Ireland: Betrachtung Ausgewaehlter Klavierwerke*. Diplomarbeit, Hochschule fuer Musik und Theater 'Felix Mendelssohn Bartholdy', Leipzig, 2001.

BANFIELD, Stephen D. *Solo Song in England, 1900 to 1940*. DPhil, Oxford University, 1979.

CAIRNS, Valérie. *British Romantic Piano Music at the Beginning of the Twentieth Century: A Study of Four Representative Composers*. MLitt, Newcastle Upon Tyne University, 1979
[The four composers are John Ireland, Cyril Scott, Arnold Bax and William Baines.]

COOKE, Margaret Winifred. *John Ireland (1879–1962): A Biographical and Critical Study with Special Reference to the Work Involving Piano*. MA, University of Wales, Bangor, 1972.

CROFT, Gordon Simon. *The Piano Works of John Ireland: Contexts for Study*. MPhil, Birmingham University, 1995.

DAVENPORT, Dennis. *A. E. Housman and English Song*. 2 vols. MA, Birmingham University, 1974.

HEIM, Norman Michael. *The Use of the Clarinet in Published Sonatas for Clarinet and Piano by English Composers from 1880–1954*. MM, University of Rochester, Eastman School of Music, 1954.
[Ireland Sonata pp. 159–201.]

JUSPIN, Richard Michael. *Gerald Finzi and John Ireland: A Stylistic Comparison of Compositional Approaches in the Context of Ten Selected Poems by Thomas Hardy*. DMA, State University of New York at Potsdam, December 2005.

KEIR, P. *John Ireland – A Practical Guide to Selected Works for Piano*. Master of Music, Royal College of Music, 1990.

KUYKENDALL, J. B. *The English Ceremonial Style circa 1887–1937 and its Aftermath*. PhD, Cornell University, 2005.

LAUNDON, Vivian. *British Library Additional Manuscripts 52900 and 52901: A Survey of the Compositional Process and Some Unpublished Works of John Ireland*. MA, University of London, 1989.

LESLIE, K. *The Chamber Music of John Ireland*. MA, University of Wales at Cardiff, 1976.

McCRAY, James Elwin. *The British Magnificat in the Twentieth Century*. PhD (Music), University of Iowa, 1968.
[John Ireland pp. 67–71.]

NESBITT, Sheelagh Margaret. *The Piano Trios of John Ireland*. Royal Northern College of Music, 1998.

ONO, Mariko. *John Ireland's Piano Works: Towards an Informed Performance*. PhD, Leeds University, 2009.

RANKIN, W. D. *The Solo Piano Music of John Ireland*. DMA, University of Boston, 1970.

RENOUF, D. F. *Thomas Hardy and the English Musical Renaissance*. DPhil, Trent Polytechnic, 1987.

RICHARDS, Fiona. *Meanings in the Music of John Ireland*. PhD, Birmingham University, 2000.
[Includes 'Ireland and Songs'; Ireland and Ravel's *Gaspard de la Nuit*'; 'Ireland and Debussy's Preludes'; 'Ireland and English Composers'.]

ROBERTS, David. *Alexander Ireland (1810–1894) – A Middleman of Letters in the Cultural Life of Nineteenth Century Manchester*. PhD, Sheffield University, 1985.

SMALLEY, D. *John Ireland's Chamber Music*. MA, University of Wales at Aberystwyth, 1982.

WHITMIRE, M. A. *Songs by John Ireland and Benjamin Britten to Poems by Thomas Hardy.* DMA, University of Maryland, 1991.

YENNE, V. L. *Three Twentieth Century English Composers: Peter Warlock, E. J. Moeran and John Ireland.* DMA, University of Illinois, 1969.

Articles

ANDERTON, H. O. 'Cameo Portraits No 22 – Ariel Enmeshed'. *Musical Opinion*, August 1922, pp. 953–5

BANFIELD, Stephen. 'Introduction: The Uses of Technique – Style and Personal Symbolism in John Ireland'. In his *Sensibility and English Song: Critical Studies of the Early 20th Century.* Cambridge: Cambridge University Press, 1985, vol. 1, pp. 159–78.

——'Megaliths in English Art Music'. In *The Sounds of Stonehenge,* ed. Stephen Banfield. Chombec Working Papers no. 1/BAR British Series 504. Oxford: Archeopress, 2009. pp. 46–55.

BENNETT, Rodney. 'Ireland's Songs'. *Bookman*, March 1922, pp. 282–5.

——'Ireland's Songs'. *Music Teacher*, November 1926, pp. 690–1.

BROOK, Donald. 'John Ireland.' In his *Composers' Gallery: Biographical Sketches of Contemporary Composers.* London: Rockliff, 1946, pp. 78–81.

COOPER, Martin. 'John Ireland et Arnold Bax'. In his *Les Musiciens anglais d'aujourd'hui.* Paris: Librarie Plon, 1952, pp. 61–73. (Translated by Frans Dury from the original English text, which was never published.)

CROSSLEY-HOLLAND, Peter. 'Ireland, John N.' *Grove's Dictionary of Music and Musicians*, 5th edn, ed. Eric Blom. London: Macmillan, 1954, pp. 533–44.

——'John Ireland', ed. Lewis Foreman. *Manchester Sounds*, vol. 7 (2007–8), pp. 4–73.
[First publication of a text originally written to be one of Louise B. M. Dyer's 'British Contemporary Composers' series for her Éditions de L'Oiseau-Lyre in the late 1940s, but never issued.]

DEMUTH, Norman. 'John Ireland'. In his *Musical Trends in the 20th Century.* London: Rockliffe, 1952, pp. 124–6.

DICKINSON, A. E. F. 'The Progress of John Ireland'. *Music Review*, vol. 1 no. 4 (November 1940), pp. 343–53.

DOCHERTY, B. 'The Murdered Self: John Ireland and the English Song, 1903–13'. *Tempo*, no. 171 (December 1989), pp. 18–26.

EGGAR, Kathryn. 'The Pianoforte Music of John Ireland'. *Music Teacher*, June 1922, pp. 465–7.

EVANS, Edwin. 'John Ireland'. *Musical Quarterly*, vol. 5 no. 2 (April 1919), pp. 213–20.

——'Ireland, John'. In *Cobbett's Cyclopedic Survey of Chamber Music,* ed. Walter Willson Cobbett. Vol. 2. London: Oxford University Press, 1930, pp. 20–4.

——'John Ireland'. *The Chesterian*, March 1930, pp. 133–40.

FOX, Stephen. 'The Clarinet Trio of John Ireland'. *Clarinet and Saxophone*, Winter 2007, pp. 18–20 (later reissued in The Clarinet, June 2008).

FRANK, Alan. 'John Ireland'. In his *Modern British Composers*. London: Dennis Dobson, 1953, pp. 15–20.

GOWER, Robert. 'John Ireland's Organ Music'. *Musical Times*, August 1979, pp. 682–3.

HERBAGE, Julian. 'John Ireland and the Orchestra'. *The Listener*, 4 June 1959, p. 1001.

HILL, Ralph. 'John Ireland'. In *British Music of Our Time*, ed. A. L. Bacharach. New edition. Harmondsworth: Pelican Books, 1951. pp. 97–110.

HOLBROOKE, Joseph. 'John Ireland'. In his *Contemporary British Composers*. London: Cecil Palmer, 1925, pp. 72–82.

HOLD, Trevor. 'John Ireland'. In his *Parry to Finzi: 20 English Song Composers*. Woodbridge: Boydell Press, 2002, pp. 185–212.

HUGHES, Eric. 'John Ireland Discography'. *Recorded Sound*, no. 53 (January 1974), pp. 258–62.

L.N. 'John Ireland Memorial Window'. *Musical Times*, January 1964, p. 38.

MICHON, Jacques. 'John Ireland'. In his *La Musique anglaise*. Paris: Librairie Armand Colin, 1970, pp. 285–7.

MITCHELL, Donald, and Phillip READ. *Letters from a Life – Selected Letters and Diaries of Benjamin Britten*, vol 1. London: Faber & Faber, 1991, pp. 132–47.

MOORE, Gerald. 'John Ireland – Sea Fever'. In his *Singer and Accompanist*. London: Methuen, 1953, pp. 108–10.

OLDROYD, George. 'Violin Sonata'. *Monthly Musical Record*, July 1918, pp. 150–1.

OTTAWAY, Hugh. 'The Piano Music of John Ireland'. *Monthly Musical Record*, December 1954, pp. 258–66.

PILKINGTON, Michael. 'John Ireland'. In his *Gurney, Ireland, Quilter and Warlock*. London: Duckworth, 1989, pp. 43–75.

PRICE, Bernard. 'John Ireland'. In his *Creative Landscapes of the British Isles*. London: Ebury Press, 1983. pp. 150–1

——'Profile: Dr John Ireland'. *The Observer*, 15 August 1954, p. 3.

RENNERT, Jonathan. 'The Church and the Organ Music of John Ireland'. *English Church Music*, 1979, pp. 8–16.

RICHARDS, Fiona. 'An Anthology of Friendship: The Letters from John Ireland to Father Kenneth Thompson'. In *Queer Episodes in Music and Modern Identity*, ed. Sophie Fuller and L. Whitesell. Urbana: University of Illinois Press, 2002, pp. 245–67.

ROWLANDS, Alan. 'John Ireland 1879–1962'. *RCM Magazine*, vol. 58 no. 3 (Autumn 1962), pp. 70–1.

——'John Ireland: a significant composer?' *RCM Magazine*, vol. 89 no. 2 (Summer 1992), pp. 18–24; vol. 90 no. 1 (Spring 1993), pp. 13–19.

RUTLAND, Harold. 'John Ireland'. *Recorded Sound*, nos. 50–51 (April–July 1973), pp. 190–8.

SUCKLING, Norman. 'John Ireland and the Piano'. *The Listener*, 24 December 1953, p. 1101.

TOWNSEND, N. 'The Achievement of John Ireland'. *Music and Letters*, vol. 24 no. 2 (April 1943), pp. 65–74.

VARCOE, Stephen. 'John Ireland'. In his *Sing English Song*. London: Thames Publishing, 2000, pp. 154–7.

Index of Works by John Ireland

This index includes variant titles, colloquial usage and individual movements of multi-movement works. Solo songs appear at the end in a separate sequence. Underlined references indicate an illustration or music example on that page.

Songs

General Index

Underlined references indicate an illustration or music example on that page.

Historical Recordings of
John Ireland and his Music

A guide to the recordings on the accompanying CD

The Voice of John Ireland: talking about his life and music
(Transcriptions of John Ireland's own copies of his broadcast talks)

1. Recollections of Stanford (*BBC Music Magazine*, 24 March 1949)

2. My introduction to Beethoven (*BBC Music Magazine*, 16 December 1945)

3. *Concertino Pastorale* – 'Eclogue' only, Boyd Neel Orchestra/Boyd Neel (from Decca X 253–5, r. February 1940)

John Ireland as pianist in his own music from broadcasts

4. *The Towing Path* (off-air acetate, 28 May 1948)

5. *Chelsea Reach* (*London Pieces* no. 1) (off-air acetate, 28 May 1948)

John Ireland as pianist in his own music from piano rolls

6. *Amberley Wild Brooks* (Duo-Art D 577, r. 1924)

7. *Ragamuffin* (*London Pieces* no. 2) (Duo-Art D 0211, r. 1924)

John Ireland: Sonatina played by Helen Perkin (19 June 1951)

8. *Moderato*

9. *Quasi Lento*

10. Rondo (*Ritmico, non troppo allegro*)

Songs by John Ireland recorded in his lifetime on 78s

11. *Hope the Hornblower* with orchestral accompaniment, Thomas Case with orchestra (Parlophone R 552, r. c. 1930)

12. *The Bells of San Marie* with piano quintet, Hubert Eisdel (Columbia L 1333, r. 1919)

13 *When Lights Go Rolling Round the Sky*, Peter Dawson/ Madam Amani, pf (HMV B 1337, r. 31 May 1920)

14. *Sea Fever*, Fraser Gange (HMV E3, r. July 1919)

15. *Sea Fever*, Betty Chester/ Melville Gideon, pf (HMV B 1445, r. November 1922)

16. *The Soldier*, Roy Henderson/ Ivor Newton, pf (Decca M 526, r. 1943)

John Ireland conducts his own music (fragment)
(The only surviving recording of John Ireland conducting)

17. *The Forgotten Rite* (from 3 after B (p. 6) to 3 after G (p. 18)), BBC Symphony Orchestra/John Ireland (Queen's Hall, 10 January 1935)

All except the following are from the Archives of the John Ireland Trust, courtesy of Bruce Phillips: 3, 11, 16 from the collection of Lewis Foreman; 12 and 13 from David Michell; 14 and 15 from Timothy Massey; 17 originally from the National Sound Archive T 11461W1 C1 courtesy John Ireland Trust. The piano rolls are courtesy of The Pianola Institute. All have been copied and remastered by Michael J. Dutton, to whom many thanks. Copies and/or originals of all John Ireland Trust archive recordings have been deposited in the National Sound Archive at the British Library.

OTHER BOOKS AND THESES ON MUSIC BY LEWIS FOREMAN

A Catalogue of Full and Miniature Scores in Stock at Ealing Central Library (1966)

Havergal Brian: A Collection of Essays (1969)

The British Musical Renaissance: A Guide to Research (diss, 1972)

Discographies: A Bibliography (1973)

Archive Sound Collections (1974)

Systematic Discography (1974)

Factors Affecting the Preservation and Dissemination of Archives Sound Recordings (diss, 1975)

British Music Now (1975)

Havergal Brian and the Performance of his Orchestral Music (1976)

Arthur Bliss: Catalogue of the Complete Works (1980)

The Percy Grainger Companion (1981)

Bax: A Composer and his Times (1983, 1988)

Oskar Fried: Delius and the Late Romantic School (1984)

From Parry to Britten: British Music in Letters (1987, 1988)

Farewell, My Youth and Other Writings by Arnold Bax (1992)

Lost and Only Sometimes Found: A Seminar on Music Publishing and Archives (1992)

British Music 1885–1920 (1994)

Koanga: The 1935 Production of Frederick Delius's Opera in the Context of its Performance History (1995)

Vaughan Williams in Perspective (1998)

Elgar & Gerontius: The Early Performances (1998)

British Choral Music (2001)

Oh My Horses! Edward Elgar and the Great War (2001)

Information Sources in Music (2003)

London: A Musical Gazetteer (with Susan Foreman) (2005)

English Music 1860–1960: Its Reception, Revival and Recording (diss, 2005)

Bax: A Composer and his Times. Third edition expanded and reset (2007)

Unexpected Paradise: The Story of Reclaiming a Repertoire (forthcoming)

Felix: The Diaries and Selected Musical Writings of Felix Aprahamian (edited with Susan Foreman) *(forthcoming)*